HOLLYWOOD Songsters

Hollywood Songsters

Singers Who Act and Actors Who Sing

A Biographical Dictionary

2nd Edition

Volume 1: Allyson to Funicello

James Robert Parish and Michael R. Pitts

Routledge
New York and London

Published in 2003 by
Routledge
29 West 35th Street
New York, NY 10001
www.routledge-ny.com

Published in Great Britain by
Routledge
11 New Fetter Lane
London EC4P 4EE
www.routledge.uk.co

10 9 8 7 6 5 4 3 2 1

Library of Congress Cataloging-in-Publication Data is available from the Library
of Congress.

Parish, James Robert and Pitts, Michael R.
Hollywood songsters : singers who act and actors who sing.
ISBN: 0-415-93775-2 (set: alk. paper).
ISBN: 0-415-94332-9 (vol. 1: alk. paper)
ISBN: 0-415-94333-7 (vol. 2: alk. paper)
ISBN: 0-415-94334-5 (vol. 3: alk. paper)

for

Kate Smith (1907–1986)

The Songbird of the South

Contents

Volume 1

Volume 2

Volume 3

Authors' Note

As indicated by the title, *Hollywood Songsters* includes performers who have had success both as singers and as film stars of American-made movies. In compiling this volume, we have tried to include a variety of personalities who have been popular since the introduction of sound to movies in the late 1920s. Naturally, some of those included have had more success than others and some are associated more with singing than acting, or vice versa, but all have had an impact in both performance arts.

While we have included 112 performers in this updated and expanded edition of the 1991 original book—and this new edition now includes CD as well as LP discographies for each singer—we realize that not every singer who has worked successfully in United States motion pictures is represented with an individual entry. If you find that a favorite songster is missing, please contact us (in care of the publisher) and tell us so. Also, we welcome additions and corrections for this book. Given the space limitations, we could not offer minute details on all aspects of the lives and careers of the people included. However, we hope we have provided well-rounded coverage of their show business activities, especially in relation to their music and films.

James Robert Parish
Michael R. Pitts

Keys to Abbreviations

LP and CD Album Discography Key

Cap	Capitol Records		Par	Paramount Records
CIF	Classic International Filmusicals Records		SRO	Standing Room Only Records
Col	Columbia Records		ST	Soundtrack (film)
Har	Harmony Records		ST/R	Soundtrack (radio)
Mer	Mercury Records		ST/TV	Soundtrack (television)
MGM	Metro-Goldwyn-Mayer Records		UA	United Artists Records
OC	Original Cast		WB	Warner Bros. Records

Notes

- In the LP section of each discography, the listing 10″ in front of the company name refers to a ten-inch, long-playing record; all others are twelve-inch LPs. The LP section does not include 78s, 45s, EPs, 8-tracks, or audio cassettes. However, CD albums—but *not* CD singles—have their own separate discographic listing following the LP section in each appropriate entry.

- When two code numbers are given for a particular LP listing, the first one is for the monaural release; the second one for the stereo release.

- As for LP reissues, the original LP issue company and code number are listed first, followed by any reissues by other labels. The one exception to this rule is some of the soundtracks from MGM musical films, which have had as many as a half dozen reissues. In that case, we have listed the first issue *only*. When a title first was issued on a ten-inch LP we listed it first, followed by the first twelve-inch LP release (if any). However, an LF album that has the same title but does *not* contain the same tracks as a prior LP release of the performer is listed separately in alphabetical order by title (and subsorted by label name) within the LP section of the songster's discography.

- We had to draw the line on some album listings where one of the *Hollywood Songsters* does not do the entire record. Basically, if a performer is given substantial billing on the disc cover, we listed it, and tried to include any other performers on the release as well.

- In the LP record listings, Amalgamated Records is an umbrella title for a host of small, independent labels. We have used the Amalgamated code numbers for such releases.

- In the CD disc listings for a performer, as in the LP section of each subject's discography, reissues of a particular album by other labels are included as part of the same entry. However, as in the LP section, albums that have the same title but do *not* contain the same tracks as a prior release of the performer are listed separately in alphabetical order by title (and subsorted by label name) within the CD section of the songster's discography.

Filmography Key

AA	Allied Artists		MGM/UA	Metro-Goldwyn-Mayer/United Artists Pictures
ABC	American Broadcasting Corporation		NBC	National Broadcasting Corporation
AIP	American International Pictures		NG	National General Pictures
Aus	Austrian		Par	Paramount Pictures
Avco Emb	Avco Embassy Pictures		PBS	Public Broadcasting System
Br	British		PRC	Producers Releasing Corporation
Braz	Brazilian		Rep	Republic Pictures Corporation
BV	Buena Vista		RKO	RKO Radio Pictures
CBN	Christian Broadcasting Network [later The Family Channel]		(s)	Short Subject
CBS	Columbia Broadcasting System		Soundies	Soundies Distributing Corporation of America (SDCA)
Cin	Cinerama Releasing Corporation		Sp	Spanish
Col	Columbia Pictures		Tif	Tiffany Film Corporation
Emb	Embassy Pictures Corporation		20th-Fox	Twentieth Century-Fox Film Corporation
Fox	Fox Film Corporation		UA	United Artists Pictures
FN	First National Pictures (Warner Bros.)		UI	Universal-International Pictures
Fr	French		Univ	Universal Pictures
Ger	German		Unk	Unknown Distributor
GN	Grand National Pictures		Vita	Vitaphone Corporation (Warner Bros.)
Ir	Iranian		WB	Warner Bros. Pictures
It	Italian		WB-7 Arts	Warner Bros.–Seven Arts Pictures
Lip	Lippert Films			
MGM	Metro-Goldwyn-Mayer Pictures			

Notes

Film titles in brackets following a listing are the alternate release title, reissue title, or British release title for the given film.

Television/Cable Key

ABC	American Broadcasting Corporation		NBC	National Broadcasting Corporation
BBC	British Broadcasting Corporation		NN	Non Network
CBN	Christian Broadcasting Network [later The Family Channel]		PBS	Public Broadcasting System
CBS	Columbia Broadcasting System		Synd	Syndicated
Fox	Fox Broadcasting Corporation		TNN	The Nashville Network

Notes

Made-for-television or made-for-cable feature films (telefilms/cable features) are listed with all the other films as part of the appropriate individual filmography.

Acknowledgments

Thanks to: Academy of Motion Picture Arts and Sciences—Margaret Herrick Library, Larry Billman (Academy of Dance on Film), Billy Rose Theater Collection of the New York Public Library at Lincoln Center, Stephen Bourne, John Cocchi (JC Archives), Stephen Cole, Tony Cooper (Frankie Laine International Appreciation Society), Ernest Cunningham, Eleanor Knowles Dugan, Echo Book Shop, Dr. James Fisher, Karin Fowler, Gary Giddins, Laura Gwaltney, Richard K. Hayes (Kate Smith Commemorative Society), Jane Klain (Museum of Television & Radio), Alvin H. Marill, Doug McClelland, Jim Meyer, Donn Moyer, Albert L. Ortega (Albert L. Ortega Photos), Barry Rivadue, Margie Schultz, André Soares, Les Spindle, Allan Taylor (copy editor), George Ulrich, Laura Wagner, Ray White.

Special thanks to literary agent Stuart Bernstein and to our editors, Richard Carlin and Sara Brady.

June Allyson

(b. Ella Geisman, South Bronx, New York, October 7, 1917)

Portraying the twinkly-eyed girl next door became June Allyson's movie forte. During the 1940s she was America's idealized image of the wholesome young woman left behind. On-screen she was always one step away from a tear, with that telling catch in her husky voice belying her brave smile. Fans (if not always the critics) liked her best when she teamed in romantic fluff with bobby-soxer idol Van Johnson (he was six feet two inches, she was five feet one inch, and he had even more freckles than she). Infrequently, she would be permitted to sing and dance in pictures. On these occasions she radiated such verve that she stole the limelight from better-known musical performers. But then it would be back to the Peter Pan collars and more saccharine, sappy roles, though she nonetheless demonstrated a surprising dramatic flare in *The Shrike* (1955). Off-camera, Allyson proved what a gritty lady she really was, overcoming several personal tragedies and always reemerging into the public arena.

Allyson was born Ella Geisman in a three-room tenement on 143rd and Third Avenue in New York's South Bronx on October 7, 1917. (Later, MGM publicists would subtract as much as a decade from her real age.) She was the second child of Clara and Robert Geisman; her father, a building janitor, left her mother when Ella was six months old, taking her older brother Henry to live with his mother. Clara Geisman went to work in a print shop, while Ella was sent to stay with her maternal grandparents. Whenever enough money was scraped together, Clara would rent a cheap railroad flat apartment so she and Ella could be together. Then, when money ran out again, Ella was shipped back to her grandparents or passed around to other relatives. When Ella was eight, she was racing down the neighborhood street one Sunday with a little wirehaired terrier. They stopped beneath a tree to rest, and a large limb came loose, landing on Ella and the animal. The dog was killed while Ella suffered a fractured skull and a broken back. She was injured so badly that she had to wear a heavy steel brace from her neck to her hips for four years.

"My whole youth was a nightmare," the actress recalled. "I grew up wanting to escape from everyone and everything that had made it so." Thus she concocted an elaborate story that she had been born in tree-lined Lucerne, New York; that in high school (after her injury from running down a hillside and tripping over a concealed log) she had become a swimming star; and that her home life had been rosy. In retrospect, she rationalized, "I told myself that movie audiences wouldn't respect a girl from the tenement side of New York City."

Part of her escape from her precarious childhood was going to the movies, especially thriving on the screen magic of Fred Astaire and Ginger Rogers. She dreamed of becoming an entertainer, and this strong determination—plus exercise—helped her to regain her strength. By the time Ella entered Theodore Roosevelt High School, her mother had remarried (Arthur Peters) and she had a half-brother named Arthur. With the household finances more stable, Ella took lessons at Ned Wayburn Dancing Academy. As Elaine Peters, she entered neighborhood amateur night contests

June Allyson and Peter Lawford in *Good News* (1947).
[Courtesy of JC Archives]

in the Bronx. Although she never won, she enthusiastically continued dancing. When her stepfather died, Ella quit high school (after only two and one-half years), determined to enter the world of professional show business.

She managed to get, eventually, a $60 per week tap-dancing job at the Lido Club in Montreal and later appeared, inconspicuously, in several short subjects for Vitaphone (Warner Bros.) and Educational that were filmed in New York. Then, she landed a chorus job in Harold Rome's Broadway musical revue *Sing Out the News* (1938). It closed after 105 performances, and ultra-aggressive Ella (already billing herself as June Allyson) joined the Copacabana Club chorus line. Always auditioning, she next was cast in *Very Warm for May* (1939), a Jerome Kern–Oscar Hammerstein II musical, in which she hoofed in the chorus line. Although this show folded after 59 performances, it led to June being hired for Rodgers and Hart's *Higher and Higher* (1940). She recalled, "I've been in more flops than you can imagine. I couldn't dance, and Lord knows I couldn't sing, but I got by somehow. It was Richard Rodgers who was always keeping them from firing me, as every dance director wanted to do." Next came Cole Porter's *Panama Hattie* (1940), starring Ethel Merman. June was in the chorus along with roommate Betsy Blair (who married Gene Kelly). The latter recalled, "She was the smallest girl and the last in the line—and on our exit, she would pretend to trip. When she picked herself up, everyone would applaud out of sympathy, which was just what she wanted." Chorine June also understudied bombastic ingénue Betty Hutton. When Hutton was ill with the measles, June went on for five performances, and in the audience one of those nights was Broadway director George Abbott, who cast her in the musical *Best Foot Forward* (1941). June was earning $125 a week and had by now moved into the American Women's Club in Manhattan and was dating singer Tommy Mitchell (who had been in *Sing Out the News*). *Best Foot Forward* closed after a 326-performance run, with June and Nancy Walker being among those cast members contracted by Metro-Goldwyn-Mayer for the film version.

According to Allyson, it was producer Joe Pasternak who had convinced MGM studio head Louis B. Mayer to look at her screen audition. Pasternak urged, "Please look at this test and do just two things. Look at her eyes and listen to her voice. Don't pay any attention to anything else about her. These are distractions we can iron out." In the Technicolor *Best Foot Forward*, which starred Lucille Ball as a movie star visiting a military academy as a publicity stunt, June repeated her role as Ethel, who—along with Nancy Walker and Gloria DeHaven—was on campus for the big prom. She joined in the numbers "The Three B's" and "Buckle Down Winsocki." This film proved an adequate feature debut for June, a perky redhead with an unexpectedly husky voice (due to recurrent bronchitis and enlarged vocal cords). Next she did a specialty number in the musical *Girl Crazy* (1943) in which she sang "Treat Me Rough" in a Manhattan nightclub scene while manhandling a bewildered Mickey Rooney. In *Thousands Cheer* (1943) the trio of June, Gloria DeHaven, and dead-pan Virginia O'Brien performed "Spanish Town" to the accompaniment of Bob Crosby and His BobCats Band.

June's professional turning point was *Two Girls and a Sailor* (1944), which boasted a bevy of guest stars: José Iturbi, Lena Horne, Gracie Allen, Xavier Cugat's Orchestra, and Harry James's Orchestra. It showcased June and Gloria DeHaven as song-and-dance sisters performing at a posh New York club. Up to this picture, it was a toss-up at MGM whether the studio would promote Allyson or DeHaven as their newest ingénue star. Oddsmakers favored more conventionally attractive DeHaven, but in *Two Girls and a Sailor* it was June (originally cast in the other role) who stole the show and won the on-camera love of leading man Van Johnson. This star-making assignment was preceded by a supporting part in *Meet the People* (1944), starring Lucille Ball and Dick Powell.

During the making of this film she renewed her acquaintanceship with crooner/actor Powell, who had seen one of her Broadway performances and met her backstage after the show. Allyson and the older Powell (who was ending his marriage to movie star Joan Blondell) became a Hollywood item, and they were wed on August 19, 1945, despite the strong objections of Louis B. Meyer, who feared it might interrupt June's promising movie career. The bitterness Blondell felt over losing Powell to Allyson translated into a nasty portrayal of her rival in Blondell's thinly veiled autobiographical fiction, *Center Door Fancy* (1972).

June was pushed into three 1945 releases. She was the weepy orchestra cellist whose husband is away at war in *Music for Millions*, outsobbed only by Margaret O'Brien as her little sister. Allyson also cried her way through *Her Highness and the Bellboy* as the invalid who adores bellhop Robert Walker who, in turn, is overwhelmed by the beauty of visiting royalty (Hedy Lamarr); and she and Walker reteamed for *The Sailor Takes a Wife*. June and Kathryn Grayson were *Two Sisters From Boston* (1946), a musical concoction that corralled Lauritz Melchior, Jimmy Durante, and Peter Lawford into the same film! In the star-crowded *Till the Clouds Roll By* (1946), June was seen demurely dueting the title tune with Ray McDonald, was noticeably sprightly in her fine rendition of "Leave It to Jane," and downright spunky in her singing and cavorting to "Cleopat-terer."

MGM, who frequently used June as a "threat" to recalcitrant Judy Garland, was now insistent that Allyson belonged in romantic fabrications, especially those costarring Van Johnson. The sweetheart team made *High Barbaree* (1947), a failed wartime fantasy, followed by the madcap comedy *The Bride Goes Wild* (1948). In between, June actually starred in a musical, a reworking of the 1920s' campus romp *Good News* (1947), matched with Peter Lawford. She was already thirty, but she came across on-camera as a high-spirited, much younger woman. Her last musical assignment under contract to the studio was singing a sparkling "Thou Swell" in *Words and Music* (1948). Also in this year, and much against her will (she hated the idea of parading in period costumes), she played Lady Constance opposite Gene Kelly in *The Three Musketeers*, while domestically she and Powell adopted a baby girl they named Pamela. Powell's children (Ellen and Norman) by Joan Blondell sometimes lived with he and June.

After assuming Katharine Hepburn's role of Jo in a remake of *Little Women* (1949), June was in *The Stratton Story* (1949) as the spunky miss who encourages her baseball-playing husband (James Stewart) after he loses a leg in a hunting accident. It was Powell who urged her to take the stereotyped assignment that proved to be one of her most popular parts. Powell wanted to borrow his wife to costar in United Artists' *Mrs. Mike* (1949), but Metro said no. Instead, they signed the actor to costar with June in two mild home lot productions: *The Reformer and the Redhead* (1949) and *Right Cross* (1950). It was also this year (December 25) that she gave birth to Richard Jr., which caused her to be replaced by Jane Powell opposite Fred Astaire in the musical *Royal Wedding* (1951).

With her continuing popularity, June should have been getting better assignments. Instead, she was rematched with Van Johnson (already becoming passé) in *Too Young to Kiss* (1951), posing as a child prodigy pianist. In the tepid *The Girl in White* (1952) she was a dedicated female doctor, and in the absurd Korean War romance *Battle Circus* (1953), she replaced Shelley Winters as an Army nurse in love with "Doctor" Humphrey Bogart. Her final big screen appearance with Johnson was in *Remains to Be Seen* (1953), a whodunit that played on the wrong half of double bills. When

MGM, now run by Dore Schary, gave the promised lead comedienne role in *The Long, Long Trailer* (1954) to Lucille Ball and asked Allyson to take a pay cut, Allyson announced she would leave the studio.

Her first freelance picture was the extremely popular *The Glenn Miller Story* (1954), which again teamed June with Jimmy Stewart and capitalized effectively on her image as the weepy, loving wife. She was supposed to do *The Gibson Girl* for Dick Powell, but the project did not jell, and it was Jane Russell not Allyson (the studio's earlier choice) who played opposite Jeff Chandler in *Foxfire* (1955) at Universal. Instead, June was among the all-star gathering in MGM's *Executive Suite* (1954); here she was William Holden's loyal spouse. More fun for her was Twentieth Century-Fox's CinemaScope comedy *Woman's World* (1954), where she excelled as Cornel Wilde's well-meaning helpmate. Paramount cast her opposite Jimmy Stewart yet again for *Strategic Air Command* (1955), and she was with equally short Alan Ladd in *The McConnell Story* (1955) at Warner Bros. On-camera, she was the wife of a stressed-out jet pilot Ladd, while off-camera she and Alan had a very personal relationship. Meanwhile, she wangled the title role in *The Shrike* (1955) opposite José Ferrer; it was an effective acting stretch by June, but the stark drama did not attract a large number of moviegoers.

What followed was a period of being Hollywood's Queen of Remakes. At $150,000 salary, she had the Norma Shearer role in MGM's musical rehash of *The Women* (1939), now known as *The Opposite Sex* (1956—in which her husband's ex-wife, Joan Blondell had a featured role). She took over Claudette Colbert's Oscar-winning assignment from *It Happened One Night* (1934) in the poor revamping of that classic film, *You Can't Run Away From It* (1956). She was the lead in *Interlude* (1957), a tearjerker revision of Irene Dunne's *When Tomorrow Comes* (1939), and in *My Man Godfrey* (1957), opposite David Niven, she inherited Carole Lombard's classic screwball comedy lead from 1936. Thereafter, it was two years before she was back on-camera, now as the woman who defies all for Jeff Chandler in Universal's *Stranger in My Arms*. It was her finale as a motion-picture leading lady. (In the interim June had rejected doing 1957's *The Three Faces of Eve*, which won an Oscar for Joanne Woodward.)

Like others before her, most notably Loretta Young, June turned to television to revive her career. (Dick Powell had already become a major force in the TV industry as an actor/director/producer.) As Allyson gained national media exposure for her anthology series, *The DuPont Show With June Allyson* (CBS-TV, 1959–61), she became more candid in her career observations. "I want to be me. During all those years at MGM, everything was done for me. The publicity department told me what to say on every interview. They stuck my neck into a Peter Pan collar, and Peter Pan and I were stuck together like glue . . . I have a temper like everybody else and I get mad sometimes. But as June Allyson I wasn't allowed to get mad . . . I see a camera, any kind of camera, and I automatically smile."

In 1961 she underwent a kidney operation and later throat surgery (which, for a time, left her with a soprano voice). She and Powell, who had a seesawing marriage with various separations (because he was too busy with his Four Star Productions), reconciled. By then he had developed cancer, and he died on January 2, 1963, leaving a $2 million estate. Ten months later (October 12, 1963), June married Glenn Maxwell in Florida. He owned barbershops and had been Powell's hair stylist. They divorced in 1965, were rewed in 1966, and divorced yet again (but still lived together). The latter divorce was prompted by the terms of Powell's will: she would receive $4,000 monthly if she was unmarried, $700 monthly if she was not.

In the early 1960s June had appeared frequently on her husband's teleseries (*The Dick Powell Show* and *Zane Grey Theater*) and was a guest on pal Judy Garland's variety series in 1963. In 1967 Allyson attempted a nightclub act comeback with Donald O'Connor in Las Vegas, and in 1968 she and Van Johnson were reunited on the "High on a Rainbow" episode of the teleseries *Name of the Game*. She was scheduled to star in a duo of Spanish Westerns in 1969 that did not materialize, and in 1970 she was among those who succeeded Julie Harris in the long-running Broadway romantic comedy *Forty Carats*. She went on national tour in 1972 with Judy Canova and Dennis Day in the revival of the old musical *No, No Nanette*. There was heightened media attention when June returned to MGM to appear in the James Garner detective thriller *They Only Kill Their Masters* (1972), because she was cast as a lesbian. Two years later she was among the MGM alumni promoting the studio's documentary *That's Entertainment!* That same year she toured (as she had in 1968) with Dick Powell Jr. in the comedy *My Daughter, Your Son*.

In the 1980s June, still looking youthful and trim, cropped up in telefeatures (*The Kid With the Broken Halo*, 1982) and in episodes of such teleseries as *The Love Boat* (1983—teamed once with Van Johnson) and *Murder, She Wrote* (1985). She became even more noticeable in the mid-1980s when she became spokesperson for an adult diaper product. Wed to Dr. David Ashrow since October 1976, she authored her autobiography, *June Allyson* (1982) with Frances Spatz Leighton in which she admitted, "Today I am a woman. I'm not the scared little girl anymore . . . Peace."

In 1993 Allyson was in the news again when she charged comedian/actors' agent Marty Ingels with harassing her with phone calls about alleged overdue commissions from commercials he had reputedly obtained for her. The defendant pleaded no contest in court and served 120 hours of community service. For the long-delayed-into-release *That's Entertainment! III* (1994), June was one of the cohosts. In July 1997 the actress was part of the contingent who appeared behind the footlights in New York City for *Carnegie Hall Celebrates the Glorious MGM Musicals*, joined by such fellow studio alumnae as Leslie Caron, Kathryn Grayson, Van Johnson, and Mickey Rooney. Similarly, in January 2000 June was among those at the Pasadena (California) Civic Theater, where she joined Cyd Charisse, Tony Martin, Gloria DeHaven, and Betty Garrett onstage for *A Celebration of the Classic Hollywood Musicals*. Meanwhile, in April 1999, Allyson, along with Dick Van Dyke, was honored in Beverly Hills by the Professional Dancers Society for her many years in show business.

Filmography

Swing for Sales (Vita, 1937) (s)
Pixilated (Educational, 1937) (s)
Dime a Dance (Educational, 1937) (s)
Hal LeRoy's Ups and Downs (Vita, 1937) (s)
Dates and Nuts (Educational, 1938) (s)
The Prisoner of Swing (Vita, 1938) (s)
Sing for Sweetie (Educational, 1938) (s)
Not Now (Educational, 1938) (s)
The Knight Is Young (Vita, 1938) (s)
Rollin' in Rhythm (Vita, 1939) (s)

All Girl Revue (Vita, 1939) (s)
Best Foot Forward (MGM, 1943)
Girl Crazy (MGM, 1943)
Thousands Cheer (MGM, 1943)
Meet the People (MGM, 1944)
Two Girls and a Sailor (MGM, 1944)
Music for Millions (MGM, 1945)
Her Highness and the Bellboy (MGM, 1945)
The Sailor Takes a Wife (MGM, 1945)
Two Sisters From Boston (MGM, 1946)

Till the Clouds Roll By (MGM, 1946)
The Secret Heart (MGM, 1946)
High Barbaree (MGM, 1947)
Good News (MGM, 1947)
The Bride Goes Wild (MGM, 1948)
The Three Musketeers (MGM, 1948)
Words and Music (MGM, 1948)
Little Women (MGM, 1949)
The Stratton Story (MGM, 1949)
The Reformer and the Redhead (MGM, 1949)
Right Cross (MGM, 1950)
Too Young to Kiss (MGM, 1951)
The Girl in White [So Bright the Flame] (MGM, 1952)
Battle Circus (MGM, 1953)
Remains to Be Seen (MGM, 1953)
The Glenn Miller Story (Univ, 1954)
Executive Suite (MGM, 1954)
Woman's World (20th-Fox, 1954)
Strategic Air Command (Par, 1955)

The McConnell Story [Tiger in the Sky] (WB, 1955)
The Shrike (Univ, 1955)
Screen Snapshots: Hollywood, City of Stars (Col, 1956) (s)
The Opposite Sex (MGM, 1956)
You Can't Run Away From It (Col, 1956)
Interlude (Univ, 1957)
My Man Godfrey (Univ, 1957)
Stranger in My Arms (Univ, 1959)
See the Man Run (NBC-TV, 12/11/71)
They Only Kill Their Masters (MGM, 1972)
Letters From Three Lovers (ABC-TV, 10/3/73)
Curse of the Black Widow (ABC-TV, 9/16/77)
Three on a Date (ABC-TV, 2/17/78)
Vega$ (ABC-TV, 4/25/78)
Blackout (New World, 1978)
The Kid With the Broken Halo (NBC-TV, 4/5/82)
That's Entertainment! III (1994) (cohost)

Broadway Plays

Sing Out the News (1938)
Very Warm for May (1939)
Higher and Higher (1940)

Panama Hattie (1940)
Best Foot Forward (1941)
Forty Carats (1970) (replacement)

TV Series

DuPont Show With June Allyson (CBS, 1959–61)

Album Discography

LPs

Best Foot Forward (Caliban 6039) [ST]
Girl Crazy (Curtain Calls 100/9-10) [ST]
Girl Crazy (Hollywood Soundstage HS-5006) [ST]
Good News (10″ MGM E-504; MGM E-3229, Sandy Hook SH-2074, Sountrak 111, Vertinge 2001) [ST]
Judy Garland and Friends (Minerva MIN LP-6JG-FNJ) [ST/TV] w. Steve Lawrence
That's Entertainment! (MCA MCA2-11002) [ST]
Thousands Cheer (Amalgamated 232, Hollywood Soundstage 409) [ST]

Till the Clouds Roll By (10″ MGM E-501, MGM E-3231, Metro M/S-578, Soundtrak 115, Vertinge 2000) [ST]
Two Girls and a Sailor (Hollywood Sound Stage HS-2307) [ST]
Very Warm for May (AEI 1156) [OC]
Words and Music (10″ MGM E-505, MGM E-3233, Metro M/S-580) [ST]
You Can't Run Away From It (Decca DL-8396) [ST]

CDs

The Belle of New York/Good News/Rich, Young and Pretty (EMI 794869) [ST]
Girl Crazy (Turner Classic Movies/Rhino R2-72590) [ST]
Good News (Columbia AK-47025, MGM/EMI MGM-23) [ST]
That's Entertainment! (Sony Music Special Products A2K-46872) [ST]

That's Entertainment, Part 2 (Angel CDQ-555215) [ST]
Till the Clouds Roll By (MGM/EMI MGM-24, Sandy Hook CDSH-2080, Sony Music Special Products AK-47029) [ST]
Two Girls and a Sailor (Great Movie Themes 60023) [ST]
Words and Music (MGM/EMI MGM-14, Sony Music Special Products AK-47711) [ST]

Don Ameche and Al Jolson in *Swanee River* (1939).
[Courtesy of JC Archives]

Don Ameche

(b. Dominic Felix Amici, Kenosha, Wisconsin, May 31, 1908; d. Scottsdale, Arizona, December 6, 1993)

Don Ameche celebrated more than a half century in show business by making one of filmdom's biggest comebacks when he won an Academy Award for his performance in the science-fiction hit *Cocoon* (1985). Although he had remained professionally active for years, Ameche had been considered a figure from Hollywood's nostalgic past, a personality best known (and teased) for his title role in *The Story of Alexander Graham Bell* (1939). His reemergence on the movie scene as a major box-office figure in his seventies brought the actor a new generation of followers. Although he appeared in some fifty feature films, Don had a very diverse career, which also included radio, Broadway, and television. In the 1930s and early 1940s, the dapper and droll Ameche was also a movie crooner who sang in many of the films in which he appeared. While he had a more than passable singing voice, vocalizing was to become the least of his screen accomplishments, whereas he was equally adept, or better, as a light comedian and a dramatic performer. In retrospect, this breezy, polished leading man should have fought harder for showcase vehicles during his prime years as a star during World War II.

Don Ameche was born Dominic Felix Amici in Kenosha, Wisconsin, on May 31, 1908, the son of an Italian immigrant father and a German-Irish mother; he was the second of eight children. He was educated in Catholic schools and at Columbia Academy in Dubuque, Iowa, where he was to meet his future wife, Honore Prendergast. After earning his school diploma, the young man acceded to his father's wishes and studied law at Washington, DC's, Georgetown University, but later transferred to the University of Wisconsin, where he became interested in dramatics. Thanks to his impressive work in college plays, he won a part in the touring show *Excess Baggage*. He dropped out of school and went to New York City, where he obtained a small part in the Broadway show *Jerry for Short* (1929), billing himself as Don Ameche, the phonetic pronunciation of his name.

After the Broadway experience, Ameche became a singer in Texas Guinan's traveling vaudeville show; but she disliked his stage presence, and he was let go in Chicago. He quickly got a part in the play *Illegal Practice* and then headed back to Manhattan, where he landed radio work. In the next few years he acted in such radio programs as *The Empire Builders, Betty and Bob, Foreign Legion, The Little Theater Off Times Square, Grand Hotel*, and *Rin-Tin-Tin*. However, his best-known role was as the host of the NBC series *The First Nighter* in the early 1930s. Don's brother, Jim, also became a radio announcer and performer and stayed with the medium to become one of its best-known voices during the next two decades. Meanwhile, Don was doing so well financially that he and Honore Prendergast were wed in 1932, and over the next several years they had five children. In 1933 he made his film debut in the short subject, *Beauty at the World's Fair*.

Ameche made a Hollywood screen test for MGM in 1935 that did not impress them. However, Darryl F. Zanuck at the newly formed Twentieth Century-Fox saw the test and offered the radio actor a seven-year contract. His first major appearance was as one of Jean Hersholt's sons in *Sins of Man* (1936). Don made such a favorable impression he was cast as the male lead in the Technicolor remake of *Ramona* (1936) as the Indian who weds a half-breed girl (Loretta Young) only to have them both suffer racial prejudice. Ameche was one of a trio of suitors in *Ladies In Love* (1936) and first displayed his trademark thin mustache when he costarred with Sonja Henie in her film debut, *One In a Million* (1936). In this delightful musical comedy he is the newsman who falls in love with Henie and croons to her during the proceedings.

By now Twentieth Century-Fox realized that Ameche's handsome features, able singing voice, and likable personality were a definite plus for the studio. He was used by his employer in a diverse number of roles (several of them thankless) over the next few years, always providing the studio with good box-office returns. In his first thirty-three motion pictures, he was only loaned out on three occasions. The five features Don performed for the studio in 1937 well exemplified the tone of his career during his tenure with the Zanuck organization, which always favored their blondized female stars over contract leading men. *One In a Million* and *You Can't Have Everything* (the first of a half dozen screen pairings with Alice Faye) were tuneful musicals that offered him dashing, if one-dimensional, leading man roles with a chance to croon a bit. *Love Is News* had him as a romantic contender who loses Loretta Young to handsome Tyrone Power. *Fifty Roads to Town* found him winning the girl in a light comedy, while *Love Under Fire* presented him in a dramatic role (although he did sing a song!) as a Scotland Yard detective caught in Spain during its civil war. In 1937 Don also began one of his best-known assignments, that of host of NBC radio's *The Chase and Sanborn Hour* with Edgar Bergen and Charlie McCarthy. Even after he became one of the top two dozen stars in Hollywood he retained this post into the early 1940s and was often a part of the famous radio duels between McCarthy and W. C. Fields.

During 1938 Ameche had several key roles at Twentieth Century-Fox that helped to solidify his growing Hollywood popularity. For example, the period melodrama *In Old Chicago* had him as a crusader at odds with crooked brother Tyrone Power over politics and Alice Faye. *Josette* was a delightful comedy about brothers (Ameche and Robert Young) both pursuing Simone Simon, while the Irving Berlin songfest, *Alexander's Ragtime Band*, showcased Don as a pianist who wins singer Alice Faye only to lose her to bandsman Tyrone Power. The latter film provided Ameche and Faye with a good duet on "Now It Can Be Told."

The next year, 1939, proved to be his peak movie year. *The Three Musketeers* was a rousing rendition of the Dumas swashbuckling classic with Ameche as D'Artagnan to the Ritz Brothers' comedic musketeers, while in his first loanout he was a Parisian cabdriver who finds love with a beautiful woman (Claudette Colbert) in Paramount's grand comedy *Midnight*. Next came Ameche's most enduring film role, the title assignment in the contrived biography *The Story of Alexander Graham Bell*. So completely identified was Ameche with Bell that it became a national joke that it was Don Ameche who actually invented the telephone! In *Swanee River* Ameche portrayed the famous nineteenth-century American composer Stephen Foster. This film gave Ameche occasion to sing some of Foster's famous songs (although most were done by Al Jolson as E. P. Christie). Despite the fact that Ameche recurrently sang in films, he never recorded commercially at the time because studio mogul Darryl F. Zanuck had a prohibition against studio stars making records, except for Alice Faye. Ameche and Faye were teamed for the fifth occasion in *Lillian Russell* in 1940 in which he portrayed the famous stage star's first spouse. Later that year, in the sprightly Technicolor musical *Down Argentine Way*, he was the horse-breeder who carries the torch for Betty Grable in South America.

Don began 1941 with another colorful song-and-dance entry, *That Night in Rio*, where he was involved in a mistaken identity case as a singer and a bank president; he and Alice Faye performed "Chica, Chica, Boom Chic," but the song was cut. At MGM he was a college professor/ writer whose wife (Rosalind Russell) becomes jealous of his chic editor (Kay Francis) in *The Feminine Touch*, and *Confirm or Deny* had him back in the dramatic vein as a reporter who uncovers a Nazi plan to invade England. *The Magnificent Dope* (1942) offered Don a good part as a con artist. Ameche's favorite picture assignment came in 1943 in the classic *Heaven Can Wait*, Ernst Lubitsch's wry period comedy, which cast him as a droll sinner reliving his zesty life. Ameche had another solid dramatic role as an Air Force officer in the fine war drama *Wing and a Prayer* (1944), and in a lighter vein, he was a composer who finds love with Vivian Blaine in the less-than-stellar musical *Greenwich Village* (1944), his last contract feature for Twentieth.

Freelancing (and as a financial investor), the actor again costarred with Claudette Colbert as a war correspondent in the comedy *Guest Wife* (1945). In another comedy—more strained than amusing—*That's My Man* (1947), he was a bookkeeper who becomes a horse race fanatic. For the modestly budgeted thriller *Sleep, My Love* (1948), he attempted to drive wife Claudette Colbert mad.

Ameche had benefited professionally during the World War II years by not being called into active service. However, his film career faded in the late '40s as demobilized stars and younger players claimed the spotlight. Moreover, in the public's eye Don had been too typecast in frothy musicals, which were drifting out of fashion in the postwar years. Ameche again returned to radio, guesting on programs like Mutual's *Mother's Day Special* in 1947 and *Mail Call* and *The Spike Jones Show* in 1949. During the 1946–47 season he costarred with Frances Langford and Pinky Lee on NBC's *The Drene Program* on which he and Ms. Langford did their famous "The Bickersons" (feuding husband-and-wife characters created originally on *The Chase and Sanborn Hour*). In 1947 and 1948 they starred as *The Bickersons* on CBS radio.

In 1950 Don Ameche and his family moved to New York City, where he became actively involved in television. From October to December 1950, he emceed the NBC-TV quiz show *Take a Chance*, and from 1950 to 1951, he was the hotel manager in ABC-TV's *Holiday Hotel*, later called *Don Ameche's Musical Playhouse*. He starred in the religious film *The Triumphant Hour* in 1950, and in the summer of 1951, he and Frances Langford reprised *The Bickersons* on CBS radio. The year 1953 found him a regular on NBC-TV's *Coke Time With Eddie Fisher*. In 1954 he starred in two early TV movies, *Phantom Caravan* and *Fire One*.

Don successfully made his leading-man debut on Broadway in *Silk Stockings* (1955), Cole Porter's sophisticated musical version of the film *Ninotchka* (1939). The hit show cast Ameche as a hedonistic Frenchman in love with a beautiful Communist (Hildegarde Neff); he sang the title song and "All of You," and the play ran for a year. (Fred Astaire did the screen version in 1957.) On TV Ameche starred with Nanette Fabray in the NBC-TV special version of *High Button Shoes* in 1956, and the next year he reappeared on Broadway in the middling comedy, *Holiday for Lovers*, as well as starring with Joan Bennett in a version of *Junior Miss* on CBS-TV's *Dupont Show of the Month*. In 1958 he played underworld figure Albert Anastasia on CBS-TV's *Climax* and hosted the syndicated TV series *Don Ameche Theater*. He also returned again to Broadway in the musical about early movie making, *Goldilocks*, with Elaine Stritch and Margaret Hamilton. This show had a good run but Ameche was less successful with the Hawaiian-set musical *13 Daughters* (1961). He costarred with Joan Bennett in the shortlived 1959 NBC-TV comedy series *Too Young to Go*

Steady, and into the early 1960s, he was a frequent panelist on the CBS-TV quiz program *To Tell the Truth*.

In 1961 Don relocated to California and appeared as a senator in the political thriller *A Fever in the Blood* and narrated an episode of NBC-TV's *Our American Heritage* before commencing a five-season run as the urbane host of that network's Friday night series *International Showtime*. This successful series had him traveling in Europe to film the various circus acts he introduced. Back home he and Frances Langford were reunited on Columbia Records for two best-selling LPs about their Bickersons' characters. Following the *International Showtime* run, Ameche guest-starred on such TV series fare as *The Greatest Show on Earth* and *Burke's Law*. He returned to films in *Rings Around the World* (1966), repeating his circus introductions, and in the tawdry murder mystery *Picture Mommy Dead* (1966), he was a father whose daughter (Susan Gordon) is supposedly haunted by the specter of her murdered mother (Zsa Zsa Gabor).

Don was back on Broadway in 1967's *Henry, Sweet Henry*, a failed musical version of Peter Sellers's popular film comedy *The World of Henry Orient* (1964). After that it was back to TV for guest shots on programs like *Alias Smith and Jones, Julia, Columbo*, and TV movies such as *Shadow Over Elveron* (1968) and *Gidget Gets Married* (1972), as well as featured roles in two 1970 theatrical comedies—*Suppose They Gave a War and Nobody Came* and *The Boatniks*—in both of which he played a military officer. He was onstage in 1974 for a tour with Evelyn Keyes in *No, No Nanette* and then another tour in the same show with Ruby Keeler. The next year he and Alice Faye reunited for a very successful road revival of *Good News*, and Ameche guest-starred on the *McCloud* and *Ellery Queen* teleseries.

Outside of sporadic TV guest shots in such series as *The Love Boat, Quincy, Fantasy Island, Mr. Smith, Not in Front of the Kids*, and *Detective in the House*, Ameche remained fairly inactive until 1983 when he costarred in the Eddie Murphy comedy *Trading Places* and nearly stole the movie with his deft, underplayed humor. As a result he was cast as one of the Florida retirees who has his youth restored mystically in *Cocoon* (1985), the film that netted him an Academy Award as Best Supporting Actor. He then costarred with Bob Hope in the feckless TV movie comedy *A Masterpiece of Murder* (1986) and had a featured part in the good-natured *Harry and the Hendersons* (1987), about a family trying to domesticate a Bigfoot monster. In the TV movie *Pals* (1987) he and another retiree (George C. Scott), living in a trailer park, stumble across hidden cash (drug-related proceeds) and discover money is not everything, especially when it engenders problems.

The next year brought Ameche his second-favorite movie role, that of Italian immigrant Gino who goes to prison for the Mafia after having his dream of owning a fishing boat fulfilled in *Things Change*, directed by playwright David Mamet. "Working with David Mamet and Ernst Lubitsch are the only two great, great joys I've ever had," Ameche said. (In the fall of 1988 Ameche shared the Venice Film Festival's Best Actor Award with Joe Mantegna for their performances in *Things Change*.) He closed out the year repeating his Oscar-winning role in *Cocoon: The Return*, and early 1989 found him on Broadway taking over the role of the Stage Manager in yet another revival of *Our Town*.

In his early eighties, Don Ameche credited his good health and lengthy, successful career to his religious faith. "I'm a deeply religious man, a Catholic—and without my religion I don't think I could have handled this business. More than once I've been at the pinnacle of success—and plunged into the depths . . . For many people, to have climbed those mountains and then fallen so far would have created such bitterness they couldn't have survived. But I always had my God for comfort. In the good years I said an awful lot of prayers that helped keep my feet on the ground. And in the bad times, I always felt God was there watching over me." Regarding his discipline in keeping himself mentally and physically active in his senior years, he pointed out, "How many actors in their twenties and thirties have two pictures being released by major studios right now?"

In the early 1990s Ameche moved from Santa Monica, California, to live with his son Don Jr., in Scottsdale, Arizona. He continued to appear in movies like *Oddball Hall* (1990), *Oscar* (1991), and *Folks!* (1992) before being diagnosed with prostate cancer. He continued to work, however, finishing his role in *Corinna, Corinna* (1994) just weeks before his death at his son's home on December 6, 1993.

Following his passing, Charles Champlin wrote of the actor in the *Los Angeles Times* (December 8, 1993), "The rediscovery of Don Ameche gave heart to everyone who imagined that life and recognition had passed them by. He lent hope to all those who had thought there was nothing left but solitaire and the vacant stare after age 65 . . . Don Ameche worked very nearly to the end of his days, adding to a legacy of more than a half-century's frequently charming work."

Filmography

Beauty at the World's Fair (Unk, 1933) (s)
Clive of India (Fox, 1935)
Dante's Inferno (Fox, 1935)
Sins of Man (20th-Fox, 1936)
Ramona (20th-Fox, 1936)
Ladies in Love (20th-Fox, 1936)
One in a Million (20th-Fox, 1936)
Love Is News (20th-Fox, 1937)
Fifty Roads to Town (20th-Fox, 1937)
You Can't Have Everything (20th-Fox, 1937)
Love Under Fire (20th-Fox, 1937)
Screen Snapshots #8 (Col, 1937) (s)
In Old Chicago (20th-Fox, 1938)
Happy Landing (20th-Fox, 1938)
Josette (20th-Fox, 1938)
Alexander's Ragtime Band (20th-Fox, 1938)
Gateway (20th-Fox, 1938)
The Three Musketeers [The Singing Musketeer] (20th-Fox, 1939)
Midnight (Par, 1939)
The Story of Alexander Graham Bell [The Modern Miracle] (20th-Fox, 1939)
Hollywood Cavalcade (20th-Fox, 1939)
Swanee River (20th-Fox, 1939)
Lillian Russell (20th-Fox, 1940)
Four Sons (20th-Fox, 1940)
Down Argentine Way (20th-Fox, 1940)
That Night in Rio (20th-Fox, 1941)
Moon Over Miami (20th-Fox, 1941)
Kiss the Boys Goodbye (Par, 1941)
The Feminine Touch (MGM, 1941)
Confirm or Deny (20th-Fox, 1942)
The Magnificent Dope (20th-Fox, 1942)

Girl Trouble (20th-Fox, 1942)
Heaven Can Wait (20th-Fox, 1943)
Happy Land (20th-Fox, 1943)
Something to Shout About (20th-Fox, 1943)
Wing and a Prayer (20th-Fox, 1944)
Greenwich Village (20th-Fox, 1944)
It's in the Bag! [The Fifth Chair] (UA, 1945)
Guest Wife (UA, 1945)
So Goes My Love [A Genius in the Family] (Univ, 1946)
That's My Man [Will Tomorrow Ever Come?] (Rep, 1947)
Sleep, My Love (UA, 1948)
Slightly French (Col, 1949)
The Triumphant Hour (Peyton, 1950)
Hollywood Night at 21 Club (Col, 1952) (s)
Phantom Caravan (Princess, 1954)
Fire One (Princess, 1954)
A Fever in the Blood (WB, 1961)
Rings Around the World (Col, 1966)
Picture Mommy Dead (Emb, 1966)
Shadow Over Elveron (NBC-TV, 3/5/68)
Suppose They Gave a War and Nobody Came (UA, 1970)
The Boatniks (BV, 1970)
Gidget Gets Married (ABC-TV, 1/4/72)
Won Ton Ton, The Dog Who Saved Hollywood (Par, 1976)
Trading Places (Par, 1983)
Cocoon (20th-Fox, 1985)
A Masterpiece of Murder (NBC-TV, 1/26/86)
Harry and the Hendersons (Univ, 1987)
Pals (CBS-TV, 2/28/87)

Things Change (TriStar, 1988)
Cocoon: The Return (20th-Fox, 1988)
Coming to America (Par, 1988)
Oddball Hall (Cannon, 1990)
Oscar (BV, 1991)

Folks! (20th-Fox, 1992)
Sunstroke (Wilshire Court Productions, 1992)
Homeward Bound: The Incredible Journey (BV, 1993) (voice only)
Corinna, Corinna (New Line Cinema, 1994)

Broadway Plays

Jerry for Short (1929)
Silk Stockings (1955)
Holiday for Lovers (1957)
Goldilocks (1958)

13 Daughters (1961)
Henry, Sweet Henry (1967)
Our Town (1989) (revival) [replacement]

Radio Series

The Empire Builders (NBC Blue, 1929–31)
Household Program (NBC Blue, 1930)
The First Nighter (NBC Blue, 1931–37)
Beau Bachelor (CBS, 1932)
Captain Jack (CBS, 1932)
Story Behind the Song (CBS, 1934–35)

The Chase and Sanborn Hour (NBC, c. 1937–1940s)
What's New (NBC Blue, 1943–44)
The Bickersons (NBC, 1946–47; CBS, 1947–48; CBS, 1951)
Your Lucky Strike (CBS, 1948–49)
The Eddie Fisher Show (NBC, 1953)

TV Series

Take a Chance (ABC, 1950)
Holiday Hotel (ABC, 1950–51)
Star Time (Dumont, 1950–51)
Don Ameche's Musical Playhouse (ABC, 1951)
The Frances Langford-Don Ameche Show (ABC, 1951–52)

Coke Time with Eddie Fisher (NBC, 1953)
Don Ameche Theater (CBS, 1958)
Too Young to Go Steady (NBC, 1959)
To Tell the Truth (CBS, c. 1960–61)
International Showtime (NBC, 1961–65)

Album Discography

LPs

Alexander's Ragtime Band (Hollywood Soundstage 406) [ST]
The Bickersons (Col CL-1692/CS-8492) w. Frances Langford
The Bickersons (Radiola 115) w. Frances Langford
The Bickersons Fight Back (Col CL-1883/CS-8683) w. Frances Langford
The Bickersons Rematch (Col G-30523) w. Frances Langford
Don Ameche—Co-Star (Co-Star 112)
Down Argentine Way (Caliban 6003, Hollywood Soundstage 5012) [ST]
The Further Radio Adventures of Larson E. Whipsnade and Other Taradiddles (Col KC-33240) w. W. C. Fields

Goldilocks (Col OL-5340/OS-2007) [OC]
The Great Radio Feuds (Col KC-33241) w. W. C. Fields
Greenwich Village (Caliban 6026) [ST]
Henry, Sweet, Henry (ABC OC/SOC-4) [OC]
Lillian Russell (Caliban 6016) [ST]
Mae West—Original Radio Broadcasts (Mark 56 643)
Mae West on the Chase and Sanborn Hour (Radiola 126)
Moon Over Miami (Caliban 6001) [ST]
The Return of the Bickersons! (Radiola 3MR-4) w. Frances Langford
Silk Stockings (RCA OC-1016, RCA LOC/LSO-1102) [OC]
That Night in Rio (Curtain Calls CC-100/14) [ST]
You Can't Have Everything (Titania 508) [ST]

CDs

Alexander's Ragtime Band (Hollywood Soundstage 4011) [ST]

Best of Radio Comedy: Ozzie & Harriet/The Bickersons (Laserlight 12–689) w. Frances Langford

The Bickersons (Radiola CDMR-1115) w. Frances Langford

Goldilocks (Sony Broadway SK-48222) [OC]

Henry, Sweet, Henry (Varese Sarabande VSD-5631) [OC]

Moon Over Miami/Broadway Melody of 1938 (Great Movie Themes 60030) [ST]

Silk Stockings (RCA Victor 1102-2-R) [OC]

You Can't Have Everything/Go Into Your Dance/You'll Never Get Rich (Great Movie Themes 60014) [ST]

Julie Andrews in *Star!* (1968).
[Courtesy of JC Archives]

Julie Andrews

(b. Julia Elizabeth Wells, October 1, 1935, Walton-on-Thames, Surrey, England)

At the height of her tremendous popularity in the mid-1960s, *Time* magazine effused, "To grown men, Julie Andrews is a lady; to housewives, she's the girl next door; to little children, the most huggable aunt of all. She is a Christmas carol in the snow, a companion by the fire, a laughing clown at charades, and a girl to read poetry to on a cold winter's night." Such high praise was not untypical for this perfect-pitch soprano from England who had sung winningly on Broadway in *The Boy Friend, My Fair Lady*, and *Camelot*. She had gone on to claim an Oscar as the screen's *Mary Poppins* (1964) and followed it with the enormously commercial *The Sound of Music* (1965) and the very successful *Thoroughly Modern Millie* (1967). However, within a few years, as big-budget movie musicals proved unmarketable to the general public, Andrews became a star in desperate search of a proper vehicle. She attempted a TV variety series and a return to films, but they were typically comedies or dramas, and her presence—while still welcome—was often a case of nepotism, because her filmmaker husband (Blake Edwards) was making the project.

Much of the career backlash was not Julie Andrews's fault. It was an instance of an overly successful personality being overhyped by the media. The public eventually grew weary of this "perfect" person who apparently had everything. (As did Julie, who in the 1980s admitted that she had spent years in therapy adjusting to her image, her fame, and her career crises.) For a while Julie chose to devote herself to her family life and other pursuits rather than fight the odds. Despite her continued professionalism, she never quite made that anticipated return to the top. Ironically, she became a more satisfying performer in middle age than in her glory years. She expanded her acting range, and with her mature warmth and strength, she registered far more true as a person and less as a manufactured star.

Andrews was born Julia Elizabeth Wells on October 1, 1935, in Walton-on-Thames in Surrey, England. Her father (Edward C. "Ted" Wells) was a metalcraft teacher, and her mother (Barbara Morris) was an amateur pianist who acted as rehearsal and performance accompanist in her sister Joan's dance school. Because Barbara could not afford a babysitter, Julie, as she became known, was taken along to the dance classes, thus developing an affinity for song and dance early in her life. When she was two, Julie began taking ballet and tap classes from Joan and was soon participating in the school's musical presentations. At age four, Julie's parents divorced, with her younger brother John going to live with her father. Her mother married Canadian-born tenor Ted Andrews (who billed himself as "The Canadian Troubadour: Songs and a Guitar"), and the Andrews moved to London. They began touring the provinces with their act, and in 1943 the family relocated to Beckenham, Kent. The Andrews would have two sons of their own: Donald and Christopher.

Ted Andrews was convinced that young Julie, with her four-and-one-half octave soprano range, had a calling in show business. He arranged for concert singer Madame Lilian Stiles-Allen to train the girl and later for Julie to enroll in a London performing arts school. By 1946, the family had moved back to Walton-on-Thames and Julie was appearing occasionally with her parents' vaudeville act in concert and on radio. In 1947 Ted Andrews introduced Julie to Val Parnell, head of the important Moss Empire theatrical booking circuit. That October she made her professional debut singing the "I Am Titania" aria from the opera *Mignon* by Ambrose Thomas in the Starlight Roof revue at London's Hippodrome Theater. As a result of her excellent reviews, Julie came to the attention of MGM producer Joe Pasternak who considered testing her for a screen career in Hollywood, but had second thoughts. She also met theatrical manager Charles Tucker during the show's run; he would have a strong influence on her budding career. More importantly, she was requested to appear in a Royal Command Performance (November 1, 1948) at the London Palladium for which Danny Kaye headlined the bill. It was also in 1948 that fifteen-year-old Julie met fourteen-year-old Tony Walton (her future husband). She was appearing in *Humpty Dumpty* at the London Casino, and he was in the audience.

In 1950, Julie became a regular performer on the British Broadcasting Company's radio comedy series, *Educating Archie*. It gained instant popularity for her throughout England, and she stayed with the program through 1952. Meanwhile, Julie continued concert appearances (with and without her parents), provided the voice for the princess character in the dubbed version of the Italian-made animated feature *La Rosa di Baghdad* [The Rose of Baghdad], and was much in demand for an array of holiday pantomime productions: *Little Red Riding Hood* (1950), *Jack and the Beanstalk* (1952), and *Cinderella* (1953). It was during the latter—at the London Palladium—that Vida Hope, the director of the hit London musical spoof *The Boy Friend*, visited her backstage and offered her the lead of Polly Browne in the Broadway edition. Julie rejected the assignment initially, despite the protests of her family and Charles Tucker. Instead, she accepted the role of a ruined Southern belle in *Mountain Fire,* which played the provinces in the spring of 1954. When the show closed in August that year, Julie accepted the New York City assignment reluctantly, demanding that her contract be for one year only. Meanwhile, her parents had separated and her own romance with Tony Walton had faltered due to her infatuation with her *Mountain Fire* costar Neil McCallum.

The Americanized *The Boy Friend* opened on Broadway on September 30, 1954, the evening before Julie's nineteenth birthday. The infectious musical caught on immediately, and its ingénue (being paid $400 weekly) became a Broadway figure. It led to television and radio guest appearances for her. Because of her short-term *Boy Friend* contract, Julie was invited to audition for other upcoming Broadway musicals. She was rejected for Rodgers and Hammerstein II's *Pipe Dream* (1955), but won the interest of Alan Jay Lerner and Frederick Loewe who were preparing a musical (*My Fair Lady*) based on George Bernard Shaw's *Pygmalion*. Less than a month before Julie was scheduled to return to England, she was contracted to play the lead female role of Eliza Doolittle opposite Rex Harrison as Professor Henry Higgins. After leaving *The Boy Friend* she joined Bing Crosby in a much-touted television musical special of Maxwell Anderson's fanciful *High Tor* (CBS-TV, March 10, 1956).

Much has been written about the pre-Broadway hazards of transforming *My Fair Lady* into a magical show, and how Julie Andrews was almost discharged for not bringing conviction to her role of the Cockney flower girl who is transformed into an aristocratic lady. Director Moss Hart devoted a full weekend to a crash course of coaching and practice. The drilling worked. *My Fair*

Lady opened on March 15, 1956, at the Mark Hellinger Theater. The show was a smash hit, and Julie was the new toast of Broadway. The *New York Times* enthused, "Miss Andrews acts her part triumphantly," and a few weeks later she was on the cover of *Life* magazine. During the show's run, Julie's weekly salary escalated from $1,000 to $1,250. While in *My Fair Lady* she finally worked with Rodgers and Hammerstein II, this time for their original TV musical *Cinderella* (CBS-TV, March 31, 1957) with Jon Cypher as the Prince. On April 30, 1958, *My Fair Lady* opened at the Drury Lane Theater with Julie and Rex Harrison re-creating their star assignments. Once again they and the show were a major hit. On May 10, 1959, Julie and Tony Walton (now a magazine art designer) were married in Outlander, Waybridge, England, and that August she left the British cast of *My Fair Lady*.

Julie had rejected a small featured role in the film version of George Bernard Shaw's *The Devil's Disciple* (1959) because she wanted a more advantageous assignment for her screen debut. Instead, she agreed to star in Lerner and Loewe's new Broadway musical, based on T. H. White's classic of King Arthur, *The Once and Future King*. *Camelot* was to be a big, lavish production with Richard Burton as the wistful King Arthur and Julie as his Queen Guenevere. The expensively mounted costume show opened on December 3, 1960, to mixed reviews but to a solid ($3 million) advance sale. Andrews again enjoyed impressive reviews. Meanwhile, her husband, Tony Walton, was successful as the costume designer for the Broadway comedy hit, *A Funny Thing Happened on the Way to the Forum*. One of Julie's most engaging performances occurred when she teamed with friend Carol Burnett in the CBS-TV special *Julie and Carol at Carnegie Hall* (June 11, 1962). Each played delightfully against type and worked extremely well together. The show received an Emmy as Best Musical Program. On November 27, 1962, in London, Julie gave birth to Emma Kate Walton.

Julie Andrews's first major career setback occurred when Warner Bros. studio head Jack L. Warner hired Audrey Hepburn (a non-singer) to star in the movie of *My Fair Lady* (1964). Walt Disney was wise enough, however, to sign Andrews to play the lovable, flying nanny in *Mary Poppins* (1964), his screen musical based on the series of children's books by Pamela (P. L.) Travers. It caught filmgoers' fancy and became an enormous box-office champion. (The LP album from *Mary Poppins* won a Grammy Award as Best Album for Children.) More importantly, in the Oscar race, Julie won the Best Actress Award. When she received the Golden Globe Award as Best Actress for the same movie, she quipped, "My thanks to Jack L. Warner for making all this possible." By now she had already signed for two additional pictures. *The Americanization of Emily* (1964) was a stark, satirical antiwar entry that cast Andrews in a dramatic role opposite flippant James Garner. Neither she (being too stiff) nor the picture were liked by the public. Fortunately, her next picture was a commercial bonanza. Robert Wise's *The Sound of Music* (1965) was an expansion of Rodgers and Hammerstein II's Broadway megahit that had starred Mary Martin. Julie was just right as the irrepressible Sister Maria caught up in romance and strife in World War II Austria while tending a flock of motherless children. Her renditions of "The Sound of Music" and "My Favorite Things" helped to make the film the highest-grossing feature up to that time, and its film soundtrack became the best-selling LP to that date, superseding the Broadcast cast recording of *My Fair Lady*.

Hoping to break her mold as the screen's prim miss, Julie made *Torn Curtain* (1966), an Alfred Hitchcock Cold War thriller. It is most noteworthy for the scene that finds Andrews in bed with costar Paul Newman. For *Hawaii* (1967), based on portions of James Michener's historical epic novel, Julie was the 1820s' New England girl who weds a religious fundamentalist (Max Von Sydow) and sails for Hawaii. She sang the Academy Award–nominated song "My Wishing Doll" in the course of the melodrama. Neither project lived up to expectation. By this time she was separated from her husband and was dating producer/director Blake Edwards. In addition, she had begun work on her third screen musical, Ross Hunter's *Thoroughly Modern Millie* (1967). In this 1920s' lark, she sang, danced, and performed slapstick, abetted by Carol Channing, Beatrice Lillie, and Mary Tyler Moore. The picture was a big earner, and for the third year (1967) in a row, Julie was named the top box-office attraction in the United States. Unknowingly, her career had peaked.

Andrews reunited with *The Sound of Music* director Robert Wise for *Star!* (1968) at Twentieth Century-Fox. The magic was gone, and this $12 million biography of British stage star Gertrude Lawrence failed to recoup its cost. It was later reedited to remove many of the song numbers. Her downward career trend continued in Blake Edwards's *Darling Lili* (1970), a $16.7 million spoof of World War I espionage with Rock Hudson as Julie's vis-à-vis. Edwards blamed its failure on the studio's massive editing; the truth was the public had tired of musicals. In the interim, Julie married Edwards on November 12, 1969, in Beverly Hills. He had two children by a prior marriage.

Movie musicals and Julie on-screen had become passé, and MGM shelved plans to star her in *She Loves Me* (based on the Broadway show) and *Say It With Music*. However, there was still television. She was seen on *An Evening With Julie Andrews and Harry Belafonte* (NBC-TV, November 9, 1969) and then enjoyed a return matching with Miss Burnett in *Julie and Carol at Lincoln Center* (CBS-TV, December 7, 1971). Less popular was her *The Julie Andrews Hour*, a variety format teleseries produced by England's Sir Lew Grade. The show debuted on ABC-TV in September 1972, and despite a roster of top guest stars, good reviews, and several Emmy Awards, the program was cancelled after one season. As part of her deal with Grade she starred in *The Tamarind Seed* (1974), a tepid spy romance with Omar Sharif. By now Julie and Edwards had relocated to Switzerland, with a London house as well. They would adopt two Vietnamese children, Amy and Joanne. Andrews authored two children's books: *Mandy* (1971) and *The Last of the Really Great Whangdoodles* (1974), which traded more on her star reputation than on their contents. There were a series of specials, and in 1976 she had a popular concert stand at the London Palladium, followed by a not-so-well-liked cabaret engagement in Las Vegas the same year. A 1977 concert tour took her across the United States and to Japan.

Except for providing the off-camera voice for the song "Until You Love Me" for a sequence in Blake Edwards's *The Pink Panther Strikes Again* (1976)—she was billed as Ainsley Jarvis—Julie had been off the screen for five years. She returned in her husband's comedy hit *10* (1979). Charming as she was, it was costars Dudley Moore and Bo Derek who received the most attention. In the fourth screen version of *Little Miss Marker* (1980) she was in definite support of Walter Matthau and moppet actress Sara Stimson, and for a change she was not directed by her husband. *S.O.B.* (1981) was Edwards's long-festering attack against Hollywood for the fate of *Darling Lili*. It was biting, bitter, and sometimes hilarious. Its plot premise required Julie to bare her breasts on-screen.

Much more popular was *Victor/Victoria* (1982) in which Andrews played an actress masquerading as a man who plays a woman onstage. She sang "The Shady Dame From Seville," "Le Jazz Hot," "Crazy World," and dueted "You and Me" with Robert Preston. She received a Best Actress Academy Award nomination, and it seemed as if her career was now on an upturn. However, this judgment was premature. She was a patient psychiatrist in Burt Reynolds's *The Man Who Loved Women* (1983) and was again under Edwards's aegis in the overlooked *That's Life* (1986), in which she sparkled as the patient wife of self-centered Jack Lemmon. (Both her daughter Emma and her stepchild Jennifer appeared in the picture.) Andrews was reunited with *Hawaii* costar Max Von Sydow in *Duet for One* (1986), which featured stark theatrics about a lady cellist suffering from multiple sclerosis. Nothing seemed to revive her star impetus.

In 1987, Andrews made another concert tour of major U.S. cities and continued to appear in occasional TV specials (her 1987 Christmas outing won an Emmy) and guest appearances (such as the *American Film Institute Salute* to Jack Lemmon in 1988). Plans to translate *Victor/Victoria* to the stage fell through at this time, while talk of a London revival of *Lady in the Dark* continued to surface. In the late 1980s she hoped to make a film based on the story of Yvette Pierppaoli, the French woman who helped war-torn children in 1966 Cambodia. In 1989 she cut an album—*Love, Julie*—in which critics found a new sexiness to her voice as she sang such standards as "Tea for Two," "How Deep Is the Ocean," and "Come Rain or Come Shine." In the spring of 1989 she recorded a special Christmas album for Hallmark Cards with the London Symphony Orchestra as well as taping a new holiday special. In Los Angeles in June 1989, Andrews and Carol Burnett taped a new special for ABC-TV, and then Andrews embarked on a six-week series of concerts. The *Love, Julie* tour (which was taped for a PBS-TV telecast in early 1990) included a two-night engagement at Hollywood's Greek Theater in late July 1989. It was her first Los Angeles solo concert in a decade. She told the press: "Now, I can't do the coloratura any more. But my voice was so quiet and thin then [as a young performer]—now it's mature, and I can do more varied things with it."

With her husband and children as major priorities, Julie and the Edwards family continued to reside at their villa in Gstaad, Switzerland. But her presence continued to be a force on (American) TV. On December 13, 1989, the ABC-TV network aired *Julie and Carol: Together Again*, the third matching of Andrews and Burnett in a television special, which was well received. In the controversial TV movie *Our Sons* (ABC-TV, May 19, 1991) Julie and Ann-Margret were cast as two contrasting types of women/mothers whose sons (played by Hugh Grant and Zeljiko Ivanek, respectively) are lovers, with Ivanek's character dying of AIDS. The *Hollywood Reporter* concluded of this well-intentioned telefeature: "While Andrews and Ann-Margret go about their jobs with praiseworthy finesse, not even their performances can triumph over *Our Sons'* overwrought manner." Also in 1991 Andrews was seen in *A Fine Romance* (1991) based on a West End/Broadway play *Tchin Tchin*. The faltering farce teamed her with Italy's Marcello Mastroianni but received little distribution or public interest.

The songster had long wanted to try another television series, and after many starts and stops she did a sitcom entitled *Julie*. The trouble-plagued sitcom presented her as a TV variety show star who quits lush Beverly Hills to wed a Sioux City, Iowa veterinarian/widow. Dropped several times from the CBS network lineup, it finally debuted on May 30, 1992. *Daily Variety* judged: "Andrews exudes graciousness under pressure; otherwise, *Julie* is just another sitcom with a gimmick." *TV Guide* was more forthright in its assessment, describing it as "something that came out of a time capsule buried around 1972." To no one's surprise the lackluster property faded from sight as of July 4, 1992.

Reaching out in new directions, Julie headlined a musical revue (*Putting It Together*) an off-Broadway show that opened April 1, 1993, at the Manhattan Theater Club in New York City.

The show was a composite of Stephen Sondheim songs and was so eagerly anticipated that scalpers were charging as much as $750 for a pair of tickets. The production received high marks from the critics and theatergoers. Meanwhile Andrews had recorded *The King and I* (with Ben Kingsley as the King) in 1992. Although the Phillips label release received mixed reviews, it was a bestseller and led to such other albums as *The Music of Richard Rodgers* (1994) and *Here I'll Stay: The Words of Alan Jay Lerner* (1996). In talking with the press she noted that she had undergone psychotherapy for years to deal better with a childhood that was devoted to the stage. She claimed to have gained stability and security through her lengthy marriage to Blake Edwards. She also noted about her British reserve: "I think somewhere I'm probably rather shy. I guess I don't want to impose on my family. When you're in the public eye, I think it's very hard for them. I'm always trying to protect them. I just hope that through my music, you'll know who I am."

On October 25, 1995, Andrews was the subject of a PBS-TV special titled *Julie Andrews: Back on Broadway*. The show's title referred to her finally bringing *Victor/Victoria* to the New York stage. After many false starts and dealing with the death of songwriter Henry Mancini (who had written the musical's score), *Victor/Victoria* was translated into a stage musical, with additional songs by Fran Wildhorn with Leslie Bricusse. With direction by Blake Edwards, it featured Tony Roberts and Michael Nouri respectively in the Robert Preston and James Garner roles from the 1982 movie version. While many critics severely panned the production (but not Andrews's vivacity and charm in front of the footlights) when it opened in October 1995, the vehicle was, nevertheless, a huge hit because of Julie's drawing power. When she was nominated for a Tony award for her *Victor/Victoria* performance, she refused to accept her nomination because other key talents in her stage production were not so cited. Julie's audacity made headlines, especially when she won the award as Best Actress in a Musical. (While the Queen of Broadway was not present at the June 2, 1996, Tony broadcast, actor Nathan Lane stopped the prize-giving show in its tracks when he came out onstage dressed in a copy of Julie's key *Victor/Victoria* costume.) In spring 1996, after days of suffering in silence so she would not miss any performances of her stage show, Andrews was hospitalized for an emergency gallbladder surgery. Thereafter, her fragile health (including laryngitis) led to her leaving the production on June 8, 1997. (Raquel Welch took over the lead, but the show closed soon thereafter.)

Soon after departing her Broadway vehicle, Andrews underwent surgery to remove noncancerous throat nodules. After the operation she discovered she had "lost" her singing voice. The star kept the information quiet until it was (accidentally) revealed to the media by Edwards. As the result of the severe trauma of her career-threatening throat condition, she underwent grief therapy at an Arizona rehab clinic and also sued the New York surgeons who had performed the medical procedure on her. (The case ended in 2000 with a huge settlement in Julie's favor.)

While working to retrain her singing voice, Andrews teamed yet again with James Garner, this time for the TV movie *One Special Night* (CBS-TV, November 28, 1999), which concerned two contrasting strangers who meet on a cold winter's night. The *New York Times* reported of the duo: "Time (and other interventions) may have rearranged their familiar faces a little, but these actors can slip so easily into their expected personals—she's a bit too flinty for her own good; he's a bit too pigheaded for his—that you'll be charmed." By the time that telefeature aired she had filmed another movie, *Relative Values* (2000), based on a 1951 Noël Coward play. (It opened to lukewarm notices in England.) Julie had also published her third children's book, *Little Bo: The Story of Bonnie Boadicia*, and was at work on her memoirs. (Her next children's book, *Little Bo in*

France, appeared in spring 2002.) By this juncture Andrews and Edwards were frequently living apart.

In 2000 the home-video edition of 1995's *Victor/Victoria*, made originally for Japanese pay-per-view TV, was released in home video/DVD in the United States. In December 2000, PBS-TV aired a concert (*Leading Ladies of Broadway*), which was shot on September 28, 1998, at Carnegie Hall. Andrews hosted the star-studded event. She did similar chores on *My Favorite Broadway: The Love Songs*, which played for one night (October 18, 2000) at New York's City Center Theater and which was broadcast in 2001. Meanwhile on May 16, 2000, Andrews attended a ceremony at Buckingham Palace where she was made a dame commander of the Order of the British Empire. Having retained her British citizenship while living in the United States for many years, she told the English press: "What a thrill to be honored by your own country, to get a recognition of some kind . . . I consider myself English first and foremost and am very, very proud to be so."

Turning to TV again, Andrews joined with her *The Sound of Music* colead Christopher Plummer in a live performance of the Broadway play/Hollywood movie *On Golden Pond* that aired on CBS-TV on April 29, 2001. The *New York Times* observed that the costars "with admirable finesse, brought a crisp astringency to the proceedings, which made the play's sentimentality bearable." Far better received was the Walt Disney Studio comedy *The Princess Diaries* (2001), in which Andrews appeared as a queen who must ensure that her granddaughter (Anne Hathaway) accepts her royal birthright. The Garry Marshall–directed G-rated comedy did extremely well at the box office (grossing over $108 million in domestic distribution) and earned Julie excellent notices. Next, Julie joined Rupert Everett, Kathy Bates, and Lynn Redgrave for *Who Shot Victor Fox* (2002), a tale of the repercussions when a pop star is murdered. On December 2, 2001, Julie was among the quintet (which also included actor Jack Nicholson and composer/music producer Quincy Jones) to receive the prestigious twenty-fourth annual Kennedy Center Honors. The event was televised on December 26, 2001. In 2002, besides her acting chores, Andrews was arranging to have her own book imprint at a major publisher for a children's book series, was planning to produce a TV film, and was hoping to try directing (in the theater).

Still praying that her famed singing voice would eventually return, Andrews said that if it did not, "I think it will change something inside me forever." Nevertheless, her standard still remains to be "an original, to be myself and not a pale copy of anyone else." As Julie once stated, "Hopefully, one never stops growing and learning. I'd like to lose certain restrictions I put on myself when I work, be able to loosen up a little bit more, be a little bit easier in my skin at times. My passion all my life has been to do as much that is varied as possible. So, inasmuch as there's a lot out there that I haven't tried, I guess you could say that's my goal."

Filmography

Rose of Baghdad (La Rosa di Bagdad/The Singing Princess) (Artisti Associati, 1952) (voice) (U.S. release by Trans National in 1967)
Mary Poppins (BV, 1964)
The Americanization of Emily (MGM, 1964)
The Sound of Music (20th-Fox, 1965)
Torn Curtain (Univ, 1966)
Hawaii (UA, 1967)
Thoroughly Modern Millie (Univ, 1967)

Star! (20th-Fox, 1968)
Darling Lily (Par, 1970)
The Tamarind Seed (Avco Emb, 1974)
The Pink Panther Strikes Again (UA, 1976) (voice)
10 (Orion, 1979)
Little Miss Marker (Univ, 1980)
S.O.B. (Par, 1981)
Victor/Victoria (MGM, 1982)
The Man Who Loved Women (Col, 1983)

That's Life! (Col, 1986)
Duet for One (Cannon, 1986)
Our Sons (ABC-TV, 5/19/91)
A Fine Romance [Cin Cin] (Castle Hill, 1992)
Victor/Victoria (Image Entertainment, 1995) (direct to video)

One Special Night (CBS-TV, 11/28/99)
Relative Values (Alliance Atlantic, 2000)
On Golden Pond (CBS-TV, 4/29/2001)
The Princess Diaries (BV, 2001)
Who Shot Victor Fox (New Line, 2002)

Broadway Plays

The Boy Friend (1954)
My Fair Lady (1956)

Camelot (1960)
Victor/Victoria (1995)

TV Series

The Julie Andrews Hour (ABC, 1972–73)

Julie (ABC, 1992)

Album Discography

LPs

The Boy Friend (RCA LOC-1018) [OC]
Broadway's Fair Julie (Col CL/CS-1712)
Camelot (Col KOL/KOS-5620) [OC]
Christmas Treasure (RCA LPM/LSP/3829)
Christmas With Julie Andrews (RCA PRS-290)
Cinderella (Col OL-OS/2005) [ST/TV]
Darling Lili (RCA LSPX-1000) [ST]
Don't Go into the Lion's Cage Tonight (Col CL/CS-8686)
An Evening With Julie Andrews (RCA SX-281) [released in Japan only]
Firestone Presents Your Favorite Christmas Carols, Starring Julie Andrews (Firestone SLP-7012/MLP-7012)
Hawaii (UA-LA283) [ST]
High Tor (Decca DL-8272) [ST/TV]
Julie and Carol at Carnegie Hall (Col OL-5840) w. Carol Burnett [ST/TV]
Julie and Carol at Lincoln Center (Col S3115) w. Carol Burnett [ST/TV]
Julie Andrews (RCA ANL1-1098)
Julie Andrews Sings (RCA LPM/LSP-1681)

The Lass With the Delicate Air (RCA LPM/LSP-1403)
A Little Bit in Love (Har H-30021)
Love, Julie (USA JA)
Love Me Tender (Julie 1)
Mary Poppins (Buena Vista 4026) [ST]
My Fair Lady (Col OL-5090/OS-2015) [OC]
The Pink Panther Strikes Again (UA UA-LA-694-G) [ST] (billed as Ainsley Jarvis)
Rose Marie (RCA LOP/LSO-1001)
Secret of Christmas (Embassy 31237/31522)
Silver-Voiced Super Star (Suffolk Marketing)
The Sound of Music (RCA LSOD/LSPD-2005) [ST]
Star! (20th Century-Fox 5102) [ST]
The Story Behind "My Fair Lady" (Radiola 1122)
Tell It Again (Angel 65041) w. Martyn Green
"10" (WB BSK-3399) [ST]
Thoroughly Modern Millie (Decca DL-71500, MCA 1723) [ST]
TV's Fair Julie (Har KH-31958)
Victor/Victoria (MGM MG-1–5407) [ST]
The World of Julie Andrews (Col KG-31970)

CDs

The Best of Julie Andrews: Thoroughly Modern Julie (Rhino R2-72881)
The Boy Friend (RCA 60056-2-RG) [OC]
Broadway: The Music of Richard Rodgers (Philips 442603-2)
Broadway's Fair Julie/Heartrendering Ballad and Raucous Ditties (Musicrama 78822)
Camelot (Col CK-32602) [OC]
A Christmas Treasure (RCA 3829-2-R, BMG Special Products 44685) w. Andre Previn

Christmas With Julie Andrews (Col 4891862, Legacy CK-65940)
Cinderella (Col CK-02005) (ST/TV)
Classic Julie Classic Broadway (Uptown/Univ 468593)
Come Rain or Shine (Going for a Song) [no additional data available]
Darling Lili (RCA 74321-66500-2) [ST]
Doctor Doolittle (First Night Cast 68) [OC]
Greatest Christmas Songs (RCA 07863-67971-2, Camden 74321-77871-2)

Here I'll Stay: The Words of Alan J. Lerner (Philips 446-219)

The King and I (Philips 438007-2) [OC]

Love, Julie (Prestige Elite 5000, USA Music Group 539) w. Bob Florence

Mary Poppins (Walt Disney 60842-2) [ST]

My Fair Lady (CBS CK-02015, Col CK-05090, Legacy CK-66128) [OC]

Putting It Together (RCA 09026-61729-2) [OC]

Relative Values (Silva Screen FILMCD-337) [ST]

The Sound of Music (RCA 07863-66587-2, RCA 07863-66588-2) [ST]

Star! (Fox 07822-11009-2)

Tea for Two (Hallmark 309522)

Thoroughly Modern Millie (MCA MCAD-10062) [ST]

Victor/Victoria (GNP Crescendo GNPD-8038) [ST]

Victor/Victoria (Philips 446-919-2) [OC]

Lee Bowman (far left, standing), Maxene, Patty, and LaVerne Andrews, and Alan Curtis (far right, standing) in *Buck Privates* (1941). [Courtesy of JC Archives]

The Andrews Sisters

(LaVerne, b. July 6, 1911; d. May 8, 1967, Brentwood, California. Maxene, b. January 3, 1916; d. October 22, 1995, Hyannis, Massachusetts. Patricia [Patty], b. February 16, 1918. All born in Minneapolis, Minnesota.)

Sister acts have long been an intriguing show-business staple. There were the Cherry Sisters, the Dolly Sisters, and the Duncan Sisters in vaudeville; the sisters Boswell, Dinning, King, and DeMarco on radio; and on television, the Lennons and McGuires. But when harmonizing siblings are discussed, the group that comes to mind immediately is the Andrews Sisters. During the Swing Era (late-1930s to mid-1940s), they were the reigning jive queens of song. They were natural singers, solid musicians, and always fun. They performed in many types of media: radio, cabarets, recordings, and in several motion pictures, becoming an indelible symbol of the World War II years.

Viewing their mostly low-budget feature films today may be an experience in true camp, but despite their unstylish outfits, frizzy coiffures, and naive dramatics, the Andrews Sisters' gusto and harmonics remain supreme. Their distinctive vocal blend carried them through years of tremendous popularity, and when in the early 1970s, Bette Midler rerecorded their famous "Boogie Woogie Bugle Boy of Company B," a whole new generation developed a fascination with the distinctive singing sisters. Here was a group who really knew how to sell a song. As Maxene once detailed, "Until we came along, all harmony groups put their heads together to get a blend, and because music was such a part of our lives, we had to move! We were the first harmony group that ever moved onstage. Other groups just sang."

The Andrews Sisters came of immigrant stock. Their Greek father (Peter) and Norwegian mother (Olga "Ollie" Sollie) operated the Pure Food Café on Hennepin Avenue in Minneapolis, Minnesota. LaVerne was born on July 6, 1911; Maxene on January 3, 1916; and Patricia (Patty) on February 16, 1918. The little girls spent a great deal of time at a vaudeville theater that was located near the little restaurant while their parents worked at the café. Mrs. Andrews came from a musical background and instilled a love of song and dance into her daughters. LaVerne, who had learned to play the piano, paid for the sisters' dancing lessons by playing for the sessions. (Over the years, only LaVerne of the sisters could read music.) It was from listening to the Boswell Sisters (with Bing Crosby) on the radio that LaVerne picked up songs that she then taught to her sisters. The girls entered kiddie talent contests. Among the several competitions they won was first prize at Minneapolis's Orpheum Theater on the same bill with a then-unknown ventriloquist named Edgar Bergen. In the audience one night was bandleader Larry Rich who, months later, hired the girls to perform with his troupe. They toured with his orchestra, performing on the vaudeville circuit and living in cheap theater hotels. Although they were paid next to nothing, they learned the art of putting over a song and winning audiences' enthusiastic attention.

After eighteen months with Larry Rich, the trio joined Joe E. Howard's vaudeville act and later, in the mid-1930s, sang with Ted Mack's band. While singing in Chicago at nightclubs, they were heard by Leon Belasco, who signed the trio, at $225 a week, to sing with his band. With the Belasco unit the Andrews Sisters made their first recordings on Brunswick Records on March 18, 1937, singing "Jammin'," "There's a Lull in My Life," "Turn Off the Moon," and "Wake Up and Live." Later, while performing at the Mayfair Hotel in Kansas City, a fire backstage destroyed the band's equipment, costumes, and arrangements. Belasco quit the band business and became a character actor in films. The girls, in turn, decided to try New York City. Their father sold the family restaurant to finance the expedition, and the parents soon relocated to Manhattan to be with their ambitious daughters.

Accepting any and every play date they could muster, the sisters managed a radio assignment at $15 weekly with the Billy Swanson Band, which was broadcast from the Hotel Edison. They were fired after two air dates. However, two men had heard them performing "Sleepy Time Down South": Dave Kapp (who, along with his brother Jack, operated Decca Records) and struggling booking agent Lou Levy. Levy brought the sisters to Decca Records, where they were signed to a recording contract ($50 per record with no royalties). Their initial Decca session on October 18, 1937, produced "Just a Simple Melody" and "Why Talk About Love?" The results were negligible, but the next session proved to be their breakthrough.

By now Levy had abandoned his other clients, and he taught the girls the lyrics to an old Yiddish song, "Bei Mir Bist Du Schoen." He convinced the Kapp Brothers to record it with "Joseph, Joseph" on the flip side. That 78 rpm was not released because the Kapps wanted a more universal approach to the lead song. Sammy Cahn was hired to prepare English lyrics for "Bei Mir Bist Du Schoen," and on November 24, 1937, the sisters cut the record for Decca with "Nice Work If You Can Get It" as the new flip side. "Bei Mir Bist Du Schoen" made the team an overnight hit, and the sisters were given a new Decca contract that paid them from 2¢ to 5¢ royalty on each disc sold. The Andrews Sisters would remain with Decca Records for almost seventeen years. They would record over four hundred songs that would collectively sell over eighty million records. (For the record, LaVerne was the tall, quiet redhead on the right; Patty was the blonde lead singer in the center, who belted out the tunes and provided the barrelhouse comedy; and Maxene, on the left, was the snappy brunette, considered the prettiest of the group.)

Lou Levy continued to pick hits for his sensational client team. With Vic Schoen providing customized (brassy) arrangements, the Andrews Sisters turned out pop hit after pop hit for Decca, including "The Beer Barrel Polka, "Hold Tight, Hold Tight," and "Well, All Right." They were guest performers on several major radio programs and quickly became an American institution.

As America moved closer to World War II, Hollywood began a resurgence of diversionary musical movies. The studio that churned out the most—even though in low-budget, assembly-line fashion—was Universal (which later absorbed Decca Records). Through Decca's Jack Kapp, who was friendly with Universal Pictures' head, Nate Blumberg, the Andrews Sisters were hired by this studio where Deanna Durbin reigned as the singing star. Without any preparation, they were tossed into their debut picture, *Argentine Nights* (1940). They portrayed an impoverished singing trio who, abetted by their managers (the Ritz Brothers), head south of the border to avoid their creditors. The quickie production was trite and pretty awful (Argentina banned the film and the *Harvard Lampoon* named it the most frightening movie of the year), but the Andrews Sisters were sensational in their singing. They performed "Hit the Road," "Oh, He Loves Me," and

"Rhumboogie," which they later recorded for Decca. Giving audiences the chance to see the fun sisters on-screen certainly boosted their record sales. Later in the year they had top recordings of "Beat Me Daddy, Eight to the Bar," "I'll Be With You in Apple Blossom Time" (which became their signature song), and "Mean to Me."

The year 1941 found the sisters in three films with the comedy team of Bud Abbott and Lou Costello. *Buck Privates* was the movie that made Abbott and Costello a big success. In this laugh fest, the Andrews Sisters provided musical interludes, singing "Bounce Brother, With a Solid Four," "You're a Lucky Fellow, Mr. Smith," and one of the sisters' greatest hits, "Boogie Woogie Bugle Boy From Company B." After recording all these tunes for Decca, the trio joined Abbott and Costello for *In the Navy*, along with crooner Dick Powell, and sang three undistinguished numbers, including "Hula Ba Lua." Their next assignment with Abbott and Costello was *Hold That Ghost*, in which they delivered zesty renditions of "Aurora" and "Sleepy Serenade."

With Patty singing the leads, LaVerne reading the music for the group, and Maxene explaining, "We sing what we feel—from the heart," their professional momentum continued unabated. There were more guest-starring assignments on radio variety shows, record-breaking engagements at New York's Paramount Theater, personal appearances throughout the United States, and in March 1941, Maxene married the trio's manager, Lou Levy.

Their lively, if unsophisticated, film romps continued. *What's Cookin'?* (1942) was a bit of nonsense about youngsters wanting to break into show business with the sisters three doing "What to Do?" *Private Buckaroo* (1942), was a celluloid jam session uniting the singing team with Harry James and His Music Makers, giving the Andrews Sisters occasion to harmonize on "Three Little Sisters" and "Don't Sit Under the Apple Tree With Anyone Else But Me" (which became one of their quintessential theme songs). In *Give Out, Sisters* (1942) they harmonized on "The Pennsylvania Polka," which became one of their prime hit tunes.

Between performing at military bases both in the United States and, later, in France and Italy, and embarking on war bond tours, the sisters made two 1943 releases including *How's About It?* in which they socked across "The Beer Barrel Polka." In 1944, the sisters were at their most prolific, with four releases. Among their projects were the celebrity-packed *Hollywood Canteen* (at Warner Bros.). In the tuneful mini-Western *Moonlight and Cactus*, they wore cowgirl garb and put across such numbers as "Send Me a Man, Amen."

World War II ended in 1945, and so did the Andrews Sisters' contract with Universal. The studio had never figured out how to use them effectively on-screen; their costuming, makeup, and hairstyles were generally atrocious. Having exploited them, the company now dropped them. (According to the team, they dropped the studio, finding a loophole in their contract and getting even for the studio's refusal to let them move over to Twentieth Century-Fox.) Despite their movie interlude, the Andrews Sisters remained extremely popular through their recordings and their radio series, the *Eight-to-the-Bar Ranch*. The latter had begun broadcasting over the ABC network in 1944 and moved to CBS for the 1945–46 season.

Back in 1944 they had recorded vocal backing ("Johnny Fedora and Alice Blue Bonnet") for the "A Love Story" segment of Walt Disney's cartoon feature *Make Mine Music!*, which was released finally in 1946. The next year they were featured, attractively photographed, in a shipboard sequence of Paramount's *The Road to Rio* (1947). They sang "You Don't Have to Know the Language." Their song mate was crooner Bing Crosby, with whom they had first teamed on Decca Records on September 20, 1939, singing "Cirbiribin" and "Yodelin' Jive" backed by Joe Venuti's orchestra. Despite the success of that hit record, it was not until late 1943 that song stylist Crosby was reunited with the sisters for "Pistol Packin' Mama." Thereafter, they were heard together frequently on radio and on records, with their final waxing sessions being "Cool Water" and "South Rampart Street Parade" on September 5, 1952. (The Andrews Sisters also would perform often in the 1940s with Dick Haymes and with Guy Lombardo and His Orchestra.)

In 1948 the Andrews Sisters repeated their voice-over chores for Walt Disney in his animated *Melody Time*, this time singing "Little Toot" in the segment about a little tugboat heroically saving a big steamer from a heavy storm. That year LaVerne married Lou Rogers, and their mother, Ollie Andrews, died (followed shortly thereafter by their father's passing). Meanwhile, they and their arranger Vic Schoen split. During September 1948 Maxene and Lou Levy separated, and they divorced in March 1949. Meanwhile, in 1949, Patty had a solo record hit with "I Can Dream, Can't I?" Also in 1949, in August, Patty separated from agent Martin Melcher, whom she had wed in October 1947. (They divorced in March 1950, and the next year he wed Doris Day.)

During 1950 the Andrews Sisters went to London for a successful Palladium engagement. Maxene and Lou Levy divorced, with Maxene being awarded custody of their children Peter and Aleda Ann. When Maxene underwent major surgery in 1951, Patty and LaVerne completed their prearranged bookings, appearing as a duo for the first time. Lou Levy continued as their agent, with Maxene explaining, "We love our work too much to break up, and each of us has too great an investment to sacrifice it. We sisters are a corporation, with Lou and each of us owning an equal amount of stock." On Christmas Day 1951 Patty wed Walter Wechsler, the group's accompanist, and that same week the sisters played Las Vegas.

There had been rumors of strife between the Andrews Sisters for years, and in 1954, Patty devised her own act with Wechsler. She signed with Capitol Records. That November Patty brought legal action against LaVerne (who had received one-half of her mother's estate; in contrast to Patty and Maxene's one-fourth share), demanding a proper settlement of the estate. The court denied Patty's suit. On December 21, Maxene was in the headlines for an apparent suicide attempt brought on by the family discord. Maxene denied it, and LaVerne insisted, "She loves life too much to want to end it!"

Thereafter, the sisters reunited, broke up, and reunited again for recording, club, and television sessions, but their popularity had peaked. When LaVerne developed cancer, Patty and Maxene performed as a duo (sometimes as a trio using Joyce DeYoung) and on May 8, 1967, LaVerne died at her Brentwood, California, home, survived by her husband Lou Rogers. The next year Maxene retired to teach in the Drama and Speech Department of Nevada's Tahoe Paradise College, becoming dean of women there. Patty continued in show business, explaining, "Show business is my life. I'll never leave it!" She teamed with Lucille Ball and Lucie Arnaz to make a new singing trio on an episode of the *Here's Lucy* show, and she was among the veteran personalities trapped in the *The Phynx* (1970), concocted as part of the nostalgia craze by Warner Bros. In 1971, Patty was contracted for the stage musical *Victory Canteen*, which opened at Hollywood's Ivar Theater on January 27, 1971. "I've never done a book show before," she told the press. "It's one phase of show business we promised each other we'd never do. I'm not worried about it, though. I was always the one doing the talking when the sisters worked and that was like doing a show. Musically too, I'm right at home. This is a play about the '40s and canteen life. Well, let me tell you, we lived it." The show soon folded.

In the early 1970s, Bette Midler's dynamic renditions (onstage and on record) of "Boogie Woogie Bugle Boy from Company B" and "In the Mood" refocused American audiences—including the younger set—on the unique talent that was the Andrews Sisters. Their recordings received new popularity in yet more reissues, and Kenneth Waissman and Maxine Fox, who had produced *Victory Canteen*, developed a new book show (by Will Holt) entitled *Over Here!* Both Maxene and Patty joined the musical comedy, which had a long shakedown on the road and opened on Broadway on March 6, 1974. Looking a bit plumper than in their heyday, but still peppy and in wonderful voice, they trucked, boogied, and harmonized through numbers like "The Big Beat," "We Got It!," and "Wartime Wedding." However, the highlight of the evening came after the final curtain when the two sisters appeared onstage in shimmering gowns and Patty bubbled to the audience, "Do you want to hear some of the old ones?" *Over Here!* closed in January 1975, but a projected road tour of the musical hit was cancelled because the two sisters were feuding with the producers. Later they agreed to re-create the show for summer stock. They announced plans to do an autobiography of their career, but it never appeared.

In the mid-1970s both Maxene and Patty were living in Encino, California, but neither sister was speaking to one another, although neither one would admit to the exact nature of the rift. Patty and her husband Wechsler began working on their own act again, and Maxene reconsidered—once more—retirement. However, in 1979 she thought again about having a solo career and began experimenting in the recording studios again. She tested her solo club act (which included a slide show tracing the trio's career) at Reno Sweeney's in New York. *Variety* reported: "Andrews is a pro. She knows how to involve the crowd with song as well as with spoken word, as she has a distinguished musical background. The session is both pleasant and rousing." Also in Manhattan the solo Andrews performed at the Copacabana and the Bottom Line. Meanwhile, not to be outdone, Patty showcased her own club in New York at Les Mouches in Manhattan in winter 1980. When interviewed by the press at this time, Patty insisted it was Maxene who had caused a splinter between the sisters, while in her own interview, Maxene stressed she had made several attempts at a reconciliation.

In the early 1980s both Maxene and Patty continued their separate cabaret performing around the United States. In addition, Patty teamed with various groupings of show-business veterans—including Eartha Kitt, Lainie Kazan, Vivian Blaine, and Dorothy Lamour—for club revues. In August 1982 Maxene suffered a near-fatal heart attack and underwent quadruple-bypass surgery. Always the trooper, five weeks later she was performing in Denver. "I had a desire to continue singing," she said. "It's the only thing I know how to do. Singing is my whole life." Maxene's solo album *Maxene—An Andrews Sister*, appeared in 1985, and thereafter the two surviving sisters—singly, never together—were seen occasionally on TV nostalgia documentaries syndicated on the PBS network. A rare occasion where the two siblings were at the same place at the same time occurred on October 1, 1987, when the sisters received their star on Hollywood's Walk of Fame. The occasion was to commemorate their fifty years in the recording field. That same year Maxene was bestowed the Medal for Distinguished Pubic Service, a high honor from the U.S. government. In early 1989 Maxene sold her Encino home and moved closer to Nevada.

In 1993 there appeared the anecdotal book *Over Here, Over There: The Andrews Sisters and the USO Stars in World War II*, authored by Maxene along with Bill Gilbert. In fall 1995 Maxene performed for a month at the Blue Angel club in New York in a revue she called *Swingtime Canteen*. When her engagement ended, she agreed to return to the venue to perform during the December holidays. After flying to Honolulu to participate in ceremonies denoting the fiftieth anniversary of V-J Day, Maxene vacationed on Cape Cod. There, on October 22, 1995, she died of a massive heart attack at a hospital in Hyannis, Massachusetts. She was seventy-nine years old. Patty, who had mostly retired, occasionally performed—with her husband as her pianist/conductor—on cruise lines for their nostalgia cabaret shows. In fall 1998, the Andrews Sisters were inducted into the Vocal Group Hall of Fame. Patty did not attend the ceremony in Sharon, Pennsylvania. By now she had found a new passion: her respect for the military personnel she and her sisters entertained so devotedly during World War II led her to join in an effort to have a World War II memorial erected on the National Mall in the nation's capital. In 2000, there appeared John Sforza's book *Swing It! The Andrews Sisters Story*, which detailed the trio's career and offstage lives. On Christmas day 2001, Patty and her husband Wally Wechsler celebrated their fiftieth wedding anniversary.

Once, when asked to define the phenomenon of their 1940s' fame, Patty Andrews offered, "We were such a part of everybody's life in the Second World War. We represented something overseas and at home—a sort of security."

Filmography

Argentine Nights (Univ, 1940)
Buck Privates (Univ, 1941)
In the Navy (Univ, 1941)
Hold That Ghost (Univ, 1941)
What's Cookin'? [Wake Up and Dream] (Univ, 1942)
Private Buckaroo (Univ, 1942)
Give Out, Sisters (Univ, 1942)
Always a Bridesmaid (Univ, 1943)
How's About It? (Univ, 1943)

Swingtime Johnny (Univ, 1944)
Follow the Boys (Univ, 1944)
Hollywood Canteen (WB, 1944)
Moonlight and Cactus (Univ, 1944)
Her Lucky Night (Univ, 1945)
Make Mine Music! (RKO, 1946) (voices only)
Road to Rio (Par, 1947)
Melody Time (RKO, 1948) (voices only)
The Phynx (WB, 1970) (Patty only)

Broadway Plays

Over Here (1974)

Radio Series

Eight-to-the-Bar Ranch [The Andrews Sisters Show] (ABC, 1944–45; CBS, 1945–46)

Album Discography

LPs

The Andrew Sisters

The Andrews Sisters (Decca DL-8360)
The Andrews Sisters (EEC DMC 42-796)
The Andrews Sisters (Rediffusion ZS153)
The Andrews Sisters at Their Very Best (Pair PDL2-1159)
The Andrews Sisters: Christmas (CA 20415)
The Andrews Sisters Go Hawaiian (Dot 3632/25362)

The Andrews Sisters: Golden Greats (MCA MCM-5015)
The Andrews Sisters Greatest Hits (Decca DL-74919)
The Andrews Sisters Greatest Hits (Dot 3406/25406)
The Andrews Sisters Greatest Hits, Vol. 2 (Dot 3543/25543)

The Andrews Sisters in Hi-Fi (Cap W-790)

The Andrews Sisters: In the Mood (Famous Twinsets PAS-20123)

The Andrews Sisters Live (Amalgamated 210)

The Andrews Sisters Live (Andros 4566)

The Andrews Sisters on Radio (Radiola 1033)

The Andrews Sisters on the Air (Pelican 123)

The Andrews Sisters Present (Dot 3529/25529)

The Andrews Sisters Show (Radiola MR-1033) w. Bing Crosby, Gabby Hayes

The Andrews Sisters Sing World War II . . . And Win! (Official 1208)

The Andrews Sisters: Swinging Sweethearts (German MCA 52021)

The Andrews Sisters: The Fabulous Century (Joker 3240)

The Andrews Sisters: Their Greatest Hits (MSM-35117)

The Andrews Sisters: Twenty Greatest Hits (Scana GH-83001)

At the Microphone (Take Two TT-305)

Beat Me Daddy, Eight to the Bar (Music for Pleasure 50556)

The Best of the Andrews Sisters (MCA 2-4024)

The Best of the Andrews Sisters, Vol. 2 (MCA 2-4093)

Bing Crosby and the Andrews Sisters (MCA Coral 804)

Bing Crosby and the Andrews Sisters, Vols. 1-3 (Coral 80, 91, 112)

Boogie Woogie Bugle Girls (Par 6075, MCA 27082)

Collection of Favorites (10″ Decca 5120)

The Dancing Twenties (Cap T-973/Cap ED-2604178, EMI 417)

Dick Tracy in B-Flat (Curtain Calls 100/1) [ST/R]

Don't Sit Under the Apple Tree (Pickwick 3904)

The Early Years 1937-42 (Official 12005)

The Early Years 1938-1941 (Official 12011)

Favorite Hymns (Hamilton HL-154/12154)

Follow the Boys (Hollywood Soundstage 5012) [ST]

Fresh and Fancy Free (Cap T-860)

Give Out, Sisters (Vertinge 2004) [ST]

Great Country Hits (Dot 3567/25567)

Great Golden Hits (Contour 2870-169)

Great Performers (Dot 3807/25807)

Greatest Golden Hits (Dot DLP 3452D/DLP-25452)

The Greatest of the Andrews Sisters Vols. 1–2 (Telehouse TH-2-164 SLB-6935)

Hits of the Andrews Sisters (Cap T/DT-1924)

Hollywood Canteen/Stage Door Canteen (Curtain Calls 100/11-12) [ST]

I Love to Tell the Story (10″ Decca DL-5306)

In the Mood (Par 1002)

Irving Berlin Tunes (Decca DL-5263)

Jingle Bells (Decca DL-8354)

The Jumpin' Jive (MCA 1789)

More Hits of the Andrews Sisters (MCA Coral 8030)

My Isle of Golden Dreams (Decca DL-5423)

Near You (Vocalion 3611, MCA-739)

Pennsylvania Polka (Hamilton 24/12124)

Rarities (MCA 908)

Red Sky at Morning (Decca DL-79180) [ST]

Rum and Coca Cola (Hep HN-4131)

Says My Heart (Conifer Happy Days CHD 161)

Sing, Sing, Sing (Decca DL-5438)

Sing, Sing, Sing (Music for Pleasure 5851)

Sing! Sing! Sing! (Pickwick 3382)

Sirens of Swing (Historia H-638)

Sixteen Great Performances (ABC 4003, MCA-27081)

Stage Door Canteen/Hollywood Canteen (Curtain Calls 100/11-12) [ST]

Tropical Songs (10″ Decca DL-5065)

The Very Best of the Andrews Sisters (MCA 1635)

Worth Remembering (Magic 4)

Patty and Maxene Andrews

Over Here! (Col KS-32961) [OC]

Maxene Andrews

Maxene: An Andrews Sister (Bainbridge BT 6258)

CDs

The Andrews Sisters

All-Time Favorites (EMI-Cap Special Markets 57395)

All-Time Greatest Hits (Comca 1111)

The Andrews Sisters (BCD GLD-63336)

The Andrews Sisters (The Entertainers 255)

The Andrews Sisters (Stemra—no number)

The Andrews Sisters: At Their Very Best (Cema Special Markets CDL-9478)

Andrews Sisters Christmas (Universal Special Markets 20415)

The Andrews Sisters Collection (PMT 90956)

The Andrews Sisters' Greatest Hits (Reader's Digest RBD-105CDI)

The Andrews Sisters Show (Radiola 1033)

The Andrews Sisters: Twenty Greatest Hits (Companion 6187172)

The Andrews Sisters: Twenty Greatest Hits (Scana CD-77019)

The Andrews Sisters With Glenn Miller—The Chesterfield Broadcasts (RCA 63113)

Apple Blossom Time (ASV CD-AJA-5286)

At Their Best! (Pair PCD-2-1159)

Back to Back—The McGuire Sisters and The Andrews Sisters Sing Their Big Hits (Universal Special Markets 21022)

Beat Me Daddy Eight to the Bar (ASV CD-AJA-5096)

Beat Me Daddy, Eight to the Bar (MCA/EMI CDAX-70129)

Bei Mir Bist Du Schon (Disky S1990392)

Bei Mir Bist Du Schon (Past Perfect 4322)

Bei Mir Bist Du Schon (Simply the Best 99039)

The Best of the Andrews Sisters (Blue Moon BMCD-3005)

The Best of the Andrews Sisters (CeDe International 66010)

The Best of the Andrews Sisters (Delta—no number)

The Best of the Andrews Sisters (DJ Specialist 814557)

The Best of the Andrews Sisters (Empire Music Collection 445)

The Best of the Andrews Sisters (Masters 503772)

The Best of the Andrews Sisters (MCA MCAD-2-4024)

The Best of the Andrews Sisters, Vol. 2 (MCA MCAD-2-4093)

The Best of the Andrews Sisters (MCI MCCD-445)

The Best of the Andrews Sisters (Music Club MCCCD 199)

Bing Crosby and the Andrews Sisters—Their Complete Recordings (MCA MCAD-11503)

Blitz Hits (UMTV 5443102)

Boogie Woogie Bugle Boy (HMK 30514)

Boogie Woogie Bugle Boy (Javelin HADCD-173)

Boogie Woogie Bugle Boy (PRA 00506)

Boogie Woogie Bugle Boy (ProArte CDD-506)

Boogie Woogie Bugle Boy: Forty Swing Era Memories (MCA MSC3-35984)

Boogie Woogie Bugle Boy: Greatest Hits (Goldies 25424)

Boogie Woogie Bugle Boy in Sparkling Hi-Fi (Cap/EMI CDAX 70114)

Boogie Woogie Bugle Girls (MCA MCAD-27082E)

Capitol Collector's Series (Cap CDP-7-94078–2)

Christmas With the Andrews Sisters (Pickwick PWK-092)

Cocktail Hour (Columbia River Entertainment Group CRG-218035)

The Collection (PMF Records 90956)

The Cream of the Andrews Sisters (Pearl Flapper PAST-CD-9766)

Dick Tracy in B-Flat (Sandy Hook CDSH-2052) [ST/R]

The Early Years (Official 12011)

50th Anniversary Collection, Vol. 1 (MCA MCAD-42044)

50th Anniversary Collection, Vol. 2 (MCA MCAD-10093)

Follow the Boys/To Have and Have Not/Star Dust/Waterloo Bridge (Great Movie Themes 60032) [ST]

Golden Sounds (Public Music 9015)

The Great Andrews Sisters (BCD GLD-63131)

The Great Andrews Sisters (Redx RXBOX-31043)

Greatest Hits (Curb D21K-77400)

Greatest Hits: The 60th Anniversary (MCA MCAD-11727)

Hold Tight, It's the Andrews Sisters (Prism DBCD-12)

Hollywood Canteen (Great Movie Themes 60024) [ST]

Hollywood Canteen/Stage Door Canteen (Curtain Calls 100/11–12) [ST]

The Immortal Hits of the Andrews Sisters (ETN 255)

Just a Simple Melody (All Star ALS-23101)

L'Art Vocal, Vol. 17: 1937–44 (Melodie 17)

The Magic of the Andrews Sisters (ABM ABMMCD-1054)

The Magic of the Andrews Sisters (EMI G-5219822)

The Magic of the Andrews Sisters (Parade OAR-2963)

Memories (Samba MTLCD-5035)

A Merry Christmas With Bing Crosby & the Andrews Sisters (MCA MCAD-112337)

Mister Five by Five (Empress 869)

My Greatest Songs (MCA MCD-18766)

Portrait of the Andrews Sisters: 1938–44 (MCI Gallerie 401)

Radio Days (Memories of Yesteryear 5055)

Rarities (MCA MCAD-22012, MCA Special Markets 22012, Universal Special Markets 31036)

Red Sky at Morning (Decca DL-79180) [ST]

Rum and Coca Cola (Eclipse 64002-2/Eclipse 64041-2)

Rum and Coca Cola (Golden Options—no number)

Rum and Coca Cola (Golden Stars 5105)

Rum and Coca Cola (Remember RMB 75018)

Selection of the Andrews Sisters (Gold Sound GSS-0808)

Sing! Sing! Sing! (MFP/EMI CD-6044)

Sixteen Original World Hits (MCA 8.620231.Z)

A Sure Score (Magic 49)

Their All-Time Greatest Hits (MCA 11121)

Tico Tico (Magic 49)

20th Century Masters: The Millennium Collection (MCA 112230)

Ultimate Collection (Prism PLATCD-477)

Unforgettable! The Andrews Sisters: Sixteen Golden Classics (Castle UNCD-250)

V-Disc Recordings (Collectors' Choice Music 6662)

The Very Best of the Andrews Sisters (ABM ABMMCD1054)

The Very Best of the Andrews Sisters (Half Moon HMNCD-309)

The Very Best of the Andrews Sisters (Pickwick 064)

The Very Best of the Andrews Sisters (Polygram HMNCD-39)

The Very Best of the Andrews Sisters (Roadg SUMCD-4047)

Yes, My Darling Daughter—The Best of the Andrews Sisters (Castle Communications MAD-CD-318)

Patty & Maxene Andrews

Over Here! (Sony Broadway SK-32961) [OC]

Maxene Andrews

An Andrews Sister (DRG CDSBL-5218)

An Evening With Frank Loesser (DRG 5169)*

*Compilation album

Ann-Margret in the early 1960s.
[Courtesy of Echo Book Shop]

Ann-Margret

(b. Ann-Margret Olsson, April 28, 1941, Valsjöbyn, Jämtland, Sweden)

To successfully make the transition from sex kitten to polished cabaret performer and dramatic actress is a far greater career jump than most sex symbols ever contemplate, let alone accomplish. Ann-Margret burst into show business prominence in the early 1960s as Hollywood's latest sex bomb. She was a little less than five feet five inches, with whispery reddish brunette hair and a voice described as "feathers falling on whipped cream." She had as many curves to her shapely figure as she did to her much-mocked breathless singing. By the mid-1960s she was labeled a "lewd mechanical doll" who had passed the peak of her fad. However, via a sharp career shift (sponsored by her agents and her husband, Roger Smith) she made an impressive professional turnabout. Gradually, she emerged as a respected screen performer and a strong cabaret attraction. In clubs she became an electric personality whose dancing, singing, and rapport with her audience attracted customers in droves.

In the early 1970s Ann-Margret survived a near-fatal onstage accident; later on, she displayed great dignity in helping her actor husband cope with his ongoing precarious health (which was the result of a debilitating disease). It gave added dimension to her persona as she moved into middle age. More recently, in the 1980s, in films and on television, she proved repeatedly that noteworthy performances in *Carnal Knowledge* (1971) and *Tommy* (1975) were not flukes of a sex goddess. In the 1980s she emerged as one of Hollywood's most accomplished dramatic actresses. Fighting the bias against giving screen and TV roles to mature women, she retained her prominence in show business.

She was born Ann-Margret Olsson in Valsjöbyn, Järnland, Sweden, some 185 miles north of Stockholm. She was the only child of Gustav and Anna (Aronsson) Olsson. Her electrician father had spent fourteen years in the United States and returned to America when his daughter was just a year old. He settled near Chicago, where he obtained work with the Johnson Electrical Company, hoping to save enough money to send for his family. Because Mrs. Olsson was hesitant to leave her homeland, several years passed.

At the age of four Ann-Margret discovered music and rhythm. Her uncle played the accordion, and she would dance around and sing; her mother taught her Swedish children's songs. In 1946, Mrs. Olsson and Ann-Margret, neither of whom could speak English, came to America to be united with Mr. Olsson. The family settled in Fox Lake, forty miles northwest of Chicago. Even though funds were low, Mrs. Olsson insisted that her daughter have the dancing, singing, and piano lessons she could never afford for herself back in Sweden. At one point when Gustav Olsson fell two stories at work and was disabled, Mrs. Olsson got a receptionist's job at a mortuary in Wilmette. Part of her salary included free living quarters for the family. For a time, Ann-Margret slept on a convertible couch in the mourners' room and for years was haunted by memories of the big rats that ran through the building at night. Later, Ann-Margret was enrolled in New Trier High School in nearby Winnetka.

By now Ann-Margret was singing in class plays, at churches, at charity functions, socials, and at clubs. Having won $75 in a talent contest, she competed on *Don McNeil's Breakfast Club* on a Chicago radio station. Ted Mack was the substitute host that day, and she sang "Them There Eyes." She lost to a boy who made music by blowing through a leaf. However, Mack invited her to be a guest on his New York-based *The Original Amateur Hour* (ABC-TV). During the summer of 1957, after her sophomore year in high school, she made the rounds of Chicago talent agents. Finally she won a month's engagement as a vocalist with Danny Ferguson's band at the Muehlebach Hotel in Kansas City. During 1959 she made her recording debut on *Lagniappe 1959*, an LP produced by the Boys' Tri-Ship Club of New Trier High School; she sang "Tropical Heat Wave."

After graduating from high school in 1959, Ann-Margret enrolled at Northwestern University as a speech major, with a minor in dramatics. During her first college year, she joined with three male classmates in a group called the Suttletones. On weekends they performed at Chicago area clubs. That June they drove to Las Vegas, hoping for a summer's booking/vacation at the Nevada Club. Their attempt failed, and they drove on to Los Angeles, where they made the rounds of agents. They finally obtained a three-week engagement at the Villa Marina Club in Newport Beach, California. Their new agent (Bobby Roberts) helped them find additional bookings (in Reno and Elko, Nevada), and then it was time to return to college. Ann-Margret decided to remain on the coast.

In November 1960, after she finished singing in the lounge show of the Dunes Hotel in Las Vegas, Roberts and his partner, Pierre Cossette, took Ann-Margret to meet George Burns back in Los Angeles. She auditioned for the comedian by singing "Mack the Knife" and "Bill Bailey, Won't You Come Home." He hired her for his Christmas 1960 show at the Sahara Hotel, paying her $100 nightly for the ten-evening gig. From that exposure she was hired to guest with Burns on *The Jack Benny Program* (CBS-TV, April 2, 1961) and signed a recording contract with RCA Victor. (Her song "I Just Don't Understand" reached number seventeen on the charts in the autumn of 1961.) Meanwhile, she came to the attention of Twentieth Century-Fox, who screen-tested her, as did filmmaker Frank Capra.

Capra used Ann-Margret to play the demure, convent-bred daughter of a Manhattan bag lady (Bette Davis) in his Damon Runyon fable, *Pocketful of Miracles* (1961). *Variety* acknowledged, "Ann-Margret emotes with feeling." Far more audience-grabbing was Ann-Margret's role in *State Fair* (1962), Twentieth Century-Fox's third rendering of that piece of Americana. In a cast that featured Bobby Darin, Alice Faye, and Pamela Tiffin, Ann-Margret was the high-voltage showgirl with whom farm boy Pat Boone falls wildly in love. (Originally she had been scheduled for the docile role of Boone's sister, a part taken over by Tiffin.) She soloed "Isn't It Kind of Fun?" and dueted with Boone on "Willing and Eager." With her long dark brown hair changed to red and her electric presence, Ann-Margret was the film's main attraction.

In 1961 Ann-Margret had earned $18,000; but by the next year her career was zooming and she was grossing $200,000. Her agents orchestrated an intensive publicity campaign to transform their client into a very recognizable personality. Its crescendo was on April 19, 1962, when she sang the Oscar-nominated song "Bachelor in Paradise" on the Academy Awards telecast. She recalls, "I was standing in the wings, petrified. Perspiring terribly. I heard Mr. [Bob] Hope introduce me and suddenly found myself standing there. I started to snap my fingers, and I remember saying to myself, 'I'll show them. I'll show them!' Then the music got to me and I just went." That sizzling performance, filled with bumps and grinds, made her Hollywood's hottest commodity.

Ann-Margret was already under a nonexclusive seven-year (one picture a year) contract with Fox starting at $500 per week. She now signed a three-picture deal with Columbia, which would escalate to $100,000 per movie. For Columbia she costarred in the musical *Bye Bye Birdie* (1963), easily stealing the limelight from Dick Van Dyke and Janet Leigh as the small-town high schooler who develops a wild crush on a visiting rock 'n' roll star. She sang "One Boy" with Bobby Rydell, but her highlight was performing "How Lovely to Be a Woman." *Variety* enraptured, "this is one of the most exciting fresh personalities to take the cinematic stage in some time. The magnetism of early-vintage Judy Garland is here." That soundtrack album sold well, certainly better than had her two earlier LPs (*And Here She Is—Ann-Margret* and *On the Way Up*).

Ann-Margret was among the entertainers (who included Marilyn Monroe) performing at President John F. Kennedy's forty-fifth birthday celebration in New York in 1963. (The next year Ann-Margret would sing at President Lyndon Johnson's Inaugural Gala.) She provided an off-camera voice for one episode of *The Flintstones* (ABC-TV, September 19, 1963) cartoon series. It seemed Ann-Margret could do no wrong, even if she was given the Sour Apple Award in both 1962 and 1963 for being uncooperative with the Hollywood Women's Press Club in detailing matters about her private life. Off-camera she dated Frankie Avalon, Vince Edwards, Eddie Fisher, and Hugh O'Brian and then announced (and later broke) her engagement with businessman Burt Sugarman. She made headlines when she began dating Elvis Presley, the costar of her next musical picture, *Viva Las Vegas* (1964). It was the start of a long-standing friendship, which lasted until his death in 1977 (she attended his funeral in Memphis in 1977). Later, she hosted a TV tribute to Presley.

Most of her mid-'60s motion pictures were claptrap, exploiting her sex-star image. Nevertheless, she was twice named Star of the Year by the Theater Owners of America. It would be years before she could live down *Kitten With a Whip* (1964), a horrendously shrill melodrama costarring John Forsythe. In it she was cast as a reformatory escapee. Advertisements of a slinky Ann-Margret provocatively snapping a whip made her a figure of mirth in the industry. Distinguished playwright William Inge had written the screenplay for *Bus Riley's Back in Town* (1965), but there were so many problems with the production, which featured Michael Parks as her costar, that it was held up for a year to do retakes. It was released in a severely edited, badly received version and with Inge's name removed from the credits.

In contrast, Ann-Margret was among the star lineup in MGM's superior *The Cincinnati Kid* (1965) as Rip Torn's wife who has an affair with stud poker champ Steve McQueen. Then it was back to more screen duds. She inherited Claire Trevor's old role of dance-hall girl Dallas in a bad remake of *Stagecoach* (1966) with Alex Cord as the new Ringo Kid; the Western was a box-office flop. The nadir of her career was *The Swinger* (1966), which cast her as writer Kelly Olsson who pretends to be a mod "swinger" to convince her publisher that she can write lurid prose. Ann-Margret shimmied, sung, and simpered through the trash. One reviewer said of her appearance that she is "a pale-faced creature with streaming red hair and over-inflated mammary glands who emits strange sounds through her nose." Another reviewer wrote that for New Year's he wished, "Ann-Margret would stop acting like Everyman's Erotica, blow her nose and get back to being a girl."

By 1967 Ann-Margret had earned $3 million but owed $117,000 in debts. She had worn out her show-business welcome. At this juncture she began to listen seriously to the career advice of actor/producer Roger Smith whom she had met in 1961 and had been seriously dating since 1964. He suggested that he and his talent-agency partner, Allan Carr, become her managers; she agreed, and also agreed to become Smith's wife. They were married at the Riviera Hotel in Las Vegas on May 8, 1967. He had three children by a prior marriage. As part of her professional revamping, Ann-Margret made her debut at the Riviera Hotel in July 1967 as a headliner. She went to Italy to costar with Rossano Brazzi in a film *Sette Uomini e un Cervello* [Criminal Symphony] (1968) produced by Smith and Carr. Then, she starred in *The Ann-Margret Show* (CBS-TV, December 11, 1968), the first of several hour specials she would do for television, teamed with the likes of Lucille Ball, Dean Martin, Bob Hope, and Jack Benny. In each of these lucrative, slick outings she exploited her growing versatility as a singer and dancer and sought to soften and sweeten her image. In December 1968 she returned to Vietnam (where she had gone in 1966) to entertain the troops with a USO show, this time headlined with Bob Hope.

Her agents turned down roles for Ann-Margret in *The Maltese Bippy* (1969), *Viva Max!* (1969), and *Song of Norway* (1970), but agreed to her starring in the action melodrama *C. C. and Company* (1970), where she sang and rode a motorcycle (as she did in real life). She guest-starred on a segment of Lucille Ball's *Here's Lucy* (CBS-TV, February 2, 1970). She then joined with Anthony Quinn in the embarrassing *R.P.M.* (1970), a college revolution drama produced and directed by the once-esteemed Stanley Kramer. The film was a bust, but she received respectable reviews as the grad student who falls in love with a zealous professor (Quinn).

The turning point of Ann-Margret's career was winning (over Dyan Cannon, Jane Fonda, Raquel Welch, and Natalie Wood) a key role in the Mike Nichols–directed *Carnal Knowledge* (1971). She was love-hungry Bobbie Templeton, the blowsy and busty neurotic whom Jack Nicholson eventually dumps. Critics and moviegoers alike were amazed by her serious dramatics, and she was Oscar-nominated. (She lost the Best Supporting Actress Oscar to Cloris Leachman of *The Last Picture Show,* but she did win the Golden Globe Award in the same category.) *Time* magazine noted that because of this film "her body got a degree and quality of exposure that made her overnight what for eleven years she had clumsily tried to be: a sex symbol." She was again on the cover of *Life* magazine. In 1971 she earned $2 million, part of that income from appearing in the musical spoof *Dames at Sea* (NBC-TV, November 15, 1971) in which she costarred with Ann Miller.

Ann-Margret had had accidents before. She had spilled off her motorcycle in 1968; she had fallen in Las Vegas in 1971, requiring twenty-four stitches. But these were nothing like what occurred at the Sahara Hotel in Lake Tahoe on September 10, 1972. She was performing a Carnival in Rio number for the midnight show when she tumbled from a faulty platform. She fell twenty-two feet and would most likely have died had not a stagehand heard her screams and rushed in her direction to break her fall. As it was, besides suffering a concussion, she broke her jaw, facial bones in five places (pieces of which were driven up into her sinuses), and her left arm. After she was rushed to a local hospital, her husband flew her in their private jet to UCLA Medical Center where a team of five doctors, including a plastic surgeon who had done wonders on comedienne Phyllis Diller, operated on her for two hours. Her jaw was wired from the inside; it was a very painful procedure, but one that ensured no scars.

Scarcely ten weeks later, Ann-Margret was back performing. (Part of her drive to recover was to prove to her dying father that she was okay.) When asked what drove her, Ann-Margret explained,

"If I don't work I climb the walls. You see, entertaining is what I do. I've been doing it since I was four, and I don't do anything else. If I stop, the world might not come apart. But I would." When she played on the Las Vegas stage she now had a specialty number, "Return of the Kitten With a Whip," which teased her former sex-cat image. She ended the show with a teary rendition of "When You're Smiling." On April 4, 1973, she had another television special *Ann-Margret: When You're Smiling* (NBC-TV). On her TV studio dressing room door was posted the sign "Nothin' Stops the Champ!"

Ann-Margret had made *The Train Robbers* (1973) with John Wayne *before* her accident, and, on January 23, 1975, she was back with another NBC-TV special: *Ann-Margret Olsson*, which included tributes to Marilyn Monroe, Betty Grable, Rita Hayworth, and Esther Williams. In the bizarre, vulgar Ken Russell–directed rock opera *Tommy* (1975) Ann-Margret played the mother of Roger Daltrey (of the rock group the Who). Even though, musically, Elton John (with "Pinball Wizard") and Tina Turner (with "Acid Queen") were more outrageous, Ann-Margret was Oscar-nominated for her (over)strong dramatics. (She lost the Best Supporting Actress Academy Award to Louise Fletcher of *One Flew Over the Cuckoo's Nest*.) Also in England, she costarred in *Joseph Andrews* (1976), a rowdy restoration sex adventure, playing the earthy Lady Booby.

Ann-Margret's films at home and abroad continued being a mixed bag, ranging from the failed adventure satire *The Last Remake of Beau Geste* (1977), to Neil Simon's commercial private-eye spoof, *The Cheap Detective* (1978), to the ignored Western burlesque, *The Villain* (1979). They were stopgaps in her career, which also included annual club tours and more TV specials, such as *Ann-Margret . . . Rhinestone Cowgirl* (NBC-TV, April 26, 1977) on which Perry Como, Bob Hope, Minnie Pearl, and Chet Atkins were guests. Much more substantial was the film *Middle Age Crazy* (1980) in which she was the wife of a Houston building contractor (Bruce Dern) who was undergoing male menopause on his fortieth birthday. (Ann-Margret had costarred previously with Dern in the confusing Claude Chabrol–directed *Folies Bourgeoises*, 1976.)

Now in her forties, Ann-Margret played a succession of understanding women on-screen. In *Looking to Get Out* (1982; shot in 1980), coproduced and cowritten by costar Jon Voight, Ann-Margret was seen as an ex-hooker (now living with a wealthy Las Vegas hotel owner) who is sympathetic to her old lover/loser (Voight). She was tremendously effective as the terminally ill (with cancer) mother of ten in the telefeature *Who Will Love My Children?* (1983), and the next year, she was handpicked by playwright Tennessee Williams to play Blanche Dubois opposite Treat Williams's Stanley in the telefilm version of *A Streetcar Named Desire*. Some critics compared her favorably to Vivien Leigh's benchmark performance. For *Twice in a Lifetime* (1985) she was the striking barmaid who falls in love with Seattle steelworker Gene Hackman, who is suffering the blues from his thirty-year marriage to Ellen Burstyn. The picture and Ann-Margret's resilient performance received much critical attention, but insufficient public response.

For every artistic appearance Ann-Margret made, there was a calculated commercial effort such as *The Two Mrs. Grenvilles* (NBC-TV, February 8–9, 1987) based on Dominick Dunne's best-seller. In this slick, four-hour miniseries, she played the Kansan from the wrong side of the tracks who marries a handsome sailor (Stephen Collins) only to be rebuffed by her upper-crust East Coast in-laws and to end up a drunk after shooting her husband. Ann-Margret was Emmy-nominated for her role. In *A New Life*, (1988), written and directed by and costarring Alan Alda, she was his overly patient spouse who, after twenty-six years of marriage, strikes out on her own.

Said the *Los Angeles Times*, "As always, it is special pleasure to watch Ann-Margret, who has become that rarity in American films, a glamorous star who is also an impeccable ensemble player."

Since 1980, her husband Roger Smith had been suffering from myasthenia gravis (a nerve disease that weakens the muscles), and much of Ann-Margret's career had been subordinated to accommodating his illness, as she had devoted time to raising her three stepchildren. In October 1988, Ann-Margret returned to performing onstage in Las Vegas after a five-year absence. The spectacular floor show at Caesars Palace was successfully geared to remind audiences why Ann-Margret had been known as "Queen of the Strip" for many years. She informed the opening-night audience that George Burns remained her inspiration and that it was he who advised her to continue doing "all that dramatic [movie] stuff but get back onstage." It was the beginning of a new club act, which saw her performing in Las Vegas, Atlantic City, and Lake Tahoe.

In October 1988 the Thalians' thirty-third anniversary ball in Los Angeles honored Ann-Margret and raised $600,000 for charity. Debbie Reynolds was cohostess of the event, and June Haver, the previous year's honoree, made the presentation to Ann-Margret. In December 1988, Ann-Margret was among four Southern Californians awarded the Swedish Royal Order of the Polar Star for their efforts to promote Sweden in the United States.

Ann-Margret made a return to movies in the controversial telefeature *Our Sons* (ABC-TV, May 19, 1991), cast as a bigoted mother living in an Arizona trailer park who learns that her son is dying of AIDS. She is helped to deal with her offspring's lifestyle and his pending death by the mother (Julie Andrews) of the young man's lover. The unsuccessful big-screen musical *Newsies* (1992) found Ann-Margret in the superfluous role of a musical-comedy stage performer who helps newsboys in 1899 New York with their strike against newspaper owners. Much more appropriate to the actress's fiery image was her role in the 1993 TV miniseries *Queen*. With Halle Berry in the title role, Ann-Margret was Sally Jackson in this story of the Old South based on an Alex Haley story. In another TV miniseries, also set in the same locale, Ann-Margret played Belle Watling (the bordello madam with a heart of gold) in *Scarlett* (1994) the sequel to the classic Civil War–set movie *Gone With the Wind* (1939). Also in 1994 her long-anticipated autobiography (*Ann-Margret: My Story*), written with Todd Gold, was published. In the tome the usually privacy-prone entertainer discussed (for the first time publicly) her relationship with Elvis Presley, which had begun when they made *Viva Las Vegas* (1964) and, after the romance ended, continued as a friendship till the end of his life. According to Ann-Margret: "We were extremely alike; it was uncanny. I get so angry, because there have been so many negative things written about him. So I wanted to celebrate his life." The actress also discussed her bouts with alcoholism—especially in the 1970s—a propensity handed down from her heavy-drinking father. She said of her current life: "I'm real happy. I feel really blessed at this point in my life to be with Roger [Smith] . . . I have three [step]children that I'm very, very proud of—and three grandchildren who all call me Grandma Smith. I love it!"

In *Grumpy Old Men* (1993), which reunited the comedy team of Walter Matthau and Jack Lemmon, Ann-Margret was the feisty widow who causes competition between Minnesota retirees anxious to gain her attention. The successful release led to the sequel *Grumpier Old Men* (1995) in which the formula was spiced by the addition of Sophia Loren as Matthau's love interest while Ann-Margret continued to intrigue Lemmon's on-screen character. Always searching for a new type of screen persona, she played a plain-Jane lonely widow on a journey of self-discovery in the 1994 TV movie *Following Her Heart*. In contrast, in the two-part *Seduced by Madness [The Diane*

Borchardt Story] (NBC-TV, February 25–26, 1996), she portrayed a Wisconsin school teacher who convinced three of her teenage students to kill her husband (Peter Coyote). Reviewing the two-part movie, the *New York Times* decided, "It's Ann-Margret who gives the production its compelling tension with her portrait of a woman in diabolical control of the world as she sees it. Her Diane is on a par with all the classic horror movies you've ever seen."

Also in 1996 the veteran entertainer had an RCA album (*Let Me Entertain You*) in release. *Entertainment Weekly* rated the disc a "B+" reasoning, "The kicky-cool shots of Ann-Margret gracing this collection of vintage Vegasy performances tells you everything you need to know about the slinky, coquettish music within. Ann-Margret may sing some notes flat, and miss some entirely. But this kitten with a whip will still leave her mark on you." Reportedly, making the telefeature *Blue Rodeo* (CBS-TV, October 20, 1996)—in which she costarred with Kris Kristofferson in a drama about a mother coping with a troubled son who goes deaf—was such a heavily dramatic experience that it left the actress in a depressed mode for weeks thereafter. Then in winter 1997 she dealt with the progressively worsening affects of her husband's battle with myasthenia gravis when he had to be hospitalized to monitor his condition.

Long in the works, Ann-Margret's TV series *Four Corners* finally premiered on February 24, 1998, on CBS-TV. On the weekly hour-long show, she played the matriarch of a California ranching family that is in the midst of unsettling transitions. Poorly received, the program was cancelled a month later. She had much better success starring in *Life of the Party: The Pamela Harriman Story* (ABC-TV, 10/7/98) cast as the twentieth-century courtesan whose marriages included unions with Broadway producer Leland Hayward and politician Averell Harriman. It includes her years as an ambassador to France and her death in 1997. For her work in this entry, she received an Emmy and a Golden Globe nomination. In 1999's *Happy Face Murders* (Showtime Cable, September 5, 1999), she was seen as an eccentric grandmotherly older woman (self-)implicated in the murder of a young retarded girl. As a change of pace from this entry Ann-Margret took a one-woman show on the road (including stopovers in Canada) to present an evening of clips from her movies and reminiscences about her movie-star life. (She had given up touring with her dancing/singing stage act five years earlier.)

Continuing into the new century, Ann-Margret played Queen Cinderella in the lavish TV movie fantasy *The Tenth Kingdom* (NBC-TV, February 27, 2001) and was among those in *Blonde* (CBS-TV, 5/31/2001), a telefeature about the life of Marilyn Monroe; she played Della Monroe, Monroe's loving grandmother. In *The Last Producer* (USA Cable, September 20, 2001)—which sat on the shelf for two years—she was the spouse of an old-time film producer (Burt Reynolds) with the latter wanting to get back into the movie-making game.

Now into her sixties, Ann-Margret still continued to ride motorcycles even after a bad accident in August 2000 resulted in three broken ribs and a fractured shoulder. In fall 2001 she headlined a nationwide tour of *The Best Little Whorehouse in Texas* that ran into 2002. Always seeking the next creative challenge, Ann-Margret had the perspective to say of life to that point: "No one gets everything he or she wants, but I'm really a very lucky lady."

Filmography

Pocketful of Miracles (UA, 1961)

State Fair (20th-Fox, 1962)

Bye Bye Birdie (Col, 1963)

Kitten With a Whip (Univ, 1964)

Viva Las Vegas [Love in Las Vegas] (MGM, 1964)

The Pleasure Seekers (20th-Fox, 1964)

Bus Riley's Back in Town (Univ, 1965)

Once a Thief (MGM, 1965)

The Cincinnati Kid (MGM, 1965)

Made in Paris (MGM, 1966)

The Swinger (Par, 1966)

Stagecoach (20th-Fox, 1966)

Murderers' Row (Col, 1966)

The Tiger and the Pussycat [Il Tigre] (Emb, 1967)

Il Profeta [The Prophet/Mr. Kinky] (It 1967) (released in the United States in 1976)

Sette Uomini e un Cervello [Criminal Affair/Criminal Symphony] (It/Arg, 1968)

Rebus [The Puzzle] (It/Sp/Ger, 1968)

C.C. and Company (Avco Emb, 1970)

R.P.M. (Col, 1970)

Carnal Knowledge (Avco Emb, 1971)

The Train Robbers (WB, 1973)

The Outside Man [Un Homme Est Mort] (UA, 1973)

Tommy (Col, 1975)

Joseph Andrews (Par, 1976)

Folies Bourgeoises [The Twist] (Fr, 1976)

The Last Remake of Beau Geste (Univ, 1977)

The Cheap Detective (Col, 1978)

Magic (Avco Emb, 1978)

The Villain [Cactus Jack] (Col, 1979)

Ken Murray Shooting Stars (Royal Oaks, 1979) (documentary)

Middle Age Crazy (20th-Fox, 1980)

I Ought to Be in Pictures (20th-Fox, 1982)

Lookin' to Get Out (Par, 1982) (made in 1980)

Who Will Love My Children? (ABC-TV, 2/14/83)

A Streetcar Named Desire (ABC-TV, 3/4/84)

Twice in a Lifetime (Yorkin, 1985)

The Return of the Soldier (European Classics, 1985) (made in 1982)

52 Pick-Up (Cannon, 1986)

The Two Mrs. Grenvilles (NBC-TV, 2/8–9/87)

A Tiger's Tale (Atlantic Releasing, 1988)

A New Life (Par, 1988)

Our Sons (ABC-TV, 5/19/91)

Newsies (BV, 1992)

Grumpy Old Men (WB, 1993)

Nobody's Children (USA Cable, 3/3/94)

Following Her Heart (NBC-TV, 11/28/94)

Grumpier Old Men (WB, 1995)

Seduced by Madness [Seduced by Madness: The Diane Borchardt Story] (NBC-TV, 2/25–26/96)

Blue Rodeo (CBS-TV, 10/20/96)

Life of the Party: The Pamela Harriman Story (ABC-TV, 10/7/98)

Happy Face Murders (Showtime Cable, 9/5/99)

Any Given Sunday (WB, 1999)

Perfect Murder, Perfect Town (CBS-TV, 2/27/2000)

The Tenth Kingdom (NBC-TV, 2/27/2000)

A Woman's a Helluva Thing (Regent Moonstone, 2000)

The Last Producer (USA Cable, 2/9/2001)

Blonde (CBS-TV, 5/31/2001)

Interstate 60 (Fireworks Entertainment/Redeemable Features, 2002)

TV Series

Queen (CBS, 2/14, 2/16, 2/18/93 (miniseries)

Scarlett (CBS, 11/13–17/94) (miniseries)

Album Discography

LPs

And Here She Is—Ann-Margret (RCA LPK/LSP-2399)

Ann-Margret (MCA 3226)

Ann-Margret and John Gary Sing David Merrick's Hits From Broadway Shows (RCA LPM/LSP-2947)

Bachelors' Paradise (RCA LPM/LSP-2659)

Beauty and the Beard (RCA LPM/LSP-2690) w. Al Hirt

Bye Bye Birdie (RCA LOC/LSO-1081) [ST]

The Cowboy and the Lady (LHI 12007) w. Lee Hazelwood

Dames at Sea (Bell System K-4900) [ST/TV]

Hits and Rarities (Teenager 604)

Hits and Rarities, Vol. 2 (Teenager 615)

It's the Most Happy Sound (WB 1285) w. the Ja-Da Quartet

The Many Moods of Ann-Margret (Raven RVLP 1009)

On the Way Up (RCA LPM/LSP-2453)

The Pleasure Seekers (RCA LOC/LSO-1101) [ST]

Songs From *The Swinger* and Other Swing Songs (RCA LPM/LSP-3710)

State Fair (Dot DLP-29011) [ST]

The Swinger (RCA LPM/LPS 3710) [ST]
Three Great Girls (RCA LPM/LSP-2724) w. Kitty
    Kallen, Della Reese
Tommy (Polydor 2-9502) [ST]

Va-Va Voom (Rhino RNTA 1999)
Viva Las Vegas! (Lucky LR-711) [ST]
The Vivacious One (RCA LPM/LSP-2551)

CDs

And Here She Is/Vivacious One (Laser 399)
Ann-Margret 1961–66 (Bear Family BCD-16248)
And Here She Is (RCA Japan BVCJ-1012)
Bachelor's Paradise (RCA BVCJ-7364)
Beauty and the Beard (RCA Japan BVCJ-7471,
    RCA Spain 52732) w. Al Hirt
The Best Little Whorehouse in Texas (Fynsworth
    Alley 062–117) [OC]
Best Selection (RCA Japan BVCP-2629)
Bye Bye Birdie (RCA 1081-2-R) [ST]
Cowboy and the Lady (Smells Like Records 41) w.
    Lee Greenwood

Hits and Rarities (Teenager Records)
Hits and Rarities, Vol. 2 (Teenager Records)
Let Me Entertain You (RCA 07863-66882-2)
Lovely Ann-Margret—Hits & Rarities (Marginal
    MA-072)
On the Way Up (RCA Japan BVCJ-35022)
State Fair (Varese Sarabande 302-066075-2) [ST]
Tommy (Polydor P48P-25062) [ST]
The Very Best of Ann-Margret (BMG/RCA)
The Very Best of Ann-Margret (RCA 69389)
The Vivacous One (RCA Japan BVCJ-7371)
Viva Las Vegas/Roustabout (RCA 07863-66129-2,
    RCA Japan BVCP-621) [ST]

George Burns, Gracie Allen, and Fred Astaire in *Damsels in Distress* (1937).
[Courtesy of JC Archives]

Fred Astaire

(b. Frederick Austerlitz, Omaha, Nebraska, May 10, 1899; d. Beverly Hills, California, June 22, 1987)

A show-business legend, Fred Astaire made cinema history with his elegant dancing style and aristocratic, smooth personality. While everything he accomplished on-screen, and in other facets of show business, appeared to be effortless, in reality he was a tremendously hardworking craftsman who toiled long and hard to make his work appear so natural. In addition to becoming the movies' best-known dancer, Astaire was also a fine actor and a more-than-fair vocalist who had a distinctive knack for lyric phrasing. Because of his ten screen teamings with vivacious Ginger Rogers, Fred Astaire is most frequently thought of in context with the blonde actress, although most of his screen endeavors were without her. Astaire was beloved by audiences and coworkers alike, and, in 1949, the Academy of Motion Picture Arts and Sciences presented him with a special Oscar for his "unique artistry and his contributions to the technique of musical pictures."

The future dancing star was born Frederick Austerlitz in Omaha, Nebraska, on May 10, 1899, the son of an Austrian immigrant beer salesman. His sister, Adele, was a year and one-half older than he, and when she began taking dancing lessons, he accompanied her and also took up the art. As children they performed locally and, in 1906, their mother enrolled them in the Ned Wayburn School of Dance in New York City. When Fred was five, he and Adele made their vaudeville debut in Keyport, New Jersey, and their dancing act was so good they obtained steady work and began using the surname Astaire. ("Austerlitz sounded too much like a battle," Astaire said later.)

After eleven years on the road, with their only academic schooling being their mother's tutoring, the brother-and-sister act was booked into New York City, and their notices were so gilt-edged they landed a part in the Broadway musical *Over the Top* (1917) the next year. This was followed by such Great White Way productions as *The Passing Show of 1918* (1918), *Apple Blossoms* (1919), and *The Love Letter* (1921), before having *For Goodness Sake* written for them in 1922. This was followed in the same year by Jerome Kern's *The Bunch and Judy*, and in 1924 they starred in George Gershwin's sensational musical *Lady Be Good!* (Gershwin had done the additional music for *For Goodness Sake*.) In the interim, between the Kern and Gershwin shows, the Astaires took *The Bunch and Judy* to London as *Stop Flirting* in 1923, and they became the toast of the British capital. They returned to London in 1926 for a run there in *Lady Be Good!*, and in 1927 they headlined still another Broadway triumph that George Gershwin wrote for them, *Funny Face*.

While in England in 1923, Fred and Adele made their recording debuts doing two songs from *Stop Flirting* on HMV (His Master's Voice) Records. In 1926, accompanied by George Gershwin on the piano, they recorded two *Lady Be Good!* selections: "Hang on to Me" and "Fascinatin' Rhythm" for Columbia. At the same time Fred did his first solo record vocal on "The Half of It Dearie Blues," also from the Gershwin show. In 1928 brother and sister also recorded a quartet of tunes from *Funny Face* in London for Columbia.

In 1930 the Astaires returned to America to headline the Broadway musical *Smiles*, and the next year they costarred in *The Band Wagon*. Their successful teaming came to a sudden halt, however, in 1932 when Adele married Lord Charles Cavendish, the second son of the duke of Devonshire, and retired from show business. Going it alone Fred took the lead in the musical *Gay Divorce* in 1932, introducing Cole Porter's song "Night and Day," and after a 248-performance run, took the show to London.

After filmmaker Samuel Goldwyn signed and then released Fred from a screen contract, he was hired by RKO to star in a new musical. However, that project was slow in developing, and he was loaned to MGM, where he made his feature debut in the 1933 Joan Crawford musical *Dancing Lady*. The *New York Times* commented, "The dancing of Fred Astaire and Miss Crawford is most graceful and charming. The photographic effects of their scenes are an impressive achievement" (although Astaire thought "My God, I looked like a knife" in his film debut). By now RKO had its project, *Flying Down to Rio* (1933), ready, and Astaire was teamed with Ginger Rogers (a replacement for Dorothy Jordan) as featured dancers in the elaborate picture starring Dolores Del Rio and Gene Raymond. The duo caused a sensation dancing "The Carioca." Realizing there was money to be made from their teaming, the studio quickly starred them in *The Gay Divorcee* (1934), a screen version of Astaire's stage musical, *Gay Divorce*. This light and elegant story of an American dancer romancing a pretty young woman in London introduced the dance "The Continental," and Astaire and Rogers (despite the fact Fred never wanted to be teamed with anyone again) were a hot box-office property.

In 1935, Astaire and Rogers costarred with Irene Dunne and Randolph Scott in the screen version of *Roberta*, in which they were essentially wasted. This situation was remedied by *Top Hat* the same year, where they were again romancing in London and executing such beautiful songs as "No Strings," "Isn't It a Lovely Day," "Cheek to Cheek," "The Piccolino," and "Top Hat, White Tie and Tails." The picture grossed over $3 million at the box office. Astaire and Rogers opened 1936 with *Follow the Fleet*, with Fred as a sailor romancing dance-hall girl Ginger, and it contained Irving Berlin's song "Let's Face the Music and Dance."

Next came *Swing Time* (1936), perhaps their best screen pairing, with its songs "A Fine Romance" and "The Way You Look Tonight" and Fred's solo on "Bojangles of Harlem" and his hoofing on "Never Gonna Dance." (In November 2001, a workshop version of a new musical, *Never Gonna Dance* was performed in New York City. It was based on *Swing Time* and featured Noah Rayce and Nancy Lemenager in the Astaire-Rogers roles.) While the plot of *Shall We Dance?* (1937) appeared to be mostly warmed-over leftovers from some of the screen team's earlier scripts, the film was alive with great George Gershwin songs like the title tune, as well as "Let's Call the Whole Thing Off," "They All Laughed," and "They Can't Take That Away From Me" plus a delightful roller-skating sequence. In 1937, without Ginger in the proceedings, Fred made *Damsel in Distress*. It cast him as a composer in love with a pretty British lass (Joan Fontaine), and sported such good Gershwin songs as "A Foggy Day" and "Nice Work If You Can Get It."

However, the public did not react favorably to Fred *without* Ginger, and in 1938 they were rematched for the eighth time in *Carefree*, with Astaire as a psychiatrist who finds himself in love with his patient (Rogers). It contained the song "Change Partners" but its nearly $2 million budget was not recouped at the box office. The couple's final RKO pairing was in the biopic *The Story of Vernon and Irene Castle* (1939), tracing the lives of the famous husband-and-wife ballroom dancing team of the pre–World War I era, but it lacked a good score and again failed to return its production costs. At this point Astaire, then earning $150,000 per film, and RKO came to a parting.

During the period of the Astaire-Rogers musicals in the 1930s, Fred recorded many of the songs from their films for Brunswick records, and in addition, the duo performed most of their joint films in radio versions. Also the star headlined the one-hour *The Fred Astaire Show* on NBC radio from 1936–37. On a personal note, Fred had one of the happiest marriages in Hollywood, having wed New York socialite divorcée Phyllis Baker Potter in 1933. They later had two children: Fred Jr. (born in 1941) and Ava (born in 1942).

Fred Astaire's first real dancing partner without Ginger Rogers was tap-dancer Eleanor Powell in MGM's *Broadway Melody of 1940* (1940). She proved more than a match for Astaire, but they had no on-camera chemistry. He next danced with Paulette Goddard in Paramount's *Second Chorus* (1941), in which Fred and Burgess Meredith, the latter as an Artie Shaw bandsman, both romanced the leading lady. At Columbia, Astaire was teamed with Rita Hayworth and Cole Porter music for *You'll Never Get Rich* (1941). The two stars worked well together, plus the film offered the song "So Near and Yet So Far." After vying with Bing Crosby for Marjorie Reynolds in Paramount's expensive *Holiday Inn* (1942), Fred reteamed with Hayworth for *You Were Never Lovelier* in 1942. This time the duo had a screen romance against the backdrop of such Jerome Kern songs as "I'm Old Fashioned" and "Dearly Beloved," both of which Astaire recorded for Decca Records. He then returned to RKO for the unremarkable *The Sky's the Limit* (1943), which cast him as a service pilot on leave in Manhattan who falls for a pretty magazine photographer (Joan Leslie). It offered the Harold Arlen songs "One for My Baby," "I've Got a Lot in Common With You," and "My Shining Hour," but was not popular at the box office.

In 1944 the much-matured Astaire thought his film career was over, but MGM's Arthur Freed (and members of his production) unit urged that he be signed with the studio for more musicals. He inaugurated the association with *Ziegfeld Follies* (not released until 1946), where he danced the "Limehouse Blues" and "This Heart of Mine" with Lucille Bremer and teamed with Gene Kelly for "The Babbitt and the Bromide" number. The latter dance vehicle found the two very disparate dancers blending their unique styles surprisingly well together. In the bland, whimsical fantasy musical *Yolanda and the Thief* (1945), Fred again danced with Lucille Bremer. He reteamed with Bing Crosby in 1946 for *Blue Skies* at Paramount, which cast them as two rival performers who were once partners. They performed the number "A Couple of Song and Dance Men," while Astaire soloed on "Puttin' on the Ritz." As in their last joint offering, it was Crosby who won the heart of the film's leading lady (this time, Joan Caulfield).

Since MGM could not smooth out a script of *The Belle of New York* for Astaire and Judy Garland, he decided now was the right time to retire. Two years later he was wooed back to MGM to replace Gene Kelly, who had suffered a broken ankle, in *Easter Parade* (1948). The Irving Berlin songfest cast him as a dancer who is lovelorn over a stage star (Ann Miller) but teams with a new singer (Judy Garland). He soloed on "Steppin' Out With My Baby," and he and Garland performed a duo on the novelty number "A Couple of Swells." The result was a smash hit. When Garland was unable to take the lead in *The Barkleys of Broadway* in 1949, Ginger Rogers replaced her, and the vehicle, while not one of their best, was a pleasant, nostalgic reunion for the performers. The reprised song "They Can't Take That Away From Me" was better than the thin plot about feuding husband-and-wife performers.

In the late 1940s and early 1950s, Fred was a guest on radio shows that starred Bing Crosby and Bob Hope. He kicked off the 1950s with the MGM musical *Three Little Words* (1950) costarring Vera-Ellen. This biopic of songwriters Bert Kalmar and Harry Ruby had Fred singing the title song and dancing with Vera-Ellen. Next he went to Paramount for the overlong *Let's Dance* (1950), which mismatched the elegant Astaire with the rambunctious Betty Hutton. In *Royal Wedding* (1951), back at MGM, his dancing on the ceiling highlighted this tale of a dancer (Astaire) and his sister (Jane Powell) each finding love in London at the time of Queen Elizabeth II's coronation.

Next Astaire finally made *Belle of New York* (1952) with Vera-Ellen, but this mundane period fantasy was unpopular. In contrast, the Vincent Minnelli–directed musical *The Band Wagon* (1953) proved to be his best film in some time with its story of washed-up movie actor Astaire hoping for success on Broadway. It featured songs like "That's Entertainment" and "Dancing in the Dark," plus the Mike Hammer ballet spoof "The Girl Hunt" that he performed with his soon-to-be-favorite screen partner, Cyd Charisse. As a result of *The Band Wagon's* popularity, Astaire signed a new contract with MGM for three more films at $100,000 per picture, but when nothing developed he thought again of retiring and then moved over to Paramount. He rejected a costarring role (which went to Danny Kaye) with Bing Crosby in *White Christmas* (1954) and turned down *Papa's Delicate Condition* (later made with Jackie Gleason).

Meanwhile, his wife Phyllis died in 1954, and as therapy Astaire did a musical remake of *Daddy Long Legs* (1955) at Twentieth Century-Fox with Leslie Caron. Made on a modest budget, it was a profitable picture and had the hit tune "Something's Gotta Give." He made another May-September musical romance in Paramount's *Funny Face* (1956), a top-notch production that cast him as a chic fashion photographer who makes a star out of a young model (Audrey Hepburn) against a Parisian setting. For his final MGM musical he teamed with Cyd Charisse for Cole Porter's *Silk Stockings* (1957), a song-and-dance version of *Ninotchka* (1939), where Fred performed the role done by Don Ameche in the Broadway musical. Astaire and Charisse danced well together, but the storyline was worn and the score essentially mediocre.

With his screen dancing seemingly behind him, Astaire accepted a dramatic (supporting) role in the science-fiction film *On the Beach* (1959), about a group of Australians awaiting the end of the world following a nuclear holocaust. As the veteran race-car driver, he proved adept in a telling straight acting assignment. In 1961 Fred was urbane and lighthearted when he costarred in Paramount's drawing room comedy *The Pleasure of His Company* as a man who returns to visit his grown daughter (Debbie Reynolds) and causes family havoc. At Columbia he was wasted in the Kim Novak–Jack Lemmon British-set comedy *The Notorious Landlady* (1962).

Astaire came to TV in 1957 in a dramatic role on *General Electric Theater*, and he did another episode in the CBS series in 1959. His biggest TV splash, however, was in 1958 in the special *An Evening With Fred Astaire* on NBC-TV, which won nine Emmy Awards. Beautiful Barrie Chase was his astute dancing partner in the special, as she would be in the two equally good follow-ups, *Another Evening With Fred Astaire*, in 1959 and 1960's *Astaire Time*. In the fall of 1961, Astaire hosted ABC-TV's anthology dramatic series *Alcoa Premiere* for two years and during the decade made guest appearances on *The Bob Hope Chrysler Theater*, *Dr. Kildare*, and *It Takes a Thief*, the latter on ABC-TV in 1969. This last guest appearance led a year later to a recurring role for Astaire as Robert Wagner's debonair detective father. He made his TV movie debut late in 1970 with

ABC-TV's *The Over-the-Hill Gang Rides Again*, which concerned a group of old lawmen who reteam to take on an outlaw gang. In 1971 he did a voice-over on the ABC-TV special *Santa Claus Is Coming to Town*.

In 1968, Fred returned to the big screen in *Finian's Rainbow*, an overlong musical with Petula Clark, but it was a good showcase for his singing and dancing in what proved to be his final movie musical. It was certainly superior to the British-made *Midas Run* (1969), which had him plotting a big bank heist. (His son had a brief role as an aviator in this feature.) Over the years, Astaire continued to make records, and in the 1950s and 1960s he made LPs for such labels as MGM, Kapp, and Verve. (The Verve albums he made in the 1950s were highly praised and considered highlights of Fred's illustrious career.) In the 1970s Astaire cut two albums for United Artists, and he and Bing Crosby did a pleasant duet album for that label called *A Couple of Song and Dance Men*.

In 1974 Astaire was one of the several on-screen hosts of the excellent compilation film *That's Entertainment!*, made up of footage from vintage MGM musicals, and two years later he and Gene Kelly teamed to host the sequel *That's Entertainment, Part II* (1976). In 1978 Fred and Helen Hayes costarred in the telefeature *A Family Upside Down* on NBC-TV, about how the elderly can become overly dependent on their children. Always anxious to try new things, Fred guest starred on ABC-TV's *Battlestar Galactica* science-fiction series. Later that year he was in the NBC-TV movie *The Man in the Santa Claus Suit*, which gave him seven (!) different roles. In this production about how Santa Claus affects the lives of several people, he sang the title theme. Fred's final film appearance came in *Ghost Story* (1981) in which he was one of four elderly men who are haunted by the vengeful spirit of the girl they used and murdered a half century before. That year Fred also received the American Film Institute's Life Achievement Award.

Phyllis Astaire had died in the fall of 1954, and Astaire did not remarry until the summer of 1980, when he wed thirty-five-year-old jockey Robyn Smith. Despite the age difference (which caused much media speculation), they led a quiet, happy life together in Astaire's Beverly Hills home. Adele Astaire died in the early 1980s. Fred, who once claimed he would live to be one hundred, remained in fairly good health until he was stricken with pneumonia and died at the age of eighty-eight in mid-1987. He was buried on June 24, 1987, seven years to the day into his second marriage. In June 1989 he was elected posthumously to the Academy of Television Arts and Sciences' Hall of Fame.

Filmography

Dancing Lady (MGM, 1933)
Flying Down to Rio (RKO, 1933)
The Gay Divorcee [The Gay Divorce] (RKO, 1934)
Roberta (RKO, 1935)
Top Hat (RKO, 1935)
Follow the Fleet (RKO, 1936)
Swing Time (RKO, 1936)
Shall We Dance? (RKO, 1937)
A Damsel in Distress (RKO, 1937)
Carefree (RKO, 1938)
The Story of Vernon and Irene Castle (RKO, 1939)

Broadway Melody of 1940 (1940)
Second Chorus (UA, 1941)
You'll Never Get Rich (Col, 1941)
Holiday Inn (Par, 1942)
You Were Never Lovelier (Col, 1942)
The Sky's the Limit (RKO, 1943)
Yolanda and the Thief (MGM, 1945)
Blue Skies (Par, 1946)
Ziegfeld Follies of 1946 (MGM, 1946)
Easter Parade (MGM, 1948)
The Barkleys of Broadway (MGM, 1949)
Three Little Words (MGM, 1950)
Let's Dance (Par, 1950)

Royal Wedding [Wedding Bells] (MGM, 1951)
The Belle of New York, (MGM, 1952)
The Band Wagon (MGM, 1953)
Daddy Long Legs (20th-Fox, 1954)
Funny Face (Par, 1956)
Silk Stockings (MGM, 1957)
On the Beach (UA, 1959)
The Pleasure of His Company (Par, 1961)
The Notorious Landlady (Col, 1962)
Paris When It Sizzles (Par, 1964) (voice only)
Finian's Rainbow (WB-7 Arts, 1968)
Midas Run [A Run on Gold] (Cin, 1969)

The Over-the-Hill Gang Rides Again (ABC-TV, 11/17/70)
The Towering Inferno (20th-Fox, 1974)
That's Entertainment! (MGM, 1974) (cohost)
The Amazing Dobermans (Golden, 1976)
That's Entertainment, Part 2 (MGM, 1976) (co-host)
Un Taxi Mauve [Purple Taxi] (Fr/It/Irish, 1977)
A Family Upside Down (NBC-TV, 4/9/78)
The Man in the Santa Claus Suit (NBC-TV, 12/23/79)
Ghost Story (Univ, 1981)

Broadway Plays

Over the Top (1917)
The Passing Show of 1918 (1918)
Apple Blossoms (1919)
The Love Letter (1921)
For Goodness Sake (1922)
The Bunch and Judy (1922)

Lady Be Good! (1924)
Funny Face (1927)
Smiles (1930)
The Band Wagon (1931)
Gay Divorce (1932)

Radio Series

The Fred Astaire Show (aka The Packard Hour) (NBC, 1936–37)

TV Series

Alcoa Premiere (ABC, 1961–63)

It Takes a Thief (ABC, 1969–70)

Album Discography

LPs

Annie Get Your Gun/Easter Parade (MGM E-3227) [ST]
Another Evening With Fred Astaire (Chrysler Corp K80P-1087-8) [ST/TV]
The Astaire Story (DRG 1102)
Astaire Time (Chrysler M80P-1003) (ST/TV)
Astaireable Fred (DRG 911)
Attitude Dancing (UA LA-580-G)
The Band Wagon (MGM E-3051) [ST]
The Band Wagon (X LVA-1001) [OC]
The Barkleys of Broadway (MGM SES-51ST) [ST]
The Belle of New York (10″ MGM E-108, Stet 15004) [ST]
The Best of Fred Astaire (Epic LN-3137)
Best of Fred Astaire from MGM Classic Films (MCA 25985)
Blue Skies (10″ Decca DL-5042, Decca DL-4259) w. Bing Crosby
Blue Skies (Sountrak 104) [ST]

Broadway Melody of 1940 (CIF 3002) [ST]
Cavalcade of Dance (Coral CRL-57008)
A Couple of Song and Dance Men (UA LA-588-G) w. Bing Crosby
Crazy Feet! (ASV 5021)
Daddy Long Legs/The Story of Vernon & Irene Castle (Caliban 6000) [ST]
Damsel in Distress/The Sky's the Limit (Curtain Calls 100/19) [ST]
Easter Parade (10″ MGM E-402, MGM E-3227) [ST]
Easy to Dance With (Verve 2114)
An Evening With Fred Astaire (Chrysler Corp) [ST/TV]
Finian's Rainbow (WB 2550) [ST]
Flying Down to Rio/Carefree (CIF 30040) [ST]
Follow the Fleet (Caliban 6024) [ST]
Follow the Fleet/Damsel in Distress (Scarce Rarities 5505) [ST]

Fred Astaire (Lion 70121)

Fred Astaire (Vocalion 3716)

Fred Astaire (VSP 23-24)

Fred Astaire and Ginger Rogers (EMI 184-95807/8)

Fred Astaire Live! (Pye 5542) [ST/TV]

Fred Astaire Now! (Kapp 1165/3049)

Fred Astaire Sings (MCA 1552)

Fred Astaire Sings and Swings Irving Berlin (MGM PR-1) (ST/TV)

Fred Astaire Sings Gershwin "Nice Work" (Saville 199)

The Fred Astaire Story (Clef 1001-04)

From Classic MGM Films (MCA 25985) [ST]

Funny Face (Monmouth-Evergreen 7037) [OC]

Funny Face (Verve 15001, Stet 15001) [ST]

The Gay Divorcee/Top Hat (Sountrak 105) [ST]

The Golden Age of Fred Astaire (Music for Pleasure 5827)

Holiday Inn (Decca DL-4256) w. Bing Crosby

Holiday Inn (Sountrak 112) [ST]

Lady Be Good (Monmouth-Evergreen 7036) [OC]

The Legendary Fred Astaire (Murray Hill 15532)

Let's Dance (Caliban 6017)

Mr. Top Hat (Verve 2010)

Never Before—The Songs From Original Soundtracks 1933-48 (Oxford 3038) [ST]

Nothing Thrilled Us Half as Much (Epic FLM-13103/FLS-15103)

Original Recordings 1935-40 (CBS 66316)

Pennies From Heaven (Warner Bros. 2HW-3639) [ST]

Roberta (Amalgamated 218) [ST]

Roberta/Top Hat (Star-Tone 204) [ST/R]

Royal Wedding (10″ MGM E-543, MGM E-3235) [ST]

Santa Claus Is Comin' to Town (MGM E/SDE-4732)

Second Chorus (Hollywood Soundstage 404) [ST]

A Shine on Your Shoes (MGM 2353-112)

Shoes With Wings On (MGM E-3413)

Silk Stockings (MGM E-3542) [ST]

The Special Magic of Fred Astaire (MGM 2317-082)

Starring Fred Astaire (Col C2-44233)

Starring Fred Astaire (Col SG-34272)

The Story of Vernon and Irene Castle (Caliban 6000) [ST]

Swing Time/Shall We Dance? (Sountrak 106) [ST]

Swing Time/The Gay Divorcee (EMI 1010) [ST]

Swing Time/The Gay Divorcee/Top Hat/Shall We Dance? (Pathé 184-95807-08) [ST]

S'Wonderful, S'Marvelous, S'Gershwin (Daybreak DR-2009) [ST/TV]

That's Dancing! (EMI America SJ-17149) [ST]

That's Entertainment! (MCA MCA2-11002) [ST]

That's Entertainment, Part 2 (MGM MG-1-5301, MCA 6155) [ST]

They Can't Take That Away From Me (UA 29918)

They Can't Take These Away From Me (UA 29941)

Three Evenings With Fred Astaire (Ava 1, Choreo 1, DRG 518) [ST/TV]

Three Little Words (10″ MGM E-516, MGM E-3229, Metro M/S-615) [ST]

Top Hat/Shall We Dance? (EMI 102) [ST]

Top Hat, White Tie and Golf Shoes (Facit 142) w. Bing Crosby, Ginger Rogers

Top Hat, White Tie and Tails (Saville 184)

Yolanda and the Thief/You'll Never Get Rich (Hollywood Soundstage HS-5001) [ST]

You Were Never Lovelier (Curtain Calls 10/24) [ST]

Ziegfeld Follies of 1946 (Curtain Calls 100/15-16) [ST]

CDs

Astaire Sings Gershwin (Saville 199)

Astaire Story (Verve 35649)

The Band Wagon (Sony Music Special Products AK-46197, Turner Classic Movies/Rhino R2-72257) [ST]

The Belle of New York (Sony Music Special Products AK-47701) [ST]

The Belle of New York/Good News/Rich, Young and Pretty (EMI 794869) [ST]

Best of Bing Crosby and Fred Astaire—A Couple of Song and Dance Men (Curb D21K-77617)

Best of Fred Astaire—18 Timeless Recordings (MCL 204)

Blue Skies (Great Movie Themes 60025, MCA MCAD-25989, Sandy Hook CDSH-2095) [ST]

Broadway Melody 1936-40 (Great Movie Themes 60007) [ST]

Cheek to Cheek (Pegasus) w. Ginger Rogers

Cocktail Hour (Columbia River Entertainment Group CRG-21806)

Complete London Sessions (EMI G-5200452)

Cover Girl/You Were Never Lovelier (Hollywood Soundstage 4005) [ST]

Crazy Feet (ASV CD-AJA-5021)

Crazy Feet (Empress 856)

The Cream of Fred Astaire (Pearl 7013)

The Dancing King (PMF Music Collection 90752)

Easter Parade (Sony Music Special Products AK-45392, Turner Classic Movies/Rhino R2-71960) [ST]

An Evening With Fred Astaire (Project 3 PRD-5120)

An Evening With Fred Astaire (Spectrum U4096)

An Evening With Fred Astaire (Warwick U-2050)

Fascinating Rhythm (Blue Moon BMCD-3029)

Fascinating Rhythm (Fremeaux 172)

Fascinating Rhythm—The Complete Recordings, Vol. 1 (Naxos Nostalgia NX8.12051)

A Fine Romance—Fred Astaire (ProArte CD 458)

Flying Down to Rio/Hollywood Hotel (Great Movie Themes 6008) [ST]

Fred Astaire (AWS 12204)

Fred Astaire (L'Art Vocal 16)

Fred Astaire at MGM—Steppin' Out (Columbia CK-47712)

Fred Astaire and Ginger Rogers at RKO (Rhino 72957)

Fred Astaire—Cheek to Cheek (ProArte CDD 431)

The Fred Astaire Collection—The Golden Greats (Déjà Vu S022-2)

Fred Astaire in Hollywood (Avid 570)

Fred Astaire Now (Official 12010)

Fred Astaire Sings (MCA 1552, Universal Special Marketing 1552)

From MGM Classic Films (MCA 33175)

Funny Face (DRG 15001, Stet CDSBL-15001, Verve 31453-12312) [ST]

Ginger Rogers and Fred Astaire, Vol. 1 (Chansons 005)

Ginger Rogers and Fred Astaire, Vol. 2 (Chansons 006)

Ginger Rogers and Fred Astaire, Vol. 3 (Chansons 007)

The Great Fred Astaire (Redx RMGR-0030)

Hit the Deck/Royal Wedding (MGM/EMI MGM-15) [ST]

Holiday Inn (Soundtrack Factory 33551) [ST]

Holiday Inn/Blue Skies (Vintage Jazz Classics VJC-1012) [ST]

Holiday Inn/Road to Morocco (Great Movie Themes 60027) [ST]

How Lucky Can You Get! Fred Astaire and Bing Crosby (EMI 789312)

The Incomparable Fred Astaire—Love of My Life (Halcyon 124)

Irving Berlin Songbook (Verve 829172)

The King of Jazz/King of Burlesque/Going Places/Carefree (Great Movie Themes 60019) [ST]

Legendary Fred Astaire (Dressed to Kill 404)

Let's Face the Music (Avid 577)

Let's Face the Music and Dance (ASV CD-AJA-5123)

Let's Face the Music and Dance (Prism PLACTCD-125)

Let's Sing and Dance With Fred Astaire (Great Music Themes 60015)

Love of My Life (Halcyon 124)

My Greatest Songs (MCA MCAD-1876)

Nice Work—Fred Astaire Sings George Gershwin (Saville CDSVL 199)

Night and Day: The Complete Recordings, Vol. 2 (Naxos Nostalgia NX-8.120519)

Pick Yourself Up (ABM ABMMCD1069)

Portrait of Fred Astaire (Gallerie 414)

Puttin' on the Ritz (Golden Stars 5106)

Puttin' on the Ritz (Remember 75010)

Quintessential (Sound Touch Factory 33515)

Rain Man (Capitol C2Y-91866) [ST]

Rarities (RCA 2337-2-R)

Royal Wedding (Sony Music Special Products AK-47028) [ST]

Shall We Dance (ABC 36043)

Silk Stockings (EMI 94251, Sony Music Special Products AK-46198) [ST]

The Sky's the Limit (Grand Movie Themes 60010) [ST]

Song and Dance Man (Classic Hits CDCD-1075)

Songs and Pictures 1928–44 (EPM Musique 066-983452-2)

Starring Fred Astaire (Col C244233)

Starring Fred Astaire (The Entertainers 405)

Steppin' Out—Astaire Sings (Verve 523006)

Stepping in Paradise (The Entertainers 246)

Swing Time/Shall We Dance (Radiola 2028) [ST]

That's Entertainment, Part 2 (Sony Music Special Products A2K-46872) [ST]

That's Entertainment! III (Angel CDQ-555215) [ST]

Three Little Words (EMI 794159) [ST]

Top Hat Hits From Hollywood (Legacy CK-64172)

Top Hat (Soundtrack Factory SFCD-33557) [ST]

Top Hat/Shall We Dance (Great Movie Themes 60042) [ST]

Top Hat, White Tie and Tails (Masters 503992)

Top Hat, White Tie and Tails (Saville 184)

Universal Legends Collection (MCA 1122662)

You Can't Have Everything/Go Into Your Dance/You'll Never Get Rich (Great Movie Themes 60014) [ST]

Yolanda and the Thief/You Were Never Lovelier (Hollywood Soundstage HSCD-4005) [ST]

Ziegfeld Follies of 1946 (Rhino R2-71959) [ST]

Gene Austin

(b. Eugene Lucas, Gainsville, Texas, June 24, 1900; d. Palm Springs, California, January 24, 1972)

Forever associated with the song "My Blue Heaven," Gene Austin was a smooth-sounding crooner whose phonograph records sold some 86 million copies during the 1920s and early 1930s. With his pleasing tenor voice, a propensity for hitting high notes, and an easygoing musical style, Gene Austin was the antithesis of the Jazz Age that spawned him. Starting out as a country singer, he changed his style under the guidance of Nathaniel Shilkret at Victor Records, and along with his close friend Nick Lucas, he made crooning a vogue. His success paved the way for Rudy Vallee, Bing Crosby, Dick Powell, and other romantic songsters. In addition to his singing, Austin composed many songs and found success in other media. Although he sang of "a little nest that nestles where the roses bloom," he was a vagabond who kept on the move throughout his life, often claiming, "I never want to nest anywhere."

He was born Eugene Lucas in Gainsville, Texas, on June 24, 1900, but he grew up in Yellow Pine and Minden, Louisiana. His father died when he was small, and Gene's mother later remarried, to Jim Austin. Music came easily to the youth, and by the time he was a teenager he had the urge to roam. At age fifteen, he ran away from home with a circus and, while traveling with the aggregation, he learned to play the calliope. Lying about his age, he joined the Army in 1916 and saw service with General John J. Pershing in the Mexican Punitive Expedition; during the First World War he was stationed in France. After the war Gene returned home to study both dentistry and law and, for a time, he was enrolled at the University of Baltimore. However, his love of music became the driving force behind his career efforts, and he began working as a professional singer.

In the early 1920s Gene Lucas changed his name to Gene Austin to avoid confusion with another rising music performer, Nick Lucas. At this time Austin teamed with Roy Bergere, and billed as Austin and Bergere, they performed a comedy duet in vaudeville in the East and Midwest. In the spring of 1924 they made their recording debut for Vocalion Records performing "A Thousand Miles From Here." The duo also composed the song "How Come You Do Me Like You Do?" which became a national favorite in 1924. While working at Vocalion, Austin was asked to team with George Reneau, "the Blind Musician of the Smoky Mountains." Together they cut a series of successful records for that label as well as for Edison while Austin also continued working with Roy Bergere.

Early in 1925, popular Victor recording star Aileen Stanley recorded Gene Austin's tune "When My Sugar Walks Down the Street," and she insisted he accompany her on the record. The label next teamed him with Carson Robison on a duet of "Way Down Home." In the spring of 1926 Gene Austin had his first solo Victor best-seller, "Yearning," and he was to remain with the label for six more years, developing into one of the top two (the other was Nick Lucas) record sellers in the nation. His Victor bestsellers included such numbers as "Yes Sir, That's My Baby,"

Gloria Stuart, Gene Austin, and Ruth Etting in *Gift of Gab* (1934).
[Courtesy of Michael R. Pitts]

"Five Foot Two, Eyes of Blue," "Bye Bye Blackbird," "One Sweet Letter From You," "The Sweetheart of Sigma Chi," "Carolina Moon," "I Can't Give You Anything But Love," and "Ain't Misbehavin'." His two biggest sellers for Victor were "My Blue Heaven" and "Ramona." The former was done in 1927 and eventually sold over 8 million copies, while "Ramona" came out the next year and had sales in excess of 3 million platters.

Like most popular recording artists of the day, Gene Austin toured in vaudeville, plugging his latest records and making a good living from the stage. In 1927 he also had a successful stand in London, and during the rest of the 1920s he became a very wealthy man thanks to his vaudeville appearances and record royalties. He and Nathaniel Shilkret composed the song "The Lonesome Road" in 1927, and it was a bestseller for Austin on Victor Records. In 1929 the composition was used in the Universal film *Show Boat*.

While the Roaring Twenties brought Gene Austin his greatest success the bubble burst with the coming of the Depression. As his career began to fade with dwindling record sales, he turned to radio but was unable to obtain a sustaining network series. In 1931 he began cutting records for the American Record Company, which sold its product on a variety of labels (Banner, Conqueror, Oriole, Perfect) in dime stores. In the early 1930s he was a vocalist on the *California Melodies* radio show before touring in musical revues like *Broadway Rhapsody* and *Going Places*. In the mid–1930s he teamed with bass player Candy Candido and guitarist Otto "Coco" Heimel, who were billed as Candy and Coco, and he had a career resurgence. He returned to Victor in 1934 to record his own song "Ridin' Around in the Rain," and it sold well.

It was in 1934 that Austin made his film debut with Candy and Coco in the Joan Crawford vehicle, *Sadie McKee,* at MGM. During a cabaret sequence, Austin sings a hot rendition of "After You've Gone." That year also found him with Candy and Coco in the Universal musical *Gift of Gab* performing "Blue Sky Avenue," which failed in its attempt to repeat the success of his "My Blue Heaven." He also appeared briefly in Mae West's ribald *Belle of the Nineties* (1934) singing "My American Beauty" while one of his compositions, "When a St. Louis Woman Comes Down to New Orleans," was performed by Miss West. That same year he appeared in the first of four short subjects in which he would star for RKO, beginning with *Ferry-Go-Round*, where he crooned "My Blue Heaven," "Pretty Lady," "Baby, Won't You Please Come Home," "Dear Old Southland," and "Nobody Loves Me No More." In the 1935 RKO short *Night Life*, Austin performed a number of songs including "My Melancholy Baby" and his standard "My Blue Heaven."

Mae West had taken a shine to Austin, and she hired him to write the songs for her sassy *Klondike Annie* (1936), and he created for the film such tunes as "I'm an Occidental Woman in an Oriental Mood for Love," "Little Bar Fly," and "Mr. Deep Blue Sea." He also had a featured role in this Paramount release playing a singing evangelist, performing "You'll Feel Better in the Morning" and "It's Better to Give Than to Receive." He also made two additional RKO shorts, *Bad Medicine* (1936) and *Trailing Along* (1937). In the former he sang "Smoke Rings," "When My Sugar Walks Down the Street," "Sweet Sue," and "Git Along," while *Trailing Along* found him doing numbers like "Trailing Down the Highway" and "You've Got to Get That Mellow Jive." By now Russell Hall had replaced Candy Candido in the Candy and Coco backup act for Gene.

The quickie *Songs and Saddles* (1938) was Austin's only Western feature. It was made to cash in on the popularity of the Gene Autry musical-cowboy pictures. Austin was seen as himself as he and his musical troupe attempt to stop a gang of land-grabbers. He handled the rugged role surprisingly well and also composed a number of tunes he sang in the feature, including "Song of the Saddle," "I Fell Down and Broke My Heart," "I'm Comin' Home," and "That Rootin' Tootin' Shootin' Man From Texas." To help the box-office grosses on the picture, Austin and his touring company appeared with the film when it was shown on the road in the South. Meanwhile, from early in 1937 until late in 1938, Gene Austin was the featured vocalist on comedian Joe Penner's CBS radio program.

By the late 1930s, Gene Austin's greatest following was in the South. During this period, he had a group, including Candy and Coco and Joan Brooks, that toured with a musical revue financed by Mae West. Late in the decade, though, matters slipped so bad financially for Austin that, for a time, he broadcast from a Mexican border station at Del Rio using the name Bob Bennett. Mae West, however, brought him back to Hollywood in 1940 for a brief appearance as himself leading a band, including Candy and Coco, as she sang "Willy of the Valley" in *My Little Chickadee* (1940).

In the early 1940s, Gene Austin starred in a batch of three-minute musical shorts for Soundies Distributing Corporation of America and Murray Hollywood Productions; several of these featured singer Doris Sherrell, to whom he was married at the time. He also sang "My Blue Heaven" in the inconsequential Universal musical *Moon Over Las Vegas* (1944) starring Anne Gwynne, and in the East Side Kids comedy *Follow the Leader* (1944) he performed his composition, "Now and Then." He reprised "My Blue Heaven" yet again in the Universal short *Pagliacci Swings It* (1944) and in the 1945 Soundies' musical *My Blue Heaven*.

During the late 1930s Gene had recorded for Decca Records as well as for Standard and Thesaurus Transcriptions. In the mid-'40s he resumed his recording career for the Four Star and Universal labels as well as forming his own record firm, Gene Austin Records. (During the 1920s and early 1930s, he had also operated Gene Austin, Incorporated, a music publishing company.) He made guest appearances on such radio shows as those of the Andrews Sisters and *Philco Radio Hall of Fame*. Another aspect of his activities was Austin's penchant for purchasing a nightclub, starring himself as its main attraction, and then selling the business for a profit. It was a practice he would continue on and off throughout the remainder of his career. In the late 1940s, Gene ceased performing for a time after he (incorrectly) was reported to be missing at sea. The rumor even spawned a memorial service conducted for him. The incident disturbed him greatly.

The early 1950s found the veteran performer resuming his career, and in 1954 he cut a long-playing album, *Blue Heaven*, for RCA Victor. His career really rebounded in 1957 after NBC-TV aired "The Gene Austin Story" on *The Goodyear Television Playhouse* (April 20, 1957), with George Grizzard playing the title role and Gene dubbing the vocals. At the end of the hour show Austin appeared and sang his latest composition "Too Late," and his RCA single of it put him back on the record charts for the first time in a quarter of a century.

After that success, Gene appeared on such TV shows as those of Ed Sullivan, Jimmy Dean, Red Skelton, Dave Garroway, *The Woolworth Hour*, and Patti Page's *The Big Record*. In 1958, he returned to London for a successful engagement. He also cut albums for RCA and Dot and toured the nation with his club act. Austin entered politics in 1962 when he opposed Nevada governor Grant Sawyer in the Democratic primary (he had been a Las Vegas resident since the 1940s and had operated a gambling casino called "My Blue Heaven" there); but he and running mate Eddie Jackson (of Clayton-Jackson-Durante fame) lost to Sawyer and his running mate, former film star Rex Bell. After that Gene moved to Florida, where he operated still another "My Blue Heaven" club, and in the late 1960s he settled in California.

Austin's last years were spent like his previous ones, traveling with his club act and writing songs. Early in 1971 he appeared on Merv Griffin's CBS-TV tribute to popular composers, and later in the year he assisted in establishing the Museum of Jazz in New Orleans. By now, however, he was suffering from cancer, and his final appearance was at the Jack London Club in Palm Springs, where he brought in the year 1972 performing his old favorites. Three weeks later, on January 24, 1972, at the age of seventy-one, he died in a Palm Springs hospital. He was survived by his fifth wife, Gigi, and two daughters from previous marriages: Charlotte (who, as Charlotte Austin, starred in several 1950s' movies) and Ann, and three grandchildren. It is ironic that although Gene Austin wanted originally to become a country singer, his godson (David Houston) and cousin (Tommy Overstreet) both became popular country singing stars in the 1960s and 1970s.

Filmography

Show Boat (Univ, 1929) (song only)
Sadie McKee (MGM, 1934)
Ferry-Go-Round (RKO, 1934) (s)
Bad Medicine (RKO, 1934) (s)
The Gift of Gab (Univ, 1934)
Belle of the Nineties (Par, 1934) (also song)
Night Life (RKO, 1935) (s)
Klondike Annie (Par, 1936) (also songs)
Trailing Along (RKO, 1937) (s)
Songs and Saddles (Colony, 1938) (also songs)
My Little Chickadee (Univ, 1940)
One Dozen Roses (Soundies, 1942) (s)
That Rootin' Tootin' Shootin' Man from Texas (Soundies, 1942) (s)
I Hear You Knockin' But You Can't Come In (Soundies, 1942) (s)

Take Your Shoes Off Daddy (Murray Hollywood Productions, 1943) (s)
I Hear You Knockin' But You Can't Come In (Murray Hollywood Productions, 1943) (s)
You're Marvelous (Murray Hollywood Productions, 1943) (s)
Boogie Woogie Wedding (Murray Hollywood Productions, 1943) (s)
My Melancholy Baby (Murray Hollywood Productions, 1943) (s)
I Want to Be Bad (Soundies, 1944) (s)
I Want to Lead a Band (Soundies, 1944) (s)
Moon Over Las Vegas (Univ, 1944)
Imagine (Soundies, 1944) (s)
Follow the Leader (Mon, 1944) (also song)
Pagliacci Swings It (Univ, 1944) (s)
My Blue Heaven (Soundies, 1945) (s)

Radio Series

Gene Austin (NBC, 1931; NBC, 1932)

California Melodies (CBS, 1932–34)
The Joe Penner Show (CBS, 1937–38)

Album Discography

LPs

All-Time Favorites by Gene Austin (Vik LX-998, X LVA-1007)
Blue Heaven (10″ RCA LPM-3200)
Folk Singers (10″ Victor LPT-6) w. Jimmie Rodgers, Vernon Dalhart
Gene Austin and His Lonesome Road (Fraternity 1006)

Gene Austin's Great Hits (Dot 3300/25300)
My Blue Heaven (Decca DL-8433)
My Blue Heaven (RCA LPM-2490)
Old Pals Are the Best Pals (Sunbeam 507)
Restless Heart (RCA LPM-1547)
This Is Gene Austin (RCA VPM-6056)

CDs

Gene Austin (Sounds of Century 1802)
A Time to Relax (Take Two TT-414CD)
The Voice of the Southland (ASV CD-AJA-5217)

Sterling Holloway, Gene Autry, and Bert Dodson (of Cass County Boys) in *Twilight on the Rio Grande* (1947). [Courtesy of JC Archives]

Gene Autry

(b. Orvon Gene Autry, Tioga, Texas, September 29, 1907; d. Studio City, California, October 2, 1998)

Gene Autry started the craze of the singing movie cowboy in the mid-1930s, and he utilized his enormous popularity with the public to develop a number of lucrative business interests. In 1988 *Forbes* magazine named him one of the richest people in America with assets of $230 million. While many critics insist Autry was a less-than-mediocre actor (he was) and only a mediocre singer (he was actually a very good vocalist), the performer was so consistently popular, especially in the South and Midwest, that he single-handedly changed the image of the American cowboy forever. He devised a Cowboy Code of Clean Living as a model for the country's youth, and he forever espoused the American dream. Gene Autry's tremendous show-business success not only encompassed motion pictures but also radio, personal appearances, records, television, songwriting, and all types of merchandising. Even long after he retired from performing (and had become a man of business and baseball), his fans remembered him fondly as the clean-cut cowboy who crooned the songs of the plains.

The future cowboy hero was born Orvon Gene Autry on September 29, 1907, in Tioga, Texas, the son of Delbert and Elnora Ozmont Autry. He was the eldest of four children, having two younger sisters and a brother. His grandfather, a minister, taught young Autry to sing at age five and, thereafter, the boy sang in the local church choir. At the age of twelve, Autry received his first guitar, and during one summer while a teenager he worked in a medicine show. After high school he became a telegraph operator in Chelsea, Oklahoma, for the Frisco Line, but show business had become his passion. He developed his guitar technique after coming under the influence of popular singer-guitarist Nick Lucas's recordings. Gene practiced singing while on the job during the day and also wrote songs with fellow telegrapher Jimmie Long. One evening when Will Rogers stopped by Autry's office to send his syndicated newspaper column, he heard Gene singing and suggested he perform on radio. This led to work on station KVOO in Tulsa as "The Oklahoma Yodeling Cowboy," for which he performed gratis.

Gene cut a single for Paramount Records in 1927, but the company went bankrupt before it was issued. Autry then relocated to New York City, where he looked up two Oklahoma men, Johnny and Frankie Marvin. Johnny had been very successful onstage and in recordings in the mid-to-late 1920s and had a vaudeville act with his brother. They befriended young Autry and tried to get him bookings as well as a recording contract. In the fall of 1929 Gene managed to get a session with Victor Records and recorded two tunes, "My Dreaming of You" and "My Alabama Home," the latter written by Johnny Marvin. Autry then began recording for a number of dime-store labels like Champion, Clarion, Conqueror, Diva, Harmony, Perfect, and Velvet Tone, under his own name as well as using such pseudonyms as Bob Clayton, Johnny Dodds, John Hardy, Overton Hatfield, Sam Hill, Gene Johnson, Tom Long, and Jimmie Smith.

In 1930 Autry signed with Art Satherley's new American Record Corporation (ARC), and the next year he and Jimmie Long had a best-selling record of "That Silver Haired Daddy of Mine," a tune they had written. In spring 1931, Gene married Long's niece, Ina Mae Spivey. The best-selling song also changed Autry's singing style to a more urban, pop format. (His earlier recordings had reflected the influence of then-popular country singer Jimmie Rodgers.) The year 1930 also found Gene working in Chicago at the *National Barn Dance* radio show on WLS, a station that reached listeners in most of the Midwest. As a result of the radio program, personal appearances, and more best-selling records (like "Mexicali Rose") Gene Autry quickly became a household name in the Midwest. In 1932, Sears Roebuck began marketing the Gene Autry Guitar, and Autry was being featured on sheet music and songbooks.

In 1934, Autry, Smiley Burnette, and Frankie Marvin came to Hollywood, where they appeared in the barn dance sequence in the Ken Maynard Western *In Old Santa Fe* for Mascot Pictures. Gene was especially impressive in his brief singing appearance and landed a small acting part in another Maynard-Mascot production, the serial *Mystery Mountain* (1934). When Ken Maynard quit Mascot in 1935, studio chief Nat Levine took a chance and toplined the screen newcomer as the lead in the science-fiction/Western cliffhanger, *The Phantom Empire* (1935). It proved to be a great success.

Also in 1935, Mascot merged with Monogram and several other studios to form Republic Pictures. Autry was signed to star in the Western feature *Tumbling Tumbleweeds* (1935) with Smiley Burnette as his pal Frog Millhouse. Despite Autry's lack of acting acumen, he proved to be a sensation in the film and quickly became Republic's most popular action-film star. From 1936 to 1954 he was in the *Motion Picture Herald's* poll of Top Ten Money-Making Western Stars, except for 1943–45, when he was off the screen; and he topped the poll from 1937–42. From 1940–42 he was also ranked in the poll's Top Ten Money-Making Stars, the only "B" Western star to make that chart in those years.

Gene's Republic pictures were slickly made standardized affairs, with Autry as the hero who saves the heroine from the villains and sings a number of songs along the way. His movies were particularly popular with rural audiences and youngsters. Despite the fact his movies were consistent moneymakers, he was paid very little by Republic, his initial contract calling for only a salary of $150 per week. In the late 1930s Autry walked out on Republic, and the studio threatened to replace him with Roy Rogers; but a new contract had him making $12,500 per picture. More lucrative, however, were personal appearances, and Autry was popular on the rodeo circuit. When he toured the British Isles in 1939 some 750,000 people showed up in Dublin, Ireland to see him in a parade. By now Autry was recording for Okeh Records, and he had many bestsellers, some from his films, like "Tumbling Tumbleweeds," "Nobody's Darlin' But Mine," "There's a Gold Mine in the Sky," "You Are My Sunshine," "Rainbow on the Rio Colorado," "Have I Told You Lately That I Love You," "South of the Border," "Amapola," and "That Little Kid Sister of Mine," in addition to his theme song, "Back in the Saddle Again," written with Ray Whitley.

In 1940 Gene came to network radio with his *Melody Ranch* program on CBS; it was one of his few media activities that did not include his beautiful horse Champion. That year also found him the subject of the newspaper comic strip *Gene Autry Rides*, and late in 1941 the first Gene Autry comic book appeared. Comic books about him were on the newsstands until 1959. In the 1930s and 1940s, he was also the subject of Whitman Publishing's fictional Better Little Books for Children, and in the 1950s he was featured in the company's Little Golden and Tell-a-Tale books. In addition, from 1944 to 1957 he was featured in eight novels published by Whitman.

Late in 1941 a town in Oklahoma was named for Gene, and as the year ended he volunteered for military service and was inducted on a *Melody Ranch* radio broadcast. At first he entertained troops and sold war bonds, but after earning his pilot's license he flew cargo and men in North Africa and the Far East for the duration of World War II. After the war, Autry returned home to resume his film career, but he found his number-one cowboy status had been usurped by Roy Rogers (of Republic Pictures) in his absence. In 1946 Autry returned to the screen in *Sioux City Sue*, but he was no longer happy at Republic and left the studio in 1947 to produce his own pictures at Columbia. He also continued on radio, made personal appearances, and had several best-selling records for Columbia, including the children's favorites "Here Comes Santa Claus," "Peter Cottontail," and "Rudolph, the Red-Nosed Reindeer" (which sold over 10 million records).

In 1950 Gene came to television with *The Gene Autry Show*, which ran on CBS-TV for over ninety episodes through 1955. Costarring with him on the program was Pat Buttram, with whom he had worked at WLS in the 1930s. In fact, Autry was instrumental in bringing many of his WLS coworkers to Hollywood, including Lulu Belle and Scotty Wiseman, Patsy Montana, Max Terhune, the Cass County Boys, and the Maple City Four. Smiley Burnette was Autry's costar in scores of films, and Frankie Marvin appeared in nearly all of his pictures as well as writing songs for them. In addition, Johnny Marvin composed many songs for Autry's movies and handled some of his business affairs until Marvin's death in 1944.

Although now more portly, Autry continued to make feature films until 1953, when he left the screen after *The Last of the Pony Riders*. He had starred in eighty-nine features and one serial plus having appeared in the two Ken Maynard productions. In 1958 Autry appeared on NBC-TV's *Wide, Wide World* program in a tribute to Western movies. The show was partially telecast from Gene Autry's Melody Ranch Movie Location in Newhall, California. He had purchased the ranch in 1940 (and it would burn down in 1962). In 1959 Autry returned to the screen for the last time for a guest bit in Bob Hope's *Alias Jesse James*. (Contrary to reports, Autry did not appear in the unissued 1969 film *The Silent Treatment*.) Autry continued to record for Columbia Records well into the 1950s, and then he formed his own company, Republic Records, which also owned Challenge Records. He recorded for both labels. In 1962 he cut his final album, *Gene Autry's Golden Hits*, for RCA. In 1956 his radio show *Melody Ranch* left the air after broadcasting for sixteen years. The show format returned to TV from 1961 to 1972 over Autry's Los Angeles TV station KTLA and was hosted by his radio costar Johnny Bond. Autry made occasional appearances on the program, which was also syndicated.

Around 1960 Gene began to ease himself out of show business in deference to his many other lucrative financial activities. Since the mid-'40s he had been involved in broadcasting with his Golden West Broadcasting Corporation, and he controlled several radio and television stations throughout the country. Moreover, he owned several hotels, including Palm Springs' Gene Autry Hotel. During the 1950s, in addition to his own TV series, Gene Autry's company produced a number of TV Western series, including *The Adventures of Champion, the Wonder Horse; Buffalo Bill Jr.; Annie Oakley; The Range Rider*; and the first season of *Death Valley Days*. Perhaps his most noted enterprise was his purchase of the California Angels baseball team late in 1960. In 1966 the team moved to a new stadium in Anaheim. In 1969 Gene Autry was inducted into the Country Music Hall of Fame.

During the 1970s Gene made occasional guest appearances on TV shows like *Hee Haw* and *The Tonight Show*, but primarily he kept involved in his assorted commercial activities. Nevertheless, he was always available for interviews, happily and openly talking about the past and his long career. During that decade his record label, Republic, was revived, and several albums by Autry made up of "Melody Ranch" radio songs were issued to good sales. In 1977 some of his recordings were used in the feature film *Semi-Tough*, and in 1978 his autobiography, *Back in the Saddle Again*, written with Mickey Hershowitz, was published by Doubleday. The next year Henry Crowell Jr. portrayed Autry in the television tribute, *Gene Autry, An American Hero*. In 1980 the veteran star was inducted into the Cowboy Hall of Fame of Great Westerners in Oklahoma City, Oklahoma, but in the spring of that year his wife of forty-eight years, Ina Mae, died. In accordance with her will, Autry sold several of his properties, including KTLA.

The decade of the 1980s found Gene Autry making a somewhat surprising return to the limelight. On July 19, 1981, he wed thirty-nine-year-old banking executive Jackie Ellam, whom he had known through various business transactions since 1964. He received plenty of publicity when the California Angels won the baseball pennant in the mid–1980s, and in 1987 Autry returned to television, with Pat Buttram, hosting *Melody Ranch Theater* on The Nashville Network. On the show, the two partners showed Autry's old films and discussed various aspects of his career. Late in 1988 the Gene Autry Western Heritage Museum in Los Angeles' Griffith Park was opened to much fanfare. The museum was designed as a permanent shrine for Gene Autry memorabilia and to the heritage of the American frontier.

Gene Autry made his final recording in 1989, reciting "The Cowboy Code" with Erich Kunzel and the Cincinnati Pops Orchestra on the CD *Happy Trails: Round-Up 2* for the Telarc label. Meanwhile, *Happy Trails Theater* ended its run on TNN cable in 1991.

Autry's famed horse Champion died May 9, 1990, at the star's Melody Ranch at Newhall, California. During the 1990s Gene kept busy with his business interests and promoting the Gene Autry Western Heritage Museum, which had a value of $54 million. By mid-decade the star was worth in excess of $320 million, although he was no longer listed as one of *Forbes* magazine's four hundred richest Americans. He was the subject of the 1994 documentary *Gene Autry, Melody of the West*, narrated by Johnny Cash. In the spring of 1996 the Walt Disney Company bought a 25 percent interest in Autry's baseball team and renamed it the Anaheim Angels later that year. Following a bout with pneumonia, Gene died October 2, 1998, at his Studio City, California, home, two days after his ninety-first birthday.

Despite all the success and wealth Gene Autry attained from the business world, he will always be best remembered as the singing cowboy hero. It is to this image that he owed his success, and despite all it brought him, he never took that perception too seriously. He once summed up his successful film career by stating, "We had to have a decent story, good music, comic relief, enough action with chases and gunfights, and a little romance. But we had to treat that love angle real careful. Almost no clinches or embraces. I could put my arm around the girl only if it was necessary to stop her falling off a cliff."

Filmography

In Old Santa Fe (Mascot, 1934)
Mystery Mountain (Mascot, 1934) (serial)
The Phantom Empire (Mascot, 1935) (serial)
Tumbling Tumbleweeds (Rep, 1935)
Melody Trail (Rep, 1935)
Sagebrush Troubador (Rep, 1935)
The Singing Vagabond (Rep, 1935)
Red River Valley (Rep, 1936)
Comin' Round the Mountain (Rep, 1936)
The Singing Cowboy (Rep, 1936)
Guns and Guitars (Rep, 1936)
Oh, Susannah! (Rep, 1936)
Ride, Ranger, Ride (Rep, 1936)
The Old Corral (Rep, 1936)
Round-Up Time in Texas (Rep, 1937)
Git Along, Little Dogies [Serenade of the West] (Rep, 1937)
Rootin' Tootin' Rhythm [Rhythm on the Ranch] (Rep, 1937)
Yodelin' Kid From Pine Ridge [The Hero of Pine Ridge] (Rep, 1937)
Public Cowboy No. 1. (Rep, 1937)
Holiday Greetings (Unk, 1937) (s)
Boots and Saddles (Rep, 1937)
Manhattan Merry-Go-Round [Manhattan Music Box] (Rep, 1937)
The Old Barn Dance (Rep, 1938)
Gold Mine in the Sky (Rep, 1938)
Man From Music Mountain (Rep, 1938)
Prairie Moon (Rep, 1938)
Rhythm of the Saddle (Rep, 1938)
Western Jamboree (Rep, 1939)
Home on the Prairie (Rep, 1939)
Mexicali Rose (Rep, 1939)
Blue Montana Skies (Rep, 1939)
Mountain Rhythm (Rep, 1939)
Colorado Sunset (Rep, 1939)
In Old Monterey (Rep, 1939)
Rovin' Tumbleweeds (Rep, 1939)
South of the Border (Rep, 1939)
Rancho Grande (Rep, 1940)
Shooting High (20th-Fox, 1940)
Gaucho Serenade (Rep, 1940)
Carolina Moon (Rep, 1940)
Rodeo Dough (MGM, 1940) (s)
Ride, Tenderfoot, Ride (Rep, 1940)
Melody Ranch (Rep, 1940)
Ridin' on a Rainbow (Rep, 1940)
Meet Roy Rogers (Rep, 1941) (s)
Meet the Stars—Stars at Play (Rep, 1941) (s)
Meet the Stars—Stars Past and Present (Rep, 1941)(s)
Meet the Stars—Variety Reel No. 4 (Rep, 1941)(s)
Back in the Saddle (Rep, 1941)
The Singing Hills (Rep, 1941)

Sunset in Wyoming (Rep, 1941)
Under Fiesta Stars (Rep, 1941)
Down Mexico Way (Rep, 1941)
Sierra Sue (Rep, 1941)
Cowboy Serenade [Serenade of the West] (Rep, 1942)
Heart of the Rio Grande (Rep, 1942)
Home in Wyomin' (Rep, 1942)
Stardust on the Sage (Rep, 1942)
Call of the Canyon (Rep, 1942)
Bell of Capistrano (Rep, 1942)
Screen Snapshots #108 (Col, 1942) (s)
Sioux City Sue (Rep, 1946)
Trail to San Antone (Rep, 1947)
Twilight on the Rio Grande (Rep, 1947)
Saddle Pals (Rep, 1947)
Robin Hood of Texas (Rep, 1947)
The Last Round-Up (Rep, 1947)
The Strawberry Roan [Fools Awake] (Col, 1948)
Loaded Pistols (Col, 1949)
The Big Sombrero (Col, 1949)
Riders of the Whistling Pines (Col, 1949)
Rim of the Canyon (Col, 1949)
Screen Snapshots #129 (Col, 1949) (s)
The Cowboy and the Indians (Col, 1949)
Riders in the Sky (Col, 1949)
Sons of New Mexico [The Brat] (Col, 1949)
Mule Train (Col, 1950)
Beyond the Purple Hills (Col, 1950)
Cow Town [Barbed Wire] (Col, 1950)
Indian Territory (Col, 1950)
The Blazing Sun (Col, 1951)
Gene Autry and the Mounties (Col, 1951)
Texans Never Cry (Col, 1951)
Whirlwind (Col, 1951)
Silver Canyon (Col, 1951)
Hills of Utah (Col, 1951)
Valley of Fire (Col, 1951)
The Old West (Col, 1952)
Night Stage to Galveston (Col, 1952)
Apache Country (Col, 1952)
Wagon Team (Col, 1952)
Blue Canadian Rockies (Col, 1952)
Barbed Wire [False News] (Col, 1952)
Winning of the West (Col, 1953)
On Top of Old Smoky (Col, 1953)
Goldtown Ghost Riders (Col, 1953)
Pack Train (Col, 1953)
Memories in Uniform (Col, 1953) (s)
Saginaw Trail (Col, 1953)
Last of the Pony Riders (Col, 1953)
Hollywood Cowboy Stars (Col, 1954) (s)
Alias Jesse James (UA, 1959)
Gene Autry, Melody of the West (Galen Film Productions, 1994) (documentary)

Radio Series

National Barn Dance (WLS, 1930–34)

Gene Autry's Melody Ranch (CBS, 1940–56)

TV Series

Gene Autry Show (CBS, 1950–56)

Melody Ranch Theater (TNN, 1987–1991)

Album Discography

LPs

Back in the Saddle Again (Encore P-14380)
Back in the Saddle Again (Har HL-7399/HS-11276)
Christmas Favorites (Col Special Products P-15766)
Christmas With Gene Autry (Challenge 600, Republic 6018)
Christmastime With Gene Autry (Misletoe 1207)
Country and Western Memories (Cattle CAT-8008)
Country Music Hall of Fame (Col CL-1035)
Cowboy Hall of Fame (Republic 6012)
Everyone's a Child at Christmas (Col Special Products P-15767)
Famous Favorites/His Golden Hits (Suffolk Marketing)
Gene Autry and Champion Western Adventures (Col CL-677, Har HL-9505)
Gene Autry at the Rodeo (Col JL-8001)
Gene Autry Classics, Vol. 1 (Republic 6021)
The Gene Autry Collection (Murray Hill 17079)
Gene Autry—Columbia Historic Edition (Col FD-37465)
Gene Autry Favorites (Republic 6013, Birchmont 562)
Gene Autry Favorites/Live from Madison Square Garden (Republic 1968/69)
Gene Autry—50th Anniversary (Republic 6022)
Gene Autry Live (Amalgamated 118)
Gene Autry Sings (Hallmark HM-582)
Gene Autry Sings (Har HL-7399/HS-11199)
Gene Autry's Christmas Classics (Starday SD-1038)
Golden Hits (RCA LPM/LSP-2623)
Great Western Hits (Har HL-7332)
Greatest Hits (Col CL-1575)
Holiday Time With Gene Autry (Republic 1966)
Little Johnny Pilgrim and Guffy the Goofy Gobbler (10″ Col MJV-83)

Live From Madison Square Garden (Republic 6014, Bulldog 1024)
Melody Ranch (Golden Age 5012)
Melody Ranch (Melody Ranch 101) w. Johnny Bond
Melody Ranch (Radiola 1048)
The Melody Ranch Show (Murray Hill 897296)
Merry Christmas With Gene Autry (10″ Col CL-2547)
Peter Cottontail (10″ Col CL-2568, Har HL-9555)
Rudolph the Red-Nosed Reindeer (Design DLPX-5, Grand Prix KSX-11, Hurrah HX-11)
Rudolph the Red-Nosed Reindeer and Other Children's Christmas Favorites (Har HL-9550)
Rusty the Rocking Horse and Bucky, the Bucking Bronco (10″ Col MVJ-94)
The Singing Cowboy (Republic 1967)
Songs of Faith (Republic 6107)
Sounds Like Jimmie Rodgers, Vol. 2 (Anthology of Country Music AMC-19)
South of the Border (Republic 6001, Bulldog 1021)
South of the Border/All American Cowboy (Republic 6011)
Stampede (10″ Col JL-8009)
The Story of the Nativity (10″ Col MJV-82)
20 Golden Pieces (Bulldog 2013)
Twenty-Two All-Time Favorites (GRT 2103-720)
The Very Rarest of Young Autry (Peace Maker 01)
Western Classics (10″ Col CL-6020)
Western Classics (10″ Col HL-9001)
Western Classics, Vol. 2 (10″ Col HL-9002)
The Yellow Rose of Texas (Bear Family 15204)
The Young Gene Autry (Six Gun Singers 69)
The Young Gene Autry, Vol. 2 (Prairie Justice 70)
The Young Gene Autry, Vol. 3 (Prairie Justice 71)

CDs

Always Your Pal, Gene Autry (Sony Wonder LK-63422)
At the Melody Ranch (Collector's Choice 1009)
Back in the Saddle Again (Country Stars)
Back in the Saddle Again (Sony Music Special Products AZ4302)
Back in the Saddle Again—22 Country Songs (BCD CTS-55430)

The Best of Gene Autry (Heartland Music 5983-2)
Best of Gene Autry (St. Clair 219)
Best of Gene Autry—South of the Border (Castle MACCD-219)
Best of the Singing Cowboys (Soundwaves SWNCD020) w. Roy Rogers
Blues Singer 1929-31 (Legacy KG-4987)
Christmas Album (Legacy Entertainment 3)

Christmas Cowboy (Laserlight 15-460)

Christmas Favorites (Sony Music Special Products 15766)

Christmas for Kids (Exclusive 65001) w. Von Trapp Family

Country Christmas (Mastertone) w. Faron Young

Country Music Hall of Fame 1965 (King 3819)

Cowboy's Christmas (KRB Music Companies KRB-8060-2)

Deep in the Heart of Texas (Pegasus 831)

The Essential Gene Autry 1933-46 (Legacy CK-48957)

Gene Autry (Sounds of a Century 1702)

Gene Autry at Melody Ranch (Heartland Music 12749-2)

Gene Autry Christmas (Legacy CK-57904)

Gene Autry Show: Complete 1950s Television Recordings (Varese Sarabande VSD-66190)

Gene Autry Sings Gene Autry and Other Favorites (Bescol 62)

Gene Autry With His Little Darlin' Mary Lee (Varese Sarabande VSD-5910)

Gene Autry With Legendary Singing Groups (Varese Sarabande VSD-5841)

Goin' Back to Texas (Varese Vintage 66272)

Greatest Hits (Evergreen 2690772)

Greatest Hits (Sony Music Special Products A18874)

Here Comes Santa Claus (Varese Vintage 6034)

His Christmas Album (Legacy International 40; Bescol CD-40)

His Greatest Hits (Bescol 325)

Historic Edition (Columbia CK-37465)

The Last Roundup: 25 Cowboy Classics (ASV CD-AJA-5264)

Love Songs (Varese Sarabande VSD-5991)

Melody Ranch/Hopalong Cassidy (Radiola CDMR-1048)

The Melody Ranch Radio Show (Good Music Company UKD-105)

Private Buckaroo (Bronco Buster CD-9009)

Rudolph the Red-Nosed Reindeer (Pilz Entertainment 445449-2)

Sing, Cowboy, Sing (Rhino R2-72630)

Singing Cowboy, Chapter One (Varese Sarabande VSD-5840)

Singing Cowboy, Chapter Two (Varese Sarabande VSD-5909)

Sleepless in Seattle (Epic Soundtrax EX-53764) [ST]

That's How I Got My Start: Jimmie and the Cowboys (Jasmine JASMCD-3527)

20 Golden Cowboy Hits (Teevee Records 6028)

20 Great Movie Hits (Varese Sarabande VSD-5990)

22 Legendary Hits: Portrait of an Artist (Sony Music Special Products A24533)

25 Cowboy Classics—Back in the Saddle Again (ASV CD-AJA-5188)

Tumbling Tumbleweeds (Prism PLATCD-244)

The Western Collection (Varese Vintage 66271)

Yodelin' Gene Autry—The Life of Jimmie Rodgers (Bronco Buster CD-9017)

Frankie Avalon and Alan Ladd on the set of *Guns of the Timberland* (1960).
[Courtesy of JC Archives]

Frankie Avalon

(b. Francis Thomas Avallone, Philadelphia, Pennsylvania, September 18, 1939)

In the late 1950s there were (apparently) three requisites to becoming a teenie bopper rock 'n' roll star: (1) be born in South Philadelphia, (2) have clean-cut good looks, and (3) be able to carry a tune—just barely. Frankie Avalon, like two of his pals (Fabian and Bobby Rydell), fulfilled these qualifications and then some.

Avalon was an instinctive musician whose goal had been to become a professional trumpeter, so he had studied music and understood it. Singing was a lark that he fell into and did not take seriously (he used to sing in a nasal twang as a joke) until he had become a national rage with a series of hot-selling pop tunes. Like Ricky Nelson, Connie Francis, Tommy Sands, and Fabian, he became part of the Hollywood cycle that found its new movie "talent" among the singers who guested repeatedly on TV's *American Bandstand*. (This tremendously popular television show began as a Philadelphia local show in 1952. Before long the program hosted by Dick Clark had national airing, giving its cluster of visiting recording stars who sang and plugged their latest tunes great visibility with teen TV watchers.) The film factories counted on these *American Bandstand* performers to draw millions of their enthusiastic fans into cinemas. The gimmick had worked with Elvis Presley and Pat Boone, and it did with Frankie Avalon—for a while.

Just when it appeared his career was burning out in the early 1960s, Avalon was teamed with ex-Mouseketeer star Annette Funicello in a batch of low-budget beach party musicals that found box-office favor. They were examples of sunny foolishness that, over the years, have become tremendously important escapist memories to a great many moviegoers of that generation. On the strength of those sand-and-song flicks, the very aggressive Avalon carried his career through subsequent decades of nostalgia revivals, including a very well liked sequel, *Back to the Beach* (1987). However, as with most of his confreres yanked into premature stardom, it was not all sugar and spice. *The Idolmaker* (1980), loosely based on the rise and fall of personalities like Frankie Avalon and Fabian, made all that painfully clear.

He was born Francis Thomas Avallone on September 18, 1939 in South Philadelphia, the son of Nicholas and Mary Avallone. His father was a machinist, and his mother was a tailor-shop seamstress. There were two other children, Frankie's sisters. From his earliest days, Frankie wanted to be a somebody. After winning a red scooter in a talent contest for singing "Give Me Five Minutes More," he thought show business would be his entree to a better life. Then he became intrigued with boxing. However, after seeing the Kirk Douglas–Doris Day movie *Young Man With a Horn* (1950), he was determined to become a trumpeter. Avalon remembers, "It inspired me so much. I asked my father if I could get a trumpet. He was elated, being a frustrated musician himself. So not having money to buy me a horn, he borrowed the money and went to a pawn shop, where he bought my first trumpet for $15." After four hours of self-teaching, Frankie could play "Music, Music, Music." Later he took lessons from Seymour Rosenfeld, a member of the Philadelphia Symphony Orchestra.

By the time he was twelve, Frankie and his family had aspirations for him becoming a professional musician. Performing for singer Al Martino at a neighborhood block party opened career doors that led to the teenager doing instrumental recordings for X Records, one of RCA Victor's budget labels. Avalon appeared on the Philadelphia-based *Paul Whiteman's TV Teen Club* (ABC-TV), where neighborhood pal Bobby Rydell was already a regular guest performer. It was Whiteman who suggested Avalon as a new surname for the boy. Later, Frankie was taken to New York, where he was snuck into a midnight penthouse audition for Jackie Gleason. The Great One was so impressed by the boy's trumpeting that he hired him to guest on *The Jackie Gleason Show* (CBS-TV). Other TV variety show appearances (Pinky Lee, the Dorsey Brothers) followed.

Avalon attended Vare Junior High School in South Philadelphia and during summer vacations was the trumpeter for Bobby Boyd and the Jazz Bums. He also formed Frankie Avalon's Teen and Twenty Club, sponsored by two older businessmen (Bob Marcucci and Peter DeAngelis) from the neighborhood. During the academic year, Frankie was a member of the band Rocco and the Saints, led by one of his school teachers, Rocco de Laurentis. Occasionally, they had gigs at Murray's Inn in South Camden, New Jersey. Although the group had two vocalists, Avalon typically sang at least one number per performance. One day Bob Marcucci called Avalon and told him he was forming a record label (Chancellor Records) and needed new talent. Did Avalon know of any? "I told him that I was in a band and a couple of guys sang. So he came in one night to hear us. I did a couple of songs, and after the set, he said he wanted to make a record with the band doing an instrumental on one side and me singing on the other. That's how it got started."

At the time Frankie was determined to promote his trumpet playing, not his "singing." But recalls Marcucci, with whom Avalon would have a long-standing love-hate relationship, "Frankie never understood that trumpet prodigies sound better at eleven than they do at seventeen." Marcucci signed Rocco and the Saints to record "Cupid" / "Jivin' With the Saints." Marcucci also negotiated for Rocco and the Saints to be among the teen groups hired by Warner Bros. for *Jamboree* (1957). In eighty-five minutes of inglorious black-and-white, this quickie film trotted forth twenty-one disc jockeys (including Dick Clark), and an amazing array of recording artists ranging from Count Basie and His Orchestra to Fats Domino, Jerry Lee Lewis, and Connie Francis. Avalon's solo was "Teacher's Pet." As a single, neither that nor "Cupid" made any chart marks, but at local record hops, Avalon proved he had charisma with the gals. This was not lost on Marcucci.

Marcucci continued to record Frankie (as he was doing with Fabian and others). Marcucci and Peter DeAngelis had written a song that they insisted Frankie should record. If it failed, he could go back to his trumpet playing. Frankie was not impressed by the song's beat and, as a lark, began holding his nose as he rehearsed the lyrics. Marcucci and DeAngelis recorded Avalon singing like that, and the result was the nasal "Dede Dinah." It was on the hit charts for eleven weeks, rising to number seven in early 1958. "Ginger Bread," sung in the same twangy way, rose to number nine that summer. "I'll Wait for You," was a more conventional ballad—and sung more romantically. It rose to number fifteen that fall. Avalon went on a tour to Australia with the Platters and Tommy Sands.

By now songwriters were coming to Frankie with new numbers to record. One of them, Ed Marshall, brought him an item that Al Martino had been considering for an album. Avalon was drawn to the song and three days later recorded it. A short time later when he was doing a live telephone interview with Dick Clark (*American Bandstand*—ABC-TV) he said he had just recorded a new song that he was sure would be a hit. The song was "Venus," and in early 1959 it rose to number one on the charts, staying there for five weeks. It would become the song most closely associated with Frankie. Throughout 1959 he created jukebox magic with "Bobby Sox to Stockings," "A Boy Without a Girl," and "Just Ask Your Heart."

His manager, Marcucci, engineered several movie deals for his hot young talent, who was now taking acting and voice lessons. Avalon was hired for Alan Ladd's *Guns of the Timberland* (1960). It was a modestly conceived actioner of northwestern lumbering camps, produced by the star and featuring the actor's real-life daughter, Alana. Frankie was the wholesome young man drawn to her. Three song numbers (including "Gee Whizz Whillikens Golly Gee") were forced into the screenplay to appease Avalon's fans. Said *Variety*, "Avalon turns in some respectable work."

While Avalon's song "Why?"—his last really big hit—was reaching the number one spot on the charts in December 1959, he was on four months' location in Racketville, Texas for John Wayne's *The Alamo* (1960). It was a $15 million spectacle about Colonel Davy Crockett (John Wayne), Colonel James Bowie (Richard Widmark), and the defenders of the Alamo, who for thirteen days in 1836 staved off General Santa Anna (Ruben Padilla) and his Mexican troops, before succumbing. In the Mexicans' siege, Frankie was cast as Smitty, the exuberant young friend of Bowie. The picture was disliked by the critics, but it made money eventually. For Avalon, it was an important career boost to be in a major production.

In quick order (and without any career direction or particular studio backing) Frankie supplied one of the off-camera voices in the Japanese cartoon *Alakazam the Great!* (1961), supported Robert Wagner and Ernie Kovacs in the middling service comedy *Sail a Crooked Ship* (1961—Avalon sang "Opposites Attract"), was among the underwater crew in *Voyage to the Bottom of the Sea* (1961), and played one of Ray Milland's teenage children in the science-fiction entry *Panic in the Year Zero* (1962).

While Avalon's screen career and television guesting (ranging from a *Shirley Temple Theater* to an *Eleventh Hour* and a *Jack Benny Program*) was exploiting his popularity, his record successes were winding down. In 1960 he had hit songs with "Swinging on a Rainbow" (from his only top-forty album, *Swinging on a Rainbow*), "Don't Throw Away All Those Teardrops," "Where Are You," and "Togetherness." He had no charted hits in 1961, and in mid-1962 he had his final best-selling single, "You Are Mine." Meanwhile, he had passed the age of twenty-one. In teen parlance, he was "over the hill."

Avalon went to Spain to film a dreary costume picture, *The Castilian* (1963), which worked in a few Bob Marcucci songs for its youthful costar. This was followed by the inept jungle actioner *Drums of Africa* (1963)—in which he sang "The River Love" by Marcucci and Russell Faith and by a slight tale of a World War II underwater demolition team titled *Operation Bikini* (1963), in which he vocalized "The Girl Back Home," by Marcucci and Faith.

By 1963 the singer was twenty-four years old. He was supposed to have $250,000 in trust-fund accounts. However, through a series of bad investment deals, owed back taxes, and a subsequent mid-'60s breakup with Marcucci (which cost him an estimated $100,000 to sever the relationship), Frankie had exhausted most of his financial resources. That year he was a guest on several TV shows (*Rawhide, Burke's Law,* and *Mr. Novak*) and married dental technician Kay Deibel. They would have eight children.

Just as too much exposure and the coming of the British Invasion (the Beatles, etc.) combined to make Avalon and his peers passé, he suddenly fell into another show-business break. It was American International's *Beach Party* (1963), made on a $500,000 budget. Frankie had already made several pictures for the economy company, and no one had any particular expectations for this project when he and Annette Funicello (still under Walt Disney contract) were hired to be the youthful love interest in a hack account of an anthropologist (Bob Cummings) studying the mating habits of the Southern California surf set. With Avalon, Annette, and Dick Dale and the Del-Tones delivering the bubble-brained songs ("Promise Me Anything," "Treat Him Nicely," and "Don't Stop Now"), Harvey Lembeck and crew doing a Three Stooges' version of a motorcycle gang, and the presence of healthy young adults frolicking on the beach doing the rest, *Beach Party* was a surprise hit. *Variety* perceived, "*Beach Party* has the kind of direct, simple-minded cheeriness which should prove well nigh irresistible to those teenagers who have no desire to escape the emptiness of their lives."

With such a bankable formula, American International turned out a slew of these beach party romps. They all had the same recipe: a mix of forgettable pop rock tunes, a bevy of shapely young women, a few old-timers for the adult segment, and always Frankie (known as surfing champ "Big Kahuna") pursuing Annette (who always insisted virtuously "Not without a ring"). They would surf (against a process screen), her hair would be sprayed frozen to offset her decorous bathing suit, and Avalon would realize, at the last moment, that waiting for Annette was far better than succumbing to the wiles of the latest seductive siren of the sands. Most of these minifilms were shot in ten days, and Avalon received $30,000 per film.

Sometimes American International teamed Avalon with another costar in a new setting, such as Deborah Walley in *Ski Party* (1965), or starred him in a different genre: the service comedy *Sergeant Deadhead* (1965), also with Walley, or the science-fiction farce *Dr. Goldfoot and the Bikini Machine* (1965, with Susan Hart). However, Frankie always was the same on-camera: convivial, wholesome, and usually spouting a song now and again. Occasionally, he would be cast in a major production, such as United Artists' *I'll Take Sweden* (1965), a lesser Bob Hope comedy in which guitar-strumming Frankie romanced hyperactive teenager Tuesday Weld. By 1966 he and Funicello had made their last joint teen outing, *Fireball 500*. Having exhausted the beach scene, they were placed in a race-track environment with Fabian tossed in for good measure. The cycle had run its course.

Frankie had a growing family to support, and he accepted jobs wherever he could. He had no recording contract, so he continued testing a club act, trying to cross over into the adult marketplace with his "hat and cane" routine. He recalled of this period, "I'd been leading a man's life since I was sixteen. When I was 25–26, I was still playing nineteen-year-old kids. It's a long struggle . . ." In the summer of 1966, he costarred with Yvonne De Carlo in a stock version of *Pal Joey*, and in 1967 he was back in court dealing with suits and countersuits on his disagreement with Marcucci. He still had his American International Pictures contract, and they used him for the exotic *The Million Eyes of Su-Muru* (1967) and *Horror House* (1970). For Paramount, he was in Otto Preminger's big-budgeted comedy misfire *Skidoo* (1968) in a cast that included Groucho Marx, Carol Channing, and Avalon's one-time booster, Jackie Gleason. Off-camera, family-man Avalon was noted as a great golfing advocate and seemed to be low key about his show-business career. However, because he had no other trade, he was determined to survive financially in the business.

There were occasional TV guest spots (*Love, American Style, Here's Lucy*) and a syndicated minor television event (*Frankie Avalon's Easter Special,* 1969). Avalon hoped to star in a biopic of *The Willie Pep Story,* but the project's backer died. Instead, he auditioned for Sean Connery's *The Anderson Tapes* (1971), but director Sidney Lumet rejected him for this caper feature. In his early thirties, Avalon was considered a congenial carryover from a past era. He was always good for a quote. In 1970 he said, "It isn't like the old days. There isn't the excitement. Nobody has it today. People come in, go out in thirty days." In 1974, he showed up in a police melodrama (*The Take*) starring Billie Dee Williams. Avalon portrayed the shifty-eyed stoolie and in his three scenes gave a resourceful account of himself.

In the mid-1970s several artists from the 1950s (e.g., Frankie Valli, Neil Sedaka, Paul Anka, and Bobby Vinton) were making a nostalgic comeback. Fourteen other record companies had already turned Avalon down when De-Lite Records signed him up. Since disco was the then-current rhythm fad, the label released a disco version of "Venus" that became popular briefly in late 1975. It was enough to convince Avalon to abandon plans to move with his family to Hawaii to take a permanent singing job at a hotel there. Things seemed to be improving, even if someone wrote to the *Los Angeles Times* that year and asked, "I would like to know if Frankie Avalon is dead or alive." He recorded a few other singles ("Daydream Sunday") but they made no impact.

At the urging of longtime friend Dick Clark, CBS-TV took a chance on Avalon for a comeback in *Easy Does It . . . Starring Frankie Avalon.* Debuting on August 25, 1976, the four-week half-hour series costarred him with Annette Funicello. Together they sang, did skits, and joked about their old images. Two years later Frankie and Annette (for their fans, first names always sufficed) shot a Dick Clark–produced comedy pilot, *Frankie and Annette: The Second Time Around.* It aired November 18, 1978, on NBC-TV, but the series did not sell. (Nor did an earlier NBC-TV pilot *The Beach Girls* that was aired early in 1978.) Much more important to his career was his appearance in the blockbuster nostalgia musical movie, *Grease* (1978). John Travolta and Olivia Newton-John were the stars, but Avalon made a strong impression with his "Beauty School Dropout" number that, from the soundtrack album, earned him a Grammy nomination.

Avalon was still playing the club circuits in 1980 when United Artists released *The Idolmaker.* It was a thinly veiled account of record producer/agent Bob Marcucci (played by Ray Sharkey) and his discovery/promotion of Philadelphia sound talent, especially two rival rock 'n' roll stars whose looks and career moves paralleled Frankie Avalon and Fabian Forte. It led to a round of fresh interest in Fabian and Avalon. Frankie said of his on-camera act-alike, "So the character that was supposed to be me made me out a real heel . . . That's the movies. They went strictly for a Hollywood-type cliché story, and that's exactly what came out."

Throughout the years, Avalon was constantly promoting new ventures (music-publishing companies, film projects). He wanted to film *Rock Garden,* about young rock and rollers back in 1958–59, but could find no backing. In 1981 he toured with Dick Clark and his nostalgia rock 'n' roll show. In 1982 Frankie traveled with a fourteen-piece band, starred in a low-budget splatter movie called *Blood Song* in which he was an ax murderer, guested on TV's *Happy Days,* and was in the syndicated TV special *Rock 'n' Roll: The First 25 Years.* He organized a touring act with Fabian and Bobby Rydell called "Golden Boys of Bandstand" and continued to boost a project that he had had in mind for years: another reunion of the Beach Party gang, with he and Annette as middle-aged marrieds. Finally, in 1987, it became a reality. At a cost of $9 million and an eight-and-a-half-week shooting schedule, *Back to the Beach* had Avalon as an Ohio car agency dealer who with his wife (Annette) and their fourteen-year-old son fly to Los Angeles to track down their daughter, who is living in Malibu with a surfer. With Connie Stevens as the femme fatale, a guest appearance by Pee Wee Herman, and lots of lighthearted digs about the stars' pedigree (the son says, "A long time ago my parents were the most popular teenagers in the world"), the musical comedy found a surprising appeal with the public.

After *Back to the Beach*, Avalon continued to play eighty one-nighters yearly, sometimes teamed with such contemporaries as Fabian and Bobby Rydell. With the latter two, Frankie appeared on the *All-Star Salute to the President* (ABC-TV, January 19, 1989). Also on television, in the spring of 1989, Avalon hosted the two-part syndicated special *Frankie Avalon Presents Surfs Up*. Meanwhile, in Frankie's personal life, the oldest of his and Kay Avalon's eight children (four girls and four boys), Diana, was married in May 1987. The Avalons, who became first-time grandparents in August 1991, continued to live in a six-bedroom house in Malibu Canyon.

In March 1991 Frankie reunited yet again with Annette Funicello for a guest-starring appearance on the TV sitcom *Full House*. This engagement led the still-popular duo to plan a joint TV sitcom and/or to do a follow-up feature film to their *Back to the Beach*. However, these hopes were shattered when Annette later announced that she was suffering from multiple sclerosis, a disease that already had begun its crippling effects on her. (In later years, Avalon reunited with the disease-ravaged Funicello for public appearances to thank her loyal fans for their continued support during her progressive illness.)

Returning to club engagements, Frankie also found time to hawk his line of tanning products first on an 800 number and later, in 1994, on the Home Shopping Network. In the mid-'90s he played himself in cameos in such varied big-screen projects as the direct-to-video youth film *The Stoned Age* (1994) and Martin Scorsese's *Casino* (1995). He also made a cameo appearance as himself in the TV movie *A Dream Is a Wish Your Heart Makes: The Annette Funicello Story* (CBS-TV, 10/22/95.) Continuing onward into the new millennium with his nostalgia-club act, Avalon, usually teamed with Bobby Rydell, performed at venues throughout the United States, especially in Las Vegas. He also hosted such syndicated concert specials for television as *Let's Do It Again* (2001).

Reflecting on his lengthy career, Avalon once said, "Sure the average Joe probably thinks of us as these pretty boys who were turned into marketable packages, but I'll tell you something. There weren't that many of us guys who happened to hit and become successful in a business that is very difficult to become successful in." He also observed about his decades in the entertainment industry: "You've got to look at the games being played and step back and put them in perspective. It's vital to keep a level head. Don't take anything in Hollywood seriously, especially yourself."

Filmography

Jamboree [Disc Jockey Jamboree] (WB, 1957)
Guns of the Timberlands (WB, 1960)
The Alamo (UA 1960)
Alakazam the Great! (AIP, 1961) (voice only)
Sail a Crooked Ship (Col, 1961)
Voyage to the Bottom of the Sea (20th-Fox, 1961)
Panic in the Year Zero! [End of the World, Survival] (AIP, 1962)
The Castilian [Valley of the Sword] (WB, 1963)

Operation Bikini (AIP, 1963)
Drums of Africa (MGM, 1963)
Beach Party (AIP, 1963)
Muscle Beach Party (AIP, 1964)
Dr. Goldfoot and the Bikini Machine [Dr G. and the Bikini Machine] (AIP, 1965)
Beach Blanket Bingo [Malibu Beach] (AIP, 1965)
Ski Party (AIP, 1965)
How to Stuff a Wild Bikini (AIP, 1965)

Sergeant Deadhead (AIP, 1965)
I'll Take Sweden (UA, 1965)
Fireball 500 (AIP, 1966)
The Million Eyes of Su-Muru [Sumuru] (AIP, 1967)
Skidoo (Par, 1968)
Horror House (AIP, 1970)
The Take (Col, 1974)
Grease (Par, 1978)

Blood Song (Summa Vista/Allstate/Mountain High, 1982)
Back to the Beach (Par, 1987)
Troop Beverly Hills (Col, 1989)
The Stoned Age [Tack's Chicks] (Trimark, 1994) (direct to video)
Casino (Univ, 1995)
A Dream Is a Wish Your Heart Makes: The Annette Funicello Story (CBS-TV, 10/22/95)

TV Series

Easy Does It . . . Starring Frankie Avalon (CBS, 1976)

Album Discography

LPs

Alakazam the Great! (Vee Jay 6000) [ST]
And Now Mr. Avalon (Chancellor 5022)
Avalon Italiano (Chancellor 5025)
Back to the Beach (Col SC 40892) [ST]
Born on the Fourth of July (MCA 6340) [ST]
Christmas Album (Chancellor 5031)
Fabian and Frankie Avalon: The Hit Makers (Chancellor 5009)
Facade (Chancellor 68901)
Fifteen Greatest Hits (UA 6382)
Frankie Avalon (Chancellor 5001)
Frankie Avalon Sings "Cleopatra" Plus 13 Other Great Hits (Chancellor 5032)
Grease (RS RS-2-4002) [ST]
The Greatest of Frankie Avalon and Fabian (MCA 27097)

I'll Take Sweden (UA 4121) [ST]
Jamboree (WB—label number unk) [ST]
More Frankie Avalon (Sunset 5244)
Muscle Beach Party and Other Motion Picture Songs (UA 3371)
She's Out of Control (MCA 6281) [ST]
Sixteen Greatest Hits (ABC X-805)
Summer Scene (Chancellor 5011)
Swingin' on a Rainbow (Chancellor 5004)
Venus (De-Lite 2020)
The Very Best of Frankie Avalon (UA LA-450)
Whole Lotta Frankie (Chancellor 5018)
You Are Mine (Chancellor 5027)
The Young Frankie Avalon (Chancellor 5002)
You're My Life (De-Lite 9504)

CDs

Back to Back (K-tel 3019-2) w. Annette Funicello
Back to the Beach (CBS SCT-40892) [ST]
The Best of Frankie Avalon (Repertoire REP-4831WG)
Christmas Album (Taragon 1023)
A Dream Is a Wish Your Heart Makes: The Annette Funicello Story (WEA 520564) [ST]
The EP Collection (See for Miles 699)
The Fabulous Frankie Avalon (Ace CDFAB-007)
The Frankie Avalon Story (EMI Plus 5760180)
Frankie Avalon's Good Guys (GNP/Crescendo 3010)
Grease (Polydor 825-095-2) [ST]
Grease: 20th Anniversary (Polydor 044041-2) [ST]
Greatest Hits (Curb/Atlantic 77757-2)

New Recordings of Old Favorites (Unidisc A6EK-2149)
Rock and Roll Hall of Fame: New Recordings of Frankie Avalon (EMI/Capitol Special Markets 56923)
Teen Idol (Madacy 3441)
Teen Idols (Madacy 3466) w. Fabian
Teen Idols: The Very Best of Frankie Avalon (Music Club Records 50030)
Venus (Unidisc SPLK-7159)
Venus: The Very Best of Frankie Avalon (Collectables COL-CD-6297)
Venus: The Very Best of Frankie Avalon (Varese Sarabande VSD-5594)
When the Good Guys Used to Win (GNP/Crescendo 1415)

Harry Belafonte, Milo O'Shea, and Zero Mostel in *The Angel Levine* (1970).
[Courtesy of JC Archives]

Harry Belafonte

(b. Harold George Belafonte Jr., Harlem, New York, March 1, 1927)

Harry Belafonte first came to musical prominence through the mid-1950s' calypso craze with such favorites as "Matilda," "Jamaica Farewell," and "Banana Boat." But he was really a folk singer. Along with Pete Seeger and the Weavers, Belafonte helped to carry folk music into the popular arena of American musical taste. His particular brand of folk music combined West Indian African, American pop gospel, and folk strains into a warm universal blend. As a velvety song interpreter, Belafonte was one of the first folk singers to discard the guitar to use his hands for expression. His trademark open-necked (to the navel) silk performance shirts became a symbol for the trend away from formal attire in concert performance. It was in the concert arena that he made his greatest dramatic impact, merging purpose, dramatic intensity, and imagination into his performances. One critic once noted of his sexy stage presence, "Like a cat, he is never caught in an ungraceful posture."

Nevertheless, Belafonte's impact went beyond his decades of successful concertizing and recording. He starred in Broadway shows and performed as a dramatic actor and variety entertainer on television. Unlike his friend Sidney Poitier who persevered to find suitable roles for a black man in white Hollywood, Belafonte only acted in a relatively few motion pictures. Under other circumstances, this handsome, six-feet two-inches performer might have continued in filmmaking. Instead, he chose to devote a great deal of his time and concern to issues of integration (as an entertainer he broke several "color lines") and to other humanitarian causes.

He was born Harold George Belafonte Jr. in the Harlem section of New York on March 1, 1927. His father (Harold George Belafonte Sr.) was a cook in the British Royal Navy. His mother (Melvine [Love] Belafonte) was a dressmaker/domestic. His father, from Martinique, became a British subject during World War I. His mother was from Jamaica. Belafonte's paternal grandfather and his maternal grandmother were white. Harold Sr. and Melvine would have a second son, Dennis. Before Harry was six, his father had deserted the family. Belafonte was a troubled youth, greatly upset about the racial tension in his neighborhood and angry that he was poor. When he was nine, Mrs. Belafonte moved with her two sons to Kingston, Jamaica. By the time he was thirteen, his mother, who had remarried, moved her family back to Harlem. Harry was in his second year of high school (at George Washington High in the Bronx) in 1944 when he enlisted in the Navy, believing that serving in World War II (even as a black man) would be better than continuing with the frustrations at home. He received training at the Navy's Storekeeper School at Hampton, Virginia, and was later transferred to the West Coast. Without ever going overseas, he was discharged in 1945 at war's end.

By late 1945 Belafonte was living in Harlem again and working as a maintenance man for his stepfather. It was in December 1945 that he saw his first play, *Home Is the Hunter*, presented by the American Negro Theater in Harlem. He suddenly realized he wanted to become a performer, and he began to hang around the American Negro Theater, first as a volunteer stagehand, then as an actor and singer. In *On Striver's Row* he had the juvenile lead. To improve his craft, he used his GI Bill of Rights to pay for a drama workshop at the New School for Social Research in Manhattan's Greenwich Village. Among his fellow students were Marlon Brando and Sidney Poitier (who also had been at the American Negro Theater). Meanwhile, Belafonte began dating Frances Margurite Byrd, whom he had initially met when he was in the Navy and she was a student at Hampton Institute in Newport News. She had since come to New York to attend New York University, where she would later teach child psychology. She and Belafonte were married on June 18, 1948.

After working at a summer camp in Pennsylvania and briefly in Manhattan's garment district, Belafonte stopped in one night at the Royal Roost, a midtown jazz club. Its owner, Monte Kay (who later married Diahann Carroll), had heard Belafonte sing before when he was at the New School. Kay had been impressed then and now auditioned him live in front of the club audience. The test was successful, and Belafonte was hired to sing for a week at $70 in January 1949. He was so popular that he stayed at the Royal Roost for nineteen additional weeks. During this period, Kay became his manager and Harry was among the jazz musicians appearing in a Carnegie Hall concert. He made his first recordings, "Lean on Me" and "Recognition" (which he had written), which were distributed by a local record company without much impact. By now, the Belafontes' first daughter, Adrienne, had been born.

Briefly, Belafonte and Sidney Poitier thought of forming a comedy team and rehearsed an act. They both concluded they were not born comedians. Meanwhile, Kay promoted his client as the new Billy Eckstine, and Belafonte performed as a jazz and/or pop singer in clubs around the country. Although he did not enjoy singing this type of music, he hoped this exposure would lead to acting assignments. In 1949 he was signed to a contract by Capitol Records and recorded "They Didn't Believe Me" and "How Green Was My Valley." Neither these numbers, nor a later session at the end of December (in which he sang such songs as "Sometimes I Feel Like a Motherless Child"), created much of an impression. He was dropped by the label. Among the club engagements Kay arranged for him was a month's stay at Cafe Society Downtown in Greenwich Village. *Variety* ranked Belafonte as "a vocalist of promise." From September 13, 1949, to October 20, 1949, he appeared with Timmy Rogers and the Jubileers in a half-hour CBS-TV series *Sugar Hill Times* (*Uptown Jubilee*), a variety show featuring black entertainers. By Christmas of 1950, Harry's frustration at singing a type of music that was not meant for him culminated in his walking out of his contract at Martha Raye's Five O'Clock Club in Miami Beach. He was then earning $350 a week.

To help support his family (his wife was still teaching), he opened a Greenwich Village restaurant, the Sage, with two friends; eight months later it failed. Meanwhile, Harry had established the restaurant as a bohemian Mecca for musicians, folk singers in particular. By now his interest in folk music had expanded tremendously, and on weekends he would travel to the Library of Congress in Washington, DC, to research in their folk-music archives and to listen to folk records. Belafonte's friends, novelist Bill Attaway (who collaborated on many of Belafonte's later folk adaptations) and guitarist Millard Thomas (who later became his accompanist), worked together to build a repertoire of old and new folk ballads. By 1951 Belafonte had polished his skills as a folksong singer and was booked into the Village Vanguard. He remained there for fourteen weeks at $225 weekly. From there he moved uptown to the Blue Angel, where he stayed for sixteen weeks at $300 weekly. Millard Thomas had become his official accompanist, leaving Harry free to use his hands while performing for "dramatic treatment." After an engagement in Philadelphia, Belafonte returned to the Village Vanguard in June of 1952.

After an MGM talent scout saw Harry perform, Belafonte was brought to Hollywood to be screen-tested. He was hired for *Bright Road* (1953), a sensitive but slight tale of a fourth-grade student helped by his understanding teacher (Dorothy Dandridge) to acclimate to his academic routine. Belafonte had the subordinate role of the school principal. Within the sixty-eight minute film, he sang "Suzanne," a song he and Millard Thomas had written. Unfortunately neither the movie nor Harry received much attention; *Variety* gave him a brief mention: "Harry Belafonte is satisfactory as school principal. . . ." While on the West Coast, he appeared at the Mocambo Club in Beverly Hills and at the Thunderbird Hotel in Las Vegas. Throughout this period, Belafonte experienced a great deal of racial discrimination.

By 1953, Harry had signed a recording contract with RCA Victor, and by his third session, his songs ("Shenandoah" and "Scarlet Ribbons") began meeting with commercial success. It was his recording that year of a Japanese folk-style song "Gomen-Nasai" that made a mark in record sales, and RCA renewed his contract. He had a successful stand at the Black Orchid Club in Chicago as well as a popular return engagement at the Boulevard Club in Queens. *Billboard* magazine chose Belafonte to be among their prestigious "Talent Showcase of 1954." He was also signed to appear with Hermione Gingold, Billy De Wolfe, and others in *John Murray Anderson's Almanac*, which opened on Broadway on December 10, 1953. Within the revue, he sang "Acorn in the Meadow" and "Hold 'Em Joe," but his most dramatic number was a song rendering of "Mark Twain." The show lasted for 229 performances, and Belfaonte won both a Tony and the Donaldson Award as Best Supporting Actor. While performing in the show, Harry also appeared in the East Side Manhattan club, La Vie en Rose.

Filmmaker Otto Preminger saw Harry in *Almanac* and hired him for the role of Joe the soldier in his all-black film musical *Carmen Jones* (1954). Like costar Dorothy Dandridge, Belafonte's singing voice was dubbed (his by Levern Hutcherson), but at least he had the opportunity to express his dramatic talent. When released, the CinemaScope production was considered heavy-handed, yet he received good reviews. "Harry Belafonte's Joe is a clean-cut American youth, handsome and guileless." (*New York Herald-Tribune*). While on the West Coast, he made his second appearance at the Cocoanut Grove Club, his most popular number being "Noah." The Belafontes became parents for a second time in September 1954, with the birth of Shari (who would become a film and TV actress).

In early 1955, Harry, with Marge and Gower Champion, toured for three months for ninety-four one-night engagements of the pre-Broadway production of *3 for Tonight*. The show opened in New York on April 17, 1955. Belafonte performed fourteen numbers (folk songs and spirituals) in the revue; the *New York Times* reported that he "sings every song with the fierce conviction of an evangelist." The show itself lasted only 85 performances but was transformed into a CBS-TV special (June 25, 1955). That year Harry also played club engagements in Los Angeles, Las Vegas, Chicago, San Francisco, and at the Empire Room of the Waldorf-Astoria in New York. He began expanding the size and range of his backup musicians and did further research into folk music around the country. He continued recording for RCA, and on television he made the first of five appearances on NBC-TV's *Colgate Variety Hour*. On November 6, 1955, he costarred with Ethel Waters in *Winner by Decision*, a drama of a young fighter, on *G.E. Theater* (CBS-TV). As a prolific, much-in-demand talent, he earned $350,000 in 1955.

In 1956 Belafonte worked on *Sing, Man, Sing*, a musical in which he played Everyman from the Garden of Eden to contemporary times. The show was performed a few times at the Academy of Music in Brooklyn in April 1956 and later at the Shubert Theater in Chicago, but it did not reach Broadway. However, it was in this year that Harry's recordings broke into the mainstream. In the first half of 1956, he had three albums on the top-ten charts: *Mark Twain and Other Folk*

Favorites, Belafonte, and *Calypso*. The latter contained "Banana Boat (Day-O)" that in early 1957 rose to number five on the charts. Later in 1956, such songs as "Jamaica Farewell" and "Mary's Boy Child" were in the top fifteen on the singles chart. He also appeared in June 1956 at a sold-out, open air concert at Lewisohn Stadium in the Bronx. In July, he appeared at the Greek Theater in Los Angeles, bringing in $145,000 in two weeks, which was $30,000 above previous records. Harry reportedly turned down a ten-year TV contract that would have brought him $200,000 in salary because he did not like the terms; he also rejected a role in a new Tennessee Williams play. By late 1956 he and his wife ended their troublesome marriage, and they were divorced in early 1957. His companion of recent years, Julie Robinson (a white, Jewish dancer), became his wife in March 1957 in Mexico. (They would have two children, David and Gina.) The interracial marriage caused a great deal of controversial publicity.

Because of the huge success of the *Calypso* album (it remained in the number-one spot for thirty-one weeks), Belafonte was concerned that he would be caught in a mold (which happened to a degree as he became famous as the King of Calypso). He tried to diversify. He was hired by Twentieth Century-Fox to costar in *Island in the Sun* (1957), a tawdry, multistoried drama of the Caribbean in which he has a controversial interracial romance with Joan Fontaine. He sang two songs in the picture, "Island in the Sun" and "Lead Man Holler," both of which appeared in his album *Belafonte Sings of the Caribbean* (1957). Although the exploitive film was popular, neither it nor Belafonte (now considered a "matinee idol") received many favorable reviews.

In 1958, Belafonte underwent three corrective eye surgeries, made his first European tour, and turned down a lead role in *Porgy and Bess* (1959) because he felt the movie would compromise his race. He had formed his own production company (Harbel) and hoped to do a film biography of Martin Luther King; however, neither this nor a project called *The Brothers* materialized. In 1959, in a deal between his company and United Artists, he starred in the low-budget ($1.4 million) science-fiction morality tale *The World, The Flesh and the Devil*. Set in postholocaust New York, Harry portrays a Pennsylvania coal miner who is tempted by a white woman (Inger Stevens) and pitted against a bigoted seaman (Mel Ferrer). In the course of the picture, he sang the ballad "Fifteen." The movie received more attention for its stridently handled interracial issues than for its effectiveness as a film. Also in 1959, Belafonte appeared successfully in two one-man concerts at Carnegie Hall (which led to a live album), recorded a version of *Porgy and Bess* with Lena Horne, and starred in a variety special *Tonight With Belafonte* (CBS-TV, December 10, 1959) on which Bonnie McGee, Sonny Terry, and Odetta were his guests. For this program, Belafonte won an Emmy Award.

During this time, Belafonte produced and starred in *Odds Against Tomorrow* (1959). It was another racially themed picture, but this time the plot was a superior crime caper. It costarred Robert Ryan and Shelley Winters and gave to Belafonte a part as a member of a disparate trio robbing an upstate New York bank of $150,000, with ironic results. Despite the fine performances, this film noir was not popular, and it was the actor's last movie for a decade. (Plans to star in a Western, *The Last Notch*, or in the life of the Russian poet Alexander Pushkin did not materialize.) Additionally in 1959, he produced on Broadway the short-lived French comedy *Moonbirds*, starring Wally Cox.

He had another TV special on November 20, 1960—*Belafonte, New York* (CBS-TV)—with Gloria Lynne as his guest. He continued recording for RCA, never able to get away from the calypso beat in his folk albums. His *Belafonte Returns to Carnegie Hall* (1960) was one of his "live" albums and featured such guest artists as Miriam Makeba, Odetta, and the Chad Mitchell Trio.

Throughout the years, Belafonte would do much to foster new talent, especially artists from South Africa. He performed frequently in tandem with Miriam Makeba, and later Lette Mbulu, Nana Mouskouri, Hugh Masekela, and Falumi Prince. His album *Swing Dat Hammer* (1961) won a Grammy, as did his later *An Evening With Harry Belafonte and Miriam Makeba* (1965). The last time Harry made the top-forty album charts was in 1964 with his album *Belafonte at the Greek Theater*. After his three 1966 albums (*An Evening With Mouskouri, In My Quiet Room*, and *Calypso in Brass*), he did not record any further discs until 1970. Nevertheless, both here and abroad, he continued to perform extensive club engagements. On November 9, 1969, he was starring in an NBC-TV special *An Evening With Julie Andrews and Harry Belafonte*, and the next year he reunited with friend Lena Horne for *Harry and Lena* (ABC-TV, March 22, 1970).

In the 1950s, Belafonte had been accused by some African-American factions of trying frequently to acclimate too much with the white world. In the 1960s, he became a strong advocate of racial integration and a great supporter of the work of Dr. Martin Luther King. After the latter's assassination and its discouraging aftermath for race relations, Belafonte was among the personalities featured in the documentary *King: A Filmed Record . . . Montgomery to Memphis* (1970). (By then Harry was an executor of King's estate.) In the symbolic fantasy *The Angel Levine* (1970), the multitalented performer played an angel, the soul of a black street hustler, who is sent to earth by God to help an elderly Orthodox Jewish tailor (Zero Mostel) regain his failing faith. It was another Belafonte production, more noteworthy for its message than for its entertainment value.

Far more commercial was Belafonte's participation in *Buck and the Preacher* (1972), a Western coproduced and directed by Sidney Poitier. With a cast that included Ruby Dee, *Buck and the Preacher* was a high-grade entry in Hollywood's cycle of black action pictures. Belafonte excelled as the bogus preacher in post–Civil War days who claimed to be of the High and Low Orders of the Holiness Persuasion Church. The Western was hugely successful (with the public, not the critics), and as the rollicking rogue, Belafonte stole the show. *Variety* noted, "Never let it be said that Sidney Poitier and Harry Belafonte will sit still for being typecast." Two years later, the duo reteamed for another buddy picture, *Uptown Saturday Night* (1974), this time a comedy also featuring Bill Cosby, Flip Wilson, Richard Pryor, and Roscoe Lee Browne. In the course of the shenanigans, Poitier and Cosby must recover a stolen winning lottery ticket. They appeal to ghetto gang lord Geechie Dan (Belafonte) for help. Once again, with his boisterous performance (this time in a gruff-voiced, puff-cheeked imitation of *The Godfather*'s Marlon Brando), Harry was the focal comedy spot of the very successful film. However, Belafonte did not participate when Poitier and Cosby combined for their next joint outing, *Let's Do It Again*, 1976.

Since he could earn a million dollars with one of his frequent European tours, Harry abandoned filmmaking once again. In 1980 he and Sidney Poitier planned to make a film together in Africa, but that did not happen. Also that year, he received the Sixth Annual Paul Robeson Award for Humanitarianism from the Actors Equity Association. On October 4, 1981, he costarred in the NBC-TV telefeature *Grambling's White Tiger*. Based on a true-life event, he portrayed Eddie Robinson, football coach at Grambling College in Louisiana, who trains quarterback Jim Gregory (Bruce Jenner), the only white student at the all-black college. Although he received good reviews, it was his last such effort to date. He explained, "Anyone who does it [TV movies] is masochistic and anyone who continues to do them is sadistic." In 1982 he received the Tenth Annual Martin Luther King Nonviolent Peace Prize.

In the mid-'70s Belafonte had ended his recording association with RCA and then, after a six-year hiatus, returned on other labels, including CBS Records. But for him, recording was now an exception, not the rule. He insisted, "I've been on enough charts and played that game. But I wasn't won over by the game. I haven't lost the vitality because I haven't been burned out by the industry. I haven't played their game." On May 2, 1983, he was among the Parade of Stars Playing the Palace, a benefit staged at New York's Palace Theater for the Actors' Fund of America; it was televised in abbreviated form as an ABC-TV special. When asked in 1983 why he was not acting in more films, he said, "To be very honest, those who make movies and TV decisions nowadays are not aware of my existence, nor do they care. We have nothing in common." In 1984 he coproduced *Beat Street*, a musical film starring Rae Dawn Chong that exploited the rap and break-dancing craze. Plans to produce a docudrama film on Nelson Mandela remained unrealized.

In 1985 Harry was part of the USA for Africa delegation that went on a sixteen-day tour of the famine-stricken continent. As a fund-raiser to help Africans, he was one of the key participants in the celebrity-filled group, which recorded the hugely popular song "We Are the World." The next year he considered (but decided against) running for U.S. senator from New York on the Democratic ticket. In April 1987 he was coproducer of *Asinamali!*, a stage drama set in a prison cell at Leeuwkop Prison near Johannesburg, South Africa. The play lasted only twenty-nine performances on Broadway. Thereafter, he continued with an abbreviated concertizing schedule, which included his traditional annual appearance at the Greek Theater in Los Angeles. On September 14, 1988, he was a singing guest on *Live! Dick Clark Presents* (CBS-TV). Also in 1988 his song "Banana Boat" was featured in the Michael Keaton comedy film *Beetlejuice*, which gave him a fresh audience with new generations. While his wife Julie (a former Katherine Dunham dancer) was planning to produce *The Katherine Dunham Story* for Home Box Office, both she and Belafonte were active in mid-1989 in trying to start a new film festival in Cuba.

When Harry made his return to Los Angeles's Greek Theater in July 1989, *Daily Variety* reported, "Musically, Belafonte remains in excellent voice . . . the rich vibrant tone that made him a hit three decades ago is still there, seemingly as resilient as ever and able to take full advantage of any vocal line." Regarding his singing of such politically oriented songs as "We Are the Wave," "Global Carnival," and "Paradise in Gazankula," the trade paper noted, "There are few entertainers who can deliver this message with as much sincerity and good fellowship as Belafonte."

Harry devoted much of the early 1990s to humanitarian work, occasional concerts, and a few film appearances. He played cameos for director Robert Altman's *The Player* (1992) and *Prêt-à-Porter* [Ready to Wear] (1994), and for the same filmmaker Harry took on a full-sized role as a mob boss in *Kansas City* (1996). Belafonte also teamed with John Travolta in *White Man's Burden* (1995), a film set in a fictional United States in which African Americans are the rich majority. The offbeat production was not popular with moviegoers. Meanwhile Harry formed a new band (Djoliba) to perform African and Third World music, and the group toured. (In this period Belafonte also gave several solo concerts.)

The veteran singer was sidelined in spring 1996 when he underwent surgery for prostate cancer. His ordeal led him to become a spokesperson for awareness about the disease. (His humanitarian chores already included being a goodwill ambassador for UNICEF since 1987.) He returned to acting in 1999's *Swing Vote*, dealing with the U.S. Supreme Court reviewing a case involving abortion. The star continued his interest in civil rights issues by serving as executive producer of the TV documentary *Parting the Waters* (2000). At century's end he helped to produce *The Long Road to Freedom: An Anthology of Black Music*, which was launched in 1961 and finally completed and released in 2001. The multimedia project (containing five CDs, a coffee-table book, and a

DVD of Belafonte and others discussing the making of *The Long Road*) traced the history of black music.

While Harry Belafonte had many noteworthy artistic accomplishments in his prolific career, it was his humanitarian and political activities (on behalf of racial equality) of which he was always most proud.

Filmography

Bright Road (MGM, 1953)
Carmen Jones (20th-Fox, 1954)
Island in the Sun (20th-Fox, 1957)
The World, The Flesh and the Devil (UA, 1959) (also coproducer)
Odds Against Tomorrow (UA, 1959) (also producer)
The Angel Levine (UA, 1970) (also producer)
King: A Filmed Record . . . Montgomery to Memphis (Commonwealth, 1970) (documentary)
Buck and the Preacher (Col, 1972) (also coproducer)
Uptown Saturday Night (WB, 1974)
Grambling's White Tiger (NBC-TV, 10/4/81)
Beat Street (Orion, 1984) (coproducer/co-songs only)
We Shall Overcome (California Newsreel, 1989) (s) (documentary)

Eyes on the Prize II (PBS-TV, 1990) (documentary)
The Player (Par, 1992)
Prêt-à-Porter [Ready to Wear] (Miramax, 1994)
White Man's Burden (20th-Fox, 1995)
The Affair (HBO-cable, 10/14/95) (executive producer only)
Hank Aaron: Chasing the Dream (Turner, 1995) (documentary)
Kansas City (Fine Line, 1996)
Jazz '34 [Robert Altman's Jazz '34] (Rhapsody, 1996) (documentary)
Danny Kaye: A Legacy of Laughter (PBS-TV, 1996) (documentary)
Swing Vote (ABC-TV, 4/19/99)
Fidel (Unk, 2001) (documentary)

Broadway Plays

John Murray Anderson's Almanac (1953)
3 for Tonight (1955)

Moonbirds (1959) (producer only)
Asinamali! (1987) (coproducer only)

TV Series

Sugar Hill Times (CBS, 1949)

Parting the Waters (Synd, 2000) (executive producer only) (documentary)

Album Discography

LPs

Abraham, Martin and John (Camden ACL1-0502)
Ballads, Blues and Boasters (RCA LPM-LSP-2953)
Belafonte (RCA LPM-1150)
Belafonte at Carnegie Hall (RCA LOC/LSO-6006)
Belafonte at the Greek Theater (RCA LOC/LSO-6009)
Belafonte Live (RCA VPSX-6077)
Belafonte on Campus (RCA LPM/LSP-3779)
Belafonte Returns to Carnegie Hall (RCA LOC/LSP-6007)

Belafonte Sings Five Early Songs (Coronet CX-CSX-115)
Belafonte Sings of Love (RCA LPM/LSP-3938)
Belafonte Sings of the Caribbean (RCA LPM-1505)
Belafonte Sings the Blues (RCA LOP-1006/LPM-1972)
By Request (RCA LSP-4301)
Calypso (RCA LPM-1248)
Calypso Carnival (RCA LSP-4521)
Calypso in Brass (RCA LPM/LSP-3658)

An Evening With Belafonte (RCA LPM/LSP-1402, RCA ANL1-1434)

An Evening With Belafonte and Miriam Makeba (RCA LPM/LSP-3420)

An Evening With Belafonte and Nana Mouskouri (RCA LPM/LSP-3415)

Fabergé Presents Harry and Lena (RCA PRS-295) [ST/TV] w. Lena Horne

Harry (Camden CAS-2599)

Homeward Bound (RCA LSP-4255)

In My Quiet Room (RCA LPM/LSP-3571)

Jump Up Calypso (RCA LPM/LSP-2388)

Love Is a Gentle Thing (RCA LPM/LSP-1927)

Loving You Is Where I Belong (Col FC-37489)

The Many Moods of Belafonte (RCA LPM/LSP-2574)

"Mark Twain" and Other Folk Favorites (RCA LPM-1022)

The Midnight Special (RCA LPM/LSP-2449)

My Lord, What a Morning (RCA LPM/LSP-2022)

Play Me (RCA ANL1-0094)

Porgy and Bess (RCA LOP/LSOL-1507) w. Lena Horne

Pure Gold (RCA ANL1-0979)

Streets I Have Walked (RCA LPM/LSP-2695)

Swing Dat Hammer (RCA LPM/LSP-2194)

This Is Harry Belafonte (RCA VPS-6024)

To Wish You a Merry Christmas (RCA LPM/LSP-1887)

The Warm Touch (RCA LSP-4481)

CDs

All-Time Greatest Hits, Vol. 1 (RCA 6877-2-R)

All-Time Greatest Hits, Vol. 2 (RCA 8555-2-R)

All-Time Greatest Hits, Vol. 3 (RCA 9771-2-R)

Banana Boat Song (Sony Music World MRC-1054, Starlite CDS-51020)

Belafonte (Grandprix CSJ-586)

Belafonte at Carnegie Hall (RCA 6006-2-R)

Belafonte '89 (EMI E21Y-92247)

Belafonte Returns to Carnegie Hall (RCA 07863-62690-2, Mobile Fidelity MFCD-10-00782)

The Belafonte Songbook (Pair PCD-2-1060)

The Best of Harry Belafonte (RCA BVCM-37007, RCA 74321-78948-2)

Calypso From Jamaica (Music of the World 12505)

Calypso Night (RCA 07863-53801-2, Back Biter 61089)

Carmen Jones (RCA 1881-2) [ST]

Collection (BMG 74321-66057-2)

Day-O (Golden Stars GSS-5153)

Day-O (MSI 353)

Day-O and Other Hits (RCA 07863-52082-2)

An Evening With Belafonte/Mouskouri (BMG ND-89844, Musicrama 610182) w. Nana Mouskouri

An Evening With Harry Belafonte (Island 524-384)

Folk Songs From the World (Music of the World 12512)

Folk Standards (BMG Special Products 7551-744676-2)

Folk Standards: The Encore Collection (Laserlight 46-137)

Gold (Gold GOLD-072)

Golden Records, Vol. 1 (RCA/BMG 74321-13952-2)

Golden Records, Vol. 2 (RCA/BMG 74321-13853-2)

Great (BCD GLD-63214)

Greatest Hits (RCA 07863-67403-2)

Harry Belafonte (Delta 6075)

Harry Belafonte (Eagle EAB-CD-036)

Harry Belafonte (RCA 74321-66057-2)

Harry Belafonte (Weton 97032)

Harry Belafonte/Miriam Makeba/Odetta (Music of the World 12518)

His Greatest Hits (Disky WMCD-5643)

The Hit Collection (Scana 95010)

I Grandi Successi (BMG 74321-55805-2)

Island in the Sun (Armour ARM19)

Island in the Sun (BMG 74321-43683-2)

Island in the Sun (Laserlight 15-094)

Island in the Sun (Pair PDC-2-1295)

Jump Up Calypso (RCA 07863-52388-2)

Jump Up Calypso/Midnight Special (RCA 74321-29454-2)

The Legend (RCA PD-89796)

A Legendary Performer (RCA 52469-2)

Live at Carnegie Hall (BMG 74321-15713-2)

A Man and His Music (RCA ND-90462)

My Greatest Songs (RCA/BMG 74321-10730-2)

My Lord What a Mornin' (BMG 74321-26049-2, MSI/UNI 2064)

Paradise in Gazankulu (EMI-Manhattan E21Y-46971)

Pure Gold (RCA 07863-53860-2)

Scarlet Ribbons (Camden 74321-33948-2)

Simply the Best (Woodford WMCD-5643)

Skin to Skin (EMI CDR-2029992)

36 All-Time Greatest Hits (RCA 1130-15250-2)

This Is Harry Belafonte (RCA ND-89195)

3 Originals (BMG 74321-77952-2)

To Wish You a Merry Christmas (RCA 2626-2-R)

20 Golden Songs (Remember RMB-75089)

The Very Best of Harry Belafonte (Reader's Digest B93001)

The Very Best of Harry Belafonte (Scranta SACD-1203)

Ann Blyth

(b. Ann Marie Blyth, Mt. Kisco, New York, August 16, 1928)

Beautiful, talented Ann Blyth—proficient as a dramatic actress and an accomplished singer—had a rather checkerboard career during her many years as an entertainer. Her show-business achievements ranged from appearing in Universal Pictures low-budget pictures at the start of her screen years in the mid-'40s, quickly reaching an apex with her Academy Award nomination in 1945 for *Mildred Pierce*, and transversing a succession of more standard film roles (although she was notable in a strong dramatic assignment in *Another Part of the Forest*, 1948). Then she settled down to a series of glossy MGM musicals in the mid–1950s where she proved to be a sweet soubrette. Unfortunately movie musicals were going out of vogue, and her career came to a near halt. Thereafter, she mostly retired, choosing a family over fame. However, it was a busy retirement, and her face remained a familiar one via a variety of television work.

Ann Marie Blyth was born in Mount Kisco, New York, on August 16, 1928. Her parents separated when she was still an infant, and her mother took her and her older sister Dorothy to live in New York City. The family lived in a walk-up flat on New York's east side, and Mrs. Blyth earned a meager living by doing ironing for the Park Avenue elite. As a little girl, Ann, a child prodigy, dreamed of a show-business career, and despite the financial difficulty, her mother always managed to have the necessary money for her singing, dancing, and dramatic lessons. While older sister Dorothy worked as a secretary, Ann, at age eight, was singing on radio station WJZ while attending Catholic schools and the New York Professional Children's School. Ann also did dramatic work on radio and undertook opera at the San Carlo Opera Company.

At age thirteen, Ann received her first solid break when she was cast as Babette, the daughter of a freedom fighter (Paul Lukas), in the Broadway production of Lillian Hellman's *Watch on the Rhine* (1941). She remained with the hit drama for nearly a year before going on tour with the patriotic melodrama. In the interim she had dinner at the White House, and while she was on tour, a Universal Pictures talent scout saw Ann and had her signed to a seven-year studio contract. Ann made her motion-picture debut as a society snob who vies with Peggy Ryan for Donald O'Connor's affections in the musical comedy *Chip Off the Old Block* (1944). This vehicle was quickly followed by another musical, *The Merry Monahans* (1944). This low-budget imitation of the Judy Garland–Mickey Rooney MGM musicals cast Ann as the daughter of a singer (Rosemary De Camp) who meets her former lover (Jack Oakie) who has two grown children (O'Connor, Ryan). Next Ann and Peggy Ryan costarred as two teenagers staging a benefit show in *Babes On Swing Street* (1944), followed by the studio's all-star musical *Bowery to Broadway* (1944). This quartet of innocuous fluff proved that Ann was not destined to be the replacement for the studio's now-adult Deanna Durbin.

Ann was loaned to Warner Bros. for the most telling role of her screen career, that of self-centered teenager Veda, the willful daughter of a restaurateur (Joan Crawford) who murders her

Ann Blyth in the mid 1950s.
[Courtesy of JC Archives]

mother's lover (Zachary Scott) after having an affair with him, in *Mildred Pierce* (1945). James Agee (*The Nation*) found Blyth's performance "as good an embodiment of all that is most terrifying about native contemporary adolescence as I ever hope to see." Ann earned an Academy Award nomination for the part, and her motion picture career was on its way.

Following the completion of *Mildred Pierce*, Ann and Zachary Scott were reunited for *Her Kind of Man* (1946). However, after two weeks of shooting, Ann was involved in a toboggan accident at Snow Valley in the San Bernardino Mountains. It left her with a broken back and what appeared to be the end of her acting career. While in a body cast, she worked at graduating from high school with her studio class. She also found spiritual reward from the accident. She wrote later, "The busy exciting world I had known faded away and my life slowed down to little things. But even here I found myself blessed, for a new sense of prayer began to unfold to me. Now there were not the busy times of telling Him what I needed but rather, times of listening, communion, of gathering strength, when my human strength and courage seemed to ebb away." After seven months in the cast, Ann was told she would be able to walk again, but she spent seven more months in and out of a wheelchair before she was able to swim, attend a preview of *Mildred Pierce*, and play golf.

In her first film after the accident, Ann was cast by Universal as a small-town girl in love with a newly arrived con man (Sonny Tufts) in *Swell Guy* (1946). This budget entry was followed by a guest role as a young adult who loves a convict (Howard Duff) in the taut prison melodrama *Brute Force* (1947). In between these assignments, her mother died. A loanout to MGM followed with the role of boxer Mickey Rooney's romantic interest in *Killer McCoy* (1947); that, in turn, was followed by Universal's *A Woman's Vengeance* (1947), in which she portrayed a shop girl whose lover (Charles Boyer) is tried for poisoning his wife.

Next the studio gave her a strong dramatic role, that of young Regina Hubbard in Lillian Hellman's *Another Part of the Forest* (1948), which examined the early years of the ruthless Southern clan Ms. Hellman had made famous in her play *The Little Foxes*. The role Ann played was done in the earlier play by Tallulah Bankhead onstage and by Bette Davis in the 1941 screen version of *The Little Foxes*. Unfortunately, Regina Hubbard was to be Ann's last substantial screen part, although she was to make more than twenty feature films in the next decade.

In 1948 Blyth garnered lots of publicity as the aquatic object of William Powell's affection in the pleasant comedy-fantasy *Mr. Peabody and the Mermaid*, but this was followed by such conventional studio fare as the Western *Red Canyon* (1949), the arch comedy *Free For All* (1949), and the small-town doings of *Katie Did It* (1951). Bing Crosby chose her as his leading lady in the pedestrian *Top o' the Morning* (1949), and Samuel Goldwyn borrowed her for the soap opera *Our Very Own* (1950). Her career received a tremendous boost by being cast as Mario Lanza's leading lady in *The Great Caruso* (1951) at MGM, a part that would have gone to Metro's own Kathryn Grayson had she not objected so strongly to costarring again with the boorish Lanza. Complete with new makeup, Ann made a strong impression in this colorful biographical musical and got to sing the picture's best song, "The Loveliest Night of the Year." Universal provided Ann with a solid role as a convicted murderess who takes refuge in a convent during a storm in *Thunder on the Hill* (1951), and whose innocence is believed by one of the nuns (Claudette Colbert).

At this time the actress also worked on radio, being heard on such series as *Guest Star* and *The Louella Parsons Show*, as well as in the "Ultimately Yours" segment of the 1950 syndicated program *Voice of the Army*. On January 11, 1951, she and Jeff Chandler costarred in the CBS radio adaptation of "Shadow of a Doubt" on *Hollywood Soundstage*.

Ann's early 1950s' movies were a motley assortment, like Universal's *The Silver Horde* (1951), and Twentieth Century-Fox's *I'll Never Forget You* (1951) opposite Tyrone Power. She was Gregory Peck's love interest in *The World in His Arms* (1952), and then joined Edmund Gwenn in the light comedy *Sally and Saint Anne* (1952). When Claudette Colbert bowed out of the Korean War melodrama *One Minute to Zero* (1952) at RKO, Ann Blyth replaced her.

In 1952, Ann's Universal contract expired, and she moved over to MGM, which had long wanted her on their roster. They promised to star her in the type of screen fare she longed to do: musicals. Instead, her initial Metro contract outing was the rugged seafaring actioner *All the Brothers Were Valiant* (1953). Then she was given the Jeanette MacDonald part in the wide-screen remake of *Rose Marie* (1954) opposite Howard Keel in the Nelson Eddy role. The picture was colorful and glossy but hardly up to the well-remembered 1936 version, as Ann sang "Free to Be Free" and dueted with Fernando Lamas on "Indian Love Call."

Next Blyth replaced Jane Powell as the barmaid loved by a prince (Edmund Purdom) in the operetta *The Student Prince* (1954), with the overweight Mario Lanza (originally set for the lead) dubbing Purdom's singing. Ann was then thrust into the bland swashbuckler *The King's Thief* (1955), also with Purdom. Next she and Howard Keel were reunited for a color remake of *Kismet* (1955), which was well produced but surprisingly vapid. Ann soloed on "Baubles, Bangles and Beads" and performed duets with Keel and Vic Damone. By now MGM was abandoning musicals and going in a new direction. She closed out her MGM tenure with the smut magazine exposé *Slander* (1956).

At Paramount she was reunited with Donald O'Connor, who had the title role in *The Buster Keaton Story* (1957), with Ann playing the loyal Mrs. Keaton. Her final movie proved to be the title part in *The Helen Morgan Story* (1957), in which she gave a finely honed performance as the torch singer who sinks into alcoholism. While Ann's natural singing voice was very much like that of Helen Morgan's, Warner Bros. chose to have the songs dubbed on the film's soundtrack by full-voiced Gogi Grant. The resultant movie, shot in black-and-white, was not popular.

In 1953 Ann had married Dr. James McNulty, the brother of Irish tenor/comedian Dennis Day, and it was on the latter's program, *The RCA Victor Show*, that the actress made her television debut in June 1953. The next year she appeared on CBS's *Video Theater* and then took a hiatus from TV work while making her MGM features. (One of the projects that Ann rejected was 1957's *The Three Faces of Eve*, which won Joanne Woodward an Oscar.) In 1959 Blyth came back to TV for a *Wagon Train* segment, and during the next four years she would guest-star three additional times on that program. She also appeared on such small-screen series as *Dick Powell Theater, Twilight Zone, Burke's Law, Kraft Suspense Theater*, and *The Name of the Game*. In 1960 she headlined the ABC-TV production of *The Citadel*, and in 1963 she guest-starred in an interesting segment of NBC-TV's *Saints and Sinners* show called "The Year Joan Crawford Won the Oscar."

More important than Ann's career, however, was her family. She had five children: Timothy Patrick (born in 1954), Maureen Ann (born in 1955), Kathleen Mary (born in 1957), Terence Grady (born in 1960), and Eileen Alana (born in 1963). The McNultys lived in a large home in Toluca Lake, and in addition to her family and charity work, Ann, a devout Catholic, made time to participate in church activities. In 1973 she and her husband were invested with the rank of Lady and Knight of the Holy Sepulcher by Cardinal Cooke in New York City.

During the 1970s Ann Blyth was seen frequently on television promoting Hostess cupcakes and other Hostess products, and her three youngest children often appeared in the commercials with their still-famous mother. In 1974 she did the one-minute CBS-TV spot detailing the history of Santa Claus in the network's *200 Years Ago Today* series, and late in 1975 she did a guest star role in that network's series *Switch*. During the decade, she also performed yearly tours with various Light Opera companies in musicals such as *Bittersweet, The King and I, South Pacific,* and *The Sound of Music.* For *South Pacific* in 1973 she was given the coveted "Show Stopper Plaque," because all the show's performances were SRO ("standing room only") in every city in which it was staged. In 1978 she guest-starred on the NBC-TV series *Quincy,* and in 1983 she returned again to the detective show. In 1985 Blyth turned up on the CBS-TV show *Murder, She Wrote.* In 1988 Ann was given the "Angel Award" for her work with St. Anne's Maternity Home.

By the 1990s Ann and her husband—who were several times grandparents—had moved to Rancho Santa Fe near San Diego and also had a home in Capistrano Beach. In May 1992 Ann, teamed with singer/soap opera actor Bill Hayes, made their Las Vegas debut at the Dunes Hotel. The duo performed their much-praised cabaret act in New York that November. Four years later, in April, Blyth headlined a revue (which included Constance Towers, Bill Hayes, and John Raitt) at the Performing Arts Center at Cal-State Northridge. In 1999 Ann supplied an audio commentary for a mini film clip tribute on cable's Turner Classic Movies to her once movie costar, Joan Crawford.

Although Ann Blyth never reached the screen heights suggested by her performances in *Mildred Pierce* and *Another Part of the Forest,* she did have a well-rounded and satisfactory show-business career. Unlike many of her contemporaries, she displayed no bitterness toward the film capital. She reasoned, "Hollywood has been very good to me. I was never hurt by the town or the profession." Still, personal happiness far outweighed a career in Ann Blyth's mind, and because of her husband and children she could contentedly say, "I consider myself a blessed woman." She also admitted, "If I were a teenage actress today, I don't think I would go to present-day Hollywood to shoot for a career. It's very different. I've seen some very interesting work, but I don't always see the kind of discipline that I had to have at a very early age, and that we all generally need in life anyway. I see a definite lack of that."

Filmography

Chip Off the Old Block (Univ, 1944)
The Merry Monahans (Univ, 1944)
Babes on Swing Street (Univ, 1944)
Bowery to Broadway (Univ, 1944)
Mildred Pierce (WB, 1945)
Swell Guy (Univ, 1946)
Brute Force (Univ, 1947)
Killer McCoy (MGM, 1947)
A Woman's Vengeance (Univ, 1947)
Another Part of the Forest (Univ, 1948)
Mr. Peabody and the Mermaid (Univ, 1949)
Red Canyon (Univ, 1949)
Once More, My Darling (Univ, 1949)
Top o' the Morning (Par, 1949)
Free for All (Univ, 1949)
Our Very Own (RKO, 1950)

The Triumphant Hour (Peyton, 1950)
The Great Caruso (MGM, 1951)
Katie Did It (Univ, 1951)
The Golden Horde (Univ, 1951)
Thunder on the Hill [Bonaventure] (Univ, 1951)
I'll Never Forget You (20th-Fox, 1951)
The World in His Arms (Univ, 1952)
Sally and Saint Anne (Univ, 1952)
One Minute to Zero (RKO, 1952)
All the Brothers Were Valiant (MGM, 1953)
Rose Marie (MGM, 1954)
The Student Prince (MGM, 1954)
Kismet (MGM, 1955)
The King's Thief (MGM, 1956)
Slander (MGM, 1957)
The Buster Keaton Story (Par, 1957)

The Helen Morgan Story [Both Ends of the
  Candle] (WB, 1957)

Broadway Plays

Watch on the Rhine (1941)

Album Discography

LPs

The Emperor Waltz/Top o' the Morning (10″
  Decca DL-5272) w. Bing Crosby
Hail, Mary (Everest 5113/1113)
Kismet (MCA-1424, MGM E-3281, Metro M/S-
  526) [ST]

Rose Marie (MCA 25009, 10″ MGM E-229,
  MGM E-3228, Metro M/S-616) [ST]
Rose Marie/Seven Brides for Seven Brothers (MGM
  E-3769, MGM 2SES-42ST) [ST]

CDs

Kismet (MCA MCAD-1424, Sony Music Special
  Products AK-45393, EMI 854536) [ST]
Rose Marie (MCA MCAD-25009) [ST]

John Boles

(b. John Boles, Greenville, Texas, October 28, 1895; d. San Angelo, Texas, February 27, 1969)

During the late 1920s, John Boles seemed everything that a film matinee idol could or should be: he was tall, good-looking, and an understated actor. When talkies swamped Hollywood, he demonstrated not only a fine, cultivated speaking voice for the screen, but also an admirable singing one as well! Therefore, in the studios' crush to churn out all-talking, all-singing, all-dancing pictures he was a tremendous asset, especially in operettas. Even before the musical craze died out, industry executives had concluded that he was (like George Brent) the perfect type of leading man to play opposite strong screen actresses, because he never overshadowed them but provided a well-bred vis-à-vis who allowed the *star* the full limelight. Thus he was in great demand to appear with the likes of Irene Dunne, Gloria Swanson, Loretta Young, Rosalind Russell, and Barbara Stanwyck, and he even survived several pictures with that ace scene-stealer Shirley Temple. Nevertheless, some critics did not succumb to his Southern gentility and well-modulated voice; they found his movie persona banal, artificial, and passive. However, John was a trouper (four decades on the screen), who proved himself repeatedly onstage, on-screen, and off.

Boles was born on October 28, 1895, in Greenville, Texas. During his childhood, he spent summers in a neighboring town with his grandparents, who encouraged him to sing. Throughout his school years, John was an avid vocalist and was often the lead performer at Friday afternoon "entertainments." Planning on either joining the family banking business or becoming a surgeon, he attended the University of Texas at Austin, where he graduated in June 1917. Two days later he wed his college sweetheart, Marcelite Dobbs; it was a union that would last fifty-two years. Not long thereafter, he was detailed to the Criminal Investigation Department of the American Expeditionary Force, where his mastery of French and German (learned during childhood from a Greenville matron) made him useful in secret missions in Bulgaria and Turkey during World War I. After the Armistice, he attended the Peace Conference in Paris.

Returning to Greenville from his eighteen months overseas, Boles abandoned the idea of a medical career and turned to the cotton industry. When vocal coach/performer Oscar Seagle was passing through Austin on a concert tour, John maneuvered a private audition. Seagle was so impressed he encouraged the young man to become his student back in upstate New York. With a $1,000 loan from his father, Boles and his wife relocated to Schroon Lake in the Adirondacks. When funds ran out, John taught French and music at a nearby high school to pay for his singing lessons and to support his wife. When his mentor urged him to pursue his studies in Paris, the enterprising young man organized a band of musical students. Serving as their business manager, Boles paid for his passage to France. Accompanied by his spouse and young daughter (Frances), he studied for two years with renowned operatic tenor Jean de Reszke.

Returning to New York City, John tried Broadway. After three months of bad luck, he auditioned for producer L. Lawrence Weber and was assigned to replace Jay Velie in the Broadway

Frances Drake and John Boles in *She Married an Artist* (1937).
[Courtesy of JC Archives]

musical hit *Little Jesse James* (1923), which featured Miriam Hopkins. Boles sang "I Love You" and dueted with Louise Allen on "Little Jack Horner." It was no little feat to be a leading man in his debut professional appearance. After *Little Jesse James* closed, Boles made his screen bow in Metro-Goldwyn's comedy drama *So This Is Marriage?* (1924)—starring Eleanor Boardman, Conrad Nagel, and Lew Cody—which was filmed in New York and featured Technicolor sequences. In a second Metro feature made in New York, John was the fifth lead in the farce *Excuse Me* (1925) featuring Norma Shearer, Conrad Nagel, and Renee Adorée. He was back on Broadway in *Mercenary Mary* (April 13, 1925), which lasted for thirty-two performances. Next he was signed to play opposite the legendary Geraldine Farrar in her operetta debut in Franz Lehar's *Romany Love*, which opened and closed in November 1926 in New Haven, Connecticut, as *The Love Spell*. Years later, Boles admitted, "She was, possibly, the grandest personality I shall ever encounter!"

John reappeared on Broadway in *Kitty's Kisses* (May 6, 1926), a musical with a book by Otto Harbach and lyrics by Con Conrad and Gus Kahn. Film superstar Gloria Swanson attended one of the show's forty-six performances and chose Boles to be her leading man in her first United Artists production. The exotic feature, *The Love of Sunya* (1927), which opened New York City's Roxy Theater, was a showcase for Miss Swanson, but the New York–lensed feature allowed room for Boles to shine as the man she marries eventually.

Impressed by his screen presence, Universal signed Boles to a studio contract. Boles and his family (which now included a second daughter, Janet) moved westward. He was cast initially by the studio in a supporting role in the society drama *We Americans* (1928), which starred Patsy Ruth Miller. Then he made several 1928 loanouts, including *Fazil* at Fox, in which he was in support to Charles Farrell and Greta Nissen; Paramount's Zane Grey Western *The Water Hole*, starring Jack Holt and Nancy Carroll, in which Boles's screen character goes crazy in the desert heat; and Pathé's *Man Made Woman* as Leatrice Joy's husband. In First National's *The Shepherd of the Hill*, based on Harold Bell Wright's oft-filmed melodrama, he was Young Matt.

With so many varied picture assignments to his credit, Universal used him in two 1929 part-talking features (*The Last Warning, Scandal*), both starring Laura La Plante. But the film that was to change his screen future was made when he was on loan to Warner Bros. *The Desert Song* cast him as Pierre Birbeau, who masquerades as "The Red Shadow," the masked leader of the Riffs. It was Hollywood's first sound operetta. With a score by Sigmund Romberg, a bright leading lady (Carlotta King), and Technicolor sequences, the musical was a big hit. The *New York Times* endorsed, "John Boles . . . has a voice that is quite pleasing." Universal announced that Boles would star in *Moonlight Madness* and *The Song of Passion*, but instead he went to RKO for their plush screen operetta, *Rio Rita* (1929), starring Bebe Daniels and featuring the frantic comedy of (Bert) Wheeler and (Robert) Woolsey. At Warner Bros., Boles starred in *Song of the West* (1930), based on the Broadway musical *Rainbow* and dealing with 1840s California. Vivienne Segal made her screen debut in this Technicolor feature, with Boles as her manly hero. In November 1929 he recorded this movie's three songs (by Vincent Youman-Oscar Hammerstein II, Grant Clarke, and Harry Akst) for Victor Records.

Finally, Universal utilized their valuable singing star in a home-lot musical, originally to be titled *La Marseillaise*. It was started by director Paul Fejos, but completed by John Stuart Robertson and released as *Captain of the Guard* (1930), with Boles singing love songs to Laura La Plante against a setting in Louis XVI's France. He recorded two of the film's songs ("You, You, Alone" and "For You") for the Victor label. Following the example of the other Hollywood studios, Universal produced an extravaganza Hollywood revue in Technicolor called *The King of Jazz* (1930). It boasted Paul Whiteman and His Orchestra, Bing Crosby and the Rhythm Boys, many vaudeville artists, and Boles teamed yet again with Laura La Plante. He sang the film's big hit song ("It Happened in Monterey"), and because Bing Crosby had been jailed for drunken driving when "The Song of the Dawn" was due to be lensed, John took over that spotlight number as well. He recorded both these songs for Victor. Meanwhile, Boles was loaned to United Artists to appear opposite English actress Evelyn Laye in her U.S. movie debut, *One Heavenly Night* (1930).

By the end of 1930 Hollywood had oversaturated moviegoers with song-and-dance pictures, and Boles's singing talents were no longer wanted. However, he was already an established screen name, and Universal starred him in a remake of Leo Tolstoy's story *Resurrection* (1931). Neither he nor his South American costar, Lupe Velez, were credible as the doomed Russians. The studio promoted the idea that Boles would have the lead in Preston Sturges's *Strictly Dishonorable* (1931), but Paul Lukas was borrowed for that assignment and, instead, Boles appeared in *Seed* (1931). Here he was seen to advantage as the average American male frustrated by the marriage trap. *Variety* reported, "John Boles emerges here much more finished in camera bearing and extremely the better actor than when seen before." It opened a new career vista for the handsome leading man. Also at the studio he appeared as Dr. Frankenstein's (Colin Clive) loyal friend in the classic *Frankenstein* (1931), and then moved over to Fox for two bread-and-butter features.

Producer Carl Laemmle Jr. realized Fannie Hurst's enduring soap opera *Back Street* (1932) required a top production. He borrowed Irene Dunne from RKO to star as the self-sacrificing heroine and cast Boles as the upper-crust married man, Walter Saxel, who keeps a mistress (Dunne) on the side. Under John Stahl's direction, Irene shone in this woman's picture, and John was serviceable in his cardboard, subordinate role. With that characterization, the screen mold was set for Boles. After joining Nancy Carroll in Columbia's *Child of Manhattan* (1933) and Lilian Harvey in Fox's *My Lips Betray* (1933), Universal put him in another tearjerker, *Only Yesterday* (1934), in which he played Margaret Sullavan's lover.

Fox's *Music in the Air* (1934) was based on Jerome Kern's stage hit and reteamed Boles with Gloria Swanson in her movie comeback. The operetta won no plaudits from critics or moviegoers, who found it too old-fashioned. In Fox's revue, *Stand Up and Cheer* (1934), Boles played himself in support of the studio's moppet star, Shirley Temple, whom he reunited with for *Curly Top* (1935—he sang the title song to her) and *The Littlest Rebel* (1935). Diplomatic Boles said of the little megastar, "I'd rather work with Shirley than anyone I know." Meanwhile, he was also doing *Back Street*–type chores yet again, such as performing opposite Ann Harding in RKO's *The Life of Vergie Winters* (1934). During this period John was a much-in-demand guest star on radio shows, performing scenes from well-known plays and movies.

John was paid $50,000 by Paramount to portray the undercover federal agent in the musical *Rose of the Rancho* (1936) with Metropolitan Opera diva Gladys Swarthout. He admitted enthusiastically his preference for the genre: "And now musicals have begun to come back and I've had a chance to do some first class singing in *Rose of the Rancho*." Paramount intended to costar the two singers in *Madame Butterfly*, but the mild reception to *Rose of the Rancho* quashed those expansive plans.

If Boles was ill at ease in the Twentieth Century-Fox action drama *A Message to Garcia* (1936) with Wallace Beery and Barbara Stanwyck, he was adequate (some critics, however, judged him "dismal") as the much-nagged husband in *Craig's Wife* (1936). This landmark film, directed by Dorothy Arzner and starring Rosalind Russell as the shrewish spouse, left little room for audience sympathy for John as the Milquetoast who finally rebels. He was back in form as Stephen Dallas in Samuel Goldwyn's elaborate remake of *Stella Dallas* (1937), in which Barbara Stanwyck (as the self-sacrificing mother) and Anne Shirley (as the daughter) shone. The star trio repeated their assignment for *Lux Radio Theater* on October 11, 1937.

After more than a decade in Hollywood, Boles's career ground down. His three 1938 releases were run-of-the-mill entries at best, including *Romance in the Dark*, which reteamed him in infelicitous comedy with Gladys Swarthout and in which Boles's attempts at broad farce were almost embarrassing.

By the summer of 1939, forty-three-year-old Boles was performing "in person" at assorted theaters around the country, singing such career-associated songs as "Rio Rita," "One Alone," and "I See Your Face Before Me." He continued such appearances during the next three years. Meanwhile, in the summer of 1940 he was dashing as Gaylord Ravenal in a revival of *Show Boat* that played Los Angeles and San Francisco. Norma Terris re-created her Broadway role as Julie; Paul Robeson was Joe; Guy Kibbee portrayed Cap'n Andy; and for the Los Angeles engagement, Helen Morgan was Julie.

It was quite a comedown for Boles when he reemerged on-screen in Monogram's *Road to Happiness* (1942). In this poverty-row entry he was the divorced dad overcoming obstacles in making a home for his son (Billy Lee). He was in support of chic Kay Francis in Universal's *Between Us Girls* (1942), which spotlighted Diana Barrymore, and he was properly charming as Kathryn Grayson's Army colonel father in MGM's star-filled *Thousands Cheer* (1943).

Back on Broadway Boles costarred with fellow Texan Mary Martin and Kenny Baker in *One Touch of Venus* (1943), directed by Elia Kazan. In this Kurt Weill musical, he sang "West Wind" and several other numbers. After the show closed in February 1944, Boles and Martin took the hit on the road for a year. In 1948 he appeared at London's Palladium in a musical revue, *Sky High*, and later made a concert tour of the British Isles.

In September 1950, Boles returned to the legitimate stage in the West Coast production of *Gentlemen Prefer Blondes*, starring Gertrude Niesen. What proved to be his cinema farewell was the low-budget United Artists release, *Babes in Bagdad* (1952), shot in Spain. It was an embarrassing costume satire starring the aging Paulette Goddard and Gypsy Rose Lee. John would admit later that anyone who failed to see it certainly "didn't miss much."

Perceiving the handwriting on the wall, Boles wisely chose to retire, returning home to San Angelo, Texas, and becoming involved in the oil business. In late 1954 he was a founder of the Pipecote Service Company, Incorporated, which serviced pipelines. As he explained in the mid-'50s, "When my career started to slow down, I didn't want to sit around. So when the opportunity came to get into the oil business, I jumped at it. All the fun appears to have gone out of making movies. In the old days, we used to enjoy ourselves!" John did make one final return to Hollywood in 1961 when his old studio remade *Back Street* yet again and asked the veteran star to publicize the new picture.

On February 27, 1969, Boles died of a stroke in San Angelo, Texas, at the age of seventy-three. He was survived by his wife Marcelite, by his daughters Frances (Mrs. Daniel Queen) and Janet (Mrs. Robert Fullerton), and by seven grandchildren. His autobiography, which he had been working on, was never completed or published.

It was a typically candid Boles who had said years before about his chosen profession, "Why attempt to kid the public? When a screen actor tells you his art, business, profession, or whatever he chooses to call it, is a serious, dignified pursuit, he is either spouting 'poppycock' or just taking himself too seriously."

Filmography

So This Is Marriage? (Metro-Goldwyn, 1924)
Excuse Me (Metro-Goldwyn, 1925)
The Love of Sunya (UA, 1927)
We Americans [The Heart of a Nation] (Univ, 1928)
The Shepherd of the Hills (FN, 1928)
The Bride of the Colorado (Pathé, 1928)

Fazil (Fox, 1928)
The Water Hole (Par, 1929)
Virgin Lips (Col, 1928)
Man-Made Woman (Pathé, 1928)
Romance of the Underworld (Fox, 1928)
The Last Warning (Univ, 1929)
The Desert Song (WB, 1929)

Scandal (Univ, 1929)
Rio Rita (RKO, 1929)
Voice of Hollywood #1 (Tif, 1929) (s)
Song of the West (WB, 1930)
The King of Jazz (Univ, 1930)
One Heavenly Night (UA, 1930)
Captain of the Guard (Univ, 1930)
Queen of Scandal (UA, 1930)
Resurrection (Univ, 1931)
Seed (Univ, 1931)
Frankenstein (Univ, 1931)
Good Sport (Fox, 1931)
Voice of Hollywood #6 (Tif, 1931) (s)
Careless Lady (Fox, 1932)
Back Street (Univ, 1932)
Six Hours to Live (Fox, 1932)
Hollywood on Parade #2 (Par, 1932) (s)
Child of Manhattan (Col, 1933)
My Lips Betray (Fox, 1933)
Hollywood on Parade #9 (Par, 1933) (s)
Only Yesterday (Univ, 1933)
I Believed in You (Fox, 1934)
Music in the Air (Fox, 1934)
Beloved (Univ, 1934)
Bottoms Up (Fox, 1934)

Stand Up and Cheer (Fox, 1934)
The Life of Vergie Winters (RKO, 1934)
Wild Gold (Fox, 1934)
The Age of Innocence (RKO, 1934)
The White Parade (Fox, 1934)
Orchids to You (Fox, 1935)
Curly Top (Fox, 1935)
Redheads on Parade (Fox, 1935)
The Littlest Rebel (Fox, 1935)
Screen Snapshots #8 (Col, 1935) (s)
Rose of the Rancho (Par, 1936)
A Message to Garcia (20th-Fox, 1936)
Craig's Wife (Col, 1936)
Screen Snapshots #13 (Col, 1936) (s)
As Good as Married (Univ, 1937)
Stella Dallas (UA, 1937)
Fight for Your Lady (RKO, 1937)
Holiday Greetings (Unk, 1937) (s)
She Married an Artist (Col, 1938)
Romance in the Dark (Par, 1938)
Sinners in Paradise (Univ, 1938)
The Road to Happiness (Mon, 1942)
Between Us Girls (Univ, 1942)
Thousands Cheer (MGM, 1943)
Babes in Bagdad (UA, 1952)

Broadway Plays

Little Jessie James (1923)
Mercenary Mary (1925)

Kitty's Kisses (1926)
One Touch of Venus (1943)

Album Discography

LPs

Jerome Kern 1934–38 (Box Office Productions 19747)*
The King of Jazz (Caliban 6025) [ST]
Music in the Air (World T-121)*

Stars of the Silver Screen 1929–30 (RCA LPV-538)*
*Compilation album

CDs

The King of Jazz/King of Burlesque/Going Places/ Carefree (Great Movie Themes 60019) [ST]
Memories (Crystal Stream Audio IDCD30)*

Movie Musicals, Vol. 2: 1930-38 (ABC 838-440-2)*
Year: Hits of 1930 (ASV CD-AJA-5195)*
*Compilation album

Pat Boone

(b. Charles Eugene Boone, Jacksonville, Florida, June 1, 1934)

Pat Boone will forever be typecast as the clean-cut singer wearing white buck shoes who provided an alternative for Elvis Presley at the dawn of the mid-1950s' rock 'n' roll era. While still in his twenties, Pat Boone became the idol of millions, both teenagers and adults, and he sold over 20 million records, starred in several successful films, was a TV star, and a best-selling author. Yet by the time he was thirty, Pat Boone's popularity had begun to erode, and he never recaptured his legion of followers. Still, his career was a steadily successful one, although from the 1970s on he mainly worked in show business as a spokesman for Fundamentalist Christianity through his music. Today many chroniclers of rock music are reluctant to allow Pat Boone his due credit in being a founder of the genre, declaring that much of his early recording success was geared on making "white," gentler versions of songs originally recorded by African-American artists, which many radio stations refused to air at the time. In actuality, while many (especially adults) were turned off by Elvis and his ilk, the good looks and fine baritone voice of Pat Boone made many converts to the rock 'n' roll movement, paving the way for several of its later stars. Without Pat Boone, rock music may never have found the mainstream following it needed to succeed in the United States.

He was born Charles Eugene Boone, the son of Archie and Margaret Boone, in Jacksonville, Florida, on June 1, 1934, one of four children who included two sisters and a younger brother named Nick. His family traced its lineage to pioneer Daniel Boone. Archie Boone was a building contractor, while Margaret was a registered nurse. When Boone was six, the family moved to Nashville, and by the age of ten the young man was performing in public. Always religious, he was baptized in the Church of Christ not long after he was thirteen. He attended David Lipscomb High School, where he excelled in sports and worked on the school newspaper as a reporter and a cartoonist. He also appeared in school dramatics, was elected president of the student body, and was voted the "most popular boy" in school. During his junior year he met Shirley Foley, daughter of country music star Red Foley, and they fell in love.

After high school, Pat, as he had been called since he was a small boy, attended David Lipscomb College and had his own radio show on Nashville WSIX called *Youth on Parade*. He also made his television debut on *The Original Amateur Hour* with Ted Mack on ABC-TV, and he was one of the show's few three-time winners, becoming a semifinalist in their big contest. Meanwhile, when he appeared on *Arthur Godfrey's Talent Scouts* on CBS-TV and won, he was disqualified from being a finalist on the *Amateur Hour* because he was now a professional. Meanwhile, he and Shirley eloped and were married on November 7, 1953.

Boone next accepted a job at WBAP-TV in Fort Worth, Texas, and he enrolled at North Texas State College in Denton intending to become a school teacher. When Arthur Godfrey fired Julius LaRosa from his TV show, Pat was hired as his replacement on *Arthur Godfrey's Talent Scouts*. Already the young singer had been signed by record producer Randy Wood for his Dot

Debbie Reynolds and Pat Boone in *Goodbye Charlie* (1964).
[Courtesy of JC Archives]

Records label, where he would remain for thirteen years. (His brother Nick would later record on the Dot label under the name Nick Todd.) Boone's first single for Dot, "Two Hearts," did well, and in the summer of 1955 he had his first big seller, the rocker "Ain't That a Shame," followed by "At My Front Door." Moving to New York City to appear on the Godfrey program, Pat enrolled at Columbia University as a junior. However, he soon had to take a leave of absence, as Twentieth Century-Fox Pictures production chief Buddy Adler (who predicted Boone would be the biggest star in Hollywood since James Stewart) signed him to a studio contract. (It was at this studio that Elvis Presley made his screen debut in 1956's *Love Me Tender*.)

Pat had best-selling single records of "Friendly Persuasion," "Chains of Love," "Don't Forbid Me," "I Almost Lost My Mind," "I'll Be Home," and "Anastasia" in 1956, but the year 1957 proved to be the high-water mark of his career with several hit records, two big money-making movies, and his own network TV show. His hit records that year included "I'm Just Waiting for You," "Love Letters in the Sand" (which sold over a million copies and remains Boone's most successful single), "Remember You're Mine," "There's a Goldmine in the Sky," "Why Baby Why," and the themes to his hit movies, *Bernadine* and *April Love*. The former cast Boone as a teenager facing life's problems, and it brought Oscar winner Janet Gaynor back to the screen. Peculiarly the project was conceived as a nonmusical, and only belatedly did the studio decide that their hit vocalist/leading man should have song numbers in the picture. So two were added: "Bernadine" and "Love Letters in the Sand."

April Love provided the star with a meatier role, that of a juvenile delinquent who is placed in the custody of his aunt (Jeanette Nolan) and uncle (Arthur O'Connell). Thanks to his winning way with horses, he not only redeems himself with his relatives, but also finds love with pretty farm girl Shirley Jones. In the wholesome movie Boone sang "Clover in the Meadow," "Give Me a Gentle Girl," and the title song, while he and Shirley Jones dueted on "Do It Yourself" and "The Bentonville Fair." During the shooting of *April Love*, Pat Boone received a great deal of fan magazine copy by refusing (for religious reasons) to kiss Shirley Jones on-screen. In addition, due to his attractive family (he and his wife Shirley would have four daughters: Cheryl, Linda, Debbie, and Laura), he was one of the most written-about stars both in fan and family-type magazines.

Boone left the Arthur Godfrey television show in 1957, and in the fall of that year, his *The Pat Boone–Chevy Showroom* weekly program debuted on ABC-TV as a prime-time variety show on Thursday nights. The series featured Pat and guest performers singing without expensive production trimmings, and each program typically closed with an inspiration number. While a *TV Guide* critic complained that the show was "about as exciting as a milkshake with two straws," it found an immediate audience that sustained it for three seasons.

Although Pat was extremely active during this period, he turned down many lucrative offers in order to continue his education. In 1958 he graduated from Columbia University magna cum laude with a Bachelor of Science degree. At the time he explained, "Too many teenagers want to quit school. I can't set a bad example. Besides I'll need an education to support my family if this bubble ever bursts." In that period, there was no need to worry, because in 1958 Boone continued his string of hit records for Dot (by now he was the label's top-selling artist) with "Cherie, I Love You," "For My Good Fortune," "I'll Remember Tonight," "It's Too Soon to Know," "That's How Much I Love You," and another million seller, "A Wonderful Time Up There."

Pat's movie and TV contracts called for him to be paid $1 million annually, and he was also involved in product endorsements (such as Pat Boone shoes, watches, and so on). He also had many investments, such as oil wells; two music-publishing companies; a restaurant in Denton, Texas; and two radio stations. The year 1958 saw the publication of his first book, the best-selling *Twixt Twelve and Twenty* (which remained a good seller well into the 1970s), and he starred in his third Twentieth Century-Fox feature, *Mardi Gras*. He portrayed a military school cadet who wins a raffle, the prize being a date with film star Christine Carere. Pat was top-billed as Alec McEwen in the Technicolor adventure film *Journey to the Center of the Earth* (1959) from the Jules Verne novel, which exploited Boone's physique in scant clothing. That year he continued to churn out hit records for Dot with "Beyond the Sunset," "Fool's Hall of Fame," "Good Rockin' Tonight," "Twixt Twelve and Twenty," and "With the Wind and Rain in Your Hair." His top-selling long playing albums for the company included *Howdy!, Pat, Stardust, Pat Boone Sings,* and *Tenderly*.

Buddy Adler, Pat's movie mentor at Twentieth Century-Fox, died in the summer of 1960, and it was the beginning of the end of Boone's superstardom. He made no pictures that year, and his TV show had already ended. However, he still had chart records (albeit not at the top), such as "Alabam," "Candy Sweet," "Dear John," "New Lovers," "Spring Rain," and "Walkin' the Floor Over You" along with the album *Moonglow*. In 1961 his pop recording of "Moody River" and the album of the same title were big sellers, while his other singles that year included "Big Cold Wind," "The Exodus (Theme) Song," and "Johnny Will." That year also found him back on-screen for Twentieth as he and Buddy Hackett played two sailors out to find romance in the breezy service comedy *All Hands on Deck*. The next year, he starred as farm boy Wayne who journeys with his family to the local *State Fair* (1962), where he encounters the girl of his dreams (Ann-Margret). Unfortunately, this pale remake did little to bolster Boone's sinking screen career.

In 1962 Boone did have a good-selling record for Dot with "Speedy Gonzales," but his other releases—like "I'll See You in My Dreams," "Pictures in the Fire," and "Ten Lonely Guys"—did not have long chart stays. In an attempt to change his clean-cut image, Boone headlined *The Yellow Canary* for Fox in 1963 as a self-centered pop singer who changes his ways when his child is kidnapped, and in the British-made *The Main Attraction* as a drifter who finds trouble and romance with a traveling circus. Neither film caused much of a box-office stir. While in England he also made the horror comedy entry *The Horror of It All* (1964) as an American tourist trapped in a spooky old house. However, by now his marquee allure was so tepid that the latter movie ended up on the lower half of a double bill. Receiving even less release was another programmer he made in London for Allied Artists called *Never Put It in Writing* (1964), in which he played a man out to retrieve an embarrassing letter that could cost him his job. Back in Hollywood, Boone ended his Twentieth Century-Fox contract by costarring in the abysmal farce *Goodbye Charlie*, about a murdered gangster who is reincarnated as a beautiful woman (Debbie Reynolds).

During the 1960s, the maturing Pat suffered the low point of his career. His records rarely made the charts, with only "Wish You Were Here Buddy" in 1966 doing well, and he attempted to become a nightclub star. But, as he later admitted, he looked "like a choirboy imitating Liberace." He did well by his cameo role as the Young Man at the Tomb in United Artists' *The Greatest Story Ever Told* (1965), and in 1967 a TV pilot he made was expanded into a theatrical film called *The Perils of Pauline*, where he played a globe-trotter out to find his lost sweetheart (Pamela Austin). In 1969 he guest-starred on the TV series *The Beverly Hillbillies* and *That Girl*, and that year he was in the TV movie *The Pigeon* for ABC-TV as a man involved with a detective (Sammy Davis Jr.) on a complicated case. In 1971 Boone was on TV's *Night Gallery*, and two years later he was in an *Owen Marshall* segment.

The 1970s brought a distinct change in Boone and in his show-business career. He abandoned "trying to round myself out as an actor" and began devoting most of his energies to religious-oriented entertainment. In 1970 he made *The Cross and the Switchblade*, directed by actor Don Murray, a biography in which Boone portrayed country minister Reverend David Wilkerson, who comes to Manhattan to combat gang wars, drugs, and racial disharmony. The production proved successful not only in theaters but also on the religious circuit, where it continues to be shown.

At that time, Pat also formed his own record company, Lamb and Lion (which in 1988 filed for protection in the U.S. Bankruptcy Court), and he recorded a number of religious albums, some with his wife and daughters, as well as producing LPs with such performers as Stuart Hamblen, Del Wood, and Johnny Bond. Although he sometimes performed at rock festivals, Boone mostly kept his personal appearances to religious congregations, and he also recorded for various labels such as Motown, Word, MGM, Tetragrammaton (co-owned by Bill Cosby), Thistle, and Hitsville. He returned to the record charts in the 1970s, but now in country music, with "I'll Do It." Recorded in 1975 for Melodyland Records, the song was followed by two 1976 singles for Hitsville, "Oklahoma Sunshine" and "Texas Woman," and in 1980 for Warner Bros./Curb he charted a single with "Colorado Country Morning." In addition, Boone, already well published (*Between You, Me and the Gatepost*, 1960; *The Care and Feeding of Parents*, 1967), continued to author a number of books, most of them on religious topics, like *The Real Christmas* (1972), *Joy* (1973), *A Miracle a Day Keeps the Devil Away* (1974), *Dr. Balaam's Talking Mule* (1975), *Get Your Life Together* (1978), *Pray to Win* (1980), and *A New Song* (1981). *The Honeymoon's Over* (1977) and *The Marriage Game* (1984) were both coauthored with his wife Shirley. In the late 1970s Pat made a number of joint appearances with his daughter Debbie, who won a Grammy Award as Best New Artist of the Year in 1977 for the hit song "You Light Up My Life."

In the early 1980s, the still-youthful-looking Boone resumed hosting a television program on the Christian Broadcasting Network (CBN) with the weekly *Together With Pat and Shirley Boone*, and was also a frequent TV personality, guesting on religious programs and charity telethons. In 1989, now a grandfather, he produced *Gospel America*, a touring show of rock gospel singers, and he was cofounder/owner and host of Shop Television Network on cable TV, as well as part owner of a television station in Anaheim, California. That year he also appeared as himself in the documentary-comedy *Roger and Me*. Since 1984 he has headlined *The Pat Boone Show*, a syndicated radio series heard weekly on over 140 stations worldwide. The program has won a number of awards, including NRB Program of the Year Award and Seven Angels Awards.

In the 1990s Boone hosted the religious TV show *Gospel America* on the Trinity Broadcasting Network. In 1997, however, the program was suddenly pulled from the lineup after Boone appeared that year at the nationally televised American Music Awards dressed in a leather vest and studs, promoting his spoof album, *Pat Boone in a Metal Mood: No More Mr. Nice Guy*. While the compact disc returned the singer to the pop record charts for the first time in decades, it alienated some of his religious followers. A poll conducted by the Trinity network resulted overwhelming in Pat's favor, but his show was never reinstated.

As a result of the controversy, Pat was in great demand and continued to make personal appearances, hosting his syndicated radio show and engaging in various business enterprises. One of these was the record company Gold Label, which not only released material by Boone but also by such singers as Connie Francis, Roy Clark, and Steve Lawrence and Eydie Gorme, as well as reissuing popular hits of the past. A member of the Christian Coalition, he was a spokesman for the faith-based Mercy Corps International, the Israeli Tourism Department, and the Easter Seals Society. In the 1990s Pat also guested on TV shows like *Space Ghost Coast to Coast* and *Second Noah* as well as appearing in a "Weird Al" Yankovic video. He was back on-screen in 2000 typecast as a Christian entertainer in *The Eyes of Tammy Faye*, a documentary on Tammy Faye Baker. He also began hosting a second weekly radio series, *Then and Now*, on the Music of Your Life Radio Network.

While some music critics complained that Pat Boone built his career on recording rhythm-and-blues songs that mainstream radio stations in the 1950s would not play otherwise, the singer countered, "I was not a rip-off artist." He told a 1997 interviewer, "I call myself a midwife of rock 'n' roll. I was not, like Elvis, a watershed performer; he was a white boy who could legitimately sing black music. But I provided the necessary transition. I was a bridge."

Filmography

Bernadine (20th-Fox, 1957)
April Love (20th-Fox, 1957)
Mardi Gras (20th-Fox, 1958)
Journey to the Center of the Earth (20th-Fox, 1959)
All Hands on Deck (20th-Fox, 1961)
State Fair (20th-Fox, 1962)
The Yellow Canary (20th-Fox, 1963)
The Main Attraction (20th-Fox, 1963)
The Horror of It All (20th-Fox, 1963)
Never Put It in Writing (AA, 1964)

Goodbye Charlie (20th-Fox, 1964)
The Greatest Story Ever Told (UA, 1965)
The Perils of Pauline (Univ, 1967)
The Pigeon (ABC-TV, 11/4/69)
The Cross and the Switchblade (Gateway, 1970)
Seven Alone (Doty-Dayton, 1974) (voice only)
Matilda (American International, 1978) (voice only)
A Better Way (Daughters of St. Paul, 1988) (s)
Roger and Me (WB, 1989)
The Eyes of Tammy Faye (Lions Gate Films, 2000) (documentary)

Radio Series

The Pat Boone Show (Syndicated, 1984–)

Then and Now (Music of Your Life Radio Network, 2000–)

TV Series

Arthur Godfrey and His Friends (CBS, 1955–57)
The Pat Boone–Chevy Showroom (ABC, 1957–60)
The Pat Boone Show (NBC, 1966–67)

Together With Pat and Shirley Boone (CBN, 1982)
Gospel America (Trinity Broadcasting, 1994–97)
The Osbournes (MTV, 2002–) (voice only)

Album Discography

LPs

Ain't That a Shame (Dot 3573/25573)
All in the Boone Family (Lamb and Lion 1008)
April Love (Dot 9000) [ST]
The Best of Pat Boone—22 Original Hits (Warwick WW-5089)
Blest Be the Tie (Dot 3601/25601)
Born Again (Lamb and Lion 1007)

Boss Beat (Dot 3594/25594)
Canadian Sunset (Pickwick 3123)
Christian People (Lamb and Lion 1005)
Christmas Is a-Comin' (Dot 25770)
The Cross and the Switchblade (Light 5550) [ST]
The Country Side of Pat Boone (Motown 6-501)
Departure (Tetragrammaton 118)

The Family Who Prays (Lamb and Lion 1006)
Favorite Hymns (Pickwick 3145)
First Nashville Jesus Band (Lamb and Lion 1004)
The General Motors Fiftieth Anniversary Show (RCA LOC-1037) [ST/TV]
Golden Era of Country Hits (Dot 3626/25626)
Golden Hits (Dot 3455/25455)
Golden Hits—15 Hits (Dot 3814/25814)
Great, Great, Great! (Dot 3346/25346)
Great Hits (Pickwick 3597)
Greatest Hits (Paramount 1043)
Greatest Hits of 1965 (Dot 3685/25685)
Greatest Hymns (Paramount 1024)
He Leadeth Me (Dot 3234/25234)
How Great Thou Art (Dot 3798/25798)
Howdy (Dot 3030)
Hymns We Love (Dot 3068/25068)
Hymns We Love (Word 8664)
I Love You More and More (MGM SE-4899)
I Was Kaiser Bill's Batman (Dot 3805/25805)
I'll See You in My Dreams (Dot 3399/25399)
In the Holy Land (Lamb and Lion 5000)
It's Time to Pray, America! (House Top HTR-702) [ST/TV]
Jivin' Pat (Bear Family BFX-15230)
Just the Way I Am (Lamb and Lion 1039)
Look Ahead (Dot 25876)
The Lord's Prayer (Dot 3582/25582)
Love Me Tender (Pickwick 3101)
Magic of Lassie (Peter Pan 155) [ST]
Memories (Dot 3748/25748)
Moody River (Dot 3384/25384)
Moonglow (Dot 3270/25270)
My God and I (Dot 3386/25386)
Near You (Dot 3606/25606)
1965 (Hamilton 153/12153)
The Old Rugged Cross (Pickwick 3568)
Pat (Dot 3050)

Pat Boone (Dot 3012)
Pat Boone (MCA 2-6020)
The Pat Boone Family (Word 8536)
Pat Boone Reads From the Bible (Dot 3402)
Pat Boone Sings (Dot 3158/25158)
Pat Boone Sings Golden Hymns (Lamb and Lion 1001)
Pat Boone Sings Irving Berlin (Dot 3077/25077)
Pat Boone Sings the New Songs of the Jesus People (Lamb and Lion 1002)
Pat's Great Hits (Dot 3071/25071)
Pat's Great Hits, Vol. 2 (Dot 3261/25261)
A Pocketful of Hope (Thistle 1005)
Rapture (Supreme 2060)
The Romantic Pat Boone (Pickwick 2006)
S-A-V-E-D (Lamb and Lion 1013)
Side by Side (Dot 319/25199) w. Shirley Boone
Sing Along With Pat Boone (Dot 3513)
Sixteen Great Performances (ABC 4006, MCA AB-4006)
Something Supernatural (Lamb and Lion 1017)
Songs From the Inner Court (Lamb and Lion 1016)
Speedy Gonzales (Dot 3455/25455)
Star Dust (Dot 3118/25118)
The Star Spangled Banner (Word 8725)
State Fair (Dot 9011) [ST]
Tenderly (Dot 3180/25180)
Tenth Anniversary With Dot (Dot 3650/25650)
Texas Woman (Hitsville 40551)
This and That (Dot 3285/25285)
The Touch of Your Lips (Dot 3546/25546)
True Love (Pickwick 3079)
Twelve Great Hits (Hamilton 118/12118)
White Christmas (Dot 3222/25222)
Winners of the Reader's Digest Poll (Dot 3667/25667)
Wish You Were Here, Buddy (Dot 3764/25764)
Yes, Indeed (Dot 3121/25121)

CDs

April Love (BCI Music 64547)
April Love: The Best of Pat Boone (Laserlight 12-121)
The Best of Pat Boone (Fat Boy FATCD-143)
The Best of Pat Boone (Prism PLATCD-434)
The Best of Pat Boone—The Millennium Collection (MCA 112394)
Best of the Best of Pat Boone (Legacy Entertainment ATP074)
Collection of Personal Favorites (Homeland 9709)
A Date With Pat Boone (Pair PCD-2-1311)
The EP Collection (See for Miles 487)
Fifties: Complete (Bear Family BCD-15884)
Gold Collection (Gold Label 8000)
Golden Treasury of Hymns (Gold Label 8003)
Greatest Hits (Curb D21K-77298)
Greatest Hits (Curb D21K-77655)

Greatest Hits (MCA MCAD-10885)
Greatest Hymns (Curb 77808-2)
Hymns We Love (Universal Special Markets 21139)
I Remember Red—A Tribute to Red Foley (Laserlight 12-384)
I'll be Home (ABM ABMMCD1036)
In a Metal Mood—No More Mr. Nice Guy (Hip-O Record 40025)
In a Symphonic Mood (Gold Label 9036)
Inspirational Collection (Varese Vintage VSD-5903)
Israel Oh Israel (Gold Label 1500)
Love Letters in the Sand (Golgram GC-007)
Love Letters in the Sand (Hallmark 31229)
Love Letters in the Sand (Masters 503322)
Love Letters in the Sand (Promo Sound)

The Masters (Eagle Rock 408)
More Greatest Hits (Varese Vintage VSD-5522)
Our Recollections (Word 5413)
Pat Boone (Castle Communications MAT-CD-306)
Pat Boone Family Christmas (Laserlight 12-289)
Pat's 40 Big Ones (PID 646462, Conno SDVSOP-328)

Remember (PCI Eclipse 64700)
State Fair (Varese Sarabande 66090) [ST]
20 Classics (Summit 4081)
The Very Best of Pat Boone (Big Eye Music 4049)
The Very Best of Pat Boone (Pegasus PEG076)
White Christmas (Universal Special Products 20049)

Bobby Breen

(b. Robert Borsuch, Montreal, Canada, November 4, 1927)

For a time in the latter 1930s, one child star rivaled Shirley Temple in popularity. He was Bobby Breen, a Canadian youth who appeared with extraordinary success in a series of mawkish RKO low-budget musicals, all showcasing his amazingly cultivated soprano voice. These wafer-thin scenarios displayed curly-haired little Bobby coping with life's vagaries, always singing and always finding happiness by the picture's finale. Detractors insisted he presented a very syrupy, sissified image. In real life, his voice changed in 1939 and his movie career faded immediately. Thereafter, he devoted decades to avoiding and/or capitalizing on his tremendous childhood fame.

He was born in Montreal, Canada, on November 4, 1927, the son of Hyman and Rebeccah Borsuch [Borsuk], who had fled from Kiev, Russia during one of the many anti-Jewish pogroms of the 1910s. (Mrs. Borsuch's father, a violinist/cellist, had been killed in the Bolshevik fighting.) The Borsuches arrived penniless in Western Canada, first living in Regina, Saskatchewan, and then resettling in Montreal. There were already three older children (Gertrude, seventeen; Michael [Mickey], fifteen; and Sally, nine) when Bobby was born. Hoping for better, the Borsuch family moved to Toronto, where they operated a tiny candy store, with the family packed into crowded living quarters in the back. Hyman Borsuch was a garment cutter usually too sick to work.

Young Michael Borsuch had already displayed a fine singing voice, but it paled in comparison to little Bobby's. When Bobby was still a tyke, his doting sister Sally took him to amateur contests. The sight of this precocious child with light yellow curly hair singing in a surprisingly mature lyrical treble quickly won for him a series of first prizes. When Sally was fourteen she called the Silver Slipper, a Toronto restaurant, and bargained for a waitress job for herself. After she had worked there for a while, she asked whether she could bring her little brother in for the Silver Slipper's Wednesday-night radio amateur programs. Bobby won a prize. Thereafter she escorted him to the restaurant weekly for this event, and for nearly two years he sang on the program. Later little Bobby performed at the Savarin Restaurant for nearly a year. By now Sally had changed the family name to Borene and then to Breen. In the summertime, Sally (who also sang and danced) and Bobby toured the outskirts of Toronto, entertaining at estate parties. At the Canadian National exposition, Bobby sang and Sally modeled.

Sally, who had assumed the role of being her brother's devout stage mother, dreamed of transforming her little sibling into a stellar show-business attraction. With money saved from various jobs, she (now sixteen) took Bobby to Chicago. Through a man who had managed her brother Mickey as a "concert singer," she was given an entree to stage producer Louis Lipstone of the Balaban and Katz Theater circuit. He auditioned Bobby and hired him to sing at the Oriental Theater in the same variety revue as Milton Berle, with Bobby being promoted as Berle's nephew. Next, Breen appeared at the Chicago Theater, where he was on the same bill as Gloria Swanson.

Marion Claire and Bobby Breen in *Make a Wish* (1937).
[Courtesy of JC Archives]

During this six-month period in late 1933/early 1934, Bobby was heard also on Chicago radio programs.

Wanting greater opportunities for Bobby, Sally determined to move to New York City. Lipstone provided her with a letter of introduction to Boris Morros, then in Manhattan in charge of the Paramount Theaters' stage prologues. Morros was so impressed with the youngster's abilities that he underwent a great deal of trouble (obtaining a special work permit for the young boy) to employ him for two weeks at the flagship Paramount Theater. Meanwhile, Sally—who had a job as a cigarette girl at the Hotel Edison—enrolled Bobby at the New York Professional Children's School. When vocalist/actor Harry Richman was preparing the Broadway musical *Say When* (November 1934), he contacted the school to send over some kids to audition for a small role in the show. Bobby was among the seventy-six who tried out, and he was hired to be the newsboy son of a drunk (Bob Hope). *Say When* lasted for a brief seventy-six performances. Later, Breen had an appearance on Alexander Woollcott's radio program.

More determined than ever for the success of her younger brother, Sally led him on the endless rounds of casting agents, including Ben Holtzman, then Eddie Cantor's manager. Bobby auditioned for Cantor, who was impressed but did not hire him for his network radio show as Sally had hoped. The steadfast girl prophetically advised the superstar, "Some day Mr. Cantor, you will ask this little boy to sing with you."

Now reduced to living on $7 a week, Sally and Bobby moved from one boardinghouse to another, always a step down. At one theatrical lodging, a neighbor led Sally to showman Arthur Levy, who in turn, called in agent William Shapiro, who signed the talented boy (now seven) to a three-month trial-period contract. Sally and Bobby moved to Hollywood. Near the end of the three months, Mike Hoffman of Pathé suggested that Sally take Bobby to audition for Sol Lesser, a former movie exhibitor who in the 1930s turned to producing low-budget films and serials. More importantly, Lesser had experience in promoting/exploiting child performers (such as Baby Peggy Montgomery).

Lesser was impressed by Bobby's voice, presence, and wholesome youthfulness. To confirm his hunch, he had young Breen perform for famed vocal coach Dr. Mario Marafioti (he numbered Grace Moore among his clients), who endorsed the boy's potential. Lesser next arranged for Bobby to perform in an outdoor program at the Uplifters Club in suburban Los Angeles. Eddie Cantor was at the concert, and he soon hired Bobby to sing on his NBC network radio program. Bobby had just turned eight. For Cantor's Christmas show, Bobby sang "Santa, Bring My Mommy Back to Me." Audience response was so enthusiastic that Cantor hired Breen to be a permanent member of his radio troupe, along with another Canadian prodigy, Deanna Durbin. On the air Bobby referred to Cantor as "Uncle Eddie," and listeners were convinced the two were indeed relatives.

Meanwhile, Sol Lesser, through his Principal Pictures, which released its product via RKO Pictures, rushed Bobby into his first feature picture, *Let's Sing Again* (1936). It contained every saccharine ingredient that would become standard for Breen vehicles. Here he is a supposed orphan who runs away from the orphanage to join a circus, ending up in New York City and being reunited with his long-lost tenor father (George Houston). Besides the title tune, there were such items as "Lullaby," "Farmer in the Dell," and "La Donna e Mobile." *Variety* decided, "Young Breen makes a decidedly promising shove off. He has a voice which is sweet. . . . He reads his lines naturally. . . . " The *New York Times* dubbed him "the most curious voice in a generation of vocal curiosities" and reported, "Bobby's dwarf tenor also appears to excite rapturous feminine murmurs in his audience."

The die was cast, and Bobby Breen was now a movie star. His next vehicle—a period piece—was his most popular. *Rainbow on the River* (1936) finds the winsome boy in short pants melting the cold heart of his grandmother (May Robson) and being reunited with his loving mammy (Louise Beavers). The maudlin movie contained Breen's signature tune, "Rainbow on the River," and the low-budget musical featured the Hall Johnson choir.

As a moppet star, Breen was earning $50,000 a year just from testimonials, plus the income from pictures and radio and, in addition, up to $500 weekly for personal appearances. Sister Sally was on Sol Lesser's payroll at $75 per week, and Bobby was attending Los Angeles' Black Foxe Military Academy, along with such fellow students as Charlie Chaplin's two boys and Paul Whiteman's son. By now Breen's awestruck parents had moved to Hollywood, where their youngest child was supporting them. (The father would die in 1954 and the mother in 1957, at which time there would be a squabble as to which offspring deserved the $60,000 estate.)

Make a Wish (1937) was set at a boys' summer camp, with smiley Bobby acting as matchmaker between his mother (Marion Claire) and a Broadway composer (Basil Rathbone) who is writing a new operetta. Among the musical interludes were "Make a Wish," "Music in My Heart," and "Old Man Rip." *Hawaii Calls* (1938) boasted exotic settings (via process screen) with stowaway bootblack Breen on a vessel headed for the tropical paradise, with such tunes as "Hawaii Calls," "That's the Hawaiian in Me," and "Down Where the Trade Winds Blow." *Breaking the Ice* (1938) displayed sensitive Breen running away from home yet again—this time to Philadelphia, where he performs in an ice-skating show, his coperformer being precocious Irene Dare (touted as the world's youngest skater). The songs this go-around included, "Telling My Troubles to a Mule," "Put Your Heart in a Song", "The Sunny Side of Things," and "Happy As a Lark."

The year 1939 was Bobby Breen's busiest on-camera, as he was in three releases. *Fisherman's Wharf* used San Francisco as a backdrop and had the support of such stalwarts as Leo Carrillo, Henry Armetta, and Slick the Seal. When not running away from home yet again, Breen was busy singing "Sell Your Cares for a Song," "Songs of Italy," and "Fisherman's Chantie." *Way Down South* was laid in the pre–Civil War South, with Louisiana youth Breen almost fleeced of his inheritance, but aided by a kindly New Orleans innkeeper (Alan Mowbray) and a happy (!) slave (Clarence Muse). The Hall Johnson Choir supported Bobby in some of his numbers, including "Louisiana" and "Good Ground." Breen's finale film for the year was *Escape to Paradise* (1939), a meandering study of a South-American port youth who convinces a lazy playboy (Kent Taylor) that getting a job is the best way to win a beautiful localite (Marta Shelton). The lackluster songs were, "Tra-La-La" ("youngster's soprano warbling is shrill on the high notes," *Variety* alerted) "Ay, Ay, Ay," and "Rhythm of the Rio."

By now, twelve-year-old Bobby was experiencing a severe career crisis. His voice was changing. At the first signs of his vocal maturity (in late 1938), he had been dropped from Eddie Cantor's radio program, and as 1939 concluded, Sol Lesser announced gravely, "Bob's voice is changing, and he has been warned to do no more singing for at least two years." Breen had just had his tonsils and adenoids removed, a surgical procedure much delayed for fear of what it would do to his voice. After graduating from high school he went to UCLA, where in his year plus there, he majored in music and drama. (Later, he reflected, "I suppose I should have learned something else, business for instance, but I was waiting for my voice to settle down so I could get started again.")

He became the California State oratorical champ six successive times and had a brief flurry as guest pianist with the NBC (radio) Symphony Orchestra.

Meanwhile, Breen's career eclipse ended briefly in 1943 when he appeared with several other onetime child stars (Jane Withers, Carl "Alfalfa" Switzer, Spanky McFarland, and Cora Sue Collins) in a minimusical at Republic Pictures. In this entry, *Johnny Doughboy*, Bobby was given *no* songs to sing.

During World War II Breen served in the Army, sometimes in the infantry and sometimes appearing in jeep shows to entertain Allied troops in Europe, often appearing with Mickey Rooney. In February of 1946 he was demobilized and entered the American Academy of Dramatic Arts in New York City. He later had a local fifteen-minute variety TV show and began playing nightclub engagements. He was much in the national news in November 1948 when he and a pilot/hunter friend were traveling from Waukesha to Haywood, Wisconsin, in a small plane that was reported missing. After a massive twenty-four-hour search, Bobby and his pal were found to be safely resting in a Glidding, Wisconsin, hotel, unharmed. The search-party sheriff suggested the entire episode could have been a publicity gimmick dreamed up by the former child star.

In the 1950s Breen, now a full-bodied tenor who was finding decent engagements hard to find, was the first to admit, "Thank God my folks put away some of the money I made as a kid. I've never been hungry. I'm trying to prove to producers and agency people that I still have talent as a grownup. That child star label never stops haunting me. The notion is that a child star isn't supposed to have talent when he grows up." In November 1952, he and Brooklyn model Jocelyn Lesh were married. They would have a son Keith, separate in 1958, and be divorced in 1961.

Breen spent much of the 1950s in and out of show business. "I wasn't getting ahead fast enough. I was insecure in an insecure business." When he was not performing his club act (based on the old style of entertainment) he was a real-estate seller or produced TV commercials. To continue performing he had to go far from home, sometimes overseas. Regarding his audiences, he admitted, "They expect me to come onstage still wearing short pants. It takes a lot of work out there to make them believe I'm grown up. They resent it somehow. It's something I have to fight every single performance."

By the early 1960s, Breen had relocated to Miami, Florida, and was signed to Thunderbird Recordings to do albums. Later he would make a pact with Motown Records, which also failed to revive his career. There were occasional club engagements, but more often Breen was occupied as a talent booker. There was a nostalgic reunion with Eddie Cantor in 1964, shortly before the latter's death. Cantor's advice to the once-star, "No matter what happens, keep going." Breen did.

In 1971 Breen appeared at the London nitery The Plough, and that same year, when beginning a New Jersey club engagement, he badly scratched his eyes with defective contact lens and was nearly blinded. Later in the 1970s, Breen, now rewed (to Audra, who had two sons, Paul and Ronald, by a prior marriage), was performing a minimusical stage version of *The Jazz Singer*, doing the numbers in the Al Jolson style. According to his wife, it was she who helped Breen change his stage image. "I made him put on sports clothes and throw away his elevator shoes."

Even in the 1980s Florida-based club booker Bobby Breen (head of Bobby Breen Enterprises) had mixed feelings about his long-ago successes. "As a child I had pretty nearly everything—except a childhood. The demands of a career—the practicing, rehearsals and appearances on radio and film—just didn't allow for it." When interviewed by TV's *Entertainment Tonight* (December 1985) from his Fort Lauderdale home, Breen commented, "If I couldn't make it really big again, super big, like I was when I was a kid, I'd rather go in other businesses." He ended his brief appearance on the television show by singing "The Best of Times." After that, the onetime child star disappeared from the national limelight.

Filmography

Let's Sing Again (RKO, 1936)
Rainbow on the River (RKO, 1936)
Make a Wish (RKO, 1937)
Hawaii Calls (RKO, 1938)
Breaking the Ice (RKO, 1938)

Fisherman's Wharf (RKO, 1939)
Way Down South (RKO, 1939)
Escape to Paradise (RKO, 1939)
Johnny Doughboy (Rep, 1943)

Broadway Plays

Say When (1934)

Radio Series

The Eddie Cantor Show (NBC, c. 1935–38)

Album Discography

LPs

Bobby Breen: Songs at Yuletide (10″ London 270)
Radio Memories, Number 3 (Bergen 1476-69)*

Those Wonderful Thirties, Vol. 1 (Decca DEA-7-1)*
*Compilation album

CDs

Bobby Breen (Sounds of a Century 1867)
Chris Barber at the BBC (Upbeat Jazz URCD-158)*
Memories (Crystal Stream Audio IDCD05)*

Movie Memories, Vol. 2, 1930-38 (ABC 838-440-2)*
To Mother, With Love (ASV CD-AJA-5351)*
*Compilation album

Judy Canova

(b. Juliette Canova, Starke, Florida, November 20, 1913; d. Los Angeles, CA, August 5, 1983)

Decades before such popular TV shows as *The Beverly Hillbillies, Petticoat Junction, Green Acres,* or *Hee Haw,* there was Judy Canova. Long before country western's Minnie Pearl became a U.S. institution, there was Judy Canova. It was Judy Canova, in the 1930s to 1950s, who made hillbilly humor a national pastime through her successful work on the Broadway stage, films, recordings, and especially on radio. As the energetic country hick spouting good-natured humor, she became an entertainment landmark. Yet beneath her trademark braided pigtails, oafish ankle boots, sloppy socks, and checkered blouse was a far more versatile performer than her public (or even she) would allow. Fans remember her best for that bellowing (yet melodic) voice that seemed forever geared to yodeling and guffawing. When Judy sang, her public expected it would be a countrified ballad like "Wabash Blues" or "Tons of Love." However, Judy Canova had an operatic-trained voice that was professionally adept at all types of music. And when given that rare opportunity, the "canyon-mouthed, pigtailed girl" could be a wow at dramatics.

She was born Juliette Canova in Starke, Florida, on November 20, 1913, the daughter of Joe (a cotton broker) and Henrietta Perry Canova (a former concert singer). There were three older Canova children: Anne, Zeke, and Pete. In the 1920s, Anne, Zeke, and Judy were heard as the Canova Cracker Trio on WJAX in Jacksonville, Florida. Meanwhile, Judy, the most effervescent of the trio, was performing in talent shows and in any other venue she could find for her show-business ambitions. Coming to terms with her plain looks, she admitted later, "I got smart and not only accepted my lack of glamour, but made the most of it." Both Anne and Zeke had attended the Cincinnati Conservatory of Music, and Judy had hoped to study there as well. However, her father died in 1930, and there was no money for tuition. Instead, Judy and her mother went to New York City, where Judy studied tap-dancing with Tommy Nip. Later she returned to Florida, where she taught contortion dancing at Orlando's Ebsen School.

Determined to prosper as an entertainer, Judy saved her money and returned to New York. Joined by Anne and Zeke, she won a job at Jimmie Kelly's Club and later at the Village Barn. It was during these engagements that she introduced her cornpone character to audiences. It was a successful novelty in Gotham, and she expanded the rubber-faced comedy aspect of her act. Rudy Vallee used her in a spot on his radio show, which led to a regular assignment on orchestra leader Paul Whiteman's NBC radio program. It gave her a much wider audience for her developing brand of country humor and singing. In time away from her radio commitments, she played the country in vaudeville tours.

Judy made her Broadway debut in *Calling All Stars,* which opened at the Hollywood Theater on December 13, 1934. Besides Martha Raye, Mitzi Mayfair, and Phil Baker, the revue featured

Eddie Foy Jr. and Judy Canova in *Joan of Ozark* (1942).
[Courtesy of Michael R. Pitts]

Anne, Pete, and Zeke Canova. Judy's best moment was a sketch entitled "Last of the Hillbillies" in which she sang "If It's Love." Unfortunately, the show ran for only 36 performances.

Calling All Stars had been financed by Warner Bros. Pictures, and when that show folded, the studio contracted the Canovas to come to California. Judy's screen debut proved to be her most memorable film moment. *In Caliente* (1935) was a musical potpourri with choreography by Busby Berkeley and songs by Harry Warren, Al Dubin, Mort Dixon, and Allie Wrubel. In the film's elaborate production number "The Lady in Red," Winifred Shaw sang the lead, and in the midst of an ensemble of shapely chorines, suddenly angular Judy Canova popped up to yodel nasally her variation of the lilting torch song. Later in the movie, the Canova quartet had a hillbilly musical spot, but it was Judy's superb burlesque of "The Lady in Red" that grabbed audience attention. In *Broadway Gondolier* (1935), the Canovas performed a brief specialty number, while in *Going Highbrow* (1935), Judy was cast without her family and played a dumb waitress. When the studio allowed their contract to lapse, the Canovas returned to New York City.

Without her family, Judy was hired to play in *The Ziegfeld Follies of 1936*, which opened at the Winter Garden Theater on January 30, 1936. The Lee Shubert production had Ira Gershwin lyrics and an ensemble that included Fanny Brice, Bob Hope, Josephine Baker, and Eve Arden.

The revue ran for 115 performances before closing for the summer, with Judy receiving solid revues for her antics and parodies. However, when the show reopened that fall, she was no longer part of the production. She had negotiated a radio contract with NBC/WJZ radio for the *Ripling Rhythm Revue*, which gave her family parts in the show. The program was on the airwaves for the 1936–37 season.

Paramount now offered the Canovas a film contract, and the group (minus Pete who had entered business management) reported back to Hollywood. In *Artists and Models* (1937), Anne and Zeke were part of the Canova act, but it was Judy who had a featured role and a specialty number, "Pop Goes the Bubble" (a send-up of bubble bath songs). It was also during this "new" Hollywood period that Judy gained much publicity with her (staged) fracas with Edgar Bergen, the ventriloquist, who, in tandem with dummy Charlie McCarthy, was starring on radio's *Chase and Sanborn Hour*. Judy confessed publicly that she and Bergen were no longer an item (she could not compete with the dummy). Bergen retorted that he had never met Canova. Unpublicized was the fact that Judy was already wed, having married New York insurance man Robert Burns in Maryland in 1936.

In *Thrill of a Lifetime* (1937), Paramount cast Judy as the sex-starved, clumsy sister of Eleanore Whitney and Johnny Downs, who is courted by Ben Blue. She, Anne, and Zeke sang a hillbilly song. Paramount dropped their option, which ended their $6,000 weekly paycheck. Judy assessed later, "I would have done better getting eighteen bucks a week and a good part."

The Canovas returned to vaudeville, where they had developed an enthusiastic following, and played a two-week engagement at London's Café de Paris. They then joined Edgar Bergen on his NBC radio *Chase and Sanborn Hour* for thirteen weeks in 1938, for which they received $4,300 weekly for their efforts. On May 3, 1939, the Canova clan appeared on an experimental NBC-TV program, making them the first hillbilly act ever seen on television.

It was on Broadway in *Yokel Boy* (July 6, 1939) that Judy Canova reached a career peak. The comedy featured Phil Silvers, Buddy Ebsen, Dixie Dunbar, and Anne and Zeke Canova. Judy starred as the hillbilly who becomes an "overnight" movie star. The *New York Times* enthused about Judy: "A rowdy mixture of Beatrice Lillie and other comediennes along parallel lines in the general direction of Fannie [sic] Brice ... Quite a girl on the whole." *Yokel Boy* ran for 208 performances, and Hollywood took notice of Judy Canova for the third time.

Herbert J. Yates, head of Republic Pictures, offered Judy a contract. She reasoned that her rustic bumpkin specialty would be better utilized at a studio noted for its "horse-opry" stars (Gene Autry and Roy Rogers) and that here, without the competition of glamorous leading ladies under contract, she would better shine. Her Republic debut was *Scatterbrain* (1940), in which she portrayed a hillbilly who is transformed into a movie starlet. She performed slapstick (washing her kitchen floor on roller skates with brushes tied to them) and sang "Benny the Beaver (You Better Be Like That, Yeah, Yeah)." The *New York Daily News* reported, "The gags are good, the situations funny, and Judy Canova herself a riot in her first starring role for the screen."

As part of her five-year Republic pact (which called for three films annually), Judy made *Sis Hopkins* (1941), featuring Charles Butterworth, Jerry Colonna, and a rising newcomer, Susan Hayward. This movie, more than any other of her pictures, displays Judy's vocal virtuosity. She did selections ranging from an operatic aria from Giuseppe Verdi's opera *La Traviata* to Frank

Loesser–Jule Styne's "It Ain't Hay (It's the U.S.A.)," and on to "Cracker Barrel County," showing that she could handle a swing number (with Bob Crosby's band) admirably. The film produced her trademark expression, "You're telling I."

Judy Canova was now a star of sorts. Republic had bought the screen rights to *Yokel Boy* as a Canova vehicle, but she and the studio had a disagreement, and she was replaced in the screen version (1942) by Joan Davis. MGM asked to borrow her services, and Judy responded, "I don't want any more big studios for a while. You get lost." Instead, Judy and Republic renegotiated her contract, which now provided she be part-owner of her features made for them. Meanwhile, Judy, divorced since 1939, made headlines in June 1941 while on a Honolulu vacation. On June 10 she and a hometown Florida friend, Army Corporal James H. Ripley, became engaged, and they were wed on June 14. That same evening, he was arrested for being AWOL. Judy soon returned to the mainland and on October 8, 1941, she annulled the marriage.

Puddin'head (1941) was more of the same profitable Judy Canova bucolic shenanigans. She sang "Minnie Hotcha," "Hey, Junior!," "Manhattan Holiday," and "You're Telling I" (a duet with Eddie Foy Jr.). Her busiest screen year was 1942, with three releases. For Republic's *Sleepytime Gal*, she was a cake decorator at a Miami hotel and sang "Barrelhouse Bessie," "I Don't Want Anybody at All," "Sleepytime Gal," and "The Cat's Away." On loan to Paramount for *True to the Army*, she was a circus tightrope walker who witnesses a killing and flees to Fort Bragg, where her boyfriend (Jerry Colonna) is a GI. Judy did her stock-in-trade hillbilly gambits, while Ann Miller tap-danced and Allan Jones crooned. Back at Republic, she was paired with equally big-mouthed funster Joe E. Brown in *Joan of Ozark*, a spy farce, and she got to warble "Backwood Barbecue," "The Lady at Lockheed," and "Wabash Blues." Judy and Brown would re-create their roles for radio's *Screen Guild Playhouse* in February 1945.

By now Canova had guested on most of the top radio variety programs, and on July 6, 1943, she began *The Judy Canova Show* on the CBS network. The humor remained strictly hillbilly, with Judy braying forth with backwoods jokes. ("Is this a room with bath?" "Hoo," Judy replies, "the only thing we got here is a room with a path.") *Variety* reported, "Miss Canova, when given to songs, spreads her style from scat to rhythm to plain hog calling, but it was all entertaining." Her show was a big hit. Earlier in the year, on March 14, 1943, Judy wed Private Chester B. England in Newton, New Jersey. She had met him in London during her 1938 club engagement in England.

Chatterbox (1943) rematched her with Joe E. Brown in a satire of the radio industry and Western movies. The Mills Brothers and Spade Cooley performed musical specialties, and Judy sang "Why Can't I Sing a Love Song?" In *Sleepy Lagoon* (1943) Judy is a radio singer who is made mayor of her hometown and must endure the hazards of an amusement park's fun house. She vocalized "I'm Not Myself Anymore" and, with Joe Sawyer, harmonized "You're the Fondest Thing I Am of." It was her last film at Republic for several years because she and the studio were in constant disagreement over properties and budgets for her projects.

During the World War II years, Judy was active in war-bond tours and entertaining at Army camps. On August 24, 1944, she gave birth to her first child, Julieta. Two weeks later, her husband went overseas for active military duty. That same month also marked her first Columbia Pictures' effort, *Louisiana Hayride*. She portrayed a hillbilly debutante and got to vocalize "You Gotta Go Where the Train Goes," "Rainbow Road," "I'm a Woman of the World," "Put Your Arms Around Me Honey," and a smattering of "Short'nin Bread." If her Republic properties had been economy-conscious, Judy's three Columbia projects were shoddy programmers tossed out to exploit the popular Canova image with rural audiences. *Hit the Hay* (1945) presented Judy in dual roles. Besides belting out "Old MacDonald Had a Farm" and "No Other Love," the versatile songstress provided arias from such operas as *Rigoletto, The Barber of Seville,* and *La Traviata.* In *Singin' in the Corn* (1946), she is a carnival fortune-teller who inherits great wealth and must deal with a ghost town. Her numbers included "Pepita Chiquita," "I'm a Gal of Property," "Ma, He's Making Eyes at Me," and "An Old Love Is a True Love."

If her films were mired in an uncreative rut, Judy was faring far better on radio. Having been off the air since June 1944, she returned to the airwaves on January 6, 1945, for NBC with a new Saturday night program. The lineup included a host of talented players: Verna Felton, Joe Kerns, Ruby Dandridge, and Mel Blanc. Using a comedy-variety format, she continued to garner howls as the back-country miss from Unadella, Georgia, who had relatives out west in Cactus Junction and who had a rich Aunt Agatha in the big city. Judy would regale audiences with humorous tales of her cousin Ureenus who fancied chopped-liver ice cream and her nonsensical interchanges with Pedro the gardener. She would close each show by singing "Go to Sleepy Little Baby." As with her films, Judy's production company owned a percentage of her show. Meanwhile, Judy's mother, age eighty, died on August 30, 1949.

In the following years (until 1952), radio was Judy's primary medium. She made a nightclub tour of Latin America in 1947 (the same year her brother Pete died). In February 1950, she divorced Chester B. England and, in July 1950, married Filiberto [Philip] Rivero, a Cuban musician and ardent Cuban nationalist who had had his band in Havana. (It would prove to be a stormy marriage; they divorced in 1964, and Rivero died in 1971.) She made personal appearances at large fairs throughout the Southwest. One of her biggest career disappointments was not being considered seriously by MGM for the lead in the musical *Annie Get Your Gun* (1950). (She had been considered for the lead in the Broadway production, but at the time she was making movies at Columbia Pictures.)

In 1951, Herbert J. Yates lured Judy back to Republic Pictures for more pictures. Her first was in Trucolor (the studio's own film color process), *Honeychile* (1951), and her singing ranged from an operatic version of "Rag Mop" to "Tutti Frutti." *Oklahoma Annie* (1952) could have been a half-hour TV Western, with Canova at her best singing "Blow the Whistle." *The WAC From Walla Walla* (1952) was a service comedy, and her four songs included "If Only Dreams Came True." Also in 1952, on November 2, she made her major television debut on *The Colgate Comedy Hour* (NBC), along with Anne and Zeke Canova. She was off the screen in 1953 due to the birth of her daughter Diana (June 1). Plans for a *Judy Canova Show* TV series did not materialize, but she was back on-camera in the black-and-white *Untamed Heiress* (1954), singing, among others, "A Dream for Sale." It was a family affair, for Canova's daughter Julieta played Judy as a youngster, and five-month-old Diana had a bit in this caper. *Carolina Cannonball* (1955) was very thinly produced, with Judy singing the title song; and *Lay That Rifle Down* (1955) had such novelty tunes as "I'm Glad I Was Born on My Birthday." Because Republic was moving out of theatrical filmmaking, Judy and the studio ended their contract.

The late 1950s were a fallow period for the country star. She guest-starred occasionally on TV, such as in *The Danny Thomas Show* (March 17, 1958), and in July 1958 Tops Records released *Judy Canova in Hi-Fi,* an LP compilation of such Canova singles as "Blow Whistle Blow," "Butcher Boy," and "Ain't Gonna Grieve My Lord." On May 29, 1960, she returned to television, making her dramatic TV debut on *Alfred Hitchcock Presents* in the episode "Party Line." She proved that she was far more than a comedienne. In the feature film, *The Adventures of Huckleberry Finn* (1960), she had a brief scene as the sheriff's wife. She was also among those in the low-budget *Hillbilly Jamboree* (1960).

Canova, whose slapstick talents should have made her a rival to television's Lucille Ball, unfortunately could never grab a proper foothold in the medium. She made several pilots for unsold TV series: *Cap'n Ahab* (1965), *Li'l Abner* (1967), and *The Murdocks and the McClays* (1970), as well as doing commercials. However, she could not regain the momentum of her star years, an ironic situation since country western was becoming so fashionable in the United States. In late December 1971, Judy, although suffering from emphysema, returned to the stage, taking the maid's role in the national road tour of the revived *No, No Nanette*. Her costars were June Allyson and Dennis Day, and she mugged to full audience approval. Later there were more TV commercials, a role as the mom of a buffoonish country-western singer in *Cannonball* (1976), and guest appearances on *Police Woman* (1974) and *The Love Boat* (1977). Plans to write a cookbook and an autobiography never materialized. In 1980 her brother Zeke died. Judy's last public appearance was at a showing of a trio of her films at a Hollywood-revival theater in September 1982.

Judy Canova died of cancer on August 5, 1983. Her body was cremated, and the ashes were placed in an urn that rests in the Columbarium of Eternal Light section at Forest Lawn Memorial Park in Glendale. (Her memorial plaque is inscribed "Judy Canova: 1913–1983—Love and Laughter.") The veteran star was survived by her daughters Julieta, in the mortgage business, and Diana, an actress who starred in several teleseries: *Soap, I'm a Big Girl Now, Foot in the Door*, and *Throb*.

Filmography

In Caliente (WB, 1935)
Going Highbrow (WB, 1935)
Broadway Gondolier (WB, 1935)
Artists and Models (Par, 1937)
Thrill of a Lifetime (Par, 1937)
Scatterbrain (Rep, 1940)
Sis Hopkins (Rep, 1941)
Puddin'Head [Judy Goes to Town] (Rep, 1941)
Meet Roy Rogers (Rep, 1941) (s)
Joan of Ozark (Rep, 1942)
True to the Army (Par, 1942)
Sleepytime Gal (Rep, 1942)
Chatterbox (Rep, 1943)
Sleepy Lagoon (Rep, 1943)
Louisiana Hayride (Col, 1944)

Screen Snapshot #2 (Col, 1945)(s)
Hit the Hay (Col, 1945)
Singin' in the Corn (Col, 1946)
Famous Hollywood Mothers (Col, 1946) (s)
Radio Characters of 1946 (Col, 1946) (s)
Honeychile (Rep, 1951)
Oklahoma Annie (Rep, 1952)
The WAC From Walla Walla [Army Capers] (Rep, 1952)
Untamed Heiress (Rep, 1954)
Carolina Cannonball (Rep, 1955)
Lay that Rifle Down (Rep, 1956)
The Adventures of Huckleberry Finn (MGM, 1960)
Hillbilly Jamboree (Ronnie Ashcroft, 1960)
Cannonball [Carquake] (New World, 1976)

Broadway Plays

Calling All Stars (1934)
The Ziegfeld Follies of 1936 (1936)

Yokel Boy (1939)

Radio Series

The Kraft Music Hall (NBC, c. 1933–34)
Rippling Rhythm Revue (NBC, 1936–37)
The Chase and Sanborn Hour (NBC, 1938)

The Judy Canova Show (CBS, 1943–44; NBC, 1945–52)

Album Discography

LPs

Country Cousin (Crown CLP-239)
Country Cousin Sings (Coronet CX/CSX-239)
Favorite Songs (10″ Royale 6108)
Featuring Judy Canova (Viking 8802)
Judy Canova (Camden CAL-662)

Judy Canova and the Hoosier Hot Shots (Hurrah HS-1051)
Judy Canova/Esmerldy (Sutton SSU-296)
Judy Canova in Hi-Fi (Tops L-1613)
Miss Country, U.S.A. (Craftsmen 8062)
Thrill of a Lifetime (Caliban 6046) [ST]

CDs

Judy Canova (Simitar 5568)
Judy Canova (Sounds of a Century 1879)

Judy Canova and the Canova Family (Sounds of a Century 1779)

Eddie Cantor in the early 1940s.
[Courtesy of Echo Book Shop]

Eddie Cantor

(b. Isidor Iskowitch, New York City, January 31, 1892; Beverly Hills, California,
October 10, 1964)

Eddie Cantor was one of the more fabulous show-business phenomenons of the first half of the twentieth century. Honing his craft in vaudeville, he rose to stardom on Broadway, motion pictures, radio, television, and recordings. Often appearing in blackface (like fellow star Al Jolson), the dapper, five-feet seven-inches Cantor was known as Banjo Eyes, an endearing term referring to his oversized brown orbs that gazed in perpetual surprise at life's perplexing realities. The hyperenergetic performer was a sight to behold, prancing about onstage with arms akimbo and hands clasped in bemusement. His singing of such ditties as "Ida," "If You Knew Susie" (his trademark song), "Dinah," "Mandy," "My Baby Just Cares for Me," "You'd Be Surprised" (his top seller), "Ma, He's Making Eyes at Me," or his indelible "Making Whoopee," were unforgettable moments of entertainment.

Cantor's professional guise was often seemingly ineffective and indelibly boyish, but his heart was always set on winning the ingénue and outmaneuvering his city-slicker opponents. Like equally beloved comedians Al Jolson and Jack Benny, Cantor traded heavily on his Jewish background and made lighthearted ethnic remarks a part of the national vocabulary. His trademark song became "I'd Love to Spend This Hour With You," and throughout five decades as a performing star, he introduced and guided such new talent as Deanna Durbin, Bobby Breen, Dinah Shore, and Eddie Fisher.

Eddie was born on January 31, 1892, to Russian immigrants Michael and Maite (Minnie) Iskowitch in a crowded tenement flat over a Russian tearoom on New York's lower east side. A year later, Minnie succumbed in childbirth; the violin-playing Michael died in 1894 of pneumonia. The orphaned Isidor Iskowitch was raised by his maternal grandmother, Esther Kantrowitz. She was sixty-two years old, and supported both of them by peddling wares door-to-door and, later, by running her own employment agency.

Izzy had a sparse formal education at best, never completing grade school. When he won a $5 (top) prize as "Edward Cantor" while impersonating current show-business greats at Miner's Bowery Theater Amateur Night, his career was decided. He made his professional vaudeville bow in 1907 at the Clinton Music Hall teamed with Dan Lipsky. The latter, Eddie's lifelong friend, would become the future vice president of Manufacturers Trust Company in New York City.

Cantor's fledgling stage years were erratic. He was stranded in Shenandoah, Pennsylvania, on Christmas Eve 1908, when Frank B. Carr's burlesque unit, *Indian Maidens*, folded there. At Carey Walsh's Coney Island saloon, he worked as a singing waiter, accompanied by a big-nosed, ragtime piano player named Jimmy Durante. He played for sixteen weeks, at $20 weekly, in the four-house vaudeville circuit owned by Adolph Zukor, Marcus Loew, and Joseph and Nicholas

Schenck (all future film magnates). This People's Vaudeville Company circuit offered Cantor additional bookings if he would revamp his act. His stratagem was to blacken his face with burnt cork as done in the minstrel shows and to heighten his performance with more physical comedy and ad libs. The gimmicks succeeded, and he soon became the featured "stooge" with the popular team of Bedini and Arthur, performing at Hammerstein's Victoria Theater on Broadway.

Concluding nearly two years with Bedini and Arthur, Eddie next signed with promoter Gus Edwards and was featured in his *Kid Kabaret* touring show in 1912. Fellow performers included Lila Lee, Eddie Buzzell (later a film director) and George Jessel. Cantor recalled, "It was not first class vaudeville, but the best and only acting school of its kind, where poor young boys and girls could learn the art of entertainment in all its forms and get paid for learning." He stayed with this popular act for two years, playing a black butler. Eddie left the show to wed his childhood sweetheart, Ida Tobias. They were married in Brooklyn on June 9, 1914, and sailed to England for their honeymoon. Shortly after arriving in London, Cantor paired with Sam Kessler for a week's engagement at the Oxford Theater, and then joined Andre Charlot's revue *Not Likely at the Alhambra* where he sang the show-stopping tune, "I Love the Ladies."

Back in the United States, Eddie teamed in a vaudeville act, Master and Man, with straight man Al Lee, and for almost two years they played the circuits. The pair split when Cantor was hired to be in *Canary Cottage*, which opened its tour in the spring of 1916 in San Diego, California. He had the supporting role of a black chauffeur, but built up his role with ad libs. By now the Cantors had two children: Marjorie (1915) and Natalie (1916). Returning to New York, Cantor extended a one-night tryout in Florenz Ziegfeld's *Midnight Frolics* (atop the New Amsterdam Theater) into a twenty-seven-week turn. The delighted Ziegfeld cast him in his new *Follies* at $400 weekly. The revue show opened on June 12, 1917, and lasted 111 performances, with a star-studded roster including Will Rogers, W. C. Fields, Bert Williams, Fanny Brice, and Cantor. Eddie remained with various editions of the *Follies* through 1919, during which period his grandmother died (on his birthday, January 31, 1917) and he and Ida had a third daughter, Edna (1919). It was in the 1919 *Follies* that the team of Van and Schenck introduced the song "Mandy" that Cantor adopted later as his own.

Cantor and Ziegfeld had a falling out when the former supported the great Actors' Equity strike (August 6, 1919). Thus he went to work for the Shubert Brothers in *Broadway Brevities of 1920* and starred for the same producers in *The Midnight Rounders* (1921). The Cantors' fourth daughter, Marilyn, was born in September 1921. After touring with *The Midnight Rounders* (which featured a sketch of an enterprising Jewish tailor), Cantor revamped much of the material into the revue *Make It Snappy*, which bowed on Broadway on April 13, 1922. He was also busy recording for Brunswick Records under a new pact (signed in 1920), which paid him a total of $220,000. It was reportedly the biggest such contract to that date. When Cantor opened a new vaudeville tour at the Orpheum Theater in Brooklyn (June 1923), *Variety* noted, "Eddie Cantor is an entertainer with a capital 'E.' He is value received for vaudeville."

A chastened Ziegfeld petitioned Cantor to return to the fold by offering him a "book" show in which he would have the lead as a Florida golf caddie/club bootlegger. *Kid Boots* debuted on New Year's Eve 1923 and played on Broadway and on tour well into 1926. By this time, Paramount Pictures had acquired the screen rights to the hit production, along with Cantor's services as star.

Cantor supposedly (although some sources dispute his participation) made his motion-picture debut circa 1913 when he and George Jessel appeared in an experimental talking picture, *Widow at the Races*, for Thomas Edison. Then, around 1923, he had made a short subject for the DeForest Phonofilm Company. For the silent *Kid Boots* (1926), which costarred Billie Dove and Clara Bow, Cantor was paid a healthy $3,000 weekly. Audience response to Cantor was positive, and the studio contracted him for *Special Delivery* (1927), directed by William Goodrich (better known as Roscoe "Fatty" Arbuckle). Because this comedy was unsuccessful, Paramount abandoned plans to feature Cantor in picture versions of Rodgers and Hart's *The Girl Friend* or a comedy to be called *Help*.

Eddie returned to Broadway for his last *Follies* (1927), and that same year his fifth and final daughter, Janet, was born. *Whoopee!* (1928), based on the stage hit comedy *The Nervous Wreck*, costarred Ruth Etting and ran for a resounding 379 performances on Broadway. The stock market crash of 1929 wiped out most of Cantor's savings, and he recounted his bad luck in the amusing book, *Caught Short*, which was made into a 1930 MGM movie comedy with Marie Dresser and Polly Moran. It was just one of several humorous tomes and autobiographies the comedian wrote during this period. In other venues, Cantor continued to tax his physical endurance. He was appearing onstage, making talkie short subjects for Paramount at its Astoria, Long Island studio, and repeating his antic tailor-shop sketch in Ziegfeld's Technicolor film, *Glorifying the American Girl* (1929). Meanwhile Eddie continued to make short subjects, several of which—especially *Insurance* (1930)—were quite popular with filmgoers.

In mid-1930 Cantor announced his stage retirement. He reasoned, "I've enough money and I've reached the peak of a theatrical career. Why shouldn't my family and children enjoy my companionship? . . . What does a performer work for? Only two things—money and applause. If I still want to remain before the public how long does it take to make a picture? In two or three months I can make one and then I'm through for the rest of the year to do as I darn please."

Eddie went to Hollywood to star in the Samuel Goldwyn–Florenz Ziegfeld production of *Whoopee!* (1930) filmed in two-color Technicolor. The *New York Times* enthused, "It is a picture in which one never tires of Mr. Cantor . . . One looks forward to another chance to chuckle and giggle at the ludicrous conduct of the 'nervous wreck.'" Cantor negotiated a profitable contract with Goldwyn to star in five additional United Artists releases. First came *Palmy Days* (1931), a gangster farce set in a candy factory. It was cowritten by Cantor and costarred angular, high-kicking comedienne Charlotte Greenwood. *Time* magazine analyzed, "Eddie Cantor belongs to the school of clowns whose humor derives from ineffectuality; a certain eccentric excitability makes him sometimes hilariously funny . . . He is a culprit from a comic strip and no one would be surprised if, when something hit him on the head, it gave the sound of 'plop' or 'zowie!'" In *Palmy Days* (1931), which boasted the by-now-obligatory Goldwyn chorus girls and Busby Berkeley's geometric choreography, Cantor sang "My Baby Says Yes, Yes" (which became part of his repertoire) and "There's Nothing Too Good for My Baby" (which he cocomposed). On October 31, 1931, Eddie was reunited with George Jessel on Broadway at the Palace Theater in a bill that included Burns and Allen. Originally scheduled to last two weeks, the hugely popular engagement was extended through New Year's Eve. Cantor was paid $8,000 weekly.

Goldwyn lavished a $1 million budget on *The Kid From Spain* (1932), directed by Leo McCarey, in which Eddie was an ersatz bullfighter on the lam from the law. Then, the setting was ancient Rome for *Roman Scandals* (1933), an extravaganza featuring Cantor with the likes of Ruth Etting, Gloria Stuart, and Edward Arnold. In this show, stuffed with hokum, low comedy, and very scantily clad chorines, the star put across such numbers as "Build a Little Home." Because the star "tampered" with the film's story and dialogue, authors George S. Kaufman and Robert Sherwood brought legal action and won a judgment against producer Goldwyn.

For *Kid Millions* (1934), Eddie was a Brooklyn dock worker who inherits $77 million and sails to Egypt to claim his rewards. Ethel Merman and Warren Hymer portrayed preying con artists, while Ann Sothern and George Murphy (in his film bow) played the young lovers. The nonsense plot worked in a blackface number ("I Want to Be a Minstrel Man") for the star. He also got to sing Irving Berlin's "Mandy." The Brooklyn ice-cream factory finale was shot in Technicolor. *Strike Me Pink* (1936) proved to be Eddie Cantor's sixth and final Goldwyn motion picture. Despite a hoard of scripters, it proved to be pretty thin stuff about a tailor who takes over an amusement park and must deal with greedy gangsters out to control the slot-machine concession. The Harold Arlen–Lew Brown score was unremarkable, with Eddie dueting "Calabash Pipe" with Ethel Merman and leading "The Lady Dances" with the Goldwyn Girls and Rita Rio. Because Cantor's performing style (which he was not about to change) was now considered out of sync with Hollywood's new wave of musicals, he and Goldwyn parted company.

If he was no longer a king of movie musicals, Cantor was still very much a star of radio, where his folksy, neighborly persona was a soothing tonic for Depression-weary listeners. (During the 1930s Eddie—more so than most radio stars—underlined a charitable spirit to his radio broadcasts, which well reflected America's New Deal message to combat the Depression.) Cantor had begun on the medium on January 6, 1929, being heard on CBS' *Majestic Theater of the Air* with Ruth Etting. After guesting on Rudy Vallee's radio program in February 1931, Eddie started a long-running show on NBC network radio (September 13, 1931) that would stretch almost unbroken to 1954, with a year (1938–39) on CBS. (He was taken off the air in 1939 for his outspoken remarks at the New York World's Fair accusing particular government officials of being "fascists," but he returned to NBC in 1940, thanks to the intervention of his pal Jack Benny.) Eddie was one of the first to use a live audience for his shows; in fact he had a habit of previewing the new script in a dress rehearsal for the studio audience and leaving in the jokes they liked the best. His enormous appeal on the airwaves was reflected by the $7,000 a show salary he earned from Texaco when he began a new season under their sponsorship in September 1936.

Twentieth Century-Fox, hoping to duplicate Goldwyn's box-office successes with Cantor, hired Cantor for the high-budgeted *Ali Baba Goes to Town* (1937), in which he was a tramp who falls asleep on an Oriental movie set and dreams that he is the savior of old Baghdad using "New Deal" know-how to succeed. He pranced, sang ("Swing Is Here to Stay"), cavorted with Gypsy Rose Lee—one of the Sultan's (Roland Young) 865 wives—and played nursemaid to the romantic lead (Tony Martin). For too many, the merriment seemed a watered-down version of *Roman Scandals*, and Fox lost interest in pursuing more films with Cantor. Movie offers became scarce. In 1939, MGM announced it would team Eleanor Powell and Cantor in *Girl Crazy*, but court battles over the screen rights delayed production. (The musical was made finally in 1943 with Mickey Rooney and Judy Garland.) Instead, the studio put Cantor into a mild, sentimental comedy, *Forty Little Mothers* (1940), as a college professor protecting an abandoned baby. Busby Berkeley directed this tepidly received quasi drama.

Again, Eddie returned to Broadway, this time to star in a musical version of the old comedy hit *Three Men on a Horse*. As *Banjo Eyes*, the show bowed on December 25, 1941, with the veteran star cast as a meek greeting-card writer who is a wow at selecting winning race horses. Eddie performed his usual shtick of singing and prancing about in blackface, straw hat, and white-rimmed spectacles. It was amazing bravado for a new generation of theatergoers. (In the spirit of America's recent entry into World War II, the star included a patriotic song entitled "We Did It Before" in the show. It became popular beyond the show itself.) Despite glowing reviews, the entry lasted only 126 performances, because Cantor had to withdraw from the vehicle because of illness. Meanwhile, with America involved in World War II, Cantor repeated his volunteer efforts of World War I by entertaining troops and raising enormous funds through selling war bonds. During one twenty-four-hour radio marathon he hosted in 1944, the war cause netted $41 million in sales of war bonds.

In 1943, Cantor was the focal point of *Thank Your Lucky Stars*, an all-star musical concocted by Warner Bros. for its stable of luminaries. In the plot ploy tying together the sketches, he was featured as both studio tour guide Joe Simpson and as himself and sang "We're Staying Home Tonight." For many viewers, such a double dose of Cantor was too much for one picture. In the same studio's personality-filled *Hollywood Canteen* (1944), he dueted "We're Having a Baby" with Nora Martin. That same year, with his very good friend slapstick comedienne Joan Davis, Cantor costarred in RKO's *Show Business*, a modestly budgeted picture that he produced. It was a clichéd but fond tribute to vaudeville and showcased the leads well, especially in their burlesque of Anthony and Cleopatra. In the finale, Cantor reprised his trademark "Makin' Whoopee" number.

After financing a failed Broadway musical, *Nellie Bly* (1945) with Marilyn Maxwell and Victor Moore, Eddie returned to the silver screen producing RKO's *If You Knew Susie* (1948), a benign comedy with zany Joan Davis costarring as his effervescent screen spouse. Cantor rolled his eyes, mugged, and sang the title tune and other standards. *Variety* warned, "There's little here that Cantor hasn't done in one form or another for many years, whether it's been in radio, musicomedy or pictures." The picture failed at the box office.

Ever since Columbia Pictures' profitable *The Jolson Story* (1946) and *Jolson Sings Again* (1949), Hollywood had been on a cycle of screen biography about show-business legends. Warner Bros. induced Cantor to appear as himself in the uninspired *The Will Rogers Story* (1952) starring the late legend's look-alike son. The next year, the studio paid Cantor a reported $1 million (over a ten-year period) for the rights to make *The Eddie Cantor Story*. The unimaginative biography featured Keefe Brasselle as the legendary star with Cantor dubbing in the singing. Eddie, along with his wife Ida, appeared in a brief epilogue to the picture, in which having just seen a screening of the film, he turns to the movie audience and says, "I never looked better!"

Milton Berle may have been dubbed "The King of Television," but many other ex-vaudeville and burlesque stars became mainstays of the new medium as well—including Eddie Cantor. "I didn't jump into TV," he would explain. "I waited until 1950, the year 5,000,000 more television sets were sold . . . After all, Cantor likes to play to full houses." He had a four-year engagement (1950–54) as one of the revolving hosts of the popular NBC network variety show *The Colgate Comedy Hour*. It afforded him ample opportunity to dust off many of his old routines and to sing all of the songs that had become associated with him through his lengthy show-business career. As the *New York Times*'s Jack Gould termed it, "a sort of Cavalcade of Cantor." In 1955 he hosted the Ziv Television Programs Company's syndicated half-hour show, *The Eddie Cantor Comedy Theater*, performing sketches and songs in some of the offerings. In one of his rare dramatic appearances on TV, he starred with Farley Granger on CBS's *Playhouse 90* (October 18, 1956) in "Seidman and Son."

Eddie's final stage appearances were at New York's Carnegie Hall on March 21; on September 30, 1950, in *My Forty Years in Show Business;* and in 1951 and 1952 with *An Evening With Eddie Cantor.* As a show-business luminary, he received a constant flood of testimonials and awards. On January 31, 1952, the State of Israel Bond Committee hosted a gala Eddie Cantor Sixtieth Birthday Party in the grand ballroom of New York's Hotel Commodore, in which 1,800 guests honored his remarkable efforts in selling $60 million worth of bonds for Israel. He dealt with the event in his published booklet, *I'm Glad I Spent Those Sixty Years.* (Previously he had authored, among other books, *My Life Is in Your Hands* [1928]. Later, he wrote, *Take My Life,* [1957]). At the 1956 Academy Awards, he was given a special honorary Oscar for his distinguished services to the film industry, including his work as head of the Screen Actors Guild. (He had been a founder of Actors' Equity and of the American Federation of Radio Artists [later AFTRA].) Backstage at the Awards, Cantor suffered a mild heart attack after receiving his Oscar.

Eddie and Ida Cantor celebrated their thirty-ninth wedding anniversary on national TV on Sunday, June 7, 1953, reenacting their marriage vows. Cantor's protégée, Dinah Shore, served as matron of honor, with Jack Benny, Ralph Edwards, and George Jessel as ushers. In August of 1962, two years before their golden anniversary, Ida died of a heart attack. This, combined with the earlier death (1959) of daughter Marjorie, took its toll on Eddie, who had first been stricken with a heart ailment himself in September 1952. The State of Israel awarded Cantor the Medallion of Valor in 1962 for his many "extraordinary achievements" on behalf of that country, and in 1964 he was given the U.S. Service Medal from President Lyndon Johnson for his devotion to the United States and to humanity (e.g., fostering such charitable causes as the March of Dimes charity, which he had founded).

On October 10, 1964, seventy-two-year-old Cantor died of a sudden coronary occlusion at his Beverly Hills home. What this energetic and beloved comedian once said of his career as a funster personified him as an entertainer: "Laughter is the world's oxygen tank."

Filmography

Widow at the Races (Edison, c. 1913) (s)*
A Few Moments With Eddie Cantor (DeForest Phonofilms, c. 1923) (s)
Kid Boots (Par, 1926)
The Speed Hound (Bray Studios, 1927) (s)
Special Delivery (Par, 1928)
Glorifying the American Girl (Par, 1929)
That Party in Person [That Certain Party] (Par, 1929) (s)
Untitled Short (Unk, 1929) (s)
Midnite Frolics (Par, 1929) (s)
Getting a Ticket (Par, 1929) (s)
Caught Short (1930) (screen story only)
Insurance (Par, 1930)
The Cockeyed News #1 (Par, 1930) (s)
Whoopee! (UA, 1930)
Minstrel Days (Vita, 1930) (s)
Screen Snapshots #18 (Col, 1930) (s)
Mr. Lemon of Orange (Fox, 1931) (dialogue only)
Palmy Days (UA, 1931) (also script, cosong)
The Kid From Spain (UA, 1932)

Roman Scandals (UA, 1933)
Kid Millions (UA, 1934)
Hollywood Cavalcade (Unk, 1934) (s)
Screen Snapshots #11 (Col, 1934) (s)
The Hollywood Gad-About (Educational, 1934) (s)
Strike Me Pink (UA, 1936)
Ali Baba Goes to Town (20th-Fox, 1937)
Forty Little Mothers (MGM, 1940)
Thank Your Lucky Stars (WB, 1943)
Hollywood Canteen (WB, 1944)
Show Business (RKO, 1944) (also producer)
Screen Snapshots #2 (Col, 1945) (s)
For All the People (Selznick International/National Conference of Christians and Jews, 1946) (s)
Screen Snapshots #10 (Col, 1946) (s)
We Must Not Forget. A Personal Message From Eddie Cantor (United Jewish Appeal, 1947) (s)
If You Knew Susie (RKO, 1948) (also producer)
Eddie Cantor in Israel (United Jewish Appeal, 1950) (s)

Memorial to Al Jolson (Col, 1951) (s) (documentary)
Eddie Cantor in Front Line '52 (United Jewish Appeal, 1952) (s)
The Story of Will Rogers (WB, 1952)
The Eddie Cantor Story (WB, 1953)

Eddie Cantor Birthday [Israel Bond Appeal] (United Jewish Appeal, 1957) (s)
Hollywood Hist-or-Rama: Eddie Cantor (Jaymark Films, 1961) (s) (documentary)
*Some sources dispute Cantor's participation in this experimental short subject

Broadway Plays

The Ziegfeld Follies (1917)
The Ziegfeld Follies (1918)
The Ziegfeld Follies (1919)
Broadway Brevities of 1920 (1920)
Make It Snappy (1922)
The Ziegfeld Follies (1923)*
Kid Boots (1923)
The Ziegfeld Follies (1927)

Whoopee! (1928)
Banjo Eyes (1941)
* Having mended his differences with producer Florenz Ziegfeld, Cantor, along with dancer Ann Pennington, appeared in some performances of 1923's *The Ziegfeld Follies*, after the show opened on October 20, 1923 and before he debuted in *Kid Boots* (December 31, 1923).

Radio Series

The Eddie Cantor Show (NBC, 1931–34; CBS, 1935–39; NBC 1940–49, 1951–54; Synd, 1956)

Ask Eddie Cantor (Synd, 1961)

TV Series

The Colgate Comedy Hour (NBC, 1950–54)

The Eddie Cantor Comedy Theater (Synd, 1955)

Album Discography

LPs

The Best of Eddie Cantor (Vik LX-1119, Camden CAL/CAS-531)
A Date with Eddie Cantor—The Carnegie Hall Concert (Audio Fidelity 702)
The Eddie Cantor Album (Top Ten 5)
Eddie Cantor on the Silver Screen, 1934–35 (Sandy Hook 2039)
The Eddie Cantor Show, Vols. 1–2 (Memorabilia 702-03)
Eddie Cantor Sings (10″ Decca DL-5504)
Eddie Cantor Sings Ida, Sweet as Apple Cider (Camden CAL/CAS-870)
The Eddie Cantor Story (10″ Cap L-467) [ST]
Harry Richman and Eddie Cantor Live (Amalgamated 127)
Hollywood Canteen (Curtain Calls 100/11-12) [ST]
Immortals: Al Jolson and Eddie Cantor (Epic LN-1128)

Jimmy Durante/Eddie Cantor Sings (Ace of Hearts 25)
Kid Millions/Roman Scandals (CIF 3007) [ST]
The Legends of Al Jolson, Jimmy Durante and Eddie Cantor (Ambassador Artists 1003-3)
The Living Legend (Show Biz 1004)
Memories (MCA 1506)
Ol' Banjo Eyes Is Back (Pelican 134)
Rare Early Recordings, 1919-21 (Biograph 12054)
Show Business (Caliban 6034) [ST]
Songs He Made Famous (Decca DL-4431)
Thank Your Lucky Stars (Curtain Calls 100/8) [ST]
Tweedle De Dee and Tweedle De Dum (Heidi Ho 5501)
Whoopee! (Smithsonian 0349, Meet Patti 1930) [ST]
The Ziegfeld Follies of 1919 (Smithsonian R009/P14272) [OC]

CDs

Cantor Loves Lucy/All Star Show (Original Cast)

Cantor Meets Jolson (Original Cast 9753) w. Al Jolson

Carnegie Hall Concert (Original Cast 9217)

A Centennial Celebration: The Best of Eddie Cantor (RCA 07863-66033-2)

Cocktail Hour (Columbia River Entertainment Group CRG-218025)

The Columbia Years 1922–40 (Legacy C2K-57148)

Early Days 1917–21 (Original Cast 9872)

Eddie Cantor (Sounds of a Century 1808)

The Eddie Cantor Show (Original Cast 8715)

The Eddie Cantor Show (Original Cast 9494)

The Eddie Cantor Show (Original Cast 9617)

Eddie Cantor, Vol. 1, 1917-19 (P&L 18342)

Eddie Cantor, Vol. 2, 1919-20 (P&L 22260)

Eddie Cantor, Vol. 3, 1920-24 (P&L 10301)

Eddie Cantor, Vol. 4, 1929-30 (P&L 213-B)

Eddie Cantor, Vol. 5, 1932-34 (P&L—no number)

Eddie Cantor, Vol. 6, 1934-50 (P&L 30-0310)

I Remember Jolson (Original Cast 2073)

Makin' Whoopee (ProArte/Fanfare CDD-460) w. Fannie Brice

Makin' Whoopee With Banjo Eyes (ASV CD-AJA-5357)

Pals (Original Cast) w. George Jessel

The Radio Shows 1930s (Storyville 3019)

The Show That Never Aired (Original Cast 9347)

Thank Your Lucky Stars (Sandy Hook CDSH-2012) [ST]

Whoopee! (Jasmine JASCD-116)

Diahann Carroll

(b. Carol Diahann Johnson, Bronx, NY, July 17, 1935)

There was a gilt-edged quality about show-business veteran Diahann Carroll long before she gained renewed popularity as the chic but evil Dominique Devereaux on TV's *Dynasty* (1984–87). For years, whether singing on Broadway, in clubs, or on the air, this svelte five-feet six-inches entertainer projected herself as an aloof, sophisticated chanteuse. She always seemed more comfortable interpreting old standards than performing contemporary pop or rock music. Like the earlier Lena Horne, she was a superior technician. But also like that performer, her mixed reactions to becoming a leading black star (and role model) in a white world of show business caused her to erect an invisible shield between herself and audiences. (Both of these entertainers dropped the protection, in varying degrees, as they reached middle age.)

The multitalented Diahann Carroll, long noted for her elegant living style, could also be quite outspoken. When she became the first African-American actress in the 1960s to star in a major American TV sitcom, *Julia*, she used her power position to speak out against racial iniquity. She was quite direct in assessing her token-figure status in the "new" Hollywood. Later, as a leading cabaret attraction, she teamed with her longtime friend and, later husband, singer Vic Damone. Thereafter, once again single, she continued to act in films and TV movies and to be a vocal spokesperson about cancer survival, a disease she had combated in the 1990s.

She was born Carol Diahann Johnson on July 17, 1935, in the Bronx, New York, the older daughter of subway conductor John Johnson and his nurse wife Mabel. There would be a younger sister Lydia. As a child she was musically inclined, and by the age of six was performing in school plays. She also became a member of the Tiny Tots choir at Adam Clayton Powell's Abyssinian Baptist Church. She was ten years old when she won a music scholarship from the Metropolitan Opera, but she abandoned the singing lessons because it interfered with being a normal little girl on the ghetto block. She went to Public School #46 and to a local junior high (which she has referred to as "my own blackboard jungle"). However, the High School of Music and Art was "a wonderful, beautiful oasis." When she was fifteen, she began a career modeling clothes for Johnson Publications, which published black-oriented magazines. She also made an appearance on *Arthur Godfrey's Talent Scout* (CBS-TV) and was heard on his radio show as well.

To appease her parents, who wanted her to attend Howard University, she enrolled at New York University, planning to become a psychiatric social worker. However, she continued her singing and dancing lessons—and modeling—while attending school. She understood that show business could open doors and create a new lifestyle for her in preintegration America. But this realization also produced internal conflicts. She knew her career path would separate her from her background: "The conflict first took the form of music. The music we all listened and danced to, rhythm and blues . . . I never sang that kind of music. I never had a jazz feeling, a blues feeling, and I still don't. I had a very strong resistance to that kind of music because it was racial. I saw

Diahann Carroll in the 1960s.
[Courtesy of JC Archives]

the other kind, my kind, as a move to assimilation." To balance her growing attraction to the mainstream, she became a modest spokeswoman for black causes, allying herself with SNICK (Student Nonviolent Coordinating Committee). Later in her career, she would testify before a U.S. Congressional hearing that she was proof of discrimination in America and in show business.

While still a college freshman, Carroll auditioned for Lou Walters's all-black revue *Jazz Train*, but the show never came to be. However, Walters (father of TV interviewer Barbara) got her an audition for Dennis James's talent show, *Chance of a Lifetime* (ABC-TV). She won three weeks in a row, earning $1,000 in prize money. By now she was known professionally as Diahann Carroll. She quit college, promising her parents that if she did not become a successful entertainer within two years, she would return to the university. Walters booked her into the Latin Quarter, where, despite an extreme case of stage fright, she was successful. Later he negotiated for her to sing at Ciro's and at the Cloister in Los Angeles, as well as for club dates in Chicago, Miami, Philadelphia, Paris, and at New York's Persian Room (Hotel Plaza) and the Waldorf-Astoria Hotel.

Her film debut came in *Carmen Jones* (1954), the all African-American version of Georges Bizet's opera *Carmen* as adapted by Oscar Hammerstein II. On film, as in the 1943 Broadway version, the characters were nondimensional. Making the movie even more artificial were director Otto Preminger's heavy-handed touches. Because he demanded a certain look and yet a different sound, most of the main players (including Dorothy Dandridge, Harry Belafonte, and Joe Adams), but excluding Pearl Bailey, had their voices dubbed. Bernice Peterson provided the singing voice for Diahann's character of Myrt. Diahann recalled that for one of her costumes she was given a hand-me-down, red-fringed gown once worn on-screen by Bonita Granville. It was not an auspicious screen beginning for Carroll.

Much more successful was her Broadway bow. On December 30, 1954, at the Alvin Theater, she joined with Pearl Bailey, Juanita Hall, Ray Walston, and Frederick O'Neal in *House of Flowers*, a Harold Arlen–composed musical based on a Truman Capote's story set in the West Indies. As Ottilie the innocent bordello girl, she sang such numbers as "House of Flowers" and "A Sleepin' Bee" and earned a warm critical reception, despite the show's mixed reviews. The *New York Herald-Tribune* judged her "a plaintive and extraordinarily appealing ingénue." While the show lasted only 165 performances, she had made a favorable debut both onstage and on the original cast album released by Columbia Records. She returned to club work and began making guest appearances on TV variety shows both in the United States. (*The Red Skelton Show, The Jack Paar Show, The Steve Allen Show*) and abroad. In September 1956, Diahann married Monte Kay, the white casting director of *House of Flowers* who became manager for the Modern Jazz Quartet and other jazz musicians, and later for Flip Wilson. Their daughter, Suzanne Patricia Ottilie, was born in 1961. Meanwhile, on September 27, 1957, Diahann, along with Louis Armstrong, Peggy Lee, Ethel Merman, Carol Channing, and others were featured on the Rex Harrison TV special *Crescendo* (CBS-TV).

Composer Richard Rodgers had been delighted with Diahann's abilities in *House of Flowers* and had promised her that he would create a role for her in one of his next Broadway shows. He attempted to cast her in *Flower Drum Song* (1958), but regardless of what type of costuming effects they tried, she did not look Oriental. They abandoned the effort. Thereafter, for producer Samuel Goldwyn, Diahann return to moviemaking in *Porgy and Bess* (1959), based on the classic Broadway operetta with songs by George and Ira Gershwin. The film was plagued with problems ranging from the July 1958 studio fire that razed all the sets to the firing of director Rouben Mamoulian and the hiring of Otto Preminger. The cast included several members from *Carmen Jones*, with Dorothy Dandridge in the title role, Pearl Bailey as Maria, and others such as Sidney Poitier as Porgy and Sammy Davis Jr. as Sportin' Life. The story was set in the early 1900s on Catfish Row in Charleston and had Diahann as Clara, the wife of a fisherman who is lost at sea. Once again, the decision was made to dub the singing of many of the film's leads, from Poitier to Dandridge to Carroll. Despite Diahann's reputation as a songstress, her vocal range was deemed too low to handle the character's big number, "Summertime." Thus Caucasian soprano Loulie Jean Norman provided her singing voice. *Porgy and Bess*, which cost over $6 million to make, met with lukewarm reviews and did not recoup its costs. Although Diahann did not sing on the soundtrack album, she later recorded a United Artists LP on which she sang *Porgy and Bess* numbers, backed by the Andre Previn Trio.

It was during the making of *Porgy and Bess* that Diahann and Sidney Poitier, both of them married, began an affair that lasted off and on for nine years. In his autobiography, *This Life* (1980), Poitier describes Diahann as "an independent woman who shifted emotional gears quickly." When their relationship terminated finally, Poitier wrote, "Regrets? Yes, I'll have a few." Diahann would comment of her famous beau, "I think he felt confounded by what actually happened. Unfortunately, there's no way for me to be confounded." Carroll's marriage to Monte Kay, who was informed about the affair by Diahann, ended in divorce in 1963. (He died of a heart attack in May 1988 at the age of sixty-three.)

In 1961, Sidney Poitier joined with Paul Newman in making *Paris Blues*, a study of two jazz musician expatriates living in post–World War II Paris. Saxophonist Poitier falls in love with American tourist Diahann, as Newman does with Carroll's pal Joanne Woodward. Before the conclusion of this somber screen romance, Diahann convinces Poitier to return to the United States to marry her and to confront the racial bigotry that drove him away originally. The Duke Ellington score and Louis Armstrong's exuberant, if brief, appearance playing jazz received better notices than the actors. While on Paris location for this feature, Diahann made a cameo appearance in another United Artists release, *Goodbye Again* (1961). She was the chic club chanteuse attracted to Anthony Perkins, and she sang "Say No More, It's Goodbye" and "Love Is Just a Word."

According to Diahann, it was seeing her TV guest appearance on a *Jack Paar Show* in 1961 that led Richard Rodgers to remember his original promise to build a show around her. When they lunched and talked about the project, she suggested doing a musical in which the leading character, a black woman, falls in love with a white man, and they play through the usual boy-girl situations without making skin color a stated problem. Thus came about *No Strings*, which opened at the 54th Street Theater in New York on March 15, 1962. The story was set in Paris, and Diahann played Barbara Woodruff, the high-fashion model who falls in love with an ambivalent Pulitzer Prize novelist (Richard Kiley) from Maine. What made the intimate show special was not Samuel Taylor's mundane book, but the staging that established the musicians behind a scrim curtain upstage (sometimes strolling into the action) and the personal messages of the touching songs. The *New York Times* said of the star, "Miss Carroll brings glowing personal beauty to the role of the model, and her singing captures many moods." Critics were quick to notice the special attention she gave to interpreting the lyrics (a trademark quality of her showmanship). "To do justice to a song," she explained, "a singer should have a feeling for dramatic interpretation as well as an ear for musical sound. You must be able to create a mood, to make the audience feel that the words have meaning to the singer. . . ." The show lasted 580 performances. For Diahann, who had already been named Entertainer of the Year in the late 1950s as a club singer, it brought new tributes. She won a Tony Award.

After *No Strings*, which was mentioned for some time as a possible film project for Frank Sinatra (and maybe Diahann), she returned to club work and guest appearances on television. She had several dramatic appearances on the small screen, appearing on *Peter Gunn* (NBC-TV, March 7, 1960) and on *Eleventh Hour* (NBC-TV, October 23, 1963). For her performance on the "A Horse Has a Big-Head—Let Him Worry" segment of *Naked City* (ABC-TV, November 21, 1962) she was Emmy-nominated. On *ABC Stage '67* she was in "A Time for Laughter" (April 6, 1967) a review of black humor in America, which featured Harry Belafonte, Sidney Poitier, Redd Foxx, Richard Pryor, and others. The next year she and the 5th Dimension were Sinatra's guests on his special *Francis Albert Sinatra Does His Thing* (CBS-TV, November 25, 1968).

Carroll returned to Hollywood to appear in Otto Preminger's tasteless, steamy shenanigans of the contemporary South, *Hurry Sundown* (1967). Carroll was the prim Georgia schoolmarm who helps fellow black Robert Hooks to prove his ownership of a piece of property coveted by grasping, bigoted Michael Caine. The movie was specious trash, more noted for the disturbing acts of racisms by Louisiana locals during the filming and for costar Jane Fonda's phallic fondling of a saxophone in one of the picture's more lurid moments. Also during that year, Diahann costarred with Jim Brown (the ex–football player turned movie-hunk-of-the-year) in a robbery caper called *The Split*. It was one of the first black action pictures. She was the ex-wife of ex-convict Brown who is killed by her lust-driven landlord (James Whitmore). It was an earthy role for the songstress.

In a mid-1960s' article, *TV Guide* magazine reported, "[Diahann Carroll] is Negro first and Diahann Carroll second." This anti-individuality description of the singer was certainly not unique to African-American performers—then or even now. However, it reflected Carroll's continual struggle between being regarded as a voice for her people and being thought of as a talented vocalist who just happened to be black. The conflict was not eased when she was cast in a TV sitcom to play Julia Baker, the twenty-six-year-old widow of an air force captain killed in Vietnam. As a nurse, she attempts to make a new life for herself and her six-year-old son. Produced by Twentieth Century-Fox, *Julia* debuted on September 24, 1968. The program was highly touted as "a new experience in television," the first weekly series built around a contemporary black character. During its popular three-season run, Carroll existed in a no-person's land: criticized by many in the black community for not reflecting black life accurately, and yet discriminated against by whites for daring to be a success in their world. Trying to balance these ironies, she told the press candidly, "The moneyed people, the managers, know they can deal with me. I'm 'acceptable.' In fact I'm sure that's why I got the part of Julia. I'm a black woman with a white image. I'm as close as they can get to having the best of both worlds. The audience can accept me in the same way, and for the same reason. I don't scare them."

In 1970 Diahann was dating black actor Don Marshall (of *Land of the Giants*) and was on the international best-dressed list for the second time. She continued playing the cabaret circuit globally and starred in *The Diahann Carroll Show* (NBC-TV, April 5, 1971), in which her guest stars were Harry Belafonte, Tom Jones, and Donald Sutherland. For two years in the early 1970s she dated British show-business figure David Frost and then, in 1973, married Las Vegas business-man Freddie Glusman. She described her three-month marriage as "another mistake." Her best feature film to date was Twentieth Century-Fox's *Claudine* (1974). She was the down-to-earth single mother of six children trying to keep everything going in her working-class environment. She is romanced by robust garbage collector James Earl Jones, who eventually overcomes his fear of a long-term commitment. Coming in the midst of the blaxploitation craze, *Claudine* was praised for its range of wholesome, respectful, and loving characters. Diahann was Oscar-nominated, but lost the Best Actress Academy Award to Ellen Burstyn (of *Alice Doesn't Live Here Anymore*).

In 1975, Diahann married Robert DeLeon, managing editor of *Jet* magazine. (In retrospect she assessed, "I set about finding a relationship that would punish me for being successful.") She was forty; he was twenty-four. Because he had business interests in Oakland, they moved there. He would die in an auto crash on Mulholland Drive in Los Angeles in March 1977. The marriage was stormy and depleted much of her savings. Meanwhile, with her career taking secondary interest to her personal life, Carroll appeared in the telefeature *Death Scream* (ABC-TV, September 26, 1975) as Betty May, one of fifteen neighbors who witnesses a young woman's murder. She had a four-week variety series on CBS-TV, *The Diahann Carroll Show*, an hour-long program that debuted on August 14, 1976. She allowed her then-husband to produce the series; his inexperience she says, caused the shows to be an embarrassment. As therapy after DeLeon died, she costarred with Cleavon Little in June 1977 in the comedy, *Same Time, Next Year* at the Huntington Hartford Theater in Los Angeles.

The next few years found Diahann Carroll at a low ebb. She admits the industry had come to regard her as risky, believing she had not taken her career seriously enough during the 1970s. They were unwilling to take a chance on her; besides she was over forty. As such, acting opportunities for the African-American star became more infrequent. However, when she was given the opportunity to emote, she shone. She was on the February 23, 1979, segment of the miniseries *Roots: The Next Generations* (ABC-TV) playing Zeona, the wife of Simon Haley (Dorian Harewood). In the telefeature *I Know Why the Caged Bird Sings* (CBS-TV, April 28, 1979) she joined with Ruby Dee, Roger E. Mosley, Paul Benjamin, Esther Rolle, and Madge Sinclair in an eloquent study of a gifted youngster (Constance Good) growing up in the 1930s' South.

Diahann had appeared on several Bob Hope television specials, and in September 1980 she played with him in a concert to open the new Amphitheater at Universal Studios in California. She credited Hope as one of the few to take a "chance" on her when she needed it. John Berry had already directed Carroll in *Claudine*, and in 1979 he helmed the telefeature *Sister, Sister*, filmed largely in Montgomery, Alabama. It was not shown on NBC-TV until June 7, 1982. Diahann was one of three sisters (with Rosalind Cash and Irene Cara) who reunite to sell the family home. She was cast as the inflexible spinster loved by local club owner Paul Winfield. For a week in the fall of 1982, she replaced Elizabeth Ashley as Dr. Livingston in the Broadway drama *Agnes of God*, which proved to be a rewarding dramatic stretch for Carroll. Because she thrived on the New York lifestyle so much, she moved back to Manhattan.

Not since *Julia* had Diahann Carroll enjoyed so much professional exposure as she did in her next stint when portraying the velvet vixen Dominique Devereaux. She first showed up on the "New Lady in Town" segment (ABC-TV, May 2, 1984) episode of *Dynasty*. In future installments of this plush, prime-time soap opera, it was revealed that her character, a black singer who had arrived in Denver with her record-mogul husband (Billy Dee Williams), was actually the illegitimate stepsister of patriarch Blake Carrington (John Forsythe). She remained with the hit series until

1987 and also made crossover appearances in late 1985 and early 1986, again as the scheming Dominique, on the spin-off series *The Colbys* (ABC-TV).

In 1980 Carroll had been commissioned to write her memoirs, but it was not until 1986 that *Diahann!*, written with Ross Firestone, appeared. She confessed to problems in preparing the book: "It has meant digging up a lot of painful things as part of the process of trying to tell the truth about my life, its struggles and what it's been like as a single working woman raising a child." *People* magazine called it "a spicy read" and the trade journal *Publishers Weekly* judged it "engrossing and frank." She dedicated her autobiography "To my mother, Mabel, and my daughter, Suzanne. From where it came, to where it is going." In 1989 she turned up as one of the mothers of the college girls on the *A Different World* (NBC-TV) series, and in the two-part Grand Guignol suspense telefeature, *From the Dead of Night* (NBC-TV, February 27–28, 1989), starring Lindsay Wagner. She was Maggie, who runs the fashion house in which Lindsay Wagner is the chief designer.

Diahann and white singer Vic Damone had met several years earlier, but it was in 1984 that she and Damone renewed their acquaintance while performing in a Palm Springs' show. They were married on January 3, 1987, in Las Vegas and thereafter performed together frequently in a cabaret act throughout the country. He was still recording albums and tried to persuade her to do likewise. However, she insisted, "I've always considered myself primarily a visual artist. I just don't like to listen to my records." (She would later change her mind and return to recording.) Of matrimony the fourth time around (for both of them) she said, "This business of learning how to be married is taking up a great deal of my time; no one told me that. Once I learn how to handle it, without feeling like I'm juggling five balls at the same time, I'd like to move toward producing." Regarding her next career moves, she offered, "I want something to test me, to make me want to jump out of bed in the morning."

Carroll started the 1990s with an appearance in *Murder in Black and White* (CBS-TV, January 7, 1990), one of several telefeatures starring Richard Crenna as a New York City police detective. Diahann played his interracial love interest in this entry. She had a subordinate role in filmmaker Robert Townsend's *The Five Heartbeats* (1991) an underappreciated study of a 1960 singing group. She was window dressing in the Perry Mason TV movie entry *The Case of the Lethal Lifestyle* (NBC-TV, May 10, 1994). During this period she lived mostly in Los Angeles with her singer husband Damone, but still maintained her nine-room co-op apartment in New York City. From 1994 to 1995, she portrayed Ida Grayson in the TV entry *Lonesome Dove: The Series*. She was seen as the black settler in the Dakota Territory who takes a young white man (Scott Bairstow) as her partner so she can buy a local hotel.

To much hoopla, on October 15, 1995, the veteran talent began her run as the insane former movie star Norma Desmond in the Canadian premiere engagement of Andrew Lloyd Webber's *Sunset Boulevard*. The dramatic musical opened at the Ford Center for the Performing Arts in Toronto. Carroll continued with the show for the next two years. During this period her marriage to Vic Damone ended in divorce. In the fall of 1997, Diahann sold her Beverly Hills home of more than twenty years and purchased a Beverly Hills–area condominium.

After several years' absence, Carroll returned to feature filmmaking in the ensemble cast of *Eve's Bayou* (1997). This effective drama dealt with a Creole family in the early 1960s told from the point of view of a ten-year-old. Also that year the performer had a new CD (*The Time of My Life*) on the Sterling label. The warmhearted 1998 cable TV movie *The Sweetest Gift* found Diahann in a leading role opposite Helen Shaver. They played Florida neighbors—one black, one white—who are each single parents bringing up their children to their best abilities while dealing with poverty and racial prejudice.

In late April 1998 a routine medical checkup revealed that Diahann had a small cancerous growth on her breast. On May 14, she underwent surgery, followed by weeks of radiation treatment. Recovering from the ordeal, the star observed, "Something like this brings your life into perspective. Cancer isn't glamorous, but it is important that people realize they don't have a special exemption from reality." As part of her recovery process, she became an advocate for early detection of the disease through regular examinations. Returning to her active schedule, she accepted a Lucy award from the group Women in Film in recognition of her career achievements in television. She undertook a cross-country concert tour in *An Evening With Lerner and Lowe* and launched her own Signature Brand Fashion Collection.

In the late 1990s Diahann had a choice TV movie role when she joined with Ruby Dee to play the long-living African-American sisters in *Having Our Say: The Delany Sisters' First 100 Years* (CBS-TV, April 18, 1999) for which both actresses were nominated for Image Awards. Carroll played the mother of a black slave who has a relationship with President Thomas Jefferson in *Sally Hemings: An American Scandal* (CBS-TV, February 13, 2000), and was the wife of Nat "King" Cole in the biographical drama about the Cole's songstress daughter in *Livin' for Love: The Natalie Cole Story* (NBC-TV, December 10, 2000). During this period, Carroll also had a line of clothing distributed through J. C. Penney stores.

When the A&E cable channel premiered its *Biography* episode (July 20, 2000) on Diahann Carroll, the *Hollywood Reporter* observed of the subject: "the impenetrable hide that Carroll has cultivated is endemic to black performers of her generation. She . . . had to develop robust survival skills merely to endure the institutional racism of the mid-20th century." The reviewer observed, "there is simply no pigeonholing this lady. She is at once wildly insecure and boldly self-assured. Yet Carrol is still gliding through life with that same regal bearing, indicating that maybe she has finally succeeded in bringing a certain harmony to an existence plagued by perpetual imbalance."

Filmography

Carmen Jones (20th-Fox, 1954)
Porgy and Bess (UA, 1959)
Goodbye Again (UA, 1961)
Paris Blues (UA, 1961)
Hurry Sundown (Par, 1967)
The Split (MGM, 1968)
Claudine (20th-Fox, 1974)
Death Scream [The Woman Who Cried Murder] (ABC-TV, 9/26/75)
I Know Why the Caged Bird Sings (CBS-TV, 4/28/79)
Sister, Sister (NBC-TV, 6/7/82)
From the Dead of Night (NBC-TV, 2/27–28/89)

Murder in Black and White (CBS-TV, 1/7/90)
The Five Heartbeats (20th-Fox, 1991)
Perry Mason: The Case of the Lethal Lifestyle (NBC-TV, 5/10/94)
Eve's Bayou (Trimark, 1997)
The Sweetest Gift (Showtime cable, 2/28/98)
Having Our Say: The Delany Sisters' First 100 Years (CBS-TV, 4/18/99)
Jackie's Back! (Lifetime-cable, 6/14/99)
Courage to Love (CBS-TV, 1/24/2000)
Sally Hemings: An American Scandal (CBS-TV, 2/13/2000)
Livin' for Love: The Natalie Cole Story (NBC-TV, 12/10/2000)

Broadway Plays

House of Flowers (1954)
No Strings (1962)

Agnes of God (1982) (replacement)

TV Series

Julia (NBC, 1968–71)
The Diahann Carroll Show (CBS, 1976)

Dynasty (ABC-TV, 1984–87)
Lonesome Dove: The Series (Synd, 1994–95)

Album Discography

LPs

"A" You're Adorable (Disque 398-2)
Best Beat Forward (Vik LX-1131)
Cole Porter in Paris (Bell Telephone 36508) [ST/TV]
Diahann Carroll (Har HS-11347)
Diahann Carroll (Motown 805)
Diahann Carroll Accompanied by the Andre Previn Trio (Sunset 5293)
Diahann Carroll and Andre Previn (UA 6069)
The Fabulous Diahann Carroll (UA UAL-3229/UAS-6229)

Fun Life (Atlantic 8048)
Goodbye Again (UA UAL 4091/UAS 5091) [ST]
Harold Arlen Songs (RCA LPM-1467)
House of Flowers (Col OL-4969/OC-2320) [OC]
Love Songs for Children (Golden 141)
No Strings (Cap O/SO-1695) [OC]
Nobody Sees Me Cry (Col CL-2571/CS-9371)
The Persian Room Presents Diahann Carroll (UA 6080)
Porgy and Bess (UA UAL-4021/UAS-5021)
Showstopper! (Camden CAL/CAS-695)

CDs

Diahann Carroll and the Duke (Delta 79168) w. Duke Ellington
Diahann Carroll Sings Harold Arlen Songs (RCA Spain 74321-47869-2)
House of Flowers (Col CK-2320) [OC]
No Strings (Broadway Angel ZDM-64694) [OC]
Nobody Sees Me Cry—The Best of the Columbia Years (Collectables COL-CD-6688)

Side by Side (Sony Music Special Products CK-32972) w. Michele Lee
Sunset Boulevard (Polydor 529757) [OC]
The Time of My Life (Sterling S-1015-2)
A Tribute to Ethel Waters (Bainbridge BCD-6101, Laserlight 15-294)

Johnny Cash in *Road to Nashville* (1966).
[Courtesy of JC Archives]

Johnny Cash

(b. John R. Cash, Kingsland, Arkansas, February 26, 1932)

One of the legends of country music, deep-voiced Johnny Cash sustained his popularity for nearly a half century in a successful career that has not only encompassed music but also films and television. The composer of many country songs, Cash also delved into movie production with his self-conceived religious feature *Gospel Road* (1973). For many devotees this famous "man in black" was long regarded as the epitome of a country-music star. Ironically, Cash was held in higher regard by noncountry fans than by followers of this type of music. Around 1970, when Cash's national popularity was at its height due to his ABC-TV program and several top-selling singles and LPs, a poll was taken in the Nashville area to determine the most popular country-music performer. The winner was Marty Robbins, not Johnny Cash. When Cash was inducted into the Country Music Hall of Fame in 1980 there was some grumbling around Nashville that many country pioneer performers had been overlooked in deference to Cash. The resentment in Music City was due, mostly, to his association with country rock and the "Country Jesus" crowds. Still, Johnny Cash's accomplishments have been many, such as in 1969 when he was the first performer to receive six awards from the Country Music Association. Although he participated in more than a dozen feature films in various capacities over the years, acting was one of the least of his many abilities.

Born John R. Cash in Kingsland, Arkansas, on February 26, 1932, he was the son of poor cotton sharecroppers, Ray and Carrie Cash. With his brothers and sisters, Cash worked in the fields when he was old enough, but he was also attracted to music, especially the country sounds he heard via the radio (the only form of entertainment available to the family). When he was three, the family moved to the Dyess Colony, a government resettlement community, and by 1940 the Cash family included seven children with the birth of son Tom (who later became a popular country singer, Tommy Cash).

As a boy, Johnny started writing poems and songs, and in high school he sang over a local radio station while his older brother Roy Cash formed a band called the Delta Rhythm Ramblers. Cash graduated from high school in 1950 and moved to Detroit to work in an auto plant. He also took other manual-labor jobs before enlisting in the Air Force that summer and spending the next four years in West Germany. While in the military, Cash learned to play the guitar, and he composed a number of songs. In 1954, after leaving the Air Force as a staff sergeant, Cash wed Vivian Liberto (who was part Italian—in later years, she was branded a mulatto by the Ku Klux Klan, who boycotted Cash's performances), and they moved to Memphis where he sold electrical appliances. In Memphis, Cash met musicians Luther Perkins (guitar) and Marshall Grant (bass), and along with brother Roy Cash, the four began performing together, mostly Hank Snow songs and religious numbers. This led to some unpaid radio work and an audition at Sun Records for Sam Phillips, who had just launched Elvis Presley.

Signing with Sun Records proved to be the professional launching pad for Cash and the Tennessee Two (made up of Perkins and Grant). Their first single, Johnny's compositions of "Cry, Cry, Cry" / "Hey Porter," sold well, and this was followed by the even more popular "Folsom Prison Blues" and the gold disc "I Walk the Line." Thereafter Cash had a string of bestsellers, becoming Sun's most popular recording star, and he began his round of seemingly endless one-night stands as well as becoming a regular on the *Louisiana Hayride* radio show in 1955 and the *Grand Ole Opry* in 1957. Next, Hollywood called, and Johnny Cash starred in his first feature film, *Five Minutes to Live*, a poverty-row effort for Sutton Pictures that was filmed in 1958 but not issued until 1961. In it, Cash was a third-rate country singer who joins a gang of crooks in abducting a woman (Cay Forester) in order to get ransom money from her rich husband (Donald Woods). In the feature, Cash sang the title song and "I've Come to Kill," both of which he cocomposed with Gene Kauer. In the mid 1960s, new footage was added to this exploitation thriller (by this time Cash had lost so much weight due to pill addiction that the new footage did not match the old), and American International reissued it as *Door-To-Door Maniac* in 1966.

Next, Cash and his group successfully toured Australia and Canada. In 1958, they switched to the Columbia label, where Cash would remain for three decades. His singles and albums for the company sold well, and he did a number of theme LPs for the label, such as the pro–Native American *Bitter Tears*, his narration of Ferde Grofé's *Grand Canyon Suite* with Andre Kostelanetz, and a tribute to the railroad, *Ride This Train*. By 1960 drummer W. S. Holland had been added to his backup group, now called the Tennessee Three, and they began playing clubs in addition to some three hundred one-nighters each year. The grind of constant travel became so great that Cash began using prescription drugs to keep going, and within a few years, he was hopelessly addicted to pills. In 1961, June Carter joined the Cash troupe, and the next year his heavy schedule included a month in Korea and a failed Carnegie Hall concert. He also starred in the Western featurette *The Night Rider* (1962), with Eddie Dean, Merle Travis, Johnny Western, and Gordon Terry, the latter two often a part of his touring shows.

In 1963 he performed in the undistinguished low-budget MGM feature *Hootenanny Hoot*, directed by ex-dancer/singer Gene Nelson and also featuring Sheb Wooley and the Brothers Four. Cash expanded his musical horizons by appearing with Bob Dylan at the Newport Folk Festival in 1964, but by the next year Cash was in trouble with the law. He received a suspended sentence and a fine for narcotics violations, and in 1965 he was arrested in Georgia for carrying illegal drugs. When Carl Perkins (who had alcohol problems and with whom Cash had toured along with Elvis Presley in 1954 when all three were on the Sun label) joined his troupe in 1966, both Cash and Perkins agreed to seek medical help for their addictions. Cash was able to kick his pill habit and resume his career, but his wife, Vivian, divorced him in 1966. (They had two daughters, one of whom, Roseanne, later toured with her dad and then became a country star in her own right in the 1970s.)

Despite his health problems, Johnny Cash continued to have hit records for Columbia like "Ring of Fire," "The Ballad of Ira Hayes," "I Got Stripes," "In the Jailhouse Now," "It Ain't Me, Babe," and "Understand Your Man." From 1959 to 1962 Cash was heard singing the title theme, "The Ballad of Johnny Yuma" (also a hit for him on record), for the ABC-TV series *The Rebel*. Early in 1960, he guest-starred in a segment of that series, followed by an appearance on NBC-TV's *The Deputy* in 1961. In 1967 Johnny Cash and June Carter won a Grammy for their duet on the song "Jackson," and the next year (March 1968) they were married. (June daughter's Carlene, by a previous marriage to country singer Carl Smith, would also have a singing career in the '80s and '90s.)

Following highly successful albums of his group's appearance at Folsom Prison in 1968 and at San Quentin Prison in 1969, the singer came to national television with the very popular *The Johnny Cash Show* on ABC-TV, which ran from 1969 to 1971. As a result of the success of the program he was the subject of the documentary film *Johnny Cash! The Man, His World, His Music* (1969). (He had appeared briefly in the 1966 country-music feature *The Road to Nashville* singing "I Walk the Line.") In 1970, he appeared on *NET Playhouse*'s production of "The Trail of Tears" and had a guest shot on the ABC-TV series *The Partridge Family*. For his first major Hollywood film, Cash was cast as an old-time gunman in *A Gunfight* (1971), in which he agrees to shoot it out with a rival (Kirk Douglas) with admission fees charged for the deadly event. The less said about Cash's performance, the better.

Following the demise of his teleseries in 1971, Johnny resumed his heavy touring schedule, although by now he and his wife June had a son, John Carter Cash, to care for. Besides the Tennessee Three, Carl Perkins, and Gordon Terry, the package tour group with Cash included not only his wife but also her mother, Maybelle Carter, and her sisters Anita and Helen—all of whom had worked with Cash since the early 1960s as well as having performed on his TV variety show. In 1970 Cash provided the songs and sang many of them on the soundtracks of the features *I Walk the Line* and *Little Fauss and Big Halsy*, and he began performing at Billy Graham religious crusades.

A visit to the Holy Land in 1972 resulted in the feature film *Gospel Road*, the script of which Cash cowrote. In addition, he coproduced the movie with his wife (who played Mary Magdalene in it), sang its songs, as well as serving as on-screen narrator. While this motion picture was a very personal statement on religion by the star, it did not do well in theaters and finished being road-shown for church viewing.

Cash did a guest appearance on the network TV program *Columbo* in 1974 and starred in a well-regarded TV "documusical" *Ridin' the Rails—The Great American Train Story*, for which he wrote songs. He was a guest on the TV series *Little House on the Prairie* in 1976, and that year he came back with four episodes of the CBS-TV music show *Johnny Cash and Friends*.

By the mid-'70s, however, despite a regular touring schedule, Cash's records were no longer selling well except for an occasional duet with more currently popular sellers like Waylon Jennings. Nevertheless, Cash was much in evidence, appearing frequently on his own TV specials (usually celebrating Christmastime and always with June and other members of his entourage). In 1978, Cash and Bo Hopkins played two vagabonds in the CBS-TV telefeature *Thaddeus Rose and Eddie*, in which June Carter Cash also appeared. It was the first of several of his made-for-television features. In May 1980, he hosted a ninety-minute CBS-TV special (*Johnny Cash: The First 25 Years*), a salute to his many years in show business. The next year found him going to London to appear in concert (a performance released later on videocassette). Also, in 1981, he starred as an illiterate who wants an education in *The Pride of Jesse Hallan* for CBS-TV. In it Cash and his wife sang the telefeature's songs.

Murder in Coweta County, for CBS-TV in 1983, offered Cash the part of a stubborn Southern lawman determined to prove a murder charge against a powerful businessman (Andy Griffith), with June cast as an eccentric soothsayer. *The Baron and the Kid* (1984), for the same network, showcased Cash as a pool hustler who meets the son (Greg Webb) he has never known. This TV movie provided the star with a moderate record seller, *The Baron*. Meanwhile, health problems arose for Cash again in 1984 when ulcer surgery resulted in problems with morphine. Again overcoming a near drug addiction, he resumed his career activities. Also in 1984, the videocassette *The Other Side of Nashville* was released. It contained old performance clips and interviews with Johnny Cash, Kris Kristofferson, Chet Atkins, Carl Perkins, Willie Nelson, Hank Williams Jr., and several other country stars.

In 1986, Johnny Cash, by now portly and leather-faced, starred in two TV Western features: *The Last Days of Frank and Jesse James* and *Stagecoach*. In the former he was Frank James to Kris Kristofferson's Jesse, while June Carter Cash portrayed their mother! In the third feature-length version of *Stagecoach*, Cash was the least impressive of a bevy of country singers (Willie Nelson, Kris Kristofferson, Waylon Jennings, and John Schneider) in dramatic roles; Cash played a lawman while wife June and son John had brief assignments as way station owners. Two years later, Cash was on hand as Davy Crockett in the NBC-TV Disney telefilm *Rainbow in the Thunder*. In 1989, he returned to feature-film acting in *Tennessee Nights*, an unimpressive entry that was issued directly to home video.

Late in 1988, Cash blacked out while arriving in Bristol, Virginia, for a charity concert and was diagnosed as having a blocked heart artery. He underwent successful surgery, but complications arose that sidelined him for several weeks. Ironically, his country-singer friend Roy Orbison had died of a heart attack just a few days before, and Waylon Jennings (a onetime roommate of Cash in Nashville in the 1960s), who was also on the Bristol show, had undergone surgery after suffering a heart attack en route to the same concert. After a long recuperation, Cash resumed his activities, saying, "It's a wonderful life and I'm not going to miss a second of it. I want to enjoy every precious moment with my family."

The decade of the 1990s brought both further fame and severe health problems to the country-music star. From 1993 to 1997 he enacted the role of King Cole in four episodes of the TV series *Dr. Quinn, Medicine Woman*. His disc career had a major resurgence when he began working for the American Recording label in the mid-'90s. It was during this period, however, that he was diagnosed with a Parkinson's-like disease, and he had several near-fatal episodes with pneumonia. In 1996, Cash was honored with the Kennedy Center Award, but his movies during the decade consisted of work in only three documentaries: *Radio Star—Die AFN Story* (1994), a German production; he was narrator and performer in *Gene Autry, Melody of the West* (1994); and he guested in *All My Friends Are Cowboys* (1998). Although health problems forced Johnny to stop touring after nearly forty years on the road, he continued to record, and in 2001, after another near-fatal bout with pneumonia, he was given the Grammy Award for Best Male Country Performer, his eleventh Grammy. That year he was also inducted into the Country Music Association Hall of Fame. (He had been made a member of the Country Music Hall of Fame in 1980, and a decade later he was given the Academy of Country Music's Pioneer Award and a Grammy Legend Award.)

Filmography

Five Minutes to Live [Door to Door Maniac] (Sutton Pictures/Astor Pictures/AIP, 1961) (also co-songs)

The Night Rider (Parallel, 1962) (s)

Hootenanny Hoot (MGM, 1963)

The Road to Nashville (Crown International, 1966)

Festival (Peppercorn-Wormser, 1967) (documentary)

Johnny Cash All-Star Extra (Road Show, 1969) (s)

I Walk the Line (Col, 1970) (voice, songs)

Little Fauss and Big Halsy (Par, 1970) (voice, songs)

Johnny Cash! The Man, His World, His Music (Continental, 1969)

A Gunfight (Par, 1971)

The Nashville Sound (John F. Bradford, 1972)

Eat the Document (Pennebaker Associates, 1972) (documentary)

The Gospel Road (20th-Fox, 1973) (coproducer, coscripter, co-songs, narrator)

Thaddeus Rose and Eddie (CBS-TV, 2/24/78)

The Pride of Jesse Hallan (CBS-TV, 3/3/81)

Murder in Coweta County (CBS-TV, 2/15/83)

The Baron and the Kid (CBS-TV, 12/21/84)

The Last Days of Frank and Jesse James (NBC-TV, 2/16/86)

Stagecoach (CBS-TV, 5/18/86)

Illegally Yours (MGM/UA, 1988) (voice, co-songs)

Rainbow in the Thunder (NBC-TV, 11/20/88)

Tennessee Nights [Black Water] (Academy Video, 1989)

Radio Star—Die AFN Story (Film und Teleclub, 1994) (documentary)

Gene Autry, Melody of the Plains (Galen Film Productions, 1994) (narrator) (documentary)

All My Friends Are Cowboys (1998) (documentary)

Radio Series

Louisiana Hayride (Synd, 1955)

Grand Ole Opry (Synd, 1957)

TV Series

Ranch Party (Synd, 1958)

The Johnny Cash Show (ABC, 1969–71)

Johnny Cash and Friends (CBS, 1976)

Album Discography

LPs

The Adventures of Johnny Cash (Col FC-38094)

All Aboard the Blue Train (Sun 1270)

America: A 200 Year Salute in Story and Song (Col KC-31645)

Anniversary Collection (Imperial House 3570)

Any Old Wind That Blows (Col KC-32091)

Ballad of a Teenage Queen (Hallmark SHM-862)

Ballads of the American Indian (Har KH-32388)

Ballads of the True West (Col C2L-28/2CS-838, CBS Embassy 31520)

The Baron (Col FC-37179)

Believe in Him (Word 8333)

A Believer Sings the Truth (Cachet CL3-9001, Priority 38074)

The Best of Johnny Cash (CBS 65846)

The Best of Johnny Cash (7″ Reader's Digest RDJC-761/65)

The Best of Johnny Cash (Tripp TLX-8500)

Big River (Hilltop JS-6118)

Big River (Longines) w. Jeannie C. Riley

Big Town (Atlantic 81769-1) [ST]

Biggest Hits (Col FC-38317)

Biggest Hits (Embassy 32304)

Bitter Tears (Col CL-2248/CS-9048, Bear Family BFX-15127)

Blood, Sweat and Tears (Col CL-1930/CS-8730)

The Blue Train (Share 5002)

Born to Sing (Longines LS-205A&B)

A Boy Named Sue (Embassy 31827)

Carryin' On (Col CL-2728/CS-9528) w. June Carter

The Children's Album (Col C-32898)

Christmas Spirit (Col CL-2117/CS-8917)

Christmas With the Johnny Cash Family (Col C-31754)

The Class of '55 (Mer/Polygram 830-002-1) w. Jerry Lee Lewis, Carl Perkins, Roy Orbison

Classic Cash (Mer/Polygram 834-526-1)

Classic Christmas (Col JC-36866)

Columbia Records 1958–86 (Col C2-40637)

Country Classics (Columbia Special Products P-16915)

Country Cousins (Sears SPS-109)

Country Gold (Power Pak PO-246)

Country Music—Johnny Cash (Time-Life)

Country's Round-Up (Hilltop 6010) w. Billy Grammer, the Wilburn Brothers)

Destination Victoria Station (Columbia Special Products VS-150)

A Diamond in the Rough (Word WST-9629)

Dukes of Hazzard (Scotti Bros. FZ-37712) [ST/TV]

The Electrifying Johnny Cash (Columbia Special Products P4S-5406)

Encore (Col FC-37355)

Everlasting (Out of Town Distributors 8019)

Everybody Loves a Nut (Col CL-2492/CS-9292)

The Fabulous Johnny Cash (Col CL-1253/CS-8122, Columbia Special Products P-11506)

The First Years (Allegiance 5017)

Five Feet High and Rising (Col C-32951)

Folk Songs of Trains and Rivers (Music Disc 30CV-1320)

Folsom Prison Blues (Grand Prix GP-10002)

Folsom Prison Blues (Hallmark SHM-822)

Folsom Prison Blues (NGLP 4002)

Folsom Prison Blues (Share 5001)

Friend to Friend (Album Globe 2360) w. Jeannie C. Riley

From Sea to Shining Sea (Col CL-2647/CS-9447)

Gentle Giant of Country Music (Sun International 6641-161)

Get Rhythm (Sun 105)

Give My Love to Rose (Har KH-31256) w. June Carter

Golden Sounds of Country Music (Har HS-11249)

Gone Girl (Col KC-35646)

The Gospel Road (Col KG-32253, Priority 32253) [ST]

Gospel Singer (Priority 38503)

Grand Canyon Suite (Col MS-7425) w. Andre Kostelanetz

Great Johnny Cash (Hallmark SHM-696)

Great Songs of Johnny Cash (Pickwick PD-50004)

Greatest! (Sun 1240)

Greatest Hits (Col CL-2678/CS-9478)

Greatest Hits, Vol. 2 (Col PC-30887)

Greatest Hits, Vol. 3 (Col KC-35637)

The Greatest Hits (Share 5003)

Greatest Hits (Spotlight SPLO-113)

The Greatest Johnny Cash (London S379267LDY)

The Greatness of Johnny Cash (Cap Record Club 93213)

Happiness Is You (Col CL-2537/CS-9337)

Harper Valley P.T.A. (Plantation PLP-700) [ST]

The Heart of Johnny Cash (Col STS-2004)

Hello, I'm Johnny Cash (Col KCS-9943)

Hello, I'm Johnny Cash (Encore P-13832)

Heroes (Col 40327) w. Waylon Jennings

Hi, I'm Johnny Cash (Longines LWGF-8)

Highwayman (Col 40056) w. Willie Nelson, Waylon Jennings, Kris Kristofferson

The Holy Land (Col KCS-9766)

Hot and Blue Guitar (Charity CRM-2013)

Hot and Blue Guitar (Sun 1220)

Hymns by Johnny Cash (Col CL-1284/CS-8125)

Hymns From the Heart (Col CL-1722/CS-8522)

I Believe (Arrival NU-3870)

I Forgot to Remember to Forget (Hallmark SHM-884)

I Love Country (CBS 54938)

I Love You Because (Spotlight SPLO-105)

I Walk the Line (Accord 7134)

I Walk the Line (Album Globe 9206)

I Walk the Line (Col CL-2190/CS-8490)

I Walk the Line (Col S-30397) [ST]

I Walk the Line (Hallmark SHM-849)

I Walk the Line (Hilltop JS-6097)

I Walk the Line (Longines) w. Jeannie C. Riley

I Walk the Line (Nashville 2108)

I Walk the Line (Share 5000)

I Would Like to See You Again (Col KC-35313)

I'm So Lonesome I Could Cry (Hallmark SHM-3027)

In God We Trust (Good Music Company JNR)

Inside a Swedish Prison (Bear Family BFX-15092)

International Superstar (CBS 67284)

It's Time to Pray, America! (House Top HTR-702) [ST/TV]

Jackson (Col CL-2728/CS-9528, Columbia Special Products P-11507)

John R. Cash (Col KC-33370)

Johnny and June (Bear Family BFX-15030) w. June Carter Cash

Johnny Cash (Embassy 31039)

Johnny Cash (Everest FS-278)

Johnny Cash (Har HS-11342)

Johnny Cash (HMB 7001)

Johnny Cash (Pickwick PTP-2045)

Johnny Cash (Pickwick PTP-2052)

Johnny Cash (Pickup PU-14006)

Johnny Cash (Suraphon 113-1926ZD)

Johnny Cash (Syndicate NC-401)

Johnny Cash (Time-Life TLCW-03)

Johnny Cash and Friends (Columbia Special Products C-10777)

Johnny Cash and His Woman (Col KC-32443) w. June Carter Cash

Johnny Cash and Jerry Lee Lewis Sing Hank Williams (Sun 125)

Johnny Cash at Folsom Prison (Col CS-9639)

Johnny Cash at Folsom Prison and San Quentin (Col CG-33639)

Johnny Cash at Osteraker Prison (CBS 65308)

Johnny Cash at San Quentin (Col CS-9827)

The Johnny Cash Collection (Col KC-30887)

The Johnny Cash Collection (Pickwick PDA-005)

The Johnny Cash Collection, Vol. 2 (Pickwick PDA-033)

The Johnny Cash Collection, Vol. 3 (Pickwick PDA-062)

Johnny Cash Family Christmas (Col KC-31754)

Johnny Cash in Prague—Live (Suraphon 1113-3278)

Johnny Cash Is Coming to Town (Mer/Polygram 837-031-1)

The Johnny Cash Show (Col KC-30100)

Johnny Cash Sings Hank Williams (Sun 1245)

Johnny Cash Sings With Goodpasture Christian School (BCG)

The Johnny Cash Songbook (Har KH-31602)

Johnny Cash Special (CBS 80811)

Johnny Down West (Reader's Digest 7033)

Johnny in Jail (Reader's Digest 7036)

Johnny in Love (Reader's Digest 7034)

Johnny 99 (Col FC-38696)

Johnny on Sunday (Reader's Digest 7035)

Johnny on the Railroad (Reader's Digest 7032)

Johnny's Big Hits (Reader's Digest 7031)

The Junkie and the Juicehead Minus Me (Col KC-33086)

Keep on the Sunny Side (Col CL-2152/CS-8952, Columbia Special Products P-11504) w. the Carter Family

The King and Queen (Col Musical Treasury P2S-5418) w. Tammy Wynette

The King and the Queen (Columbia Special Products P4S-5376) w. Tammy Wynette

King of Country Music (Festival FT-174)

The Last Gunfighter Ballad (Col KC-34314)

The Legend (Sun 2-118)

Legends and Love Songs (Col DS-363)

Little Fauss and Big Halsy (Col S-30285) [ST]

Lonesome Me (London HAS-8253)

Look at Them Beans (Col KC-33814)

The Lure of the Grand Canyon (Col CL-1622/CS-8422) w. Andre Kostelanetz

Magnificent Johnny Cash (Hallmark SHM-277)

The Man Behind Johnny Cash (CBS 64892)

The Man in Black (Col C-30550)

The Man, the World, His Music (Sun 2-216)

Mean as Hell (Col CL-2446/CS-9246)

More of Old Golden Throat (Bear Family BFX-15073)

Names and Places (Embassy 31548)

Now Here's Johnny Cash (Sun 1255)

Now There Was a Song (Col CL-1463/CS-8254)

Old Golden Throat (Bear Family BFX-15072)

Old Golden Throat (Charly CR-30005)

One Piece at a Time (Col PC-34193)

Orange Blossom Special (Col CL-2309/CS-9109)

Original Golden Hits, Vol. 1 (Sun 100)

Original Golden Hits, Vol. 2 (Sun 101)

Original Golden Hits, Vol. 3 (Sun 127)

The Original Johnny Cash (Charly CR-30113)

The Original Sun Sound (Sun SLP-1275)

Portrait Einer Legende (Prisma CBS-28214)

Previous Memories (Col C-33087, Priority 33087)

Ragged Old Flag (Col KC-32917)

Rainbow (Col 39951-4)

The Rambler (Col KC-34883)

Ride This Train (Col CL-1464/CS-8255)

Riding the Rails (CBS 88153)

Ring of Fire (Col CL-2053/CS-8255)

Rock Island Line (Hilltop JS-6101)

Rock Island Line (Longines LS-205C) w. Jeannie C. Riley

Rockabilly Blues (Col 36779)

The Rough Cut of Country Music (Sun 122)

Show Time (Sun 106)

Silver (Col JC-36086)

The Singing Story Teller (Buckboard BBS-1021)

The Singing Story Teller (Sun 115)

Songs of Life and Love (Columbia Special Products P-16657)

Songs of Our Soil (Col CL-1339/8148, Columbia Special Products P-11505)

The Songs That Made Him Famous (Sun 1235)

The Sons of Katie Elder (Col OL/OS/6420) [ST]

The Sound Behind Johnny Cash (Col C-30220) w. the Tennessee Three

The Sound of Johnny Cash (Col CL-1802/CS-8602)

Souvenir Album (Sun International NL-361/62)

Story of a Broken Heart (Design SDLP-610)

Story of a Broken Heart (Hallmark SHM-897)

Story Songs of Trains and Rivers (Sun 104)

Strawberry Cake (Col KC-34088)

The Sun Sessions (NGLP 4000)

The Sun Story, Vol. 1 (Johnny Cash) (Sunnyvale 9330-901)

The Sun Story, Vol. 1 (Spotlight SPLO-125)

The Sun Years (Charly 103)

Sunday Down South (Sun 119) w. Jerry Lee Lewis, Charlie Rich

Sunday Morning Coming Down (Col KC-32240)

Superbilly (Sun 1002)

The Survivors (Col FC-37961) w. Jerry Lee Lewis, Carl Perkins

A Thing Called Love (Col KC-31332)

This Is Johnny Cash (Har HS-11342)

The Two of Us (Sun International ELD-975)

Understand Your Man (Har KH-30916)

The Unforgettable Johnny Cash (DGR 1003)

The Unissued Johnny Cash (Bear Family BFX-15016)

The Very Best of Johnny Cash (Sun International HJS-166)

The Vintage Cash (Rhino 70229)

The Walls of Prison (Har HC-15053, Har KH-30138)

Water From the Wells of Home (Mer/Polygram 834-778-1)

Welcome to Europe (CBS 53658)

The World of Johnny Cash (Col GP-29)

CDs

All American Country (Polygram 5525582)

American Recordings (American Recordings 69402)

American III: Solitary Man (American Recordings 69691)

At Folsom Prison (Legacy CK-65955)

At Folsom Prison and San Quentin (Col CGK-33639)

Back to Back (K-Tel 3193-2) w. George Jones

Ballad of Ira Hayes (Goldies 63236)

The Best of Johnny Cash (Castle Communications MAC-CD-58344)

The Best of Johnny Cash (Col 519792)

The Best of Johnny Cash (Curb D21K-77494)

The Best of Johnny Cash and Willie Nelson—37 Outlaw Country Classics (Master Song 550312)

Best of the Best (Federal 6548)

The Best of the Sun Years (Reper RR-482)

Biggest Hits (Col CK-38317)

Bitter Tears: Ballads of the American Indian (Legacy CK-66507)

Bitter Tears/Blood, Sweat and Tears (Legacy CK-64812)

Blood, Sweat and Tears (Legacy CK-66508)

Boom Chick a Boom (Mer 842155-2)

Christmas Spirit (Sony Music Special Products 24082)

Class of '55 (Polygram 550838) w. Jerry Lee Lewis, Roy Orbison, Carl Perkins

Classic Cash (Mer 834526-2)

Classic Christmas (Sony Music Special Products 20726)

Columbia Records 1958-86 (Col CGK-40637)

Come Along and Ride This Train (Bear Family BCD-15563)

Complete Live From San Quentin (Legacy 66017)

Complete Original Sun Hits (Varese Vintage 66056)

Country Cash (Hallmark 308352)

Country Christmas (Laserlight 14-417)

Country Classics (Hallmark 33023)

Country Greatest (EMI P-5760382)

Country Music Hall of Fame 1980 (King 3823)

Crazy Country (Sony Music Special Products 2879)

Dead Men Walking (Col CK-67522) [ST]

Doin' My Time (Delta 47026)

The EP Collection (See for Miles 719)

The Essential Johnny Cash 1955-73 (Legacy C3K-65557)

The Essential Sun Collection (PID 547732)

The Fabulous Johnny Cash (K-Tel 75024-2)

The Fabulous Johnny Cash/Songs of Our Soil (Sony 4948962, Globetrotter 753112)

Years Gone By (Accord 7208)

Famous Country Music Makers (Pulse PLS-CD-602)

Faraway, So Close! (SBK K21X-27216) [ST]

Folsom Prison Blues (BCD GSS-5132, Master 2502922)

Folsom Prison Blues—The Concert Collection (Prism PLATCD-1130)

Get Rhythm (Classic Country CDCD-1054)

Get Rhythm/Story Songs of Trains (Collectables COL-CD-6427)

Giant Hits (Sony Music Special Products 15713)

God (Col 65545)

Give My Love to Rose (ABM ABMMCD1139)

Gold Collection (Retro R2CD40-56) w. Boxcar Willie

Golden Hits (ITC Masters 1236)

Gospel Collection (Legacy CK-48952)

Gospel Glory (Sony Music Special Products 21608)

Great (BDC GLD-63189, Redx RXBOX-31056)

Greatest Hits (CSI CLASSICS-40105)

Greatest Hits: Finest Performances (Sun 700)

Greatest Hits of Johnny (Platinum Disc 15222)

Greatest Hits of Johnny Cash I (Platinum Disc 1498)

Greatest Hits of Johnny Cash II (Platinum Disc 1499)

Greatest Hits/Sings (Collectables COL-CD-6438)

Hello, I'm Johnny Cash (Sony Music Special Products 13832)

Here's Johnny (Sony Music Special Products 23702) w. Johnny Horton, Johnny Paycheck

Heroes (Razor & Tie Music 82078) w. Waylon Jennings

Highwayman (BCD GLD-25380) w. Willie Nelson, Waylon Jennings, Kris Kristofferson

Highwayman (Col FCT-40056) w. Willie Nelson, Waylon Jennings, Kris Kristofferson

Highwayman 2 (Col CK-45240) w. Willie Nelson, Waylon Jennings, Kris Kristofferson

Hits (Mer Nashville 534665)

Holy Land (Har 1786)

It's All in the Family (Bear Family BCD-16132)

I Walk the Line (Delta 6186)

I Walk the Line (Golgram GG-011)

I Walk the Line (Prism PLACT-515)

I Walk the Line (Spectrum U4065)

I Walk the Line/Folsom Prison Blues (Collectables COL-CD-6437)

I Walk the Line/Little Fauss and Big Halsey (Bear Family BCD-16130) [ST]

I Walk the Line—Very Best of Johnny Cash (Collectables COL-CD-6010)

I Would Like to See You Again (DCC Compact Classics DZS-192)

Johnny Cash (CD Sounds CDFX-6757)

Johnny Cash (Pegasus PEG078)

Johnny Cash (Sony Music Special Products A-8122)

Johnny Cash (Valmark 1171)

Johnny Cash Collection (Madacy 820)

Johnny Cash Is Coming to Town (Mer 832031-2)

Johnny Cash Sings His 20 Best (Teevee Records 6006)

Johnny 99 (Koch 7980)

Just As I Am (Vanguard 79530)

The Legend at His Best (Collectables 50)

Legends Collection (Dressed to Kill 58)

Live and on the Air (Double Gold 53054)

Live Recording (Fat Boy FATCD-235)

Living Legend (Teevee Records 6029)

Love (Col 65544)

Love and a .45 (Immortal EK-66632) [ST]

Love God Murder (Col 63809)

The Man in Black (KRB Music Companies KRB7024-2)

Man in Black—His Greatest Hits (Col 65712)

Man in Black, Vol. 1 (Bear Family BCD-15517)

Man in Black, Vol. 2 (Bear Family BCD-15562)

Man in Black, Vol. 3 (Bear Family BCD-15888)

The Many Sides of Johnny Cash (Sony Music Special Products 19845)

Maximum Audio Biography (Griffin Music 76)

The Mercury Years (Spectrum 5443262)

Murder (Col 65543)

The Mystery of Life (Mer 848051-2)

Now There Was a Song! (Legacy CK-66506)

Original Golden Hits, Vols. 1 and 2 (Collectables COL-CD-6435)

Patriot (Col CK-45384)

A Perfect World (Reprise 9-45516-2) [ST]

Personal Christmas Collection (Legacy CK-64154)

Return to the Promised Land (Renaissance 235) w. June Carter Cash

Ride This Train (Sony Music Special Products A-8255)

Ride This Train (K-Tel 75026-2)

Ring of Fire (Bear Family BCD-25345)

Ring of Fire (Goldies 25345)

Ring of Fire (Polygram 5509322)

Ring of Fire and Other Great Hits Live (BCD CTS-55441)

Ring of Fire—Best of Johnny Cash (Legacy CK-66890)

Ring of Fire/Blood, Sweat and Tears/Johnny Cash Sings the Ballads of the American Indian (Legacy C3K-64812)

Roads Less Traveled (Varese Sarabande 66214)

Rockabilly Blues (Koch 7979)

Showtime/Original Golden Hits, Vol. 3 (Collectables COL-CD-6433)

Simply the Best (Col 4837259)

Singing Storyteller/Rough Cut King of Country Music (Collectables COL-CD-6432) w. the Tennessee Two

Sings Ballads of the True West (DDC Compact Classics DZS-176)

Sings the Greatest Hits/Sings the Blue Train (Collectables COL-CD-6438)

16 Biggest Hits (Legacy CK-69779)

16 Biggest Hits, Vol. 2 (Legacy CK-85726)

The Sun Years (Original Sun Recordings 41005)

The Sun Years (Rhino R2-70950)

Sunday Down South/Sings Hank Williams (Collectables COL-CD-6432) w. Jerry Lee Lewis

Sunday Morning Comin' Down (DDC Compact Classics DZS-173)

Super Hits (Col CK-66773) w. June Carter Cash

The Survivors (Razor and Tie Music 82077) w. Jerry Lee Lewis, Carl Perkins

There You Go (Pegasus Flight Productions 409)

Things to Do in Denver When You're Dead (A&M 31454-0424-2) [ST]

30 Essential Hits (Heartland Music 1196-2)

39 Great Performances (Prism PLATBX-2203)

Unchained (American Recordings 69404)

Up Through the Years 1955-57 (Bear Family BCD-15247)

The Very Best of the Sun Years (Metro 45)

VH1 Storytellers (American Recordings 69416) w. Willie Nelson

Wanted Man (Mer 314-52279-2)

Wanted Man—The Very Best of Johnny Cash (TEN 654502)

Water From the Wells of Home (Rebound 520510; Rebound/Excelsior 440-060-3110)

The Wonderful World of Johnny Cash (BCD WMO-90319)

Cher and Sonny Bono on TV's *The Sonny and Cher Comedy Hour* in the early 1970s.
[Courtesy of JC Archives]

Cher

(b. Cherilyn Sarkisian, El Centro, California, May 20, 1946)

The outrageous Cher went through many dramatic career stages in her transformation from the trash queen to the queen of class. She was first a teenage backup singer; then, from the mid-'60s through the early '70s, the prettier half of the pop team of Sonny and Cher, noted for their sweet harmony. By the 1970s she had become an exotic (self-satirizing) sex symbol on TV, famed for her glamorous costumes, zany exhibitionism (especially the display of her navel), and sly humor. Then, having split from Sonny Bono in private life, she became a solo contralto singing act. She amazed the public when she moved her career into a new direction as a dramatic performer. After her solid emoting in *Silkwood* (1983) and *Mask* (1985), she struck gold with her Oscar-winning starring role in the romantic comedy *Moonstruck* (1987).

The blatantly direct Cher was far closer in temperament to the "me" generation of hard-rock stars than to any sultry vocalist of bygone eras. Once emancipated from Sonny, Cher became a brash solo attraction insisting on a self-sufficient lifestyle. Then, afterward, there seemed to be two Chers. There was the energetic middle-age woman (still displaying plenty of bare skin and tattoos), vying to remain contemporary in her singing and to out-trash the trashier of today's rock stars in her performance style. Equally dominant was the other Cher, whose self-determination shaped her into a charismatic screen presence. Tying together these wildly divergent personalities was the offstage, rebellious Cher. She was filled with excessive frankness, hyper emotions (ranging from super toughness to charming vulnerability), and an ever-present overpowering belief in herself.

She was born Cherilyn Sarkisian on May 20, 1946, in El Centro, California, the daughter of truck driver George Sarkisian and his teenage wife Jackie Jean (Crouch) Sarkisian. He was of Armenian descent; she was part Cherokee Indian. George Sarkisian was scarcely around when Cherilyn was a little child, and he and Jackie eventually divorced (they would marry and divorce twice more over the years). With her next husband, Jackie had another daughter named Georgeanne, and by then they were living in Los Angeles. Jackie was pursuing an acting career (while being a waitress) and changed her name to Georgia Holt. As Georgia Holt, she earned small roles in films and on television. (Some accounts have that she obtained her young daughters extra parts in such TV shows as *Ozzie and Harriet*.) As Jackie married and divorced, the family moved from place to place (including New York, Texas, and California). The girls also transferred from school to school, including a stay at Mother Cabrini's High School in the San Fernando Valley of California. It was Georgia's fifth husband, Gilbert LaPiere, who adopted both Cherilyn and Georgeanne. (Georgia would marry three more times.) He was a wealthy banker, and the girls attended private school. However, in 1962, at age sixteen, Cher dropped out of the educational system. She recalled later, "I was never really in school. I was always thinking about when I was grown up and famous." (Years later, she realized that she had been dyslexic as a child.) Cher moved out of her mother's house and in with a girlfriend in Hollywood, supporting herself with menial jobs.

With her long black hair, pronounced nose, and very thin legs, the bohemian Cher was more exotic than intriguing when she first met Sonny Bono in November 1962 at a Hollywood coffee shop. Born Salvatore Philip Bono in Detroit Michigan in 1935, he had been married (and was now separated) and had a four year-old daughter (Christy). He was a struggling songwriter/singer/promoter who could not make a success of the various recording-company ventures he had begun. He was then working as a subordinate to Hollywood-based pop-music entrepreneur Phil Spector. It was not long before the five-feet six-inches Sonny and the five-feet seven-inches Cher were living together. Cher began hanging around at Gold Star, and Phil Spector eventually used her to sing backup vocals for several of his performers, including the Ronettes, the Crystals, and Darlene Love. On some of these sessions, Sonny played percussion.

When Georgia Holt learned of Cher's new living arrangement, she demanded that her daughter return home. As a compromise, Cher moved to a women's residence and later, for a time, stayed in Arkansas with her mother and Georgeanne. Throughout this period, Cher continued dating Sonny and being part of the pop-music scene. In early 1964, deep-voiced Cher recorded the song "Ringo, I Love You" for Phil Spector's Annette Records to cash in on the early days of Beatlemania. However, Sonny, who had become her controlling influence, demanded that she use an alias for this recording (which he thought atrocious). Thus it was released as a (novelty) single featuring "Bonnie Jo Mason." Soon thereafter, Sonny, now divorced, began moving away from Spector's influence. He and Cher (billed as "Caesar and Cleo") recorded such singles as "The Letter" and "Love Is Strange," which received some air play. On October 27, 1964, Sonny and Cher were married in Tijuana, Mexico. (It later developed that this was an unofficial ceremony, and reportedly they renewed on December 13, 1965. Other sources state they were not married legally until 1969, just before the birth of their child.)

In November 1964, Sonny and Cher were hired as the opening act for Ike and Tina Turner at Hollywood's Purple Onion Club. Soon thereafter, Sonny arranged a recording contract for Cher with Imperial Records. In early 1965, Sonny and Cher were on concert tour, playing mostly one-night stands for $350 weekly. For Reprise, the team of Sonny and Cher sang "Baby Don't Go," a song he had written; it rose to number eight on the charts by the fall of 1965. Meanwhile, in mid-1965, Sonny negotiated a joint contract for the singing team of Sonny and Cher with Atco Records, a division of Atlantic Records. Their first Atco hit single was "I Got You Babe" (written by Bono). It rose to number one on the charts in the summer of 1965, beating out the latest songs of the Rolling Stones, Tom Jones, and Herman's Hermits for the top spot.

Suddenly the warm harmony and smooth sound of Sonny and Cher was "in," and the duo competed successfully with the British Invasion of the Beatles and the Motown Sound of the Supremes. Sonny and Cher had hits with the singles "But You're Mine" (1965) "What Now My Love" (1966), and "Little Man" (1966). Their joint album *Look at Us* (1965) was number two on the charts. Meanwhile, as a single performer on the Imperial label, Cher had a top-twenty hit with "All I Really Want to Do" (1965—the album of the same title was also in the top twenty), and her "Bang Bang (My Baby Shot Me Down)" was number two on the scoreboard in the spring of 1966. As a result of their prosperity, Sonny and Cher moved from a shabby Hollywood apartment to a $75,000 model home in Encino and thereafter to a thirty-one room Holmby Hills mansion with fancy cars and motorcycles.

Then came "The Beat Goes On," which rose to number six on the charts in early 1967. Along with "I Got You Babe," it was one of the two songs most associated with Sonny and Cher.

The team made several appearances on the teen-pop showcases *Hullabaloo* (NBC-TV) and *Shindig* (ABC-TV). They guested, along with Mitzi Gaynor and Jim Nabors, on Danny Thomas's NBC-TV special in January 1966. They were now instant celebrities adored by their young fans and invited to participate in jet-set partying. Cher expanded her range by designing a line of marketed wardrobe.

In 1965, Cher had sung the theme song for the Michael Caine movie *Alfie*. Together with Sonny, she had made a fleeting appearance in the independently produced *Wild on the Beach*, released by Twentieth Century-Fox. In this minor sand-and-music flick, Sonny and Cher sang "It's Gonna Rain," written by Bono. This movie and their performance had been so completely ignored that when they starred in Columbia Pictures' *Good Times* in the spring of 1967, it was promoted as their screen debut. Within *Good Times* they played themselves, with Sonny's character more interested than Cher's in expanding themselves into screen careers. In the scenario, they have several fantasy sequences as they imagine themselves starring in a variety of movie genres. The film was the debut feature directed by William Friedkin, who made a name for himself later with *The French Connection* (1971) and *The Exorcist* (1973). *Variety* reported, "Sonny and Cher are natural enough in their acting, but expectedly excel in their song numbers which they sock over in their customary style." Among their nine numbers were "I Got You Babe," "Good Times," and "I'm Gonna Love You." The movie was a flop, as was the album soundtrack.

Before *Good Times* was released Sonny and Cher had undertaken a European concert tour. After the movie failed, they attempted to resurrect their recording/concertizing career in the United States—it had been on hold during the many months of planning and filming their feature. The duo's "Plastic Man" (1967) never got beyond seventy-fourth position; however Cher's solo "You Better Sit Down Kids" (1967, written by Bono) reached number nine in the winter of 1967. It was her last single hit for four years. Almost as fast as they had risen to popularity, Sonny and Cher seemed to become passé by 1968. Their records were no longer selling, and their club dates and concert tours began to come from the bottom of the barrel. To reverse their career decline (and their overextended finances), Sonny wrote a screenplay to star Cher. When no Hollywood studio showed interest in the project, he mortgaged everything to raise the $300,000-plus needed to finance the venture. American International Pictures agreed to distribute it. The film, *Chastity* (1969), with music by Sonny, traced the maturation of an unhappy young woman (Cher) who takes to the roads in the Southwest. Despite meeting a succession of men, she remains chaste, always haunted by her troubled childhood. The arty movie, shot in Phoenix, Arizona, was a commercial dud that put the couple $190,000 in debt with back taxes. However, a few critics noted that deadpan Cher demonstrated traces of good instinctive acting. It was also in 1969 that Cher gave birth to their child, also named Chastity.

At a low professional ebb, Sonny determined they should try nightclubs, complete with a new image that moved away from their hippie costumes into more mainstream outfits. By 1970 the couple was booked into the Empire Room of the Waldorf-Astoria Hotel in New York City, and a good part of the act was focused on Cher's sexy gowns and her put-down wisecracks to her partner. In April 1971, as one of their frequent TV guest performances, they were substitute hosts on *The Merv Griffin Show* (CBS-TV). Network officials were sufficiently impressed by the duo to offer them a contract to star in *The Sonny and Cher Comedy Hour*. The summer replacement show debuted on August 1, 1971, and ran for six episodes. Because it did well enough in the ratings, the couple returned that December with a full-time show that enjoyed a three-season run. The weekly sixty minutes was filled typically with blackout skits, a recurring visit to "Sonny's Pizzeria," a stopover at the laundromat where housewife Cher chatted with her friend (Teri Garr), a satirical newscast portion, and a segment devoted to Cher portraying assorted "vamps" throughout history. And, of course, the couple sang a wide assortment of songs, always ending their show with "I Got You Babe." As contrasting images, Sonny was blithely optimistic and energetic; Cher—in her increasingly ridiculous outré fashions (by Bob Mackie)—was constantly putting her mate down with sardonic humor.

Now recording for MCA, the team's joint albums (including 1971's *All I Ever Need Is You* and 1972's *A Cowboy's Work Is Never Done*) did well. As a solo Cher had number-one hits with "Half-Breed" (1973) and "Dark Lady" (1974). Her solo album *Gypsys, Tramps and Thieves* (1971), which had been a number-one single hit, reached the number-sixteen spot on the charts. Sonny and Cher played Las Vegas clubs successfully.

Since the fall of 1972, Sonny and Cher had been romantically separated, and she dated, among others, record producer David Geffen. In February 1974, Sonny filed for legal separation from his wife of nine years. Fifty-eight hours later (February 22, 1974), they did their last TV series episode show together. That summer, the now-single Cher explained that when she had first met Sonny, "I was lonely. I was shy. I had absolutely no confidence. Son brought me up with a whole new set of values. . . . He was more of a mother to me than my own mother. But," she added, "now I have to break out. And Sonny's not willing to make the transition with me." Meanwhile, her ex-spouse sued her for contractual default.

Sonny floundered both on television (*The Sonny Comedy Revue* flopped on ABC-TV in the fall of 1974) and as an actor. Cher continued to record for Warner Bros. with unspectacular results. She also became the star of her own variety series, *Cher,* which debuted on February 16, 1975, on CBS. Somehow the magic was missing in her solo effort. Frequently her daughter Chastity appeared on the show, as did Sonny. One month after her show faded in January 1976, *The Sonny and Cher Show* began in February 1976 and would survive through mid-1977. But things were not the same. Cher had married rock singer Gregg Allman (a year her junior) three days after her divorce (June 27, 1975) from Sonny became final. She was soon involved in highly publicized separations and reconciliations with her new husband, who had a much-touted drug problem. She had his child (Elijah Blue) in July 1976, and thereafter their relationship was very much on-again, off-again. They were termed one of show business's strangest married couples till their union finally ended in 1978. All this adverse publicity, added to Cher's much-reported high style of living, had created a public backlash that contributed a great deal to the failure of the revived Sonny and Cher teaming.

By now Cher had developed renewed interest in acting. She was among those considered for the lead role in the remake of *A Star Is Born* (1976). However, once Barbra Streisand expressed a desire for the part, Cher (as well as nearly everyone else) was out of the running. In the late 1970s, Cher dated Gene Simmons of the rock group KISS. She signed with Casablanca Records, and in 1979 her song "Take Me Home" was number eight on the charts. The album of the same title, which contained some rock numbers, rose to number five. A later LP that year, *Prisoner,* featured an album cover photo of a nude Cher bound in chains. She had reached her peak of outlandishness. She sang in the major clubs of Las Vegas. (One of her routines used two female impersonators to team Cher with "Diana Ross" and "Bette Middler.") She had begun making music videos, such as "Hell on Wheels" a single from the *Prisoner* disc. Her friendship with Gene Simmons ended, and he began a romance with Cher's pal Diana Ross. She had a relationship with rock guitarist

Les Dudek, with whom she performed in the group Black Rose and with whom she made an album (that failed) in 1980. During this period, she starred in three TV specials (1978, 1979, and 1983).

Tiring of being "just" a splashy Las Vegas star (at $320,000 weekly) noted for high-fashion costumes and exotic living, Cher tried stage acting. She auditioned for and was signed by producer/director Robert Altman (whose wife was a friend of Cher's mother) for the Broadway stage production of *Come Back to the 5 and Dime, Jimmy Dean, Jimmy Dean* (1982). It dealt with five former members of a Jimmy Dean fan club having their twentieth anniversary reunion in a rundown Texas town of 1975. She played Sissy, the dime-store waitress with a broken heart. The show ran for sixty performances, and shortly after it closed Altman filmed a shoestring movie production of it, featuring Cher and members of the original cast (including Sandy Dennis and Karen Black). Like the play, it was considered an arty failure, more interesting for its oddball cast than for its dramatic content. Cher received a Golden Globe nomination for her on-camera performance.

One of those who had seen Cher onstage in *Jimmy Dean* was director Mike Nichols, who offered her the part (at $150,000) of Meryl Streep's lesbian girlfriend and plant coworker in the controversial motion picture *Silkwood* (1983). For her intense, unvarnished performance, Cher was Oscar-nominated but lost the Best Supporting Actress Academy Award to Linda Hunt (of *The Year of Living Dangerously*). She did win a Golden Globe for her performance. It was two years before she returned to the screen, this time in the sensitive drama *Mask* (1985), in which she was a pill-popping biker who has a lover (Sam Elliott) and is coping with her teenaged son (Eric Stoltz), who is suffering from a severe head deformity. There were as many conflicts between Cher and director Peter Bogdanovich as there were between Bogdanovich and Universal, who released the hard-to-position drama. Many felt (including Cher) that because she was so anti-Establishment, the industry bypassed her in the Oscar nominations. To show her scorn for the "system" she showed up at the Academy Awards that year in one of her most outlandish (tarantulalike) costumes. She did win the Cannes Film Festival Award as Best Actress.

Now based mostly in New York City and receiving as much attention from her health-spa commercials as from her still-controversial lifestyle, Cher returned to the screen three times in 1987. She was the star of *Suspect*, playing a dedicated public defender who is both helped and romanced by one of the jurors (Dennis Quaid) in the homicide case she is handling. Along with Susan Sarandon and Michelle Pfeiffer, she was one of three divorcees involved with Jack Nicholson, the mysterious rich visitor (from hell), who comes to a small New England town in *The Witches of Eastwick*. This horror comedy grossed $31.8 million in domestic film rentals. Even better was *Moonstruck*, a joyously romantic comedy set in Brooklyn where an Italian widow falls in love with her fiancée's headstrong younger brother (Nicolas Cage). As the focal point of this Italian-American set piece, Cher was spunky and radiant as the blossoming bookkeeper who responds so enthusiastically to her passionate young lover. This time she was Oscar-nominated and won! The movie grossed $34.393 million in domestic film rentals. She had broken her frustrating mold as part of Sonny and Cher and proved her point that "I refuse to accept other people's limitations." With her new sleek look, she made a "comeback" album for Geffen Records. *Cher* contained the hit song "I Found Someone," which was popular in both audio and music-video versions.

Now taken seriously as a dramatic actress and a bankable star (commanding $1 million per film when and if she chose one), Cher set up her own movie production firm, Isis Productions. She received a great deal of attention in 1988 for her romance with Rob Camilletti, a former doorman/bartender who was nearly twenty years her junior. He appeared in a rock video that she directed—tied in with one of her new LP albums. (The highly documented romance dissolved—temporarily—in mid-1989, and she soon activated a new romance with another younger man, a musician.) Meanwhile, in April 1988 she had appeared on the David Letterman TV late-night show in a reunion with Sonny (who had recently re-remarried and who would soon become mayor of Palm Springs, California.) They did an impromptu harmonizing of "I Got You Babe," appearing to have finally reconciled with each other and their joint past. Besides making a concert and nightclub tour, she promoted a new line of Cher perfume called Uninhibited. In addition to continuing to record, she also authored a nutrition book with Robert Haas (author of *Eat to Win*), as well as being announced to star in a new film comedy (*Mermaids*).

The much-anticipated *Mermaids* (1990), Cher's first feature in three years, told an implausible tale of a single mother who has a string of failed relationships and constantly moves to a new town always hoping to meet Mr. Right (but always being attracted to Mr. Wrong). Traipsing along with her are her two precocious daughters, a teenager (Winona Ryder) and her younger sister (Christina Ricci). Newly arrived in a Massachusetts town, the flamboyant mother meets a down-to-earth man (Bob Hoskins), while the older daughter makes a new friend, a young handyman working at a nearby Roman Catholic convent. As directed by Richard Benjamin, the movie emerged more an oddball and unrealistic entry than the touching drama intended. In reviewing the picture, Roger Ebert (*Chicago Sun Times*) noted that the leading role was "[n]ot only played by Cher, but in an eerie sense played as Cher, with perfect makeup and a flawless body that seems a bit much to hope for, given the character's lifestyle and diet. . . . [W]hat the movie is saying about Cher is as elusive as it is intriguing." Mostly due to the cachet of Cher's name, the middling entry grossed $35.4 million in domestic distribution.

The Cher of the new decade—who had just finished a glitzy Las Vegas–style eight-month *Heart of Stone* concert tour (named after her then-current album)—was, perhaps, best described by Kevin Sessums in his cover article on the vocalist for *Vanity Fair*'s November 1990 issue: "After twenty-five years of stardom, Cher is still a fascinating conundrum. She attracts men half her age, but is happiest surrounded by her 'golden girls.' She's a rocking rebel who doesn't mind that MTV banned her from daytime. She endures excruciating plastic surgery in an endless search for self-recognition. And her new movie, *Mermaids*, is a tribute to her mother—whom she's not speaking to." During the course of the profile, Cher stated of her unorthodox life in which Richie Sambora, guitarist for Jon Bon Jovi's group, was her current boyfriend: "I'm not running for office. I'm not a role model. I'm just living my life."

In 1991, when not making tabloid headlines with her bagel boy-toy Rob Camilletti, she released *Love Hurts* for David Geffen's label. She had a fitness video, *Cherfitness: A New Attitude*, that year, which became a big seller in the genre, followed by the almost as popular *Body Confidence* home video in 1992. Cher was among the myriad of stars who made cameo appearances in *The Player* (1992), Robert Altman's study of contemporary Hollywood. Two years later, the exotic actress did another cameo for Altman, this time in his less-successful *Prêt-à-Porter* [Ready to Wear]. Now forty-eight, the hip celebrity informed the media: "In the past I was always afraid, always protecting myself from showing too much to the world. But now I don't care anymore. I know who I am . . . and it's a great feeling." Having sold her ski lodge in Aspen, Colorado, she was house-hunting in France. Her boyfriend of the moment was twenty-five-year-old British actor John Barrowman.

In 1996, Cher, who had been suffering from chronic-fatigue syndrome, released her first new album (*It's a Man's World*) in five years. Writing for www.allmusic.com, Jose Probis analyzed that the disc could "safely be labeled as one of the singer's finest, as well as one of her most overlooked and underappreciated discs. Full of steamy, torchy ballads, Western-themed epics, and R&B influences, the album finds the singer sounding vocally relaxed and self-assured." Also that year the long-delayed-into-release *Faithful* emerged. In it, she and her husband (Ryan O'Neal) have been wed for twenty years, and she now discovers that he has hired a hit man (Chazz Palminteri) to eliminate her so he can collect the insurance money. It had scant release and was a box-office dud. Bringing readers up to date on Cher, *Us* magazine detailed, "The tabloid queen is still visible, defiantly ready to fight off age with younger men, plastic surgery and sass to spare. Check out those tattoos. No doubt you've also seen her ads for Equal, her infomercials for hair- and skin-care products, her perfume—Uninhibited—and her Sanctuary catalog, offering accessories in all things Gothic."

On October 28, 1996, Cher was at Radio City Music Hall for the gala celebrating *GQ* magazine's first Man of the Year Award. She sang "It's a Man's World." The event was taped for a VH1 cable TV special. Also that month the star made her directing debut by helming the "1996" segment of the controversial abortion-story trilogy *If These Walls Could Talk* (HBO cable, October 13, 1996). In her segment, which featured Anne Heche and Jada Pinkett-Smith, Cher played a physician confronted with the abortion issue.

For a change, it was not Cher who caused huge tabloid headlines in early 1998. It was the strange death of her ex-husband Sonny Bono, who had become a U.S. Congressman in the 1994 elections. He had gone skiing at Lake Tahoe with his young wife (Mary Whitaker) and their two children. Sonny had disappeared while skiing on an intermediate slope. Later his frozen body was found; he had died of massive head injuries from having skied head-on into a forty-feet-high pine tree. Thereafter it was suggested that prescription medication may have disoriented him on the slopes. At his funeral a few days later Cher provided a tearful eulogy, creating some controversy among those who felt she was trying to upstage Sonny's current wife in the grief department. In the spring, while Sonny's widow was running/winning the special election to fill Sonny's Congressional vacancy, Cher was taping her hosting chores of a one-hour TV special, *Sonny and Me,* which debuted in May 1998. That November her book, *The First Time,* written with Jeff Copion, was published. It contained short vignettes on various "firsts" in her life, which ranged from the exotic to the mundane and cheesy. Her creative output in 1998 also included the album *Believe,* and its exuberant title song single became an international hit, a big favorite at dance clubs. (The single went to the top of charts, providing Cher with number-one pop songs in four decades—an achievement not equalled by another pop singer.)

The year 1999 found Cher singing the National Anthem at the Super Bowl, and she was back on the screen in Franco Zeffirelli's autobiographical movie, *Tea With Mussolini.* She played an American adventuress and art collector caught in Florence, Italy, at the start of World War II. Regarding her role in this arty picture, she said, "It was hard for me to become someone who was downright spoiled rotten. . . . I'm used to being the heroic girl." She taped her spectacular stage show—filled with her lavish costumes and complex choreography—at the MGM Grand in Las Vegas, and it turned up as an HBO cable special on August 29, 1999.

Bouncing back and forth between her London apartment and her U.S. digs, Cher released her album *not.com.mercial,* which was available for sale only through her Internet Website. The disc contained many songs that she had penned herself. In 2001, she was still working on the (re)decoration of her Malibu home, an estate worth $25 million. In midyear, Mattel toys issued its Cher doll clad in a Bob Mackie gown. Also that year Mark Bego's biography *Cher: If You Believe* was published, detailing the star's life behind the scenes. On November 26, 2001, in London, England, the singer was one of the stars at the Royal Variety Performance, a charity-raising event. During the January 2002, American Music Awards, Cher—wearing a shoulder-length blonde wig—sang "Song for the Lonely," a tune from her latest album, *Living Proof.*

As the new century progressed, Cher continued to release new and compilation albums and most of all, remained a one-of-a-kind personality. The star of the new millennium, who over the years had had her nose, breasts, and teeth restructured, once admitted, "I do keep wondering about how much longer I'll be able to dress the way I want to dress and get away with it." (Obviously, that day has not yet arrived.) She also said, "I'm not a role model, but trust me: if I could accomplish this thing [career success] that seemed impossible, you can accomplish anything you want to do. It's not me, it's just people need symbols along the way to remind them, Yes I can do this." As to her position in the world of show business, she acknowledged, "Some years I'm the coolest thing that ever happened, and then the next year everyone's so over me, and I'm just so past my sell date."

Filmography

Cher

Alfie (Par, 1965) (voice only)
Roller Boogie (UA, 1979) (voice only)
Come Back to the 5 and Dime, Jimmy Dean, Jimmy Dean (Cinecom International, 1982)
Silkwood (Par, 1983)
Mask (Univ, 1985)
The Witches of Eastwick (WB, 1987)
Suspect (TriStar, 1987)

Moonstruck (MGM/UA, 1987)
Mermaids (Orion, 1990)
The Player (Fine Line, 1992)
Prêt-à-Porter [Ready to Wear] (Miramax, 1994)
Faithful (New Line, 1996) (made in 1994)
If These Walls Could Talk (HBO cable, 10/13/96) (also director of her segment "1996")
Tea With Mussolini (G2 Films/MGM, 1999)

Sonny and Cher

Wild on the Beach (20th-Fox, 1965) (also songs by Sonny)
Good Times (Par, 1966) (also songs by Sonny)

Chastity (AIP, 1969) (also producer, script, and music for Sonny who did not appear in this feature)

Broadway Plays

Come Back to the 5 and Dime, Jimmy Dean, Jimmy Dean (1982)

TV Series

Sonny and Cher Comedy Hour (CBS, 1971–74; 1976–77)

Cher (CBS, 1975–76)

Album Discography

LPs

Cher

All I Really Want To Do (Imperial 12292)
Backstage (Imperial 12373)
The Best of Cher, Vols. 1–2 (Liberty 10110/11)
Bittersweet White Light (MCA 2101)
Black Rose (Casablanca) w. Les Dudek
Chastity (Atco 302) [ST]
Cher (Geffen 6HS-24164)
Cher (Imperial 12320)
Cher Backstage (Imperial 12373)
Cher Superpak, Vols. 1-2 (UA 88, 94)
Cherished (WB 3046)
Dark Lady (MCA 2113)
Days of Thunder (Geffen DGC-24294) [ST]
Foxy Lady (Kapp 5514)
Golden Greats (Imperial 12406)
Greatest Hits (MCA 2127)

Gypsies, Tramps and Thieves (Kapp 3649)
Half-Breed (MCA 2104)
Heart of Stone (Geffen GHS-24239)
I Paralyze (CBS 38096)
I'd Rather Believe in You (WB 2898)
Prisoner (Casablanca 7184)
Roller Boogie (Casablanca NBLP-2-7194) [ST]
The Sonny Side of Cher (Imperial 9301/12301)
Stars (WB 2850)
Take Me Home (Casablanca 7133)
3614 Jackson Highway (Atco SD-33-298)
This Is Cher (Sunset 5276)
Two the Hard Way (WB K-3120) w. Gregg All-man [Cher billed as Woman]
The Very Best of Cher (UA 377)
With Love (Imperial 12358)

Sonny and Cher

All I Ever Need Is You (Kapp 3660, MCA 2021)
Baby Don't Go (Reprise 6177)
The Beat Goes On (Atco 11000)
The Best of Sonny and Cher (Atco 233-219)
Buster (Atlantic 81905-1) [ST]
Good Times (Atco 33-214) [ST]
Greatest Hits (Atco A2S-5178, MCA 2117)
In Case You're in Love (Atco SD-33-203)

Look at Us (Atco SD-33-177)
Sonny and Cher Live (Kapp 3654)
Sonny and Cher Live in Las Vegas, Vol. 2 (MCA 2-8004)
The Two of Us (Atco SD-2-804)
Wild on the Beach (RCA LPM/LSP-3441) [ST]
The Wondrous World of Sonny and Cher (Atco SD-33-183)

CDs

Cher

All I Really Want to Do/The Sonny Side of Cher (EMI E21Y-80241)
All Or Nothing, Part 1 (WEA-212CD)
All Or Nothing, Part 2 (WEA 398421272)
Bang Bang and Other Hits (EMI-Capitol Special Markets 56684)
Bang Bang: The Best of Cher (EMI E21Y-92773)
Bang Bang: The Early Years (Capitol/EMI 99900)
Basic—Original Hits (Disky 600532)
Behind the Door 1964-74 (Raven RVCD-108)
Believe (WB 44576, WB 47121)
The Best of Cher (EMI E21K-91838)
The Best of Cher—20th Century Masters: The Millennium Collection (MCA 112-154)
Bittersweet: The Love Songs Collection (MCA MCAD-11899)
The Casablanca Years (Casablanca/Mercury 532320)
Cher (Geffen 24164-2)
Cher and Sonny and Cher—Greatest Hits (MCA MCAD-11745)
City of Subacus (Cher Doll/Darla DRL-055CD)

Dov'e L'Amore, Part 2 (WEA 8573803932)
Favorites (Masters 1182)
Greatest Hits (MCA MCAD-922)
Greatest Hits (PID 56328)
Greatest Hits (WEA 280420)
Greatest Hits (WEA 8573804202)
Greatest Hits (WMU 751352)
Greatest Hits 1965-92 (Geffen 24439)
Gypsies, Tramps and Thieves (MCA MCAD-31376, Universal Special Markets 31376, WEA 3804702)
Gypsies, Tramps and Thieves: 25 Great Songs (BCD MPG-74017, MSI 113681)
Half Breed (Laserlight 46-140)
Half Breed/Dark Lady (Polygram 0030945MCD)
Heart of Stone (Geffen 24239-2)
Holdin' Out For Love (Plans CD7089)
I Paralyze (Col CK-38096, Varese Sarabande VSD-6039)
If I Could Turn Back Time: Cher's Greatest Hits (Geffen 24509-2)
It's a Man's World (Reprise 46179)

Living Proof (WEA 42463)

Love Hurts (Geffen GEFD-24421, Geffen Goldline CEFD-24369)

The Magic Collection (ARC EC-949049)

Maximum (Chrom ABCD029)

Maximum Audio Biography (Griffin Music 29)

Maximum Cher (Griffin Music 2872)

Millennium Edition (Inter 4905962)

not.com.mercial (Isis 0119010102)

One by One (Reprise 43643)

Original Hits (Disky BA-860222)

Outrageous (BR Music RM-1556)

Pop Giants (Polygram 5541042)

Silkwood (DRG DRGCD-6107) [ST]

Sing-A-Long (Priddis Music)

Story (EMI P-5761410)

Strong Enough (WB 44644)

Strong Enough/Believe (WEA WPCR-10224)

Strong Enough, Part 1 (WEA 398426621)

Sunny (EMI 5316982)

Take Me Home (Spectrum 5500382)

Take Me Home (Universal Special Markets 52051)

A Tribute to Cher (Big Eye)

The Way of Love: The Cher Collection (MCA 560-209)

Universal Masters Collection (Polygram 490528206069)

With Love (EMI 53172121)

With Love, Cher + Four (PID 563762)

You Better Sit Down Kids (Disky 865672)

You Better Sit Down Kids (EMI SE-865672)

Sonny and Cher

All I Ever Need Is You (Universal Special Markets 22025)

All I Ever Need Is You/MCA Anthology (MCA MCAD2-11300)

The Beat Goes On: The Best of Sonny and Cher (Atco 91796-2)

The Beat Goes On: The Best of Sonny and Cher (Rhino R2-91796)

Buster (Atlantic 81905-2) [ST]

Good Times (One Way Records OW-35140) [ST]

I Got You Babe! Rhino Special Edition (Rhino R2-71233)

In Case You're In Love (Sundazed Music 6139)

Singles (And More) (BR Music BS82142)

The Wondrous World of Sonny and Cher (Sundazed Music 6140)

Maurice Chevalier

(b. Maurice Auguste Chevalier, Paris, France, September 12, 1888; d. Paris, France, January 1, 1972)

The word "charmer" has been used to characterize many entertainers over the decades, but perhaps no one exemplified its meaning more than boulevardier Maurice Chevalier. With his bright smile, Gallic charm, and straw hat, he charmed generations of theater and moviegoers. Although Chevalier freely admitted he was a man of limited talents, he used his distinctive abilities to their utmost, and he hewed his act to perfection. He presented a picture of a happy-go-lucky Parisian who never took life seriously and always found romance. It was an image that remained with him throughout his life. Chevalier chronicler R. A. Israel summed it up, "The ease, the charm, the droll insights, the physical dexterity, the incredible ability to create meaningful characters in a seemingly effortless manner was astonishing, but not accidental."

The perennial entertainer was born Maurice Auguste Chevalier in Paris on September 12, 1888, the son of a house painter and his Flemish wife. The family was quite poor, and several of the ten offspring (Maurice was the next-to-youngest child) died at an early age. When Chevalier was eight, his father left the family, and Maurice did not see him again for nearly two decades. Life was miserable for the Chevaliers, and after only brief schooling, young Maurice had to go to work at a variety of jobs, always losing them because of his daydreaming about either becoming an acrobat or a singer. In 1900, he began working as an amateur singer, and he became a professional the next year billed as "Le Petit Chevalier," singing in cafes around Paris and its suburbs. He eventually toured the provinces and performed in Belgium. Thus he grew into manhood through the vagabond life of a cabaret entertainer, and in 1907 he became the head singer at Paris's Eldorado Club, leading to three seasons of work with the prestigious Folies Bergère. By now, he also danced and used comedy in his act, in addition to songs, and he was much in demand. In 1909, he met the esteemed French star Mistinguett, who took the much younger man as her stage partner and lover; they worked together adroitly for a decade. During this period, Maurice also began making silent films, the first being *Trop Crédule* in 1908. Starting in 1910, he appeared in a trio of movie shorts with the noted French film comedian Max Linder.

In 1913, Chevalier joined the French army, although he continued to appear in tandem with Mistinguett, and they filmed their act in a 1914 short, *La Valse Renversante*. When France joined the Allies in World War I, Chevalier's Thirty-first Infantry regiment was sent to Germany, and during an assault on a small village he was wounded and taken prisoner. He spent the remainder of the war in a prisoner-of-war camp at Alten Grabow, where he worked as a pharmacist's assistant and learned English from a British prisoner. When the Red Cross obtained an exchange-of-prisoners pact, Maurice returned home in 1916, and the next year was awarded the Croix de Guerre. In Paris, he returned to the Folies Bergère with Mistinguett, and the duo made a second film, *Une Soirée Mondaine* (1917). Two years later, he appeared in London with Elsie Janis in the revue

Maurice Chevalier and Jeanette MacDonald in *The Love Parade* (1929).
[Courtesy of JC Archives]

Hullo, America, and then returned home to do the same show as *Hullo, Paris*. By now the entertainer had split with Mistinguett and became the headliner at the Casino de Paris, also starring successfully in the operetta *Dede*. He then came to America planning to produce the show in the United States, but his efforts came to naught and he suffered a nervous breakdown.

During his recuperation, Chevalier became attached to dancer Yvonne Vallee. During the 1920s, he toured the provinces and made several feature films, most of which he produced. He and Yvonne were wed in 1926, and the next year they went to London to headline the *White Birds* revue. MGM's Irving Thalberg saw Chevalier performing at the Casino de Paris and had him test for the movies, but no studio contract was forthcoming. However, Jesse L. Lasky also saw the test, and the Frenchman was signed by Paramount, the most cosmopolitan of the Hollywood studios, to appear in talkies.

Maurice Chevalier made his sound-film debut in 1928 in the three-reel, American-shot trave-logue film *Bonjour, New York!* By now his image as the debonair, carefree Frenchman, in a tuxedo and straw hat (which was suggested by cabaret star Gaby Delys), was well established, as was his singing of the song favorite "Valentine." Hollywood would not alter the basic Chevalier image, but his half dozen years in the film capital would greatly expand his song catalog. This extension of his repertory was inaugurated by his initial English-language feature film, *Innocents of Paris* (1929), in which he sang his most famous song, "Louise." Although modestly mounted, the sentimental musical proved to be a good showcase for Chevalier, and he appealed immediately to moviegoers in America and elsewhere. *The Love Parade* (1929), the first of a quartet of very sophisticated features with Jeanette MacDonald, followed, and in it he sang the title song. In the studio's all-star revue, *Paramount on Parade* (1930), he performed "All I Want Is Just One Girl," but his biggest hit came at the film's finale when he sang "Sweeping the Clouds Away." He also headlined the French-language version of the movie. In 1930, he costarred with Claudette Colbert in the English and French editions of *The Big Pond* (a froufrou about the manufacture of liquor-flavored gum) singing "You Brought a New Kind of Love to Me." That same year, with a new contract (four films for $1 million), he starred in the English and French versions of *Playboy of Paris*, with Frances Dee, performing "My Ideal."

Chevalier sang "One More Hour of Love" in *The Smiling Lieutenant* in 1931, which again paired him with Claudette Colbert in English and French versions. Off-camera he was romancing Paramount leading ladies Kay Francis and Marlene Dietrich. Next he starred with Jeanette MacDonald, for the second time, in the urbane *One Hour With You* (1932), which gave him the popular title tune plus "Oh, That Mitzi!"; the duo (whose strong egos clashed offscreen) also made the French version. Chevalier did a guest bit as himself in Paramount's *Make Me a Star* (1932), as well as a cameo in the Masquers Club all-star detective spoof short *The Slippery Pearls* (1932). The same year, after a visit to Paris, he was seen as himself in *Battling Georges* [Toboggan], which starred his close friend, boxing champion Georges Carpentier.

Back in Hollywood, Chevalier, who was tiring of his successful but limited one-dimensional charming playboy screen roles, costarred with Jeanette MacDonald for the third time in *Love Me Tonight* (1932), which gave him the songs "Mimi" and "Isn't It Romantic?" By 1933 the stereotyping was affecting his box office. Neither *A Bedtime Story* nor *The Way to Love* (also issued in a French version as *L'Amour Guide*) gave him any memorable songs to sing. Audiences were tiring of seeing him in a succession of all-too-similar, fake Paris tales. Chevalier and Paramount ended their contract, and he moved over to MGM at the suggestion of second-in-command Irving Thalberg.

The first Metro-Goldwyn-Mayer project was to be *The Merry Widow*. Ernst Lubitsch, who had directed Chevalier's most successful Paramount vehicles, was to direct the operetta, and opera diva Grace Moore was to costar. But after a billing dispute she withdrew, and much against Chevalier's will, Jeanette MacDonald was substituted. The glittery production was extremely expensive to produce, and neither it nor its French language edition, *La Veuve Joyeuse*, could recoup the enormous expense. Chevalier was loaned to United Artists for *Folies Bergère* (1935) with Merle Oberon and Ann Sothern, and he had a trio of memorable tunes: "I Was Lucky," "The Rhythm of the Rain," and "I Don't Stand a Ghost of a Chance With You." Once again, neither it nor its French language version, *L'Homme des Folies-Bergère*, was particularly popular.

Back at MGM, the executives decided to try to team Chevalier with Grace Moore, but he preferred MacDonald. When she declined the offer and he could not decide upon a proper vehicle, his MGM contract was dissolved. He now left Hollywood and returned to Paris. His wife had left him in the early 1930s (their only child died after birth in 1927), because she did not enjoy Hollywood life, and they were divorced in 1939. During the time he was in Hollywood, Chevalier recorded most of his popular movie numbers for Victor Records, plus other songs such as "Hello Beautiful," "There Ought to Be a Moonlight Saving Time," and "Walking My Baby Back Home." Chevalier had been recording since 1919, and after returning to Paris he continued to record for Victor's British label HMV (His Master's Voice) through 1941.

Upon his return to his homeland, Chevalier appeared in two 1936 French releases, *L'Homme du Jour* and *Avec le Sourire*, and then went to England, where he topped the cast in *Break the News* (1936) and *The Beloved Vagabond* (1937), the latter of which was also produced in a French-language version. He continued to work in music halls, and in 1939 starred in Robert Siodmak's *Pièges*, his last film for the duration of World War II.

By now France was involved in the war, and Maurice remained inactive professionally, except for occasional appearances. One of these was at the German prisoner-of-war camp Alten Grabow, the same place he had been a prisoner in the previous war; he entertained French prisoners and worked for the exchange of several of his incarcerated countrymen. For his efforts he was branded a collaborator, and in 1944, published reports insisted he had been killed. When the war was over, Chevalier was exonerated of charges of aiding the Nazis, but the stigma stayed with him for a long time.

In 1947, Maurice returned to filmmaking in Rene Clair's comedy *Le Silence Est d'Or*, which found him in a new persona, that of the older man who loses the girl to someone her own age; in the United States it was shown as *Man About Town*. That year also saw him make a triumphant return to the United States, taking his one-man show to New York City. It was his first Gotham appearance since working in vaudeville there a dozen years before. While in the United States, he newly recorded his standards "Louise" and "Valentine" for RCA Victor with Henri Rene and His Orchestra, and he also appeared on several network radio shows such as *Philco Radio Time* with Bing Crosby. In 1949, he starred in the Mutual radio series *This Is Paris*, and for the next several years he made films in France; performed his one-man show throughout Europe, England and the United States; and recorded for labels like Pathé, Vox, and London.

In 1955, the French star came to American TV with *The Maurice Chevalier Show*, a special on NBC-TV, and in 1957, he did the documentary *Maurice Chevalier's Paris*. That year also saw his return to American films in Billy Wilder's bittersweet comedy *Love in the Afternoon*, which found him as an engaging detective whose pretty daughter (Audrey Hepburn) becomes attracted to an older American (Gary Cooper). This picture gave Chevalier a good song—its theme—"Fascination." In 1958, sixty-year old Maurice Chevalier had one of the biggest successes of his career, the role of the roué playboy uncle in *Gigi*. It provided him with two additional trademark songs: "Thank Heaven for Little Girls" and "I'm Glad I'm Not Young Anymore," plus a poignant duet with Hermione Gingold on "I Remember It Well."

The MGM musical's success (and multiple Oscar wins) catapulted Chevalier into the kind of stardom he had not enjoyed since his U.S. film debut nearly three decades earlier. As a result, he made a string of long-playing record albums for MGM Records, as well as appearing on a variety of TV shows, including *The Lucille Ball–Desi Arnaz Comedy Hour* and a CBS-TV presentation of his one-man show (February 4, 1960). On February 23, 1967, he starred on the ABC-TV special *C'est la Vie*, the first American-French program from Paris in color.

Gigi also revitalized Maurice Chevalier's movie career, although now he mainly acted as a character star. For MGM he did the comedy *Count Your Blessings* (1959), followed by the gaudy musical *Can-Can* (1960), with Shirley MacLaine and Frank Sinatra, in which he sang "Just One of Those Things" and "I Love Paris." He provided support to Sophia Loren and John Gavin in *A Breath of Scandal* (1960) and appeared as himself in *Pepe* (1960). He had a fine acting assignment in *Fanny* (1961) as the older man who marries the young daughter (Leslie Caron) of his friend (Charles Boyer) so her unborn child will have a father. Chevalier enthused about the part, "In *Fanny* for the first time I've done a character far away from Maurice Chevalier. I found it enjoyable to create a man with a personality not my own." *Jessica* (1962) gave him the opportunity to both sing and act as a priest who advises the curvaceous title character (Angie Dickinson) on the dangers of lust.

For Walt Disney, he made the well-executed *In Search of the Castaways* (1962) as a scientist searching for a missing sea captain, and he appeared as himself in the Paul Newman–Joanne Woodward romantic comedy *A New Kind of Love* (1963). In the mediocre comedy *Panic Button* (1964), he was a divorced man romancing a younger woman (Jayne Mansfield), while in *I'd Rather Be Rich* (1964), he inherited an old Charles Laughton role as Sandra Dee's grandfather who pretends to be terminally ill in order to see her married. This well-mounted but mostly overlooked film, reteamed him with Hermione Gingold. His final two features were for Walt Disney: *Monkey, Go Home!* (1967) cast him as a priest who aids a young American (Dean Jones) who has inherited an olive farm and plans to use monkeys to harvest the crop; while in the cartoon feature *The Aristocats* (1970) he sang the title song.

After numerous "farewell tours," Chevalier retired from the stage in 1968 following several concerts in Paris. He spent the remainder of his life on his country estate outside Paris, with his companion, Odette Meslier-Junet, and her young mute daughter, Pascale. Maurice died January 1, 1972, at the age of 83, as the result of a kidney ailment. The entertainer left an estate valued at $20 million and many awards, including France's Legion d'Honneur and Ordre Merite National, Belgium's Order of Leopold, and a special 1959 Academy Award. He also left behind four engaging volumes of published memoirs, *The Man in the Straw Hat* (1949), *With Love* (1960), *I Remember It Well* (1970), and *My Paris* (1972).

In 1993, two new biographies of the famed entertainer were published: Edward Behr's *The Good Frenchman: The True Story of the Life and Times of Maurice Chevalier* and David Bret's *Maurice Chevalier: On Top of a Rainbow*. In 1997, Gustav Vintas was performing *Merci Maurice*, his one-man show based on the life and music of the legendary Chevalier.

Filmography

Trop Crédule (Fr, 1908) (s)
Un mariée Qui Se Fait Attendre (Fr, 1911) (s)
La Mariée Récalcitrante (Fr, 1911) (s)
Par Habitude (Fr, 1911) (s)
La Valse Renversante (Fr, 1914) (s)
Une Soirée Mondaine (Fr, 1917) (s)
Le Mauvais Garçon (Fr, 1922)
Le Match Criqui-Ledoux (Fr, 1922)
Gonzague (Fr, 1923)
L'Affaire de la Rue de Lourcine (Fr, 1923)
Jim Bougne, Boxeur (Fr, 1923)
Par Habitude (Fr, 1924)
Bonjour, New York! (Fr, 1928) (travelogue)
Innocents of Paris (Par, 1929)*

The Love Parade (Par, 1930)*
Paramount on Parade (Par, 1930)*
The Big Pond (Par, 1930)*
Playboy of Paris (Par, 1930)*
The Smiling Lieutenant (Par, 1931)*
El Cliente Seductor (Sp, 1931) (s)
One Hour With You (Par, 1932)*
Make Me a Star (Par, 1932)
Battling Georges [Toboggan] (Fr, 1932)
Hollywood on Parade #5 (Par, 1932) (s)
Love Me Tonight (Par, 1932)
The Stolen Jools [The Slippery Pearls] (Masquers Club, 1932) (s)
Stopping the Show (Par, 1932) (s) (voice only)

A Bedtime Story (Par, 1933)
The Way to Love (Par, 1934)*
The Merry Widow (MGM, 1934)*
Folies Bergère [The Man From the Folies Bergère] (UA, 1935)*
The Beloved Vagabond (Br, 1936)*
L'Homme du Jour [The Man of the Hour] (Fr, 1936)
Avec le Sourire [With a Smile] (Fr, 1936)
Break the News (Br, 1938)
Pièges [Personal Column] (Fr, 1939)
Paris 1900 (Fr, 1946) (documentary)
Le Silence Est d'Or [Man About Town] (Fr, 1947)
Paris 1900 (Fr, 1948) (documentary)
Le Roi [A Royal Affair] (Fr, 1949)
Ma Pomme [Just Me] (Fr, 1950)
Schlager-parade (Ger, 1953)
Jouons le Jeu . . . l'Avarice (Fr, 1953) (s)
Chevalier de Menilmontant (Fr, 1953) (s)
Caf'Conc (Fr, 1953) (s)
Cento Anni d'Amore [A Hundred Years of Love] (It, 1954)
J'Avais Sept Filles [My Seven Little Sins] (Br, 1955)

Sur Toute la Gamme (Fr, 1954) (s) (narrator)
Rendez-vous avec Maurice Chevalier (Fr, 1956) (documentary)
The Heart of Show Business (Col, 1956) (s)
Love in the Afternoon (AA, 1957)
The Happy Road (MGM, 1957) (voice only)
Gigi (MGM, 1958)
Count Your Blessings (MGM, 1959)
Can-Can (20th-Fox, 1960)
Un, Deux, Trois, Quatre! [Black Tights] (Fr, 1960) (narrator)
A Breath of Scandal (Par, 1960)
Pepe (Col, 1960)
Fanny (WB, 1961)
Jessica (UA, 1962)
In Search of the Castaway (BV, 1962)
A New Kind of Love (Par, 1963)
Panic Button (Gorton Associates, 1964)
I'd Rather Be Rich (Univ, 1964)
Monkeys, Go Home! (1967)
The Aristocats (BV, 1970) (voice only)
Le Chagrin et la Pitie [The Sorrow and the Pity] (Fr, 1972) (documentary)
*Also starred in the French-language version

Radio Series

This Is Paris (Mutual, 1949)

Album Discography

LPs

A La Chevalier (AEI 2125)
The Art of Maurice Chevalier (London International 91183)
Bing Crosby, Groucho Marx and Maurice Chevalier—Live (Amalgamated 221)
Black Tights (RCA FOC/FSO-3) [ST]
Bravo Maurice! (ASV 5034)
A Breath of Scandal (Imperial 9132) [ST]
Can-Can (Cap W/SW-1301) [ST]
Chevalier Chante Paris (RCA 540-036)
Chevalier's Paris (Col CL-1049)
Deux Fois Vingt Ans (EMI/Pathé 240-356)
The Early Years (World Record Club SH-120)
Encore Maurice! (ASV 5016)
Franco-American Hits (9CBS 63447)
Gigi (Col WL-158) [ST—French]
Gigi (MGM/E-SE-3641) [ST]
Hollywood, 1929-32 (EMI/Pathé 240-639)
In Search of the Castaways (Disneyland 3916) [ST]
Jessica (UA UAL-4097/UAS-5096) [ST]
Lerner and Loewe and Chevalier (MGM E/SE-4015)
Life Is Just a Bowl of Cherries (MGM E/SE-3801)
Love Me Tonight (Caliban 6047) [ST]

Love Parade/One Hour With You/Love Me Tonight (Ariel CMF 23) [ST]
Maurice (EMI/Pathé C162-1186/9)
Maurice Chevalier (Col CL-568)
Maurice Chevalier (Emidsic CO48-50656)
Maurice Chevalier (Pickwick 3161) w. Paul Mauriat
Maurice Chevalier (10″ RCA LPT-3042)
Maurice Chevalier (Time S/2072)
Maurice Chevalier at 80 (Epic FXS-15117)
Maurice Chevalier Sings (Metro M/S-533)
Maurice Chevalier Sings (Vox 30020)
Maurice Chevalier Sings Broadway (MGM E/SE-3738)
Maurice Chevalier Sings Early Movie Hits (World Record Club SH-156)
Maurice Chevalier, Vol. 1 (RCA LPV-564)
The Merry Widow (Hollywood Soundstage 5015) [ST]
The Merry Widow/The Love Parade (Amalgamated 240) [ST]
A Musical Tour of France (Disneyland 3940)
One Hour With You (Caliban 6011) [ST]
Originals, 1935-47 (10″ HMV CLP-1640)

Paramount on Parade (Caliban 6044) [ST]

Paris Je T'Aimee (10″ Vox 3180)

Paris to Broadway (MGM E/SE-4120)

Pepe (Colpix 507) [ST]

Playboy of Paris/The Way to Love/The Beloved Vagabond (Caliban 6013) [ST]

Poemes de Jehan Rictus (London International 91065)

Quatre Fois Vingt Ans (EMI/Pathé 240-732)

Rendezvous a Paris, Vols. 1-3 (London International 91078-80)

A Royal Affair (10″ Audio Archives 0026) [ST]

A Salute to Al Jolson (Metro M/S-595)

Sixty Years of Song (London 56001-4)

Souvenir, 1928-48 (Cap SPBO-10549)

Teen Street (Buena Vista 3313) w. Hayley Mills

Thank Heaven for Girls (MGM E/SE-3835)

Thank Heaven for Maurice Chevalier (RCA LPM-2076)

That's Entertainment! (MCA MCA2-11002) [ST]

That's Entertainment, Part 2 (MGM MG-1-5301) [ST]

This Is Maurice Chevalier (RCA VPM-6055)

Today (MGM E/SE-3703)

Toujours Maurice (Camden CAL-579)

A Tribute to Al Jolson (MGM E/SE-3773)

Trois Fois Vingt Ans (EMI/Pathé 240-170)

The Very Best of Maurice Chevalier (MGM E/SE-4205)

We Remember Him Well (MGM 2353-055)

Yesterday (MGM E/SE-3702)

Yesterday and Today (MGM 2E/2SE-5)

You Brought a New Kind of Love to Me (Monmouth Evergreen 7028)

The Young Maurice Chevalier (Cap T-10360)

CDs

Au Temps Du Charleston (EMI 7868402)

Au Temps Du Charleston (Music Memoria 30218)

Best Recordings (BMG UN3-411)

Can-Can (Cap 91248, Cap C21K-92064) [ST]

The CD Collection (OR 0086)

The Charmer—Maurice Chevalier (JHE HADCD-158)

Chevalier (Cine Stars CIN-302607)

Cocktail Hour (Columbia River Entertainment Group G-218021)

D'Hollywood a Adrole de Guerre (Virgin 7868412)

Early Movie Hits (DRG 5575)

Encore Maurice! (ASV CD-AJA-5016)

Etoiles de la Chanson (Etoiles de la Chanson 85591)

Etoiles de la Chanson (Disky FS-855912)

Fleur de Paris (Hallmark 306272)

Forever Gold (St. Clair 5727)

Gigi (EMI 838115, Sony Music Special Products AL-45395, Turner Classic Movie Music R2-71962) [ST]

Gold Collection (MSI 4061)

Gold Collection (Retro R2CD40-61)

High Society/Can-Can/Pal Joey (EMI 8140792, MSI/EMD 28433) [ST]

The Hollywood Years (Crystal Stream Audio IDCD56)

Jazz Archives (PMF Records 90725)

Les Legends D'Or (Disky FS-1610942)

Louise (ASV CD-AJA-5233)

Louise (BMG G-03833)

Louise (Golden Options)

Ma Cherie (ProArte CDD-438)

Ma Pomme (ARC TOP-943003)

Ma Pomme Chansons 1935-46 (Naxos Nostalgia NX-8.120508)

Maurice Chevalier (Accord ACD-100792)

Maurice Chevalier (Best Music International 88377)

Maurice Chevalier (BMG CD-321)

Maurice Chevalier (Les Chansons Eternelles 388803)

Maurice Chevalier (Musicdisc MUS-331522)

Maurice Chevalier (Music Memoria 8399352)

Maurice Chevalier (PIN PASTCD-9711)

Maurice Chevalier (Records 125210)

Maurice Chevalier (Socadisc 109-722-2)

Maurice Chevalier (Sounds of a Century 1809)

Maurice Chevalier: The Collection (Prism PLATCD-641)

Maurice Chevalier, Vol. 1 (Fremeaux 162)

Les Meilleurs (EMI 8559652)

Les Meilleurs (FDC FDC-883772)

Moi Evec une Chanson (PCI 8372192)

On Top of the World (Pearl Flapper 9711)

Paris By Moonlight (A Play 102912)

Paris, Paris (BMG MDF-102608)

Paris Sera Toujours Paris (BCD MDF-102.608)

Paris Sera Toujours Paris (Mudisque de France 102608)

Pepe (Collectors' Choice Music CCM-113-2, DRG 113) [ST]

Portrait of Maurice Chevalier (MCI Galleric 416)

Le Roi Du Music Hall (Forlane FRL-19055)

The Romance of Paris (Going for a Song)

Valentine (Arkadia 75102)

Valentine (St. Clair 3911)

Petula Clark and Peter O'Toole in *Goodbye, Mr. Chips* (1969).
[Courtesy of JC Archives]

Petula Clark

(b. Petula Sally Olwen Clark, West Ewell, Surrey, England, November 15, 1932)

Said to be the most collectable of all female singing stars, Petula Clark's career was noteworthy for both its longevity and diversity. Despite having appeared in over thirty feature films, motion pictures have been but one aspect in her career of many decades that successfully spanned personal appearances, radio, television, stage, composition, and recordings. The British songstress became an international star whose popularity was worldwide and who had over 150 top-forty charted recordings, not only in English but also in French, German, Italian, and Spanish. By the new millennium her record sales internationally surpassed 70 million. A star since childhood, Clark continued into the twenty-first century enchanting audiences, as she had done for many generations with her gutsy, belting voice.

Petula Sally Olwen Clark was born November 15, 1932, in West Ewell, Surrey, England, to Leslie Norman and Doris (Phillips) Clark. At an early age, she showed a talent for singing and entertaining. Managed by her protective father, the child's first break came in entertaining troops on the home front during World War II, where she became a favorite with both British and American soldiers. By the age of nine, she had done over two hundred shows for servicemen and was promoted as having "a voice as sweet as chapel bells." "Pet," as she was affectionately called, made her first record in 1944, and when the war ended, she was asked to sing at Trafalgar Square for a victory celebration. During the war, she also appeared on radio, and she made her film debut in 1944's *Medal for the General.*

Following the war, Petula continued her career, dividing time between concerts, radio, and film. In the latter medium, she had juvenile roles in a variety of features, including playing the daughter in a trio of entries in the *Huggetts* comedy series. In 1949, she began recording in earnest for the Polygon label, where she remained for six years, charting in England with "Where Did My Snowman Go" (1952), "The Little Shoemaker" (1954), and "Majorca" (1955). On film, she had a good role as a spoiled teen in *Don't Ever Leave Me* in 1949, and the next year, she left juvenile parts when she portrayed a fun-loving factory girl in *Dance Hall.* Another aspect of her career came with television; she did experimental programs for the BBC in 1946, and from 1949 to 1952 she headlined the series, *Pet's Parlour.* In 1950, Petula received the Silver Microphone Award as the Most Outstanding Female TV Personality of the Year from the London *Daily Mail.* That year she also made her dramatic stage debut in *Sauce for the Goose,* and four years later she appeared as Tessa with John Gregson in *The Constant Nymph,* both productions being staged at the Q Theater, Kew Bridge.

Petula continued to star in British movies for most of the 1950s. By now a leading lady, her features included *Made in Heaven* (1952), a comedy in which she is a newlywed whose efforts to win a national contest are nearly thwarted by jealousy, and *The Card* (1952), an Alec Guinness comedy in which she played the girl who wins her man away from a countess and a gold digger.

The Happiness of Three Women (1954) found her as a village girl whose life is helped by a postal delivery man.

In the United States, probably the most known of her 1950s' features was Republic's *Track the Man Down* (1954), in which she is an innocent whose sister's (Ursula Howells) lover (George Rose) takes the loot from a racetrack robbery. Clark is stuck with the money and being pursued by a newsman (Kent Taylor). In 1955, Petula Clark guest-starred on the television series *The Vise*, which was shown in the United States on ABC-TV. Also that year she began recording with the Pye Nixa label and charted in England with "Suddenly There's a Valley," followed by "With All My Heart" and "Alone" in 1957 and "Baby Lover" the next year. By 1961, the label was simply called Pye, and she had hits that year with "Sailor," "Something Missing," and "Romeo," followed by "I'm Counting On You" and "Ya Ya Twist" in 1962, and the two-sided hit "Casanova" / "Chariot" in 1963. By this time, the songstress was also recording and charting records in other languages, having been a continental star since her first appearance in France at the Olympia Theater in 1957.

In 1961, Clark wed French record producer Claude Wolff (they had three children: Barra, Kate, and Patrick), who took over the management of her career, causing a break with her father, who had guided her professionally for over twenty years. She appeared as Petula in the 1963 French film *A Couteaux Tires*, issued in the United States on TV as *Daggers Drawn*, and she also wrote its music.

Clark first came to the United States in 1959, where she made an album for Imperial Records, although it was not issued stateside until 1965, when she enjoyed her first big hit in the United States with the song "Downtown," which was released by Warner Bros. Records. It went to the top of the pop charts and earned her a Grammy Award. It also marked the beginning of a fruitful working relationship with composer–record producer Tony Hatch, who wrote a number of top best-sellers for the star. (Petula, herself, to date has composed over one hundred songs, with lyrics in five languages.) "I Know a Place" in 1965 brought her a second Grammy, and she followed it with a string of record-charting Warner Bros. releases (she was still on the Pye label in England), including: "My Love," and "'Round Every Corner" in 1965; "A Sign of the Times" and "Who Am I" in 1966; "Color My World" and "The Other Man's Grass Is Always Greener" in 1967; "Kiss Me Goodbye" and "American Boys" in 1968; and "Happy Heart" and "No One Better Than You" in 1969. Screen comedian legend Charlie Chaplin composed "This Is My Song," which was also a hit for Petula in England and France in 1967; he wrote another number for her, but it was lost following his death. From 1965 to 1970, she had eleven record albums on the Warner Bros. label, with *Downtown* in 1965 staying on the charts for over six months; *I Know a Place* (1965), *My Love* (1966), *Color My World* and *These Are My Songs* (1967), *Petula* (1968), and *Petula Clark's Greatest Hits* (1969) each spent at least three months on the top-selling album charts. She also sang in two 1965 movie musicals: *The Big T.N.T. Show* and *Questa Pazzi, Pazzi Italiani*.

With her success in records, Petula Clark became a highly paid concert performer in the United States in such venues as the Copacabana (New York City), the Cocoanut Grove (Los Angeles), and Caesars Palace (Las Vegas). She was also much in demand as a guest star on American TV, where she appeared on scores of musical programs as well as headlining her own NBC-TV specials *Petula* in 1968 and *Portrait of Petula* in 1969. (In her homeland in 1966, she starred in the six-episode variety TV series *This Is Petula Clark*). The late 1960s also brought Petula Clark back to motion pictures. Although she wisely turned down *Valley of the Dolls* (1967), she did star as Sharon McLongergan in *Finian's Rainbow* (1968), an old-fashioned but fun musical that had her singing such favorites as "How Are Things in Glocca Mora?" "Look to the Rainbow," "If This

Isn't Love," "That Great Come-and-Get-It Day," and "Old Devil Moon." She then played a showgirl who falls in love with a British schoolmaster (Peter O'Toole) in the musical remake of *Goodbye, Mr. Chips* (1969), which gave her seven songs, the best being "Walk Through the World" and "You and I." After the lukewarm reception to these two big-budget musicals, Petula backed away from movies to concentrate on her successful career as an international chanteuse and TV/recording star.

During the 1970s, Clark continued to make numerous guest appearances on American TV, and late in 1970 starred in the ABC-TV special *Petula*. In England from 1972 to 1974, she headlined eighteen musical programs, including two Christmas specials. In 1977, she starred in the syndicated television special *Petula Clark in Concert*, and she also did a number of TV commercials. She continued to star in Las Vegas, as well as making concert appearances in France and Canada, and she guested on various European TV programs. Record-wise she charted in England on the Pye label with "The Song of My Life" in 1971 and "I Don't Know How to Love Him" in 1972, and in the United States she had hits on MGM with "My Guy" and "Wedding Song," also in 1972. In 1979, she hosted the TV special *Carnival in Rio* and starred in Britain in Independent Television's musical *Traces of Love*. Petula also sang "On the Road" in the 1970 French feature *Dame dans l'Auto avec des Lunettes et un Fusil* and appeared as herself in the 1977 Gallic comedy *Drôles de Zèbres*.

The 1980s found Petula Clark back in movies, playing the part of Aunt Bee in *Never Never Land* (1980), and she was Lady Elizabeth in the 1981 French TV series *Sans Famille*. Petula returned to the stage as Maria, later Baroness Von Trapp, in the London West End revival of *The Sound of Music*, which ran for over a year from 1981 to 1982. She also did an original cast album of the show for CBS/Epic Records in England. In 1982, she was back on the record charts in the United States with the country hit "Natural Love" for Scotti Brothers Records, and in 1983, she had the dramatic title role in *Candida* in Guildford, England. Not only did Clark continue her worldwide concert tours, but in 1988 she returned to the British record charts with a remix of her 1964 classic "Downtown" on the PRT label, making her the longest-charted singing star in British record history. Late in 1989, Petula starred in a British tour of the dramatic musical *Someone Like You*, for which she wrote the original story with Ferdie Pacheco and also the show's music. It had a brief run at the Strand Theater in London in the spring of 1990.

During the 1990s, the British songstress found further success. By now her older recordings were being reissued on a myriad of international labels, and she continued her popular concerts. In 1993 Petula teamed with David and Shaun Cassidy in the dramatic Broadway musical *Blood Brothers*, which ran for nine months, followed by a nine-month British tour that ended in the spring of 1995. Following that production, Clark headlined one of her most successful ventures, Andrew Lloyd Webber's musical version of *Sunset Boulevard*, which offered her as faded screen icon Norma Desmond, the part Gloria Swanson made famous in the classic 1950 Paramount feature film. Petula first did the role for six weeks in the fall of 1995 at London's Adelphi Theater, substituting for Elaine Paige, but took over the lead for good in January 1996 and stayed with it to critical acclaim until April 1997. In 1998 Queen Elizabeth presented Clark with the Commander of the Order of the British Empire (C.B.E.). In November 1998, Petula embarked on an American tour of a streamlined version of *Sunset Boulevard*, which lasted through the spring of 2000, before resuming the role on the British stage. In the fall of 2000, she opened in a new show, a concert highlighting her long career, at the St. Denis Theater in Montreal, Canada. She continued to tour with this showcase production into 2001. The songstress closed out 2001 by headlining the PBS-TV special, *Petula Clark in Concert: A Sign of the Times*.

Filmography

Medal for the General (Anglo-American, 1944)

Strawberry Roan (Anglo-American, 1944)

I Know Where I'm Going! (General Film Distributors, 1945)

Murder in Reverse (Anglo-American, 1945) (U.S.: Query)

London Town (Eagle-Lion, 1946) (U.S.: My Heart Goes Crazy)

Trouble at Townsend (General Film Distributors, 1946)

Vice Versa (General Film Distributors, 1948)

Here Come the Huggetts (General Film Distributors, 1948)

Easy Money (General Film Distributors, 1948)

Vote for Huggett (General Film Distributors, 1949)

The Romantic Age (General Film Distributors, 1949) (U.S.: Naughty Arlette)

The Huggetts Abroad (General Film Distributors, 1949)

Don't Ever Leave Me (General Film Distributors, 1949)

Dance Hall (General Film Distributors, 1950)

White Corridors (General Film Distributors, 1950)

Tin Pan Alley (Pathé Pictorial, 1951) (documentary) (s)

Madame Louise (Butchers, 1951)

Made in Heaven (General Film Distributors, 1951)

The Card (General Film Distributors, 1952) (U.S.: The Promoter)

The Runaway Bus (Eros, 1954)

Track the Man Down (Rep, 1954)

The Happiness of Three Women (Adelphi, 1954)

The Gay Dog (Eros, 1954)

The Woman Opposite (Monarch, 1957) (U.S.: City After Midnight)

6–5 Calling [Calling All Cars] (Anglo-Amalgamated, 1958)

À Couteaux Tirés (1963) (Filmatec/Francois Sweerts, 1963) (U.S. TV: Daggers Drawn) (also music)

Questa Pazzi, Pazzi Italiani (ASACAM, 1965)

The Big T.N.T. Show (American International, 1966)

Finian's Rainbow (Warner Bros.–7 Arts, 1968)

Goodbye, Mr. Chips (MGM, 1969)

Dame dans l'Auto avec des Lunnettes un Fusil [The Lady in the Car With Glasses and a Gun] (Col/Lira Films, 1970) (voice only)

Drôles de Zèbres (Alexia, 1977)

Never Never Land (Sharp Pictures, 1980)

Twin Town (Gramercy Pictures, 1997) (voice only)

Billy's Hollywood Screen Test (Trimark, 1998) (voice only)

Girl Interrupted (Col, 1999) (voice only)

Simpatico (Fine Line Features, 1999) (voice only)

Radio Series

A Cabin in the Cotton (BBC, 1947)

Calling All Forces (BBC, 1951–52)

A Life of Bliss (BBC, 1954)

TV Series

Petula Clark (BBC, 1946)

Pet's Parlour (BBC, 1949–52)

This Is Petula Clark (BBC, 1966)

The Sound of Petula Clark (BBC, 1972–74)

Album Discography

LPs

Beautiful Sounds (Pet Projects PP-2)

The Best of Petula Clark (Pye NPL/NSPL-18282)

The Best of Petula Clark (Pye/Reader's Digest RDS-6704)

Call Me (Vogue POP-7512)

C'est le Refrain de Ma Vie (Vogue SLD-773)

C'est Ma Chanson (Vogue CLD-706.30)

Ceux Qui Ont un Coeur (Vogue LD-623-30)

La Chanson de Marie-Madeleine (Vogue SLD-831)

Color My World/Who Am I (WB W/WS-1673)

Come on Home (Polydor 2383-3033)

Comme une Priere (Vogue LDM-30140)

La Dame dans l'Auto avec des Lunnettes et un Fusil (Vogue SLD-755) [ST]

Destiny (CBS 82608)

Die Grossen Erfolge (Vogue 6-24590)

Downtown (WB W/WS-1590)

Downtown '88 (Carrere/PRT 66681)

The Early Years (2-PRT PCL-101)

The English Sound (Premier PM/PS-9016) w. Barbara Brown and the Supermarine Spitfires

Finian's Rainbow (WB B/BS-2550) [ST]

Give It a Try (Jango JA-LP-779)

Goodbye, Mr. Chips (MGM S1E-19ST) [ST]

Grandes Hits de Petula Clark (Vogue MV-30-175)

Greatest Hits (Applause APLP-1015)

Hello Paris (Pye VRL-3016)

Hello Paris (Pye VRL-3019)

Hit Parade (Pye NSLP-18159)

Hits . . . My Way (WB 93215)

The Hits Singles Collection (PRT PYL-7002)

An Hour in Concert With Petula Clark and the London Philharmonic Orchestra (Music for Pleasure MFP-5636)

I Couldn't Live Without Your Love (WB W/WS-1645)

I Grandi Successi di Petula Clark (Penny Oro RPO/ST-72020)

I Know a Place (WB W/WS-1598)

I'm the Woman You Need (Polydor 2382-324)

In Love (Laurie 2032)

In Other Words (Pye NPL-18070)

The International Hits (WB W/WS-1608)

Les James Dean (Vogue LDS-650-30)

Je Reviens (CBS 81986)

Just Pet (WB W/WS-1823)

Just Petula (Polydor 2384-068)

Live at the Royal Albert Hall (GNP Crescendo 2069)

Live in London (Pye 2383-303)

Memphis (WB W/WS-1862)

A Musicorama (Vogue VPV-76005)

My Love (WB W/WS-1630)

Noel (Pet Projects PP-1)

Now (MGM SE-4859)

The Other Man's Grass Is Always Greener (WB W/WS-1719)

Le Palmares (Vogue LVLXS-81-30)

A Paris (Vogue 180)

Petula (AZ STEC-151)

Petula (Kebec Disc KD-916)

Petula (Roulette Special Products RSP-1)

Petula (Vogue CLD-721)

Petula (Vogue LDV-17001)

Petula (Vogue PC1 NPL-18098)

Petula (WB W/WS-1743)

Petula Au Canada (Vogue PC2)

Petula '65 (Pye VRL-3010)

Petula '71 (Pye NSPL-18370)

Petula Clark (Pye 11PP-01)

Petula Clark (Vogue COF-6)

Petula Clark (Vogue LD-692-30)

Petula Clark (Vogue CLD-721)

Petula Clark (Vogue CLD-726)

Petula Clark (Vogue VRLS-3041)

The Petula Clark Album (Pye PET-1)

Petula Clark in Hollywood (Pye Nixa NPL-18039)

Petula Clark Story (Golden Hour GH-539)

Petula Clark Today (Pye Special PKL-5502)

Petula Clark's Greatest Hits (WB W/WS-1765)

Petula Italiana (Vogue/Trans Canada TF-382)

Portrait in Stereo (Vogue LDVS-17153)

Portrait of Petula (WB W/WS-1789)

Prends Mon Coeur (Vogue VPV-76-008)

Rendez-Vous avec Petula Clark (Vogue VPV-76017-30)

Sings for Everybody (Laurie 2043)

Le Soleil dans les Yeux (Vogue PC1)

Song of My Life (Pye NSPL-18363)

The Sound of Music (CBS/Epic EPC-70212) [OC]

Tête-à-têtes avec Petula Clark (Vogue VPV-76-105)

These Are My Songs (WB W/WS-1698)

This Is My Song Album (Dino Music DMLP-1167)

This Is My Song/Personne Ne Veut Mourir (Vogue VF-47029)

This Is Petula Clark (Sunset SUM-1101/SUS-5101)

Timex Presents Opryland U.S.A.—The American Music Scene tête-à-tête (Timex) [ST/TV]

Today (Pye PKL-5502)

A Touch of Petula Clark (Vogue LDVS-17175)

12 Succes de Petula Clark (Mondio Music/Vogue MM-115)

12 Succes de Petula Clark, Vol. 2 (Mondio Music/Vogue MM-136)

20 All Time Greatest (K-Tel NE-945)

20 Fantastic Hits (Kel-Tel NC-454)

Uptown (Imperial 9281/11281)

Warm and Tender (WB W/WS-1885)

The World's Greatest (WB W/WS-1608)

Windmills of Your Mind (RPC PET-1)

You Are My Lucky Star (Pye Nixa NPL-18007)

CDs

Les Annees Petula . . . (Vogue BMG-7321360032)

Anthologie, Vol. 1 (Anthology ANT-3039572)

Anthologie, Vol. 2 (Anthology ANT-3039562)

Anthologie, Vol. 3 (Anthology ANT-990606)

Anthologie, Vol. 4 (Anthology ANT-991008)

Anthologie, Vol. 5 (Anthology ANT-200215)

Anthologie, Vol. 6 (Anthology ANT-3060712)

Beautiful Sounds (Castle CMRD-059)

Best of Petula Clark (BCI Music BCCD-307)

Best of Petula Clark (BMG 360032)

Best of Petula Clark (Cameo CD-3064)

Best of Petula Clark (Castle MAT-CD-206)

Best of Petula Clark (Kaz EUK-CD-910)

Best of Petula Clark (PO CAMECD-3564)

Best of Petula Clark (Sequel PDS-CD-529)

Blood Brothers (Relativity 88561-1539-2) [OC]

Blue Lady: The Nashville Sessions (Varese Sarabande VSD-5610)

Castle Masters Collection (Castle Communications CMC-3042)

CD Collection (BMG 74321462382)

C'est Ma Chanson (Vogue VG-671-670042)

Ceux Qui Ont un Coeur (PID 557342)

Ceux Qui Ont un Coeur (RCA NEMCD-0000461)

Classic Collection (Pulse PBX-CD-404)

Classic Hits (Excelsior EXL-7067)

Classic Hits (Masters 1067)

Colour My World (Cedar GFS-132)

Colour My World/The Other Man's Grass is Always Greener (Castle CMRCD-061)

Come on Home (Chronicles 314-539-078-2)

Complete Golden Hits (PID 444122)

Complete Golden Hits Collection (Castle SEKCD-508)

Conversations in the Wind (Castle Music NEMCD-459)

Die Deutschen Erfolge (Castle Communications CHC-7057)

Downtown (Abracadabra AB-3006/AB-3308)

Downtown (Carnaby CD-552001)

Downtown (Castle Communications CD-290-133)

Downtown (Castle Communications PRC-10133)

Downtown (Karussell KA-506, Spectrum 550-773-2)

Downtown (Laserlight 15-103)

Downtown (Legend WZ-9017)

Downtown (Life Time LT-5117)

Downtown (Maverick Music 1-173)

Downtown (Musicrama 750262)

Downtown (Rainbow RCD-421)

Downtown (Sequel NEB-CD-661)

Downtown (Success 2203-CD)

Downtown '88 (Carrere-PRT 96681)

Downtown: Greatest Hits (RCA 744650996712)

Downtown/I Know a Place (Sequel NEMCD-390)

Downtown: The Best of Petula Clark (BMG PDSCD-519)

Downtown: The Best of Petula Clark (Century CECC-00718)

Downtown: The Best of Petula Clark (Kaz PDS-CD-529)

Downtown: The Greatest Hits of Petula Clark (Buddha 99671)

Downtown: The Hit Singles Collection (Teldec-PRT 8.26945)

Downtown: The Petula Clark Collection (PRT PYC-17)

Downtown to Sunset Boulevard (Hip-O Records 012-157-455-2)

Downtown: 20 Greatest Hits (Green Line-PRT EEC)

En Vogue—Le Bent en Français (Castle CMDDD-214)

The EP Collection (See For Miles SEECD-306)

The EP Collection, Vol. 2 (See For Miles SEECD-381)

Forever Classic (Master 0300)

Give It a Try (Jango JA-CD-779)

Gold (Gold 130)

Golden Greats (Starburst CD-STB-8655)

Golden Hits (Flash 8351-2)

Golden Hits (Masters MACD-61067-2)

Golden Hits (Prima Musik PMM-0537-2)

A Golden Hour of Petula Clark, Vol. 1 (Knight KGHCD-130)

A Golden Hour of Petula Clark, Vol. 2 (Knight KGHCD-151)

Les Grande Nemeros 1 (PID 480882)

Greatest Hits (A Play Collect 10052-2)

Greatest Hits (Applause APCS-1015-2)

Greatest Hits (BR Music BRCD-55)

Greatest Hits (Castle CMDDD-151) w. Sandie Shaw

Greatest Hits (Cleo CLCD-00315)

Greatest Hits (Galaxy Music 3885132)

Greatest Hits (Lasertech 956D, Pickwick PICD-3105)

Greatest Hits (Tring International GRFO83)

Greatest Hits (WEA 0630175032)

Greatest Hits of Petula Clark (GNP/Crescendo GNPD-2170)

Hello Paris (LASTC 3039562)

Her Greatest Hits (Snapper SMD-CD-195)

Here for You (Varese Sarabande VSD-5978)

The Hits Collection (Telly Disc TEL-CD-36)

The Hits Singles Collection (PRT PYC-7002)

The Hits Singles Collection (Teldec-PRT 8.26837)

I Know a Place (Sequel NEBCD-660)

I Love to Sing: Pye 35th Anniversary 3 CD Box Set (Sequel CD-265)

I'm the Woman You Need (Chronicles 314-539-080-2)

In Concert With Petula Clark (EMI CDB-7-97493-2)

In Hollywood/In Other Words (Sequel NEMCD-389)

Inoubliables . . . (Perfil CD-5456/TC-16)

International Collection (Bear Family BCD-16212)

International Hits/These Are My Songs (Castle CMRCD-6060)

Jumble Sale: Rarities and Obscurities (Sequel NEC-CD-198)

Just Pet (Sequel 902)

Just Pet/Petula '71 (Castle CMRCD-216, PID 699832)

Just Petula (Chronicles 314-539-081-2)

Legendary (3-BMG 74321785692, PID 643232)

The Little Tramp (WB 4281) [OC]

Live at the Copacabana (Sequel NEB-CD-653)

Live at the Copacabana/Live at the Royal Albert Hall (Castle CMRCD-217)

Live at the Royal Albert Hall (GNP/Crescendo GNPD-2069)

Live in London (Chronicles 314-539-079-2)

Live '65 (Magic 5295402)

Love Songs (Pickwick Music PWK-080)

Memphis (Sequel NEB-CD-901)

Memphis/The Song of My Life (Castle CMRCD-215)

Merry Christmas/Joyeux Noel (Sequel NEMCD-945)

Most of Petula Clark (EMI 8142152)

Music: Pye Anthology, Vol. 2 (Sequel NE-CD-392)

My Greatest (Madacy SA-2-6401)

My Love (Sequel NEMCD-658)

My Love/I Couldn't Live Without Your Love (Sequel NEMCD-391)

The Nixa Years, Vol. 1 (RPM 138)

The Nixa Years, Vol. 2 (PRM 144)

Now (Chronicles 314-539-077-2)

Original Hits (Polytel 8487072)

Os Grandes Successos de Petula Clark (Som Livre CD-401-0047)

The Other Man's Grass Is Always Greener/Petula—Kiss Me Goodbye (See For Miles 435)

Petula Clark (BMG-France)

Petula Clark (Classic World Productions CWP-9923)

Petula Clark (Legends LECD-104)

Petula Clark Collection (Elite 5128352)

Petula Clark Collection (Object Enterprises OR-0056)

Petula Clark Gold (Disky Gold 207)

Petula Clark Interview (VOXPOP VP-002)

Petula [Pink Album]/Portrait of Petula (Castle CMRCD-062)

Petula '65/Petula '66 (Sequel NEMCD-462)

Pick of the Hits (Spectrum 544332)

The Polygon Years, Vol. 1 (RPM 130)

The Polygon Years, Vol. 2 (RPM 131)

Portrait of a Song Stylist (Knight HARCD-119)

Portrait of Petula/Happy Heart (Sequel NEMCD-6)

The Pye Years: Don't Sleep in the Subway/Petula Clark Sings International Hits (RPM 146)

The Pye Years, Vol. 2: Wind of Change (RPM 159)

The Pye Years, Vol. 3: I Couldn't Live Without Your Love/Colour My World (RPM 170)

Sailor (Castle/Pye PIESCD-242)

Sailor, Romeo and Other Romantic Notions (Castle Music CMRCD376)

Ses Plus Belles Chansons—Best of Petula Clark (WAGR 3060962)

Showstoppers (PID 513832)

A Sign of the Times (UNI/Varese Sarabande—no number)

Sixties EP Collection (Sequel NXTCD-338)

Songbird (Pickwick PWKM-4094)

Songs of Petula (Castle Communications ACSCD-025)

The Sound of Petula Clark (Spectrum 5444332)

The Special Collection (Castle Communications CCSCD-236)

The Spirit of Today (Castle Music CMRCD377)

Super Hit Collection (Conquistador CONQ-010)

These Are My Songs (Start STFCD-5)

These Are My Songs—The Ultimate Collection (BMG 74321564622)

This Is My Song (Delta 47035)

This Is My Song (FMCG FMC-007)

This Is My Song (Skyline CDSL-812)

This Is My Song Album (Dino Music DNCD-1167)

Today (Sequel NEBCD-943)

Treasures, Vol. 1 (Scotti Bros. 72392-75260-2)

20 Greatest Hits (Vogue VG-651-600058)

The Ultimate Collection, Vol. 1. (NZ-no number)

Very Best of Petula Clark (BCI Music 307)

Very Best of Petula Clark (BMG PKSCD-156)

Very Best of Petula Clark (Cris CRMCD-201)

Very Best of Petula Clark (Musicrama 676057)

Very Best of Petula Clark (Prism PLATCD-114)

Very Best of Petula Clark (Raijon Entertainment RJSUC-16268)

Very Best of Petula Clark (Rainbow 2RCD-013-014)

Very Best of Petula Clark (RDCD 2481-3)

Very Best of Petula Clark (Success 16268CD)

Warm and Tender (Sequel NEBCD-944)

Wedding Song (Rebound 520496)

Where the Heart Is (Conno VSOPCD-249)

You Are My Lucky Star (C5 Records C5CD-551)

You Are My Lucky Star (Sequel NEMCD-460)

Rosemary Clooney in *Red Garters* (1954).
[Courtesy of Echo Book Shop]

Rosemary Clooney

(b. Rosemary Clooney, Maysville, Kentucky, May 23, 1928, d. Beverly Hills,
California, June 29, 2002)

In the early 1950s, attractive band singer Rosemary Clooney rose to "overnight stardom" with a string of novelty tunes hits ("Come On-a My House," "Mambo Italiano," "This Old House") recorded in her husky, bouncy manner. It made music lovers wonder if that was her limit. But as the star of TV and radio variety programs—and in other types of recordings—she demonstrated a versatility and musicianship that soon ranked her as a top female vocalist of the period, along with Patti Page, Peggy Lee, and Jo Stafford. In her brief film career (Paramount envisioned her as Betty Hutton's successor), Rosemary Clooney was comely, pert, and direct. A few more motion-pictures assignments and her acting stiffness would certainly have evaporated. But her private life intervened: she was grappling with raising a large family and dealing with a troublesome marriage. When she could no longer muddle through it all, she had a severe nervous breakdown. As part of her therapy, which included a revealing autobiography and a telefeature based on the book, she made her private life very public.

When the "new" Rosemary Clooney emerged professionally—boosted by her long-time friend Bing Crosby—she was no longer svelte, and her singing was not the same: It had improved! There was a smoky edge to her remarkable voice that enhanced her expert phrasing. Critics ranked her in the caliber of Ella Fitzgerald, Frank Sinatra, and Mel Tormé at their jazz peak. In a series of highly regarded albums for a small label, she took familiar material by great songwriters (Cole Porter, Irving Berlin, and Ira Gershwin) and, without distortion, gave them fresh meaning. It was Bing Crosby who said, "To me, Rosemary Clooney is a unique lady in many respects. She combines the ability to deliver a song with an unquenchable sense of humor."

She was born on May 23, 1928, in Maysville, Kentucky, the daughter of Andrew and Frances (Guilfoyle) Clooney. Her father was a housepainter and a heavy drinker. There was a brother (Nick), a half-brother (Andrew, who died in a drowning accident after World War II), and a sister (Betty). When Rosemary was very young, her parents began a recurring pattern of separating and reconciling. Frances Clooney went to Lexington, where she worked in a dress shop. The Clooney children were farmed out to different relatives, sometimes living with their paternal grandfather, Andrew J. Clooney. When he was campaigning for reelection as mayor of their small Ohio river town, Rosemary and Betty (three years younger than Rosemary) would sing frequently at his political rallies. They also sang in amateur contests. Grandmother Clooney died when Rosemary was nine, and they were sent to live with their widowed Grandmother Guilfoyle. Later, when Frances Clooney remarried a sailor and left for California, Andy Clooney tried to make a home for his children, but it did not work out. Thereafter, the kids were shunted from relative to relative, resulting in Rosemary attending four different schools. The only consistencies in life were Rosemary and Betty's love of music, and during their high school years they sang with a local band.

When Rosemary was sixteen she learned that Cincinnati radio station WLW was holding auditions to discover new talent. Rosemary and Betty responded and were hired to sing on a local show nightly at $20 each weekly. They continued singing (as the Clooney Sisters) at the station for nearly two years. In the interim, Cincinnati bandleader Barney Rapp (with whom Doris Day had once sung) hired the girls to sing with his group. The summer after Rosemary graduated from Our Lady of Mercy Convent, Rapp introduced the sisters to bandleader Tony Pastor, who was passing through town on tour in 1945; he hired them to join his band. Their uncle George Guilfoyle went with them on the tour; Pastor's star singer (Dolly Dawn) taught the girls how to apply onstage makeup. In the post big-band boom, Pastor and his group had to settle for mostly one-night stands as they played across country in theaters, at proms, in hotel ballrooms, at barn dances. In July 1946, they were performing at the Steel Pier in Atlantic City. Because Rosemary had the better middle-range voice, she sang solos for the sister team.

Rosemary's first recording with the Pastor group was "I'm Sorry I Didn't Say I'm Sorry When I Made You Cry Last Night" (Columbia Records). Disc jockeys took note of her "revolutionary" styling (she was so scared she was whispering) and predicted a good future for her. Rosemary admitted later that recording so frightened her that she avoided any more sessions for a long time. (Other recordings she and Betty did make with Pastor's group were "Saturday Night Mood," "Bread and Butter Woman," and "The Secretary Song.") In the spring of 1949, Betty got fed up with the pressures of the business. During intermission one night in Elkhart, Indiana, she quit, packed her bag, and went home. Now on her own, Rosemary blossomed into a more polished, assertive songstress, enhancing her industry reputation. Later in 1949, Rosemary decided it was time to leave Pastor and go out on her own. Through Joe Shribman, then Tony Pastor's manager (and soon to become Rosemary's), Clooney gained an entree to Mannie Sacks of Columbia Records in New York City. He signed her to a recording contract. Its terms guaranteed her only eight sides a year at $50 per side.

In between recording sessions, she made club, radio (especially with Vaughn Monroe on the *Camel Caravan*) and television appearances. She was on *Arthur Godfrey's Talent Scouts* (CBS-TV) in early 1950 and won first prize. This led to her being hired for *Songs for Sale* (CBS-TV), which debuted on July 7, 1950. The program was a showcase for aspiring songwriters, and there were two permanent show vocalists: Rosemary and Tony Bennett (who soon left and was replaced by Richard Hayes). The show was simulcast on radio and television. During late January 1951, Clooney was also on the short-lived daily variety program, *The Johnny Johnston Show* (CBS-TV). Meanwhile, her singles of "The Kid's a Dreamer" and especially "Beautiful Brown Eyes" gained her recognition at Columbia Records, where Doris Day and Dinah Shore were the top contract recording artists.

One of Rosemary's (known as Rosie) biggest boosters at Columbia Records was artist and repertoire man Mitch Miller, who insisted, "Rosie can sing anything and in any style. Then she always sings as if she's singing just to you. But her most important asset springs straight from the girl's character. To Rosie, everything is rosy." To prove her versatility, Miller requested her to record a novelty number that William Saroyan and Ross Bagdasarian had adapted from an old Armenian folk song. She refused; he insisted. The song was "Come On-a My House" and became a huge hit, selling over a million copies. It was followed by such pop hits as "Botcha Me" and "Suzy Snowflake." She made the ballad "Tenderly" a big seller. And she began to record children's records ("Little Johnny Chickadee," "Me and My Teddy Bear"), which had a distinct appeal because she understood "the arrangements can be cute, but your diction has to be perfect. Kids have to understand every single word. . . ." Clooney also continued to perform on radio, TV, and in concert and clubs.

On a TV talk show in 1950, Rosemary had met stage-film actor José Ferrer, a man much acclaimed for his talent, his acerbic wit, and his large ego. He was then separated from his stage-actress wife, Phyllis Hill. Subsequently, Ferrer won an Academy Award (*Cyrano de Bergerac*) and divorced. On July 13, 1953, he and Rosemary Clooney were married in Durant, Oklahoma, which was near to Dallas, where Ferrer was starring in *Kiss Me Kate* at the state fair. They bought a house in Beverly Hills; it had once belonged to famed crooner Russ Colombo (he died in the den there) and later to George Gershwin, and then to singer Ginny Simms. Meanwhile, Bing Crosby had become a big fan of Clooney's straightforward song style, and it was he who recommended to Paramount production head Don Hartman that she be screen-tested. The studio was having problems with their blonde bombshell star, Betty Hutton, and was looking for a backup/replacement. Paramount contracted Clooney to make pictures.

She made her screen debut in *The Stars Are Singing*, which premiered in her hometown of Maysville, Kentucky, in early 1953. Clooney was cast as a New York vaudevillian who, with the aid of her neighbor (portrayed by opera tenor Lauritz Melchior) and others, helps to hide an illegal alien (Anna Maria Alberghetti). The Technicolor film was slim going, but it was a strong showcase for peppy Rosemary, who among other numbers reprised her hit, "Come On-a My House." *Variety* reported that she "bounces about with considerable gusto in a part that doesn't allow for much show of histrionic talent." More zesty was *Here Come the Girls* (1953), one of Bob Hope's best 1950s' vehicles. Set in a theater environment where the comedian/singer is being stalked by a slasher, it featured Arlene Dahl as the leading lady of the show within the movie and Tony Martin and Clooney (once again refreshingly attractive) as the production's singing leads. Rosemary sang "When You Love Someone" and the more frantic "Ali Baba Be My Baby," as well as dueting with Hope on "Ya Got Class."

The studio had high hopes for its satirical musical Western *Red Garters* (1954), a project originally planned for Betty Hutton. There were stylistic flat sets and garish costumes, and all the expected genre conventions were overturned (the hero did not always win the gunfights, and so on). Clooney was the saloon owner who takes advantage of cowpoke Guy Mitchell to make her lawyer boyfriend (Jack Carson) jealous. She sang "Red Garters" and dueted "Man and Woman" with Mitchell. The picture was a flop. In contrast, *White Christmas* (1954), shot in wide-screen Vista-Vision and costarring Bing Crosby, Danny Kaye, and Vera-Ellen, was an enormous hit. Its show-business story was a loose reworking of Crosby's *Holiday Inn* (1942), and Crosby not only reprised his megahit "White Christmas" but scored well with "Count Your Blessings Instead of Sheep." Clooney's solo number was "Love, You Didn't Do Right By Me," and she was credited by critics for her more relaxed presence and improved dramatics. This film is now a holiday tradition, telecast every Yule time. Coming at year's end was *Deep in My Heart*, made on loanout to MGM. The picture was an overproduced biopic of Sigmund Romberg, with José Ferrer in the title role. Among the horde of guest stars paraded forth were Rosemary Clooney, who joined with Ferrer in a rendition of "Mr. and Mrs." During this period (October 7, 1954) she had begun *The Rosemary Clooney Show* on CBS radio, which lasted for a season.

In February 1955, Rosemary gave birth to her first child, Miguel José, and on March 11, 1955, she was the subject of Edward R. Murrow's televised interview program, *Person to Person* (CBS-TV). She did not return to the screen but instead pursued her recording career, with such hits as "Hey There" and "Tenderly." With her husband, she had recorded "A Bunch of Bananas" and "Woman," and with her good friend Marlene Dietrich she dueted on "Too Old to Cut the Mustard" and "That's a Nice, Don't Fight." She was a frequent TV guest on variety shows such as *The Ed Sullivan Show, The Perry Como Show*, and *The Steve Allen Show*. She played at the London Palladium and was at the Sands Hotel in Las Vegas. That December she announced she had been granted her release (at her own request) from her Paramount film contract. She planned, she said, to freelance in pictures thereafter. However, she made no further theatrical films.

In January 1956, she was contracted by Music Corporation of America (MCA) to star in the syndicated half-hour television show *The Rosemary Clooney Show*. The well-received, intimate program featured Nelson Riddle's Orchestra and the pop-vocal group the Hi-Los. With the Hi-Los, she recorded the Columbia LP album *Now Hear This*, which rose to number nineteen on the charts in the fall of 1957. She had her own top-ten single hit, "Mangos," which was on the charts for nine weeks in the spring of 1957. That fall, on September 26, 1957, she began a new half-hour variety series on NBC-TV, *The Lux Show Starring Rosemary Clooney*, which featured Paula Kelly & the Modernaires and Frank DeVol and His Orchestra; it remained on the air for a season. By now Rosemary's divorced-again mother and her twelve-year-old stepsister Gail were living with the Ferrers (and their three children, Miguel, Maria, and Gabriel), as was José's daughter, Lettie, by his earlier marriage. Because Mitch Miller at Columbia Records and José Ferrer did not get along at all, Miller's working relationship with Clooney suffered. She had no more big hits with the label and in 1958 left them to join RCA. By now her entire career was subordinated to her family's needs and to her husband's whims. The Ferrers' fourth child, Monsita, was born in October 1958. When Ferrer decided California was no longer congenial to his talents, he ordered that they move to New York City. As Clooney's career petered out, she became more intrigued with politics, especially with the rising careers of the Kennedys. Later, the Ferrers moved back to California, and in March 1960 her fifth child Rafael was born. After his birth, Clooney became active in John F. Kennedy's presidential campaign. On radio (a dying medium at that time) she had the *Ford Road Show Starring Rosemary Clooney*, which alternated daily with Bing Crosby's program; it lasted from 1958 until 1962.

In September 1961, Clooney learned she was not the only woman in her husband's life. Over the next five years, the couple separated, divorced, remarried, and later divorced again. She had the responsibility of bringing up the children. Clooney guested on *The Losers* episode (NBC-TV, January 15, 1963) of *The Dick Powell Show* and was on Bing Crosby's CBS-TV special that February, along with Frank Sinatra, Dean Martin, and Bob Hope. She continued to play the cabaret circuit.

The year 1968 was disastrous for Rosemary. That January she ended a two-year romantic relationship with a drummer fifteen years her junior. She had been relying heavily on pills for years, and her addiction increased on her pressured concert tour of the Far East, the Continent, and Brazil. Back in New York, she contacted Robert Kennedy in California, a pal since the 1960 elections, and volunteered to work on his presidential primary campaign on the West Coast. With all else in her world failing, politicking for Kennedy became the cause in her life. She was on the election trail for him in Oakland and San Diego, California. She flew back with Kennedy and his family from San Diego to Los Angeles in early June and was with the party at the Ambassador Hotel rally the night of June 5 when he was assassinated.

Clooney could not deal with the horrible reality of his death and was hospitalized briefly, but talked her way out of having the therapy treatment she really needed. In early July she was performing at Harold's Club in Reno when singer Jerry Vale showed her the *Life* magazine cover story dealing with Robert Kennedy's murder. At her performance that night she told a stunned audience, "You can't imagine the price I've paid to be here to sing a bunch of dumb songs for you." Later, she hysterically tore up her hotel room and then fled to her Lake Tahoe apartment. Her physicians admitted her to a local hospital, and later she was flown to Los Angeles, where she managed to get released from one hospital, before relatives, friends, and her priest convinced her to check into Mount Sinai Hospital, where she remained for several weeks. She underwent extensive therapy for the next eight years.

Less than six months after her breakdown, Clooney returned to performing, but it required several years of care and therapy before she regained the confidence necessary to make her performing anything more than mechanical. Meanwhile, rock had taken over the music business, and she was considered a has-been. In December 1973, her mother died (as Clooney referred to it, "One of the great conflicts in my life ended"), and in August 1974 her father passed away. In 1975, Bing Crosby and she made several performing tours together (including playing the London Palladium), and these shows did a great deal to reestablish her both in the industry and with the public. She began recording again. Then in August 1976 her sister Betty (who had been in and out of show business over the years) died of a brain aneurysm. Shortly after, Bing Crosby died of a heart attack in October 1977. A month before Crosby died, he wrote the foreword to Rosemary's straightforward autobiography *This for Remembrance*, written with Raymond Strait. Clooney said of this therapeutic experience of writing her memoirs, "It turned out to be the best thing I could do: Tell all and learn to live with it."

A much happier, much heavier Rosemary Clooney emerged in the 1980s. She played the nightclub circuit (especially Las Vegas) and in 1982 began touring with a theater revue *Four Girls Four*, which at different times included Margaret Whiting, Helen O'Connell, Rose Marie, Martha Raye, and Kay Starr. When CBS bought the screen rights to her autobiography, it was friend Merv Griffin who suggested that Sondra Locke would be ideal for the lead in *Rosie: The Rosemary Clooney Story* (December 8, 1982). Clooney provided the soundtrack singing voices for both her character and that of her sister Betty. In 1986, she turned up on an episode of *Hardcastle and McCormick* (ABC-TV), and on January 17, 1987 she was seen in the telefeature *Sister Margaret and the Saturday Night Lady*. In this CBS-TV film about a nun (Bonnie Franklin) who operates a halfway house for ex-convicts, Rosemary was a Bible-toting murderess. In 1988, when the gangster spoof *Married to the Mob* was released, a recording of Rosemary's "Mambo Italiano" was featured in the film. Said Clooney, "I put that one to bed thirty years ago and I thought it would stay there." In April 1989, she and her brother Nick hosted the fourth annual Singers' Salute to the Songwriter in Los Angeles. It was a benefit for the Betty Clooney Foundation for Persons with Brain Injury, an organization founded by Rosemary. At the time, she concertized on tours for forty weeks a year.

Tremendously family-oriented, Clooney had a large clan that included grandchildren and even a rapprochement with ex-spouse Ferrer. ("José and I are friendly now. With five children we have to be.") Her painter son Gabriel would marry singer Pat Boone's daughter Debbie. Daughter Maria became a painter, Monsita wed a producer for the Christian Broadcasting Network, and both Miguel and Rafael became actors. Clooney's brother Nick was a TV anchorman in Cincinnati and host of the syndicated show *On Trial*. His actor son George went to Hollywood, where he began getting TV roles. Rosemary's companion was Dante DiPaolo, a dance coordinator whom she had met at Paramount during the making of *Red Garters*.

During Clooney's touring with Bing Crosby in the 1970s, their drummer had been Jake Hanna, who was the house drummer for Concord Jazz Records where, by the end of the 1980s, Clooney had recorded thirteen albums. Most of the Concord releases used small jazz groups to accompany Rosemary, although one album united her with Woody Herman's Orchestra. She was praised consistently as one of this country's leading jazz vocalists. As she explained her craftsmanship, "You know, an awful lot of very good jazz singers do things with a melodic line within the chord, the improvisation. I don't have that ability. But I can read a lyric well, and I understand it. As Crosby used to say, 'You have three minutes as an actor to create that mood and tell your story, and that's all the time you've got.' "

In the 1990s Rosemary continued to record albums for Concord Jazz. Meanwhile, on January 26, 1992, her former husband José Ferrer passed away, ending another chapter in her complex life. October 1993 saw Pacific Pioneer Broadcasters host a luncheon tribute in honor of Clooney. She had a cameo in the comedic period whodunit *Radioland Murders* (1994), and that same year the trouper appeared at the Rainbow and Stars club in New York City. When not on the road, Rosemary and her longtime companion, Dante DiPaolo, divided their time between Beverly Hills and a Kentucky house she had restored years ago. On August 18, 1994, the singer was the featured performer at *Jazz at the* (Hollywood) *Bowl. Daily Variety* reported, "She's a thoroughly jazz-grounded stylist now; for example, her lightly swinging 'Hey There' today is eons removed from her sweetly crooned hit version 40 years ago, and is much the better for it. She also has the power to burrow deeply into a ballad; witness her hushed, vulnerable 'September Song.' "

Thanks to her nephew George Clooney—then starring on the hit NBC-TV series *ER*—Rosemary showed up in September and December 1994 in two episodes of that medical drama. On both occasions she played Mary Cavanaugh, a disoriented, lonely woman wandering about Chicago's County General Hospital. The plotline on each segment allowed her to sing snatches of songs in her inimitable style. (For one of these appearances, the actress/songster was Emmy-nominated.) When Concord Jazz released Rosemary's *Demi-Centennial* album in early 1995, *People* magazine was effusive, "Quite simply, Clooney, who is celebrating her 50th anniversary as a 'girl singer,' has no peer . . . Clooney's vibrato has narrowed, and she can no longer stretch some notes. But her taste, musicianship, simplicity and directness, the voice that's equal parts sun and seductiveness—they are all here and accounted for." As part of celebrating her fifty years in show business, A&E cable network presented (November 11, 1995) a 90-minute concert starring Rosemary. The dedicated performer was doing her act at Manhattan's Rainbow and Stars club on February 28, 1996. She was up for a Grammy award (her third in a row) that evening, but she lost in the Pop Vocalist category to Frank Sinatra (*Duets II*). In July that year, Rosemary shared the bill with pianist/vocalist Michael Feinstein at the Greek Theater in Los Angeles. On December 6 that year, Clooney was among those at Carnegie Hall singing/celebrating the centennial of Ira Gershwin.

In early 1997 Rosemary, whose weight had ballooned over recent decades, underwent knee replacement surgery at the Mayo Clinic but was back performing at Manhattan's Rainbow and Stars club that May. The *New York Times* enthused that she "invests song lyrics with such a powerful sense of emotional solidity that she can make trite-sounding phrases seem profound." On November 7, 1997, Rosemary wed her longtime sweetheart Dante DiPaolo in her tiny hometown of Maysville, Kentucky, at St. Patrick's Church. In late 1997, Concord Jazz released *White Christmas*, her twenty-first recording for the label and her first official Christmas album. In March 1998, while in New York City for a concert, Clooney collapsed and was rushed to the hospital suffering from a bout of meningitis. After recouping, she returned to business as usual: concertizing. In May 1998 she made her tenth annual appearance at New York City's Rainbow and Stars. A few days after the stint ended, she was the star attraction at Carnegie Hall, the acts at which included the Count Basie Orchestra and her own sextet led by John Oddo. On October 8, 1998, she received the Ella Lifetime Achievement Award from the Society of Singers at the Beverly Hilton Hotel; she was presented with the accolade by her nephew George.

In her follow-up autobiography *Girl Singer* (1999), written with Joan Barthel, Rosemary acknowledged that on her honeymoon with José Ferrer she learned he was cheating on her. In her candid tome, she also discussed her eventual separation from Ferrer and how she turned to composer/conductor Nelson Riddle for comfort. He, like she, was still married at the time, and they eventually broke apart, much to her regret. Meanwhile, Rosemary continued to concertize around the United States. On May 31, 2001, "Rosemary Clooney: Girl Singer" was the subject of a *Biography* episode on the A&E cable network. In mid-January 2002, the veteran entertainer underwent successful surgery for lung cancer at the Mayo Clinic in Rochester, Minnesota. A month later she received a Lifetime Achievement Award at the Grammy Awards, but could not attend as she was still hospitalized with a post-operative infection. In June Rosemary's cancer returned, and the seventy-four-year old talent died at her Beverly Hills home on June 29, 2002. She was survived by her husband (Dante DiPaolo), her five children, and her grandchildren.

Evaluating her lengthy career as a songstress, Rosemary wrote in her second memoir: "There's a great loneliness in a woman getting ready to go on the stage. You're sitting alone in a dressing room, looking at a face you know all too well . . . You're hearing all the noise outside . . . Everybody is in it together, except you're absolutely apart. You're not a part of it at all. Until you set foot onstage. And then you are."

Filmography

The Stars Are Singing (Par, 1953)
Here Come the Girls (Par, 1953)
Red Garters (Par, 1954)
White Christmas (Par, 1954)
Deep in My Heart (MGM, 1954)

Rosie: The Rosemary Clooney Story (CBS-TV, 12/8/82) (voice only)
Sister Margaret and the Saturday Night Ladies (CBS-TV, 1/17/87)

Radio Series

Songs for Sale (CBS, 1950–51)
The Rosemary Clooney Show (CBS, 1954–55)

The Ford Road Show With Bing Crosby and Rosemary Clooney (CBS, 1958–62)

TV Series

Songs for Sale (CBS, 1950–51)
The Johnny Johnston Show (CBS, 1951)
The Rosemary Clooney Show (Synd, 1956–57)

The Lux Show Starring Rosemary Clooney (NBC, 1957–58)

Album Discography

LPs

Blue Rose (Col CL-872, Col Special Products EN-13085) w. Duke Ellington

Children's Favorites (Col CL/2569)

Clap Hands, Here Comes Rosie (RCA LPM/LSP-2212, RCA International 89315)

The Clooney Sisters (Epic LN-3160) w. Betty Clooney

Clooney Tunes (Col CL-969)

Come On-a My House (Col Special Products 14382)

Country Hits from the Heart (RCA LPM/LSP-2565)

A Date With the King (10″ Col CL-2572) w. Benny Goodman

Deep in My Heart (MGM E-3153, MGM 2SES-54ST, MCA 5949) [ST]

Everything's Coming up Rosie (Concord Jazz CJ-47)

Fancy Meeting You Here (RCA LPM/LSP-1854, RCA International 89461) w. Bing Crosby

The Ferrers Sing Selections from "Oh Captain!" (MGM E-3687) w. José Ferrer

Greatest Hits (CBS 32263)

Greatest Hits (Embassy 31389)

Here's to My Lady (Concord Jazz CJ-81)

Hollywood Hits (Har HL-7213) w. Harry James

Hollywood's Best (10″ Col CL-6224, Col CL-585, Col Special Products EN-13083) w. Harry James

Hymns from the Heart (MGM E/SE-3782)

Look My Way (UA 29918)

Love (Reprise 6088)

Mixed Emotions (Har HL-7454/HS-11254)

Now Hear This (Col CL-1023) w. the Hi-Los

Red Garters (10″ Col CL-6282, Phillips B07652R) [ST]

Rendezvous (Camden CAS-2330) w. Bing Crosby

Ring Around Rosie (Col CL-1006) w. the Hi-Los

Rosemary Clooney and Dick Haymes (Exact 232)

Rosemary Clooney in High Fidelity (Har HL-7123)

Rosemary Clooney Onstage (Col CL-2581)

Rosemary Clooney Sings Ballads (Concord Jazz CJ-282)

Rosemary Clooney Sings the Lyrics of Ira Gershwin (Concord Jazz CJ-112)

Rosemary Clooney Sings the Lyrics of Johnny Mercer (Concord Jazz CJ-333)

Rosemary Clooney Sings the Music of Cole Porter (Concord Jazz CJ-195)

Rosemary Clooney Sings the Music of Harold Arlen (Concord Jazz CJ-210)

Rosemary Clooney Sings the Music of Irving Berlin (Concord Jazz CJ-255)

Rosemary Clooney Sings the Music of Jimmy Van Heusen (Concord Jazz CJ-308)

Rosemary Clooney Swings Softly (MGM E/SE-3834)

Rosie Sings Bing (Concord Jazz CJ-60)

Rosie Solves the Swingin' Riddle (RCA LPM/LSP-2265)

Rosie's Greatest Hits (Col CL-1230)

Show Tunes (Concord Jazz CJ-364)

Songs for Children (Har HL-9501)

The Story of Celeste (MGM E-3709, MGM CH-111, Leo the Lion CH-104)

Stepping Out (CBS, 1950)

Swing Around Rosie (Coral 57266, Jasmine 1502)

Tenderly (10″ Col CL-2525)

Thanks for Nothing (Reprise 6108)

That Travelin' Two Beat (Cap T/ST-2300) w. Bing Crosby

A Touch of Tabasco (RCA LPM/LSP-2133) w. Perez Prado

The Uncollected Rosemary Clooney (Hindsight HSR-234)

While We're Young (10″ Col CL-6297)

White Christmas (10″ Col CL-6338)

With Love (Concord Jazz CJ-144)

Young at Heart (Har HL-7236)

CDs

At Long Last (Concord Jazz CDD-4795) w. Count Basie

Bing Crosby on Broadway (Bing Crosby at the London Palladium) (UA/K-Tel NE-951) w. Bing Crosby, the Crosby Family [OC]

Blue Rose (Legacy CK-65506, Mobile Fidelity MFCD-10-00850) w. Duke Ellington

Brazil (Concord Jazz CDD-4884) w. John Pizarelli, Jr., Diana Krall

Christmas Classics (CMU 102)

Christmas Kind of Season (KRB Music Companies KRB8068-2)

Christmas Present (Sony Music Special Products CK-26826)

Clap Hands Here Comes Rosie/Fancy Meeting You Here (Taragon 1060)

The Classic Rosemary Clooney (RCA 68001)

Cocktail Hour (Columbia River Entertainment Group CRG-218014)

Come On-a My House (Bear Family BCD-15895)

Come On-a My House (Columbia Special Products CK-15895)

The Concord Jazz Heritage Series (Concord Jazz CDD-4812)

Dedicated to Nelson (Riddle) (Concord Jazz CDD-4685)

Deep in My Heart (Sony Music Special Products AK-47703) [ST]

Deep in My Heart/Words and Music (MCA MCAD-5949) [ST]

Demi-Centennial (Concord Jazz CCD-4633)

Do You Miss New York? (Concord Jazz CDD-4537)

The Essence of Rosemary Clooney (Legacy CK-53569)

Everything's Coming Up Rosie (Concord Jazz CDD-4047)

Everything's Rosie 1952/1963 (Hindsight HCD-255)

Fancy Meeting You Here (RCA R25J-1003) w. Bing Crosby

For the Duration (Concord Jazz CDD-4444)

Girl Singer (Concord Jazz CDD-4496)

Greatest Hits (RCA 63693)

Greatest Songs (Curb 77752)

Hey Look Us Over (Jasmine JASCD-318) w. Bing Crosby

Love (Warner Bros. 46072-2)

Many a Wonderful Moment (Bear Family BCD-15927)

Memories of You (Bear Family BCD-15914)

More of the Best (Laserlight 12-634)

Mothers and Daughters (Concord Jazz CDD-4754)

My Buddy (Concord Jazz CDD-4226) w. Woody Herman

Patti Page/Rosemary Clooney (Dominion 703-2)

Radioland Murders (MCA MCAD-11159) [ST]

RCA 100th Anniversary Series (BMG/RCA 68001)

Red Garters/Irving Berlin's White Christmas (Collectables COL-CD-6685)

Rendezvous (RCA Camden Classics 6128) w. Bing Crosby

Ring Around the Rosie/Hollywood's Best (Collectables COL-CD-6460) w. the Hi-Lo's, Harry James

Rosemary Clooney (The Entertainers 303)

Rosemary Clooney Sings Ballads (Concord Jazz CDD-4282)

Rosemary Clooney Sings Rodgers and Hammerstein (Concord Jazz CDD-4405)

Rosemary Clooney Sings the Lyrics of Ira Gershwin (Concord Jazz CDD-4112)

Rosemary Clooney Sings the Lyrics of Johnny Mercer (Concord Jazz CDD-4333)

Rosemary Clooney Sings the Music of Cole Porter (Concord Jazz CDD-4185)

Rosie Sings Bing (Concord Jazz CDD-4060)

Rosie Solves the Swingin' Riddle (Koch 7991)

Sentimental Journey (Concord Jazz CDD-4952)

70: A Seventieth Birthday Celebration (Concord Jazz CDD-4804)

Show Tunes (Concord Jazz CDD-4364)

Silver Bells of Christmas (KRB Music Companies KRB0870-2) w. Bing Crosby

16 Bigget Hits (Legacy CK-63553)

16 Most Requested Songs (Legacy CK-44403)

Some of the Best (Laserlight 12-633)

Songbook Collection (Concord Jazz CDD-4933)

Songs from the Girl Singer—A Musical Autobiography (Concord Jazz CDD-4870)

Songs from White Christmas (Legacy CK-65278)

Still on the Road (Concord Jazz CDD-590)

Swing Around Rosie (Coral MVCJ-19227, MSI 496982)

Swing Softly (MGM POCJ-2655)

Tenderly (Columbia Special Products CK-22542)

That Travelin' Two Beat/Bing Crosby Sings Great Country Hits (Collectors' Classic Music CCM-221-2) w. Bing Crosby

Things to Remember Me By (Jasmine JASCD-335)

A Tribute to Billie Holiday (Concord Jazz CDD-4081)

The Uncollected Rosemary Clooney 1951-52 (Hindsight HSR-234)

White Christmas (Concord Jazz CDD-4719)

With Love (Concord Jazz CDD-4144)

Wonderful Together (New Sound—no number) w. Bing Crosby

You Started Something (Sony Music Special Products CK-26085) w. Tony Pastor

June Knight, Russ Columbo, and Roger Pryor in *Wake Up and Dream* (1934).
[Courtesy of JC Archives]

Russ Columbo

(b. Ruggiero Eugenio di Rodolfo Columbo, San Francisco, California, January 14, 1908; d. Los Angeles, California, September 2, 1934)

Russ Columbo's image as a romantic crooner—perhaps the epitome of the word—has lived on despite the fact that he has been dead for more than a half century and his legacy has been retained only in a handful of recordings and films. In 1931, Al Dubin and Joe Burke wrote a popular novelty song that pinpointed correctly the three top singing idols of the day, called "Crosby, Columbo and Vallee." While Bing Crosby and Rudy Vallee went on to become show-business immortals, Russ Columbo's tragic death in 1934 made him a legend.

Ruggiero Eugenio di Rodolfo Columbo was born in San Francisco, California, on January 14, 1908, allegedly the twelfth child of a twelfth child of a twelfth child. When he was five, Columbo's family moved to Philadelphia, where his father had a low-paying job in a private bank in the Italian ghetto. A next-door neighbor taught young Columbo to play the guitar. After the family returned to the West Coast, where the elder Columbo now worked in the construction field, the boy took up the violin and studied opera. While still in high school, Russ earned money as a violinist, and he found jobs playing background music during the making of silent films. In this capacity, he came to the attention of screen siren Pola Negri, who thought he resembled Rudolph Valentino. She got him more music work as well as bits and extra work in motion pictures. After graduating from Belmont High School in Los Angeles, where he had been the school band's first violinist, Columbo obtained work with George Eckhart and His Orchestra at the Mayfair Hotel in Los Angeles. Next he worked with Slim Martin's Band at the Pantages Theater and then took a job at the Roosevelt Hotel in Hollywood with Professor Moore and His Orchestra. He played violin in all these groupings, but with Moore he also was a substitute singer, and in that capacity sang in a nationwide hookup on CBS radio.

Russ's first substantial show-business break occurred in 1928 when he signed with Gus Arnheim and his Orchestra at the Cocoanut Grove Club in Los Angeles. Again Columbo played violin and was backup vocalist to Bing Crosby, although the two future singing idols often sang together. This exposure with Arnheim led to Columbo getting small parts in sound films, beginning with *Street Girl* in 1929, in which he appeared with the Arnheim aggregation. This was followed by a straight acting role as a Latin type in *Wolf Song* (1929). Next came *Wonder of Women* (1929), in which he sang "Ich Liebe Dich," popularized that year by Nick Lucas on Brunswick Records. In Cecil B. DeMille's first talkie, *Dynamite* (1929), Columbo was cast as a Mexican prisoner, and he introduced the popular Dorothy Parker–Jack King song "How Am I to Know?" that Gene Austin made popular on Victor Records.

In 1930, Columbo also made his recording debut with Gus Arnheim on Okeh Records, singing "Back in Your Own Backyard" and "A Peach of a Pair" for Victor. He then went on a tour of the East with the band, but left in the summer of 1930 to return to Hollywood for roles in more films: *Hello, Sister* (1930), in which he had a small part as well as being credited as the composer of the film's background music; *The Texan* (1930), in which he played a cowboy singing around a campfire; and *Hellbound* (1931).

Columbo next formed his own band and, after a brief tour, played the Silver Slipper Club in Los Angeles, but when it closed he opened his own night spot, the Club Pyramid on Santa Monica Boulevard. It was there he came to the attention of songwriter Con Conrad, who believed that Columbo had a real future as a singing star. In the summer of 1931, Russ cut a test record for Victor of "Out of Nowhere," with Conrad at the piano. After many attempts, Conrad landed Columbo a fifteen-minute, four-week show on NBC radio in New York City after Rudy Vallee introduced Columbo to network executives. After the month was up, Columbo was dropped, but when the network failed to sign Bing Crosby for a series, they rehired Columbo and put him on the NBC Blue network. Within a matter of weeks, his fan mail soared and he was soon dubbed "The Romeo of Radio." In September 1931, Columbo began recording for Victor Records, and he had several best-sellers including "You Call It Madness (But I Call It Love)," which became his theme song, and "Prisoner of Love," both of which he wrote with Con Conrad. There were also such hits as "You Try Somebody Else," "Time on My Hands," "Save the Last Dance for Me," "Just Friends," and "Paradise." Columbo also composed such songs as "Let's Pretend There's a Moon," "Too Beautiful for Words," "My Love," "Just Another Dream of You," and "When You're in Love."

The success Columbo had on radio and in records soon spilled over into vaudeville and personal appearances, including a ten-week run at the Brooklyn Paramount Theater. Con Conrad constantly churned out publicity for the new star, including alleged romances with Pola Negri and Greta Garbo. In reality, Russ did date actresses Dorothy Dell, Sally Blane, and Carole Lombard and was said to be particularly close to the latter two blondes. Within a year after becoming associated with Con Conrad, Russ Columbo was able to command as much as $7,500 per week. During this period the musicians who worked in Columbo's band included Benny Goodman, Gene Krupa, Joe Sullivan, Babe Russin, Jimmy McPartland, Perry Botkin, and Leo Arnaud.

While performing in New York City, Columbo returned to moviemaking, starring in the Vitaphone/Warner Bros. two-reeler *That Goes Double* (1933), in which he portrayed himself and his look-alike, an office employee whom he hires to take his place in hectic personal appearances. In the short, Columbo sang "My Love," "Prisoner of Love," and "You Call It Madness." The crooner then went to Hollywood to star in United Artists' *Broadway Thru a Keyhole* (1933). In this, his first major role, he was a crooner whose girlfriend is kidnapped, with the case being solved with the aid of a Walter Winchell radio broadcast. Not only did Columbo receive solid reviews, but the feature gave him an opportunity to sing a song thereafter closely associated with him, "You Are My Past, Present and Future." Next Columbo was featured with the Boswell Sisters in the musical numbers for the Constance Bennett marital comedy, *Moulin Rouge* (1934) for Twentieth Century Pictures and United Artists release. While Ms. Bennett sang "Boulevard of Broken Dreams," Russ pleasingly crooned "Coffee in the Morning and Kisses at Night."

With his newfound success in motion pictures, in addition to radio, records, and personal appearances, Columbo had become one of the most popular singers of the Depression era. He and Con Conrad formed a music-publishing company, Rusco, Incorporated, and after Russ returned to Hollywood, the singer debuted a Sunday-night NBC radio program hosted by gossip columnist Jimmie Fidler. In 1934 Columbo signed a long-term, lucrative contract with Universal Pictures to star in a series of musicals for the studio (including James Whale's production of *Show Boat*), but he was to make only one for them, *Wake Up and Dream*. Columbo starred as Paul Scotti, a singer who forms a vaudeville act with two partners (Roger Pryor, June Knight), and the trio becomes a star act. Columbo cowrote the trio of songs he performed in the film: "When You're in Love," "Too Beautiful for Words," and "Let's Pretend There's a Moon," which he also recorded for Brunswick Records. He told interviewers at the time, "I find that I have just about everything I want from life and am pretty happy about the way things have worked out for me." The much-anticipated musical was released to positive reviews in October 1934, but by that time, the twenty-six-year-old was dead.

On September 2, 1934, Columbo was visiting his close friend, Hollywood portrait photographer Lansing V. Brown Jr. in the latter's home. The two were talking and looking at Brown's collection of Civil War dueling pistols when Brown struck a match on one of the weapons. A long-forgotten charge in the pistol exploded from the barrel, ricocheted off a table, and hit Russ in the left eye. The corroded ball was lodged in his brain. He was rushed to Los Angeles' Good Samaritan Hospital, where he died without gaining consciousness. Sally Blane was at the hospital when he passed away. Columbo was buried in Los Angeles, and among his pallbearers were Bing Crosby, Gilbert Roland, Zeppo Marx, Carole Lombard's brother Stuart, Walter Lang, and Lowell Sherman (who had directed him in *Broadway Thru a Keyhole*).

Oddly enough, Columbo's mother was never told of his death by his seven surviving brothers and sisters. Mrs. Columbo had suffered a heart attack two days before her son's tragic demise, and she was nearly blind. The family was afraid the shock of hearing about his passing would kill her. They concocted a story about Columbo being on a five-year tour abroad, and money from his life-insurance policy was used to support her; they even made up letters to their mother allegedly written by the singer. The loving deception was continued for a decade until her death. In her will, she bequeathed part of her estate to Russ.

Over the years there have been a number of tribute albums to Columbo, including those of Jerry Vale, Steve Mason, Gordon Lewis, Paul Bruno, and Tiny Tim. Several singers—including Johnny Desmond, Tony Martin, Perry Como, and Don Cornell—were, at one time or another over the decades, considered for the lead role in a yet-to-be-made movie based on Columbo's life. A TV drama with Tony Curtis playing the crooner also failed to materialize in the 1950s.

Some people feel that, if he had lived longer, Russ might have remained as popular as Bing Crosby or, possibly, may even have eclipsed that famed crooner. Regardless of this speculation, Russ Columbo still continues to be remembered fondly by his fans for what he did during his too-short but successful life.

Filmography

Wolf Song (Par, 1929)
Street Girl (Radio, 1929)
Wonders of Women (MGM, 1929)
Dynamite (MGM, 1929)
The Texan (Par, 1930)
Hello, Sister (Sono Art–World Wide, 1930)

Hellbound (Tif, 1931)
Broadway Thru a Keyhole (UA, 1933)
That Goes Double (Vita, 1933) (s)
Moulin Rouge (UA, 1934)
Wake Up and Dream (Univ, 1934)

Radio Series

The Russ Columbo Show (NBC, 1931–33)   The Jimmy Fidler Show (NBC, 1934)

Album Discography

LPs

Columbo, Crosby and Sinatra (10″ RCA LPT-5) w. Bing Crosby, Frank Sinatra

The Films of Russ Columbo (Golden Legends 2000/2) [ST]

A Legendary Performer (RCA CPL1-1756)

The Long Lost 1932 Broadcasts (Broncoli Gegend 32134)

Love Songs by Russ Columbo (X LVA-1002, RCA LPM-2072)

Prisoner of Love (Pelican 141)

Russ Columbo 1930–34 (Sandy Hook 2006)

Russ Columbo on the Air (Totem 1031)

Russ Columbo on the Air—The Romeo of Radio 1933-34 (Sandy Hook 2038)

CDs

Prisoner of Love (ASV CD-AJA-5234)

Russ Columbo (Sounds of a Century 1891)

Save the Last Dance for Me (Take Two TT-409CD)

Perry Como

(b. Pierino Roland Como, Canonsburg, Pennsylvania, May 18, 1912; d. Jupiter, Florida, May 12, 2001)

The art of crooning originated in the 1920s with Nick Lucas and Gene Austin, who sold millions of records, and it reached its apex in 1929 with the romantic song stylings of Rudy Vallee, who was followed by Bing Crosby, Russ Columbo, Dick Powell, and many others. In the 1940s, Frank Sinatra was still regarded as a crooner, but the vogue came to a halt as the decade waned. The last major exponent of the art of crooning was extremely clean-cut, very congenial Perry Como, whose smooth baritone voice appealed to generations of listeners. From his beginnings as a band singer through his many years on radio and TV, plus his assorted hit records (he sold over 100 million records) and a brief motion-picture interlude, Como retained his ultrarelaxed singing style as well as the reputation of being one of the nicest people ever to find success in show business.

Born Pierino Roland Como on May 18, 1912, in Canonsburg, Pennsylvania, and called Perry, the future star was the son of Pietro and Lucia Como and the first of their thirteen children to be born an American citizen; he was the seventh son of a seventh son. Canonsburg was a mill and mining town, and Como's father was a mill hand, but with thirteen children to raise, all the siblings who were old enough had to go to work. So young Perry, at age eleven, began an apprenticeship in a barbershop making 50¢ a week. His duties included opening the shop, lighting the stoves, and keeping the floors and mirrors constantly cleaned; the owner also taught him how to cut hair. When Como was fourteen, his father developed a debilitating heart condition, so he set his son up in his own barbershop and the young man began earning his own living cutting hair. When business was slow, he picked up a guitar and sang. Within six years he was making $40 a week as a barber, and he married his blonde childhood sweetheart Roselle Belline on July 31, 1933.

On vacation in Cleveland, Ohio, Roselle talked her husband into auditioning as a singer for bandleader Freddy Carlone. The bandsman liked what he heard and offered the young man $25 per week to sing with his group. Como would recall later, "That was the end of my making an honest living. But it began seven years of one-night stands, climbing on and off buses, living in flea bag hotels."

Como began working with Freddy Carlone in 1933, mostly touring southwestern Pennsylvania. One night in 1936 while Perry was performing in a casino in Warren, Ohio, bandleader Ted Weems came in to gamble and, upon hearing Como croon, offered him a job; Como accepted on the spot. In the spring of that year in Chicago, Perry made his recording debut with Weems on Decca Records vocalizing "You Can't Pull the Wool Over My Eyes" and dueting with Elmo Tanner on "Lazy Weather."

For the next six years, the younger singer continued to tour and record with the Weems Orchestra, and among their Decca recordings were "Picture Me Without You," "Rainbow on the

Perry Como in the 1940s.
[Courtesy of JC Archives]

River," "Simple and Sweet," "May I Never Love Again," and "Angeline." In 1939 Como sang the vocal on Weems's bestseller for Decca, "I Wonder Who's Kissing Her Now?" From 1940 to 1941, Perry was the featured singer with Weems on the NBC radio program *Beat the Band*. By the time the Weems group disbanded in 1942 due to several members being drafted into World War II service, Como was making $125 a week. However, he was tired of the touring grind and wanted to settle down, especially since he and Roselle were expecting their first child. (Their son Ronnie was born that year.) Como decided to return to Canonsburg and open another barbershop, but he received a call from General Artist Corporation in New York City offering him $76 a week to star in his own sustaining program on radio, and his wife convinced him that he should accept the job.

The Perry Como Show debuted on CBS radio on Sunday nights in 1943 and was an immediate hit. As a result, Como was given a singing engagement at the Copacabana in New York, and he was a big success. The *New York World Telegram* judged that Como was "darkly handsome, pleasantly wholesome and mercifully unaffected. His voice is a clear, full-throated baritone, and when he sings he appears to be suffering no pain at all." In 1943, he also began recording for RCA Victor with the song "Goodbye Sue," but sales were minimal. As he continued to record, RCA producer Eli Oberstein urged Como to put more volume in his singing, and the result was his hit recording "Till the End of Time." It would become the biggest-selling single record of 1945.

By now, Hollywood had already latched onto Como, hoping to repeat his singing success on film, as with Frank Sinatra and Dick Haymes. In the next three years, Como appeared in a trio of Twentieth Century-Fox musicals with Vivian Blaine and Carmen Miranda, all directed by Lewis Seiler, but they failed to establish him as a popular screen crooner. (He was too mild a personality to make a vivid impression.) The first film of the three was *Something for the Boys* (1944), a watered-down movie version of Cole Porter's popular stage musical. This was followed by *Doll Face* in 1945, based on a Gypsy Rose Lee play. In it he sang "Here Comes Heaven Again" and "Dig You Later (A Hubba-Hubba-Hubba)," which he also recorded successfully for RCA Victor. While Como's debut movie was in Technicolor, the second one was in economy black and white, as was his final Fox musical, *If I'm Lucky* (1946), a mild remake of *Thanks a Million* (1935) that had starred Dick Powell and Ann Dvorak. Here Perry performed the title tune and "One More Kiss," which also featured Harry James and his band. In 1948 Como, who had still to develop a dimensional screen persona, made his final movie appearance, a brief song cameo (singing "With a Song in My Heart") in MGM's *Words and Music*, a specious screen biography of composers Richard Rodgers (Tom Drake) and Lorenz Hart (Mickey Rooney).

In 1944, Como and Jo Stafford became cohosts of the weeknight radio series *The Chesterfield Supper Club* on NBC, and they would continue this chore until 1949 when the series became a half-hour Thursday-night offering with Peggy Lee as Como's new cohost. During this period Como reigned as RCA Victor's top recording star with hits like "Prisoner of Love," "Temptation," "If I'm Lucky," "Because," "Some Enchanted Evening," "You Call It Madness," and "More Than You Know." Both "Prisoner of Love" and "You Call It Madness" were associated with the late crooner Russ Columbo, whom Como had once met in Cleveland. Columbo greatly impressed Como, but Perry's real idol was Bing Crosby. In fact, he guest-starred on Crosby's radio program in 1950 as well as such other series as *Guard Session* and *Guest Star*.

In 1948 Perry brought his radio show to TV, but in the early days he made little concession to the camera, which was simply planted in front of the microphone as the star and his guests performed. The fifteen-minute NBC-TV show (*The Chesterfield Supper Club*) ran in various time slots through 1950, when *The Perry Como Show* moved to CBS-TV and was seen for a quarter hour on Monday, Wednesday, and Friday nights at 7:45 P.M. The series kept this format for five seasons while his radio show was broadcast on the Mutual network in 1953 and 1954 and then simulcast with the TV show on CBS during the 1954–55 season. In 1954, Perry won the first of his several Emmy Awards as a television musical show star. In 1955, Como's easygoing TV program became an hour-long variety outing on NBC each Saturday night, and he was now one of the most popular singers on TV, famed for his unruffability and his smooth singing of middle-of-the-road ballads. He also continued to be one of RCA's biggest sellers (often vying for top position with Tony Martin and Vaughn Monroe), with records like "A Bushel and a Peck" (with Betty Hutton), "Catch a Falling Star," "Caterina," "Don't Let the Stars Get in Your Eyes," "Hot Diggity," "If," "Just Born," "Love Makes the World Go 'Round," "Magic Moments," "Maybe" (with Eddie Fisher), "Moon Talk," "More," "No Other Love," "Papa Loves Mambo," "Round and Round" (a number-one hit on the charts), "You're Just in Love" (with the Fontaine Sisters) and "Zing, Zing—Zoom, Zoom." Perry also continued to make lucrative personal appearances, and on a domestic level, he and his wife adopted two children: son David and daughter Terri.

Perry's TV show moved to Wednesday nights on NBC-TV in 1959. The one-hour program remained an audience favorite (especially because he showcased a wide variety of new, popular performers) until the 1962–63 season, when it was overwhelmed in the ratings by CBS-TV's *The Beverly Hillbillies*, and it left the air in the spring of 1963. After that Como continued to appear on television every six to eight weeks in specials, but as the years progressed, these outings came farther and farther apart until, by the end of the decade, he was only making yearly appearances on the small screen, although his ratings remained strong. Como's record sales also began to slip, although his 1963 album, *The Songs I Love*, sold well. In the fall of 1970, however, Como attained his fourteenth gold record with "It's Impossible," and he followed it up with a best-selling album of the same title; in 1973, he had the best-seller "And I Love You," which again produced a charted LP.

With a resurgence in his career, Perry continued with his TV specials, most of them scheduled at various holiday times, plus he did good business with personal appearances at venues such as the Hilton Hotel in Las Vegas and Harrah's in Lake Tahoe. (In 1976 he enjoyed a highly successful concert tour in Australia.) In the 1980s, Como appeared in a PBS-TV special with the Boston Pops Orchestra. On June 21, 1983, RCA hosted a special dinner at the Rainbow Grill at New York's Rockefeller Center to honor Como's fortieth year with RCA Victor Records and his fiftieth anniversary as a performer. (Como's last RCA album was issued in the fall of 1987.) President Reagan bestowed Como with a Kennedy Center Award in 1987 for his outstanding achievements in the performing arts. Two years later, in June 1989, he was elected to the Academy of Television Arts and Sciences' Hall of Fame.

In 1993, Perry ended his fifty-year recording contract with RCA Victor Records. He and his wife continued to divide their time between Jupiter, Florida (where, when not entertaining his grandchildren and great-grandchild, he played golf, fished, and enjoyed taking long walks) and the North Carolina mountains. In August 1998, days after she and Perry celebrated their sixty-fifth wedding anniversary, Roselle Como died of a massive heart attack at age eighty-four. Not long thereafter, the singer developed Alzheimer's disease. On May 12, 2001, while seated in a bedroom chair at his Florida home at Jupiter Inlet Colony, he closed his eyes and died.

A spiritual man, Como always maintained that religion had been the foundation for his continuing success. He said once: "Everything that's ever happened to me has been the result of faith. The faith I found in my father's house, and now find in my own house, and in my world. Sure, there are different beliefs, but as long as men believe, they believe basically the same thing. The lyrics may be different, but the music is always the same."

Filmography

Something for the Boys (20th-Fox, 1944)
Doll Face (20th-Fox, 1945)
If I'm Lucky (20th-Fox, 1946)

Words and Music (MGM, 1948)
The Odessa File (Col, 1974) (voice only)

Radio Series

Beat the Band (NBC, 1940–41)
The Perry Como Show (CBS, 1943–44)
The Chesterfield Supper Club (NBC, 1944–49)

The Perry Como Show (Mutual, 1953–54; CBS, 1954–55)

TV Series

The Chesterfield Supper Club (NBC, 1948–50)
The Perry Como Show (CBS, 1950–55)

The Perry Como Show (NBC, 1955–61)
The Kraft Music Hall (NBC, 1961–63)

Album Discography

LPs

And I Love You So (RCA APL1-0100)
The Best of Irving Berlin's Songs from "Mr. President" (RCA LPM/LSP-2630) w. Kaye Ballard, Sandy Stewart
Bing Crosby and Perry Como (Broadway Intermission 123)
Blue Skies (Pair 2-1112)
Broadway Shows (RCA LPM-1191)
By Request (RCA LPM/LSP-2567)
By Special Request (RCA Special Products DPL1-0193)
Cole Porter in Paris (Bell System PH-36508) [ST/TV]
Como's Golden Records (RCA LOP-1007, RCA LPM/LSP-1981)
Como Swings (RCA LPM/LSP-2010)
Dream Along With Me (Camden CAL/CAS-403)
Dream on Little Dreamer (Camden CAS-2609)
Dreamer's Holiday (Camden CAL-582)
An Evening With Perry Como (Camden CAL-742)
Easy Listening (Camden CXS-9002)
Easy Listening (Pair 2-1001)
For the Young at Heart (RCA LPM/LSP-2343)
Greatest Hits (RCA International 89019)

Greatest Hits, Vol. 2 (RCA International 89020)
Hello Young Lovers (Camden CAS-2122)
I Believe (RCA LPM/LSP-4539)
Inside U.S.A. (SHB 5601) [OC]
It's Impossible (RCA LSP-4473)
Just (RCA AFL1-0863)
Just for You (Camden CAL/CAS-440)
Just for You (RCA Special Products DPL1-0153)
Just Out of Reach (RCA 1-0863)
Lightly Latin (RCA LPM/LSP-3552)
A Legendary Performer (RCA CPL1-1752)
Live on Tour (RCA AQL1-3826)
Look to Your Heart (RCA LSP-4052)
The Lord's Prayer (Camden CAS-2299)
Love Makes the World Go 'Round (Camden CAL/CAS-805)
Love Moods (Pair 2-10384)
Love You So (RCA AYL1-3672)
Make Someone Happy (Camden CAL-694)
Merry Christmas (RCA LPM-51)
No Other Love (Camden CAL/CAS-941)
The Odessa File (MCA 2084) [ST]
Over the Rainbow (RCA ANL1-2969)
Perry (RCA AFL1-0585)

Perry at His Best (RCA PR/PRS-138)

Perry Como (RCA LPC-160)

Perry Como in Italy (RCA LSP-3608)

Perry Como in Nashville (RCA 1009)

Perry Como Sings Broadway Shows (RCA LPM-1191)

Perry Como Sings Christmas Music (Camden CAL/CAS-660)

Perry Como Today (RCA 6368)

Perry Como's Wednesday Night Music Hall (Camden CAL-511)

Pop Singers on the Air! (Radiola 1149) w. Vic Damone, Eddie Fisher, and Dick Haymes

Pure Gold (RCA ANL1-0972)

Relaxing With Perry Como (RCA LPM-1176)

Saturday Night With Mr. C (RCA LOP/LSO-1004, RCA LPM/LSP-1971)

The Scene Changes (RCA LPM/LSP-3396)

Seattle (RCA LSP-4183)

Season's Greetings From Perry Como (RCA LPM/LSP-2066)

Sentimental Date (RCA LPM-3035)

A Sentimental Date With Perry Como (RCA LPC-187, RCA LPM-1177)

The Shadow of Your Smile (Camden CAS-2547)

Sing to Me, Mr. C (RCA LPM/LSP-2390)

So Smooth (RCA LPM-1085)

Somebody Loves Me (Camden CAL/CAS-858)

Something for the Boys (Caliban 6030) [ST]

The Songs I Love (RCA LPM/LSP-2708)

The Sweetest Sounds (Camden ACL-0444)

This Is Perry Como (RCA VSP-6026)

This Is Perry Como, Vol. 2 (RCA VSP-6067)

Till the End of Time (RCA LPC-109)

TV Favorites (RCA LPM-3013)

We Get Letters (RCA LPM-1463)

When You Come to the End of the Day (RCA LPM/LSP-1885)

Where You're Concerned (RCA AFL1-2641)

With Love (Family 149)

Words and Music (10″ MGM E-501, MGM E-3231, Metro M/S-578, JJA 19822, Sountrak 115) [ST]

You Are Never Far Away (Camden CAS-2201)

The Young Perry Como (MCA 1805) w. Ted Weems

CDs

All-Time Greatest Hits (RCA 8323-2-R)

And I Love You So (RCA Japan R32P-1048)

And I Love You So/It's Impossible (Collectables COL-CD-2767)

The Best of Perry Como (Applause 40872)

The Best of Perry Como (Camden 74321-37838-2)

The Best of Perry Como (Caravelle ST-9045)

The Best of Perry Como (CeDe International CD-66045)

The Best of Perry Como (Masters 501372)

The Best of Perry Como (Reader's Digest PD-74589)

The Best of Perry Como II (RCA Japan BVCP-2308)

The Best of Times (RCA PD-89970)

Best Hits (RCA Japan FBCP-30286)

Best Selection (BMG BVCP-2623)

Born to Be a Hit, Vol. 1 (Castle Communications PCD-10162)

Born to Be a Hit, Vol. 2 (Castle Communications PCD-10163)

Born to Be a Hit, Vol. 3 (Castle Communications PCD-10170)

Born to Be a Hit, Vol. 4 (Castle Communications PCD-10171)

By Request (RCA Japan BVCP-1012)

By Request (Snapper SMDCD-300)

By Request/Sing to Me, Mr. C (Collectables COL-CD-2762)

Catch a Falling Star (RCA Ariola Express 295038)

Christmas Album (Camden 74321-60783-2)

Christmas With Andy Williams and Perry Como (Delta 24953)

Christmas With Perry Como (BMG Special Products 44553)

Class Will Tell (Jasmine JASCD-362) w. Ted Weems

Classic Duo (Spectrum U4020)

Close to You (Castle Communications PCD-10112)

Close to You (PCI 82)

Cocktail Hour (Columbia River Entertainment Group CRG-218002)

Cole Porter in Paris (Bell System PH-36508) [ST/TV]

Como Swings (RCA Japan R25J-1004)

Como Swings/For the Young At Heart (Collectables COL-CD-2765)

Como's Golden Records (RCA 07863-53802-2)

Dear Mr. "C"—Perry Como's Songbook (RCA Japan BVCP-7301-05)

Definitive Collection (Camden 7271121)

Definitive Collection (PID 578212)

Dream Along With Me (RCA Camden CAD1-403)

Dream On Little Dreamer (Delta 6081)

Dreamer's Holiday (Delta 6077)

Easy Listening (Pair PDC-2-1001)

The Essential Perry Como, Vol. 1 (Collectables COL-CD-106)

The Essential Perry Como, Vol. 2 (Collectables COL-CD-107)

The Essential 60s Singles Collection (Taragon 1058)

For the Good Times—Como's Golden Records (PMI Entertainment PMI-6CD)

For You (Prism PLATCD-593)

44 Greatest Hits (Gold 53083)

The Golden Hits (Pearl Flapper 07849)

Great (Redx RXBOX-31061)

The Great Vocalists—Perry Como (Ronco CDSR067, Ronco Silver 9009)

Greatest Christmas Songs (RCA 07863-67790-2)

Greatest Gospel Songs (RCA 07863-67978-2)

Greatest Hits (Delta 64022)

Greatest Hits (RCA 07863-67436-2)

Het Beste Van (EVA/BMG PD-74589)

I Believe (BMG Special Products 44664)

I Dream of You (Disky 51247772)

I Want to Thank You Folks (Jasmine JASCD-359)

I Wish It Could Be Christmas Forever (RCA 4526-2-R)

I'm Confessin' (Memoir Classics 531)

The Incomparable Perry Como (Prism PLATCD-149)

Inside U.S.A. (SHB 5601) [OC]

It's Impossible (RCA Camden CAD1-2551)

Juke Box Baby (Bear Family BCD-15306)

Legendary (BMG 74321-75312-2)

Legendary Performer (RCA 07863-51752-2)

Legendary Singers: Perry Como (Heartland Music 1212-2)

Legendary Singers: Perry Como (Time-Life CDL-9153)

Lightly Latin (RCA Japan BVCJ-2038)

The Living Legend (Arcade ARC-94632)

Long Ago and Far Away (Legacy Entertainment 106)

The Long-Lost Hits (Collector's Choice Music CCM-054)

The Lord's Prayer (Delta 6079)

The Lord's Prayer/The Shadow of Your Smile/ Dream on Little Dreamer (Delta 6078)

Love Collection (Camden 74321-39342-2)

Love Letters (Hallmark 30012)

Love Letters From Perry Como (Viper's Nest VN-152-2)

Love Songs (Delta 6036)

Love Songs (Masters PID-424722)

The Love Songs (Music Club 125)

Magic Moments (The Entertainers 243)

Magic Moments (Pickwick PWKS-4124)

Magic Moments—The Very Best of Perry Como (Reader's Digest)

Moments to Remember (New Sound NST-111)

Moon River (CeDe International CD-66066)

My Greatest Songs (RCA 74321-10725-2)

The Odessa File (MCA 2084) [ST]

A Perfect World (Reprise 9-45516-2) [ST]

Perry Como (Bellaphon 288-07-270)

Perry Como (CTA TF-44)

Perry Como (Delta 64022)

Perry Como (Emporio EMPRCD-863)

Perry Como (The Entertainers 243)

Perry Como (Laserlight 40-222)

Perry Como (Pegasus PEG082)

Perry Como (RCA R32P-1016)

Perry Como and Matt Munro (J&B Records JB-393)

Perry Como Best (RCA Japan B23D-41065)

Perry Como—CD Diamond Series (RCA CD-90126)

The Perry Como Christmas Album (RCA ND-81929)

The Perry Como Collection (Castle Communications CCDSD-202)

Perry Como in Italy (RCA Japan BVCP-1014)

Perry Como Invites You to Dream Along With Me, Vols. 1 & 2 (Beautiful Music Company DMC2-0097)

Perry Como Live on Tour (RCA Japan BVCP-1015)

The Perry Como Shows, Vol. 1 (On the Air OTA-10195)

The Perry Como Shows, Vol. 2 (On the Air OTA-10196)

The Perry Como Shows, Vol. 3 (On the Air OTA-10197)

Perry Como Sings Hits From the Broadway Shows (RCA Japan BVCP-1009)

Perry Como Sings Just for You (RCA/Special Music CAD1-440)

Perry Como Sings Merry Christmas Music (Castle Communications CXMAS-11, RCA Camden CAD1-660)

Perry Como Sings Merry Christmas Songs (Laserlight 21-722)

Perry Como Today (RCA 6368-2-R)

Perry Como's Christmas Concert (Teal Entertainment TD5001-2, K-tel ECD-3209-UK1995)

Perry Como's 20 Greatest Hits (RCA ND-89019)

Perry Como's 20 Greatest Hits, Vol. 2 (RCA ND-89020)

Perry-Go-Round (Jasmine JASCD-344)

The Platinum Collection (Star Entertainment PC-607)

Pop Singers on the Air (Radiola 1149) w. Vic Damone, Eddie Fisher, Dick Haymes

A Portrait of Perry Como (Gallerie 448)

Prisoner of Love (St. Clair 344)

Pure Gold (RCA 0972-2-R)

Round and Round and Other Hits (RCA 07863-52167-2)

Saturday Night With Mr. C./When You Come To the End of the Day (Collectables COL-CD-2763)

Season's Greetings From Perry Como (RCA 07863-61001-2)

The Shadow of Your Smile (Delta 6080)

Sing for Me, Mr "C" (RCA Japan BVCP-1011)

Sing-A-Long (Priddis Music 1176)

16 Most Requested Songs (Castle Communications 481074-2)

So Smooth (RCA Japan R25J-1039)

So Smooth/We Get Letters (Collectables COL-CD-2764)

Softly (Back Biter BB-61055)

Some Enchanted Evening (Double DBG-5083)

The Songs I Love (RCA Japan BVCP-1013)

Super Selection (Jasdac EUC-305)

Take It Easy (RCA ND-90490)

Take Me In Your Arms (Pilz 449344-2)

They Say It's Wonderful (Prism PLATCD-592)

30 Favorites (Heartland Music 12120-2)

Till the End of Time (BCD GLD-29393, Goldies 25393)

Till the End of Time (Charly CDCD-1256)

Till the End of Time (Fat Boy FATCD-259)

Till the End of Time: 1936-45, Early Hits (ASV CD-AJA-5195)

20 Greatest Hits, Vol. 1 (BMG ND-89019)

24 Karat Gold (BMG Netherlands 74321-39008-2)

Two Family House (RCA 07863-63733-2) [ST]

TV Favorites (Collectables COL-CD-2766)

The Ultimate Collection (BMG 74321-60219-2)

V-Discs Recordings (Collector's Choice 6652)

The Very Best of Perry Como (RCA 07863-67968-2)

We Get Letters (RCA Japan BVCP-1010)

World of Dreams (RCA 74321-27849-2)

Words and Music (Sony Music Special Products AK-47111, JJA 19822) [ST]

Yesterday and Today: A Celebration in Song (RCA 07863-66098-2)

You Are Never Far Away (RCA/Special Music CAD1-2201)

Bing Crosby

(b. Harry Lillis Crosby, Tacoma, Washington, May 5, 1903; d. near Madrid, Spain, October 14, 1977)

Bing Crosby, the most famous of all crooners, is considered by many critics and fans to be the most popular entertainer of all time. Certainly he was one of the most consistently active of twentieth-century performers, and he achieved monumental success in practically all aspects of show business he chose to participate in; only Broadway eluded him as he never ventured onto the stage in a play. Bing Crosby appeared in more than one hundred films, winning one Academy Award, and he is one of the all-time-best record sellers, with disc sales exceeding 200 million copies. His recording of "White Christmas," with sales of over 10 million, is the champion best-selling seasonal disc. In addition, he was a star of radio for over three decades, he mastered television successfully in a series of specials, and he was a big star in vaudeville and made numerous personal appearances throughout his more than a half century as an entertainer. Crosby's popularity seems to have been fostered equally by both his many talents and his likable personality, although the latter came under fire in such books as *Bing Crosby: The Hollow Man* (1981) by Donald Shepherd and Robert F. Slatzer and son Gary's *Going My Own Way* (1983). Nevertheless, troubadour Bing Crosby will always be thought of as the easygoing warbler who magically captivated a nation for some fifty years. In the early days, Crosby's singing style was sincere with emotion and vocal clarity. By the mid-'30s, however, he adapted the carefree, relaxed manner that included his famous "bo-bo-ba-bo" style (because he was said to have a poor memory for lyrics) as well as a penchant for whistling the chorus.

Harry Lillis Crosby was born in Tacoma, Washington, on May 5, 1903, the son of Harry Lowe and Catherine Helen (Harrigan) Crosby; he had four brothers (one of whom, Bob, became a bandleader and occasional film player) and two sisters, and he was the fourth of the seven siblings. He earned the nickname "Bing" because of his addiction to the comic strip "The Bingville Bugle" as a child. In school he played football and baseball and won medals as a swimmer. He continued his athletic pursuits at Gonzaga University, where he studied law, but he was more interested in singing and playing the drums than either his major or sports. He dropped out of college in 1921, and he and friend Al Rinker went to Los Angeles, where the latter's sister, Mildred Bailey, was a successful singer at various nightspots. The duo, billed as "Two Boys and a Piano—Singing Songs Their Own Way," got vaudeville bookings. In 1926, they joined Paul Whiteman's band unit, and the same year Crosby and Riker recorded "I've Got the Girl" for Columbia. Crosby's first solo record was "Muddy Water" for Victor in March 1927. Thereafter Whiteman added pianist Harry Barris to their act, and the trio became known as Paul Whiteman's Rhythm Boys. Under that name, they recorded many sides with the famed bandleader on Victor through 1930, with Crosby sometimes performing vocal solos.

In 1930, Whiteman and His Orchestra appeared in the Universal color musical *The King of Jazz*, and Crosby was *supposed* to be spotlighted on the tune "Song of the Dawn," but a drunk-

Frances Farmer, Bing Crosby, Bob Burns, and Martha Raye in an advertisement for *Rhythm on the Range* (1936). [Courtesy of JC Archives]

driving charge landed him in jail. The song went to John Boles, although Crosby and the Rhythm Boys did appear in the film performing a quartet of songs. The Rhythm Boys then left Whiteman in March 1930 to join Gus Arnheim's orchestra at the Cocoanut Grove, where Crosby did many vocal solos (and some duets with the band's violin player, Russ Columbo) and got national exposure via the Grove's radio broadcasts. Crosby also began recording vocals with Arnheim on Victor, and would continue to do so until the spring of 1931, when the boys broke with Arnheim. At that point, the trio dissolved, and Crosby went solo. Also in 1930, Crosby married film starlet Dixie Lee and starred in two Pathé film shorts, *Ripstitch the Tailor* and *Two Plus Fours*. As a solo, Crosby landed singing bits in two 1931 features, *Reaching for the Moon* and *Confessions of a Co-ed*.

Nineteen thirty-one was the breakthrough year for Crosby, the one that sent him on his way to superstardom. By now Bing's older brother, Everett, was managing his career. He maneuvered him into a job singing for CBS radio as well as starring in a series of comedy shorts for Mack Sennett in which Bing sang songs he recorded under his new pact with Brunswick Records and featured on the air. The radio show debuted in the late summer of 1931, and along with Kate Smith, Bing became one of the network's two most popular radio singers. He played for twenty weeks at the Paramount Theater in New York City, earning $2,500 per week for the first half of the vaudeville booking and $4,000 per week for the rest of the enormously popular stand. His Brunswick discs also began selling well, despite the Depression, and he had success with "Just One More Chance," "I Found a Million Dollar Baby," "I'm Through With Love," "Dinah," and his radio theme "When the Blue of the Night Meets the Gold of the Day." Crosby quickly became Brunswick's biggest seller, eclipsing its former champions Nick Lucas (after whom Bing patterned his crooning style) and the Mills Brothers.

Bing had become so popular that in 1932, he signed a deal with Paramount to appear in five feature films in three years for $300,000. The first movie (in which he insisted on second billing to the actual lead player, character performer Stuart Erwin) was *The Big Broadcast* (1932), the first of many features interpolating radio personalities into its plot; Bing sang one of his biggest hits, "Please," in the picture. After that Crosby was top-billed in a series of pleasant musicals including *College Humor* (1933) and *We're Not Dressing* (1934), plus a loanout to MGM to costar with Marion Davies in *Going Hollywood* (1933).

By now, Crosby was one of the film capital's top-ten box-office draws, and his 1934 CBS radio contract called for him to make $6,000 per week for thirty-nine weekly broadcasts. Also that year he became the first singer to sign with Jack Kapp's newly formed Decca Records, where he would remain for two decades. At Decca and on radio, Bing Crosby's singing style began to change from the strong-voiced romantic crooner (of which he was the best) to the easygoing "groaner" in a style that seemed to solidify his popularity with the American public. His PR also emphasized his status as an all-around family man and the father of four sons: Gary (born in 1933), twins Philip and Dennis (born in 1934), and Lindsay (born in 1937). Later, some of his sons would claim that Crosby was less than the model father he claimed to be.

In 1935, Bing joined NBC radio as host of the *Kraft Music Hall*, remaining with the show for eleven years. He continued to make popular films for Paramount, such as *Mississippi* (1935) with W. C. Fields and *Rhythm on the Range* (1936) with Frances Farmer and Martha Raye. He was loaned to Columbia Pictures for *Pennies From Heaven* (1936), and returned to his home lot to star in such frothy Paramount entries as *Waikiki Wedding* (1937) and *Sing You Sinners* (1938). Then, again, he was loaned to Universal, for *East Side of Heaven* (1939) with Joan Blondell and thereafter returned to Paramount to play vaudeville impresario Gus Edwards in *The Star Maker* (1939).

For Decca Records, Bing began turning out a host of best-selling platters like "Love Is Just Around the Corner," "Soon," "It's Easy to Remember," "I Wished on the Moon," "Red Sails in the Sunset," "Pennies From Heaven," "You Must Have Been a Beautiful Baby," and "Maybe," among many others. Often he successfully waxed songs he sang in his Paramount features. In 1936 Bing and his wife Dixie Lee recorded duets on "The Way You Look Tonight," and "A Fine Romance."

In 1940, Crosby's screen image began to change when he costarred with comedian Bob Hope in the first of their *Road* movie comedies, *Road to Singapore*. Instead of the crooning leading man, Bing became a wisecracking comedian as he and Bob made fast work of the film scripts that they peppered liberally with topical adlibs (devised by their writing staffs). These pictures also boasted exotic locales, fine music, and pretty girls, most specifically Dorothy Lamour, who appeared with them in all the *Road* entries. Crosby and Hope also earned a percentage deal on the screen series and made a bundle from the movies' immense profits.

In addition to the *Road* comedies, which kept him in the top ten at the box-office, Bing continued to appear in such musicals as *If I Had My Way* (1940) with Gloria Jean at Universal and *Birth of the Blues* (1941) with Mary Martin, and he costarred with Fred Astaire in the Yuletime classic *Holiday Inn* (1942), in which Crosby introduced Irving Berlin's "White Christmas" (which became Bing's top-selling single recording). During this World War II period, Bing was also a tireless worker for the war effort, entertaining both in the United States and overseas with the USO, and he appeared on scores of patriotic radio shows such as *Command Performance* and *Mail Call*. In 1944, he won an Oscar for his portrayal of down-to-earth Father O'Malley in Paramount's *Going My Way*, and he repeated the winning portrayal the next year for RKO's equally good *The Bells of St. Mary's* with Ingrid Bergman. In the mid-'40s, Crosby turned to film production, but his two efforts, *The Great John L.* (1945) and a remake (1946) of *Abie's Irish Rose* (1928) were not successful; he could afford the losses, though, since he was estimated to have earned $868,000 in 1946 alone.

After World War II, Bing continued to make movies and be heard on radio. He also resumed making records following the end of the ban on recording ASCAP songs in 1945. His platters continued to sell well for the rest of the decade, with hits like "If I Loved You," "Personality," "Golden Earrings," "Tallahassee" (one of a number of duets he did with the Andrews Sisters), "Memories," and "Dear Hearts and Gentle People." Wanting more free time, Crosby terminated his NBC contract and began prerecording his radio shows on tape with *Philco Radio Time* for ABC. On film he reteamed with Fred Astaire for the buoyant *Blue Skies* (1946), and he also starred in an amusing version of *A Connecticut Yankee in King Arthur's Court* (1949), along with other musicals and the continuing *Road* series with Bob Hope.

In 1949, Chesterfield Cigarettes took over the sponsorship of Bing's ABC radio show and it became *The Bing Crosby Show*, which ran until 1956. On-camera he and Jane Wyman sang Hoagy Carmichael's "In the Cool, Cool, Cool of the Evening" in *Here Comes the Groom* (1951). Increasingly, Bing was turning to dramatic roles in films like *Just for You* (1952—also with Wyman) and *Little Boy Lost* (1953). Probably one of his most inspired roles, as the drunken former stage star in *The Country Girl* (1954), earned him an Oscar nomination opposite Academy Award–winning Grace Kelly. He and Bob Hope made *The Road to Bali* (1953), their penultimate *Road* entry. By the mid-'50s, the inroads of television had greatly cut into his radio audience, and the coming of rock 'n' roll eclipsed Bing's record sales. In the late 1950s, he left Decca but continued to be an active recording artist for companies like Capitol, RCA Victor, Warner Bros. and Reprise well into the 1960s.

Although Crosby had always photographed well on film, like many big-time performers he had been leery of television, and he did not make his debut in the medium until June 1952 (at the age of fifty-one), when he and pal Bob Hope hosted a telethon for the Olympic Fund. Later that year, Bing's wife Dixie Lee died of cancer. Two years later, Bing starred in the pleasing musical comedy *White Christmas* (1954) with Danny Kaye and Rosemary Clooney. A big moneymaker in its original release, it was later always shown on TV during the year's-end holiday season. Bing ended his long-time association with Paramount with 1956's *Anything Goes* playing a faded stage star who hopes for a comeback.

Also in 1956, the singer teamed with Grace Kelly and Frank Sinatra (who had been Crosby's biggest rival as a crooner in the 1940s) for *High Society*, MGM's musical remake of *The Philadelphia Story* (1940). The bright proceedings featured longtime Crosby musical friend Louis Armstrong, and the hit movie had Crosby and Kelly dueting "True Love," which became a hugely popular single. Bing did basically dramatic roles in *Man on Fire* (1957) and *Say One for Me* (1959), the latter finding him again as a priest. (There were a few songs scattered within the drama.) He produced this latter film at Twentieth Century-Fox as he also did the college-set shenanigans of *High Time* (1960).

In 1958, Bing returned to network radio for CBS's *The Ford Road Show* with Rosemary Clooney, which ran until 1962. By now Bing was more active in television and had guested on Joan Davis's comedy series, *I Married Joan*. In 1956 he costarred with Julie Andrews on CBS-TV's elaborate production of "High Tor" on *Ford Star Jubilee*. He also began appearing on variety shows like those hosted by Jackie Gleason, Bob Hope, and Perry Como. In 1957 Crosby married young actress Kathryn Grant, and they would have three children: Harry (born in 1958), Mary Frances (born in 1959), and Nathaniel (born in 1961).

In 1962, Crosby and Bob Hope did their last *Road* picture, *Road to Hong Kong* (with only a guest bit by Dorothy Lamour). Crosby had his final dramatic role in a feature film, that of the drunken doctor in the disappointing big-screen remake of *Stagecoach*, in 1966. He also starred on the unsuccessful TV sitcom *The Bing Crosby Show* for ABC in the 1964–65 season. By this time his recordings were only sporadic, although his older material was being reissued constantly. Crosby turned down the lead role (which went to Lee Marvin) in the film musical of the Broadway hit *Paint Your Wagon* (1969) because he did not wish to go on location.

During the 1970s, Bing, now head of Bing Crosby Productions, which produced film and television projects, appeared in the telefeature *Dr. Cook's Garden* as the kindly doctor who practices euthanasia on dying patients, a part played by Burl Ives on Broadway. He was offered the lead in the *Columbo* detective teleseries, but did not wish a long-term commitment. Bing appeared in a number of well-mounted television specials in tandem with his wife and three youngest children, and as a group, they also made personal appearances, both in the United States and abroad. Most fans seemed to agree that Crosby's voice had continued to season into a fine timbre, and he recorded for labels like Pickwick, Amos, and Daybreak. For the latter, he and Count Basie did an album in 1972. Bing remained popular in England, and in the mid-'70s he recorded two LPS there for

United Artists, one with Fred Astaire. From his Solo album, Bing's single of "Tie a Yellow Ribbon 'Round the Old Oak Tree" was a bestseller in the British Isles.

On March 3, 1977, Bing had finished taping a TV special saluting his half century in show business when he fell into the orchestra pit and was sidelined for months with a ruptured disc. Despite that fall, he and his family taped his annual Christmas program, and they appeared for two weeks before SRO crowds at the London Palladium. He also recorded his final album, *Seasons*, for Polydor Records. There was serious talk of Crosby and Hope making yet another *Road* picture. After the London work, Bing went to Spain for a golfing holiday (he was a near-fanatical enthusiast of the sport), and on October 14, 1977, at age seventy-six, he collapsed and died from a heart attack on a golf course near Madrid, Spain. When Bing Crosby died he left several million dollars in a blind trust to his four oldest sons, stipulating they could not collect the money until they turned sixty-five. Only Philip lived long enough to inherit the $10 million fortune, as Lindsay and Dennis both committed suicide, the former on December 11, 1989, and the latter on May 4, 1991; Gary Crosby died of cancer on August 24, 1995. In 2001, the first volume of Gary Giddins's two-part biography of Bing appeared, *Bing Crosby: A Pocketful of Dreams—The Early Years, 1903–1940*, which emphasized the singer's jazz roots and innovative crooning.

Once when asked about his extraordinarily successful career, Bing Crosby remarked, "I wouldn't change a thing. I would do it just exactly the same way—by singing. I had a wonderful time. I would want everything to be the same."

Filmography

Ripstitch the Tailor (Pathé, 1930) (s)
Two Plus Fours (Pathé, 1930) (s)
King of Jazz (Univ, 1930)
Check and Double Check (RKO, 1930)
I Surrender Dear (Educational, 1931) (s)
One More Chance (Educational, 1931) (s)
At Your Command (Educational, 1931) (s)
Reaching for the Moon (UA, 1931)
Confessions of a Co-ed [Her Dilemma] (Par, 1931)
The Billboard Girl (Educational, 1932) (s)
Hollywood on Parade #2 (Par, 1932) (s)
Dream House (Educational, 1932) (s)
Hollywood on Parade #4 (Par, 1932) (s)
The Big Broadcast (Par 1932)
Blue of the Night (Par, 1933) (s)
Please (Par, 1933) (s)
Sing, Bing Sing (Par, 1933) (s)
College Humor (Par, 1933)
Too Much Harmony (Par, 1933)
Going Hollywood (MGM, 1933)
Just an Echo (Par, 1934) (s)
We're Not Dressing (Par, 1934)
Here Is My Heart (Par, 1934)
She Loves Me Not (Par, 1934)
Star Night at the Cocoanut Grove (MGM, 1935) (s)
Mississippi (Par, 1935)
Two for Tonight (Par, 1935)
The Big Broadcast of 1936 (Par, 1935)

Anything Goes (Par, 1936)
Rhythm on the Range (Par, 1936)
Pennies From Heaven (Col, 1936)
Waikiki Wedding (Par, 1937)
Screen Snapshots #5 (Col, 1937) (s)
Double or Nothing (Par, 1937)
Swing With Bing (Univ, 1937) (s)
Sing You Sinners (Par, 1938)
Don't Hook Now (Par, 1938) (s)
Hollywood Handicap (MGM, 1938) (s)
Dr. Rhythm (Par, 1938)
Paris Honeymoon (Par, 1938)
The Star Maker (Par, 1938)
East Side of Heaven (Univ, 1939)
Swing With Bing (Univ, 1940) (s)
Rhythm on the River (Par, 1940)
Picture People #1 (RKO, 1940) (s)
Road to Singapore (Par, 1940)
If I Had My Way (Univ, 1940)
Birth of the Blues (Par, 1941)
Road to Zanzibar (Par, 1941)
Meet the Stars—The Stars at Play (Rep 1941) (s)
My Favorite Blonde (Par, 1942) (guest)
Holiday Inn (Par, 1942)
Angel of Mercy (MGM, 1942) (s)
Road to Morocco (Par, 1942)
Star Spangled Rhythm (Par, 1942)
Dixie (Par, 1943)
The Road to Victory (WB, 1943) (s)

Show Business at War (20th-Fox, 1943) (s)
The Princess and the Pirate (RKO, 1943) (guest)
The Shining Future (WB, 1944) (s)
Going My Way (RKO, 1944)
Here Come the Waves (Par, 1944)
Road to Utopia (Par, 1945)
All Star Bond Rally (20th-Fox, 1945) (s)
Hollywood Victory Caravan (Par, 1945) (s)
State Fair (20th-Fox, 1945) (voice only)
Duffy's Tavern (Par, 1945)
Out of This World (Par, 1945) (voice only)
The Bells of St. Mary's (RKO, 1945)
Monsieur Beaucaire (Par, 1946) (guest)
Blue Skies (Par, 1946)
Screen Snapshots #9 (Col, 1946) (s)
Road to Hollywood (Astor, 1946)
Welcome Stranger (Par, 1947)
My Favorite Brunette (Par, 1947) (guest)
Road to Rio (Par, 1947)
Variety Girl (Par, 1947)
The Emperor Waltz (Par, 1948)
Rough But Hopeful (Unk, 1948) (s)
A Connecticut Yankee in King Arthur's Court [A Yankee in King Arthur's Court] (Par, 1948)
The Road to Peace (Unk, 1949) (s)
It's in the Groove (Unk, 1949) (s)
Honor Caddie (Unk, 1949) (s)
You Can Change the World (Unk, 1949) (s)
The Adventures of Ichabod and Mr. Toad (RKO, 1949) (narrator)
Down Memory Lane (Eagle-Lion, 1949)
Top o' the Morning (Par, 1950)
Riding High (Par, 1950)
Mr. Music (Par, 1950)
Here Comes the Groom (Par, 1951)
Angels in the Outfield [Angels and the Pirates] (MGM, 1951) (guest)
A Millionaire for Christy (20th-Fox, 1951) (voice only)

The Greatest Show on Earth (Par, 1952) (guest)
Son of Paleface (Par, 1952) (guest)
Just for You (Par, 1952)
Road to Bali (Par, 1952)
Little Boy Lost (Par, 1953)
Faith, Hope and Hogan (Unk, 1953) (s) (guest)
Off Limits [Military Policemen] (Par, 1953) (guest)
Scared Stiff (Par, 1953) (guest)
White Christmas (Par, 1954)
The Country Girl (Par, 1954)
Bing Presents Oreste (Par, 1955) (s)
Hollywood Fathers (Col, 1955) (s)
Anything Goes (Par, 1956)
High Society (MGM, 1956)
The Heart of Show Business (Col, 1956) (s) (narrator)
Man on Fire (MGM, 1957)
Showdown at Ulcer Gulch (Saturday Evening Post, 1958) (s)
Alias Jesse James (UA, 1959) (guest)
Say One for Me (20th-Fox, 1959)
This Game of Golf (Unk, 1959) (s)
Your Caddy Sir (Unk, 1959) (s)
Let's Make Love (20th-Fox, 1960) (guest)
High Time (20th-Fox, 1960)
Pepe (Col, 1960)
Kitty Caddy (Unk, 1961) (s) (voice only)
The Road to Hong Kong (UA, 1962)
The Sound of Laughter (Union, 1963)
Robin and the 7 Hoods (WB-7 Arts, 1964)
Bing Crosby's Cinerama Adventures [Cinerama's Russian Adventure] (Cin,1964) (narrator)
Stagecoach (20th-Fox, 1966)
Bing Crosby's Washington's State (Cinecrest, 1968) (s)
Golf's Golden Years (Unk, 1970) (s) (narrator)
Dr. Cook's Garden (ABC-TV 1/19/71)
Cancel My Reservation (WB, 1972) (guest)
That's Entertainment! (MGM, 1974) (cohost)

Radio Series

Fifteen Minutes With Crosby (CBS, 1931)
The Bing Crosby Show (CBS, 1931–35)
Kraft Musical Hall (NBC, 1935–40)
The Bing Crosby Show (NBC, 1940–46)

Philco Radio Time With Bing Crosby (ABC, 1946–49)
The Bing Crosby Show (CBS, 1949–56)
The Ford Road Show With Bing Crosby and Rosemary Clooney (CBS, 1958–62)

TV Series

The Bing Crosby Show (ABC, 1964–65)

Album Discography

LPs

Accentuate the Positive (Decca DL-4258)

Ali Baba and the 40 Thieves (Golden 20)

All the Way (Blue & Gold 1)

All-Time Hit Parade (Longines 224)

America, I Hear You Singing (Reprise 2020) w. Frank Sinatra, Fred Waring

The Andrews Sisters Show (Radiola MR-1033) w. the Andrews Sisters, Gabby Hayes

Anything Goes (Caliban 6043) [ST] (1936 version)

Anything Goes (Decca DL-4264)

Anything Goes (Decca DL-8318) [ST] (1956 version)

Around the World With Bing (Decca DL-8687)

At My Time of Life (UA 29956)

Auld Lang Syne (10″ Decca DL-5028)

Beloved Hymns (10″ Decca DL-5351)

The Best of Bing (Decca DXB-184/DXS-7184, MCA 4045)

The Big Broadcast (Sountrak 101) [ST]

The Big Broadcast of 1935 (Kasha King 1935) [ST/R]

The Big Broadcast of 1936 (10″ Decca DL-6008) [ST]

Bing—A Musical Autobiography (Decca DX-151)

Bing—A Musical Autobiography, Vols. 1–5 (Decca DL-9054, 9064, 9067, 9077, 9078)

Bing and Al, Vols. 1–6 (Totem 1003, 1007, 1013, 1015, 1016, 1017) w. Al Jolson

Bing and Bob Hope (Spokane 22)

Bing and Connee (10″ Decca Dl-5390) w. Connee Boswell

Bing and Connee Boswell (Spokane 18)

Bing and Dinah Shore (Spokane 32)

Bing and Hoppy (Critter 8901) w. William Boyd

Bing and Louis (Metro M/S-591) w. Louis Armstrong

Bing and Mary—Rhythm on the Radio (Star-Tone 225) w. Mary Martin

Bing and Satchmo (MGM E/SE-3882) w. Louis Armstrong

Bing and the Dixieland Bands (10″ Decca DL-5323, Decca DL-8493)

Bing and the Music Maids (Spokane 21)

Bing and Trudy Erwin (Spokane 23)

Bing at His Extra Special (Avenue International 1018)

Bing, Bob and Judy (Totem 1009) w. Bob Hope and Judy Garland

Bing Crosby (Going Hollywood—no number)

Bing Crosby (Metro M/S-523)

Bing Crosby and Al Jolson Duets (Amalgamated 0003)

Bing Crosby and Bob Hope (Radiola 1044) w. Dorothy Lamour

Bing Crosby and Dorothy Lamour—Live (Amalgamated 237)

Bing Crosby and Friends (Magic 3)

Bing Crosby and Friends, Vol. 2 (Magic 10)

Bing Crosby and Perry Como (Broadway Intermission 123)

Bing Crosby and Red Nichols—Together Again (Broadway Intermission 142)

Bing Crosby and the Andrews Sisters (MCA Coral 804)

Bing Crosby and the Andrews Sisters, Vols. 1–3 (Coral 80, 91, 112)

Bing Crosby and the Rhythm Boys (Arcadia 5001)

Bing Crosby at the Music Hall (Joyce 1117)

Bing Crosby Classics, Vols. 1–3 (Cap SM 11738-40)

A Bing Crosby Collection, Vols. 1–3 (Col C-35093, C-35094, C-35748)

Bing Crosby, Duke Ellington and Nat (King) Cole (Amalgamated 253)

Bing Crosby/Glenn Miller—Rare Radio (Broadway Intermission 114)

Bing Crosby, Groucho Marx and Maurice Chevalier (Amalgamated 221)

Bing Crosby—His Greatest Hits (Musidisc 30CV1356)

Bing Crosby in Hollywood (Col C2L-43)

Bing Crosby in the Thirties, Vols. 1–3 (JSP 1076, 1084, 1104)

Bing Crosby Live at the London Palladium (K-Tel 951)

Bing Crosby, Lucille Ball and Spike Jones—Live (Amalgamated 239)

Bing Crosby on the Air (Sandy Hook 2002)

Bing Crosby on the Air (Spokane 1)

Bing Crosby on the Air (Totem 1008) w. the Boswell Sisters

Bing Crosby Reads Tom Sawyer (Argo 561-63)

The Bing Crosby Show (Memorabilia 705)

Bing Crosby Sings (Vocalion 3603)

Bing Crosby Sings for Children (Vocalion 73769)

Bing Crosby Sings the Great Songs (MCA 2721)

Bing Crosby Sings the Great Standards (Verve 4129)

Bing Crosby Sings the Hits (10″ Decca DL-5520)

The Bing Crosby Story, Vol. 1 (Col Special Products 201)

The Bing Crosby Story, Vol. 1—The Early Jazz Years (Epic E2E-201)

Bing Crosby—The Best (Music for Pleasure 5814)

Bing Crosby Treasury (Longines 344)

Bing Crosby With Special Guests (Amalgamated 1007)

Bing Goes Latin (MGM 2354-028)

Bing in Paris (Decca DL-8780)

Bing in the Thirties, Vols. 1–8 (Spokane 12, 14, 24, 25, 26, 27, 28, 29)

Bing Is Back (Totem 1002)

Bing 'n' Basie (Daybreak 2014) w. Count Basie

Bing 1932-34 (Col Special Products 14369)

Bing Sings (Reader's Digest 127)

Bing Sings Broadway (MCA 173)

Bing Sings Crosby (Broadway Intermission 139)

Bing Sings While Bregman Swings (Verve 2020) w. Buddy Bregman

Bing With a Beat (RCA LPM-1473)

Der Bingle (10″ Col CL-2502)

Der Bingle, Vols. 1–5 (Spokane 5, 10, 20, 30, 32)

Bingo Viejo (Anahuac International ANC-3901)

Bing's Beaus (Amalgamated 805) w. Tallulah Bankhead, Marlene Dietrich

Bing's Music (Magic 1)

Bing's Party (Artistic 001)

Birth of the Blues (Spokane 9) [ST/R]

Bix 'n' Bing (ASV 5005) w. Bix Beiderbecke, Paul Whiteman

Blue Hawaii (Decca DL-8269)

Blue of the Night (10″ Decca DL-5105)

Blue Skies (10″ Decca DL-5042, Decca DL-4259) w. Fred Astaire

Blue Skies (Sountrak 104) [ST]

Both Sides of Bing Crosby (Curtain Calls 100/2)

But Beautiful (Decca DL-4260)

The Chesterfield Show, Vols. 1–2 (Joyce 1133, 6050)

The Chronological Bing Crosby, Vols. 1–11 (Jonzo 1-11)

Christmas Greetings (10″ Decca DL-502)

Christmas Sing With Bing (Decca-8419)

Christmas With Bing Crosby, Nat (King) Cole and Dean Martin (Cap SL-6925)

The Classic Years (BBC 648)

Cole Porter Songs (10″ Decca DL-5064)

Collection of Early Recordings, Vols. 1–2 (10″ Brunswick BL-5800-1)

Collector's Classics, Vols. 1–8 (10″ Decca DL-6088-6015)

Columbo, Crosby and Sinatra (10″ RCA LPT-5) w. Russ Columbo, Frank Sinatra

Command Performance, U.S.A. (Tulip 108)

The Complete Bing Crosby (Silver Eagle—no number)

Cool of the Evening (Decca DL-5321)

Country Girl (10″ Decca DL-5556) [ST]

Country Style (10″ Decca DL-5321)

A Couple of Song and Dance Men (UA LA-588-G) w. Fred Astaire

Cowboy Songs, Vols. 1–2 (Decca DL-5107, 5129)

The Crooner (Col C4X-44229)

Crosby Classics, Vols. 1–2 (10″ Col CL-6027, CL-6105)

Crosby, Columbo and Sinatra (10″ RCA LPT-5) w. Russ Columbo and Frank Sinatra

Crosbyana, Vol. 1–2 (Broadway Intermission 111, 116)

Day Dreaming (Coral 113)

Dick Powell—Bing Crosby (Amalgamated 162)

The Dinah Shore-Bing Crosby Show (Sunbeam 309)

Distinctively Bing (Sunbeam 502) w. Guy Lombardo

Don't Fence Me In (10″ Decca DL-5063)

Down Memory Lane, Vols. 1–2 (10″ Decca DL-5340, 5343)

Drifting and Dreaming (10″ Decca DL-5119)

The Early Bing Crosby (Ajazz 526)

Early Film Soundtracks (Biograph BLP-M-1) [ST]

Early Gold (Col Special Products P4-13153)

The Early Thirties, Vols. 1–2 (Ace of Hearts 40, 88)

East Side of Heaven (Decca DL-4253)

Easy to Remember (Saville 190)

El Bingo (10″ Decca DL-5011)

El Señor Bingo (MGM E/SE-3890)

Emperor Waltz (10″ Decca DL-5272)

The Emperor's New Clothes (Golden 79)

Fancy Meeting You Here (RCA LPM/LSP-1854, RCA International 89315) w. Rosemary Clooney

Favorite Hawiian Songs, Vols. 1–2 (10″ Decca DL-5122, 5299)

51 Good Time Songs (WB 1435)

Forever (RCA International 89535)

From Bing's Collection, Vols. 1–2 (Broadway Intermission 135, 136)

From the Forties (Joyce 6052)

George Gershwin Songs (10″ Decca DL-5081)

Go West Young Man (10″ Decca DL-5302)

Going My Way/The Bells of St. Mary's (10″ Decca DL-5052)

Golden Memories (Col Special Products P614370)

Goldilocks (Decca DL-3511) [ST/TV]

Great Country Hits (Cap T/ST-2346, Cap SM-11737)

The Greatest Christmas Show (Music for Pleasure 210)

The Greatest Hits of Bing Crosby (M.F./MCA 7007)

Happy Holiday (Spokane 6)

The Happy Prince/The Small One (10″ Decca DL-6000)

Havin' Fun (Sounds Rare 5009) w. Louis Armstrong

Here Is My Heart (Caliban 6042) [ST]

Here Lies Love (ASV 5043)

Hey Bing! (MCA 915)

Hey Jude—Hey Bing! (Amos 7001, Springboard SP-4003)

High Society (Cap W/SW-750) [ST]

High Tor (Decca DL-8272) [ST/TV]

Holiday in Europe (Decca DL-4281)

Holiday Inn (10″ Decca DL-5092, Decca DL-4256, MCA 25205) w. Fred Astaire

Holiday Inn (Sountrak 112) [ST]

Holiday Inn/The Bells of St. Mary's (Spokane 15) [ST/R]

Home on the Range (Decca DL-8210)

How Lovely Is Christmas (Golden 121)

I Love You Truly (Coral 79)

Ichabod/Rip Van Winkle (Disneyland ST-1920) [ST]

I'll Sing You a Song of the Islands (Coral 90)

In a Little Spanish Town (Decca DL-8846)

Jack Be Nimble (Golden 23)

The Jazzin' Bing Crosby (Top Classic Historia 622)

Jerome Kern Songs (10″ Decca DL-5001)

Join Bing in a Gang Song Sing Along (WB 1422)

Judy and Bing Together (Legend 1973) w. Judy Garland

Just Breezin' Along—A Tenth Anniversary Momento (EMI 1274)

Just for Fun, Vols. 1–2 (Broadway Intermission 134, 138)

Just for You (10″ Decca Dl-5417)

King of Jazz (Caliban 6025) [ST]

Kraft Music Hall, Vols. 1–7 (Spokane 2, 3, 4, 7, 11, 13, 17)

Le Bing (10″ Decca DL-5499)

A Legendary Performer (RCA CPL1-2086)

Lullaby Time (Decca DL-8110) w. Fred Waring

A Man Without a Country/So Proudly We Hail (Decca DL-89020)

Many Happy Returns (Vocalion 1)

Merry Christmas (10″ Decca DL-5019, Decca DL-8128/78128, MCA 167)

Mr. Crosby and Mr. Mercer (MCA Coral 8025, Music for Pleasure 50554) w. Johnny Mercer

Mr. Music (10″ Decca DL-5284)

Mississippi (10″ Decca DL-6008) [ST]

More Fun! (Sounds Rare 5010) w. Louis Armstrong

Music! (Grappenhauser 1001)

Music Hall Highlights, Vols. 1–2 (Spokane 16, 19)

My Golden Favorites (Decca DL-4086)

Never Be Afraid (Golden 22)

New Tricks (Decca DL-8575)

New Tricks (Memoir 202)

Old Masters (Decca DX-152)

On the Happy Side (WB 1482)

101 Gang Songs (WB 1401)

Only Forever (Decca DL-4255)

Original Radio Broadcasts (Mark 56 762)

Paris Holiday (UA 40001) [ST]

Paris Honeymoon (10″ Decca DL-6012)

Pennies From Heaven (Decca Dl-4251)

Pennies From Heaven (WB 2HW-3639)[ST]

Pepe (Colpix 507) [ST]

Pocketful of Dreams (Decca Dl-4252)

Les Poupées de Paris (RCA LOC/LSO-1090) [OC]

Radio Cavalcade of 1936 (Amalgamated 252) [ST/R]

Rare Early Recordings, 1929-33 (Biograph 13)

Rare 1930–31 Brunswick Records (MCA 1502)

The Rare Ones (Broadway Intermission 128)

Rare Style (Ace of Hearts 164)

Remembering (Happy Days 123)

Rendezvous (Camden CAS-2330) w. Rosemary Clooney

Return to Paradise Island (Reprise 6106)

Rhythm on the Range (Coral 81)

Rip Van Winkle (10″ Decca DL-6001)

The Road Begins (Decca DL-4254)

The Road to Bali (10″ Decca DL-5444) [ST]

The Road to Hong Kong (Liberty 16002) [ST]

Robin and the 7 Hoods (Reprise 2021) [ST]

St. Patrick's Day (10″ Decca DL-5037)

St. Valentine's Day (10″ Decca DL-05039)

The San Francisco Experience (S.F.E. 101)

Say One for Me (Col CL-1337/CS-8147) [ST]

Seasons (Polydor PD-1 6128)

Selections from "The Country Girl" and "Little Boy Lost" (10″ Decca DL-5556)

She Loves Me Not (Caliban 6042) [ST]

She Loves Me Not (Toten 1004) [ST/R]

Shhh! Bing (Crosbyana LLM-02)

Shillelagh and Shamrocks (Decca Dl-8207)

Show Hit Tunes (10″ Decca DL-5298)

Sing, You Sinners (Spokane 8) [ST/R]

Singularly Bing (Broadway Intermission 137)

The Small One/The Happy Prince (Decca DL-4283/74283)

Soft Lights and Sweet Music (Pelican 104)

Some Fine Old Chestnuts (10″ Decca DL-5508)

Song Hits From Hit Musicals (10″ Decca DL-5000)

Songs Everybody Knows (Decca DL-4415/74415)

Songs I Wish I Had Sung the First Time Around (Decca DL-8352)

The Special Magic of Bing (MGM 2353-101)

The Special Magic of Bing and Satchmo (MGM 2353-084) w. Louis Armstrong

Star Maker (10″ Decca DL-6013) w. Connee Boswell, the Music Maids

Star Spangled Rhythm (Curtain Calls 100/20, Sandy Hook 2045) [ST]

Stardust (10″ Decca DL-5126)

State Fair (Box Office Productions 19761, CIF 2009, CIF 3007, Sound/Stage 2310) [ST]

Stephen Foster Songs (10″ Decca DL-5010X)

Sunshine Cake (Decca DL-4261)

Swinging on a Star (Decca DL-4257)

That Christmas Feeling (Decca DL-8781/78781)

That Travelin' Two-Beat (Cap T/ST-2300) w. Rosemary Clooney

That's Entertainment! (MCA MCA 2-11002)[ST]

That's Entertainment, Part 2 (MGM 1-15301, MCA 6155) [ST]

That's What Life Is All About (UA LA-554-G)

Themes and Songs from "The Quiet Man" (10″ Decca DL-5411)

This Is Bing Crosby (RCA DPS-2066)

Thoroughly Modern Bing (Pickwick International 6802)

Three Billion Millionaires (UA UXl-4/UXS-4) [ST]

A Time to Be Jolly (Daybreak 2006)

Too Much Harmony/Going Hollywood (Caliban 6039) [ST]

Top Hat, White Tie and Golf Shoes (Facit 124) w. Fred Astaire and Ginger Rogers

Top of the Morning/The Emperor Waltz (10″ Decca DL-5272)

Traditional Carols (WLSM 1170) w. the Bonaventura Choir

Twelve Songs of Christmas (Reprise 2022) w. Frank Sinatra, Fred Waring

20th Anniversary in Show Business (Joyce 1128)

Twilight on the Trail (Decca Dl-8365)

Variety Girl (Caliban 6007) [ST]

The Very Best of Bing Crosby (MGM E/SE-4203)

The Very Best of Bing Crosby (World Record Club SHB-291-96)

The Very First Radio Broadcast (Frogbien 6309)

Victor Herbert Songs (10″ Decca DL-5355)

The Voice of Bing in the Thirties (Brunswick BL-54005)

Waikiki Wedding (10″ Decca DL-6011)

The War Years (Broadway Intermission 129)

A Warm and Wonderful Christmas Eve (Ho-Ho-Ho 1088) w. Frank Sinatra

Way Back Home (10″ Decca DL-5310)

When Irish Eyes Are Smiling (10″ Decca DL-5403)

Where the Blue of the Night Meets the Gold of the Day (Music for Pleasure 50249)

White Christmas (Decca DL-8083)

White Christmas (MCA 1777) w. Danny Kaye, Peggy Lee

Wrap Your Troubles in Dreams (RCA LPV-584)

The Young Bing Crosby (X LVA-1000, RCA LPM-2071)

Yours Is My Heart Alone (10″ Decca DL-5326)

Zing a Little Zong (Decca Dl-4263)

CDs

Academy Award Winners and Nominees 1934-60 (MCA 112274)

Alexander's Ragtime Band (All-Star ALS-23107)

All the Clouds'll Roll Away (JSP 702) w. Judy Garland

All-Time Best of Bing Crosby (Curb D21K-77340)

American Legends (Laserlight 12-732)

Beautiful Memories (Disky HR-853142)

Beautiful Memories (Golden Sounds 85314)

The Best of Bing Crosby (BMG PDSCD-532)

The Best of Bing Crosby (Castle Communications MAT-CD-253)

The Best of Bing Crosby (The Entertainers CD-248)

The Best of Bing Crosby (MCA DMCL-1607)

The Best of Bing Crosby (MSI 58354)

The Best of Bing Crosby (Promo Sound)

The Best of Bing Crosby and Fred Astaire: A Couple of Song and Dance Men (Curb D21K-77617)

The Best of Bing Crosby—Millenium (MCA 11942)

Best of the War Years (Stardust 763)

Big Band Days (Echo 12)

Big Rock Candy Mountain (Half Moon HMNCSX102) w. Burl Ives, Danny Kaye

Bing and Louis Live (Spectrum U-4016) w. Louis Armstrong

Bing—Beyond Compare (Bar One BC-013)

Bing Crosby (ABC 36172)

Bing Crosby (Ariola Express 295040-201, RCA BPCD-5092)

Bing Crosby (BCD GLD-6335)

Bing Crosby (Bella Musica BMCD-89221)

Bing Crosby (Collection OR-0084)

Bing Crosby (Direct Source 61372, Direct Source DS-75492)

Bing Crosby (Echo Jazz EJCD-12)

Bing Crosby (Intertape 500-027)

Bing Crosby (L'Art Vocal 20)

Bing Crosby (Sounds of a Century 1812)

Bing Crosby (Stage Door SDC-8087)

Bing Crosby (Timeless 004)

Bing Crosby 1926-32 (TMLS 3)

Bing Crosby 1927-34 (BBC CD-648)

Bing Crosby 1928-45 (Melodie 20)

Bing Crosby 1931-57 (MCA 10887)

Bing Crosby and Company (Memoir 548)

Bing Crosby and Friends (ASV CD-AJA-5147)

Bing Crosby and Friends (Dutton Laboratories 3000)

Bing Crosby and Friends (Empire 89)

Bing Crosby and Friends (Magic 3)

Bing Crosby and Friends (Musicrama 778772)

Bing Crosby and His Hollywood Guests (Avid 626)

Bing Crosby and Liberace—Christmas (MCA MCAD-20521)

Bing Crosby and Some Jazz Friends (Decca Jazz GRP-603, MCA GRP-16032)

Bing Crosby and the Andrews Sisters—Their Complete Recordings (MCA MCAD-11503)

Bing Crosby at the Movies (Great Movie Themes 60017)

Bing Crosby Christmas (Delta 24493)

Bing Crosby Christmas Collection (Dejavu DVCD-2078)

Bing Crosby Classic (ABC 38985)

Bing Crosby Collection (Lasertech 944D)

Bing Crosby Duets (Columbia River Entertainment Group G-218058)

Bing Crosby in Hollywood, Vol. 2 (Chansons Cinema 072-010-2)

Bing Crosby in Hollywood, Vol. 3 (Chansons Cinema 172-011-2)

Bing Crosby 1926-32 (Timeless Jazz Nostalgia CBC1-004)

Bing Crosby on Broadway (Bing Crosby at the London Palladium) (UA/K-Tel NE-951) w. Rosemary Clooney, the Crosby Family [OC]

Bing Crosby on Treasure Island (JSP 703)

Bing Crosby on V-Disc (Tokum TKCF-77061)

Bing Crosby Show (Old Time Radio BC1-CD)

Bing Crosby Show (Old Time Radio BC2-CD)

Bing Crosby Sings Again (MCA MCAD-5764)

Bing Crosby Sings Christmas Songs (MCA MCAD-5765, Universal Special Markets 5765)

The Bing Crosby Story (Dejavu DVRECD-16)

The Bing Crosby Story, Vol. 1—The Early Jazz Years (Sony Music Special Products AZ-201)

Bing Crosby Swings (Magic 48)

Bing Crosby With Ella Fitzgerald and Peggy Lee (Avid 624)

Bing Crosby With Gary Crosby and the Andrews Sisters (Starlite CDS-51058)

Bing Crosby With Judy Garland and Al Jolson (Avid 625) w. John Charles Thomas

Bing Crosby With Paul Whiteman and His Orchestra (Chansons Cinema 172-009-2)

The Bing Crosby Years (Reader's Digest RDCD-121-6)

Bing Crosby's Christmas Classics (Cap C21K-91009, Cap/EMI 21433)

Bing Crosby's Hawaii (MCA MSD-35082)

Bing Crosby's Treasury (Bar One BCT-001)

Bing: His Legendary Years 1931-57 (MCA MCAD4-10887)

Bing in Hollywood, Vol. 1 (Collectables COL-CD-68056)

Bing in Hollywood, Vol. 2 (Collectables COL-CD-6806)

Bing 'n' Basie (Emarcy 824-705-2) w. Count Basie

Bing Sings Country (Hallmark 306722)

Bing Sings Whilst Bregman Swings (Verve UDCD-670, Verve 549-367) w. Buddy Bregman

Bing Swings (Magic 48)

Bing With a Beat (RCA BVCJ-2029)

Bing's Best (Classic Hits CDCD-1071)

Bing's Buddies (Magic 41)

Bing's Gold Records (MCA MCAD-11719)

Bing's Hollywood (Bar One BC-012)

Bix 'n' Bing (ASV CD-AJA-5005) w. Bix Beiderbecke

Blitz Hits (UMTV 5442632)

Blue Skies (Great Movie Themes 60025, MCA MCAD-25989, Sandy Hook CDSH-2095) [ST]

Blue Skies/Holiday Inn (VJC VJC-1012-2) [ST]

Blue Skies/Rhythm on the River (Great Movie Themes 60025) [ST]

Cavalcade of Songs (Festival D-26291)

Christmas (Laserlight 21-359) w. Frank Sinatra

Christmas (St. Clair 2511) w. Frank Sinatra

Christmas Album (PSM 211)

Christmas Classics (ASD CDP-7910092)

Christmas Classics (BFS Entertainment and Multimedia 82500)

A Christmas Collector (Laserlight 240952) w. Elvis Presley

The Christmas Songs (Vintage Jazz Classics VJC-1017-2)

Christmas Through the Years (Laserlight 12-532)

Christmas With Bing (Pickwick PWKS-561)

Christmas With Bing and Frank (Pilz CD-44-5446-2) w. Frank Sinatra

Christmas With Frank and Bing (Laserlight 12-775) w. Frank Sinatra

Christmas With Bing Crosby (EMI-Cap Special Markets 56619)

Christmas With Bing Crosby (Telstar TCD-2469)

Christmas With Bing Crosby, Nat (King) Cole and Dean Martin (EMI-Cap Special Markets 17742)

Classic Bing Crosby 1931-38 (ABC Music ABC-CD-838985)

Classic Crosby 1931-38 (BBC CD-766)

Classic Crosby, Vol. 1 (Naxos Nostalgia NX-8.120507)

Classic Performances (Regal 1572742)

The Collection (Castle Communications CCSCD-275)

The Collection (The Revue Collection REV-406)

Collection of Classics (Legacy Entertainment ATP101)

The Complete Bing Crosby (Silver Eagle SED-10633)

Complete United Artists Sessions (EMI G-CDBING1: PID 593162)

The Crooner: The Columbia Years 1928-34 (Columbia C3K-44229)

Crosby Classics (Columbia CK-7094)

Crosby Family Christmas (Pilz CD-44-5445-2)

Dick Tracy in B-Flat (Hollywood Soundstage 4010) [ST/R]

Dream a Little Dream of Me (Ariola Express 295040)

Duets: 1947-49 (Viper's Nest 1003)

Eleven Historic Recordings (Conquistador CONQ-004)

The EP Collection (See for Miles 360)

Everything I Have Is Yours (Prime Cuts 1364, St. Clair 1364)

Everything I Have Is Yours (Tring International GRF016)

Fancy Meeting You Here (RCA R25J-1003) w. Rosemary Clooney

Feels Good, Feels Right (London 820-586-2)

50th Anniversary Concert—London Palladium (EMI G-CDMFP-6389, EMI 7243857472)

Film Favorites (Pegasus)

Forever Gold (St. Clair 5736)

Frank Sinatra and Friends (Artanis 8104) w. Frank Sinatra, Dean Martin, Sammy Davis Jr.

Fun With Bing and Louis 1949-51 (Jasmine JASCD-336) w. Louis Armstrong

Glorious Crooners (Deuce 9212) w. Robert Goulet

Going Hollywood, Vol. 1 (Jasmine JASCD-108)

Going Hollywood, Vol. 2 (Jasmine JASCD-113)

Going Hollywood, Vol. 3 (Jasmine JASCD-121/2)

The Great Bing Crosby (Redx RXBOX-31034)

Great Moments With Bing Crosby and Friends (On the Air 101978) w. Connee Boswell, the Charioteers

The Great Songs (Pickwick PWK-065)

The Great Years (Pearl Flapper 7027)

Greatest Hits 1934-43 (EMP 983002)

Greatest Hits 1939-47 (MCA MCAD-1620)

Havin' Fun (Jazz Unlimited) w. Louis Armstrong

Havin' More Fun (Jazz Unlimited 2035) w. Louis Armstrong

Heart and Soul (Memories of Yesteryear 5064)

Here Come the Waves (Great Movie Themes 60001) [ST]

Here Lies Love (ASV CD-AJA-5043)

Hey Look Us Over (Jasmine JASCD-318) w. Rosemary Clooney

High Society (Cap C21S-93787, World Star Collection WSC-99056) [ST]

The Holiday Album (Fine Tune 3301) w. Nat (King) Cole

Holiday Inn (MCA MCAD-25205, Soundtrack Factory 33551, Universal Special Markets 25205) [ST]

Holiday Inn/Blue Skies (Vintage Jazz Classics VJC-1012-2) [ST]

Holiday Inn/Road to Morocco (Great Movie Themes 60027) [ST]

Hollywood Guys and Dolls, Vol. 1 (Parrot 005)

Hollywood Guys and Dolls, Vol. 2 (Parrot 006)

How Lovely Is Christmas (Drive Archive 47121)

How Lucky Can You Get! Fred Astaire and Bing Crosby (EMI 789312)

How to Make an American Quilt (MCA MCAD-11373) [ST]

I'm an Old Cowhand (ASV CD-AJA-5160)

The Immortal Bing Crosby (Empire/Avid AVC-535)

It's a Good Day (Parrot 001) w. Peggy Lee

It's Christmas Time (Laserlight 15-152) w. Frank Sinatra and Louis Armstrong

It's Easy to Remember (ASV CD-AJA-5394)

It's Easy to Remember (Proper Box BX-829732)

The Jazzin' Bing Crosby (Affinity CD-AFS-1021-2)

Just What I Wanted (LYCD 005)

King Bing—20 Golden Favorites (Hallmark 300222)

The King of Jazz/King of Burlesque/Going Places/ Carefree (Great Movie Themes 60019) [ST]

King of the Crooners (Javelin HADCD-219)

The Kraft Shows, Vol. 1 (Lost Gold 7598)

L'Art Vocal, Vol. 20, 1928–45 (Melodie 20)

Legends of the 20th Century (EMI 5228152)

Let Me Sing and I'm Happy (Parrot 004) w. Al Jolson

A Little Bit of Irish (Atlantic 72885)

A Little Bit of Irish (Golden Olden GOR-101)

Live Duets 1947–50 (Viper's Nest 1003)

Lonely Street (Mastertone MDT-8332)

Lonely Street (Point 8332)

Lost Columbia Sides 1928–33 (Collectors' Choice Music CCM-216-2)

Love Songs (Masters 500952)

Love Songs (MCA MCAD-20971, Universal Special Markets 20971)

Mail Call (Laserlight 150413) w. Judy Garland

The Magic Collection: Bing Crosby (ARC MEC-949001)

Memories (MCA MCLD-19360)

Merry Christmas (MCA MCAD-31143)

Merry Christmas (MCA 33XD-511)

A Merry Christmas With Bing Crosby and the Andrews Sisters (MCA MCAD-112337)

Million Sellers (Prism PLATCD-295)

Moonlight Becomes You (Classic Popular CDCD-1200)

More Great Songs (Pickwick PWK-088)

More of the Best of Bing Crosby (Applause 40522)

The Most Welcome Stranger (Parade PAR-2021)

Movie Hits (Pearl CD-9784)

My Favorite Broadway Songs (MCA MCAD-21140, Universal Special Markets 21140)

My Favorite Country Songs (MCA MCAD-20982, Universal Special Markets 20982)

My Favorite Hawaiian Songs (MCA MCAD-21008, Universal Special Markets 21008)

My Favorite Hymns (MCA MCAD-21002, Universal Special Markets 21002)

My Favorite Irish Songs (MCA MCAD-21048, Universal Special Markets 21123)

My Greatest Songs (MCA MCD-18348)

My Happiness (Parrot 002) w. Ella Fitzgerald

Old Groaner (ABM—no number)

Old Groaner, Vol. 2 (ABM ABMMCD-1093)

The Old Lamplighter (Prestige-Elite Recordings 127)

Ol Man River (BMG BVCJ-37168)

Old Man River (BMG 37168)

On the Road (Vintage Jazz Band VJB-1949) w. Bob Hope, Dorothy Lamour

On the Sentimental Side (ASV CD-AJA-5072)

On the Sentimental Side (E2 55)

On the Sentimental Side (MCI ETDCD-055)

Only Forever (ASV CD-AJA-5395)

Only Forever (Empress/Empire RAJCD-802)

Out of Nowhere (London 820-553-2)

Pennies From Heaven (Golden Options)

Pennies From Heaven (ProArte/Fanfare CDD-432)

Pepe (Collectors' Choice Music CCM-113-2, DRG 113) [ST]

Please (Evasound EMD-002)

Pocketful of Dreams (ProArte/Fanfare CDD-457)

Portrait of a Song Stylist (Harmony HARCD-120)

Portrait of Bing Crosby (Charly Classics CDCD-2020)

Portrait of Bing Crosby (MCI Gallerie 403)

Profile of Bing Crosby (Profile PRO-33362)

Radio Duets (Memories of Yesteryear 5063)

Radio Years (GNP/Crescendo GNPD-9051)

Radio Years (Hallmark 303372)

Radio Years, No. 2 (GNP/Crescendo GNPD-9052)

Remembering 1927–34 (Conifer CDHD-123)

Rendezvous (RCA Camden Classics 6128) w. Rosemary Clooney

Road to Hollywood, Vol. 1 (Great Movie Themes 60045)

Road to Hollywood, Vol. 2 (Great Movie Themes 60046)

Road to Morocco (NST NSTC-029)

Robin and the 7 Hoods (Artanis ARZ-104-2) [ST]

Silver Bells of Christmas (KRB Music Companies KRB0870-2) w. Rosemary Clooney

Sinatra Crosby Christmas (Delta 24494) w. Frank Sinatra

Sing a Song of Sunbeams (Saville CDSVL-219)

16 Most Requested Songs (Legacy 472198-2, Legacy CK-48974)

16 Original World Hits (MCA 256-137-2)

Some Fine Old Chestnuts/New Tricks (MCA 19379)

Song Hits From the Movies 1930-53 (Nimbus 2013)

Songs From the Movies (Empress Recording Company 895)

Star Spangled Rhythm (Sandy Hook CDSH-2045) [ST]

Start Off Each Day With a Song (JSP 701) w. Jimmy Durante

Swinging on a Star (MCA MCAD-31367, Universal Special Markets 31367)

Swinging on a Star (Pearl PEA-CD-7065)

Swinging on a Star (Polygram 5441762)

Temptation (Masters 500962)

Tenth Anniversary Collection (Warwick 1005)

Thanks for the Memories Mr. Crosby (3-Bird 80300)

That Christmas Feeling (MCA MCAD-22079, Universal Special Markets 22079)

That Travelin' Two Beat/Bing Crosby Sings Great Country Hits (Collectors' Classic Music CCM-221-2) w. Rosemary Clooney

That's Entertainment, Part 2 (Sony Music Special Products A2K-46872) [ST]

That's Jazz (Pearl Flapper 9739)

30 Favorites (Heartland music 16848-2)

36 All-Time Greatest Hits (MCA MSD3-37079)

36 All-Time Greatest Hits (GSC Music 15354)

Too Marvelous for Words: 25 Chart Toppers (Charly CDGR-105)

Top o' the Morning: His Irish Collection (MCA 11406)

A Tribute to Irving Berlin (Columbia River Entertainment Group G-188002)

20 Golden Favorites (Masters 500942)

20 Golden Memories (Companion 6187152)

The Ultimate Showboat (Pavilion GEMS-0060) [ST]

Universal Legends Collection (MCA 1122642)

Variety Girl (Great Movie Themes CD-60034) [ST]

V-Disc Recordings (Collectors' Choice Music 3596)

The Very Best of Bing Crosby Christmas (Decca 12019)

Very Best of the War Years (Crown CRCL-8862)

A Visit to the Movies (Laserlight 15-411)

The Voice of Christmas (Decca 11840)

Universal Legends Collection (MCA 1122642)

We Must Never Say Goodbye (Parade PAK-904)

When You're Smiling (Parrot 003) w. Judy Garland

Where the Blue of the Night (London 820-552-2)

White Christmas (CA DMCL-1777) [ST]

White Christmas (Laserlight 15-444)

White Christmas (MCA MCAD-31143, Universal Special Products 31143)

White Christmas (World Star WSC-99055, Lotus CD-5001)

Wonderful Together (New Sound—no number) w. Rosemary Clooney

WWII Radio Broadcasts (Laserlight 15-934)

WWII Radio Broadcasts, Vol. 1 (Laserlight 12-298)

WWII Radio Broadcasts, Vol. 2 (Laserlight 12-299)

WWII Radio Broadcasts, Vol. 3 (Laserlight 12-300)

WWII Radio Broadcasts, Vol. 4 (Laserlight 12-301)

WWII Radio Broadcasts, Vol. 5 (Laserlight 12-302)

WWII Radio: Special Christmas Show (Laserlight 12-310)

You the Night and the Music (Avid 633)

Zip-A-Dee-Doo-Dah (Excelsior EXL-10842)

Vic Damone

(b. Vito Rocco Farinola, Brooklyn, New York, June 12, 1928)

Over several decades, handsome Vic Damone carved for himself a respectable position in show business with his fine voice and easygoing singing style. While he had success on radio, recordings, and television, the mainstay of Damone's career was his steady nightclub engagements. For nearly all of his career, he was a popular club attraction both in the United States and abroad. Like his laid-back vocalizing and pleasant personality, Vic never really made a big career splash. Instead, his success was a result of continuous hard work over the years. In the early and mid-1950s, Metro-Goldwyn-Mayer attempted to make a movie star of the singer, but while he crooned well in a handful of big-budget screen musicals, he never caught on sufficiently with filmgoers. His intimate brand of entertaining was far better geared to the more personal atmosphere of clubs.

Vic Damone's family migrated to America from Italy after World War I and settled in Brooklyn where he was born Vito Rocco Farinola on June 12, 1928. His family was musically inclined, as his mother played and taught the piano, and the boy learned Italian folk songs from his dad (who was an electrician). While in PS 163, he sang in St. Finbar's choir and performed in amateur contests and in the school glee club. He next attended Alexander Hamilton Vocational High School and Lafayette High in Brooklyn. Meanwhile, when he was fifteen, the teenager made his professional singing debut on radio station WOR's *Rainbow House* program. Then, quitting school to help the family finances, he found a job as an usher at New York City's Paramount Theater, where he saw the finest entertainers of the day at work. His next job was as an elevator operator. Legend has it that one day one of his passengers was Perry Como, for whom Damone auditioned on the spot. Como urged the young man to continue with his singing, and Vic auditioned for *Arthur Godfrey's Talent Scouts* radio show in 1945, where he was heard by Milton Berle. The comedian, too, was impressed by the young man's singing, and told him that, if he won the Godfrey show contest, he would help him get a club audition. Damone won the amateur contest and, true to his word, Berle arranged for the newcomer to audition at La Martinique. As a result, Vic Damone (his professional name by now) had a stay of eleven weeks to critical and audience acclaim.

Thanks to his working at USO canteens, church socials, and small clubs, Vic was soon signed to star at the Paramount Theater, where only a short time before he had been an usher. As a result of these winning appearances, he was signed by Mercury Records in 1948. He also contracted for his own radio series, *The Pet Milk Program*, which was heard on NBC. During the 1948–49 season, the show was on Saturday nights, while from 1949 to 1950 it was broadcast on Sundays. Also, he visited other radio programs, including those of Spike Jones, Louella Parsons, and *Guest Star*. His Mercury singles established him as a solid seller of songs, with such items as "Vagabond Shoes," "Tzena, Tzena, Tzena," "Just Say I Love Her," "My Heart Cries for You," and "April in Portugal." He headlined clubs like the Copacabana and Riviera, plus the Roxy Theater, Gotham's Waldorf-Astoria, and the Mocambo in Hollywood.

Fernando Lamas, Jane Powell, and Vic Damone in *Rich, Young and Pretty* (1951).
[Courtesy of JC Archives]

Following his success on stage, radio, and recordings, Hollywood bid on Damone's services. He signed with MGM, making his screen debut in the Technicolor musical *Rich, Young and Pretty* (1951) as André Milan, a Parisian who romances American Jane Powell, who is on a French holiday. The *New York Times* assessed, "Vic Damone, idol of the bobbysoxers, is somewhat stiff and callow in his screen debut." On the other hand, *Variety* admitted, "Vocally, Damone knows his way around a tune." Next he was cast in *The Strip* (1951), a low-budget drama about a drummer (Mickey Rooney) who fends off mobsters while trying to get Sally Forrest a movie contract. Damone was on hand as a guest star who sings "Don't Blame Me."

Before Damone's movie career could gain any momentum, he was drafted into the military service and served two years in the U.S. Army in Europe. Back in civilian life, he resumed radio and club work and returned to MGM. (Unfortunately by now, the studio, like the rest of Hollywood, was in retrenchment due to the competition of TV and expensive musicals were becoming an endangered species.) Damone next played the part of singer Johnny Nyle in the musical *Athena* (1954), a satire on health fads. It had him romancing Debbie Reynolds on-camera and performing tunes like "Imagine," "Venezia" (a pretentious production number), and "The Girl Next Door." He then made a guest appearance in the Sigmund Romberg biopic *Deep in My Heart* (1954) singing "Road to Paradise" and dueting with Jane Powell on "Will You Remember."

In 1955, Damone and Tony Martin played two sailors on shore leave looking for romance, and finding it with Jane Powell and Debbie Reynolds in *Hit the Deck*. Damone and Powell sang "I Know That You Know," and with Martin, Russ Tamblyn, and the Jubilaires he performed "Hallelujah!" If any of Vic's studio pictures could be considered a starring vehicle, it was the Technicolor musical of *Kismet* (1955), where he played a caliph in ancient Mesopotamia who romances the beautiful Marsinah (Ann Blyth), the daughter of poet/beggar Jaaj (Howard Keel). Looking stiff and uncomfortable, Damone warbled "Night of My Nights," dueted with Blyth on "Stranger in Paradise," and with Keel and Blyth sang "This Is My Beloved." *Variety* judged correctly of the Damone-Blyth love team, "their romantic pairing does not come off." It did not matter, for by now MGM was phasing out of musical-picture making, and Damone, along with many other singing personalities, was let go by the studio. It was two years before he was involved in filmmaking again. He was heard, singing over the opening credits, on the exceedingly popular title song from Twentieth Century-Fox's *An Affair to Remember* (1957), and, the next year, for the same studio, he performed similar chores for *The Gift of Love*.

In the mid-'50s, Vic Damone signed with Columbia Records, and he had best-selling single records such as "On the Street Where You Live," "An Affair to Remember," and "Gigi." His LPs for the label also sold well; particularly *That Towering Feeling!* (1956) that reached number eight on the *Billboard* charts. On December 23, 1956, he appeared in the NBC-TV special *The Stingiest Man in Town* (a version of Charles Dickens's *A Christmas Carol*) with Johnny Desmond, Basil Rathbone (as Ebenezer Scrooge), Patrice Munsel, and the Four Lads. The previous summer he had begun *The Vic Damone Show* on CBS-TV, which served as a summer replacement for the sitcom *December Bride*. This was a half-hour experimental show that dealt with Damone's "personal" life, his friends, and various guests. The next summer for CBS-TV, the program returned but as a one-hour musical variety show with Damone backed by the Spellbinders. Damone also continued to be a top nightclub attraction, and in 1960 he undertook a dramatic role on the TV anthology series, *The June Allyson Show*.

It was also in 1960 that Damone returned to movies. He was competent in his starring role in the combat film *Hell to Eternity* for Allied Artists. In it, he portrayed a soldier, Pete, involved in the U.S. action in the South Pacific during World War II, with his two buddies played by Jeffrey Hunter and David Janssen. Continuing his dramatic work, he guest-starred on the ABC-TV Western *The Rebel*, as well as episodes of the comedy series *The Dick Van Dyke Show* and *The Joey Bishop Show*. In the early 1960s, Damone signed with Capitol Records and had a best-selling album called *Linger Awhile*, and from July to September 1962 he starred in the half-hour NBC-TV musical program *The Lively Ones*. Joan Staley and Shirley Yelm cohosted the show with Damone, but when it returned for a second session on NBC-TV in the summer of 1963, Quinn O'Hara and Gloria Neil were his new cohosts.

In 1965, Vic Damone began recording with Warner Bros. Records and had good-selling singles with "You Were Only Fooling" and "Why Don't You Believe Me?" as well as the album *You Were Only Fooling*. For the label, he was also one of the first contemporary pop singers to record an entire LP of country tunes with *Country Love Songs*. On November 11, 1965, he starred in the ABC-TV special *The Dangerous Christmas of Red Riding Hood* with Cyril Ritchard, Liza

Minnelli, and the Animals. He did a dramatic role on *Jericho* on CBS-TV in 1966 and guested on such comedy and variety/talk programs as those of Danny Thomas, John Gary, Johnny Carson, Mike Douglas, and Merv Griffin. From June to September 1967, Damone headlined the NBC-TV off-season series, *The Dean Martin Summer Show Starring Your Host Vic Damone*. The one-hour weekly musical offering also featured Carol Lawrence, Don Cherry, and Gail Martin (Dean's daughter).

Vic was also back on-screen in 1967 in the independent feature *Spree*, a junk entry that spliced in portions of his nightclub act in Las Vegas, but neither he nor the film's other unhappily included stars (Juliet Prowse, Jayne Mansfield, Mickey Hargitay, and the Clara Ward Singers) were billed due to a court order prohibiting the promotion of these unwilling "guest" players. In the late 1960s, he cut a series of record albums for RCA. During the summer of 1971, Damone was back on TV in NBC-TV's *The Vic Damone Show*. However, it was composed of segments of the 1967 outing he had done for the network and *not* new material.

Throughout the last decades of the twentieth century, the singer remained a headliner through his constant club work, TV appearances, and recordings, although the latter was for minor labels (Applause, Rebecca, West Coast, etc.). While his career continued to flow like a strong and steady stream, his personal life was an emotional seesaw. On November 24, 1954, Damone had married beautiful Italian actress Pier Angeli, also under MGM contract, in what appeared to be a storybook love story. Their son Perry Rocco Luigi (named in honor of singer Perry Como) was born the next August. Thereafter there was a series of much-publicized emotional separations and reconciliations with Damone insisting that his mother-in-law was the cause of their domestic problems. He and Pier were divorced in 1959 but spent the next six years in recurring court battles over the custody of their son, each accusing the other of kidnapping the child. They finally reached a settlement in 1965. In September of 1971, Pier Angeli committed suicide by taking pills, and, three years later, Damone's second wife, Judy Rawlins, with whom he had three daughters, killed herself in the same way, although she and the singer were divorced at the time. Later, he married and divorced for a third time. For many years, Damone and songstress Diahann Carroll had been dating. On January 8, 1987, the black star and Damone were married in Las Vegas and that same weekend sang together in the showroom at the Golden Nugget Hotel. It was the fourth marriage for each, and created a great deal of publicity. They took up residence in Beverly Hills and began performing together on the nightclub circuit throughout the country. *Variety* reported of one of their joint engagements at Harrah's in Reno, Nevada, "few evenings can offer so much fine singing and pleasant personality. . . . It's what can be expected from Damone, who has always been one of the more underrated of the saloon singers."

For Damone, who has long had an unsettling personal life, tragedy struck again in 1987 when his younger sister, Sandy Boucher, was shot and killed in Miami Beach by her ex-husband Avrum Cohen, who also killed himself. In 1996, Damone's marriage to Diahann Carroll ended when he filed for divorce in Los Angeles that September. Two years later, in March 1998, he wed fashion designer Rena Rowan, in a ceremony held in Philadelphia. Meanwhile, the entertainer fulfilled a longtime wish when he had a delayed graduation from Lafayette High in February 1997. At the presentation, Vic quipped, "You have no idea how much money I've lost signing contracts I couldn't read. Now I can go to college." (In 1999, the veteran performer received a certificate of advanced study from Philadelphia University.) In April 1997, Damone's mother, Mamie, age ninety-three, died.

When Damone appeared at the Rainbow and Stars venue in Manhattan in April 1996, the *Hollywood Reporter* noted, "the veteran singer performed impeccably through a set that didn't include one song written in the past twenty years," and that the headliner "defines what classic pop singing is all about." In April 2000, Vic announced that he was planning to launch his farewell tour, which was to include a May 2001 evening at Carnegie Hall. He said, "I have had the privilege to sing professionally for 53 years . . . but I've always wanted to go out at the top of my game." However in June 2000 Damone had a mild stroke that sidelined him for several months before undertaking a limited tour.

While Vic Damone never achieved the superstar status of Bing Crosby, Frank Sinatra, or Dean Martin, nor became a singing idol like Perry Como, he did establish himself as one of the entertainment world's most reliable songsters. Although his greatest popularity came in the 1950s, thereafter he still had a solid coterie of fans who insisted that Damone was best described by one of his record album titles: *The Best Damn Singer in the World*.

Filmography

Rich, Young and Pretty (MGM, 1951)
The Strip (MGM, 1951)
Athena (MGM, 1954)
Deep in My Heart (MGM, 1954)
Hit the Deck (MGM, 1955)
Kismet (MGM, 1955)

Meet Me in Las Vegas [Viva Las Vegas!] (MGM, 1956)
An Affair to Remember (20th-Fox, 1957) (voice only)
The Gift of Love (20th-Fox, 1958) (voice only)
Hell to Eternity (AA, 1960)
Spree (United Producers, 1967)

Radio Series

The Pet Milk Program (NBC, 1948–50)

TV Series

The Vic Damone Show (CBS, 1956, 1957)
The Lively Ones (NBC, 1962, 1963)

The Dean Martin Summer Show Starring Your Host Vic Damone (NBC, 1967)
The Vic Damone Show (NBC, 1971)

Album Discography

LPs

An Affair to Remember (Col CL-1013) [ST]
All-Star TV Revue, Vol. 1 (Hollywood LPH-110) [ST/TV]
All-Star TV Revue, Vol. 2 (Hollywood LPH-126) [ST/TV]
America's Favorites (10″ Mer MG-25045)
Amor (10″ Mer MG-25174)
Angela Mia (Columbia CL-1088/CS-6046)
Arrivederci, Baby! (RCA LOC/LSO-1132) [ST]
Athena (10″ Mer MG-25202, M.P.T. 2) [ST]
The Best Damn Singer in the World (West Coast 14001)
The Best of Vic Damone (Har HL-7328)
Born to Sing (Wing PKW-2-117)

Closer Than a Kiss (Col CL-1174/CS-8019)
Country Love Songs (WB 1607)
The Damone Type of Thing (RCA LPM/LSP-3916, RCA International 89261)
Damone's Best (RCA International 89170)
Damone's Feelings (Rebecca 1212)
Damone's Inspiration (Rebecca 1213)
The Dangerous Christmas of Red Riding Hood (ABC ABC/ABCS-536) [ST/TV]
Deep in My Heart (MGM E-31530) [ST]
Deep in My Heart/Words and Music (MGM 2SES-54ST, MCA 5949) [ST]
Ebb Tide (10″ Mer MG-25194)
The Gift of Love (Col CL-1113) [ST]

Hit the Deck (MGM E-3163) [ST]

I'll Sing for You (Wing 12113/16113)

In My Own Way (Ember 5051)

Judy and Vic (Minerva 6JG-TVD) w. Judy Garland

Kismet (MGM E-3281, Metro M/S-526, MCA 1424) [ST]

Linger Awhile (Cap T/ST-1646, EMI/Cap 186741)

The Liveliest (Cap T/ST-1944)

The Lively Ones (Cap T/ST-1748, EMI/Pathé 260414)

Make Someone Happy (RCA International 5125)

Melody Parade (Mer MG-20041) w. Vincent Lopez, Lanny Ross

My Baby Loves to Swing (Cap T/ST-1811, EMI/Cap 1151)

The Night Has a Thousand Eyes (10″ Mer MG-25131)

Now and Forever (RCA International 5234)

On the South Side of Chicago (RCA LPM/LSP-3765, RCA International 89263)

On the Street Where She Lives (Columbia Special Products 11128)

On the Street Where You Live (Cap T/ST-2133)

On the Swingin' Side (Col CL-1573/CS-8373)

Over the Rainbow (Applause 1018)

Pop Singers on the Air! (Radiola 1149) w. Perry Como, Eddie Fisher, Dick Haymes

Starring Vic Damone (Premiere 9013) w. Johnny Desmond, the Stradivari Strings

Stay With Me (RCA LPM/LSP-3671, RCA International 89262)

The Stingiest Man in Town (Col CL-950) [ST/TV]

Strange Enchantment (Cap T/ST-1691, EMI/Cap 260003)

Sunny Side of the Street (10″ Mercury MG-25100) [ST]

Take Me in Your Arms (10″ Mer MG-25132)

Tenderly (Wing 12157)

That Towering Feeling! (Col CL-900)

This Game of Love (Col CL-1368/CS-8169)

20 Golden Pieces (Bulldog 2001)

Vic Damone (CBS 32371)

Vic Damone (10″ Mer MG-25028)

Vic Damone Favorites (Mer MG-20194)

Vic Damone in San Francisco (Rebecca 1214)

Vic Damone Now (RCA International 5080)

Vic Damone Sings (Har HL-7431/HS-11231)

Vic Damone Sings (Manhattan 521)

Vic Damone Sings the Great Songs (CBS 32261)

The Voice of Vic Damone (Mer MG-20194)

Why Can't I Walk Away (RCA LSP-3984, RCA International 89264)

You Were Only Fooling (WB 1602)

Young and Lively (Col CL-1912/CS-8712)

Yours for a Song (Mer MG-20163)

CDs

Again: The Young Vic Damone (ASV CD-AJA-5392)

Angela Mia/On the Swingin' Side (Sony 4930452, Globetrotter 753122)

Athena (Rhino Handmade RHM2 7768) [ST]

The Best of the Mercury Years (Polygram 532870, Polygram 552-757-2)

The Best of Vic Damone (Camden 74321-45191-2)

The Best of Vic Damone (Curb D21K-77476)

The Best of Vic Damone (Spectrum 5527572)

The Best of Vic Damone—For Once in My Life (MRA 503912)

The Best of Vic Damone Live (Ranwood RCD-8204)

Christmas With Vic Damone (KRB Music Companies KRB6123-2)

Closer Than a Kiss/This Game of Love (Sony 487190)

Cocktail Hour (Columbia River Entertainment Group CRG-218033)

Collector's Edition (Madacy 3469)

The Complete Columbia Singles Collection (Taragon 1081)

Deep in My Heart (Sony Music Special Products AK-47703) [ST]

Deep in My Heart/Words and Music (MCA MCAD-5949) [ST]

A Dreamer's Holiday (Bridge 100.059-2) w. Nelson Riddle

The Fabulous Vic Damone (Castle Pulse PLSCD-390)

The Glory of Love (RCA 07863-66016-2)

Hit the Deck (Turner Classic Movies/Rhino R2-76668, EMI 794123) [ST]

Hit the Deck/Royal Wedding (MGM/EMI MGM-15) [ST]

I'm Glad There Is You (Sony Music Special Products CK-24162)

Kismet (MCA MCAD-1424, Sony Music Special Products AK-45393, EMI 854536) [ST]

Let's Face the Music and Swing! (Pair PCD-2-1303)

Linger Awhile/By Baby Loves to Swing (EMI 123)

The Lively Ones/Strange Enchantment (Capitol 21095)

Look of Love (Hallmark 308442)

Look of Love (Prism PLATCD-667)

Love Songs (Sony Music Special Products CK-32099)

Over the Rainbow—20 Timeless Classics (Hallmark 312102)

Pop Singers on the Air (Radiola CDMR-1149) w. Perry Como, Eddie Fisher, Dick Haymes

Rich, Young and Pretty (MGM/EMI MGM-23) [ST]

16 Most Requested Songs (Sony CK-48975)
Spotlight on Vic Damone (Capitol C41F-28513)
Tender Is the Night (EMI 59136)
That Towering Feeling/On the Street Where You
 Live (Collectables COL-CD-6467)
36 All-time Favorites (GSC Music 17041)
Vic Damone (Direct Source 61582)

Vic Damone (Madacy 3453)
Vic Damone (MCPS 323)
Vic Damone (Members' Edition UAE-30752)
Vic Damone Live (Fat Boy FATCD-142)
Vic Damone Live in Concert (Classic World 9934)
Young Vic! (Flapper PASTCD-7835)

Bobby Darin in the early 1960s.
[Courtesy of JC Archives]

Bobby Darin

(b. Walden Robert Cassotto, East Harlem, New York, May 14, 1936, d. Los Angeles, California, December 20, 1973)

Few performers were so blatantly ambitious, driven, and egotistical as snarling Bobby Darin, who earned the nickname of show business's "Angry Young Man." But then few performers were as talented as this aggressive New Yorker. He was determined to make it big, and he did! Within a few short years in the late 1950s to early 1960s, he rose from teenage singing idol to respected nightclub attraction to an Oscar-nominated screen performer. (The high achiever patterned his singing persona after such vocalists as Frank Sinatra, Elvis Presley, and Ray Charles.) While Darin had charisma and sex appeal, he was not a handsome man: his face was chubby, his hairline receded, and his profile was far from classic. Nor was he a melodious singer in the traditional manner. He typically thrust out lyrics from the side of his mouth, punctuated by his snapping fingers and bolstered by his flippant demeanor. Darin was the first to admit, "Vic Damone is a singer, I'm a performer. Even on records, what I'm saying is far more important than how well I'm singing." A *TV Guide* magazine interviewer in 1961 summed it up, "All in all, Darin has little working in his favor—except that vast, imperious finger-snapping, self-confidence—and for some reason . . . this makes people stand and cheer him."

Bobby Darin's craftsmanship as a vocalist extended to songwriting, and went far beyond his most closely associated song hits: "Splish Splash," "Mack the Knife," and "Beyond the Sea." Politically he was an ardent follower of John F. and Robert Kennedy. Romantically he was loved by singing peer Connie Francis, but he married movie star Sandra Dee instead. In retrospect, a good deal of his brash, self-assertive behavior was attributed to his long-standing hunch that he would have a short life (he died at thirty-seven).

He was born Walden Robert Cassotto on May 14, 1936, in New York's East Harlem, the son of Saverio "Sam" Anthony Cassotto and Vivian "Polly" Fern (Walden) Cassotto. (Mrs. Cassotto had been in vaudeville and had been twice previously married.) There was already an older child, Vanina (Nina), born fourteen years earlier. (According to Connie Francis in her autobiography, *Who's Sorry Now* [1984], Darin would learn shortly before his own death that Nina was actually his mother, having given birth to him out of wedlock.) Cassotto, a gambler with many shady connections, died in prison from narcotic withdrawal seven months before Walden was born. The infant was a sickly baby, and from the age of eight until thirteen suffered recurring severe attacks of rheumatic fever. It was this constant illness (and pampering from his mother and married sister who fostered his love of show business) that later drove him in his obsession of becoming a star by the age of twenty-five or earlier. (As he remarked in 1972, "For thirty years I expected to die.")

Growing up in the tough part of the Bronx where any illness was considered a sign of weakness, he very quickly developed a swaggering demeanor. Because of his poor health, he was bedridden much of his early life, and his doting mother served as his teacher. He read a great deal, and by the time he entered junior high school he was an excellent student, albeit with a chip on his shoulder. It was this excellence that led to him being recommended for admission to the respected Bronx High School of Science. By then he had learned to play the drums, piano, guitar, vibraharp, and bass, none of which was appreciated by his classmates at the science-oriented high school. He admitted later, "All the arrogance you read about stems from those days in high school. It all stems from a desire to be nobody's fool again."

After graduating from high school in June 1952, Darin entered Hunter College, planning to become an actor. But after a semester, he rebelled at the regimen and competition at the New York college scene and quit. By now he had been spending his summers at Catskill resorts, serving as a singing waiter and also as a drummer in a local band there. Sometimes during these gigs, he filled in as singer, master of ceremonies, or general entertainer, sometimes doing imitations of Donald O'Connor or Jerry Lewis. Back in the city, he held a variety of odd jobs, from sweeping up scrap in a metal factory to cleaning guns for the Navy at the Navy Yard in Brooklyn. He met a thirty-one-year-old dancer (and the mother of a ten-year-old) who hired him to play drums for her on tour. Eighteen months later, she fired him and rejected him as a lover, but the association spurred on the singer in his professional endeavors. ("Before I met her I said 'I want to.' Afterwards I said 'I'm going to.' ") By now, he was Bobby Darin (having selected his new surname at random from the phone book; other sources says that it derived from his picking part of the wordage from a Chinese restaurant sign that flashed the word "man*darin*"—only the first three letters were burned out). He was living in a tenement apartment with another struggling show-business enthusiast, and was collaborating with Don Kirschner (a fellow Bronx Science classmate and later a music publisher). Together they wrote radio commercials that they sometimes sang. They used their salaries to make demonstration records of their own songs.

Kirschner took one of these records (which featured Darin singing) to George Scheck (the manager of Connie Francis, whom Darin was dating off and on at the time). Scheck, in turn, brought it to Decca Records. Decca was sufficiently impressed to sign Darin to a year's contract. Darin recorded four songs and, to plug them, he was put on the Dorsey Brothers' TV variety show *Stage Show* (CBS-TV). According to Darin, "I went on 'cold,' scared to death, and sang 'Rock Island Line.' It bombed." So did the three other ballads he had recorded; as well as four more. Decca dropped him. Meanwhile, Connie's father, fearful of losing control over his daughter, broke up her relationship with Darin and forced Scheck to end his working relationship with Bobby.

Darin went on the road singing at third-rate clubs. In Nashville, he paid for his own session to record "Million Dollar Baby." Through Kirschner's connections, the demo record was heard by executives at Atco Records (a subsidiary of Atlantic Recording Company). They signed Darin, but kept him sidelined for several months.

In 1957 Darin had earned $1,600 singing; but 1958 was far different. He earned $40,000. Among the several numbers he wrote (he would sing them on a tape recorder and someone else would transcribe them) was a rock 'n' roll item called "Splish Splash." That June he sang it on the *Bob Crosby Show* (NBC-TV) and also on Dick Clark's *American Bandstand* (ABC-TV). It became an immediate hit with teenagers, selling 100,000 copies in three weeks and rising to number three on the record charts during a thirteen-week period. Meanwhile, Darin, who thought he would be dropped from Atco as he had been from Decca, had recorded "Early in the Morning" for Brunswick Records under a different singing-group title, the Rinky Dinks. After "Splish Splash" became a runaway hit, Brunswick released their Darin item. Atco legally forced Brunswick to withdraw the single, but Brunswick rerecorded it with Buddy Holly. Meanwhile, Darin had made his acting debut on television, appearing on the "Way of the West" segment of *Schlitz Playhouse of Stars* (CBS-TV, June 6, 1958).

Unlike many other young singers of the day, Darin had an astute sense of the record business. He noted, "It's tough these days. The kids are fickle. They do more flipping over the songs than they do over any one singer." While he continued to write rock songs such as "Queen of the Hop" (which rose to number nine on the charts in October 1958), he wanted to reach beyond this categorization into the more secure adult market. "It's the only way to build a future," he said. He used his popularity to work in nightclubs and began expanding his repertoire. In his act, he sang a hip version of "Mack the Knife" from Kurt Weill's *The Threepenny Opera*. With profits from "Splish Splash" and his first LP (*Bobby Darin*), Darin financed his next album, *That's All*. "Mack the Knife" was among the numbers he recorded. Atco insisted on releasing the song as a single, and it became a smash hit, selling over two million copies. When *That's All* was released a short time later, it sold over 450,000 copies. As a result Darin won two Grammy Awards that year, including Best New Artist of 1959.

There were a lot of changes for Bobby Darin in 1959. Polly Cassotto (actually his grandmother), who had remarried and had three children, died of a stroke that February, not living to see Bobby became a star. After his "Mack the Knife" phenomenon, he signed two seven-year performing contracts with two different studios (Paramount and Universal) while turning down an offer from NBC-TV. Among his many television appearances, he was on *The Ed Sullivan Show* twice, sang "Mack the Knife" on a NBC-TV special that November, guested on an episode of the comedy series *Hennessey* (CBS-TV), was one of the guest artists on *The Big Party* (NBC), and on December 2, 1959, was the subject of *This Is Your Life* (NBC-TV). On the NBC-TV special *George Burns in the Big Time* (November 17, 1959), he joined such superstars as Jack Benny, Eddie Cantor, and George Jessel. Darin was now earning $40,000 per TV show appearance, was starring at such clubs as Los Angeles's The Cloister (which gave him exposure to the film industry), Chicago's Chez Paree, New York City's Copacabana, and had appeared in Las Vegas at the Sahara Hotel with George Burns (who became one of his mentors). Darin owned a recording company (Direction) and two music-publishing companies, and it was estimated he was currently earning $250,000 a year. (In 1960 he earned $500,000, and in 1961 he had a gross income of over $1 million.)

Describing one of his performances at the Copacabana, the *New York World-Telegram and Sun* reviewer noted, "He has a driving, pulsating style, which, combined with a impish, small boy smile, made him irresistible to his fans." Most critics chose to review his impudence rather than his voice. It led one columnist to insisting, "When Will Rogers wrote he never met a man he didn't like, he had never met Bobby Darin." Darin had his own theory: "Cocky is my favorite word. . . . I want a battle. If it's a battle, I have a chance to change people's minds." Darin was the type of club performer who when a record company executive who had once said he had no talent showed up in the audience, Darin had him removed from the audience. When a party became overly boisterous, he had their table and drinks taken away. When a drunk stumbled up and put his arm around him, the star attraction exited the stage. Because he was "the newest singing rage," he could get away with such behavior.

After his relationship with Connie Francis, Darin began dating blonde songstress Jo-Ann Campbell, and they became engaged in 1960. But then, while in Rome making his first feature film (*Come September*), Darin fell in love with his eighteen-year-old blonde costar, Sandra Dee.

The singer confessed, "I've finally found someone more important to me than myself." They were married on December 1, 1960, on the spur of the moment in Newark, New Jersey. Their son, Dodd Mitchell Cassotto, was born on December 16, 1961.

Despite having signed long-term film commitments in 1959, Darin had not rushed into making his first picture, reasoning, "I don't think I'm mature enough yet to see what one role it is I want to play but I don't want to be billed as 'Bobby Darin in Rock around the Rumble Hall.' " In the interim, he had turned down a costarring role in Columbia Pictures' *Cry for Happy* (1961) because he was contracted to perform with George Burns at the Sahara Hotel in 1960. His screen debut came casually in the star-studded *Pepe* (1960), playing himself and singing "That's How It Went All Right" with Michael Callan, Shirley Jones, and Matt Mattox. However, he made his acting motion-picture debut in *Come September* (1961). It was a lighthearted sex comedy starring Rock Hudson and Gina Lollobrigida, with Darin and Sandra Dee as the young romantic leads. Bobby was brash and cheeky and sang "Multiplication" (which he wrote, as well as the wordless title tune). *Variety* reported, "Darin does a workmanlike job, and gives evidence he'll have more to show when the parts provide him with wider opportunity." For Paramount he was in John Cassavetes's somber *Too Late Blues* (1961). He was a troubled jazz musician who endures angst to keep his band and his girlfriend (Stella Stevens). Darin gave a low-key, thoughtful performance.

His most productive year on-camera was 1962, with four movie releases. He was in the third version of Twentieth Century-Fox's *State Fair*, inheriting Dana Andrews's role as the cynical media man who falls in love with a wholesome farm girl (Pamela Tiffin). Darin's solo was "This Isn't Heaven," which summarized the picture. For Paramount, he was one of the begrimed GIs coping with World War II warfare in *Hell Is for Heroes* (1962). Steve McQueen was the star in a diverse cast that included Bob Newhart, Fess Parker, and James Coburn. Universal chose to exploit the Darin-Dee marriage by reteaming them in *If a Man Answers*, a featherweight comedy of newlyweds who overcome marital discord and become parents-to-be. Darin wrote/sang the title song as well as writing "Chantal Theme."

While most of Bobby's prior movies traded on the drawing power of his singing career, *Pressure Point* was different. This Stanley Kramer production for United Artists allowed Darin an opportunity to demonstrate his acting prowess. He gave a strong portrayal of a highly disturbed young man who, during World War II, is imprisoned as a Nazi sympathizer. Despite the efforts of a black psychiatrist (Sidney Poitier) to treat Darin, he is released only later to kill an innocent old man and himself be executed for the crime. This screen role brought Darin tremendous recognition as a dramatic performer and should have garnered him an Oscar bid. However, the picture itself was a box-office dud.

Darin had had top-twenty albums in 1960 (*This Is Darin; Darin at the Copa*) and one in 1961 (*The Bobby Darin Story*), and he continued with top-ten hits: "You Must Have Been a Beautiful Baby" (1961), "Things" (1962), and "You're the Reason I'm Living" (1963). He switched from Atco to Capitol Records in 1962 (but would return to Atlantic in 1966). However, his focus was on his movie career. He costarred with Gregory Peck and Tony Curtis in *Captain Newman, M.D.* (1963), another glossy World War II study. He played the much-decorated Corporal Jim Tompkins, who is being treated by psychiatrist Peck for a huge guilt complex based on Darin's character's belief that he deserted a pal in the midst of combat. This time he was Oscar-nominated but lost in the Best Supporting Actor category to Melvyn Douglas of *Hud*. It was the pinnacle of

Darin's relatively brief film career. Thereafter, with his fad as a movie personality waning, he accepted lesser assignments. He wrote the songs for Universal's teen romance *The Lively Set* (1964) starring singer James Darren (who sang Darin's numbers), and the next year the studio milked whatever box-office magic was left in the Darin-Dee team by pairing them in the strained comedy *That Funny Feeling* with Donald O'Connor; the singer was now telling the press, "I am an investor. I invest in me, because it's the only thing I'm absolutely sure of. Since childhood, I've always prepared for the success that I knew was going to come."

By 1966 Darin and Sandra Dee had separated yet again, and in March of 1967 they were divorced. He began dating Diana Hartford who had been married to multimillionaire Huntington Hartford since 1962. He showed up in Universal's low-budget western *Gunfight in Abilene* (1967), a remake of a 1957 film (*Showdown at Abilene*), as an ex-Confederate soldier who cannot avoid a climactic shootout. He also wrote the film score for this ignored genre piece. In the little seen, British-filmed *Cop-Out* (1967), a murder mystery starring James Mason, Bobby was a sinister ship's steward.

In the mid-'60s, Darin, while still pushing hard to become Mr. Show Business and the "new" Frank Sinatra, became politically active, being especially drawn to the ideology of Robert Kennedy. As part of his new awareness, he started to appear in his club act wearing scruffy blue jeans (instead of his usual tuxedo), sometimes mustached, usually without his toupee, and singing liberal-oriented, anti-Vietnam songs. He now called himself Bob Darin. His last big hit was "If I Were a Carpenter," which rose to number eight on the charts in October 1966, and his last top-forty hit was "Lovin' You" in February 1967. On March 2, 1967, he joined with Diana Ross and the Supremes, the Mamas and the Papas, and Count Basie and His Band for the special *Rodgers and Hart Today* (ABC-TV). Later in 1967, Darin was booed from the stage of Las Vegas's Sahara Hotel when his program consisted of political diatribes against Richard Nixon and others, freedom songs, and protest ballads. At this time, he did two folk albums that failed.

When presidential candidate Robert Kennedy, whom the singer knew slightly and for whom he had campaigned, was assassinated in June 1968, Darin went into complete shock. He attended the funeral at Arlington Cemetery, and his life was never the same. "With him in the ground, part of me went, too," Darin said. "Most people took four days to get over his death. It took me almost four years." He sold his music-publishing company (in a very unfavorable financial deal that he regretted later), divested himself of his possessions, bought a trailer, and relocated to the Big Sur area of central California. He claimed he needed time to realign his values and to find a new perspective. In the midst of this retrenchment he made one movie, United Artists' *The Happy Ending* (1969), playing a subordinate role as a gigolo who attempts to fleece an unhappily married woman (Jean Simmons). He also produced an album on his own label of soulful, thoughtful songs. It was not a big seller.

By 1971, Darin began reemerging in show business, no longer angry and no longer young. Now wearing his toupee again, he was a guest on *Ironside* (NBC-TV) and *Cade's County* (CBS-TV), and returned to nightclubs. Soon he was back performing in Las Vegas, but after closing there on February 8, 1971, he checked into a hospital to treat heart fibrillations. He underwent open-heart surgery, which took nine hours. Two plastic valves were implanted in his heart, and the recovery required a month. He continued to perform in clubs, guest on TV (including an episode of NBC-TV's *Night Gallery*), and in July 1972 he became the summer replacement for

Dean Martin on NBC-TV. The hour-long variety show, *Dean Martin Presents the Bobby Darin Amusement Company*, was relatively popular. Besides singing, Darin developed comedy skits in which he played recurring characters such as Dusty John the hippie poet, Angie the tenement dweller, Groucho, and the Godmother Socially; his constant companion was now legal secretary Andrea Yaeger, about whom he said, "I think I've been married for the past two years. We've just dispensed with the bureaucratic involvement." (They married on June 26, 1973, but separated a few months later.)

In early 1973, NBC-TV scheduled *The Bobby Darin Show* as a midseason replacement; it bowed on January 19, 1973, and lasted through the end of April. It was a continuation of the format he had used the prior summer. With very little fanfare the low-budget movie *Happy Mother's Day ... Love, George* was released in September 1973. Directed by actor Darren McGavin on location in Nova Scotia, its cast included Patricia Neal, Cloris Leachman, Ron Howard, and Darin in a very abbreviated role as Leachman's new boyfriend who sadistically beats Howard. It was a confused tale of sin, mystery, and gore in a small town, and quickly disappeared.

In 1972, Darin had joined with Motown Records and was attempting to reconfirm himself as a recording artist. He signed a $2 million, three-year contract with the MGM Grand Hotel in Las Vegas. But poor health continued to plague him. On December 10, 1973, he summoned an ambulance to take him to Cedars-Sinai Medical Center in Los Angeles. He was suffering from congestive heart failure (the implanted valves were malfunctioning), and he slipped into a coma on December 18. He died two days later following surgery. There was no funeral, because he donated his body to medical science at UCLA for research.

That longtime purveyor of the pop music scene, Dick Clark, who saw the full spectrum of the Bobby Darin phenomenon first hand, assessed, "I used to laugh when people told me how Bobby was an arrogant little son-of-a-bitch. But if you knew him, he was the kindest and gentlest person I knew. He had a great native intellect and if he were only healthy physically, he probably could have gone on to be a legend."

In January 1990, Bobby was posthumously inducted into the Rock and Roll Hall of Fame, with son Dodd accepting his late father's award. Four years later, Dodd, with Maxine Pietro, wrote *Dream Lovers: The Magnificent Shattered Lives of Bobby Darin and Sandra Dee*. It was a graphic chronicle of his parents' difficult marriage and their struggle to cope with success and its grim aftermath. In December 1998, PBS-TV aired a biography of the late star entitled *Bobby Darin: Beyond the Song*, which the *Hollywood Reporter* rated "honest and highly watchable." Meanwhile, for years there had been industry talk of a pending biopic entitled *The Bobby Darin Story*. However, the project, spearheaded by the son, has yet to come to fruition.

Filmography

Pepe (Col, 1960)
Come September (Univ, 1961) (also songs)
Too Late Blues (Par, 1961)
State Fair (20th-Fox, 1962)
Hell Is for Heroes (Par, 1962)
If a Man Answers (Univ, 1962) (also songs)
Pressure Point (UA, 1962)
Captain Newman, M.D. (Univ, 1963)

The Lively Set (Univ, 1964) (songs only)
That Funny Feeling (Univ, 1965) (also music, song)
That Darn Cat! (BV, 1965) (only voice, song)
Gunfight in Abilene (Univ, 1967) (also music)
Cop-Out [Stranger in the House] (MGM, 1967)
The Happy Ending (UA, 1969)
Happy Mother's Day ... Love, George [Run Stranger Run] (Cinema 5, 1973)

TV Series

Dean Martin Presents the Bobby Darin Amusement Company (NBC, 1972)

The Bobby Darin Show (NBC, 1973)

Album Discography

LPs

American Hot Wax (A&M SP-6500) [ST]
As Long As I'm Singin' (Jass 9)
The Best of Bobby Darin (Cap T/ST-2571)
Big Town (Atlantic 81769-1) [ST]
Bobby Darin (Atco 33-102)
Bobby Darin (Motown 753)
Bobby Darin at the Copa (Atco 33-122)
Bobby Darin, Born Walden Robert Cassotto (Direction 1936, Bell MBLL 112/SBLL 112)
Bobby Darin Sings Ray Charles (Atco 33-140)
The Bobby Darin Story (Atco 33-131)
Bobby Darin—The Star Collection (Midi 20-031)
Clementine (Clarion 603)
Commitment (Direction 1937)
Darin 1936-1976 (Motown 813VI)
Diner (Elektra E1-60107) [ST]
Doctor Dolittle (Atlantic 8154)
Dream Lover (Leedon 5026)
Earthy (Cap T/ST-1826)
Eighteen Yellow Roses (Cap T/ST-1942)
For Teenagers Only (Atco 1001)
From "Hello, Dolly!" to "Goodbye Charlie" (Cap T/ST-2914)
Golden Folk Hits (Cap T/ST-2007)
If I Were a Carpenter (Atlantic 8135)
In a Broadway Bag (Atlantic 8126)

Inside Out (Atlantic 8142)
It's You or No One (Atco 33-124)
The Legendary Bobby Darin (Candelite CMI-1959)
The Lively Set (Decca DL-9119) [ST]
Love Swings (Atco 33-134)
Multiplication and Irresistible You (Atco 33-115)
Oh! Look at Me Now (W/SW-1791)
Or No One (Atco 33-124)
Pepe (Colpix 507) [ST]
The Shadow of Your Smile (Atlantic 8121)
Something Special (Atlantic 557073)
Stardust (Arista 5000)
State Fair (Dot 9011/290112) [ST]
Tequila Sunrise (Cap C1-91185) [ST]
That's All (Atco 33-104)
Things and Other Things (Atco 33-146)
This Is Darin (Atco 33-115)
25th Day of December (Atco 33-125)
Twist With Bobby Darin (Atco 33-138)
Two of a Kind (Atco 33-126) w. Johnny Mercer
The Versatile Bobby Darin (EMI 671)
Venice Blue [I Wanna Be Around] (Cap T/ST-2322)
The Very Best of Bobby Darin (Imperial House NU-9380)
Winners (Atco 33-167)
You're the Reason I'm Living (Cap T/ST-1866)

CDs

A&E Biography . . . A Musical Anthology (Capitol/EMI 94752)
As Long as I'm Singing (Jass J-CD-4)
As Long as I'm Singing (Rhino 72206)
As Long as I'm Singin': Rare'n Darin #1 (r'n'd Productions RND-CD-1301)
The Best of Bobby Darin (Cap/EMI Special Markets 20580)
The Best of Bobby Darin (Curb D21K-77325)
Bobby Darin (Atlantic 82626-2)
Bobby Darin 1936-1977 (Motown 34763-5185-2)
Bobby Darin Sings Dr. Doolittle (Diablo 865)
Bobby Darin Sings the Standards (EMI 5325722, PID 69877)
The Bobby Darin Story (Atco 33131-2)
Capitol Collector's Series (Capitol 91025)
The Capitol Years (EMI G-CDTRBOX-348)

Classic Darin (Pair PDC-2-1189)
The Curtain Falls: Live at the Flamingo (Collectors' Choice Music CCM-131-2)
Darin at the Copa (Atlantic 82629-2)
Diner (Elektra 60107-2) [ST]
Dream Lover (Prism PLATCD-111)
From Sea to Sea (Live Gold 130013)
Goodfellas (Atlantic 82152-2) [ST]
If I Were a Carpenter/Inside Out (Diablo 864)
It Got Rhythm (EMI C-CDMP-6247)
Live at the Desert Inn (Motown 37463-9070-2)
Mack the Knife (Columbia River Entertainment Group CRG-1157)
Mack the Knife: The Best of Bobby Darin, Vol. 2 (Atco 91795-2)
The Magic of Bobby Darin (EMI G-TPM-480D)
Moods/Swing: The Best of the Atlantic Years 1965-67 (Edsel 910)

Pepe (Collectors' Choice Music CCM-113-2, DRG 113) [ST]

The Shadow of Your Smile/In a Broadway Bag (Diablo 863)

Spotlight on Bobby Darin (Cap C21Y-28512)

State Fair (Varese Sarabande 362-066075-2) [ST]

Swingin' the Standards (Varese Vintage 6004)

Tequila Sunrise (Capitol C21Y-91185) [ST]

That's All (Atlantic 82627-2)

This Is Darin (Atlantic 82628-2)

Touch of Class (Disky TC-877052)

25th Day of December (Atco 91772-2)

Two of a Kind (Atlantic 90484-2) w. Johnny Mercer

The Ultimate Bobby Darin (Warner Special Products 27606-2)

Unreleased Capitol Sides (Collectors' Choice Music CCM-079-2)

The Very Best of Bobby Darin (Varese Vintage 6007)

Wild, Cool & Swingin': The Artist Collection (Cap/EMI 7003)

You're the Reason I'm Living/I Want To Be Around (EMI 122)

Sammy Davis Jr.

(b. Harlem, New York City, December 8, 1925; d. Hollywood, California, May 16, 1990)

One of the most versatile and boundlessly energetic of all entertainers (in the true vaudevillian sense), Sammy Davis Jr. became a professional performer when he was two years old in 1927 and remained so until his death in 1990. He always termed himself a complete entertainer (*not* a complete singer). Whether tap-dancing nimbly, singing in his throaty baritone, or becoming heavily dramatic in movies, he always made a strong impression. He was long identified with such showstopping numbers as "Mr. Bojangles," "The Candy Man," and "What Kind of Fool Am I?"

In his formative years, lantern-jawed Davis rose to distinction as a member of the Will Mastin Trio. In later years, he was an on-again-off-again member of Frank Sinatra's notorious Rat Pack and thereafter functioned as part of the globe-trotting Sinatra–Liza Minnelli–Sammy Davis Jr. cabaret trio. However, through all these cycles, the five-feet six-inches Davis displayed a strong individualistic drive. Some described this trait as egocentric, while others termed his nonstop career efforts as a manic push for self-identity. (A standing joke of the 1960s had it that if Davis merely opened a refrigerator door and its lights went on, he would start performing.)

As a black man who suffered racial persecutions in his earlier years, Davis was accused later of abandoning his race (by marrying a white woman and joining the Rat Pack). He then suffered a reverse backlash when he championed the causes of integration. Davis was the first to admit it was never easy being a multiminority figure: i.e., black, Jewish (his adopted religion), and handicapped (he lost his left eye in an auto accident in the 1950s). Nor did his past excesses (decades of ostentatious flash, heavy drug usage, and drinking) make life simple for him or those surrounding him. Nevertheless, through all these highly publicized phases, his remarkable talent survived. With his abilities to blow hot trumpet licks, display solid drum rhythm, dance, sing, and act, Davis was regarded by many as one of the last of the major American variety performers: a Renaissance man of show business.

Sammy Davis Jr. was born in Harlem, New York City, on December 8, 1925. His vaudevillian father was a lead dancer in Will Mastin's "Holiday in Dixieland" troupe; his mother—Elvera (Sanchez) Davis—was the act's lead chorus girl. When Sammy was two, his sister Ramona was born. While their parents were on the road, Ramona was brought up by maternal relatives, and Sammy was placed in the care of his paternal grandmother, Rosa B. "Mama" Davis. When he was two and a half, his parents split up and Sammy was put in his father's care. He began traveling with the Will Mastin show and soon became part of the twelve-member vaudeville act. (Although Sammy would always call Mastin "uncle," he was not a relative.) At first, Sammy would just mimic the older performers, but gradually he became an accomplished singing and dancing member of the group. In 1933, he made his film debut, appearing in two short subjects filmed at the Warner Bros.–Vitaphone studios in Brooklyn. The first, *Rufus Jones for President*, cast him as Ethel Waters's

Vicki Carr and Sammy Davis Jr. guest star on a 1972 Burt Bacharach TV variety special. [Courtesy of Echo Book Shop].

son who dreams he becomes the top executive of the United States. In the second, *Season's Greetings*, he was featured with Lita Grey.

As the effects of the Depression and competing motion pictures caused vaudeville to fade, the Will Mastin troupe was reduced gradually to the Will Mastin Trio. During the 1930s, the Trio continued to perform around the country, with Sammy befriended and tutored at one point by Bill "Bojangles" Robinson in the art of tap-dancing. In the early 1940s, Davis first met Frank Sinatra, who was then performing with Tommy Dorsey and His Band.

In late 1943, the eighteen-year-old Davis was drafted into World War II service. During his basic training in Cheyenne, Wyoming, an African-American master sergeant taught him to read. He also learned how to deal with discrimination in the service by using his fists against belligerent racists who attacked him. (Given the racial bias in the military at the time, it is a wonder it did not affect Sammy's service record.) As a member of the Special Services, he wrote and directed Army camp shows around the country. He was discharged from the Army in late 1945 and rejoined the Will Mastin Trio. Bookings were very slim, and they often found themselves playing run-down burlesque houses or seedy clubs in Los Angeles, Chicago, and elsewhere. During these many lean periods, Davis continued to expand his repertoire of impressions, his musical ability (including piano and vibes), and his flashy dancing (his father and "uncle" were now mostly background performers for the act).

In 1946, Sammy's show-business connections brought him to Capitol Records, where his recording of "The Way You Look Tonight" won recognition and led *Metronome* magazine to name him 1946's "Most Outstanding New Personality." Other friends introduced the Will Mastin Trio to Mickey Rooney, who was performing a stage revue in Boston, and they became his opening act for several weeks on the road. Later the Trio was booked into Slapsie Maxie Rosenbloom's Hollywood cabaret and began playing Las Vegas (where they could not get a hotel room except in the black part of town). They performed with Frank Sinatra at the Capitol Theater in New York in 1947 and played Ciro's in Hollywood (supporting Janis Paige). (That year Davis and the Trio appeared in the Paramount short subject, *Sweet and Low*.) Soon the Trio was making $1,250 a week on their tour with Jack Benny's stage revue, and later they appeared on *The Colgate Comedy Hour* (NBC-TV) hosted by Eddie Cantor; the Trio would be frequent guests on the show during the summer of 1954. They also played the Copacabana Club in New York City and the Apollo Theater in Harlem. For each success, however, there were several steps backward due to racial discrimination.

In June 1954, Davis signed a recording contract with Decca Records. That November, the Will Mastin Trio was performing at the New Frontier Hotel in Las Vegas at $7,500 weekly. On November 19, 1954, Davis was in an auto accident that nearly cost him his life and from which he lost his left eye. It was during this ordeal that, inspired by Jewish friends (performers Eddie Cantor and Jeff Chandler), Davis converted to Judaism. When he recovered he at first wore a patch over his eye, but later he had an artificial eye inserted instead. The accident had focused a great deal of attention on him, and he was now much in demand as a performer. He returned to entertaining with the Will Mastin Trio at Ciro's in Hollywood and at other clubs nationwide. He also was enjoying healthy record sales with his Decca LPs. His album *Starring Sammy Davis Jr.* rose to number one on the charts and *Just for Lovers* rose to number eight on the charts in mid- to late 1955. That same year, he appeared briefly as musician Fletcher Henderson in *The Benny Goodman Story* at Universal and had top-twenty singles hits with "Something's Gotta Give," "Love Me or Leave Me," and "That Old Black Magic." By now, Davis was a flashy member of Sinatra's high-living Rat Pack, which included—at different periods—Humphrey Bogart, Lauren Bacall, Dean Martin, Joey Bishop, Henry Silva, and Peter Lawford.

The only thing wonderful about the Broadway musical comedy *Mr. Wonderful* was Sammy as the energetic club performer who overcomes racial obstacles to succeed. The show opened on March 22, 1956, and also featured Sammy Davis Sr. and Will Mastin. It ran for 383 performances. By early 1957, Davis was back performing in clubs, where he was happiest, and was continuously singing his custom-written song "Give Me a Saloon Every Time." Due to insurmountable friction among the partners, the Will Mastin Trio finally disbanded, leaving Davis to perform solo.

The year 1958 marked Davis's debut performance in a TV drama on the "Auf Wiederschen" episode of *G.E. Theater* (CBS-TV, October 5, 1958). He also nearly had a substantial feature-film assignment, in *The Defiant Ones* (1958), a project Davis's friend Elvis Presley wanted to costar them both. However, Presley and his manager backed out of the interracial melodrama, fearing it might have repercussions on Presley's singing career. Instead, Davis went into the all-black *Anna Lucasta* (1958). He was the grasping, jive-talking Danny Johnson, who lusts for a streetwalker (Eartha Kitt) and almost spoils her marriage to another man. *Variety* noted, "Sammy Davis Jr. lives his role as the cocky little fellow. . . . He brings to the character a good deal of understanding and balance. . . ." The next year Davis campaigned for and won (after Cab Calloway turned down the part) the role of the dope-dealing Sportin' Life in the all-African-American operetta *Porgy and Bess* (1959). Unlike many of the film's other stars (Sidney Poitier, Dorothy Dandridge, Diahann Carroll), Davis did his own singing ("It Ain't Necessarily So"). However, ironically, on the soundtrack album Calloway sang the role of Sportin' Life because Davis was then signed to a rival recording label. Davis would later make an album of *Porgy and Bess* songs for Decca. It was also in 1959 that Davis was briefly married to black chorus girl Loray White; entertainer Harry Belafonte was best man at the ceremony.

In the early 1960s, hip Davis was at the height of his Rat Pack (and gaudy chain-wearing) period. He appeared in a trio of Frank Sinatra movies: *Ocean's Eleven* (1960), *Sergeants Three* (1962), and *Robin and the 7 Hoods* (1964), all of which were undisciplined celluloid larks. (He had been scheduled to appear in the earlier *Never So Few* [1959], but he and Sinatra had a spat at the time, and Steve McQueen inherited the Davis role.) Much more solid were Davis's performances as Wino the Halloween Bandit in the prison tale *Convicts Four* (1962), as Educated in the crime drama *Johnny Cool* (1963), and as the Ballad Singer (who performs "Mack the Knife") in *The Threepenny Opera* (1963). Sammy had the lead part of a self-defeated jazz musician in *A Man Called Adam* (1966), as the trumpet player who blames himself for the death of his family in a car accident. It was a solid dramatic performance (as were those by Cicely Tyson, Ossie Davis, and Louis Armstrong). However, the New York City–lensed picture was marred by several members of the supporting cast, which included Davis's pals and associates: Mel Torme, Peter Lawford, and Frank Sinatra Jr. In 1968, he and Rat Packer Lawford costarred in the spy spoof *Salt and Pepper*, which was popular enough, but the embarrassing sequel, *One More Time* (1970), directed by Jerry Lewis, was a bust. In Shirley MacLaine's overinflated musical *Sweet Charity* (1968), Sammy was thrown in as Big Daddy, the hippie religious cult leader who sings "Rhythm of Life."

On television, the hard-driving Davis guested on a variety of programs, including *The Dick Powell Show* (1962), *The Rifleman* (1962), *Ben Casey* (1963), and *The Patty Duke Show* (1965). The star headlined his own specials *Sammy Davis and the Wonderful World of Children* (ABC-TV, November 25, 1963) and *The Sammy Davis Jr. Special* (NBC-TV, February 18, 1965). From January to April 1966, he had his own NBC-TV variety series *The Sammy Davis Jr. Show*, which tried too hard to make the spontaneous performer conform to a regimented formula. (Moreover, after the first segment, he was not allowed to be on his own show for four weeks due to a contract with another network.)

In this period, Sammy seemed to be everywhere on the small screen, with guest appearances in *Batman* (1966), *I Dream of Jeannie* (1967), *The Beverly Hillbillies* (1969), and *The Mod Squad* (1969). He also filled in for Johnny Carson several times as host of *The Tonight Show*. On November 4, 1969, the star made his telefeature debut, starring in *The Pigeon* (ABC-TV) as a black private detective based in San Francisco. It was an early example of the black action cycle then enveloping Hollywood. However, the lighthearted show, which featured Pat Boone and Ricardo Montalban, failed to sell as a series.

Besides films, television, and continuous club work, Davis also returned to Broadway, starring in a musical version of Clifford Odets's *Golden Boy*. He was the black musician who abandoned his craft for the fast bucks of the boxing world and the love of a white woman (Paula Wayne). The show opened on October 20, 1964, to mixed reviews but, on the strength of Davis's acting, ran for 569 performances. He had top-twenty albums with *What Kind of Fool Am I?* (1962), *The Shelter of Your Arms* (1964), and *I've Gotta Be Me* (1969). Among his single hits in the top forty was "Don't Blame the Children" (1967), a spoken disc. Through much of the 1960s, he was recording for Reprise Records, a label owned by Frank Sinatra. Before his first marriage in 1959, Davis had been "linked" with Ava Gardner and later with Kim Novak, but it was Swedish actress May Britt whom he married in 1960. Together they had a daughter (Tracey) and adopted two children (Mark and Jeff). In 1968, they were divorced. Additionally, in 1965 his autobiography *Yes I Can* (written with Jane and Burt Boyar) was published, becoming a best-seller with its candid account of how Davis overcame many discriminatory odds on his road to success.

In 1970, Sammy married black dancer Altovise Gore, who once was a member of his dancing troupe. Two years later, he bought an 8-percent interest in Las Vegas's Tropicana Hotel, where he was being paid $100,000 a week to perform. He grossed $3 million in 1972. It was also that year that he had his last big hit single, "The Candy Man," which rose to number one on the charts. He continued to guest on teleseries (*All in the Family*—the famous 1972 episode where Sammy kissed the arch bigot lead character, Archie Bunker), star in TV specials (*Old Faithful*, 1973), and appear in telefeatures: *The Trackers* (1971) and *Poor Devil* (1973). He and Mickey Rooney were on almost every episode of *NBC Follies*, a variety show that ran from September to December 1973. He had his own *Sammy and Company*, a syndicated ninety-minute variety show that began its several-month run in September of 1975. He sang the theme song on the *Baretta* detective series (1975–78), and he appeared as a guest star on two network soap operas: *Love of Life* (1975) and *One Life to Live* (1979–80). Politically, the man who had endorsed John F. Kennedy and Robert F. Kennedy in the 1960s had become a supporter of Richard Nixon in the early 1970s, which caused much consternation. Having been accused in past decades of ignoring his own race, Davis exercised social consciousness in the 1960s as a follower of Dr. Martin Luther King Jr. In the musical documentary *Save the Children* (1973), he was among the black performers (Marvin Gaye, Isaac Hayes, the Staple Singers, Roberta Flack) singing at a charity concert.

Having dealt with liver and kidney trouble and chest pains in 1974 (which curtailed his assorted addictions), he appeared in a stage revue, *Sammy on Broadway*, at the Uris Theater in April 1974. Four years later (August 1978) he starred in his own version of the Anthony Newley–Leslie Bricusse musical *Stop The World, I Want to Get Off* at the New York State Theater at Lincoln Center. It was this 1960s hit show that had provided Davis with his trademark song, "What Kind of Fool Am I?" A specially taped version of the new stage production received limited distribution as the film *Sammy Stops the World* (1978).

Davis was among the guest stars in Burt Reynolds's comedy travesty, *The Cannonball Run* (1981). Said Sammy: "It was a horrible picture, I guess, but a terrific giggle." He also appeared in the sequel *Cannonball Run II* (1984, which featured Frank Sinatra in a cameo) and was one of the cohosts of the big-screen documentary *That's Dancing!* (1985). After a second and more serious bout with liver disease in 1983, he publicly swore off liquor in November 1983, and had cut down (at least by his own hectic standards) his performance schedule. Nevertheless, he still appeared in clubs and guested on television. On TV he was on *Fantasy Island* (1983 and 1984), *The Jeffersons* (1984), and in the syndicated special *Dancing in the Wings* (1985).

Sammy portrayed both the Caterpillar and Father William in the four-hour television version of *Alice in Wonderland* (CBS-TV, 1985). In 1986, he gave a concert at the Hollywood Bowl, which revealed a new, toned-down Sammy Davis Jr. Afterward, he continued to guest on a spectrum of TV outings: *The Kennedy Center Honors: A Celebration of the Arts* (1987; he was a Life Achievement medalist that year), *Evening at Pops* (1988), *A Whole Lotta Fun* (1988), *An Evening With Sammy Davis Jr. and Jerry Lewis* (1988; taped from their Las Vegas joint club act), and *Motown Returns to the Apollo* (1988). In addition, he turned up on episodes of *Hunter* (1989) and *The Cosby Show* (1989) as well as assorted talk shows and telethons.

Having turned down a role in *Beetlejuice* (1988), Davis returned to dramatic acting with *Tap* (1989) a heavy dance drama starring Gregory Hines and a host of tap-dancing greats from the past. Davis was cast as Little Mo, the father of the girl (Suzanne Douglas) ex-convict Hines adores. While the movie met with tepid audience response, Davis received uniformly solid reviews. ("[He] does a nice, unshowbizzy turn as an old hoofer"—*Newsweek* magazine.) Sammy's nonchalant reaction to his revived movie career was, "I'm a saloon entertainer who happens to make pictures."

In the late 1980s, Davis began performing again in cabarets with Frank Sinatra, and they planned an extensive international tour with Dean Martin (who dropped out and was replaced by Liza Minnelli). Of the three veteran singers, Davis received the best reviews as they crisscrossed the United States and, later, went around the world, leading to a cable network taping of their club act, *Frank, Liza & Sammy: The Ultimate Event* (Showtime Cable, May 20, 1989). In 1988, Davis underwent extensive reconstructive hip surgery, and his father died. In 1989, he continued performing in tandem with Sinatra and Minnelli, as well as doing a Las Vegas club act with Jerry Lewis. Also in 1989, his new autobiography, *Why Me?*, was published. He admitted that writing the book was painful: "The guy from 25 years ago doesn't exist anymore. The guy from 10 years ago doesn't exist anymore. And I hope 10 years from now I'll be able to say that this guy doesn't exist anymore. He's a better human being, a more caring person."

Not long after the publication of his book, Sammy was diagnosed with throat cancer. In early 1990, his many show-business friends organized a fulsome TV benefit tribute. By that point Davis was fast failing. After several months of severe pain, he passed away on May 16, 1990. His well-attended, celebrity-studded funeral service was held at Forest Lawn Memorial Park in Holly-wood Hills. He was then buried at Forest Lawn Memorial Park in Glendale in the family plot. When his estate was probated it was made known that, despite leaving assets of around $10 million, he had left huge debts, including over $5.7 million in federal (back) taxes. As part of the settlement with the government, Sammy's Beverly Hills home was sold, and much of the memorabilia he had collected over his lifetime was sold at auction. Davis's widow Altovise reached a settlement with the IRS in 1997 regarding the outstanding tax liabilities on the estate.

Since his death, the character of Sammy Davis Jr. has figured in several major movie projects. In the 1992 TV movie *Sinatra*, David Raynr portrayed the African-American entertainer, while in the theatrical film comedy *Wayne's World 2* (1993), Tim Meadows appeared as Davis. For the telefeature *The Rat Pack* (1998), Don Cheadle turned in an Emmy-nominated performance as the fast-living, hyperactive member of Frank Sinatra's talented dawn patrol. (Over the years, comedian Billy Crystal did an affectionate impersonation of Davis that also helped to keep Sammy's image alive.) In 2001, *The Sammy Davis Jr. Reader* was published. In reviewing the book edited by Gerald Early, *Entertainment Week* pointed out, "This somewhat claustrophobic compilation of everything ever printed about Davis, from his FBI file to his *New York Times* obit, reads like a history of race relations and showbiz in the U.S. at their tender point of intersection."

Once when asked his philosophy of life, Sammy Davis Jr. assessed, "You have to be able to look back at your life and say, 'Yeah, that was fun.' The only person I ever hurt was myself and even that I did to the minimum. If you can do that and you're still functioning, you're the luckiest person in the world."

Filmography

Rufus Jones for President (Vita, 1933) (s)
Season's Greetings (Vita, 1933) (s)
Sweet and Lowdown (Par, 1947) (s)
The Benny Goodman Story (Univ, 1955)
Meet Me in Las Vegas [Viva Las Vegas!] (MGM, 1956) (voice only)
Anna Lucasta (UA, 1958)
Porgy and Bess (Col, 1959)
Ocean's Eleven (WB, 1960)
Pepe (Col, 1960)
Convicts Four [Reprieve!] (AA, 1962)
Of Love and Desire (20th-Fox, 1962) (voice only)
Sergeants Three (UA, 1962)
The Threepenny Opera [Der Dreigroschenoper] (Emb, 1963)
Johnny Cool (UA, 1963)
Robin and the 7 Hoods (WB, 1964)
Nightmare in the Sun (Zodiak, 1965)
A Man Called Adam (Emb, 1966)
Salt and Pepper (UA, 1968)

Sweet Charity (Univ, 1968)
The Pigeon (ABC-TV, 11/4/69)
One More Time (UA, 1970) (also executive producer)
The Trackers (ABC-TV, 12/14/71)
Poor Devil (NBC-TV, 2/14/73)
Save the Children (Par, 1973)
Sammy Stops the World [Stop the World—I Want to Get Off] (Special Event Entertainment, 1978)
Man Without Mercy [Gone With the West/Little Moon and Jud McGraw] (International Cine Corp, 1979) (made in 1969)
The Cannonball Run (20th-Fox, 1981)
Heidi's Song (Par, 1982) (voice only)
Cannonball Run II (WB, 1984)
That's Dancing! (MGM, 1985) (cohost)
Alice in Wonderland (CBS-TV, 12/9–10/85)
Moon Over Parador (Univ, 1988)
Tap (Tri-Star, 1989)

Broadway Plays

Mr. Wonderful (1956)
Golden Boy (1964)

Stop the World, I Want to Get Off (1978) (revival)

TV Series

The Sammy Davis Jr. Show (NBC, 1966)
NBC Follies (NBC, 1973)

Sammy and Company (Synd, 1975–77)

Album Discography

LPs

All the Way and Then Some (Decca DL-8779)
Back on Broadway (Reprise 6169)
The Best of Broadway (Reprise 2010)
The Best of Sammy Davis Jr. (Decca DX-192/ DXS-7192)
Big Ones for Young Lovers (Reprise 6131)
Boy Meets Girl (Decca Dl-8490) w. Carmen McRae

California Suite (Reprise 6126)
Closest of Friends (Applause 1016)
Doctor Dolittle (Reprise 6264)
Forget-Me-Nots for First Nighters (Decca Dl-4381/ 74381)
The Goin's Great (Reprise 6339)
Golden Boy (Cap VAS/SVAS-2124) [OC]
Great (Har HS-11299)

Greatest Hits (Reprise 6291)

Here's Lookin' at You (Decca DL-8351)

Hey There! It's Sammy Davis Jr. at His Dynamite Best (MCA 4109)

I Gotta Right to Swing (Decca DL-8981/78981)

If I Ruled the World (Reprise 6159)

It's All Over but the Swingin' (Decca DL-8641)

I've Gotta Be Me (Reprise 6324)

Johnny Cool (United Artists UAL-4111/UAS-5111, Ascot ALM-30121) [ST]

Just for Lovers (Decca DL-8170)

Let There Be Love (Har HS-11365)

A Live Performance of His Greatest Hits (WB BSK-3128)

Lonely Is the Name (Reprise 6308)

A Man Called Adam (Reprise 6180) [ST]

The Many Faces of Sammy (Pickwick 3002)

The Men in My Life (Three Cherries TC 44411) w. Lena Horne, Joe Williams

Mood to Be Wooed (Decca DL8676)

Mr. Entertainment (Decca DL-4153/74153)

Mr. Wonderful (Decca DL-9032) [OC]

The Nat "King" Cole Songbook (Reprise 6164)

Now (MGM SE-4832)

Of Love and Desire (20th Century-Fox 5014) [ST]

Our Shining Hour (Verve 8605/68605) w. Count Basie

Pepe (Colpix 507) [ST]

Porgy and Bess (Decca DL-8854/78854)

Robin and the 7 Hoods (Reprise 2021) [ST]

Salt and Pepper (United Artists UAS-5187, MCA 25035) [ST]

A Salute to Nat (King) Cole (Reprise PRO-212) w. Frank Sinatra

Sammy (MGM SE-4914) [ST/TV]

Sammy Davis Jr. (Design 146)

Sammy Davis Jr. (Vocalion 3827/73827)

Sammy Davis Jr. and Count Basie (MGM SE-4825)

Sammy Davis Jr. at the Cocoanut Grove (Reprise 6063)

Sammy Davis Jr. at Town Hall (Decca DL-8841)

Sammy Davis Jr. Now (MGM 4832)

Sammy Davis Jr. Salutes the Stars of the London Palladium (Reprise 6236)

The Sammy Davis Jr. Show (Reprise 6188)

Sammy Davis Jr. Swings (Decca Dl-8486)

Sammy Davis Swings—Laurindo Almeida Plays (Reprise 6236)

Sammy Jumps With Joy (Design 22)

Sammy Steps Out (Reprise 6410)

Save the Children (Motown M-800-R2) [ST]

The Shelter of Your Arms (Reprise 6114)

Something for Everyone (Motown 710)

The Sound of Sammy (WB 1501)

Sounds of '66 (Reprise 6214)

Spotlight on Sammy Davis Jr. (Spectrum DLP-146)

Starring Sammy Davis Jr. (Decca DL-8118)

Stop the World, I Want to Get Off! (WB HS-3214) [ST]

Summit Meeting at the 500 (Souvenir 247-17) w. Frank Sinatra, Dean Martin

Sweet Charity (Decca DL-71502) [ST]

That's All (Reprise 6237)

That's Entertainment (MGM SE-4965)

Three Billion Millionaires (UA UXL-4/UXS-4) [ST]

The Threepenny Opera (RCA LOC/LSO-1086) [ST]

Try a Little Tenderness (Decca DL-4582/74582)

The Wham of Sam (Reprise 2003/92003)

What Kind of Fool Am I (Har H-30568)

What Kind of Fool Am I (Reprise 6051/96051)

When the Feeling Hits You (Reprise 6144)

CDs

All the Things You Are (Pair PCD-2-1553)

At the Cocoanut Grove (Warner Archives 74277-2)

The Best of Sammy Davis, Jr. (Curb D21K-74444)

The Best of Sammy Davis, Jr. (Empire Music Collection 140, MCI MCCD-140, Music Club Records 140)

The Best of Sammy Davis, Jr. (Phantom)

Capitol Collector's Series (Cap C21Y-94071)

The Clan in Chicago (The Entertainers 389) w. Frank Sinatra, Dean Martin

Closest of Friends (Universe 8264516)

Collection (Warner 9548339652)

The Country Side of Sammy Davis, Jr. (BCM RMB-75001)

The Decca Years (MCA MCAD-10101)

Frank Sinatra at Villa Venice, Chicago, Live 1962, Vol. 1 (Jazz Hour 1033) w. Frank Sinatra, Dean Martin

Frank Sinatra at Villa Venice, Chicago, Live 1962, Vol. 2 (Jazz Hour 1034) w. Frank Sinatra, Dean Martin

Frank Sinatra in Italy (Drive 534) w. Frank Sinatra, Liza Minnelli

From Nashville With Love (CEMA Special Products 17777)

Golden Boy (Bay Cities 3012, Broadway Angel ZDM-65024) [OC]

Golden Legends (Direct Source)

The Great Sammy Davis, Jr. (BCD G2D-63187)

Greatest Hits (The Entertainers 302)

Greatest Hits Live (Curb/Atlantic 77687-2)

Greatest Hits, Vol. 1 (Garland GR2-018)

Greatest Hits, Vols. 1 & 2 (DCC Compact Classics D2S-SPC-148)

Greatest Hits, Vol. 2 (DCC Compact Classics D2S-048)

Greatest Songs (Curb D21K-77272)

It's All Over but the Swingin'/I Gotta Be Me
(MCA MCCD-19384, MSI/UNI 19384)

I've Gotta Be Me/The Best of Sammy Davis, Jr.,
On Reprise (Reprise Archives 46416)

Johnny Cool (Ryko 10744) [ST]

The Magic Collection (ARC MEC-949012)

Mr. Bojangles (Universal Special Markets 520543,
Traditional Line TL-1384)

Mr. Wonderful (MCA Classics MCAD-10303)
[OC]

My Greatest Hits (MCA E1183542)

Our Shining Hour (Polydor 837446-2, Verve
837446) w. Count Basie

Pepe (Collectors' Classic Music CCM-113-2, DRG
113) [ST]

The Rat Pack (Armoury ARMCD-050) w. Frank Sinatra, Dean Martin

The Rat Pack (TKO Magnum CECD038) w.
Frank Sinatra, Dean Martin

The Rat Pack (TKO/United Audio Entertainment
UAE-30492) w. Frank Sinatra, Dean Martin

The Rat Pack Collection (Madacy 5315) w. Frank
Sinatra, Dean Martin

Robin & the 7 Hoods (Artanis ARZ-104-2) [ST]

Sammy & Friends (Rhino R2-75934)

Sammy Davis Jr. (Direct Source 61972)

Sammy Davis Jr., Sings and Laurindo Almeida
Plays (DCC Compact Classics DZS-055, DCC
Compact Classics 627, Sandstone D21Y-37081)

Sammy in Nashville (Hallmark)

Smokey (Auto Pilot ROGER-22)

The Sounds of '66 (DCC Compact Classics 625)
w. Buddy Rich

The Summit: In Concert (Artanis ARZ-102) w.
Frank Sinatra, Dean Martin

Sunny Side of the Street (Delta 6213) w. Frank Sinatra, Dean Martin

Ten Best Golden Greats (Cleopatra 970)

That Old Black Magic (MCA MCAD-20198, Universal Special Markets 20198)

That's All (Rhino/Warner Archives 74278)

The Wham of Sam (Warner Bros. 45637-2)

Yes, I Can: The Sammy Davis, Jr., Story (Warner
Archives/Rhino 75972-2)

Doris Day and James Cagney in *The West Point Story* (1950).
[Courtesy of JC Archives]

Doris Day

(b. Doris von Kappelhoff, Cincinnati, Ohio, April 3, 1924)

Few performers perpetuated an image longer or more successfully than Doris Day. From the start of her cinema career in the late 1940s, she was labeled as the freckle-faced, sunny, girl-next-door, and for the next several decades maintained this (not always flattering) title in films and on television. Occasionally, in her string of hit pictures, she was allowed to be spunky (*Calamity Jane*, 1953), go dramatic (*The Man Who Knew Too Much*, 1955), or be slightly risqué (*Move Over, Darling*, 1963). However, the public preferred her as the perennial screen virgin, and she obliged.

But there were always more dimensions to Doris Day as a performer than just an actress noted for her overly virtuous characterizations. After all, she was a popular big-band vocalist who made a smooth transition into becoming a leading recording artist on her own. Her voice displayed a freshness and intimate directness that overcame the cotton-candy arrangements of her singing sessions. When Day sang, the listener always felt enlivened and refreshed. Many of the numbers she recorded from her movies became hits, none so enduringly popular as "Que Sera, Sera." There was also a deeper emotional side to the singing star than being Miss Apple Pie would allow. When her therapeutic autobiography *Doris Day: Her Own Story*, written with A. E. Hotchner, was published in 1975, no one was more surprised than Day herself at the various tragedies with which she had coped and, more importantly, had survived.

She was born Doris von Kappelhoff on April 3, 1924, in Cincinnati, Ohio, the second child of Frederick Wilhelm and Alma Sophia von Kappelhoff, both of German descent. There was a three-year-older brother Paul; another child (Richard) had died at the age of two before Doris was born. Her father, a Catholic church organist/choirmaster, was a stern taskmaster, and a tyrant about other people's morals. In sharp contrast was her outgoing, amiable mother, who had named Doris after a favorite screen star, Doris Kenyon. At the age of four, Doris made her performing debut singing her rendition of "I's Gwine Down to the Cushville Hop" at a Cincinnati Masonic hall. Her mother enrolled young Doris at Pep Golden's Dance School (and at several other dance/singing schools thereafter), hoping to foster the child's interest in show business. By 1936, the von Kappelhoffs were divorced, Frederick having been caught in an affair with Alma's best friend. Doris, her brother, and mother moved to College Hill, Ohio. There Mrs. von Kappelhoff worked in a bakery, and Doris attended Our Lady of the Angels School.

Doris become intrigued with a cute teenager named Jerry Doherty, and the two formed a team as Doherty and Kappelhoff. They won a $500 prize in a dance contest sponsored by a Cincinnati department store. Inspired by this success, the two mothers took their children to Hollywood to have professional dance lessons and, hopefully, to break into motion pictures. Once on the coast and living in a Glendale, California apartment, Doris and Jerry were enrolled in classes given by Louis DaPron, a leading tap-dance teacher. The young dancers garnered a few professional appearances, but despite their mothers taking part-time jobs, the two families ran out of funds.

They returned to Ohio to convince Mr. Doherty, a dairyman, to relocate to California. He was agreeable. Meanwhile, the team of Doherty and Kappelhoff were hired to perform for a few weeks with a touring edition of the Fanchon and Marco stage show. The night before the two families were to leave for California, Doris was injured in an automobile accident in Hamilton, Ohio. Her right leg was crushed and she was hospitalized for fourteen months. With professional dancing now out of the question, she began vocalizing. Her mother focused on this new opportunity and took in sewing to pay for her daughter's singing lessons with Grace Raine.

Doris was hired to sing at the Shanghai Inn and later appeared on *Karlin's Karnival*, a local radio show over WCPO. She was given no salary for her radio chores, but she was heard by bandleader Barney Rapp, who was opening his own nightclub. He hired her in 1940 and suggested her new surname, taking it from a song, "Day After Day," that she had sung over the airwaves. Later, she sang with Bob Crosby and His Bobcats at $75 weekly and thereafter joined with the band of Fred Waring. By the summer of 1940, Day was with Les Brown and his group. *Metronome* magazine, reviewing the Brown band in 1940, noted, "Doris Day . . . for combined looks and voice has no apparent equal: she's pretty and fresh-looking, handles herself with unusual grace, and what's most important of all, sings with much natural feeling and in tune."

Meanwhile, Doris had met Al Jorden, a trombone player with Barney Rapp, who later joined drummer Gene Krupa's band. She and Jorden were married in April of 1941 at New York's City Hall, while Doris was between shows performing at Radio City Music Hall. Their son Terry (named after the radio-adventure show, *Terry and the Pirates*) was born on February 8, 1942. A year later, she and Jorden were divorced. (She later described him as a "psychopathic sadist"; he committed suicide in July 1967.) The singer and her baby returned to Cincinnati, where she sang briefly over a local radio station. Day then returned to vocalizing with Les Brown and His Band of Renown at $350 weekly, leaving her child with her mother.

Doris remained with Brown's group for three years. During this productive period she recorded many singles with his band, including "Sentimental Journey" (November 1944) for Okeh Records. It became a huge hit, as did such other tunes as "My Dreams Are Getting Better All the Time" (February 1945). On March 30, 1946, in Mount Vernon, New York, she married George Weidler (brother of child actress Virginia Weidler), who was the temporary first saxophonist with Brown's group. When the first saxophonist returned from World War II, Weidler was demoted back to third alto saxophonist, and he quit. Weidler decided to try his luck in California, and the couple moved to the West Coast, living in a mobile home (due to a housing shortage) on Sepulveda Boulevard in Santa Monica. Doris, who had sung previously for twenty weeks on *Your Hit Parade* (CBS) in New York, was hired as vocalist for the Bob Sweeney–Hal March CBS radio show. In 1947, Day and Rudy Vallee made an audition show for a radio series to be called "This Is the Mrs." It did not sell, but the show was broadcast on ABC on November 20, 1947. Later, Doris replaced Frances Langford as vocalist on Bob Hope's NBC radio program from 1948 to 1950.

In March of 1947, Doris's agent got her a job singing at Billy Reed's Little Club in New York. *Variety* reported, "Miss Day does justice by her pop chores. . . . She's more than the adequate ex-band singer. She's a fetching personality and will more than hold her own in class or mass nighteries." While performing there as a soloist, she received a letter from her husband asking for a divorce, insisting he did not want to stand in the way of her career. They were divorced in 1949.

Meanwhile Doris had recorded "Love Somebody" with Buddy Clark for Columbia Records, and it had become a big hit. When she returned to Los Angeles, her agent Al Levy took her for an interview with filmmaker Michael Curtiz. He was seeking a replacement for Paramount's Betty Hutton (then pregnant) and MGM's Judy Garland (whose studio would not release her) to star in a Warner Bros. musical called *Romance on the High Seas* (1948). Despite Day being tremendously depressed about her pending divorce (and crying through the entire interview), Curtiz was impressed sufficiently to both hire her for the picture and to sign her to a personal contract (starting at $500 weekly) with his own production company.

Romance on the High Seas was a nonsense story about an aggressive wife (Janis Paige) hiring a stand-in (Day) to take her place on a South American cruise so she can snoop on her spouse (Don DeFore) at home. Meanwhile, the husband hires a private detective (Jack Carson) to trail the wife shipboard. For the million-dollar Technicolor production, Busby Berkeley provided the choreography, with Sammy Cahn and Julie Styne writing eight songs. Unlike many other big-band vocalists, Doris was quite photogenic and even in her screen debut displayed sufficient comedy timing and adequate dramatics to carry her through the snappy production. *Film Daily* observed, "The whole show has been draped around Miss Day and she not only looks good in it but she is good." *Variety* concurred: "Pop numbers are given strong selling by Doris Day. . . . [she] clicks in her story character and should draw nifty fan response." She sang five of the eight songs, and one of them, "It's Magic," was Oscar-nominated (but lost to "Buttons and Bows").

Warner Bros., who lacked its own female singing stars (they borrowed June Haver twice from Twentieth Century-Fox in 1949), saw the box-office potential in Doris and bought her contract from Curtiz. The studio teamed her twice again (*My Dream Is Yours; It's a Great Feeling*) with Jack Carson, whom she also dated briefly. In 1950, Doris had an opportunity to test her dramatic abilities in *Young Man With a Horn*. The picture focused on an obsessed musician (Kirk Douglas) who is distracted from his career by a selfish playgirl (Lauren Bacall), but redeemed by friends, including band vocalist Jo Jordan (Day). The movie was a distortion of Dorothy Baker's fine novel, but it provided Doris with several standards to sing ("Marvelous," "The Very Thought of You") and offered her an opportunity to extend her dramatic range on-camera. The *New York Times* lauded her for her "complete naturalness."

Tea for Two (1950), an updating of *No, No Nanette*, was Day's first screen match with Gordon MacRae. They were as wholesome together as Van Johnson and June Allyson at MGM. Warner Bros. reteamed Doris and Gordon four further times on the big screen. In *The West Point Story* (1950), they supported James Cagney, who starred as the egocentric Broadway director hired to stage a show at the military academy. The screen couple was among the Warner Bros. star lineup caught in *Starlift* (1951). They came into their own in *On Moonlight Bay* (1951), which showcased them as citizens of small-town Indiana circa 1917. They were so successful in this homey musical that the studio created a sequel, *By the Light of the Silvery Moon* (1953), which followed their ingenuous path to matrimony in post–World War I days.

In the interim, Day went heavily dramatic in *Storm Warning* (1950), an expose of the Ku Klux Klan in the deep South. Photoplay magazine judged, "Songster Doris Day . . . has her first crack at dramatic acting in this violent melodrama and comes off remarkably well." *Lullaby of Broadway* (1951), originally to have starred June Haver, matched her with dancer Gene Nelson and scene-stealing Gladys George (as her mother), while *I'll See You in My Dreams* (1951) united her with Danny Thomas in a specious biography of composer Gus Kahn. Day's most unlikely leading man was dancer Ray Bolger in *April in Paris* (1952). The original songs by Sammy Cahn and Vernon Duke were a bad lot, especially in contrast to the title tune by E. Y. Harburg and Duke. For *The Winning Team* (1952), a stale interpretation of the life of baseball great Grover Cleveland Alexander, she played opposite Ronald Reagan, whom she had dated briefly in the early 1950s after he divorced Jane Wyman. By 1952, Day was earning $2,500 weekly at Warner Bros. and had surpassed Betty Grable as the United States' most popular female box-office attraction.

On April 3, 1951 (her twenty-seventh birthday), at Burbank City Hall, Doris wed her new agent, Marty Melcher. He had been married previously to Patty Andrews of the Andrews Sisters. He now took complete control of her career, as well as adopting Doris's son Terry in 1952. The best of her Warner Bros. films was the rollicking *Calamity Jane* (1953), the studio's answer to MGM's *Annie Get Your Gun* (1950). In fact, that picture's costar, Howard Keel, was borrowed from Metro to play Wild Bill Hickok to Doris's boisterous tomboy. The New York Times argued, "As for Miss Day's performance, it is tempestuous to the point of becoming just a bit frightening. . . ." However, if her emoting was overblown, her singing was on mark. She was raucous in performing "The Deadwood Stage" and was magical in stylizing "Secret Love." The latter received an Academy Award as the year's Best Song, but the movie was not the box-office bonanza anticipated. By now Day had become one of the top recording artists for Columbia Records.

Lucky Me (1954) was Doris's first wide-screen musical, a comedy set in Miami and teaming her with Bob Cummings (replacing Gordon MacRae), Nancy Walker, and Phil Silvers. She was zippy in this outing, but turned teary as the brave sister in *Young at Heart* (1954) who copes with a brash songwriter loser (Frank Sinatra). He did most of the crooning in that tearjerker, but she provided a lively rendition of "Ready, Willing and Able."

Doris had made seventeen pictures in a row for Warner Bros. when she and the studio parted company. (She had signed a new pact with the lot in 1954 before *Lucky Me*, but they could not agree on future projects, and she was displeased that Warner Bros. was using rival vocalist Peggy Lee in feature films.) Day went to MGM for $150,000, plus a percentage of the net profits, to take over the role once planned for Ava Gardner in *Love Me or Leave Me* (1955). This twisted version of the Ruth Etting story reteamed Day with James Cagney, who stole her thunder as the possessive, gimpy-legged gangster. She tried to be brassy, but there was still an air of innocence clinging to her; fortunately her song renditions of 1920s favorites were stylish. The Columbia soundtrack album rose to number one on the charts, where it stayed for seventeen weeks. (Her single "I'll Never Stop Loving You," also from the film, rose to number thirteen on the charts in the summer of 1955.) MGM signed her to a long-term pact. There was talk of she and Howard Keel joining together again for Metro's *The Opposite Sex* (1956), but instead her next feature was for esteemed director Alfred Hitchcock at Paramount. She was cast as James Stewart's distraught mate in the suspense yarn *The Man Who Knew Too Much* (1956), and her singing of "Que Sera, Sera (Whatever Will Be, Will Be)" rose to number two on the charts in the summer of 1956. She had thought the song—used to dramatic effect as a plot device in the film—"would never get out of the nursery."

Julie (1956), back at MGM, tested Doris's emotional mettle as a stewardess who must be "talked down" when she takes over piloting a disabled aircraft. She returned to Warner Bros. at a $250,000 salary to star in *Pajama Game* (1957), reprising the Broadway role done so memorably by another ex–Warner Bros. singing star, Janis Paige. Day was zesty as the determined union worker. Thereafter, she jumped around from studio to studio, focusing, however, now on comedy.

(Musicals were out, but she worked a bouncy title tune into each of her new pictures.) She turned down *An Affair to Remember* (1957; Deborah Kerr replaced her in the film that proved to be a big hit), but she was Clark Gable's young nemesis in *Teacher's Pet* (1958). Next she struggled with Gene Kelly's direction and a miscast Richard Widmark as her spouse in the suburban sex farce, *The Tunnel of Love* (1958). At Columbia she matched comic double takes with Jack Lemmon and Ernie Kovacs in *It Happened to Jane* (1959), which, like *The Tunnel of Love*, was not well received.

At this juncture of what seemed to be a sagging career, glamor producer Ross Hunter was inspired to team Doris with Rock Hudson in *Pillow Talk* (1959) at Universal. The *New York Times* termed it "One of the most lively and up-to-date comedy-romances of the year. . . ." The screenplay won an Oscar, the film did great business, and the project brought both Day and Hudson (back) to the top as box-office favorites. They starred in two additional sex farces, *Lover Come Back* (1961) and the far-less-successful *Send Me No Flowers* (1964). Meanwhile, Doris's last charted single, "Everybody Loves a Lover," rose to number six in the summer of 1958, and she had two more popular Columbia LP albums: *Day By Day* (1957) and *Listen to Day* (1960). (In the mid 1950s she had signed a new $1 million recording contract with the Columbia label.)

Day claimed that the demands of the stylish murder mystery *Midnight Lace* (1960) opposite Rex Harrison drained her; thereafter, she chose to do only comedies or musicals. She had wanted the lead in the film version of *South Pacific* (1958), but it was the less-expensive Mitzi Gaynor who garnered the plum assignment. *Billy Rose's Jumbo* (1962) was a leaden musical with Stephen Boyd, Jimmy Durante, and Martha Raye. Its financial failure cost Day the starring roles in *The Unsinkable Molly Brown* (1964) and *The Sound of Music* (1965), parts she wanted badly. She traded double takes with David Niven in *Please Don't Eat the Daisies* (1960), and was both innocent and insouciant in *That Touch of Mink* (1962) opposite Cary Grant. She and James Garner responded so well to each other's barbs and cooing in *The Thrill of it All* (1963) that when Twentieth Century-Fox fired Marilyn Monroe (and also lost Dean Martin's services) during the making of a new movie, the studio hired Day and Garner to reteam in what had been planned as a Monroe vehicle, now titled *Move Over, Darling* (1963). It was Doris's last really successful feature film.

By now, the recurrent Doris Day formula was wearing thin—and she was past forty—as she teamed twice with beefy Rod Taylor in *Do Not Disturb* (1965) and *The Glass Bottom Boat* (1966), neither of which was much appreciated. She rejected the role of Mrs. Robinson (played by Anne Bancroft) in *The Graduate* (1967) because "it offended my sense of values. . . ." *The Ballad of Josie* (1968) was a program Western, and by the making of the weak comedy *With Six You Get Egg Roll* (1968), Doris had exhausted her screen welcome. The *New York Times* carped that Day's comic talents had "over the years, become hermetically sealed inside a lacquered personality, like a butterfly in a Mason jar."

In November 1962, Doris and Marty Melcher had tried a trial separation. Later, they came to an understanding by which they would live together in name only, largely to protect their several joint business holdings. On April 20, 1968, at age fifty-two, Melcher died. It would be many months before Doris learned the ramifications of his many business decisions made on her behalf. However, she discovered right away that she had been committed (without her knowledge) to star in a TV sitcom for CBS-TV. Both as therapy and to bolster her assets (Melcher and her attorney had wiped out her $20 million in savings, and Doris found that she owed $500,000 in back taxes), she began *The Doris Day Show* (CBS-TV). It debuted on September 24, 1968, and during its five-season run, the setting changed from the family ranch to urban San Francisco. Initially she had been cast as a widow with two sons, but by the fourth season she was, in the "Mary Tyler Moore" mold, a carefree magazine staff writer. Meanwhile, she had made her first special, *The Doris Mary Anne Kappelhoff Special* (CBS-TV, March 14, 1971), with Rock Hudson as her guest star; her second special, *Doris Day Today* (CBS-TV, February 19, 1975), featured Rich Little and Tim Conway.

In 1974, Day became spokesperson for Studio Girl Cosmetics, a division of Helen Curtis, and began working on her 1975 autobiography. Among the book's many revelations was the subject's blunt statement, "After 27 years in show business my public image is that of America's la-di-da happy-go-lucky virgin, carefree and brimming with happiness. An image, I can assure you, more make-believe than any film part I ever played." She explained why in 362 pages.

On April 14, 1976, she married Barry Comden, an Eastern restaurant host eleven years her junior. They separated in 1979 and were divorced in 1981. Upset by the dissolution of her fourth marriage, she built a house near Carmel that became her permanent home. With more open space, she nurtured her caring of animals. She had been president of Actors and Others for Animals, and in 1977 she had started the Doris Day Pet Foundation. (Day said, "I'm trying with all my heart to make this world a better place for the animals.") In 1985, she was encouraged to return to television with a talk show focusing on animals, *Doris Day's Best Friends*, which aired over the Christian Broadcasting (Cable) Network for a season. Her first guest was old friend Rock Hudson, and his gaunt appearance on the show brought into public knowledge that he was dying of AIDS. She owns the Cypress Inn Hotel on the Monterey Peninsula, and via her record-producer son Terry and his second wife (Jacqueline), she is a grandmother. She insists she has no further interest in recording songs.

In 1989, Day made one of her then-rare public appearances to accept the Cecil B. DeMille Award given by the Hollywood Foreign Press Association. This Golden Globe tribute was televised on January 28, 1989. A radiantly beautiful Day received a tremendous ovation as she stepped to the dais and said, "I've been in the country and I've got to come to town more often. It's been a wonderful life and I'm not finished yet. I want to do some more. I think the best is yet to come. I really do!" However, in subsequent years, every time a project was touted as a possible new vehicle for Day, it somehow never came to be.

On November 16, 1991, the songster was the subject of a PBS-TV documentary: *Doris Day: A Sentimental Journey*, in which the star reviewed her career with the help of clips, recordings, and commentary from her son Terry, and such others as Rosemary Clooney, Betty White, and Tony Randall. In the course of the program the still-bubbling, unpretentious star said of her huge success: "If I can do it, you can do it. Anybody can."

During the '90s Day had several ongoing battles with the supermarket tabloids, which depicted her in absurd situations (e.g., reduced to living as a bag lady), which sometimes led her to sue the publications. She also continued to devote her energy to her Pet Foundation. She occasionally agreed to an interview with a major publication; for the April 1995 issue of *Vanity Fair*, she answered their questionnaire. In answer to what her great regret was, she replied, "Most of my marriages." As to when she was the happiest in life, she responded, "My childhood summers in Trenton, Ohio, and starting work at Warner Bros." By now she considered her "work with and for the animals" to be her "greatest achievement." When asked if she were to die and return as a person or thing, what might it be: "A bird. I always thought it would be wonderful to fly, but not in an airplane." In spring 1996, Doris had a new album (*The Love Album*) in release, her first in twenty years. It was a compilation of songs she recorded in the 1960s, but during a period of personal crisis (the death of husband Marty Melcher) the tapes had been misplaced and only recently found. That October, Donna Getzinger starred in her self-written *Donna's Day*, a tribute to the movies and songs of Doris Day. It was performed at a small theater in North Hollywood, California. (In 1998, another vehicle, *Definitely Doris: The Music of Doris Day*, was showcased in a small Los Angeles–area theater.) Meanwhile, Barry Comden (Day's fourth husband) allowed the tabloids to publish excerpts from his unpublished memoirs, which had unpleasant things to say about his ex-wife. One biography that was published was Michael Freedland's *Doris Day: The Illustrated Biography* (2000). It traced her life up to the present, where she was living a fairly reclusive existence in Carmel, California, fixated on animal care and rights.

When the UCLA Film and Television Archive devoted a series to Doris Day films in January 2001, it led film critic Kenneth Turan (*Los Angeles Times*) to posture, "Has there ever been another actress so popular and so ignored, so revered and so mocked? Even now, more than 30 years after here last theatrical feature, 1968's *With Six You Get Egg Roll*, she is both the darling of her die-hard fans . . . and the plaything of academics in articles with daunting titles. . . ." Turan concluded, "Seeing Day's work en masse, however, inevitably serves to underline how much of an icon she was, how much she became, in her own way, the female equivalent of John Wayne or Clint Eastwood. Not always the subtlest or most convincing of actresses . . . she was always Doris Day, and to her fans both then and now, that was enough."

Filmography

Romance on the High Seas [It's Magic] (WB, 1948)
My Dream Is Yours (WB, 1949)
It's a Great Feeling (WB, 1949)
Young Man With a Horn [Young Man of Music] (WB, 1950)
Tea for Two (WB, 1950)
The West Point Story [Fine and Dandy] (WB, 1950)
Storm Warning (WB, 1950)
Lullaby of Broadway (WB, 1951)
Starlift (WB, 1951)
On Moonlight Bay (WB, 1951)
I'll See You in My Dreams (WB, 1951)
The Winning Team (WB, 1952)
Screen Snapshots #206 (Col, 1952) (s)
April in Paris (WB, 1952)
By the Light of the Silvery Moon (WB, 1953)
Calamity Jane (WB, 1953)
So You Want a Television Set (Vita, 1953) (s)
Lucky Me (WB, 1954)
Young at Heart (WB, 1954)

Love Me or Leave Me (MGM, 1955)
The Man Who Knew Too Much (Par, 1956)
Julie (MGM, 1956)
The Pajama Game (WB, 1957)
Teacher's Pet (Par, 1958)
The Tunnel of Love (MGM, 1958)
It Happened to Jane [Twinkle and Shine] (Col, 1959)
Pillow Talk (Univ, 1959)
Midnight Lace (Univ, 1960)
Please Don't Eat the Daisies (MGM, 1960)
Lover Come Back (Univ, 1961)
That Touch of Mink (Univ, 1962)
Billy Rose's Jumbo (MGM, 1962)
The Thrill of It All (Univ, 1963)
Move Over, Darling (20th-Fox, 1963)
Send Me No Flowers (Univ, 1964)
Do Not Disturb (20th-Fox, 1965)
The Glass Bottom Boat (MGM, 1966)
Caprice (20th-Fox, 1967)
The Ballad of Josie (Univ, 1968)
Where Were You When the Lights Went Out? (MGM, 1968)
With Six You Get Egg Roll (NG, 1968)

Radio Series

Moon River (WLW, 1943) (local)
Your Hit Parade (CBS, c. 1945) (local)
The Bob Sweeney–Hal March Show (CBS, 1946)

The Bob Hope Show (NBC, c. 1948–50)
The Doris Day Show (CBS, 1952–53)

TV Series

The Doris Day Show (CBS, 1968–73)

Doris Day's Best Friends (CBN, 1985–86)

Album Discography

LPs

Annie Get Your Gun (Col OL-5960-OS-2360, Har KH-30396)
The Best of Doris Day (Spot 8533)
Billy Rose's Jumbo (Col OL-5860/OS-2260) [ST]
Bright and Shiny (Col CL-1614/CS-8414)
By the Light of the Silvery Moon (10″ Col CL-6248, Caliban 6019) [ST]
By the Light of the Silvery Moon/Lullaby of Broadway (Col Special Product 18421) [ST]
Calamity Jane (10″ Col CL-6273)
Call Me Mister/Starlift (Titania 510)
Christmas Album (Col CS-9026, Har H-30016)
Cuttin' Capers (Col CL-1232/CS-8078)
Day by Day (Col CL-942)
Day by Night (Col CL-1053/CS-8089)
Day Dreams (10″ Col CL-6071, Col CL-624)
Diamond Horseshoe (Caliban 6028) [ST/R]
Doris Day (Lots LOP 14132)
Doris Day 1940-41 (Joyce 6004)
Doris Day 1944-45 (Joyce 6005)
Doris Day Sings Do Re Mi, Que Sera Sera and Other Children's Favourites (Hallmark HM 534)
Doris Day, Vols. 1-2 (Hindsight 200, 226)
Doris Day With Les Brown and Harry James (Joyce 6013)
Duets (Col CL-1752, DRG 601) w. Andre Previn
Duets Plus (Collectables COL-CD-6860) w. Andre Previn
Great Movie Hits (Har HL-7392/HS-11192)
Greatest Hits (Col CL-1210)
Heart Full of Love (Memoir MOIR 511)
Hooray for Hollywood (Col C2L-5/CS-8006-7, Columbia Special Products 5)
I Have Dreamed (Col CL-1660/CS-8460)
I'll See You in My Dreams (10″ Col CL-6198) [ST]
I'll See You in My Dreams/Calamity Jane (Columbia Special Products 19611) [ST]
It's Magic (Har HS-11382)

Latin for Lovers (Col CL-2310/CS-9110)
Lights! Camera! Action! (10″ Col Cl-2518)
Listen to Day (Col DDS-1)
Love Him (Col CL-2131/CS-8931)
Love Me or Leave Me (Col CL-710/CS-H773) [ST]
Lucky Me (Athena LM1B-9) [ST]
Lullaby of Broadway (10″ Col CL-6168) [ST]
Lullaby of Broadway/I'll See You in My Dreams (Caliban 6008) [ST]
My Dream Is Yours/The West Point Story (Titania 501) [ST]
On Moonlight Bay (10″ Col CL-6186, Caliban 6006) [ST]
One Night Stand (Joyce 1020)
One Night Stand (Sandy Hook 2011)
One Night Stand With Les Brown 1940-45 (Sandy Hook 2078)
Pajama Game (Col OL-5210) [ST]
Pillow Talk (Universal International DCLA-1316) [ST]
Radio Soundtracks (Caliban 6047)
Romance on the High Seas/It's a Great Feeling (Caliban 6015) [ST]
Sentimental Journey (Cameo 32257)
Sentimental Journey (Col CL-2360/CS-9160)
Sentimental Journey (Encore P-14361) w. Les Brown
Show Time (Col CL-1470/CS-8261)
Softly As I Leave You (Har H-31498)
Stars of Hollywood (Avenue International AV INT 1011) w. Frank Sinatra
Tea for Two (10″ Col CL-6149, Caliban 6031) [ST]
Tea for Two/On Moonlight Bay (Columbia Special Products 17660) [ST]
Through the Eyes of Love (Memoir 123)
The Uncollected Doris Day Vol. 2: 1952-53 (Hindsight HSR-226) w. Page Cavanaugh Trio
The Uncollected Les Brown & His Orchestra 1944-46 (Hindsight HSR-103)

Victor Herbert—Beyond the Blue Horizon (Caliban 6033) [ST]

What Every Girl Should Know (Col CL-1438/CS-8234)

What Will Be, Will Be (Har HS-11282)

With a Smile and a Song (Col CL-2266/CS-9066)

Wonderful Day (Columbia Special Products 82021)

You'll Never Walk Alone (Col CL-1904/CS-8704)

Young at Heart (10″ Col CL-6106, Col CL-582, Columbia Special Products 582) [ST]

Young At Heart/April in Paris (Titania 500)

You're My Thrill (10″ Col CL-6071)

CDs

Annie Get Your Gun (Honda Music International 119) w. Robert Goulet

Beautiful Ballads (Sony Music Special Products 051523)

The Best of Doris Day (Col 4837222)

The Best of Doris Day (Music CD6056)

Best of the Big Bands (Col CK-46224) w. Les Brown

Billy Rose's Jumbo (Collectables COL-CD-6801) [ST]

Blue Skies (Hallmark 306472)

Blue Skies: The Best of Doris Day (Castle Communications MATCD-315)

Calamity Jane/I'll See You in My Dreams (Columbia Music Special Products M/P-19611) [ST]

Calamity Jane/Pajama Game (Col 467610, Sony Music Special Products 5018712) [ST]

Cocktail Hour (Col River Entertainment Group CRG-218003)

The Complete Doris Day With Les Brown (Collectors' Choice Music CCM-029)

Cuttin' Capers (Col 477593)

Cuttin' Capers (Sony Music Special Products 4775392)

A Day at the Movies (Col CK-44371)

Day by Day (Past Perfect 4330)

Day by Day/Day by Night (Col 475749, Collectables CD-COL-6489)

Daydreaming: The Very Best of Doris Day (Col 487361)

Doris Day (Golden Sound 982)

Doris Day (Javelin 315)

Doris Day: The Complete Standard Transcriptions (Soundies SCD 4109):

Doris Day Sings Broadway Hits (Blue Moon BMC-7012)

Doris Day Sings 22 Great Songs on Original Big Band Recordings (Hindsight HSR-226) w. the Page Cavanaugh Trio

Doris Day, Vol. 2 (Hindsight HSR-411)

Doris Day With Les Brown and His Orchestra (Sandy Hook CDSH-2078)

Duets (Sony 498582, Sony Music Special Products CK-8552) w. Andre Previn

The Early Days (ASV CD-AJA-5328)

The Essence of Doris Day (Legacy CK-53575)

Essential Love Songs (Col 4897162, MSI 797837)

Favorites (Planet Media PLM-1013)

The Formative Years (Avid 688)

The Girl Next Door (The Entertainers 223)

Golden Girl: The Col Recordings 1944-66 (Legacy CK-65505)

Golden Hits (Masters MCAD-61077-2)

Great Vocalist Series (Ronco Silver 9003)

Greatest Hits (Col CK-08635)

Greatest Hits (ITC Masters 1077)

Her Hollywood Hits (Blue Moon BM-7013)

Hit Singles From the Early Years (Memoir Classics 540)

Hooray for Hollywood (Globetrotter 487189)

Hooray for Hollywood, Vol. 1 (Col CK-08066)

Hooray for Hollywood, Vol. 2 (Col CK-08067)

I Have Dreamed/Listen to Day (Sony 4840312, MSI 128196)

I'll Never Stop Loving You (BUDMU CBU-67611)

I'll See You in My Dreams/Calamity Jane (Collectables COL-CD-6689) [ST]

It's Magic: Doris Day's Early Years (Turner Classic Movies/Rhino R2-15609)

It's Magic: Greatest Hits 1945-50 (Double Gold 53085)

It's Magic: The Early Years at Warner Bros. (Bear Family BCD-15609)

Latin for Lovers/Love Him (Sony 4810182)

Live It Up! (Sony Music Special Products A 26099)

Love Album (Musicrama 755152, WEA 4509999072)

Love & Magic (Recall 296)

Love Me or Leave Me (Collectables COL-CD-6490) [ST]

Love Songs (Pulse PLS-CD-370)

The Magic of Doris Day (Sony Music Special Products CK-13412)

Magic of the Movies (Sony TV79MD)

Merry Christmas From Doris Day & Dinah Shore (Laserlight 15-465)

Move Over Darling (Bear Family BCD-15800)

On Moonlight Bay/By the Light of the Silvery Moon (Collectables COL-CD-6667) [ST]

One Night Stand (Sandy Hook CDSH-2011) w. Les Brown

The Pajama Game (Collectables COL-CD-6699) [ST]

Personal Christmas Collection (Legacy CK-64153)

Pillow Talk (Bear Family BCD-15913) [ST]

Que Sera Sera (Bear Family BCD-15797)

Que Sera Sera (Pegasus PEG452)

'S Wonderful (Hindsight HSR-226)
Secret Love (Bear Family BCD-15746)
Sentimental Journey (ASV CD-AJA-5266) w. Les Brown
Sentimental Journey (Golden Sounds 24775)
Sentimental Journey (Hindsight HSR-200)
Sentimental Journey (Newsound NST-202)
Sentimental Journey (PIC 247752)
Sentimental Journey/What Every Girl Should Know (Col 493050, Globetrotter 493050)
Showtime/Day in Hollywood (Col 475750)
16 Most Requested Songs (Legacy CK-48987)
16 Most Requested Songs—Encore! (Legacy CK-64990)
16 Very Special Songs (Prism PLATCD-178)
Soundtracks (The Entertainers 342)
Tea for Two/Lullaby of Broadway (Collectables COL-CD-6690) [ST]
Through the Eyes of Love (Memoir MRMCD-123)
TV Specials (Decade DCD-101) (ST/TV)
What Every Girl Should Know/I Have Dreamed (Collectables COL-CD-6868)
With Love (Temple TMPCD032)
Young Man With a Horn (Legacy CK-65508) [ST] w. Harry James

Eddie Dean

(b. Edgar Dean Glosup, Posey, Texas, July 9, 1907; d. Thousand Oaks, California, March 4, 1999)

Along with Fred Scott and George Houston, Eddie Dean is considered one of the finest singers to have ever appeared in musical Westerns. In fact, he was one of the best vocalists to ever sing on-screen although movies were only one aspect of his multifaceted entertainment career, which included radio, recordings, and television, in addition to nearly seven decades of concerts and various types of personal appearances. Dean made over fifty feature films, most of them Westerns, and he starred in a series of sagebrush yarns for Producers Releasing Corporation (PRC) and Eagle Lion in the mid-to-late 1940s. Still it is as an overall entertainer and top-notch baritone that he is best remembered.

Born Edgar Dean Glosup in Posey, Texas, on July 9, 1907, Eddie was the seventh son of a seventh son, which caused his mother to predict that her son would find great success. He grew up on a farm and learned to sing harmony with his family. After graduating from high school, he went to Chicago in 1926 and there began calling himself Eddie Dean. The next year he sang on radio station KMA in Shenandoah, Iowa, and, two years later, he and his older brother, Jim Clifton Glosup, worked as a singing duo on WNAX in Yanton, South Dakota, and then on radio station WHBW in Topeka, Kansas. In 1931 Eddie married Lorene "Dearest" Donnelly. (They would have two children: Donna Lee and Edgar.) Two years later, he and Jim were featured on an early-morning radio show on WLS in Chicago, and then the duo became regulars on the *National Barn Dance* on the same station. In 1934, they began recording for the American Record Company (ARC), which released their records on a variety of dime-store labels like Melotone, Conqueror, and Oriole. Some of the songs they waxed were duets, others had Dean singing solo. While in Chicago, Eddie was also featured on the dramatic daytime radio serial *Modern Cinderella* on CBS.

In 1938, the Dean brothers moved to California, where Eddie made his film debut in a bit part in Gene Autry's *Western Jamboree*. For the next six years, Eddie did small parts in over two dozen cowboy movies. (These included several Hopalong Cassidy features.) In addition, he was in the Republic serial *The Lone Ranger Rides Again* (1939). Dean worked at a variety of studios with such stars as Tito Guizar, Tex Ritter, Johnny Mack Brown, and Don "Red" Barry, in addition to appearing in entries of such cowboy series as the Three Mesquiteers, the Range Busters, and Frontier Marshals.

By 1939, Eddie was recording with Decca Records, again doing solos as well as duets with his brother Jim. From 1942 to 1943, Eddie and Jim, along with Dick Rinehart, formed the Gene Autry Trio, which appeared on Autry's CBS radio program *Melody Ranch*. Rinehart had been a member of the Jimmy Wakely Trio, and Jim Dean would later join the singing group Foy Willing and the Riders of the Purple Sage. From 1943 to 1944, Eddie was the lead singer on Judy Canova's popular CBS network radio series *Rancho Canova*.

Eddie Dean, Helen Mowery, and Roscoe Ates in *Range Beyond the Blue* (1947).
[Courtesy of JC Archives]

Dean's big show-business break came in 1944, when he was signed to costar with Ken Maynard and Max Terhune in a series of musical Westerns for producer Walt Mattox. Although only one entry, *Harmony Trail* (1944), was made, it nicely showcased Eddie as a genre hero. He fit well into its medicine-show setting, which included his on-screen romancing with future star Ruth Roman. He also sang a trio of his own tunes: the title song, "Boogie Woogie Cowboy," and "On the Banks of the Sunny San Juan" (which he cowrote with Western heavy Glenn Strange; it had first been heard in *Lawless Valley* [1935] as sung by John Wayne, with Strange doing the actual singing). Robert Emmett Tansey directed *Harmony Trail*, which was reissued by Astor in 1947 as *The White Stallion*. Tansey next helmed Eddie in *Wildfire* (1945), a production starring Bob Steele, in which Dean played a singing sheriff.

Convinced that color would enhance the appeal of their "B" Westerns, PRC launched a series of such oaters starring Eddie, beginning with 1945's *Song of Old Wyoming*. While Dean patterned his screen hero after William S. Hart, he was too lanky in appearance to fulfill the needed physical requirements of a cowboy, although his acting was passable and his singing superb. The poverty-row PRC followed with four more Cinecolor (process) actioners with Dean in 1946, and that year (as well as in 1947) he placed tenth in the *Motion Picture Herald* poll of moneymaking Western film stars.

In addition to his PRC series, Eddie composed many of the songs he sang in the features, including "Wild Prairie Rose," "Lonesome Cowboy," and "Song of the Range." In 1946, Dean recorded for Majestic Records, and he had several best-sellers, including "No Vacancy," "Rainbow at Midnight," "Spring Has Come to Old Missouri," and "On the Banks of the Sunny San Juan." During this period, he made scores of radio recordings for Standard Transcriptions. Also for PRC, Dean was featured as a singer in the comedy, *Down Missouri Way* (1946), about a Hollywood film director (John Carradine) making a movie about a talking mule.

Altogether Eddie Dean starred in nineteen Westerns for PRC (which became Eagle Lion Pictures in 1947). Six of these were in Cinecolor, the last being the excellent *Wild West* (1946), which was reissued as *Prairie Outlaws* in 1948 in black and white with additional footage. Robert Emmett Tansey and Ray Taylor took turns directing Dean's features with Emmett Lynn offered as the comedy sidekick in the first three outings, followed by Roscoe Ates for the rest of the series. In the course of the features, the star utilized four different horses: War Paint, White Cloud, Copper, and Flash. Dean's Western series came to an end in 1948 with *The Tioga Kid*, since Eagle Lion wanted to concentrate on its nonmusical Westerns starring Lash LaRue. The latter had launched his own career in Dean's *Song of Old Wyoming* (1945), *Caravan Trail* (1946), and *Wild West* (1946).

With the demise of his Western movie series, Eddie concentrated on personal appearances, and was an especially big draw in southern California. In 1949 he had a hit record with his self-penned (written with his wife Dearest and Hal Blair) "One Has My Name" on the Crystal label. The next year Jimmy Wakely had a best-seller with this item on Decca, and in 1969 Jerry Lee Lewis had a number-one record with it on the Smash label. Over the years, it has been recorded by dozens of singers and is considered a standard in country music. In 1950, Eddie starred in the ABC-TV Western series *The Marshal of Gunsight Pass*, which reunited him with sidekick Roscoe Ates. It was staged live in Los Angeles and marketed to the rest of the country by kinescope. Eddie was back on-screen in 1952 singing in *Varieties on Parade*, and during the early and mid-'50s he recorded for a variety of labels, including Bel-Tone, Mercury, Coral, and Capitol. In 1955, Dean signed with Sage and Sand Records and remained with the label well into the late 1960s. That year he was back on the charts with "I Dreamed of a Hillbilly Heaven," which he cowrote with Hal Southern; in 1961 Tex Ritter had a major hit with it on the Capitol label.

Throughout the 1950s and 1960s, Eddie was active with personal appearances, and he guested on numerous radio and television programs. In 1962, he appeared in the Western short *Night Rider* with Johnny Cash, Merle Travis, Johnny Western, Gordon Terry, and Dick Jones. Also in 1962 Dean was featured on two segments of the CBS-TV program *The Beverly Hillbillies* as a singing policeman.

In the early 1970s, Eddie Dean began appearing at various Western movie conventions, as well as being a stable at North Hollywood's Palomino Club. He recorded for such labels as Western Film Collector, Shasta, Mosrite, and Nu-Sound, proving his powerful baritone voice had not eroded with time. In addition to entertaining (he could do apt impersonations of Elvis Presley, Jerry Lee Lewis, Tex Ritter, and Buck Owens), he was also an accomplished painter, carver, and golfer. In 1977, he sang the title song in *Meanwhile Back at the Ranch*, and, in 1978 he received the Pioneer Award from the Academy of Country Music. He was also inducted into the Western Music Association's Hall of Fame.

In 1990, Dean did well with the single, "A Cold Texas Beer," for the Bradley Brothers label, and he continued to do concerts and appear at Western movie conventions well into the decade. His final record session was with the Sons of the West in 1996. The cowboy star died March 4, 1999 of lung and heart disease in Thousand Oaks, California. He was survived by his wife of sixty-eight years, a son and daughter, a sister, eight grandchildren, nine great-grandchildren, and one great-great-grandchild. In March 1999, Eddie Dean posthumously received a star on the Palm Springs, California, Walk of Fame.

Filmography

Lawless Range (Monogram, 1935) (song only)
Western Jamboree (Rep, 1938)
The Renegade Trail (Par, 1939)
Range War (Par, 1939)
Law of the Pampas (Par, 1939)
The Lone Ranger Rides Again (Rep, 1939) (serial)
The Llano Kid (Par, 1939)
Santa Fe Marshal (Par, 1940)
Showdown (Par, 1940)
Hidden Gold (Par, 1940)
Stagecoach War (Par, 1940)
Light of the Western Stars (Par, 1940)
The Golden Trail (Monogram, 1940)
Ridin' Home to Texas (Monogram, 1940)
Knights of the Range (Par, 1940)
Oklahoma Renegades (Rep, 1940)
Trail of the Silver Spurs (Monogram, 1941)
Pals of the Pecos (Rep, 1941)
Kansas Cyclone (Rep, 1941)
Gauchos of El Dorado (Rep, 1941)
Fighting Bill Fargo (Universal, 1941)
West of Cimarron (Rep, 1941)
Down Mexico Way (Rep, 1941)
Sierra Sue (Rep, 1941)
The Lone Rider and the Bandit (PRC, 1942)
Raiders of the West (PRC, 1942)
Rollin' Down the Great Divide (PRC, 1942)
Stagecoach Express (Rep, 1942)
Arizona Stagecoach (Monogram, 1942)

King of the Cowboys (Rep, 1942)
Harmony Trail [The White Stallion] (Walt Mattox, 1944)
Wildfire (Screen Guild/Action Pictures, 1945)
Song of Old Wyoming (PRC, 1945)
Out California Way (Rep, 1946) (song only)
Romance of the West (PRC, 1946)
The Caravan Trail (PRC, 1946)
Colorado Serenade (PRC, 1946)
Driftin' River (PRC, 1946)
Tumbleweed Trail (PRC, 1946)
Stars Over Texas (PRC, 1946)
Wild West (PRC, 1946)
Down Missouri Way (PRC, 1946)
Wild Country (PRC, 1947)
Range Beyond the Blue (PRC, 1947)
West to Glory (PRC, 1947)
Shadow Valley (Eagle Lion, 1947)
Black Hills (Eagle Lion, 1947)
My Pal Ringeye (Col, 1947) (s)
Check Your Guns (Eagle Lion, 1948)
Tornado Range (Eagle Lion, 1948)
The Westward Trail (Eagle Lion, 1948)
The Hawk of Powder River (Eagle Lion, 1948)
Prairie Outlaws (Eagle Lion, 1948)
The Tioga Kid (Eagle Lion, 1948)
Varieties on Parade (Lippert, 1952)
Night Rider (Parallel, 1962) (s)
Meanwhile Back at the Ranch (Rancho Films, 1977)

Radio Series

WLS Barn Dance (NBC, 1934–37)
Modern Cinderella (NBC, 1936–37)

Melody Ranch (CBS, 1942–43)
Rancho Canova (CBS, 1943–44)

TV Series

The Marshal of Gunsight Pass (ABC-TV, 1950)

Album Discography

LPs

A Cowboy Sings Country (Shasta SH-537)

Dean of the West (Western Film Collector 61576)

Eddie Dean (Passaro 3326)

Eddie Dean (Showcase SSH-103-4)

Eddie Dean—In Person (Tiara TST-563) w. Cort Johnson

Eddie Dean Sings (Crown CLP-5434/CST-434)

Eddie Dean Sings Country and Western (Crown CST-583)

The Golden Cowboy (Crown CST-320)

Greatest Westerns (Sound 604, Sage & Sand C-1)

Hi Country (Sage & Sand C-5)

Hillbilly Heaven (Crown CLP-5258)

Hillbilly Heaven (Sage & Sand C-16)

I Dreamed of a Hillbilly Heaven (Castle LP-8106) (West Germany)

I Dreamed of a Hillbilly Heaven (Sutton SU-333)

Little Green Apples (Crown CST-578)

Musical Heritage of the Golden West (Cricket 33)

Release Me (Crown CST-581)

Riders of the Purple Sage: Foy Willing & Eddie Dean (10″ Royale 6987)

Saddle Up! (Tiara TMT-7562) w. Cort Johnson

Sincerely, Eddie Dean (Shasta SH-513)

A Tribute to Hank Williams (Design DLP-89/DCF-1026)

CDs

A Cowboy Sings Country (KRB Music Companies KRB-5149-2)

Eddie Dean (Branson Gold BGR-6353-2)

Eddie Dean (Simitar 55692)

1501 Miles From Heaven (Columbia River Entertainment Group 211004)

The Golden Age of Eddie Dean (Cattle CCD-233)

The Late and Great Eddie Dean (Cattle CCD-214)

On the Banks of the Sunny San Juan (Soundies SCD-4116)

The Very Best of Eddie Dean (Varese Vintage 302-066-136-2)

Marlene Dietrich in a 1930s publicity pose.
[Courtesy of JC Archives]

Marlene Dietrich

(b. Maria Magdalena Dietrich, Berlin, Germany, December 27, 1901; d. Paris, France, May 6, 1992)

One of the screen's greatest sex symbols, sophisticated and sensual Marlene Dietrich held sway in the world of entertainment for over half a century. In the process, she became an exotic living legend, the mere mention of either one of her names was sufficient for identification. She was a friend of the famous and an intellectual soul mate of some of the world's best minds. She retained her image of the inveterate femme fatale long after most of her contemporaries had chosen retirement. When her film career slackened, she continued to appear around the world as an elegant, alluring chanteuse in her one-woman showcase. It is as a singer, as well as an actress, that Marlene Dietrich established her screen siren presence, and through the years she projected this appeal successfully not only on film but also on radio, recordings, and stage. While in many ways she was limited in range as an actress and performer, Marlene coaxed the most out of her public persona thanks to her innate intelligence, Prussian fastidiousness, and the uncanny ability to retain her striking beauty well into her seventies.

Marlene Dietrich's early years are almost as much enshrouded in mystery as were the characters she later played on celluloid. She was born Maria Magdalena Dietrich on December 27, 1901, the daughter of Prussian policeman Louis Erich Otto Dietrich and Wilhelmina Elisabeth Josephine Felsing. After her father's death, while Maria was quite young, her mother remarried Edouard von Losch, an officer in the German army. At an early age, Maria took to the violin and planned a career in music, but this was cut short by a wrist injury. In 1921, she studied drama with the renowned Max Reinhardt in Berlin and had small roles in several of his Shakespearean productions. She remained with Reinhardt for two years and then began seeking work at the German movie studios. It was there she caught the eye of assistant director Rudolf Seiber, who got for her a small role in *Die Tragödie der Liebe* (1923) directed by Joe May, and starring Emil Jannings. Maria continued to have small roles in films, and in 1924 she and Seiber were married. It is intriguing to note that in 1925 she had a bit part in *Die Freudlose Gasse* directed by G. W. Pabst, which brought Greta Garbo to the attention of American filmmakers when it was issued here as *The Street of Sorrow* in 1927. In 1926 she was billed on-screen as "Marlene Dietrich" for the first time in *Eine DuBarry Von Heute* [A Modern DuBarry].

Dietrich left the entertainment field for a time in the mid-'20s after the birth of her daughter, Maria. She then returned to Max Reinhardt's company and won the lead in a stage production of *Broadway*, followed by *Es Liegt in der Luft* [Something in the Air]. In 1928, she was a chorus member of *Ensemble des Nelson-Revue* and in that capacity made her first records for the Electradisk label in Berlin. She also continued to play small roles in German movies, and in 1929 she appeared with Hans Albers in the stage production *Misalliance*, followed by the revue *Zwei Kravetten* [Two Neckties]. While appearing in this show, she came to the attention of American film director Josef von Sternberg, who had come to Berlin in 1929 at the behest of Emil Jannings to direct the German star's first sound film, *Der Blaue Engel* (1930). Marlene was one of many actresses he tested for the lead of Lola Lola, the manipulative cabaret singer, and she won the part although she did not believe she photographed well on film.

Still plumpish, Marlene Dietrich caused a sensation as the low-class cabaret trollop who seduces and marries a much older professor (Emil Jannings) and then casually casts him aside like her previous lovers. In the film, Marlene sang "Falling in Love Again" and "Lola," which she recorded in Berlin for HMV [His Master's Voice] Records. *Der Blaue Engel* was made in German, French, and English versions, and as soon as it premiered in her homeland, Marlene left with von Sternberg to come to Hollywood, where they both had been signed to make *Morocco* (1930) for Paramount. Before facing the American camera, she underwent a transformation that removed the hausfrau in her and accentuated her exotic beauty. Again, she was cast as a cabaret singer, this time with a tainted past. Her bisexual character, Amy Jolly, wore a tuxedo when she performed such numbers as "Give Me the Man" and the provocative "What Am I Bid for My Apples." In this stylistic romance, she rejects a jaded rich roué (Adolphe Menjou) for the love of a French legionnaire (Gary Cooper). At the finale, she joins with the other camp followers in plodding across the desert sands to follow her man. When the movie was released, Dietrich took Depression-weary America by storm. (She was Oscar-nominated, but lost the Best Actress Award to Marie Dressler of *Min and Bill*.) Soon the English-language version of *The Blue Angel* was also issued. The two movies established Dietrich's persona, that of an incredibly beautiful woman who is physically, but rarely mentally, attainable.

Anxious to rival MGM's foreign-bred star Greta Garbo, Paramount offered Dietrich $125,000 a picture plus artistic concessions on her productions. Marlene's now prescribed screen character was perpetuated by von Sternberg in the other five features he and Dietrich made for Paramount between 1931 and 1935. Their relationship took on the aura of a Svengali-Trilby pairing, which eventually would take its toll on both their careers. After *The Blue Angel* and *Morocco*, though, Dietrich was acknowledged to be the equal of two others of filmdom's swank sex symbols: Garbo and Constance Bennett.

Dietrich's screen popularity reached its peak in the spring of 1931 when *Dishonored* was released; in it she played a prostitute who becomes an Austrian spy in World War I and who sacrifices her life to save the Russian agent (Victor McLaglen) she loves. After it was made, Marlene returned to Berlin, and then reappeared in Hollywood with her husband and daughter, the revelation of their existence failing to make a dent in her enormous screen popularity. Dietrich and her husband would live mostly apart, he becoming a chicken farmer.

She next made *Shanghai Express* (1932) with von Sternberg, a stylishly photographed thriller in which she was cast as the notorious "China Coaster," another woman with a shady past. She is reunited with an old lover (Clive Brook) aboard the title train during a revolution. The result did little to help her box-office draw, which slipped even further with the overlong *Blonde Venus* (1932), where she portrayed a nightclub entertainer who sells herself to a playboy (Cary Grant) to obtain funds to help her ailing husband (Herbert Marshall) get well. The otherwise lachrymose film contains a wild "Hot Voodoo" production number in which Marlene appears onstage in a gorilla outfit. She broke off, temporarily, working with von Sternberg and made *The Song of Songs* (1933) with director Rouben Mamoulian. She gave a solid performance in an unbelievable plot about a poor young woman who finds brief happiness with an artist (Brian Aherne), misery with a cruel lecher (Lionel Atwill), and then lets herself go. The movie allowed her the occasion to sing "Johnny," a song associated with her since she first recorded it in Berlin in 1931. However, the most famous aspect of *The Song of Songs* was the nude life-size statue of Dietrich displayed in the film and as an advertising gimmick.

Marlene was reunited with von Sternberg for the stifling *The Scarlet Empress* (1934), in which she was the shy young girl who becomes the scheming Catherine the Great of Russia. The movie was lavish in period detail but vapid in plot. Her final production with von Sternberg was *The Devil Is a Woman* (1935), and in it she was strikingly photographed as a Spanish courtesan who romances both a younger man (Cesar Romero) and a wealthy older one (Lionel Atwill). Despite the stellar production trappings and a fine performance by Atwill as the love-smitten elder suitor, the film was sterile. The Spanish government requested the picture be withdrawn from distribution because of its "misrepresentations," and Paramount did so. It was the end of the teaming of Dietrich and von Sternberg, the latter claiming he had done as much as he could for her. Despite all its bad aspects, the picture remained a favorite with Dietrich "because I looked more lovely in that film than in any other of my whole career."

Dietrich's final Paramount contract film was *Desire* in 1936, for director Frank Borzage. She was quite good as a jewel thief who falls in love with a vacationing American (Gary Cooper) after hiding in his suit a valuable pearl necklace she has just stolen. For Paramount, she began working on *I Love a Soldier* with Charles Boyer, but after disputes with studio producer Ernst Lubitsch she left the production. Star-maker David O. Selznick thought he knew better how to showcase Marlene, and he paid her $200,000 to replace Merle Oberon in his Technicolor *The Garden of Allah* (1936) for United Artists, which cost over $2 million to produce. She was seen as a siren who seduces a Trappist monk (Charles Boyer). She earned a mammoth $375,000 for starring in the British-lensed *Knight Without Armour* (1937), which cost almost as much as the previous film. Alexander Korda produced this lavish melodrama of the Russian Revolution, with Marlene as a countess who is saved from the Bolsheviks' firing squad by her British spy lover (Robert Donat). The film was not popular at the box office.

Dietrich returned to Paramount for Ernest Lubitsch's *Angel* (1937), a confection about a titled woman (Marlene) leaving her spouse (Herbert Marshall) for a harmless fling with another man (Melvyn Douglas). It did nothing to bring back her former marquee glory. By the end of 1937, she had joined the group (which included Katharine Hepburn) labeled box-office poison. Because of this and her recurring conflicts with the Paramount filmmakers, plans for her to star in *French Without Tears* (1939) and *Midnight* (1939) did not materialize. Instead, Paramount paid her $200,000 to $250,000 *not* to make her final film for the studio.

If the public seemed tired of Dietrich, the studios were not. Both Columbia and Warner Bros. signed her for one-picture deals. She was to make the life of George Sands for the former, and do a remake of *One Way Passage* (1933) for the latter. Neither project happened with Dietrich, and she later substituted other pictures to fulfill her commitments. Meanwhile, the French cinema beckoned, and it was rumored she would star in *Dedee D, Anvers* with Jules Raimu. However, the intervention of World War II prevented her doing the vehicle.

What did bring Dietrich back as an American movie draw was *Destry Rides Again* (1939), which cast her as earthy Frenchy, a Western saloon singer who helps a gawky young man (James Stewart) tame a very corrupt frontier town. Her saloon fight with Una Merkel and her throaty singing of "The Boys in the Backroom" and "You've Got That Look" (recorded for Decca Records) were the highlights of this entertaining sagebrush tale. She had done this comeback vehicle for Universal at a very reduced rate, and now signed a contract with the studio. However, none of these subsequent films would match *Destry Rides Again*.

At Universal, she turned down *My Little Chickadee* (which Mae West did) and instead made *Seven Sinners* (1940), the first of a trio of films with John Wayne (with whom she had an off-screen affair). It cast her as a South Seas trollop bewitched by a Navy lieutenant (Wayne). She sang "I've Been in Love Before." Less enjoyable was the period piece *The Flame of New Orleans* (1941), directed by Frenchman Rene Clair in his America film debut, with Marlene as a French adventuress who ends up with a poor boatman (Bruce Cabot) instead of a rich banker (Roland Young). George Raft and Edward G. Robinson next costarred with Dietrich in *Manpower* (1941) for Warner Bros., a melodrama that did well by them as electric wire workers, but it wasted Marlene as a clip-joint hostess and the object of their heated affections. She was better served by the light comedy *The Lady Is Willing* (1942), for Columbia, which cast her as a singing star who wants to adopt a baby and seeks the aid of a pediatrician (Fred MacMurray). Back at Universal, Marlene made two rough-and-tumble melodramas with John Wayne and Randolph Scott, both movies benefiting the two male stars more than Dietrich. *The Spoilers* (1942) was the third remake of the famous 1914 classic with William Farnum (who was also in this version) and Tom Santschi, and Dietrich was cast as Alaskan saloon hostess Cherry Mallotte. *Pittsburgh* (1942) had Dietrich miscast as the girl coveted by coal-mining businessmen Scott and Wayne; the film did boast the beautiful "Garden in the Rain" as its theme number, but Marlene did not sing it.

Dietrich had become an American citizen in 1938, and when World War II broke out she was one of the most active of Hollywood entertainers in the war effort. She worked at the Hollywood Canteen, joined war-bond drives, undertook radio broadcasts in various languages for the government to send to Europe, made records (including her noteworthy "Lili Marlene") in German, which were dropped behind enemy lines, and tirelessly entertained servicemen with the USO. After the war, she received the U.S. Defense Department's Medal of Freedom for uplifting the spirits of Allied fighting men during World War II.

Marlene also worked on commercial radio. In the 1930s she had appeared on Rudy Vallee's *The Fleischmann Hour*. And in 1940 she and Fred MacMurray did a radio adaptation of *Desire* for CBS's *Gulf Screen Guild Theater*, and she and Clark Gable were heard on *Lux Radio Theater* in "Legionnaire and the Lady," an adaptation of *Morocco*. She also did radio editions of the movies *Grand Hotel* and *Pittsburgh*, the latter with John Wayne and Randolph Scott. Moreover, she guest-starred on such radio shows as Fred Allen's *Texaco Star Theater*, *The Jack Benny Program*, and *Hollywood Open House*. Having turned down the lead in Broadway's *One Touch of Venus* (1943; Mary Martin took the part), Marlene made a brief guest appearance in Universal's *Follow the Boys* (1944)—being sawed in half in a magic act performed by her off-screen friend Orson Welles—and then starred in MGM's lavish adaptation of *Kismet* (1944) as Jamilla. The highlight of the latter production was her scene where, painted in gold, she performed an exotic dance number.

After the war, Dietrich went to France, where she and her off-camera romance, Jean Gabin, were to star in *Les Portes de la Nuit*. She changed her mind and instead the two made *Martin Roumagnac* (1946), about a tart (Marlene) who is murdered by the man (Gabin) who loves her, after he learns about her many affairs. In the United States, a censored version was released as *The Room Upstairs*. Now well into her forties, Marlene found it harder to compete for starring roles in postwar Hollywood. At Paramount, she was a gypsy fortune-teller who helps a Britisher (Ray

Milland) escape from Nazi Germany in *Golden Earrings* (1947). Far more popular, and helpful for her career, was Billy Wilder's *A Foreign Affair* (1948). While Jean Arthur was the top-billed star, it was Dietrich who stole attention as the seductive German songstress with a Nazi past in postwar Berlin. She sang "Illusions" and "Black Market," both by her favorite and faithful composer, Friedrich Hollander.

In Alfred Hitchcock's *Stage Fright* (1950), lensed largely in London, Marlene was a self-centered singing star engulfed in murder. In it, she sang two of her most famous songs: "La Vie en Rose" and "The Laziest Gal in Town." Meanwhile, in 1949, Dietrich did a guest bit in *Jigsaw* (1949), and on radio she appeared in "The Lady From the Sea" on CBS's *The Philip Morris Playhouse*. By now Marlene's married daughter, Maria (who, as Maria Riva, would be a star of early television) had a child, and Dietrich was being promoted as "The World's Most Glamorous Grandmother."

In 1951, Marlene appeared at the Academy Awards presentation, and the same year performed "Anna Karenina" on radio's *MGM Theater of the Air*. That year she also costarred (again) with James Stewart in the British-made *No Highway in the Sky*, as an actress aboard a plane that may fall apart. Because she asked for "too much" ($150,000), the female lead in MGM's *The Man With the Cloak* (1951) went to Barbara Stanwyck. Instead she headlined the psychological Western *Rancho Notorious* (1952) for director Fritz Lang. She was the bawdy head of the outlaw hangout in this flat entry.

During 1952, Marlene guested on Bing Crosby's CBS radio show, and then starred in her own ABC series that year called *Café Istanbul*, a program about international intrigue. When it failed to catch on with listeners, ABC changed the format and title to *Time for Love*, and it ran into 1954. After that Marlene began her long-running one-woman show that she performed round the world for the next three decades, both in concerts and nightclubs. The outings were noteworthy for elegance, precision, and the star's fantastic devotion to meticulous detail, which always created the most glamorous mystique for her viewers. The patter between her songs continued the myths she had chosen to create and perpetuate, also a part of her grand illusion.

In 1956, Marlene played a cabaret singer in a cameo in *Around the World in 80 Days*, and in 1957 she starred with Vittorio De Sica in *The Monte Carlo Story* as a noble woman who cannot give up gambling but who finds love with a penniless count (De Sica) in the European gaming capital. She landed another plum film role in 1958 as the loyal wife in Billy Wilder's outstanding production of Agatha Christie's *Witness for the Prosecution*. In the same year she was a black-wigged fortune teller in Orson Welles's underrated *Touch of Evil*. She made a triumphant return to West Germany with her one-woman show in 1960, and the next year had her last good screen part, that of Mme. Berthholt, a Nazi general's widow, in the all-star *Judgment at Nuremberg*.

Throughout the 1950s and 1960s, Dietrich turned out a steady stream of single and long-playing records for such labels as Capitol, Columbia, Dot, Liberty, and Vox. Her recording of "Where Have All the Flowers Gone?" was especially noteworthy. She commanded high salaries for her one-woman act; i.e., in 1953, Las Vegas's Sahara Hotel paid her $30,000 a week for three weeks of work. In 1961, her book *Marlene Dietrich's ABC* was published, being in dictionary format with her comments on particular subjects. In 1967, she finally brought her act to Broadway for a successful engagement, followed by another the next year. In the 1960s, she also did two more films, as narrator of a documentary about Adolf Hitler called *The Black Fox* (1962) and a guest bit in *Paris When It Sizzles* (1964). She was persuaded to do her club show as a special for CBS-

TV in 1973. While it earned good reviews, it was too sophisticated to gain high ratings, thus negating any possible future major TV outings. She continued to tour with her stage act until sidelined by a leg injury in the mid-1970s. In 1979 she returned to films for the role of a heavily veiled madam in post–World War I Germany in *Just a Gigolo*, singing the title song, which she also recorded.

After that, Dietrich led a reclusive life in Paris, although she made it known she was available for voice-over work. In the early 1980s, the English-language version of her autobiography was rejected as not being spicy enough. (It had been published in 1979 in West Germany under the title *Nehmt Nur Mein Leben*.) She did grant offscreen interviews to actor Maximilian Schell, which he interpolated into his well-received film tribute to her, the 1984 documentary *Marlene*. It further enshrined her image as an enigmatic, disciplined soul who shrewdly manipulated her charisma into decades of international popularity.

Long out of the public eye, Marlene died on May 6, 1992, in her Paris apartment. Ten days later, she was buried in Berlin, next to her mother. The same year, her daughter, Maria Riva, wrote a controversial book about her domineering parent. Entitled *Marlene Dietrich: By Her Daughter*, the hefty tome depicted the star as cold and distant, as much caught up in her own mystique as her legion of fans. American Movie Classics cable network aired the documentary, *Marlene Dietrich: Shadow and Light*, in April 1996. In 2000, Katja Flint starred in *Marlene*, a musical biography feature film—a German-Italian coproduction—dealing with the near-mythical Dietrich. On December 27, 2001, cable TV's Turner Classic Movies debuted *Marlene Dietrich: Her Own Song*, a documentary on the dazzling icon, especially focusing on her participation as an entertainer for the Allied forces during World War II. It was directed by her grandson, David, and featured Marlene's actress daughter, Maria, in an interview. Also in this period came the coffee-table book, *Marlene Dietrich: Photographs and Memories* (2001), compiled by Jean-Jacques Naudet, with pungent captions by Maria Riva.

Perhaps it was Ernest Hemingway who summed up his longtime friend Dietrich best when he said: "If she had nothing more than her voice, she could break your heart with it. But she also has that beautiful body and the timeless loveliness of her face."

Filmography

Der Kleine Napoleon [So Sind die Männer/Napoleons Kleiner Bruder] (Ger, 1923)

Tragödie der Liebe [Tragedy of Love] (Ger, 1923)

So Sind die Manner [Der Kleine Napoleon] (Ger, 1923)

Der Mensch am Wege [Man by the Roadside] (Ger, 1923)

Der Sprung ins Leben [The Leap into Life] (Ger, 1923)

Die Freudlose Gasse [The Street(s) of Sorrow/Joyless Street] (Ger, 1925)

Eine DuBarry Von Heute [A Modern DuBarry] (Ger, 1926)

Manon Lescault (Ger, 1926)

Kopf Hoch Charly! [Heads Up, Charly!] (Ger, 1926)

Madame Wunscht Keine Kinder [Madame Wants No Children] (Ger, 1926)

Der Juxbaron [The Imaginary Baron] (Ger, 1927)

Sein Grösster Bluff [His Greatest Bluff] (Ger, 1927)

Café Electric [Wenn ein Weib den Weg Verliert/Die Liebersbörse] (Aus/Ger, 1927)

Prinzessin Olala [The Art of Love] (Ger, 1928)

Die Gluckliche Mutter (Ger, 1928) (s)

Ich Küsse Ihre Hand, Madame [I Kiss Your Hand, Madame] (Ger, 1929)

Die Frau, Nach der Man Sich Sehnt [Three Loves] (Ger, 1929)

Das Schff der verlorene Menschen [The Ship of Lost Men](Ger/Fr, 1929)

Gefahren der Brautzeit [Dangers of the Engagement Period] (Ger, 1929)

Der Blaue Engel [The Blue Angel] (Par, 1930)*
Morocco (Par, 1930)
Dishonored (Par, 1931)
Shanghai Express (Par, 1932)
Blonde Venus (Par, 1932)
Song of Songs (Par, 1933)
The Scarlet Empress (Par, 1934)
The Devil Is a Woman (Par, 1935)
Desire (Par, 1936)
The Garden of Allah (UA, 1936)
Knight Without Armour (UA, 1937)
Angel (Par, 1937)
Destry Rides Again (Univ, 1939)
Seven Sinners (Univ, 1940)
Manpower (WB, 1941)
The Flame of New Orleans (Univ, 1941)
The Lady Is Willing (Col, 1942)
The Spoilers (Univ, 1942)
Pittsburgh (Univ, 1942)
Screen Snapshots #103 (Col, 1943) (s)
Show Business at War (20th-Fox, 1943) (s)

Follow the Boys (Univ, 1944)
Kismet (MGM, 1944)
Martin Roumagnac [The Room Upstairs] (Fr, 1946)
Golden Earrings (Par, 1947)
A Foreign Affair (Par, 1948)
Jigsaw (UA, 1949)
Stage Fright (WB, 1950)
No Highway in the Sky [No Highway] (20th-Fox, 1951)
Rancho Notorious (RKO, 1952)
Around the World in 80 Days (UA, 1956)
The Monte Carlo Story (UA, 1957)
Witness for the Prosecution (UA, 1957)
Touch of Evil (Univ, 1958)
Judgment at Nuremberg (UA, 1961)
The Black Fox (MGM, 1962) (narrator)
Paris When It Sizzles (Par, 1964)
Just a Gigolo (UA, 1979)
Marlene (Zev Braun Pictures, 1984) (documentary)
*Also French- and English-language versions.

Radio Series

Café Istanbul (ABC, 1952)

Time for Love (CBS, 1953–54)

Album Discography

LPs

Ann Sheridan and Marlene Dietrich—Live (Amalgamated 249)
The Best of Marlene Dietrich (Col C-32245)
Bing's Beaus (Amalgamated 805) w. Tallulah Bankhead, Bing Crosby
The Blue Angel (Caliban 6046) [ST]
The Fabulous Marlene Dietrich (Hallmark 834)
Falling in Love Again (Regal 1078)
German Popular Songs (10″ Vox 3040)
Grand Hotel (Caliban 6040) [ST]
Her Complete Decca Recordings (MCA 1501)
The Legendary, Lovely Marlene (MCA 1685)
Lili Marlene (Col CL-1275, Columbia Special Products 1275)
Lili Marlene (MCA Coral 8002)
Magic Marlene (Cap TCL/DTCL-300)
The Magic of Marlene Dietrich (Music for Pleasure 5790)
Marlene (ASV 5039)

Marlene (Cap T/ST-10397)
Marlene (Stanyan SR-10124)
Marlene Dietrich (Decca DL-8465/DL 78465)
Marlene Dietrich and Clark Gable in "Morocco" (Amalgamated 257) [ST/R]
Marlene Dietrich at the Cafe de Paris (Col ML-4975)
The Marlene Dietrich Collection—20 Golden Greats (Dejavu 2098)
Marlene Dietrich in London (Col OL-6430/OS-2830)
Marlene Dietrich in Rio (Col WL-164/WS-316, Columbia Special Products 316)
Marlene Dietrich: Lili Marlene (Nostalgia 22005)
Marlene Dietrich Live (Malcon 5290)
Marlene Dietrich Overseas (10″ Col ML-2615)
Marlene Dietrich's Berlin (Cap T/ST-10443)
Schoner Gigolo—Armer Gigolo (Just a Gigolo) (Ariola 200-462-320)
Souvenir Album (10″ Decca DL-5100)
Wiedersehen mit Marlene (Cap T-10282)

CDs

All-Star Series: Marlene Dietrich—The Blue Angel (Patricia DL-23122)

Anthology (Chrisly CRB-1002)

The Blue Angel (ProArte CDD-517)

The Blue Angel/Morocco/Seven Sinners (Soundtrack Factory 33507) [ST]

Cocktail Hour (Columbia River Entertainment Group CRG-218015)

The Cosmopolitan Marlene Dietrich (Legacy CK-53209)

Das Lied Ist Aus (Remember 75052)

Das Musical (Die musikalischen hoehepanke) (Polydor 519-892-2)

Das War Mein Milljoeh (Col COL-471993-2)

Deja vu Moviestar collection (Suisa DVGH-701-2)

Der Mythos des "Blauen Engel" (Public Domain PD-1005-2)

Die Fruhen Aufnahmen (The Early Years) (Preiser 90032)

Die Grossen Erfolge (EMI 1563672, MCI 31288)

Die Grossen Erfolge (Electrola 1C588-156367-2)

Dietrich in Rio (CBS Special Products A-316)

Divas: The Gold Collection (Gold 4059) w. Rita Hayworth

The Essential Marlene Dietrich (Cap C21Y-96450, EMI 96450)

Etoiles de la Chanson (EMI 8401402)

An Evening With Marlene Dietrich (BMG PIESD-168)

Falling in Love Again (Beautiful Music DR)

Falling in Love Again (Goldies 25423)

Falling in Love Again (Hallmark 300332)

Falling in Love Again (Javelin HADCD-217)

Falling in Love Again (MCA MCAD-11849)

Falling in Love Again (Prism PLATCD-659)

Follow the Boys/To Have and Have Not/Star Dust/ Waterloo Bridge (Great Movie Themes 60032) [ST]

Forever Gold (St. Clair 5721)

For the Boys in the Backroom (Lafayette Music Group BSTCD-9109)

The Great Marlene Dietrich (BCD GLD-63105)

The Great Marlene Dietrich (Goldies 4598)

I Couldn't Be So Annoyed (Remember RMB-75053)

Idole: Marlene Dietrich (Polyphon 816-942-2)

Ihre Gorssen Erfoldge (ZYX ZYX-55180-2)

Immortal Songs (Galaxy Music O-NR-38881-12)

Ish Bin Von Kopf Bis Von Kauf Bis Fub (Chrisly R-81002)

La Legende (PMF 90754)

Lili Marlene (Arkadia 75104)

Lili Marlene (CBS Sony Group 28DP5348)

Lili Marlene (The Entertainers 256)

Lili Marlene (Live in London) (Castle Communications CNC-4016)

Lili Marlene (Palladium Productions RMB-75008)

Lili Marlene (Polygram 840-169-2)

Lili Marlene (St. Clair 3916)

Lili Marlene: Marlene Dietrich (Spectrum 5442932)

Marlene Dietrich (Bella Musica 5039)

Marlene Dietrich (Cine Stars CIN-302605)

Marlene Dietrich (Delta 24923)

Marlene Dietrich (Empire Disc 86603)

Marlene Dietrich (Gold Sound 929)

Marlene Dietrich (Koch CD-399-536)

Marlene Dietrich (Laserlight Digital 16-058)

Marlene Dietrich (Les Etemels 175-13025-2)

Marlene Dietrich Album (Sony MDK-47254)

Marlene Dietrich Album (Surp DCD-6529)

Marlene Dietrich at the Café de Paris (Col CK-47254)

Marlene Dietrich in London (DRG 13110)

Marlene Dietrich On-screen, Stage & Radio (Legend 6006/7)

Marlene Dietrich Sings Lili Marlene & Other Great Songs (Blue Moon 3051)

Marlene Dietrich 1928-1933 (ASV CD-AJA-5039)

Marlene: Her 18 Greatest Recordings (Music Collectors International)

More of the Best (Laserlight 12-652)

My Greatest Songs (MCA MCD-18-353)

Mythos Marlene Dietrich (EMI-Electrola CDP-538-1-59860-2)

Mythos und Legende (EMI-Electrola 7243-8-3420-26)

Platinum Series (D3 Entertainment 33338)

Portrait of Marlene Dietrich (Gallerie 445)

Sei Lieb Zu Mir (Remember 75056)

Some of the Best (Laserlight 12-651)

Universal Legends Collection (Universal 1122652)

The Dinning Sisters

(Ella Lucille "Lou" Dinning, b. Auburn, Kentucky, September 29, 1920, and twins
Virginia "Ginger" and Eugenia "Jean," b. Braman, Oklahoma, March 29, 1924)

The Dinning Sisters were one of the most popular female vocal groups of the 1940s thanks to their appearances on radio, Capitol recordings, and a series of motion pictures. In an era when female trio harmony was exceedingly popular and the field was crowded, this talented sister act managed to climb to the very top by beating out the long-popular Andrews Sisters in 1946 for not only a *Billboard* magazine award poll of jukebox operators but also the *Cashbox Magazine* Award. All three of the Dinning Sisters were very attractive, Lou a blonde and the twins dark-haired. The Dinning Sisters were more beautiful than either of their predecessors, the Boswell Sisters or the Andrews Sisters.

Success for the Dinning Sisters first came while they were still only teenagers. As they grew older, they married and eventually separated as an act. Their music appeal faded with the coming of rock 'n' roll in the mid-'50s. In the 1980s, however, thanks to the reissuance of their older recordings, a new generation began listening to and appreciating the melodious harmony of "The Sweethearts of Sunbonnet Swing."

The Dinning Sisters were the daughters of farmer John Dinning and his wife Bertha, who had a total of nine children: five girls and four boys. During the 1920s and 1930s, times were tough for farm folk, and the family moved on several occasions to farms in Kentucky, Kansas, and Oklahoma. The oldest of the singing trio, Ella Lucille "Lou" Dinning was born September 29, 1920, in Auburn, Kentucky, while her twin sisters, Virginia (called "Ginger") and Eugenia (nicknamed "Jean") were born March 29, 1924, in Braman, Oklahoma. Because their father was a church choir director and their mother sang in the choir, it was only natural for the girls to gain an appreciation of music. At an early age, they joined their mother in the church choir, and the trio also began singing together, first at home and then at social events and amateur shows. At the latter, they frequently won first prize, the money going to help feed the growing Dinning family.

By the time the girls were teenagers, they had their own noontime daily radio show over station KCRC in Enid, Oklahoma, where they were billed as "The McCormick/Deering Sisters," to accommodate their sponsors. Their fan mail was the most ever received by the station. Since their older sister, Marvis Dinning, was now a successful vocalist with Freddy Owen's orchestra, the three young ladies determined to try for the big time. Their older brother Wade drove them to Chicago in 1939, where they got a few singing jobs before having a successful audition at NBC Radio. The network executives were so impressed with the trio that they were signed to a five-year contract as NBC staff singers. They were assigned immediately to a variety of daily shows like *Don McNeil's Breakfast Club*, *Garry Moore's Club Matinee*, *The Roy Shields' Review*, and the Saturday-night favorite, *The National Barn Dance*, which already had spawned stars like Gene Autry, Patsy Montana, Max Terhune, George Gobel, the Cass County Boys, Lulu Belle and Scotty, the Hoosier

The Dinning Sisters in 1945: top: Ginger and Jean, bottom: Lou.
[Courtesy of Michael R. Pitts]

Hot Shots, and many more. Because the young performers were so outstanding, NBC also gave them their own daytime *The Dinning Sisters Show*, on which they were billed as "The Loreleis of the Airwaves." Thanks to this volume of air exposure, the trio gained national popularity quickly, and as a consequence, in 1942 they made their recording debut waxing a series of discs for Standard Transcriptions.

While working in Chicago, the Dinning Sisters met NBC staff musician Jack Fascinato, who became their pianist and arranger. They credit him with polishing their music and harmony work and helping them develop the smooth sound that was to make them the nation's favorite girl trio. They also had successful stands at the Chicago Theater and several Windy City nightspots.

In 1942, they filmed two shorts for the Soundies Corporation of America (they would do eight more for the company in 1945 and 1946). Also that year they made their feature film debut at Universal, which had a profitable policy of churning out budget musicals during the war years spotlighting the likes of the Andrews Sisters, Donald O'Connor, Peggy Ryan, Gloria Jean, and Robert Paige. The fifty-eight-minute *Strictly in the Groove* was double-bill fodder peopled with Ozzie Nelson and his Band, Mary Healy, Martha Tilton, the Jimmy Wakely Trio, Leon Errol, and Shemp Howard. At the dude-ranch setting, the Dinning Sisters sang three of the sixteen songs: "A Pretty Girl Milking Her Cow," "Be Honest With Me," and "Elmer's Tune." *Variety* noted that the trio "with similar style and delivery to the Andrews Sisters are a bright spot in their brief appearance." It was two years before they would return to feature filmmaking.

In 1944, the sisters came to Hollywood with the cast of their Saturday-night radio show to lens the low budget *The National Barn Dance* for Paramount; they portrayed themselves and also sang "Angels Never Leave Heaven," "Swing Little Indian," and "The Barn Dance Polka." Their contract with NBC ended in 1945, at which time they were signed by Johnny Mercer to record on Capitol Records. They were the premier vocal group to be contracted by the label, and they became the first performers to ever make their commercial record debut with an entire 78-rpm album. The album was an immediate success and was on the charts for eighteen weeks. As a result, the Dinnings were given the Award for Achievement by *Orchestra World* magazine and *Song Hits* magazine's Award of Merit as "The Outstanding Vocal Trio of 1945."

The late 1940s was the busiest and most fruitful period in the Dinning Sisters' career, as they guested on such top radio programs as *The Kate Smith Hour, The Kraft Music Hall,* and *The Grand Ole Opry*. They were in constant demand for personal appearances. In 1946, they appeared in the Universal Pictures short film *Takin' the Breaks* with Russ Morgan and His Orchestra, singing "Mary Lee" and "Pin Marin." That year also saw them as the featured headliners of two minor Columbia musical features: *Throw a Saddle on a Star* and *That Texas Jamboree*, both with Ken Curtis, Jeff Donnell, and Guinn "Big Boy" Williams. Ray Nazarro directed both of these economy items simultaneously. In the first entry, the girls had one acting scene and sang "Mary Lee" again and "Once in Awhile," while in *That Texas Jamboree* they had their largest screen assignment portraying the owners of a small Western town's bar and restaurant and becoming involved with the town's politics. In the latter film, they sang "I Still Remember" and "Valley of the Sun."

Next Walt Disney used the Dinning Sisters in two of his animated feature films at RKO. Providing these off-camera vocals proved to be their final movie work. In *Fun and Fancy Free* (1947) they did the song "Lazy Countryside," while in *Melody Time* (1948) they sang "Blame It on the Samba." Ironically, the Andrews Sisters, their biggest rivals who also could never harness a strong filmmaking career, sang the story of "Little Toot" in that latter feature.

In 1948, the Dinning Sisters enjoyed their strongest commercial recording success with "Buttons and Bows" for Capitol, the disc selling over one million copies. Among their other Capitol bestsellers were: "Love on a Greyhound Bus," "Brazil," "San Antonio Rose," and "Harlem Sandman." During the 1949–50 season, the trio were regulars on CBS radio's *The Spike Jones Spotlight Revue.*

By 1950, the Dinning Sisters were tiring of the show-business grind. In addition they each had distinct personal lives of their own. Ginger Dinning recalled later, "We didn't work as hard as the Andrews Sisters. We were also more centered around our husbands and raising families." Older sister Lou, who sang alto in the trio to Ginger's lead and Jean's soprano, started recording solo for Capitol; she left the group in early 1946 after marrying singer/songwriter Don Robertson and was replaced for three years by Jayne Bundesen. Lou later costarred on radio with Tennessee Ernie Ford. The family's youngest sister, Dolores, joined the trio in 1949, and, in 1952, the Dinning Sisters filmed a half dozen TV short subjects for Snader Telescriptions: *Winter Wonderland; Brazil; Mornin' on the Farm; Pig Foot Pete; You're A Character, Dear;* and *Ma, He's Makin' Eyes at Me.* In the mid-'50s Jean Dinning cut a series of singles for Essex Records, and she sang all three parts on these discs that were issued as being by the Dinning Sisters, "Featuring Jean Dinning." In the late 1950s a budget label, Somerset, released an album by the "Dinning Sisters" made up of Jean's Essex recordings.

The Dinning Sisters ceased to appear professionally in the 1950s, although they remained very close-knit as a family. Jean, who moved to Tennessee, wrote "Teen Angel," which the girls' younger brother, Mark, recorded for MGM Records, resulting in a best-selling platter. Lou remained in California, where she ceased to perform but continued to write songs, while Ginger settled in Sussex, New Jersey. In 1983, EMI Records of France issued an LP of the trio's vintage Capitol recordings, and it was so successful that another followed in 1985. A West German label, Cattle Records, released several LPs in the mid- and late 1980s made up of the Dinnings' standard transcription material thanks to a renewed interest by the public in the singing siblings. In addition the trio reunited for occasional personal appearances, such as a tribute to them held in the Ozarks in the fall of 1987, followed by a TV appearance on *Nashville Now* and their appearance singing at the *Grand Ole Opry* for the first time in over thirty-five years. In the mid-'90s, the Dinning Sisters, this time made up of Jean, Ginger, and Dolores, joined the Jordanaires in recording a CD, *Rhinestone Christian,* which contained six original songs written by Jean Dinning. For over twenty-five years, Dolores Dinning Edgin was a member of the noted country music backup group the Nashville Edition. By the new century, the Dinning Sisters appeared to be out of the limelight for good, although their music continued to be heard in the popular compilation *The Best of the Dinning Sisters,* released by Collectors' Choice Music.

Filmography

By the Light of the Silvery Moon (Soundies, 1942) (s)
Ho-Hum (Soundies, 1942) (s)
Strictly in the Groove (Univ, 1942)
The National Barn Dance (Par, 1944)
Clancy (Soundies, 1945 (s)
Pig Foot Pete (Soundies, 1945) (s)
No Can Do (Soundies, 1945) (s)
Winter Wonderland (Soundies, 1945) (s)

Takin' the Breaks (Univ, 1946) (s)
Mary Lee (Soundies, 1946) (s)
Valley of the Sun (Soundies, 1946) (s)
I Still Remember (Soundies, 1946) (s)
Pin Marin (Soundies, 1946) (s)
Throw a Saddle on a Star (Col, 1946)
That Texas Jamboree (Col, 1946)
Fun and Fancy Free (RKO, 1947) (voice only)
Melody Time (RKO, 1948) (voice only)

Radio Series

The National Barn Dance (NBC, 1940–45)

The Dinning Sisters Show (NBC, c. 1940–41)
The Spike Jones Spotlight Revue (CBS, 1949–50)

Discography

LPs

The Dinning Sisters

At the Barn Dance (Cattle LP-120)
The Dinning Sisters (10″ Cap H-318)
The Dinning Sisters (Pathé Marconi/EMI/Cap PM 231-2068-54572)
The Dinning Sisters and Friends (Cattle LP-116) w. Bob Atcher, Tennessee Ernie Ford, Tex Ritter

The Dinning Sisters, Vol. 2 (Pathé Marconi/EMI/ Cap PM231-1566261)
The Dinning Sisters and Friends (Cattle LP-116)
Songs by the Dinning Sisters (Somerset P-3800) featuring Jean Dinning
Songs We Sang at the National Barn Dance (Cattle LP-96)
Swingin' at the Barn Dance (Cattle LP-120)

Lou Dinning

Lou Dinning—Favorite Songs From the "Tennessee Ernie Ford Show" (Cattle LP-123) w. Tennessee Ernie Ford

CDs

The Dinning Sisters

Almost Sweet & Gentle (Jasmine JASCD-384)
Back in the Country Style (Jasmine JASCD-333)
The Best of the Dinning Sisters (Collectors' Choice Music CCM-045-2)

Rhinestone Christian (Gold Rhyme G90101) w. the Jordanaires

Irene Dunne in 1935.
[Courtesy of JC Archives]

Irene Dunne

(b. Irene Marie Dunn, Louisville, Kentucky, December 20, 1898; d. Holmby Hills, California, September 4, 1990)

Her singing was sweet and clear; her comedy timing was superb; her approach to dramatics was direct and understated. Because she was so versatile and excelled so effortlessly at so many screen forms, audiences frequently took beautiful Irene Dunne for granted. They enjoyed her wide range of talents, but remembered her best for her comedy roles. Thus it is for light comedies like *Theodora Goes Wild* (1936), *The Awful Truth* (1937), and *Life With Father* (1947) that durable Irene Dunne is best recalled. And with good reason: With a twinkle in her eyes, a mere tilt of her head, or the slightest inflection in her voice, she could imply so much. However, she also starred successfully in the epic Western *Cimarron* (1931); sang the lead in musicals such as *Roberta* (1935) and *Show Boat* (1936); was the dignified heroine of tearjerkers like *Back Street* (1932), *Magnificent Obsession* (1935), and *Penny Serenade* (1940); and was a regal elderly Queen Victoria in *The Mudlark* (1950).

When screen roles were no longer plentiful in the 1950s, Irene turned to politics. With her humanitarian interests, she became active at the United Nations. Of the major singing stars of Hollywood's Golden Era, it is gifted Irene Dunne whose productive and varied career demands reassessment. For a long time, many of her films (which often inspired inferior remakes) were unavailable due to copyright problems. But cable TV, VHS tapes, and DVDs have remedied that situation. This five-time Academy Award nominee is a natural treasure to be rediscovered.

She was born Irene Marie Dunn (she added the final "e" to her surname after entering show business) on December 20, 1898 (some sources list 1901, 1904, or 1907 as her birth year) in Louisville, Kentucky. She was the older child (there was a younger brother, Charles) of Joseph John Dunn and Adelaide Antoinette (Henry) Dunn. Her father built and operated Mississippi riverboats and later became a ship inspector for the federal government. Irene received a Catholic education at Saint Benedict's Academy in Louisville. When Irene was eight, her father died, and Mrs. Dunn took her two children to Madison, Indiana, to live with her parents. There Mrs. Dunn, herself an accomplished pianist, had her daughter begin lessons in voice and dance. Irene eventually entered the Conservatory Division of the Chicago Musical College in 1918, planning an opera career.

In 1920, Irene went to New York City to audition for the Metropolitan Opera. She failed the test, but on a lark (so she insisted) tried out for the lead in the road company of the musical comedy *Irene*. She was hired to tour the Midwest for four months. When no further offers developed, Irene thought of teaching music in the Chicago public schools, but her mother persuaded her to return to New York. She won a tiny role on Broadway in *The Clinging Vine* (1922), starring Peggy Wood, and when Wood became ill on the show's subsequent road tour, Irene got to star. Later, she took over the ingénue role in another musical, *Lollipops* (1924), on Broadway, and was a replacement in *Sweetheart Time* (1926). She finally played an original lead in *Luckee Girl* (1928), but that musical comedy lasted only eighty-one performances.

By this time, Irene had already wed Manhattan-based dentist Francis J. Griffin and had thought of retiring. But fate, according to the star, interceded. She was in the crowded elevator of a theatrical office building in midtown New York City. One of the other passengers was esteemed producer Florenz Ziegfeld, who was entranced by her beauty and arranged a conference. She was offered the role of Magnolia in Ziegfeld's road company of *Show Boat*. During the Chicago engagement, she won solid reviews for her singing and came to the attention of RKO Radio Pictures, which, like the other Hollywood studios, was turning out a rash of musical comedies.

Dunne was signed for the screen version of the Broadway musical *Present Arms*. However, by the time the film reached the screen in 1930, it had been retitled *Leathernecking*, and because the song-and-dance picture craze had passed, it was shorn of its musical side and turned into a straight service comedy. Plans to star Irene in a version of Victor Herbert's *Babes in Toyland* were dropped. Instead she won the lead in the expansive (131 minutes) screen adaptation of Edna Ferber's *Cimarron* (1931). For her role as the spunky Sabra Cravat—who copes with a wanderlust husband (Richard Dix) in 1880s Oklahoma—she was nominated for an Oscar. The studio then pushed her into an urbane comedy, *Bachelor Apartment* (1931), which showed she could handle that genre quite well.

It was not her home lot, but MGM that took advantage of Irene's vocal talents. She was borrowed to play the opera singer in *The Great Lover* (1931), with *Variety* reporting, "Part calls for quiet and persuasive grace, which this young actress possesses abundantly." Then it was back to romantic drama in RKO's *Consolation Marriage* (1931) opposite Pat O'Brien. This effort demonstrated that Irene could play the same weepy roles that had been the province of Ann Harding—the contract star of Pathé Pictures, which had now merged with RKO. *Symphony of Six Million* (1932) was a slick reworking of a Fannie Hearst tale with Irene as the crippled schoolteacher who falls in love with, and is cured by, a Jewish doctor (Ricardo Cortez).

But of Dunne's 1932 releases, the most important was *Back Street*, made on loan to Universal. It was a tearjerker of classical proportion with Irene as the quintessential suffering woman who cannot wed the married man (John Boles), whom she loves over the decades. She thought the film "trash," but it made her the first lady of screen soap opera and a major cinema star. After the completion of each of her pictures, Irene always returned to New York, where her husband still practiced dentistry.

For the 1933 season, RKO had Dunne suffering nobly on-camera for four pictures, including a loanout to MGM (*The Secret of Madame Blanche*). She was at her flintiest in *Ann Vickers*, the adaptation of Sinclair Lewis's novel, in which Irene was showcased as the feminist social worker who adores a salty judge (Walter Huston). By now Oscar-winning Katharine Hepburn was queen of the RKO lot, although Irene was still the more popular with filmgoers. The titles of Dunne's next films (*If I Were Free*, 1933, and *This Man Is Mine*, 1934) say all that is necessary about these celluloid exercises of noble suffering by the love-hungry heroine. She was supposed to star in *My Gal Sal*, a Gay Nineties musical, but instead was reunited with Richard Dix (as a roguish outlaw) in *Stingaree* (1934), a tale of 1874 Australia, in which she interpolated a bit of operatic singing. When Hepburn rejected *The Age of Innocence* (1934) based on Edith Wharton's satire of 1870's New York society, Irene was handed the plum role, again teamed with John Boles.

Eventually, Irene sang again on-screen when Warner Bros. borrowed her to play the lead in *Sweet Adeline* (1935), based on the Jerome Kern–Oscar Hammerstein II stage musical that had starred Helen Morgan. With her cool, high soprano, Irene sang "Don't Ever Leave Me" and "Why Was I Born?" and with Irish tenor Phil Regan, dueted "We Were So Young." For some reviewers, Dunne's patented gentility clashed with her role as the innocent daughter of a beer-garden owner. RKO finally used its singing star to headline *Roberta* (1935), which cofeatured Fred Astaire and Ginger Rogers in their third screen teaming. Dunne was the Russian princess working in a Paris dressmaking shop who is courted by a young American football player (Randolph Scott). Astaire and Rogers shone in their four dance numbers, but it was Irene who sang "Smoke Gets in Your Eyes," "Lovely to Look At," and "Yesterdays."

By the time the popular *Roberta* was in release, Irene had left RKO. She rejected Paramount's offers to join with Ann Harding in *The Old Maid* or to make *Peter Ibbetson*. (Harding made the latter for that studio in 1935, while the former became a Bette Davis–Miriam Hopkins vehicle at Warner Bros. in 1939.) Dunne chose to join with Universal on a short-time basis, with *Magnificent Obsession* (1935) as her first vehicle. "Heavy dramatic roles are essential for an actress of my type," Irene reasoned. "I know definitely that the status I have achieved has been achieved through tears. So for my career I cry." *Magnificent Obsession*, along with *Back Street* (1932), *Imitation of Life* (1934), and *Stella Dallas* (1937), remain the key tearjerkers of the 1930s. *Magnificent Obsession* featured Irene as the widow whose blindness is cured by a physician (Robert Taylor), the once-playboy who accidentally caused her husband's death.

Universal had already filmed an earlier version of *Show Boat* in 1929, removing most of the Jerome Kern–Oscar Hammerstein II score. This was remedied for the 1936 edition, which starred Irene Dunne as Magnolia Hawks and Allan Jones as dashing riverboat gambler Gaylord Ravenal. Helen Morgan re-created her stage role as the mulatto torch singer, and Paul Robeson was the muscular dockworker. Irene sang with Jones "You Are Love," "I Have the Room Above," "Why Do I Love You?" (cut from the picture), and the enchanting "Make Believe." On her own, she shuffled and trucked through a vibrant "Can't Help Lovin' Dat Man." The picture was a huge moneymaker and boosted Irene's stock with the filmgoing public. However, Irene, who was paid $100,000 for the picture, was very unhappy with the movie's director (James Whale). She commented, "There were lots of interpolations that we didn't need at all and I think the ending was stupid."

At this point, Irene chose to join Columbia Pictures on a nonexclusive basis. Studio head Harry Cohn decreed her first project should be a comedy. Irene was dubious and fled to Europe for six weeks with her husband. When she returned, she was forced to report for work on *Theodora Goes Wild* (1936). Her concerns to one side, she shone in this wacky screwball comedy as the small-town miss who writes a racy novel and is courted by her urbane book illustrator (Melvyn Douglas). "She surprises with a spirited gift for clowning," insisted the *New York Daily News*. She won her second Oscar nomination for this farce. Also in 1936, Dr. Griffin gave up his New York City practice to move to Los Angeles, and on March 17, 1936, the Griffins adopted four-year-old Anna Mary Bush. On December 17, Irene's mother, who was her constant companion, died of a cerebral hemorrhage.

For Paramount's *High, Wide and Handsome* (1937), Irene was the amorous daughter of a medicine sideshow proprietor who becomes enraptured with a farmer (Randolph Scott). The plot was complex, the artiness of director Rouben Mamoulian excessive, and the cast ranged from

Dorothy Lamour to Charles Bickford. Irene sang "Can I Forget You?" "The Folk Who Live on the Hill," and "Allegheny Al." Critics made comparisons to how MGM's diva Jeanette MacDonald might have handled the role, and *Variety* noted tactfully that Irene (now in her late thirties) was "perhaps a shade too mature" for the ingénue role. Far more successful was Columbia's *The Awful Truth* (1937), which matched her with another top farceur, Cary Grant, in a merry story of marital strife and reunion. She was Oscar-nominated for the third time, but lost (for the second time) to Luise Rainer (on this occasion for *The Good Earth*).

Irene returned to RKO to play a musical comedy star in *Joy of Living* (1938) with Douglas Fairbanks Jr. as her madcap playboy suitor and Lucille Ball as her parasitic sister. Perhaps the film's greatest ingenuity was in creating offbeat settings in which Irene could sing, including "Just Let Me Look at You" (done at the play-within-the-movie-finale and elsewhere), "You Couldn't Be Cuter" (sung in a nursery), "What's Good About Good Night? (at a radio-station broadcast), and "A Heavenly Party" (sung into a 25¢ recording device at the carnival). Sadly, *Joy of Living* was Dunne's final musical.

RKO's *Love Affair* (1939) was a sophisticated romance with Irene paired with Charles Boyer. It allowed her a chance to sing "Just Keep on Wishing." She was yet again Oscar-nominated, and later recalled it as her favorite film "not only because it was so well done, but also because we had such a good time making it." Far less felicitous was Universal's *Invitation to Happiness* (1939), with Fred MacMurray as a dumb prizefighter she comes to love, while *When Tomorrow Comes* (1939) reunited her with Boyer in a persuasive love tale.

Irene rejected a return to Broadway in *Lady in the Dark* and instead remained in Hollywood to make *My Favorite Wife* (1940) with Cary Grant. Like so many of her features, this joyous comedy would be remade, but with far lesser results—the remake of this one featured Doris Day and James Garner and was titled *Move Over, Darling* (1963). Again with Grant, Dunne was the maudlin but effective leading lady of *Penny Serenade* (1940), about a couple whose adoption of a baby reignites their love. She would comment, "I don't think I've ever felt as close to any picture. It's very much the scheme of my personal life."

After two mundane comedies (*Unfinished Business*, 1941, and *Lady in a Jam*, 1942) at Universal, Irene performed as guest vocalist with the Chicago Symphony Orchestra in their 1941–42 season, and then moved over to MGM, where her once-rival at RKO, Katharine Hepburn, was enjoying a new vogue as costar with Spencer Tracy. Irene's first assignment was *A Guy Named Joe* (1943), a patriotic war fantasy in which a deceased American pilot (Tracy) returns to "life" to help his fiancée (Dunne) fly a vital military mission. When costar Van Johnson was injured in a motorcycle accident during filming and shooting was temporarily halted, Irene began working on the elaborate *The White Cliffs of Dover* (1944). It was saccharine, full of blatant Anglo-American propaganda, but exceedingly well liked at the time.

In the mid-'40s, Irene's screen career tapered off to one picture a year. She was paired with Charles Boyer a third and final time for the romantic *Together Again* (1944) and starred in Ruth Gordon's frivolous stage hit *Over 21* (1945). In March 1945, she received an honorary degree of doctor of music from the Chicago Musical College, but learned that MGM had decided that having Greer Garson on the payroll to play noble heroines was sufficient. Irene starred at Twentieth Century-Fox with Rex Harrison in *Anna and the King of Siam* (1946), a sumptuously mounted costume feature that would later be transformed into the 1950's Broadway musical *The King and I* and later remakes (musical, nonmusical, and animated). Its success led to Irene being partnered with William Powell in bringing the long-running Broadway comedy hit *Life With Father* (1947) to the screen. In her first color feature, she was the ever-patient but addled wife Vinnie in 1890's New York and because of the nature of her sedate role was outshone by her coplayers, especially Powell. Next, Dunne rejoined her alma mater, RKO, for *I Remember Mama* (1948), as the Norwegian mother battling adversities in 1910's San Francisco. For her well-modulated characterization of the self-sacrificing, wise mother, she was Oscar-nominated for her fifth and final time but lost to Jane Wyman (*Johnny Belinda*).

Irene was off the screen in 1949, during which she was named the outstanding member of the American Catholic laity by the University of Notre Dame. In 1950, she made a tepid comedy with Fred MacMurray, *Never a Dull Moment,* and she underwent vigorous makeup changes to play the dowdy old matron Queen Victoria in *The Mudlark*. Despite her noteworthy impersonation, the picture was unsuccessful. Her last feature was Universal's *It Grows on Trees* (1952), a whimsical tale full of forced gaiety. That same year, she joined Fred MacMurray for the comedy-drama radio series *Bright Star,* in which she played a newspaper reporter and MacMurray was her editor. ZIV syndicated the fifty-two episode show.

Irene surprised many by accepting the post of hostess on CBS-TV's anthology series *Schlitz Playhouse of Stars* for a year (1952–53). Thereafter, she was seen only infrequently on television, such as "A Touch of Spring" on *Ford Theater* (NBC, 1955), "The Opening Door" segment of *The June Allyson Show* (CBS, 1959), and the "Go Fight City Hall" episode of *G.E. Theater* (CBS, 1962). On *The Perry Como Show* (NBC, 1956), she sang selections from *Show Boat*. She turned down notions of starring in her own TV series, feeling she could not do her best if she had to perform week after week.

More important for Irene in the 1950s were her political attachments. She was a staunch Republican and a supporter of General Dwight D. Eisenhower, who, as president in 1957, appointed her as an alternative delegate to the Twelfth General Assembly of the United Nations in New York. She confided, "I've played many parts, but this offers the greater challenge." After a year, she returned to Hollywood, where her daughter gave birth to her first child in 1958.

Irene's dentist husband, a shrewd real-estate investor who also was a partner in his family's Griffin Equipment Company (of New York), died on October 15, 1965. Thereafter, Irene made even fewer public appearances, preferring to continue her philanthropy work (for Saint John's Hospital in particular), supervise her vast real-estate holdings, and for a time being a member of the California Arts Commission. She was elected to the Board of Directors of Technicolor in 1965, and in 1967 was at the televised Oscar broadcast to present an award. In 1970, she was the subject of a major tribute program sponsored by the Los Angeles County Museum and the California Palace of the Legion of Honor (in San Francisco), at which festival she sang a few refrains of her *Love Affair* song. In December 1985, she was chosen one of the six winners (along with comedian Bob Hope and Beverly Sills) of the eighth annual Kennedy Center Honors for lifetime achievements. In poor health, Irene was too ill to attend the festivities. The veteran actress died of heart failure at her Holmby Hills home in the early evening of September 4, 1990, at age ninety-one. For the past year, she had been suffering from an irregular heartbeat and had been cared for by private nurses. She was survived by her daughter (now Mary Frances Gage), grandchildren Ann and Mark Shinnick, a great-granddaughter, and a niece. Irene requested that memorial donations be given to Saint John's Hospital.

Once while reminiscing, years after she had retired from show business, the always extremely private Irene Dunne claimed she never missed being a movie star: "I knew all along acting was not everything there was." Of her peak years of fame, she admitted, "I never really had time to enjoy my success. Time! All my mother wanted was me and my time. I could buy her a new car, but I couldn't go around to the shops with her. I didn't have time."

Filmography

Leathernecking [Present Arms] (RKO, 1930)

Consolation Marriage [Married in Haste] (RKO, 1931)

Cimarron (RKO, 1931)

Bachelor Apartment (RKO, 1931)

The Great Lover (MGM, 1931)

Symphony of Six Million [Melody of Life] (RKO, 1932)

The Stolen Jools [The Slippery Pearls] (Masquers Club, 1932) (s)

Back Street (Univ, 1932)

Thirteen Women (RKO, 1932)

The Secret of Madame Blanche (MGM, 1933)

No Other Woman (RKO, 1933)

The Silver Cord (RKO, 1933)

Ann Vickers (RKO, 1933)

If I Were Free [Behold We Live] (RKO, 1933)

This Man Is Mine (RKO, 1934)

Stingaree (RKO, 1934)

The Age of Innocence (RKO, 1934)

Sweet Adeline (WB, 1935)

Roberta (RKO, 1935)

Magnificent Obsession (Univ, 1935)

Show Boat (Univ, 1936)

Theodore Goes Wild (Col, 1936)

High, Wide and Handsome (Par, 1937)

The Awful Truth (Col, 1937)

Joy of Living (RKO, 1938)

Invitation to Happiness (Par, 1939)

Love Affair (RKO, 1939)

When Tomorrow Comes (Univ, 1939)

My Favorite Wife (RKO, 1940)

Penny Serenade (Col, 1940)

Unfinished Business (Univ, 1941)

Lady in a Jam (Col, 1942)

Show Business at War (20th-Fox, 1943) (s)

A Guy Named Joe (MGM, 1943)

Together Again (Col, 1944)

The White Cliffs of Dover (MGM, 1944)

Over 21 (Col, 1945)

Anna and the King of Siam (20th-Fox, 1946)

Life With Father (WB, 1947)

I Remember Mama (RKO, 1948)

Never a Dull Moment (RKO, 1950)

The Mudlark (20th-Fox, 1950)

It Grows on Trees (Univ, 1952)

Broadway Plays

The Clinging Vine (1922)

Lollipops (1924) (replacement)

The City Chap (1925)

Sweetheart Time (1926) (replacement)

Yours Truly (1927)

She's My Baby (1928)

Luckee Girl (1928)

Radio Series

Bright Star (Synd, 1952–53)

TV Series

Schlitz Playhouse of Stars (CBS, 1952–53)

Album Discography

LPs

Anna and the King of Siam (Sandpiper 3) [ST/R]
Christmas Stories From Guideposts (Guideposts) w. Dick Van Dyke
High, Wide and Handsome/Sweet Adeline (Titania 506) [ST]

Roberta (CIF 3011) [ST]
Roberta (Star-Tone 204) [ST/R]
Show Boat (Sunbeam 501) [ST/R]
Show Boat (Vertinge 2004, Xeno 251) [ST]

CDs

The Great Singing Screen Stars (Sony Musical Special Products AK-47018)*
Hits of 1935 (ASV CD-AJA-5185)*
Love Is the Sweetest Thing—Great Love Songs of the 30s (Compact Selection TQ-153)*
Makin' Whoopee—Favorites of Stage and Screen (Conifer 132)*

Musical Ladies and the Music of Jerome Kern (Encore ENBO-4/92)*
Puttin' on the Ritz (SVL 188)*
Those Sensational Swinging Sirens of the Silver Screen (Vintage Jazz Classics VJC-1002-2)*
The Ultimate Show Boat (Pavilion GEMS-060)*
*Compilation album

Judy Garland and Deanna Durbin in the short subject *Every Sunday* (1936).
[Courtesy of JC Archives]

Deanna Durbin

(b. Edna Mae Durbin, Winnipeg, Canada, December 4, 1921)

Critics and film historians have long been perplexed by the popularity of Deanna Durbin, which, at its height in the late 1930s, was credited with single-handedly saving Universal Pictures from bankruptcy. When looking objectively at the typical Deanna Durbin screen persona, it is difficult for many to discern what all the fuss was about. She usually portrayed overly precious and very meddlesome teenagers who were prone to fibbing and getting mired in all types of sticky situations. Further, she was apt to burst out in song—operatic no less—at any time, which would hardly seem to relate her to her peers. Yet, despite all, this sprightly star captured the hearts of moviegoers, who watched her mature from an awkward teenager into an attractive young woman in twenty-one Universal feature films—*all* of them moneymakers. In addition, the mystique remained after Deanna Durbin retired from the screen at age twenty-seven and thereafter lived in seclusion in France, permitting few interviews over the years.

Deanna was born Edna Mae Durbin in Winnipeg, Canada, on December 4, 1921, the second daughter (her sister Edith was eleven years her senior) of British parents, James and Ada Read Durbin. The family had moved to Canada in 1912, and in 1922 they migrated to California because of Mr. Durbin's poor health. They settled near Los Angeles, where James became a real-estate salesman. Edna showed a proclivity for music at a young age, but the family was unable to afford to pay for her voice lessons until after her older sister Edith became a teacher and helped provide the funds. Edna studied voice at Ralph Thomas's Academy in Los Angeles and sang for clubs and churches in the city.

In 1935, Durbin auditioned for MGM casting director Rufus LeMaire for the role of the young Ernestine Schumann-Heink in a biopic to be made about the famous opera singer. She impressed not only LeMaire but also MGM voice teacher Andrés de Segurola, who judged her voice to be that of a fully matured soprano. When Louis B. Mayer heard Edna sing, he signed her to a contract and her name was changed to Deanna Durbin. For their new charge, MGM maneuvered a guest spot on the *Los Angeles Breakfast Club* radio show for three appearances, and then cast her opposite another new contractee, Judy Garland, in the two-reel short *Every Sunday* (1936). The two girls played teenagers who try to save their small town's local weekly park concerts. Durbin sang "Il Bacio" and dueted with Garland on "Americana." When the studio dropped the Schumann-Heink project, MGM did not renew Deanna's contract (much to its later regret).

At this time, Rufus LeMaire moved to Universal, and he placed Deanna under personal contract at a $300 weekly salary and retained Andrés de Segurola as her vocal coach. At LeMaire's urging, producer Joe Pasternak and director Henry Koster—both recently arrived from the company's Berlin studios—cast Deanna in the comedy *Three Smart Girls* (1937). She was the youngest of three sisters (Nan Grey and Barbara Reed played the older siblings) who try to reconcile their mother (Nella Walker) and father (Charles Winninger), the latter being hotly pursued by a gold digger (Binnie Barnes) and her ambitious mother (Alice Brady). Deanna sang "Il Bacio" again, "Someone to Care for Me" (both recorded for Decca Records), and "My Heart Is Singing." During the filming, Deanna became a regular on Eddie Cantor's weekly NBC radio show, and on it she popularized "Someone to Care for Me." Also on the program was another moppet star, Bobby Breen. *Three Smart Girls* was a huge success (especially in England), which salvaged Universal's falling stock. Deanna Durbin was the nation's new sweetheart, with a large fan club, "The Deanna Durbin Devotees," and a merchandizing campaign to equal that of Shirley Temple's, with all kinds of Deanna Durbin items on the market for young people. She negotiated a new contract with Universal, which escalated her weekly salary from $1,500 to $3,000 and provided her with a $10,000 bonus per film.

Her next film, *One Hundred Men and a Girl* (1937), was even more successful than her first, continuing her association with Joe Pasternak and Henry Koster. Here she puts together a symphony orchestra and even gets famed concert conductor Leopold Stokowski to lead it, all so her unemployed musician father (Adolphe Menjou) will have a job. In the feature, Deanna sang opera (Wolfgang Amadeus Mozart's "Alleluia" and the "Libiamo" from Giuseppe Verdi's opera *La Traviata*) plus pop tunes ("It's Raining Moonbeams" and "A Heart That's Free"). In 1938, she was given a special Academy Award, and she became the first female to be sworn into the Boy Scouts.

Her first 1938 film, *Mad About Music*, cast her as a school girl who persuades a dapper composer (Herbert Marshall) to pose as her father, thus instigating a romance with her mother (Gail Patrick). She performed "Chapel Bells," "Serenade to the Stars," "There Isn't a Day Goes By," "I Love to Whistle," and Johann Bach's "Ave Maria," the latter backed by the Vienna Boys' Choir. Deanna recorded "Ave Maria" for Decca, often recording songs from her pictures. *That Certain Age* (1938) found teenager Deanna with a crush on droll war correspondent Melvyn Douglas, who has a fiancée (Nancy Carroll). This lighthearted exercise offered Durbin a half dozen musical outings, including: "My Own" (which became a bestseller on Decca) and "Les Filles de Cadiz" (by French composer Léo Delibes).

Henry Koster directed both of Deanna's 1939 pictures. *Three Smart Girls Grow Up*, a sequel to her debut feature, had the teenager guiding the romances of her two sisters (Nan Grey and Helen Parrish) and their boyfriends (William Lundigan and Robert Cummings). She also sang a quartet of songs, including "Because" and "The Last Rose of Summer." *First Love* received a great deal of hoopla because Deanna received her initial screen kiss in it from Robert Stack. The plot had her and nasty stepsister Helen Parrish both in love with handsome Stack. This time Durbin performed seven songs, including "Amapola," "Sympathy," and Giacomo Puccini's "One Fine Day" ("Un Bell Di" from the opera *Madame Butterfly*).

Deanna Durbin opened the decade of the 1940s with a new studio contract that allowed her over $300,000 per film. *It's a Date* (1940) found her as a young singer who gets the stage role coveted by her extremely chic mother (Kay Francis). Durbin's quartet of numbers included "Love Is All," "Loch Lommond," and Franz Schubert's "Ave Maria." By this time, Deanna had just graduated from high school and was busy refuting rumors that she planned to desert films for grand opera.

Spring Parade (1940) had Deanna as a Viennese peasant girl in love with a nobleman (Robert Cummings). This pleasant confection had her doing a variety of songs, including "When April Sings," "Waltzing in the Clouds," "It's Foolish, But It's Fun," and "Blue Danube Dream," whose music derived from Johann Strauss's "Blue Danube Waltz." *Nice Girl?* (1941) cast the actress as a scientist's daughter who is engulfed in a scandal with her father's rival (Franchot Tone), but she really loves her boyfriend (Robert Stack). Her songs included "Perhaps," "Love at Last," Stephen Foster's "Old Folks at Home," and the patriotic, "Thank You America." (For British release prints Durbin also sang "There'll Always Be an England," because she was the most popular box-office star at the time in that country.) After completing this entry, Deanna was a guest at the White House for President Franklin D. Roosevelt's birthday, and she also performed at various military installations. In the spring of 1941, she married Vaughn Paul in a lavish ceremony in Hollywood. By now, Deanna's screen popularity had not only generated rivals at other studios, such as Kathryn Grayson at MGM, but Universal also kept a roster of teenage girls on hand, the most successful being Gloria Jean.

Deanna culminated her association with Joe Pasternak and Henry Koster in the delightful comedy *It Started With Eve* (1941), in which she and Charles Laughton proved to be a most amiable screen team. Laughton was the dying millionaire who wants to meet his son's (Robert Cummings) fiancée, and because the girl is unavailable, Deanna substitutes. She and Laughton performed a hilarious conga dance, and Deanna sang "The Lord's Prayer," "Going Home," and "When I Sing," none of which she recorded. Instead she began recording other tunes for Decca, such as "Kiss Me Again," "My Hero," "Poor Butterfly," "God Bless America," and "The Star-Spangled Banner," along with the traditional Christmas carols, "Adeste Fideles" and "Silent Night."

Deanna Durbin made no films during 1942. Her mentor, Joe Pasternak, had left Universal in a dispute and moved over to MGM, and Universal was not sure how to guide Durbin into suitable adult roles. She refused the lead in *Boy Meets Baby* and went on suspension. She kept active singing for soldiers at USO clubs and appeared on patriotic radio shows like *Command Performance*. Amidst many production problems and the departure of French director Jean Renoir from the project, Durbin completed *The Amazing Mrs. Holliday* (1943), about a missionary trying to get nine Chinese orphans into the United States. She sang only a trio of songs, "Vissi d'Arte" from Puccini's opera *Tosca*, "Mighty Lak' a Rose," and a Chinese lullaby. By now Universal was forcing her into a standardized adult glamor mold, but, thankfully, her strong individuality still kept her screen personality unique and appealing.

Producer Felix Jackson began managing Deanna's career, and he chose for her the wartime drama *Hers to Hold* (1943), where she played a factory worker who is attracted to a dashing pilot (Joseph Cotten). Her songs included the patriotic "Say a Prayer for the Boys Over There," Cole Porter's "Begin the Beguine," and "The Kashmiri Song." With director Frank Borzage, she starred in *His Butler's Sister* (1943) as a young lady involved with a self-centered composer (Franchot Tone). In this picture, she offered a good rendition of the aria "Nessum Dorma" (normally performed by the tenor lead) from Puccini's opera *Turandot* and "When You're Away."

Durbin was bent on becoming a "dramatic" actress and pressured the studio into allowing her to star in W. Somerset Maugham's *Christmas Holiday* (1944). Even when watered down, it was a very adult subject about a young woman marrying a killer (Gene Kelly) and forced to perform in a New Orleans dive. She did sing "Always," "Spring Will Be a Little Late This Year," and "Ave Maria" (in a tearful church sequence), but her loyal fans did not care for this change of pace, despite Durbin's solid emoting. The reaction soured Durbin on moviemaking.

If Universal could not afford to buy the rights to the big Broadway hit *Oklahoma!*, it could create its own. The studio starred her in her only color picture, *Can't Help Singing*, (1944), lensed in Utah. Durbin played a plucky young lady who goes West to locate her wayward boyfriend (Robert Paige); unfortunately, the film's songs by Jerome Kern were lifeless, except for the title tune.

Having divorced Vaughn Paul (much to her fans' dismay), Deanna married Felix Jackson in the summer of 1945 in Las Vegas, and then starred in the comedy/murder mystery *Lady on a Train* (1945). It was a deft combination of the film noir and hard-boiled detective genres interpolated with crazy hijinks. Durbin played a devout murder-mystery fan who observes a killing from her train window, and in trying to convince the authorities there was a murder, she becomes potential prey for the killer. She also got to deliver "Night and Day," "Silent Night," and the Jazz Age favorite, "Give Me a Little Kiss."

The star reteamed with Charles Laughton and Franchot Tone for the amusing comedy *Because of Him* (1946), which offered her as a waitress who wants to be an actress with support from old-timer Laughton and doubts from author Tone. She did a delightful version of Francesco Paoli Tosti's "Goodbye," and the songs "Danny Boy" and "Lover," but the film was only a moderate success. Following its completion, Deanna became a mother early in 1946 with the birth of a daughter, Jessica.

Back on the screen, Durbin starred in a middling remake of *The Good Fairy* (1935), now called *I'll Be Yours* (1947), as a young woman who aids a lawyer (Tom Drake) while trying to fend off millionaire Adolphe Menjou. Despite the raggedness of the plot, Deanna was in fine voice in songs like "Granada" and "It's Dream Time." The movie was her last to be produced by her spouse Jackson. Universal was now undergoing extreme corporate changes, and the new regime decided to cut the budgets of Durbin's future entries, one way to help, supposedly, the profit margin on her projects. In both 1945 and 1947, Deanna was Hollywood's highest-paid female star.

Deanna was to star in only three more movies, beginning with *Something in the Wind* (1947), where she was a disc jockey (!) who is abducted by a millionaire's (John Dall) screwy family, who think she is his girlfriend who is gold-digging for his inheritance. Although she and Jan Peerce (in a jail scene) dueted "Miserere" from Verdi's opera *Il Travatore*, her quartet of pop selections were mediocre. Sigmund Romberg's *Up in Central Park* (1948) had been a big Broadway hit in 1945, and it deserved a well-mounted screen production, but Universal cut corners. Deanna was a young woman involved with corrupt Gotham Mayor Boss Tweed (Vincent Price), and sang "Ave, Pace, Mio Dio" from Verdi's *La Forza del Destino*.

Her screen finale was the mediocre comedy *For the Love of Mary* (1948), in which she played a White House telephone operator who involves government officials, including the president, in her romantic troubles. Its only asset was Deanna's rendering of such songs as "On Moonlight Bay," "Let Me Call You Sweetheart," "I'll Take You Home Again Kathleen," and a comical "Largo Al Factotum" from Rossini's *The Barber of Seville* (a song usually sung by the baritone lead in the opera). With no further worthwhile scripts, Deanna Durbin and Universal called it quits. (They paid her for not making three final pictures under her contract.) She and Felix Jackson were divorced that year, having been separated since 1948. At the end of 1950, she wed for the third time, to Pathé Films executive Charles David, and moved to Normandy, France. In 1951, Deanna gave birth to her second child, a son, Peter.

Durbin had long wanted to abandon her career and told her former mentor Eddie Cantor, "I don't want to have anything to do with show business ever." She insisted she hated the dieting, the fabricated screen image (which she claimed had no relationship to the private Deanna Durbin), and everything that accompanied being a screen star. (In this posture, she rejected overtures to star in the 1953 MGM screen musical, *Kiss Me, Kate.*) With her money wisely invested, she could enjoy the quiet life in France. The only time she claimed to have been tempted to return to the world of entertainment was in the 1950s, when *My Fair Lady* was being thought of as a potential Broadway musical. As she recalled, "It was still in an embryonic state, just a few songs completed when [composer] Alan Jay Lerner came to my home to play them for me. I loved them . . . but I had my ticket for Paris in my pocket, and anyway, Julie Andrews was great, and so was Audrey Hepburn in the film." In December 2001 she celebrated her eightieth birthday in Paris at her Left Bank apartment she shared with her spouse, Charles David.

Though off the screen for over half a century, Deanna Durbin retained some of her popularity thanks to reshowings of her Universal pictures and the steady reissues of her Decca recordings on both sides of the Atlantic. Unlike some of her contemporaries, Durbin saw the handwriting on the wall when she left movies, realizing that her favored screen persona had vanished as she matured and grew plumper. She was able to forsake filmdom with the satisfaction that she had both a successful career and had helped to enrich America's culture by introducing its youth to the joys of classical music.

Filmography

Every Sunday (MGM, 1936) (s)
Three Smart Girls (Univ, 1936)
One Hundred Men and a Girl (Univ, 1937)
That Certain Age (Univ, 1938)
Mad About Music (Univ, 1938)
Three Smart Girls Grow Up (Univ, 1939)
First Love (Univ, 1939)
Spring Parade (Univ, 1940)
It's a Date (Univ, 1941)
Nice Girl? (Univ, 1941)
It Started With Eve (Univ, 1941)
The Amazing Mrs. Holliday (Univ, 1943)

Hers to Hold (Univ, 1943)
His Butler's Sister (Univ, 1943)
Show Business at War (20th-Fox, 1943) (s)
Christmas Holiday (Univ, 1944)
The Shining Future (WB, 1944) (s)
Can't Help Singing (Univ, 1944)
Lady on a Train (Univ, 1945)
Because of Him (Univ 1945)
I'll Be Yours (Univ, 1946)
Something in the Wind (Univ, 1947)
Up in Central Park (Univ, 1948)
For the Love of Mary (Univ, 1948)

Radio Series

The Eddie Cantor Show (NBC, 1937)

Album Discography

LPs

All-Time Favorites (Suffolk Marketing/MCA
 MSM-35050)
America's Sweetheart of Song (The Beautiful Music
 Company AMSM-235245)
The Best of Deanna Durbin (MCA 1634)
The Best of Deanna Durbin, Vol. 2 (MCA 1729)
Can't Help Singing (Coral 43)
Can't Help Singing (Music for Pleasure 50559)
A Date With Deanna Durbin (Coral 64)

Deanna Durbin (Decca DL-8785)
Deanna Durbin Favorites (Memoir 206)
It's a Date (Coral 23)
Memories (MCA 1514)
Movie Songs (MCA 1668)
Original Voice Tracks (Decca DL-75289) [ST]
Radio Broadcast Follies of 1935 (Amalgamated
 227) [ST/R]
Souvenir Album (10″ Decca Dl-5099)

Spring Parade (Caliban 6005) [ST]
Sweetheart of Song (MCA 2579)

Three Smart Girls (Caliban 6006) [ST]

CDs

Ave Maria (Pegasus PEG629)
Can't Help Singing (ASV CD-AJA-5149)
Can't Help Singing (Jasmine JASCD-101)
Deanna Durbin (ASV CD-AJA-9781)
The Fan Club (Pearl Flapper PAST-CD-9781)
The Golden Voice of Deanna Durbin (Hallmark 308182)
Kiss Me Again (Pearl Flapper PAST-CD-7828)
Original Film Soundtracks (Movie Stars 013)

Sensational Songbird (President 567)
Sweetheart of Song (Collectors' Choice Music CCM-1007)
The Ultimate Collection: 24 Great Hits (Prism PLATCD-143)
The Very Best of Deanna Durbin (AUS IMP-752422)
With a Song in My Heart (Prestige 341)

Nelson Eddy

(b. Providence, Rhode Island, June 29, 1901; d. Miami Beach, Florida, March 7, 1967)

Although perennially associated with Jeanette MacDonald in the public's mind, Nelson Eddy had a long and illustrious career that encompassed opera, concert work, films, radio, records, television, and nightclub. He is said to have earned over $5 million alone from his movie career, which included only nineteen feature films, and some two decades after his film career faded, he was still able to command $5,000 a week for club engagements. Perhaps the ultimate romantic male lead of film operetta (an image that would be parodied by later generations), Nelson Eddy was the heartthrob of millions of women who swooned to his blond good looks and baritone voice. He was also popular with men who liked his singing and somewhat self-effacing manner.

It is not surprising that Nelson Eddy took up music as a career, because his father, William Eddy, was a choir singer and drum major of the Rhode Island National Guard's First Regimental Band. His mother, Isabel Kendrick Eddy, was also a choir singer, and her mother (Caroline Kendrick) had sung opera with some success. Eddy was born June 29, 1901, in Providence, Rhode Island, and he learned to play the drums from his father. He sang in his church choir and later did solo church work as he grew older. In 1915, Nelson's parents separated, and he went to Philadelphia with his mother, where he quit school to go to work. Later, he earned his equivalency degree through night school. He worked many odd jobs, from drummer to newspaperman (selling classified ads), but by the early 1920s he was determined to make singing his career. Lacking money for music lessons, the young man studied voice by listening to opera records. He made his stage debut in 1922 in Philadelphia in *The Marriage Tax* and then won the lead in the Gilbert and Sullivan operetta *Iolanthe*. This led to work with both the Philadelphia Civic Opera (his first role being Amonasro in Giuseppe Verdi's opera *Aida*) and the Philadelphia Operatic Society, where he especially enjoyed singing Wagner.

In the mid-'20s, Eddy, sponsored by veteran opera singer/coach Dr. Edouard Lippe, journeyed to Europe to study voice in Paris and Dresden. However, he rejected offers to work there in opera, instead opting for success in America. Back in the United States, he sang Tonio in *Pagliacci* at the Metropolitan Opera in New York City—as a guest artist with the Philadelphia Civic Opera Company—and his repertoire included over thirty roles in a half dozen languages. In the late 1920s, out of financial necessity, he left opera for concertizing, teaming with pianist Theodore Paxson, who worked with him for the rest of his life. For the next several years, Eddy eked out a living doing concerts, with an occasional foray into opera, as in 1931 when he returned to the Metropolitan Opera to be the Drum Major in Alban Berg's modern opera *Wozzeck*, which was conducted by Leopold Stokowski.

In 1933, the singer was working in San Diego and was chosen as a last-minute substitute at the Philharmonic Auditorium in Los Angeles for famed singer Lotte Lehmann, who had become

Risë Stevens and Nelson Eddy in *The Chocolate Soldier* (1941).
[Courtesy of JC Archives]

ill; he drew a warm reception when he performed in her place. Ida Koverman, Louis B. Mayer's secretary at MGM, was in the audience, and the six-feet blond so impressed her with his vocalizing and stage presence that she urged Mayer to place him under studio contract. This the mogul did when he found out other studios were also vying to sign up the handsome baritone. Then, in typical manner, MGM could not decide what to do with Eddy and limited him to performing guest song stints in *Broadway to Hollywood* (1933), *Dancing Lady* (1933), and *Student Tour* (1934). By now, the studio had lost interest in him, and Eddy returned to concert work.

In 1935, MGM was planning to produce the well-known Rudolf Friml operetta, *Naughty Marietta*, as a vehicle for its singing star Jeanette MacDonald. Upon the urging of Ida Koverman, Nelson was tested and assigned the male lead. (Allan Jones had been an earlier choice but was already obligated to stage work during the film's shooting schedule.) The slickly produced version, set in pioneer Louisiana, with Eddy as the dashing Yankee military man who comes to the aid of a princess (MacDonald), was a huge success. Eddy scored with audiences (particularly women) as he sang, "Ah, Sweet Mystery of Life," "Tramp, Tramp, Tramp," "'Neath the Southern Moon," and "I'm Falling in Love With Someone." *Naughty Marietta* was the first of seven screen teamings of Jeanette MacDonald and Nelson Eddy. It was followed the next year by *Rose-Marie*, which was originally to have teamed Eddy with Metropolitan Opera star Grace Moore. Herein, he was the handsome Canadian police officer who sang the title song and "The Mounties," while he and Jeanette MacDonald attained screen immortality with their duet of "Indian Love Call." They recorded the song for Victor at the time, and in 1959, after being in continuous print for over twenty years, it was designated as a gold record, having sold over one million copies.

The third screen teaming of Eddy and MacDonald in *Maytime* (1937) almost did not happen. Once again, the plan was to pair Eddy with Grace Moore, but when she was unavailable, Jeanette was substituted. Partway through the making of this musical epic, MGM production executive Irving Thalberg died, and the color filming was halted and scrapped. Later, with a revised script, new supporting players, and now in black-and-white, shooting started all over. *Maytime* was a schmaltzy Victor Herbert romance, set in Europe. The two stars appeared as young singers in love, but unfortunately, Jeanette was already promised to her older music teacher/sponsor (John Barrymore). This entry provided Nelson and Jeanette with two good songs, "Will You Remember?" and "Farewell to Dreams." The same year, 1937, found Eddy in his first solo-starring screen vehicle, *Rosalie*, where he played a West Point football hero who romances a princess (Eleanor Powell). The title song became one of the most requested in his repertoire.

By now Nelson Eddy was receiving over 6,000 fan letters per week, mostly from women, and he was in big demand for personal appearances. From 1937 to 1939 he was a regular on NBC radio's *The Chase and Sanborn Hour* and in 1937 and 1938 he headlined that program's summer entries.

It was no secret on the MGM lot that Nelson Eddy and Jeanette MacDonald did not especially care for one another professionally, but there was money for all concerned in their continued screen teamings. In 1938, they made two more screen operettas: *The Girl of the Golden West* and *Sweethearts*. The former showcased them as lovers, with saloon girl Jeanette playing cards with a sheriff (Walter Pidgeon) to win Eddy's freedom from the law. *Sweethearts* was MGM's first full-length Technicolor production, and the contemporary plot showcased the two stars as stage singing partners who feud, break up, and then reunite. Neither picture provided the duo with noteworthy songs, but the latter was far more popular. All during this period and later, Eddy and MacDonald frequently re-created their landmark operetta roles for radio editions.

To appease Eddy and MacDonald, who each wanted solo star billing (and to market their popularity to the maximum), MGM agreed to headline each of them in separate vehicles. In 1939 Eddy starred in two productions without Miss MacDonald and he proved he could definitely carry a vehicle on his own. Over the years, it has been fashionable to poke fun at Eddy's acting acumen, but a closer look at his pictures show he was a more-than-adequate thespian who, on several occasions, was simply overpowered by ponderous scripts. This was not the case with *Let Freedom Ring* (1939), where he was excellent as the scion of a rich family who sides with homesteaders against a corrupt land baron (Edward Arnold). A highlight of the production was his singing of "America."

Next came the glossy, but top-heavy, *Balalaika*, with Eddy as a Russian Cossack prince in love with a beautiful singer (Ilona Massey) whose father (Lionel Atwill) is a Bolshevik, all on the eve of the Russian Revolution. This overlong production did give Eddy the opportunity to sing "The Volga Boatman" and "At the Balalaika," the latter being a fine-selling record for him on Columbia Records. He had joined that company in 1938, and would continue to record for Columbia well into the 1950s, doing a variety of projects that ranged from popular songs to opera to Stephen Foster melodies to Gilbert and Sullivan patter songs.

Despite persistent rumors that he and Jeanette MacDonald were lovers off-camera, Eddy married Ann Denitz Franklin, the ex-wife of MGM film director Sidney Franklin, early in 1939, and they remained together for the rest of his life. She was three years his senior and had a son by her prior marriage.

New Moon, the first of two 1940 pairings of MacDonald and Eddy, breathed fresh life into their popularity. It was a tale set in Colonial Louisiana, with French political prisoner Eddy harbored by Jeanette, the daughter of a wealthy businessman. A quartet of Sigmund Romberg standards highlighted the story: "Stout-Hearted Men," "Softly, As in the Morning Sunrise," "Wanting You," and "Lover Come Back to Me." Not so good was the songsters' next entry, *Bitter Sweet*. With the stars as lovers in nineteenth-century Vienna, its prime asset was their dueting "I'll See You Again."

Not much better was Nelson's pairing with Metropolitan Opera diva Risë Stevens for *The Chocolate Soldier* in 1941, where the star pretended to be a Cossack to test the love of his wife (Stevens). Eddy performed the title song, "My Hero," and "Sympathy." Jeanette and Nelson were teamed for a seventh and final time on-camera in the long-delayed production of *I Married an Angel* (1942), with Jeanette in the title role romancing a wealthy count (Eddy). His recording of the title song was very successful, but the movie was vapid. Eddy explained later, "Everybody on the lot told us it was either going to be the best picture we ever did, or the worst. It was the worst. It took the studio years to figure out how to present it without offending anybody, and then they slashed it to pieces. When we finally finished it, it was a horrible mess." While the MacDonald-Eddy productions were still profitable ventures for MGM, the studio was having great difficulty in finding additional properties congenial to both stars. It was obvious on-camera that the two luminaries were no longer young, and World War II had shut out much of the lucrative overseas market. Both stars soon left MGM.

In 1943, Eddy went to Universal to star in the studio's remake of *The Phantom of the Opera*. A posh production, it gave him the opportunity to sing several opera sequences as well as romance beautiful Susanna Foster, who was lusted after by the Phantom (Claude Rains). Next he headlined *Knickerbocker Holiday* (1946) for United Artists, a disappointing film version of the Kurt Weill–Maxwell Anderson play. Eddy was a rebellious newsman in Dutch New Amsterdam at odds with Peter Stuyvesant (Charles Coburn) over politics and Constance Dowling. There was talk of RKO producing a new MacDonald-Eddy songfest, but that came to naught. It was two years before Eddy was heard on the screen again. He supplied the voice of the singing whale in Walt Disney's *Make Mine Music* (1946). Eddy, in fact, did all the voices in the film's finale sequence "The Whale Who Wanted to Sing at the Met." The star's final movie appearance came in *Northwest Outpost* (1947) for Republic, with an original screen score by Rudolf Friml, who had done the music for *Naughty Marietta* and *Rose-Marie*. The resultant movie was ponderous at best in its telling of frontier ranger Eddy fighting corrupt nobleman Joseph Schildkraut and winning the love of the latter's wife (Ilona Massey).

Nelson Eddy never again appeared on the big screen, although he continued to receive movie offers, both solo and in tandem with Jeanette MacDonald. In the 1940s, he earned up to $15,000 a week by concertizing and he continued to be quite active on radio. Not only was he a guest star on many musical programs, but during the summers of 1947 and 1948 he also headlined *The Nelson Eddy Show* on NBC as a summer replacement for the *Kraft Music Hall*. In his September 16, 1948 program, he reteamed with guest Jeanette MacDonald.

In the early 1950s, Eddy filmed a pilot for a TV series that did not sell. Then he joined with beautiful actress/soprano Gale Sherwood in doing a nightclub act that made them worldwide popular attractions. (They did the act forty weeks out of every year for the remainder of Eddy's life.) On May 7, 1955, he had the starring role in NBC-TV's production of *The Desert Song* with Gale Sherwood, and he also recorded the score for Columbia Records. On that label, Eddy had duets with Jo Stafford, and he also made guest appearances on TV's *The Danny Thomas Show* and *The Gordon MacRae Show*, the latter appearance reuniting him in song with Jeanette MacDonald. In 1958, Jeanette and Nelson recorded the album *Jeanette MacDonald and Nelson Eddy Favorites*, and it became a best-seller for RCA, becoming a gold album in 1967. When MacDonald died in 1965, Eddy sang "Ah, Sweet Mystery of Life" at her funeral. She willed him a print of *Rose-Marie* because he had never saved any memorabilia from his lengthy career.

Throughout the 1960s, Nelson Eddy and Gale Sherwood continued their club touring, commanding $5,000 per week in salary. In the early 1960s, he cut three record albums for Everest Records, one a duet with Gale Sherwood. In 1965, they appeared on ABC-TV's *The Hollywood Palace*, and Eddy's popularity was such he was still receiving an average of one hundred fan letters weekly. Early in 1967, the duo had a successful Australian tour and returned to the United States to fulfill their year's bookings. On December 31, 1966, they appeared on Guy Lombardo's New Year's Eve program, and Eddy was in top voice as he sang many of the songs associated with his long career. On March 6, 1967, Eddy and Sherwood were appearing at a Miami Beach Hotel when Nelson became ill onstage. His singing partner helped him to his dressing room; he had suffered a stroke. He died the next day as Sherwood held his hand. Eddy was survived by his wife and was buried next to his mother's grave in Hollywood's Memorial Park Cemetery (later renamed Hollywood Forever).

Unlike many singers of his day, Nelson Eddy continues to be popular through the reshowing of his movies theatrically, on television, and via cassettes and DVDs, the constant reissuance of his recordings on a variety of labels, and through the devoted efforts of the Jeanette MacDonald–Nelson Eddy International Fan Club. In 1994, Sharon Rich, president of the duo's fan club, wrote a biography of the two called *Sweethearts*. In it she claimed that Nelson and Jeanette were longtime lovers whose on-and-off but deeply passionate affair started in the mid-'30s and continued until MacDonald's death in 1965. She further alleged that both Eddy and MacDonald had sham marriages that were used to mask their romantic relationship.

Filmography

Broadway to Hollywood [Ring Up the Curtain]
(MGM, 1933)
Dancing Lady (MGM, 1933)
Student Tour (MGM, 1934)
Naughty Marietta (MGM, 1935)
Rose-Marie (MGM, 1936)
Maytime (MGM, 1937)
Rosalie (MGM, 1937)
Girl of the Golden West (MGM, 1938)
Sweethearts (MGM, 1938)
Let Freedom Ring (MGM, 1939)

Balalaika (MGM, 1939)
New Moon (MGM, 1940)
Bitter Sweet (MGM, 1940)
The Chocolate Soldier (MGM, 1941)
I Married an Angel (MGM, 1942)
The Phantom of the Opera (Univ, 1943)
Knickerbocker Holiday (UA, 1944)
Make Mine Music (RKO, 1946) (voice only)
Northwest Outpost [End of the Rainbow] (Rep, 1947)

Radio Series

Hoffman Varity Hour (Mutual, 1932)
Vick's Open House (CBS, 1935–38)
Voice of Firestone (NBC, 1935–36)
The Chase and Sanborn Hour (NBC, 1937–39)
The Charlie McCarthy Summer Show (NBC, 1937, 1938)

The Nelson Eddy Show (NBC, 1943–44)
Bell Telephone Hour (NBC, 1943–44)
The Electric Hour (CBS, 1944–46)
Kraft Music Hall (NBC, 1947, 1948, 1949)

Album Discography

LPs

The Artistry of Nelson Eddy (Everest 3292)
Balalaika (Caliban 6004) [ST]
Because (Har HL-7151)
The Best Loved Carols of Christmas (Har HL-7201)
Bitter Sweet (Amalgamated 200) [ST/R]
By Request (10″ Col ML-2037)
The Chocolate Soldier/Naughty Marietta (Columbia Special Products P-13707)
Christmas Songs (Col ML-4442)
The Desert Song (Col ML-4636, Col CL-831, Columbia Special Products ACL-831) w. Doretta Morrow
The Desert Song (Mac/Eddy JN 116) [ST/TV] w. Gale Sherwood
Gilbert and Sullivan Patter Songs (Col ML-4027)
Great Songs of Faith (10″ Col ML-2166)
Greatest Hits (Col CL-2681/CS-9481, CBS 32312)
I Married an Angel (Caliban 6004) [ST]

Jeanette MacDonald & Nelson Eddy (Mac/Eddy JN 111)
Jeanette MacDonald & Nelson Eddy (Murray Hill X14078)
Jeanette MacDonald & Nelson Eddy (RCA LPV-526)
Jeanette MacDonald & Nelson Eddy—Christmas Album (Mac/Eddy JN-119)
Jeanette MacDonald & Nelson Eddy Favorites (RCA LPM/LSP-1738, RCA ANL1-1075)
Jeanette MacDonald & Nelson Eddy—Legendary Performers (RCA CPL1-2468)
Jeanette MacDonald and Nelson Eddy: Patriotic Songs (Mac/Eddy JN 118)
Jeanette MacDonald & Nelson Eddy—Religious Songs (Mac/Eddy JN-127)
Jeanette MacDonald & Nelson Eddy—The Early Years (Mac/Eddy JN 110)
Jeanette MacDonald & Nelson Eddy—Together Again (Sandy Hook 2101)

The Lord's Prayer (Har HL-7254)

Love Songs (Everest FS-354) w. Gale Sherwood

Love Songs From Foreign Lands (10″ Col ML-2130)

Mail Call (Mac/Eddy JN-129) w. Jeanette MacDonald, Ronald Colman, George Burns, and Gracie Allen

Maytime (Pelican 121, Sandy Hook 2008) [ST/R]

Naughty Marietta (10″ Col ML-2094)

Naughty Marietta (Hollywood Soundstage 413) [ST]

Naughty Marietta (Pelican 117) [ST/R]

Nelson and the Ladies (Sounds Rare 5002) w. Jeanette MacDonald, Risë Stevens, Ann Jamison

Nelson Eddy (Empire 806)

Nelson Eddy (Scala 887) w. Gale Sherwood

Nelson Eddy & Gale Sherwood (Everest 9002/8002)

Nelson Eddy & Ilona Massey (Mac/Eddy JN-126)

Nelson Eddy & Jeanette MacDonald (Nostalgia LPF 222009)

Nelson Eddy & Jeanette MacDonald—America's Singing Sweethearts (RCA/Suffolk Marketing DVM1-0301)

Nelson Eddy Favorites (Camden (CAL-492)

Nelson Eddy on the Air (Totem 1035) w. Jeanette MacDonald

Nelson Eddy Selections From Chase and Sanborn Hour (Mac/Eddy JN 113)

The Nelson Eddy Show (Mac/Eddy JN 101, JN 102, JN 103, JN 106, JN 107)

Nelson Eddy Sings (Col CL-812)

Nelson Eddy Sings the Songs of Stephen Foster (Col ML-4090)

Nelson Eddy With Isabel Eddy and Caroline Kendrick (Mac/Eddy JN 121)

Nelson Eddy With Shirley Temple, Jane Powell, Kathryn Grayson, Lois Butler, and Norma Nelson (Mac/Eddy JN 128)

New Moon (10″ Col ML-2164)

New Moon/I Married an Angel (Pelican 103) [ST/R]

New Moon/Rose-Marie (Columbia Special Products P-13878)

Of Girls I Sing (Everest 9006/8006)

Oklahoma! (Col ML-4598, Col CL-828/CS-8739, Har HL-7364/HS 1164)

Operatic and Song Recital (OASI 610)

Operatic Recital: 1938-48 (Mac/Eddy JN 105) w. Dorothy Kirsten, Anne Jamison, Nadine Connor

Operatic Recitals II (Mac/Eddy JN 114)

Operatic Recitals III (Mac/Eddy JN 123) w. Jeanette MacDonald

Operetta Favorites by Jeanette MacDonald and Nelson Eddy (10″ RCA LCT-16)

Our Love (Sunset 11276/5176) w. Gale Sherwood

The Phantom of the Opera (Mac/Eddy 124) [ST/R]

The Phantom of the Opera (Sountrak 114) [ST]

Rose-Marie (10″ Col ML-2178)

Rose-Marie (Hollywood Soundstage 414) [ST]

Rose-Marie/Naughty Marietta/I Married an Angel/Bitter Sweet (Sandy Hook 3-SH-1) [ST]

Rose-Marie/New Moon/Naughty Marietta (Col GB-3)

Russian Songs and Arias (Mac/Eddy JN 108)

Song Jamboree (10″ Col ML-2091)

Songs We Love (Col ML-4343)

The Story of a Starry Night (Everest 9004/8004)

Stout-Hearted Men (Har HL-7142/HS-11246)

The Student Prince/The Chocolate Soldier (Col ML-4060) w. Risë Stevens

Sweethearts (The Good Music Record Company/RCA Special Products DMM2-0876) w.Jeanette MacDonald

Sweethearts (Pelican 143, Sandy Hook 2025) [ST/R]

Till the End of Time (Sunset 1143/5143)

The Torch Singer and the Mountie (Amalgamated 205) w. Helen Morgan, Gale Sherwood, Guy Lombardo

The World's Favorite Love Songs (Sunset 50261) w. Jan Peerce

CDs

Ah, Sweet Mystery of Life (Pearl PAST-CD-7026) w. Jeanette MacDonald

Always Together (Hallmark 301672) w. Jeanette MacDonald

America's Singing Sweethearts (The Beautiful Music Company/RCA Special Products DMC1-1001) w. Jeanette MacDonald

The Artistry of Nelson Eddy (Legacy International CD-370)

The Best of Jeanette MacDonald and Nelson Eddy (Sound Waves—no number)

Change Partners (Box Office Records 2793) w. Jeanette MacDonald

Cocktail Hour (Columbia River Entertainment Group 218065) w. Jeanette MacDonald

Dream Lover (Flapper PAST-CD-7824; Jasmine JASCD-2558) w. Jeanette MacDonald

Greatest Hits (Sony Music Special Products A24298)

Indian Love Call (Golden Options GO-3822) w. Jeanette MacDonald

Interviews #1 (Mac/Eddy JN-136) w. Jeanette MacDonald

Interviews #2 (Mac/Eddy JN-137) w. Jeanette MacDonald

In the Still of the Night (Laserlight 12-597)

Jeanette MacDonald & Nelson Eddy (Again LBACD-004)

Jeanette MacDonald & Nelson Eddy (Sounds of a Century 1835)

Just for Tonight (Collectors' Choice Music CCM-1023)

Legendary Performers (Great Movie Themes 60012) w. Jeanette MacDonald

Love's Old Song (Master Song 503132) w. Jeanette MacDonald

Love's Old Sweet Song (Conifer MCHD-150)

Musical Favourites (Pegasus PGNCD-8081) w. Jeanette MacDonald

Nelson Eddy & Jeanette MacDonald (The Good Music Record Company—no number)

The Night Club Act (Mac/Eddy JN-134)

Oklahoma (Sony Broadway 53326)

Ol' Man River (Mac/Eddy JN-133)

The Old Refrain (ASV CD-AJA-5409)

Opera Arias (Pearl Koch 92)

The Phantom of the Opera (Facet 8115) [ST/R]

Portrait of Nelson Eddy (Gallerie 431)

Radio Songs (Mac/Eddy JN-131)

Rose-Marie (All Star ALS-23111)

Rose-Marie (Delta—no number) w. Jeanette MacDonald

Rose-Marie (Music CD-6226) w. Jeanette MacDonald

Rose-Marie (ProArte CDD-491)

16 Classic Performances (Javelin CWN-CD-2025)

16 Most Requested Songs (Javelin CWN-CD-2042) w. Jeanette MacDonald

Smilin' Through (Memoir CDMOIR-436)

Songs for Christmas (Sony Classical SFK-60800)

Stout-Hearted Men (The Good Music Record Company CPP-SMK)

Sweethearts—20 Favorites (Prism PLATCD-140) w. Jeanette MacDonald

Sweethearts (RCA Special Products DMC1-0876) w. Jeanette MacDonald

Through the Years (ASV CD-AJA-5254)

Together Again (Sandy Hook CDSH-2101) w. Jeanette MacDonald

The Very Best of Jeanette MacDonald & Nelson Eddy (Soundwaves SWNCD005)

When I'm Calling You (ASV CD-AJA-5124) w. Jeanette MacDonald

Cliff "Ukulele Ike" Edwards

(b. Clifton A. Edwards, Hannibal, Missouri, June 14, 1895; d. Hollywood, California, July 21, 1971)

When Cliff Edwards died in the summer of 1971, he was a welfare patient whose body went unclaimed. This was the same jovial, wide-eyed man who was so proficient as a high, clear tenor singer, ukulele player, and actor that he starred on Broadway, in films, radio, television, and vaudeville, and who, as a recording artist, sold over 70 million records. With the coming of sound, Cliff Edwards came to Hollywood movies as a singing star and developed into a fine comic character performer, appearing in nearly one hundred movies.

Clifton A. Edwards was born in Hannibal, Missouri, on June 14, 1895, the son of railroad worker Edward Edwards and Nellie Farnus Edwards. He quit school while still a boy to support his family, which included three younger siblings, after his father became too ill to work. He held a variety of jobs and for several years worked in a shoe factory. During this period, he began entertaining, and he later worked in a movie house singing to lantern-slide-illustrated song programs. He also learned to make sound effects for the silent films, effects he would later use in his singing act. From St. Louis, where he had worked in the movie house, Cliff joined a carnival and then eked a meager living by singing in saloons for loose change. It was here he took up the ukulele for accompaniment and soon acquired his professional nickname. The story goes that a waiter could not remember his name and just called him Ike and, because he strummed the uke, he became known as Ukulele Ike.

By the late 1910s, Edwards was working in Chicago, singing at the Arsonia Hotel's club venue, where he met songwriter Bob Carleton. He introduced the latter's new novelty tune "Ja Da," which soon swept the nation in popularity and gave some prestige to Cliff, although he never recorded the song until 1956. Next Edwards teamed with comic Joe Frisco for a vaudeville engagement at New York City's Palace Theater, and then the pair joined the cast of *Ziegfeld Follies of 1918*. When that stage engagement ended, the performer returned alone to Chicago, where he joined with singer/dancer Pierce Keegan in an act they called "Jazz As Is." The duo subsequently appeared in Ziegfeld's new *Midnight Frolics* (atop the New Amsterdam Theater in Manhattan), and when the late-evening revue closed in 1920, the duo toured in vaudeville, even making several unissued records for the Columbia label. Next, Edwards teamed with Lou Clayton (later better known as a partner in the team of Clayton-Jackson-Durante) for a short time, and in 1922 he began making records for Gennett, a label owned by the Starr Piano Company. Cliff also made his film debut in the silent picture *Sunflower Sue* (1924), but it was never issued. Meanwhile, from 1919 to 1921 he was married to Gertrude Benson and they had a son, Clifton Jr.

Late in 1923, Cliff began recording for the Pathé Phonography and Radio Company in New York City, and during his four years with the firm he developed into one of the biggest-selling recording artists in popular music. Among his best-sellers, issued both on the Pathé and Perfect

Josephine Hutchinson, George Murphy, and Cliff "Ukulele Ike" Edwards in *The Women Men Marry* (1937). [Courtesy of JC Archives]

labels, were "Where the Lazy Daisies Grow," "When My Sweetie Puts Her Lovin' On," "June Night" (which sold over three million copies), and "I Can't Believe That You're in Love With Me."

Coupled with his newfound success on records, Cliff took Broadway by storm when he appeared with Walter Catlett and Fred and Adele Astaire in George Gershwin's musical *Lady Be Good*, singing "Fascinatin' Rhythm." The show debuted in December 1924 at the Liberty Theater and ran for 330 performances. Edwards next appeared with Marilyn Miller and Clifton Webb in *Sunny* (1925). The show was written by the team of Otto Harbach–Oscar Hammerstein II–Jerome Kern, and Cliff sang "I'm Moving Away." This was followed in August 1927 by the new edition of the *Ziegfeld Follies*, which featured Edwards performing "Shakin' the Blues Away" (also done in the revue show by Ruth Etting) and "Everybody Loves My Girl."

Following his Broadway prosperity, Edwards returned to vaudeville, earning several thousand dollars per week with his popular act. In 1928, while appearing in Los Angeles, he was signed by Metro-Goldwyn-Mayer to make two film shorts, each featuring him performing two songs. Caught up in turning out a rash of sound musical features, MGM signed him to a contract. The stocky performer made his talkie feature film debut in Marion Davies's *Marianne* (1929) as a doughboy in World War I France, singing four songs, including "Hang on to Me" and "Just You, Just Me." Edwards's biggest screen success came in *The Hollywood Revue of 1929*, in which he performed "Singin' in the Rain." He had a best-selling record of the song on Columbia Records, a label he had signed with late in 1927 after leaving Pathé. Cliff continued to have hit records for Columbia, including "Mary Ann," "Reaching for Someone," and "I'll See You in My Dreams."

Edwards continued to appear in MGM movies throughout the 1930s, but surprisingly, despite his musical talent, he was cast primarily in dramatic assignments. In most instances he played comical characters, although he occasionally won sympathetic parts, like Joan Crawford's newspaper friend who is shot in the gangster tale *Dance, Fools, Dance* (1931). *Variety* approved of his acting in this more dramatic part, stating "Cliff is good all the way and in a likable role with sentiment attached." In 1930, Edwards's second wife Irene Wylie, whom he had wed in 1923, sued him for divorce. After a headline-making trial, she was awarded all their property and one-half of Cliff's income for life. Undaunted, in 1932 he wed actress Nancy Dover, but they parted in 1936. For the rest of his working days, he would be plagued with financial problems, filing for bankruptcy on three occasions. (Edwards was noted for spending huge sums on gambling, alcohol, and cocaine.)

Despite his persistent financial woes, Cliff continued to be professionally in demand. Although his Columbia recording contract concluded in 1930, he resumed recording in 1932 for the American Record Corporation, which distributed its discs on the Brunswick label. Edwards also made regular appearances on Rudy Vallee's radio program, *The Fleischmann Hour*. In the summer of 1932, he hosted his own fifteen-minute radio show on CBS, and around this time, he signed with talent producer Ted Collins, who also managed Kate Smith. Together he and Smith appeared in the vaudeville presentation *Kate Smith and Her Swanee Music Revue* at New York's Palace Theater. When *Kate Smith's Matinee Hour* debuted on CBS radio in the fall of 1934, Cliff was a show regular. The previous spring he had worked in London, where he recorded for English Brunswick, and in October 1934, he resumed recording for the American Record Corporation, which now issued his discs on a variety of dime-store labels such as Melotone, Oriole, Perfect, Banner, and Rex. By 1936, Edwards's record fortunes had sunk so low that—without billing—he made a series of risqué party records for Novelty Record Distributors in Hollywood.

Late in 1935, Cliff made his final Broadway bow in *George White's Scandals of 1936* (he had previously had good roles in the movie musicals *George White's Scandals* [1934] and *George White's 1935 Scandals* [1935]). However, Edwards's leading role was short-lived because, upon the request of producer White, he was replaced in the key assignment by Rudy Vallee and was forced to accept a lesser role in the show. A few weeks later, Vallee and White had a fistfight backstage. During the arbitration hearing, Edwards testified against Vallee, who had by then quit the production. As a result, Edwards returned to his leading part, but the show quickly folded.

The performer continued to makes films, mostly at MGM, with interesting roles in *Saratoga* (1937), *Bad Man of Brimstone* (1938), *Maisie* (1939), and *His Girl Friday* (1940), but his part as the reminiscing soldier in *Gone With the Wind* (1939) was so tiny that Cliff was only heard and *not* seen. Another voice-only characterization, however, somewhat renewed Edwards's popularity when he supplied the voice of antic Jiminy Cricket in Walt Disney's animated cartoon feature *Pinocchio* (1940), singing the Oscar-winning song "When You Wish Upon a Star." As a result, Edwards's film career was relaunched, and he appeared in numerous films, even having sidekick parts in "B" Westerns opposite Charles Starrett at Columbia and Tim Holt at RKO Radio. One of his best-remembered performances was another voice-over, that of the crow singing "When I See an Elephant Fly" in *Dumbo* (1941).

Edwards continued to make records, for Decca in 1936 and 1939, and in 1940 and 1941, he recorded the various songs he sang in the Disney productions for Victor. In 1943, he began recording radio transcriptions (noncommercial records sold directly to radio stations) for C. P. MacGregor and Lang-Worth, and in 1944 he headlined a five-minute weekday morning show on the Mutual radio network. Also that year he recorded thirty programs called *The Cliff Edwards Show* for Tower Transcriptions, which were syndicated to radio stations throughout the country.

From March to September 1946, Edwards starred on the weekly *The Cliff Edwards Show* on ABC radio. During the late 1940s, work became less frequent for Cliff, although he had a brief record session with Mercury in 1949 and he recorded children's records for Victor in 1950. In the spring of 1949, he began a run on network television in the fifteen-minute *The Cliff Edwards Show* on CBS-TV, telecast three evenings a week. At the same time, he was a regular on another CBS show, *The 54th Street Revue*, and he made guest appearances on network TV with Ken Murray and Kate Smith. Late in 1951, Cliff embarked on a brief but successful tour of Australia, and while there he recorded two songs for the Fidelity record label.

In the mid-'50s, Cliff Edwards had a marked resurgence in his career thanks to Walt Disney's weekly television program that used his recording of "When You Wish Upon a Star" as its theme song. As a result, he became the voice of Jiminy Cricket again in numerous animated short films, and he worked on *The Mickey Mouse Club* TV show as well as appearing in the Disney feature *The Littlest Outlaw* (1955). In 1955, Cliff did television commercials for Nash cars. The next year, the veteran talent recorded an album for Disneyland Records called *Ukulele Ike Sings Again*. Edwards continued to work until the mid-'60s, by which time his alcohol addiction made him unemployable. In the late 1960s, he lived in a small apartment on Hollywood Boulevard in Tinseltown. By now he was suffering from circulatory problems in his legs. In 1969, he was moved to a nursing home as a relief patient of the Actor's Fund. He died there penniless on July 21, 1971, of heart failure. No one claimed his body, and the destitute onetime star was buried in North Hollywood. Later in the decade, his recording of "When You Wish Upon a Star" was heard on the soundtrack of *Close Encounters of the Third Kind* (1977).

Like most people who exist purely for the moment, Cliff Edwards, in later life, claimed to have had no regrets about his considerably up-and-down existence over the decades.

Filmography

Sunflower Sue (Unissued, 1924)
Ukulele Ike (MGM, 1928) (s)
Ukulele Ike #2 (MGM, 1928) (s)
Marianne (MGM, 1929)
The Hollywood Revue of 1929 (MGM, 1929)
So This Is College (MGM, 1929)
Dough Boys (MGM, 1930)

Good News (MGM, 1930)
Lord Byron of Broadway (MGM, 1930)
Montana Moon (MGM, 1930)
The Voice of Hollywood #10 (Tif, 1930) (s)
Dogway Melody (MGM, 1930) (s) (voice only)
Great Day (MGM, 1930) (unfinished)
Those Three French Girls (MGM, 1930)

Way Out West (MGM, 1930)
Dance, Fools, Dance (MGM, 1931)
The Great Lover (MGM, 1931)
Laughing Sinners (MGM, 1931)
Stepping Out (MGM, 1931)
Parlor, Bedroom and Bath (MGM, 1931)
The Prodigal (MGM, 1931)
Shipmates (MGM, 1931)
Sidewalks of New York, (MGM, 1931)
The Sin of Madelon Claudet (MGM, 1931)
Fast Life (MGM, 1932)
Hell Divers (MGM, 1932)
Paramount Pictorial #3 (Par, 1932) (s)
The World at Large (UM & M Pictorial, 1932) (s)
Young Bride (MGM, 1932)
Hollywood on Parade #12 (Par, 1933) (s)
Flying Devils (MGM, 1933)
Strange Case of Hennessy (RKO, 1933) (s)
Take a Chance (Par, 1933)
George White's Scandals (Fox, 1934)
George White's 1935 Scandals (Fox, 1935)
Red Salute (Fox, 1935)
The Man I Marry (Univ, 1936)
Bad Guy (MGM, 1937)
Between Two Women (MGM, 1937)
Saratoga (MGM, 1937)
They Gave Him a Gun (MGM, 1937)
The Women Men Marry (MGM, 1937)
Bad Man of Brimstone (MGM, 1938)
The Girl of the Golden West (MGM, 1938)
Little Adventuress (Col, 1938)
Maisie (MGM, 1939)
Royal Rodeo (Vita, 1939) (s)
Smuggled Cargo (Rep, 1939)
Ride Cowboy Ride (Vita, 1939) (s)
Gone With the Wind (MGM, 1939)
Flowing Gold (WB, 1940)
Cliff Edwards and His Musical Buckaroos (Vita, 1940) (s)
Friendly Neighbors (Rep, 1940)
Just a Cute Kid (Vita, 1940) (s)
High School (20th-Fox, 1940)

His Girl Friday (Col, 1940)
Millionaires in Prison (RKO, 1940)
Pinocchio (RKO, 1940) (voice only)
Dumbo (RKO, 1941) (voice only)
Jeannie With the Light Brown Hair (Soundies, 1941) (s)
International Squadron (WB, 1941)
Knockout (WB, 1941)
Thunder Over the Prairie (Col, 1941)
Riders of the Badlands (Col, 1941)
The Monster and the Girl (Par, 1941)
Power Dive (Par, 1941)
Prairie Stranger (Col, 1941)
She Couldn't Say No (WB, 1941)
The New Spirit (RKO, 1942) (s)
American Empire (UA, 1942)
Bandit Ranger (RKO, 1942)
Pirates of the Prairie (RKO, 1942)
Red River Robin Hood (RKO, 1942)
Bad Men of the Hills (Col, 1942)
Lawless Plainsmen (Col, 1942)
Riders of the Northland (Col, 1942)
Seven Miles From Alcatraz (RKO, 1942)
Picture People #12 (RKO, 1942) (s)
Overland to Deadwood (Col, 1942)
Sundown Jim (20th-Fox, 1942)
West of Tombstone (Col, 1942)
The Falcon Strikes Back (RKO, 1943)
Sagebrush Law (RKO, 1943)
The Avenging Rider (RKO, 1943)
Minnie, My Mountain Moocher (Soundies, 1943) (s)
Paddlin' Madeline Home (Soundies, 1943) (s)
Fighting Frontier (RKO, 1943)
Salute for Three (Par, 1943)
Between the Devil and the Deep Blue Sea (Soundies, 1944) (s)
Movieland Magic (Vita, 1945) (s)
Hollywood Wonderland (Vita, 1946) (s)
Fun and Fancy Free (RKO, 1947) (voice only)
The Littlest Outlaw (BV, 1955)
The Man From Button Willow (United Screen Arts, 1964) (voice only)

Broadway Plays

The Ziegfeld Follies (1918)
Lady Be Good (1924)
Sunny (1925)

The Ziegfeld Follies (1927)
George White's Scandals of 1936 (1935)

Radio Series

The Cliff Edwards Show (CBS, 1932, 1934)
Variety Hour (CBS, 1934)
Kate Smith's Matinee Hour (CBS, 1934)

The Cliff Edwards Show (Mutual, 1944; Synd, 1944; ABC, 1946)

TV Series

The Cliff Edwards Show (CBS, 1949)

The 54th Street Revue (CBS, 1949)

Album Discography

LPs

Cliff Edwards (10″ Bateau Chinois A-1)
Cliff Edwards and His Hot Combination 1925-26 (Fountain LFV-203)
Cliff Edwards, Vols. 1-2 (10″ Ristic 39, 42)
Dumbo (Disneyland 1204) [ST]
Fascinatin' Rhythm (Totem 1045)
I Want a Girl (Totem 1014)
I'm a Bear in a Lady's Boudoir (Yazoo 1047)
Lady Be Good (Smithsonian R-008) [OC]

The Littlest Outlaw (Disneyland DQ-1246) [ST]
Pinocchio (Disneyland 1202) [ST]
Remember (Blue Heaven 8-807)
Shakin' the Blues Away (Totem 1005)
Ukulele Ike (Glendale 6011)
Ukulele Ike Happens Again (Buena Vista 4043)
Ukulele Ike Sings Again (Disneyland 3003)
The Vintage Recordings of Cliff Edwards (Take Two TT-205)

CDs

Cliff Edwards (Sounds of a Century 1867)
Dumbo (Avex 12076, Walt Disney Records 60949-7, Walt Disney Records 860175) [ST]
Pinocchio (Walt Disney Records 60845) (ST)
Singin' in the Rain (ASV CD-AJA-5313)
Singin' in the Rain (Audiophile ACD-17)
Sunny (AEI 050) [OC]

The Vintage Recordings of Cliff Edwards (Ukulele Ike) (Take Two TT-419CD)
Ukulele Ike (Sony Music Special Products A26475)
Ukulele Ike—1930s Radio Transcriptions (Collectors' Choice CCM-018)
Ukulele Ike Sings Again (Walt Disney Records 60408CDMA)

Ruth Etting

(b. David City, Nebraska, November 23, 1896; d. Colorado Springs, Colorado, September 24, 1978)

Ruth Etting was probably the most popular female vocalist of the Roaring Twenties. Her high, clear voice and precise phrasing made her a natural for the popular tunes of the day, and coupled with her good looks, she epitomized the mature flapper of the Jazz Age. Her Columbia recordings in the last half of the 1920s sold in the millions, and she became a favorite Broadway attraction as well. In the 1930s, she also starred on radio and made dozens of appearances on the silver screen, but only a trio of these were in feature films. Lacking thespian abilities, Ruth mainly headlined short subjects, which showcased her good looks and sterling voice.

Sources vary on Etting's year of birth, placing it anywhere from 1896 to 1907, but most likely November 23, 1896, is correct. Her parents, Alfred and Winifred (Kleinhen) Etting, were farm folk, and she was born on their spread near David City, Nebraska. When Ruth was five, her mother became ill, and Ruth accompanied her to San Diego, California, where Mrs. Etting's family vainly attempted to nurse Winifred back to health. After her mother died, Ruth was brought back to live with her paternal grandparents in David City, where George Etting owned the Etting Roller Mills.

Ruth was not academically inclined, much preferring the world of show business. (Her grandfather had built the David City Opera House, and she loved to mingle with the circus and tent-show players who pitched camp on the vacant lot near the Etting Roller Mill. She sang in the Congregational Church choir, later recalling, "I sang in a high, squeaky soprano. It sounded terrible, but I didn't know I could sing in any other range.") After she graduated (barely) from high school, Ruth worked for a time in Omaha, Nebraska, in a department store and then went to Chicago to begin studies at the Academy of Fine Arts, planning to study costume design. She was interviewed by the manager of the Marigold Gardens nightclub to design costumes for the show there, but she ended up joining the chorus. She was soon featured as a singer at the Gardens. At this time, she met Moses "the Gimp" Snyder, an arrogant gangster who fell in love with her. Snyder immediately set about making her a star, and thanks to his connections, she soon was earning good bookings and salaries, none of which would have lasted had she not possessed sufficient talent on her own. She also began singing on radio, winning the title of "Chicago's Sweetheart." She married Snyder on July 12, 1922, in Crown Point, Indiana, and raised his two children from a previous marriage. Although her relationship with the hotheaded Snyder was constantly stormy, Ruth had a good rapport with her stepchildren and remained close to them throughout her life.

After the Marigold Gardens, Ruth began performing in the revue at the Rainbow Gardens and later at a variety of Chicago venues: the Green Mill, the Granada, the Terrace Gardens, and the Montmartre Café. She was heard on the Windy City's KYW radio in 1924 and began touring on the Midwestern vaudeville circuit. In the spring of 1924, Ruth made a test record for Victor

Ruth Etting in *Hips, Hips, Hooray* (1934).
[Courtesy of JC Archives]

in Chicago, and early in 1926, she had her first commercial record release on Columbia, "Let's Talk About My Sweetie" / "Nothing Else to Do."

By 1927, Moe Snyder had moved Ruth's base of operation to New York City. Years later, Ruth commented on her increasingly troublesome relationship with the obsessive underworld figure: "My sad story is that my first marriage wasn't a marriage at all. It was a mistake." Her recording career got into full swing in Gotham. For the next half dozen years, she recorded with Columbia and was soon known as "the Sweetheart of Columbia Records."

At first, she used only a piano accompanist on records, usually Rube Bloom or Arthur Shutt, but as her discs grew in popularity her arrangements became more elaborate. As the 1920s progressed, her background musicians included such jazz greats as violinist Joe Venuti, guitarist Eddie Lang, trumpeter Manny Klein, clarinetist Jimmy Dorsey, and trombonist Tommy Dorsey. Ruth always came to recording sessions well prepared, and these jazz musicians loved to work with her not only because of her professionalism but because the session usually finished early, giving them time to record their own specialty numbers. Ruth Etting had dozens of Columbia best-sellers from 1926 to 1932, including "My Blackbirds Are Bluebirds Now," "Love Me or Leave Me," "Ten Cents a Dance," and "A Faded Summer Love." She also helped to compose some of her own popular songs, like "When You're With Somebody Else."

In 1927, Ruth was appearing with Paul Whiteman and His Orchestra at the Paramount Theater in New York City. After hearing some of her recordings, leading songwriter Irving Berlin introduced her to producer Florenz Ziegfeld, who hired her at $400 weekly to appear in his new edition of the *Ziegfeld Follies*, for which Berlin was to do the music. She sang "Shaking the Blues Away" in the show and was a sensation. She kept her age a secret. "I fooled New Yorkers for a long time," she recalled years later. "They thought I was a kid. I was little and slim and blond. Very few people knew I'd been working around Chicago for almost ten years. Even Ziegfeld didn't have any idea of my age." After her success in the *Follies*, Ruth made personal appearances in Chicago (at a then enormous $8,000 weekly) and on the West Coast (at $1,000 weekly plus a percentage of the box office). The next year, she was featured in a new version of the *Ziegfeld Follies*, and during the same season she appeared on Broadway with Eddie Cantor in *Whoopee!*, popularizing the song, "Love Me or Leave Me." Next came 1929's *Ziegfeld Follies*, followed by *Simple Simon* with Ed Wynn in 1930. In the latter show, she made the Richard Rodgers–Lorenz Hart song "Ten Cents a Dance," which the composers rewrote for her, famous. Next came the brief-running the *Nine-Fifteen Revue* in 1930 and then 1931's *Ziegfeld Follies*, in which she revived the old Jack Norworth–Nora Bayes standard, "Shine On, Harvest Moon."

While appearing in *Whoopee!* in 1928, Ruth made her film debut in the Paramount one-reel talkie *Ruth Etting*, singing "Roses of Yesterday" and "Because My Baby Don't Mean 'Maybe' Now." She photographed well and sounded great, even on the primitive recording film techniques of the time, and quickly followed it with another short, *Paramount Movietone*, also shot in 1928 at the company's Astoria, Long Island, studio. In 1929, Warner Bros.–Vitaphone signed Ruth to a film contract, and in the next five years she starred in a host of one- and two-reel musical shorts for the studio. Typical of these cheaply made films is the 1930 two-reeler, *Roseland*, directed by Roy Mack and lensed at the Vitaphone Studios in Brooklyn. Here Ruth appears as a pretty dance-hall girl whose ordeals, before finding true love at the finale, permit her to sing two popular tunes, "Let Me Sing and I'm Happy" and "Dancing With Tears in My Eyes." *Artistic Temperament* (1932), also directed by Mack, has Ruth as a kitchen maid who becomes a big Broadway singing star only to a abandon it all and become a housewife for the man she adores. Along the way she warbles "That's What Heaven Means to Me," "What a Life," and "Loveable."

Coupled with her success on stage, records, and in movies, Ruth Etting ventured into radio in 1930, appearing with Walter Winchell on his first broadcast that year as well as on Rudy Vallee's *The Fleischmann Hour*. From 1932 to 1933, she headlined the *Chesterfield Satisfies* program on CBS, and in the summer of 1934 she appeared with Gus Arnheim and His Orchestra in *The Demi-Tasse Revue*. From 1934 to 1935, she was the featured attraction on another musical series on the NBC Blue network. She continued to guest-star on programs such as *The Majestic Hour, The Chase and Sanborn Hour, The Oldsmobile Show*, and *Kellogg's College Prom*.

In 1932, Ruth ended her association with Columbia Records and cut several singles for the American Record Corporation (ARC), which issued its product to various dime-store chains on labels like Melotone, Conqueror, Perfect, and Romeo. In 1933, she recorded with Brunswick (another ARC label), and after more sessions with that label the next year, she returned to Columbia, where she remained through 1935.

Ruth made her feature-film debut in the 1933 Samuel Goldwyn musical extravaganza *Roman Scandals*, starring Eddie Cantor. She was seen as Olga (a part that required very little acting) and was the centerpiece of a posh production interlude (filled with Goldwyn chorines) singing "No More Love." A second number, however, was cut after Cantor added too many comedy bits to the film's running time. *Variety* thought Ruth's handling of the Busby Berkeley–choreographed number was "socko." Two more feature films followed for Ruth, but again she was showcased in production numbers and not given dramatic parts. In *Hips, Hips Hooray* (1934), headlining the then-popular zany comedy team of Bert Wheeler and Robert Woolsey, she performed "Keeping Romance Alive." The same year she played herself in Universal's all-star radio tribute, *Gift of Gab*, singing "Talking to Myself" and "Tomorrow, Who Cares?" She was scheduled to be in RKO's *Strictly Dynamite* (1934) starring Lupe Velez, but by the time production began, her role had been written out of the scenario.

By the mid-'30s, Ruth was being dubbed "Queen of the Torch Singers" (a title she won in a national poll) and "America's Radio Sweetheart." In 1933, she signed with RKO Radio Pictures and through 1936 appeared in more than a dozen two-reelers for the studio (while continuing to appear in other companies' short-subject products). Like her previous Vitaphone miniatures, these entries were quite thin on plot but spotlighted the star in musical renditions. Still, there was repetition as Ruth sang "Shine On, Harvest Moon" in *California Weather* (1933), *A Torch Tango* (1934), and *Tuned Out* (1935) as well as on the Vitaphone shorts *The Song of Fame* (1934) and *No Contest* (1935). By the time the RKO series was winding down with *Melody in May* (1936), forty-year-old Ruth was being cast as herself on-screen but was no longer the story's love interest; here she sang "St. Louis Blues" and "It Had to Be You" and played cupid to a couple of teenagers. In 1936, Ruth went to London, and on October 1 of that year she debuted in the production *Transatlantic Rhythm* at the Adelphi Theater. While in London, during the run of the unsuccessful show, she recorded for the Rex label.

Upon her return to America late in 1936, Ruth recorded for Decca Records in New York City. At the time, she and her husband separated, and in 1937 Ruth moved to Hollywood, where she met musician/accompanist/arranger Mryl Alderman, who worked for various movie studios. Ruth had filed for divorce from Moses Snyder and did not know he had followed her to the West Coast. She and Alderman fell in love and planned to marry. Snyder forced Alderman to take him to Ruth one evening and then shot the musician while Ruth and Snyder's daughter both threatened the gangster with a gun. Snyder was arrested for kidnapping and attempted murder while Alderman recovered from his minor wounds. A sensational trial followed, with Snyder being sentenced to prison. Not long after, in December 1938, Ruth married Alderman in Las Vegas and they moved to a ranch near Colorado Springs, Colorado.

Due to the scandal, Ruth remained out of the limelight for several years, but in the late 1940s she returned to radio as a guest on Rudy Vallee's variety program, and this led to her own *The Ruth Etting Show* from WOR in New York City in 1947. Her comeback was short-lived, however, because both Ruth and Alderman, who were financially secure, preferred their private life to any kind of public life. They alternated their home life in Colorado by wintering often in Florida.

In 1955, a great deal of interest in Ruth Etting was generated when MGM filmed a version of her life story as *Love Me or Leave Me* with Doris Day as Ruth, James Cagney as Moses "The

Gimp" Snyder, and Cameron Mitchell as Mryl Alderman. Highlighted by top-notch renditions of Ruth's many song hits, the film was a treasure trove of misinformation about Ruth's stormy life, even picturing her as a dance-hall girl—something totally false. (Years later, she said about the film, "Oh what a . . . mess that was. . . . They took a lot of liberties with my life, but I guess they usually do with that kind of thing.") Following the movie's great success, Columbia Records issued an LP of Ruth's old recordings called *Love Me or Leave Me,* and she was offered a five-figure sum to sing in Las Vegas, a job she declined. She said, "I'm never going to go out there to have people in the audience say, 'Gee, I remember her when she was really something.'"

Mryl Alderman died in 1968, and Ruth moved to an apartment in Colorado Springs, where she remained for the rest of her life. She kept up correspondence with fans and wrote the liner notes to a reissue album of some of her old records, *Hello, Baby* (Biograph 11), in 1973. Although she was always available for interviews, Etting refused all requests to sing in public; those close to her insist her voice was gone. Ruth Etting died on September 24, 1978, following a long illness. In recent years a number of record albums and cassette tapes have appeared containing reissues of her vintage recordings, and her old films have been popular items on videotape and DVD.

Filmography

Ruth Etting (Par, 1928) (s)
Paramount Movietone (Par, 1928) (s)
Favorite Melodies (Par, 1929) (s)
Melancholy Dame (Par, 1929) (s)
The Book of Lovers (Illustrated, 1929) (s) (voice only)
Glorifying the Popular Song (Vita, 1929) (s)
Ruth Etting (Vita, 1929) (s)
One Good Turn (Vita, 1930) (s)
Broadway's Like That (Vita, 1930 (s)
Roseland (Vita, 1930) (s)
Old Lace (Vita, 1931) (s)
Freshman Love (Vita, 1931) (s)
Words and Music (Vita, 1931) (s)
Stage Struck (Vita, 1931) (s)
Radio Salutes (Par, 1931) (s)
Seasons Greeting (Vita, 1931) (s)
A Modern Cinderella (Vita, 1932) (s)
A Mail Bride (Vita, 1932) (s)
A Regular Trouper (Vita, 1932) (s)
Artistic Temper (Vita, 1932) (s)
Bye-Gones (Vita, 1933) (s)

Along Came Ruth (Vita, 1933) (s)
California Weather (RKO, 1933) (s)
Crashing the Gate (Vita, 1933) (s)
I Know Everybody and Everybody's Racket (Univ, 1933) (s)
Knee Deep in Music (RKO, 1933) (s)
Roman Scandals (UA, 1933)
Gift of Gab (Univ, 1934)
Hips, Hips, Hooray (RKO, 1934)
Bandits and Ballads (RKO, 1934) (s)
Derby Decade (RKO, 1934) (s)
The Song of Fame (Vita, 1934) (s)
Southern Style (RKO, 1934) (s)
A Torch Tango (RKO, 1934) (s)
Hollywood on Parade (Par, 1934) (s)
No Contest (Vita, 1935) (s)
An Old Spanish Onion (RKO, 1935) (s)
Ticket or Leave It (RKO, 1935) (s)
Tuned Out (RKO, 1935) (s)
Aladdin From Manhattan (RKO, 1936) (s)
Melody in May (RKO, 1936) (s)
Sleepy Time (RKO, 1936) (s)

Broadway Plays

The Ziegfeld Follies (1927)
Whoopee! (1928)
The Ziegfeld Follies (1928)

The Ziegfeld Follies (1929)
Simple Simon (1930)
The Nine-Fifteen Revue (1930)
The Ziegfeld Follies (1931)

Radio Series

Chesterfield Satisfies (CBS, 1932–33)
The Demi-Tasse Revue (NBC, 1934)
The Ruth Etting Show (NBC Blue, 1934–35)

College Prom (NBC Blue, 1935–36)
The Ruth Etting Show (WOR, 1947) (New York City)

Album Discography

LPs

America's Radio Sweetheart (Totem 1018, Sandy Hook 2033)
The Big Broadcast of 1935 (Kasha King 1935) [ST/R]
Encores (Take Two TT-211)
Fanny Brice, Helen Kane and Ruth Etting (Amalgamated 250)
Hello, Baby (Biograph 11)
Let Me Call You Sweetheart (Take Two TT-224)
Love Me or Leave Me (Col ML-5050)

The Original Torch Singers (Take Two TT-207) w. Fanny Brice, Libby Holman
Queen of the Torch Singers (Broadway Intermission 143)
Reflections (Take Two TT-203)
Roman Scandals (CIF 3007) [ST]
Ruth Etting Sings Again (Jay 3011)
Ten Cents a Dance (ASV 5008)
Whoopee! (Smithsonian R-012) [OC]

CDs

America's Greatest Songstress (Claremont 85074)
America's Radio Sweetheart (Sandy Hook CDSH-2033)
America's Sweetheart of Song (ASV CD-AJA-5374)
Glorifier of American Song (Take Two TT-422CD)
Goodnight My Love (Take Two TT-403CD)
Love Me Or Leave Me (Flapper 7061)

More Than You Know (Box Office ENB-CD-15/95) w. Helen Morgan
Radio Favorite (Vocalist's Showcase 17)
Ruth Etting (Sounds of a Century 1818)
Ten Cents a Dance (ASV CD-AJA-5008)
Torch Song Trio (Crystal Stream Audio IDCD61) w. Libby Holman, Helen Morgan

Dale Evans

(b. Frances Octavia Smith, Uvalde, Texas, October 31, 1912; d. Apple Valley, California, February 6, 2001)

Dale Evans, billed as "The Queen of the West," was almost always considered as part of a team with her husband, Roy Rogers, "The King of the Cowboys." While their personal and professional relationship lasted for over four decades, Evans carved for herself a distinctive and separate career in a diverse number of fields, including, radio, films, recordings, television, and concerts. In addition, she was the author of more than two dozen best-selling books, as well as being a songwriter. Religion made the main difference in Dale's life, and despite many personal tribulations, she always considered her firm faith the main reason for her enduring career success. She stated often she would have preferred to be an evangelist but that she best carried her Christian message as an entertainer and author.

A native of Uvalde, Texas, and christened Frances Octavia Smith, she was the daughter of Walter Hillman, a cotton farmer and hardware store operator, and Betty Sue Smith, who imbued her daughter with a strong Baptist heritage. Frances was born October 31, 1912, and a few years later she had a younger brother, Walter. She attended high school in Osceola, Arkansas, and it was there, at age fourteen, that she met and eloped with a young man named Tom Fox. Within a year she was the mother of a son, Tom Jr., but her husband soon deserted her, and the teenage mother supported herself and her boy by working as a secretary for an insurance firm in Memphis, Tennessee. (Later, when she was first in movies, she would introduce her son as her younger brother, on the advice of her agent, who insisted an actress with a teenage child would not be accepted by filmgoers.) When her employers discovered she was a good singer, they put her on the company-owned radio station, WMC, as a vocalist. Next she went to work for WHAS in Louisville, Kentucky, where the station's program director changed her name to Dale Evans. From there, she moved on to WFAA in Dallas, where she became quite popular and began working with touring bands, including those of Jay Mills and Herman Waldman. This led to an engagement with Anson Weeks and His Orchestra at the Chez Paree in Chicago in 1939. The next year she made her recording debut dueting with Lucio Garcia for "Help Me" with Abe Lyman and His Californians on Bluebird Records.

Besides working in Chicago nightclubs, Dale began performing on radio in the Windy City, mostly with Caesar Petrillo's Orchestra. She became so well known that her picture was often featured on sheet music of songs she had sung. During this period, she met and married pianist Dale Butts, and the two wrote a number of songs, including "Will You Marry Me, Mr. Laramie?" The song brought her to the attention of Joe Rivkin, a Hollywood talent agent, who negotiated a screen test for her at Paramount for their *Holiday Inn* (1942), but instead she ended with a twelve-month pact with Twentieth Century-Fox.

When nothing materialized in the movies for Dale, she was heard for a season on *The Chase and Sanborn Hour* on radio with Edgar Bergen and Charlie McCarthy, and then was a vocalist

Roy Rogers and Dale Evans in *Trigger Jr.* (1950)
[Courtesy of JC Archives]

with Roy Noble and His Orchestra on his radio show in 1943. The next season, she performed the same chore on *The Jack Carson Show*. She was also cast in small roles in two Twentieth Century-Fox musicals, *Girl Trouble* and *Orchestra Wives*, both 1942 releases, before her contract option was dropped. By now her manager was Art Rush, also the manager for singing cowboy star Roy Rogers. Rush got her work at Republic Pictures, where she did five feature films, the best being the John Wayne production, *In Old Oklahoma* (1943), in which she sang "Put Your Arms Around Me, Honey." Evans continued to work on radio as a regular on *The Jimmy Durante–Garry Moore Show*, and she cut four sides for Bel-Tone Records, as well as appearing at Hollywood clubs like the Mocambo and the Trocadero. Dale was also a tireless worker entertaining at Army camps, and she appeared on a number of Armed Forces Radio programs like *Personal Album, Showtime, Mail Call,* and *Radio Hall of Fame.* Her marriage to Dale Butts, now an orchestrator at Republic, ended during this period. During World War II, Dale renewed interest in her Christian faith, which grew even stronger in subsequent years.

In 1944, Dale was cast as the second female lead in the Roy Rogers Western, *The Cowboy and the Senorita,* in the part of Ysobel Martinez, singing the popular tune "Besame Mucho." She was so successful teaming with Rogers that in the next three years she appeared in nineteen more formula Westerns with him. In 1947 she was voted the first (and only!) woman to appear in the *Motion Picture Herald*'s poll of top moneymaking Western stars. Perhaps the main reason for her popularity in these action-full and glossy sagebrush musicals—besides her good looks and ability to act and sing—was the fact that her characters were not in the traditional mold of the helpless genre heroines. Dale's celluloid alter egos were independent females who were full of life and had minds of their own. Thus women and girls could empathize with Dale on the screen, and she also appealed to the men and boys in the audience.

Roy Rogers's wife, Arlene, died in 1946, following complications from the birth of their second child. After a time, Roy and Dale, who had gotten along well as costars, became involved romantically and were married in 1947. Republic, however, then removed her from Roy's pictures and instead cast her in a tepid remake of Gloria Swanson's *The Trespasser* (1947), which gave her a chance to sing Swanson's standard, "Love, Your Magic Spell Is Everywhere." Next came another remake (of a silent feature that had starred Colleen Moore). In this entry, *Slippy McGee* (1948), she was costarred with another Republic Western star, Don "Red" Barry. However, Dale then rejected the role of a bad girl in another Barry feature, *Madonna of the Desert* (1948). During this period, Dale continued to guest-star on radio shows like *All-Star Western Theater.* She also recorded for Majestic Records, waxing such Western tunes as "When the Roses Bloom in Red River Valley" and her self-penned "Aha San Antone."

Evans was finally allowed to reteam with her spouse on-camera in 1949 in Republic's *Susanna Pass,* and she was now billed as "Queen of the West." She did five more pictures with Roy through 1950 and then took a hiatus from the series to return in 1951 for his final two starring "B" Westerns, *South of Caliente* and *Pals of the Golden West.* Meanwhile, in 1949 Dale began recording with RCA Victor Records (Roy had been on the label since 1945), and she would remain with the powerful company through 1952, recording solo (often children's songs) and duets with her husband. In 1950, the duo cut the first of several religious albums, *Hymns of Faith,* for RCA. From 1950 to 1952, Dale returned to the top moneymaking Western stars poll put out by the *Motion Picture Herald.* In 1950 Dale gave birth to her second child, a daughter, Robin. The infant, however, has Down's syndrome, but Roy and Dale did not institutionalize the child. Instead they raised her at home, where she died two days before her second birthday. Out of the traumatic experience, Dale wrote the book *Angel Unaware* (1953) that became a best-seller, and its proceeds went to the National Association for Retarded Persons. The loss of their only natural child further cemented Roy and Dale's religious activities, and they worked closely with Norman Vincent Peale and Billy Graham. When the screen couple made a successful tour of Britain in 1954, they also appeared as part of Billy Graham's London crusade.

Evans had costarred with Rogers on radio since 1948, when *The Roy Rogers Show* had been broadcast on the Mutual network. The program moved to NBC in 1951 when General Foods took over its sponsorship, and late in 1951, the Western duo came to television with the half hour

The Roy Rogers Show, also on NBC. Like the radio entry, which ran on NBC through 1955, the TV edition was set in a Western locale with Dale operating a café and teaming with Roy to fight assorted villains, aided by Pat Brady and his trusty Jeep "Nellybelle," along with Roy's horse Trigger and dog Bullet. The action-full but cheaply produced series ran for nearly one hundred episodes through 1957. Its theme was "Happy Trails to You," a song written by Dale and one she and Roy recorded for RCA Victor in 1952.

During the 1950s, the Rogers guest-starred on a number of TV programs, like those of Perry Como and Milton Berle, and they were exceedingly active in personal appearances and on the rodeo circuit. In 1957, they cut another religious album for RCA, *Sweet Hour of Prayer*, and the next year they recorded still another one for RCA's subsidiary label, Bluebird, called *Jesus Loves Me*. Heard with them on this LP were their children, Linda, Dusty, Sandy, Dodie, and Debbie, the last three having been adopted. In the 1950s, Roy and Dale also made many recordings for Golden Records, mostly for children. In 1958, the Rogers were at Billy Graham's Washington, DC crusade, and attended Easter services with the President and Mrs. Dwight D. Eisenhower. In the late 1950s, Roy and Dale headlined two TV specials, and in 1962 they starred in the hour-long variety program *The Roy Rogers and Dale Evans Show* on ABC-TV. It ran for only three months due to heavy competition from Jackie Gleason on CBS-TV. That year also found them recording for Capitol Records with the duet album *The Bible Tells Me So*. In 1967, Dale recorded a gospel album for Capitol called *It's Real*, and she and Roy cut a Christmas LP, *Christmas Is Always* (Dale composed the title tune). In 1970, she and the Jordanaires made yet another gospel LP for Capitol, *Get to Know the Lord*.

Tragedy again struck the Rogers family when their nine-year-old adopted daughter Debbie was killed in a church-bus accident near San Clemente, California, in the summer of 1964. The next year Dale wrote the book *Dearest Debbie* as a remembrance to her daughter. Among Evans's other best-selling books were *My Spiritual Diary* (1955), *Christmas Is Always* (1958), and her autobiography, *The Woman at the Well* (1970), which sold over 275,000 copies in hardcover. In 1965, a third Rogers child, adopted son Sandy, died in Germany of alcoholic poisoning; Dale wrote the book *Salute to Sandy* that same year. As a further tribute to Sandy, she and Roy entertained servicemen in Vietnam in 1966, and the same year Dale was declared "the Texan of the Year" by the Texas Press Association. The next year Evans was named California's "Mother of the Year," and she and Roy opened a museum centered around their careers near their Apple Valley home. In the 1970s, the museum was moved permanently to Victorville.

By the late 1960s, Roy and Dale had settled into a life of both domestic happiness as well as joint/separate careers. Together they appeared on such TV shows as *The Hollywood Palace* and *Hee Haw* and made many personal appearances together. On her own, Dale continued to author prolifically books like *Time Out Ladies!* (1966), *Where He Leads* (1974), *Let Freedom Ring* (1975), and *Grandparents Can* (1983). In the early 1970s, she began recording for the Christian label Word Records in Waco, Texas, and for the rest of the decade she was featured on LPs like *Faith Hope and Charity*, *Heart of the Country*, *Country Dale*, and *Totally Free*, plus two duet albums with Roy: *In the Sweet By and By* and *The Good Life*. During the decade, the Rogers also hosted and were heard many times on the radio program *Country Crossroads*, sponsored by the Southern Baptist Convention.

The 1980s proved to be an active one for the seemingly indefatigable Evans, now in her seventies. She maintained a full schedule of concerts along with church visitations. In 1984, she and Roy and their son Roy Jr. (Dusty) recorded a two-record set for Teletex Records called *Many Happy Trails*, which highlighted music from their careers, with Dale doing Western, religious, and big band numbers. Earlier in the decade, in 1981, she had cut a religious album for the Manna label called *Reflections of Life*. The year 1982 found Dale Evans returning to feature films for the first time in over thirty years in *The Christian Family—A Woman's Perspective*, and two years later she was in *God in Hard Times*, made by Word Pictures and based on her book of the same title. In 1985, she and Roy started their television series, *Happy Trails Theater*, on the Nashville Network in which they screened their old Westerns and discussed them with guest stars. The same year she began appearing on her own syndicated TV program, *A Date With Dale*, at Trinity Broadcasting in Santa Ana, California. On the show, Dale discussed religious topics and interviewed guests, including members of her own family. In 1988 Word Books published her twenty-fifth volume, *The Only Star*.

A happy and fulfilled woman who found success in both her private and professional life, Dale Evans continued to be active in the 1990s. Her son Tom was a minister, and she and Roy Rogers had a large family, including grandchildren and great-grandchildren. In 1991, she joined Roy and stepson Dusty singing "Happy Trails" on her husband's *Tribute* album, which was a best-seller for RCA Records. Although their *Happy Trails Theater* ended in 1989, she continued her own TV show, *A Date With Dale*, at Trinity Broadcasting. She suffered a heart attack in 1992, but recovered, only to be partially paralyzed by another stroke in 1996. Through it all, she maintained a busy schedule that included her TV program and writing more books. Her husband Roy Rogers died in July 1998, and she said at the time, "What a blessing to have shared my life together with him for almost 51 years. To say I will miss him is a gross understatement. He was truly the king of the cowboys in my life." She suffered another heart attack in 1999, but continued to be active (her twenty-ninth book, *Rainbow on a Hard Trail*, was published that year) until her death from congestive heart failure in her Apple Valley, California, home on February 6, 2001.

Perhaps Dale Evans best summed up her feelings toward life and her deep faith in her book *Where He Leads*: "He has led me in Galilee and Judea and New York and California and everywhere I go. . . . I find the light of His countenance going before me on the common roads of home as I found it leading me there, and it lightens my journey . . . and gives me peace."

Filmography

Orchestra Wives (20th-Fox, 1942)
Girl Trouble (20th-Fox, 1942)
Here Comes Elmer (Rep, 1943)
Hoosier Holiday [Farmyard Follies] (Rep, 1943)
Swing Your Partner (Rep, 1943)
The West Side Kid (Rep, 1943)
In Old Oklahoma [War of the Wildcats] (Rep, 1943)
Casanova in Burlesque (Rep, 1944)
San Fernando Valley (Rep, 1944)
Yellow Rose of Texas (Rep, 1944)
Song of Nevada (Rep, 1944)
Utah (Rep, 1945)
Lights of Old Santa Fe (Rep, 1945)
The Big Show-Off (Rep, 1945)
The Man From Oklahoma (Rep, 1945)

Don't Fence Me In (Rep, 1945)
Hitchhike to Happiness (Rep, 1945)
Bells of Rosarita (Rep, 1945)
Sunset in Eldorado (Rep, 1945)
Along the Navajo Trail (Rep, 1945)
Song of Arizona (Rep, 1946)
My Pal Trigger (Rep, 1946)
Under Nevada Skies (Rep, 1946)
Roll on Texas Moon (Rep, 1946)
Home in Oklahoma (Rep, 1946)
Rainbow Over Texas (Rep, 1946)
Out California Way (Rep, 1946)
Heldorado (Rep, 1946)
Apache Rose (Rep, 1947)
Bells of San Angelo (Rep, 1947)
The Trespasser (Rep, 1947)

Slippy McGee (Rep, 1948)
The Golden Stallion (Rep, 1949)
Twilight in the Sierras (Rep, 1950)
Bells of Coronado (Rep, 1950)
Trigger, Jr. (Rep, 1950)

South of Caliente (Rep, 1951)
Pals of the Golden West (Rep, 1951)
Screen Snapshots #24 (Col, 1954) (s)
God in Hard Times (Word Pictures, 1984)

Radio Series

News and Rhythm (CBS, 1939–41)
Let's Be Lazy (CBS, 1940)
The Chase and Sanborn Hour (NBC, 1942–43)
Ray Noble and His Orchestra (NBC, 1943)
The Jack Carson Show (CBS, 1944)

The Jimmy Durante–Garry Moore Show (CBS, 1945–46)
The Roy Rogers Show (Mutual, 1948–51; NBC, 1951–55)

TV Series

The Roy Rogers Show (NBC, 1951–57)
The Roy Rogers and Dale Evans Show (ABC, 1962)

Happy Trails Theater (TNN, 1985–89)
A Date With Dale (Trinity Broadcasting, 1985–2001)

Album Discography

LPs

The Bible Tells Me So (Cap TST-1745, Cap SM-1745) w. Roy Rogers
A Child's Introduction to the West (Golden 7) w. Roy Rogers
Christmas Is Always (Cap ST-2818) w. Roy Rogers
Country Dale (Word 8611)
Dale Evans Sings (10″ Allegro 4116)
Faith, Hope and Charity (Word 8566)
Favorite Gospel Songs (Sacred Sounds 4505)
Get to Know the Lord (Cap ST-399)
The Good Life (Word 8761) w. Roy Rogers
Heart of the Country (Word 8658)
It's Real (Cap T/ST-2772, Word 8546)

Jesus Loves Me (Bluebird LBY-1022, Camden CAL/CAS-1022, Camden/Pickwick ACL-7021) w. Roy Rogers and Family
Many Happy Trails (Teletex C-7702) w. Roy Rogers, Roy Rogers Jr.
Peter Cottontail (Golden LP-81) w. Roy Rogers
Reflections of Life (Manna MS-2075)
16 Great Songs of the Old West (Golden 198:7) w. Roy Rogers
Sweet Hour of Prayer (RCA LPM-1439, Stetson HAT-3088) w. Roy Rogers
Sweeter As the Years Go By (Word 8583)
Totally Free (Word 8803)
Western Favorites (Evon 336)

CDs

Christmas Is Always (EMI-Capitol Music Special Markets 723435-33263-2-6)
Christmas With Roy Rogers & Dale Evans (CEMA Special Products F21X-57827) w. Roy Rogers
Lore of the West (RCA Camden CAD-11074R, Delta 6096) w. Roy Rogers, the Sons of the Pioneers, Gabby Hayes
Lore of the West/Good Old Country Music/San Antonio Rose (3-Delta 6094) w. Roy Rogers, the Sons of the Pioneers, Gabby Hayes
Our Re-Collections (Word 7013545368) w. Roy Rogers
Peace in the Valley (Pair PDC-2-1352) w. Roy Rogers

Queen of the West—Greatest Hits (Paper Moon DRC-12754)
Roy Rogers and Dale Evans (The Beautiful Music Company DMC1-1657)
Say Yes to Tomorrow (Homeland 9514-2, K-Tel International 9514, DER 2CD) w. Roy Rogers, Dusty Rogers
Sixteen Great Songs of the Old West (Drive DE2-47007) w. Roy Rogers
Songs of the Old West (MCA Special Products MCAD-21110, Universal Special Markets 21110) w. Roy Rogers

Alice Faye

(b. Alice Jeanne Leppert, New York City, May 5, 1915; d. Rancho Mirage,
California, May 9, 1998)

Alice Faye first came to Hollywood at age nineteen, and she was glamorized immediately into a platinum blonde similar to Jean Harlow. After Darryl F. Zanuck took over Fox Pictures in the mid-'30s, he recognized Alice's potential and showcased her own natural beauty and infectious, warm personality. As a result, she became Twentieth Century-Fox's top moneymaking star, and her vogue lasted well into the 1940s. She was the adorable heroine who could deliver a ballad in a tender contralto voice and make the audience really care about her yielding character. Eventually she tired of the pressures of the movie-star routine and chose instead to focus on her family life. (Betty Grable inherited her mantle as the blonde singing queen of the studio.) Although Faye never totally retired, her most successful years encompassed the thirty feature films she made from 1934 to 1943, most of which had show-business motifs, fluffy plots, pretty songs, and—best of all—the good looks and talent of Alice to put them across.

Alice Faye was born Alice Jeanne Leppert in the Hell's Kitchen section (she always referred jokingly to it as "Double Fifth Avenue") of New York City on May 5, 1915, the daughter of city patrolman Charley and Alice (Moffat) Leppert. She was the youngest of three children, being preceded by two older brothers (Charles and William). Early in life, she loved to dance, and was encouraged to perform by her maternal grandmother, who resided with her family. When she was thirteen, she quit school and won a job with *Earl Carroll's Vanities*, but was dismissed because she was underage. However, a year later—adding three years to her actual age—she obtained employment with Chester Hale's dancers at the Capitol Theater and other nightspots. She was in the chorus of *George White's Scandals of 1931*, and at a cast party, one of the production's stars, Rudy Vallee, was impressed when he heard her singing. He began featuring her on his popular variety radio show, *The Fleischmann Hour*. When the sponsor would not pay Alice's salary, Vallee did so himself; he also took her on a tour of New England with his band. During a storm, the two were in a car wreck that caused Alice to miss several broadcasts. The NBC radio network was swamped with letters asking for her, and when she recovered, the sponsor agreed to pay her radio salary. It was during this period that Vallee's second wife, Fay Webb, sued him for divorce and charged he was involved with Alice. (Vallee won the divorce settlement.)

In the fall of 1933, Alice Faye (she had taken the surname not, as legend has it, because of entertainer Frank Fay, but because she thought it pretty and that it suited her) made her recording debut with Rudy Vallee and his Connecticut Yankees, singing on "Honeymoon Hotel" and "Shame on You" for Bluebird Records. One of the songs was a duet with Vallee. Later that year, Rudy signed with Fox Pictures to star in *George White's Scandals* (1934), and he made sure Alice obtained a part in the screen musical. When his costar, European Lilian Harvey, walked out of the project because she was unhappy with the size of her role, Rudy convinced the studio to substitute Alice,

Alice Faye in 1934.
[Courtesy of JC Archives]

who got to sing the song "Nasty Man." The *New York Herald Tribune* enthused, "Miss Faye reveals, in addition to considerable personal allure, a talent for projecting a hot song number that is extremely helpful to the work." With such a successful screen debut, the studio quickly signed Alice to a long-term contract.

At the beginning of her Fox tenure, Alice was the leading lady in a trio of programmer comedies featuring the overbearing comedy team of Mitchell and Durant: *She Learned About Sailors* (1934), in which she sang "Here's the Key to My Heart"; *365 Nights in Hollywood* (1934), which had her performing "Yes to You" and "My Future Star"; and *Music Is Magic* (1935), in which she had a decent dramatic role as an aspiring actress who sings the title song and "Honey Chile." She was also featured in the gangster melodrama *Now I'll Tell* (1934) singing "Foolin' With Other Women's Men," and she played a vaudevillian in *George White's 1935 Scandals* (1935), vocalizing on "According to the Moonlight" and "Oh, I Didn't Know," which she also recorded for the American Record Company (ARC). On loan to Paramount, Alice costarred with Frances Langford and Patsy Kelly as a trio of singers seeking radio stardom in *Every Night at Eight* (1935). In this bouncy musical, she vocalized "Speaking Confidentially" and "I Feel a Song Coming On." She also made the elaborate backstage genre piece *King of Burlesque* (1935) with Warner Baxter, singing "I'm Shooting High," "Spreadin' Rhythm Around," "I Love to Ride Horses," and "I've Got My Fingers Crossed" (all recorded for ARC).

It was at this juncture in Faye's movie career that studio mogul Zanuck began softening her brassy screen image. As a result, Alice was cast in the Shirley Temple opus *Poor Little Rich Girl* (1936) as a singer who becomes a star with her partner (Jack Haley) after they add orphan Shirley to their act. Alice sang "When I'm With You" and "But Definitely," and joined Temple on "You Gotta Eat Your Spinach" and "Military Man." With her toned-down appearance, Alice seemed far more down-to-earth and, thus, easier to cast in girl-next-door parts. It did a great deal to heighten her appeal to moviegoers.

Sing, Baby Sing (1936) was Faye's tenth picture, and by now she already had first-star billing. Here she played an actress in love with a has-been performer (Adolphe Menjou). She performed the catchy title song, "Love Will Tell," and also "You Turned the Tables on Me." It is interesting to note that this picture also featured another studio hopeful, singer Tony Martin. She then returned to supporting Shirley Temple in *Stowaway* (1936), which gave Faye two of her most memorable screen songs, "Goodnight, My Love" (which she recorded for Brunswick Records) and "One Never Knows Does One." For Brunswick she also waxed a trio of songs: "I've Got My Love to Keep Me Warm," "This Year's Kisses," and "Slumming on Park Avenue," all from her next Twentieth Century-Fox film, *On the Avenue* (1937). This picture matched her with another blonde (Madeleine Carroll) and another crooner (Dick Powell).

The delightful radio satire *Wake Up and Live* (1937) provided Faye with a rich score, including "Never in a Million Years," "It's Swell of You," "There's a Lull in My Life," and the title song, all of which were recorded for Brunswick. Because Darryl Zanuck decided he wanted to focus the talents of his singing stars on-camera, he dictated that all studio stars refrain from making commercial records. As a result, Faye would not make another recording for more than a decade.

Alice was now earning $2,000 weekly at Fox. She closed out her 1937 moviemaking on the home lot with *You Can't Have Everything*, this time seen as a playwright who makes her show a success. In it, she and Tony Martin dueted on "Afraid to Dream," and she sang the title song, "Pardon Us We're in Love," as well as "Danger, Love at Work!" In *You're a Sweetheart* (1938), made on loan to Universal, she was the showgirl who warbled "My Fine Feathered Friend" (wearing feathers and crouched in a tree!), "So It's Love," and the enduring "You're a Sweetheart." In July of 1937, Alice joined Hal Kemp and His Orchestra on his half hour CBS radio show, *Music From Hollywood*. Despite her popularity on the series, Zanuck was annoyed and bought up her contract by year's end. He had decided that she should be available professionally *only* in Twentieth Century-Fox films. On September 3, 1937, she and Tony Martin were married in Yuma, Arizona.

Tony Martin was her costar in the weak show-business musical *Sally, Irene and Mary* (1938), with Faye singing "Who Stole the Jam?" "Got My Mind on Music," "This Is Where I Came In," and dueting with Martin on "Half Moon on the Hudson"(which was mostly deleted from the picture). Cut from the final print was her song "Think Twice" and her dance to "Minuet in Jazz." As an indicator of her value to the studio, Alice's last two 1938 features were big-budgeted productions and helped to put her in the top ten at the box office (as she would be the next year, too). *In Old Chicago* and *Alexander's Ragtime Band*, both with Tyrone Power and Don Ameche, established her as one of filmdom's most popular female stars. In the former, an historical drama set in the 1870s, she played a cabaret singer who performed the title song, "Carry Me Back to Old Virginny," and "I'll Never Let You Cry." The $750,000 fire sequence of the burning of Chicago was the movie's highlight. (Before starting *In Old Chicago*, Faye had said of Zanuck: "He has given me a type of role which I had not expected for at least a couple more years. It is my one big chance, and I'm just in a jittery state of nerves and elation.") *Alexander's Ragtime Band* was also a period piece (1911 to 1938) in which, as a musical comedy star, she performed such Irving Berlin tunes as "Now It Can Be Told" (written for the film), the title song, "When the Midnight Choo-Choo Leaves for Alabam'," "Everybody's Doing It," "What'll I Do," and "All Alone." Almost lost in the shuffle of twenty-six Berlin melodies was Ethel Merman in a secondary role.

After two such well-received projects, Twentieth Century-Fox wasted her as a flier (!) in the mediocre *Tail Spin* (1939) in which she sang "Are You in the Mood for Mischief?" and "Go In and Out the Window," but the latter was cut from release prints. Far better was her Fanny Brice imitation in the delightful *Rose of Washington Square* (1939), with her singing the title song, "My Man," and "I Never Knew Heaven Could Speak." However, her renditions of "I'll See You in My Dreams" and "I'm Always Chasing Rainbows" were deleted from the final print. The real Miss Brice sued the studio over this thinly veiled account of her life, which led to a curtailed distribution of the musical.

Hollywood Cavalcade (1939) was Alice's first Technicolor movie. It was a fast-paced look at the history of filmmaking as seen through the career of a once-great director (Don Ameche) who was patterned after D. W. Griffith and Mack Sennett. Alice played Molly Adair, the girl he makes a star. (Her character was based on silent screen star Mabel Normand.) Alice finished the year for Fox with the mishmash called *Barricade* (1939), which had begun two years before as *The Girl From Brooklyn*. It was a straight drama in which she was the woman falsely accused of murder. Her one song ("There'll Be Other Nights") was filmed but not used.

During the period between 1940 (the year she divorced Tony Martin) and 1943, Alice Faye starred in eight pictures for Twentieth Century-Fox, and these are the movies for which she is best remembered. Mostly in Technicolor, they were breezy romantic comedies with flashy musical numbers, and her intriguing costars included Don Ameche, Betty Grable, John Payne, Cesar Romero, Carmen Miranda, and Jack Oakie. The first of these—*Little Old New York* (1940), a biopic of steamboat inventor Robert Fulton (Richard Greene)—was the least memorable, with

Alice singing only a portion of "Who Is the Beau of the Belle of New York?" (She did, however, display a previously unseen flair for light comedy.) Far more indelible was her work in the title role of *Lillian Russell* (1940), an entertaining look at the Gay Nineties entertainer and her romances with Edward Solomon (Don Ameche), Alexander Moore (Henry Fonda), and Diamond Jim Brady (Edward Arnold). Alice sang "Come Down Ma' Evening Star," "Ma' Blushin' Rosie," and "Blue Lovebird." Then she was teamed with Betty Grable, her budding rival at the studio. While making *Tin Pan Alley* (1940), in which the two blonde actresses played a sister act in the World War I period, the women became good friends. (*Tin Pan Alley* was also her first vehicle with John Payne.) Among Alice's numbers were the "Sheik of Araby" routine with Grable and "You Say the Sweetest Things Baby" with Payne and Jack Oakie.

Alice appeared with Don Ameche for the sixth and last time while working with Carmen Miranda for the first time in the Technicolor musical *That Night in Rio* (1941), singing "They Met in Rio" and "Boa Noite." A history of radio broadcasting was the plot crux of *The Great American Broadcast* (1941), with Alice as speakeasy singer Vicki Adams who weds radio pioneer Rex Martin (John Payne) and becomes a big star in the medium. She sang "Where Are You," "I Take to You," and "Long Ago Last Night."

On May 12, 1941, in Ensenada, Mexico, Alice married bandleader-actor Phil Harris, whom she initially met when she was with Rudy Vallee's music group. After it was revealed that Harris's divorce from his first wife was not final, the couple remarried on September 22, 1941, this time in Galveston, Texas. Faye said prophetically, "My career for the first time in my life doesn't mean a thing to me. . . . I hung onto my job because I always had an idea I was going to need it some time. But now I know I'll always be taken care of as a wife should be. . . ."

Weekend in Havana (1941) had Faye again working with John Payne and Carmen Miranda in the "grandeur of Technicolor." She performed "Tropical Magic" (a well-staged production number) and "Romance and Rhumba." However, another routine, "The Man With the Lollipop Song," was snipped out. On May 19, 1942, Alice gave birth to her first child, her namesake. In this period, she was replaced on-screen by Gene Tierney in *Belle Starr* (1941), Rita Hayworth in *My Gal Sal* (1942), and Betty Grable in *Springtime in the Rockies* (1942). Faye explained her priorities: "I have always felt that motherhood is infinitely more important than any career."

The studio finally persuaded Alice to return to pictures. She was again matched with John Payne and Jack Oakie in *Hello, Frisco, Hello* (1943), a Technicolor opus set on the Barbary Coast of the early 1900s. The movie provided Alice with another memorable song, "You'll Never Know," which won an Oscar. She also performed "Why Do They Pick on Me?" and "By the Light of the Silvery Moon." Alice repeated her role of Trudy Evans on *Lux Radio Theater* and *Showtime*. The film grossed $3.4 million. Faye went contemporary in *The Gang's All Here*, issued at Christmas 1943. She and Carmen Miranda were showgirls out for romance, with Alice singing "No Love, No Nothin'," "A Journey to a Star," and "The Polka Dot Polka."

In the spring of 1944, Alice became a mother again with the birth of a second daughter, Phyllis, and she was dropped from consideration to costar in *The Dolly Sisters* (1945) with Betty Grable. (June Haver took that role in the musical biography.) Alice did appear as herself entertaining soldiers in *Four Jills and a Jeep* in 1944, reprising "You'll Never Know." This black-and-white picture proved to be her last musical while under contract to the studio.

"I became tired of playing those big musicals. . . . I felt if I could make pictures I'd be proud to show my kids some day, that would be different. . . . I wear simple dresses and tailored knits and, above all, I'm a real person—a human being—a woman with a heart. Not just a painted, doll-like dummy." So reasoned Alice Faye to columnist Hedda Hopper about her star role in the melodrama *Fallen Angel* (1945), geared by the studio as a hopeful successor to its *Laura* (1944). It was the first film under her new Twentieth Century-Fox pact. She was the wealthy woman romanced by and married to a heel (Dana Andrews) who really craves a slatternly waitress (Linda Darnell). Alice was simply too young and beautiful for the heavily dramatic part, and her only song, "Slowly," was deleted from the film. The brooding film noir picture was not a success. Faye later reflected, "I had some great scenes in it, but they ended up on the cutting-room floor. That was when they were building up Linda Darnell, and they threw the picture to her."

Having come to a parting with Fox—she never forgave Darryl Zanuck for his "betrayal"—Alice withdrew from picture making. (Over the following years, Twentieth Century-Fox offered Faye roles in such projects as *State Fair* [1945], *A Tree Grows in Brooklyn* [1945], *Greenwich Village* [1945], *Sweet Rosie O'Grady* [1945], *The Razor's Edge* [1946], *A Letter to Three Wives* (1949), *Wabash Avenue* [1950], and *I'll Never Forget You* [1951], but she was not interested.) From 1946 to 1954, Alice costarred with her husband on the popular Sunday-night radio comedy *The Phil Harris–Alice Faye Show* on NBC with Alice sometimes singing on the broadcasts. She and Harris also guested on such programs as *American Red Cross, The Bob Hope Show*, and the twentieth anniversary celebration of *One Man's Family* in the spring of 1952. She and Phil also cut a record for RCA Victor, *The Letter*.

Besides her radio offerings, Alice made only occasional public appearances, such as being on her husband's TV program in 1959. However, in 1962, with her children grown, she returned to films playing the mother in Twentieth Century-Fox's mundane remake of *State Fair*. She sang "Never Say No to a Man," "Our State Fair," and "It's the Little Things in Texas," all of which appeared on the Dot Records soundtrack album. *Time* magazine observed of her comeback, "[She] looks refreshingly real—she is middle-aged now, and she doesn't try to hide it." That year, she also recorded a long-playing album for Reprise called *Alice Faye Sings Her Famous Movie Hits*, on which she did a dozen songs from her films. (The LP was reissued in the 1970s by Stanyan Records as *Alice Faye's Greatest Hits*.)

During the 1960s, Alice appeared on TV shows such as *The Red Skelton Show* and *The Hollywood Palace*, and late in 1973 she returned to the stage with her past costar John Payne in a nostalgic revival of *Good News*. After a lengthy pre-Broadway engagement, the show opened in New York in December 1974, with Gene Nelson as her new costar. The next summer she toured with Don Ameche in the show. Her Reprise recording of "You'll Never Know" was used as the title song for the movie *Alice Doesn't Live Here Anymore* (1975), and in 1976, she was among the many former luminaries who did cameos in Paramount's *Won Ton Ton, The Dog Who Saved Hollywood* (she played a studio gate secretary). In 1978, she was seen in the family film *The Magic of Lassie* as a waitress. Said Alice, "It was fun to put on the eyelashes again." In 1979, she played art gallery proprietor Kathy in the comedy *Every Girl Should Have One*, about the theft of a million-dollar diamond.

In 1980, Alice guested on the ABC-TV show *The Love Boat*, and from 1984 to 1991 she was the Good Health Ambassador for Pfizer's "Help Yourself to Good Health" program, lecturing to senior citizens about staying fit. As a part of her talk, she appeared in the Pfizer short film, *We Still Are* (1988), which examined her career and used clips from *Wake Up and Live* and *Weekend in Havana*. In 1989 her memoirs, *Growing Older—Staying Young*, were published. On June 3,

1989, she received an honorary degree from Vincennes University in Indiana where, along with Phil Harris, she was a given a doctorate in the Performing Arts.

Phil Harris died August 11, 1995, and Alice passed away at her Rancho Mirage home on May 9, 1998, four days after her eighty-third birthday. She left an estate in excess of $5 million.

Filmography

George White's Scandals (Fox, 1934)
She Learned About Sailors (Fox, 1934)
The Hollywood Gad-About (Educational, 1934) (s)
Now I'll Tell [When New York Sleeps] (Fox, 1934)
365 Nights in Hollywood (Fox, 1934)
George White's 1935 Scandals (Fox, 1935)
Music Is Magic (Fox, 1935)
Every Night at Eight (Par, 1935)
Poor Little Rich Girl (20th-Fox, 1936)
Sing, Baby, Sing (20th-Fox, 1936)
King of Burlesque (20th-Fox, 1936)
Stowaway (20th-Fox, 1936)
Cinema Circus (MGM, 1937) (s)
On the Avenue (20th-Fox, 1937)
Wake Up and Live (20th-Fox, 1937)
You Can't Have Everything (20th-Fox, 1937)
You're a Sweetheart (Univ, 1937)
In Old Chicago (20th-Fox, 1938)
Sally, Irene and Mary (20th-Fox, 1938)
Alexander's Ragtime Band (20th-Fox, 1938)
Tail Spin (20th-Fox, 1939)

Hollywood Cavalcade (20th-Fox, 1939)
Rose of Washington Square (20th-Fox, 1939)
Barricade (20th-Fox, 1939)
Lillian Russell (20th-Fox, 1940)
Little Old New York (20th-Fox, 1940)
Tin Pan Alley (20th-Fox, 1940)
That Night in Rio (20th-Fox, 1941)
The Great American Broadcast (20th-Fox, 1941)
Weekend in Havana (20th-Fox, 1941)
Hello, Frisco, Hello (20th-Fox, 1943)
The Gang's All Here [The Girls He Left Behind] (20th-Fox, 1943)
Four Jills in a Jeep (20th-Fox, 1944)
Fallen Angel (20th-Fox, 1945)
State Fair (20th-Fox, 1962)
Won Ton Ton, The Dog Who Saved Hollywood (Par, 1976)
The Magic of Lassie (International Picture Show, 1978)
Every Girl Should Have One (Robert Fridley Productions, 1979)
We Still Are (Pfizer, 1988) (s)

Broadway Plays

George White's Scandals of 1931 (1931)

Good News (1974) (revival)

Radio Series

The Fleischmann Hour (NBC, 1931–34)
Music from Hollywood (CBS, 1937)

The Phil Harris-Alice Faye Show (NBC, 1946–54)

Album Discography

LPs

Alexander's Ragtime Band (Hollywood Soundstage 406) [ST]
Alexander's Ragtime Band (Pelican 132/Demand Performance DP-602) [ST/R]
Alice Faye (Curtain Calls 100/3)
Alice Faye and Phil Harris (Radio Archives 101)
Alice Faye—Her Famous Movie Hits (Reprise 6029)
Alice Faye in Hollywood, 1934-37 (Col CL-3068, Columbia Special Products 3068)

Alice Faye on the Air—Rare Radio Recordings (Sandy Hook 2020)
Alice Faye on the Air—Vol. 1 (Totem 1011)
Alice Faye on the Air—Vol. 2 (Totem 1032)
Alice Faye Sings Her Greatest Movie Hits (Valiant VS 122)
The Alice Faye Songbook (Amalgamated 146)
Alice Faye: Vol. 1, Outtakes and Alternates (Limited Edition, AF-1) [ST]
Alice Faye: Vol. 2, Outtakes and Alternates (Limited Edition, AF-2) [ST]

Alice Faye: Vol. 3, More Gems (Limited Editions, AF-3)

Alice Faye's Greatest Hits (Stanyon 10072/POW 3003)

Every Night at Eight (Caliban 6043)

Four Jills in a Jeep (Hollywood Soundstage HS-407) [ST]

The Gang's All Here (CIF 3003) [ST]

The Gang's All Here (Sandy Hook 2009) [ST/R]

Good News (SA 101-104) [OC]

Hello, Frisco, Hello (Caliban 6005, Hollywood Soundstage 5015) [ST]

Hello, Frisco, Hello (Pelican 126, Demand Performance DP-605) [ST/R]

Lillian Russell (Caliban 6016) [ST]

Magic of Lassie (Pickwick SHM992) [ST]

Music Is Magic (Caliban 6047) [ST]

Music, Music, Music (Take Two TT-302)

On the Avenue (Hollywood Soundstage 401) [ST]

Outtakes & Alternates, Vol. 1 (AF 1)

Outtakes & Alternates, Vol. 2 (AF 2)

Rose of Washington Square (Caliban 6002, Sandy Hook SH 2074) [ST]

Sally, Irene and Mary (Caliban 6031) [ST]

Sing, Baby, Sing (Caliban 6029) [ST]

The Songs of Harry Warren (Citadel 6004)

State Fair (Dot 9011/29011) [ST]

This Year's Kisses (Connifer CMS001)

Tin Pan Alley (Caliban 6003, Soundtrak STK 110) [ST]

Wake Up and Live (Hollywood Soundstage 403) [ST]

Weekend in Havana/That Night in Rio (Curtain Calls 100/14) [ST]

You Can't Have Everything (Titania 508) [ST]

You're a Sweetheart (Scarce Rarities 5502) [ST]

CDs

Alexander's Ragtime Band (Hollywood Soundstage 4011) [ST]

Alice Faye On-screen & Radio 1932-43 (Vintage Jazz Band VJB-1947)

Alice Faye Soundtracks (Promo Sound CD-60011)

Always the Ladies (Sound of the Movies 3109) w. Betty Grable

Best of Radio Comedy: Duffy's Tavern/The Phil Harris-Alice Faye Show (Laserlight 12-688)

Cole Porter Centennial Gala Concert (Teldec 9031-75277-2) w. Van Johnson

Film Music (Great Music Themes 6011)

The Gang's All Here (Sandy Hook CDSH-2009) [ST]

Got Music on My Mind (Jasmine JASCD-105/6)

Holiday in Mexico/Weekend in Havana (Great Movie Themes 60036) [ST]

The King of Jazz/King of Burlesque/Going Places/Carefree (Great Movie Themes 60019) [ST]

Lady Be Good/Four Jills in a Jeep (Great Movie Themes 60029) [ST]

Music From Hollywood, Vol. 1 (AFA 4) w. Hal Kemp

Music From Hollywood, Vol. 2 (AFA 5) w. Hal Kemp

On the Avenue (Soundtrack Factory SFCD-37537) [ST]

The Phil Harris-Alice Faye Show (Cliffhanger Records 805)

Rose of Washington Square (Varese Sarabande 302-066-009-2) [ST]

Rose of Washington Square/The Dolly Sisters/Gold Diggers of 1933 (Great Movie Themes 60009) [ST]

State Fair (Varese Sarabande 302-66075-2) [ST]

This Year's Kisses (Conifer CM SCD 001)

You Can't Have Everything/Go Into Your Dance/You'll Never Get Rich (Great Movie Themes 60014) [ST]

You'll Never Know (ASV CD-AJA-5303)

Susanna Foster

(b. Susanna DeLee Flanders Larson, Chicago, Illinois, December 6, 1924)

Hollywood is a world where the term "has been" is notoriously prevalent. Over the decades, hundreds of pretty ingénues were thrust aside by the studios and their production mills after their box-office potential either faded or failed to be exploited. During the late 1930s and early 1940s, blonde Susanna Foster was a bright light on the Hollywood scene. The star of a dozen feature films, she not only possessed good looks but was also an accomplished actress and a very fine soprano. Interestingly enough, it was Ms. Foster who turned her back on Hollywood, and not vice versa. When her studio contract ended in 1945, she left the movie mecca for good, never wanting to return. She said, "I want to do what I want to do and that has nothing to do with show business."

Born Susanna DeLee Flanders Larson in Chicago, Illinois, on December 6, 1924, she was still an infant when her family moved to Minneapolis, where she went to school. Gifted as a singer and quite bright in her school studies, young Susanna began being heard on local radio programs, as well as singing at theaters and conventions in the Minneapolis–St. Paul area. Her idol was Jeanette MacDonald, and she practiced to imitate that famed songstress. (Foster later said she saw 1935's *Naughty Marietta* over sixty-eight times, eagerly absorbing every nuance of her idol's performance.) Foster was impressive enough that Merle Potter, drama editor of the *Minneapolis Star*, and orchestra leader Carl Johnson persuaded the teenager to make test recordings (including "Italian Street Song" and "Ah, Sweet Mystery of Life") that were dispatched to Metro-Goldwyn-Mayer studios. Without seeing her in person, the studio signed her to a one-year contract.

Susanna and her family, which included two smaller sisters, moved to Hollywood in 1935, but an intended starring vehicle for Susanna, *B Above High C*, never materialized. When her year's contract was up, the studio dropped her. (She had refused their offer to star in a planned production of *National Velvet* because the story did not allow for her to sing.) Then, Susanna's parents separated, and it was a financial struggle for Susanna and her mother to survive. Nevertheless, the young girl studied voice with Gilda Marchetti, who helped her student strengthen her lower tones. Through Marchetti's brother Milo, Susanna later earned an audition at Paramount Pictures, where she was signed to a contract; Mr. Marchetti became her agent.

In her three years at Paramount, Susanna Foster, as she was now called, was only in four feature films, beginning with *The Great Victor Herbert*, produced in 1939 when she was fifteen. Her screen debut, however, was a good one in that the project provided her the opportunity to sing "Kiss Me Again" (hitting B flat above high C). In this biography of that great operetta composer, played by Walter Connolly, she was cast as the daughter of Allan Jones and Mary Martin. The *New York Times* forecasted, "a charming juvenile songstress, Susanna Foster, is a newcomer who is going to be very bearable to watch." On the other hand, Susanna, who was very mature for her age, was unimpressed with her noteworthy screen debut. She recalled, "When I

Turhan Bey, Susanna Foster, and Boris Karloff in *The Climax* (1944).
[Courtesy of JC Archives]

did see *The Great Victor Herbert*, and finally saw myself on the screen, all I could think was, 'My God! I'm not Jeanette MacDonald!'"

Allan Jones also costarred in Susanna's second picture, *There's Magic In Music* (1941), where she portrayed a hard-boiled burlesque singer whom Jones takes to a children's recreational camp. In 1941, Paramount released a follow-up to the beloved children's picture *Skippy* (1931) called *Glamour Boy*. Jackie Cooper, who had starred in the original movie, recreated his most famous celluloid role, while Susanna was romanced by Skippy, now a soda jerk. "Love Is Such an Old Fashioned Thing," "The Magic of Magnolias," and the aria "Sempre Libera" from Giuseppe Verdi's *La Traviata* were sung by Susanna in the movie. Her Paramount finale was a guest bit in *Star Spangled Rhythm* in 1942. The studio simply had no idea what to do with her, and much of her last year under contract was spent in idleness. Susanna, always very outspoken (she was dubbed Paramount's "Impulsive Rebel" by one fan magazine), asked for her studio release.

After leaving Paramount, Susanna, who now had Myron Selznick (the brother of famed film producer David O. Selznick) as her agent, was quickly hired by Universal. That studio was the home of much musical talent in the early 1940s. Moreover, they viewed Susanna as a good weapon to keep their reigning soprano star (Deanna Durbin) in line. Susanna appeared in eight productions for the studio, and they showcased her far better than had the Paramount films. *The Phantom of the Opera* (1943), the expensive remake of the famous 1925 Lon Chaney silent classic, was her initial Universal feature and the best one of her career. Filmed in gorgeous Technicolor with handsome production values, this Academy-Award winning opus presented her as Christine Dubois, a beautiful Parisian opera singer who is lusted after by the Phantom (Claude Rains) and romanced by her handsome leading man (Nelson Eddy). The film allowed both Susanna and Eddy ample occasion to sing opera (based on the works of Chopin and Tchaikovsky), and both were in top form in these musical sequences. Overall though, the remake was not up to the standards of the Chaney version in the terror department. Nevertheless, the production won very favorable reviews for Rains, Eddy, and Foster. She was soon known as "the Universal Nightingale." Sadly the studio did not know how to follow up properly on Susanna's success in *Phantom of the Opera*. Said Susanna: "They had a leading woman in me after *Phantom*, and most of what they gave me to do had no more to do with my *Phantom* role than the man in the moon."

Universal decided that by teaming Susanna with Donald O'Connor, they could create their own answer to MGM's very popular screen couple of Mickey Rooney and Judy Garland. Thus, Foster was cast in *Top Man* (1943), about a teenager (Donald O'Connor) who takes over the leadership of his family when his father (Richard Dix) is recalled to active duty. To aid the war effort, he and girlfriend Susanna put on a talent show at a nearby factory. The film gave her the chance to sing the popular tune "Wrap Your Troubles in Dreams," and it also brought Lillian Gish back to the screen as O'Connor's mother. Of this project, the *Los Angeles Examiner* observed, "Susanna Foster . . . is a pretty fancy dish to be high schooling around in an O'Connor film. From Nelson Eddy to Donald is quite a thing, if you know what we mean. . . ."

For her third Universal excursion, Susanna was costarred with Boris Karloff in *The Climax* (1944), which deliberately paralleled *The Phantom of the Opera*. Here she was a pretty opera singer, Angela, who resembled another performer, killed years before by mad doctor Hohner (Karloff). Again the production was in color with posh sets, and Susanna enjoyed many opera sequences, plus singing "Some Day I'll Know" and "Now At Last." Turhan Bey played her romantic interest, and *Variety* reported that Susanna "is in good voice with the several numbers handed her for delivery." Susanna was then third-billed as singer Peggy Fleming in *Bowery to Broadway* (1944), a musical drama about rival beer garden owners (Jack Oakie and Donald Cook) joining forces to produce Broadway musicals. Susanna was featured singing "There'll Always Be a Moon."

Next she had a cameo as herself in the Hollywood Victory Committee scene in *Follow the Boys* (1944). For her fourth and final release of 1944, Susanna was paired again with Donald O'Connor in *This Is the Life*, actually made in the summer of 1943. But this time she had a substantial role as fickle Angela, the singer who deserts her boyfriend (O'Connor) when she becomes attracted to a mature rival (Patric Knowles). She sang "With a Song in My Heart" and "L'Amour, Toujours, L'Amour." Increasingly, Susanna was unhappy about the quality of her screen assignments and, because she made her feelings known, became unpopular with the studio hierarchy. Following the advice of Universal peer Maria Montez, Susanna also had demanded a raise from the front office, who agreed reluctantly to give her a $5,000 bonus for each picture she made thereafter.

Universal casually thrust Susanna into the "B" Western *Frisco Gal* (1945), playing a young woman who goes West to locate her brother's killer. She sang "Beloved," "Good Little Bad Little Lady," and "I Just Go In," but the Technicolor trappings promised originally when the film was announced as *Frisco Kate* failed to materialize. Her final Universal feature—and what proved to be her last picture for decades—was *That Night With You* (1945), a screwball comedy that cast Susanna as an bubbly, ambitious singer who informs a producer (Franchot Tone) that she is his offspring from a one-day marriage. In the film she performed five numbers, including "Once Upon a Dream" (the film's working title) and a distaff version of arias from Rossini's opera, *The Barber of Seville*. The story ended happily with her succeeding on Broadway, wedding her boyfriend (David Bruce), and having many children. Off-camera Susanna was quite displeased with her role in *That Night With You*. She complained, "Imagine—singing a female version of *The Barber of Seville*! And that makeup—my eyebrows all plucked out and penciled on, a toupee widow's peak on me, a lipstick mouth that went all over my face. I looked like a made-up doll."

While working at Universal, the practical (and unhappy) Susanna had trained as a nurse's aide at the Los Angeles County Hospital and graduated with an aide's license. She then borrowed nearly $20,000 from Universal and traveled to New York and then to Europe to study voice. Upon her return, she repaid the loan. By now, however, Susanna—always pushed by her parents to further a show-business career she did not want—was totally sick of studio politics. She refused to be cast in any of the roles offered her, including that of the maid in the Sonja Henie vehicle *The Countess of Monte Cristo* (1948); she was replaced by Olga San Juan (who also replaced her in *One Touch of Venus*, 1948, starring Ava Gardner). Said the sharp-tongued Susanna, "It was the same old thing. They wanted me to sing while Sonja Henie skated. . . . She comes up to here on me. She should have been the maid!" By now, Universal, which had undergone corporate changes, was glad to terminate Foster's contract.

Now at liberty, Susanna appeared in the West Coast production of *Naughty Marietta* and fell in love with her costar, Wilbur Evans. The two were married on October 23, 1948, in Evans's hometown (Philadelphia) at the city hall and honeymooned in Atlantic City. Evans was nineteen years older than his twenty-four-year-old bride. Eventually they had two sons, Michael David (born in 1950) and Philip (born in 1952), and together they appeared in operettas with the Cleveland Light Opera Company and headed a touring company of *The Merry Widow*. Their publicity billed the husband-and-wife duo as "The Singing Lunts" and "America's Singing Sweethearts."

Later, the couple relocated to England when Evans was signed to appear opposite Mary Martin (and later Julie Wilson) in the London production of *South Pacific*. They returned to America when Evans was hired to play opposite Shirley Booth in the unsuccessful Broadway musical *By the Beautiful Sea* (1954). In 1955, Susanna sang the leads in *Brigadoon* and *Show Boat* at the Valley Forge Music Fair in Pennsylvania, where her husband was the director. The next year the couple underwent a bitter, and much publicized, divorce.

To support her sons, Susanna held a variety of low-paying jobs in New York City where she had settled. She even was heard on radio asking listeners for the whereabouts of her ex-spouse and for a part-time position to supplement her daytime employment at the brokerage firm of Merrill, Lynch, Pierce, Fenner and Smith. The feud was still in the news in April 1962 when Evans informed a court that his ex-wife had turned "beatnik," squandering a $25,000 trust fund, and that her Westside apartment was "slovenly, slipshod."

Things continued to spiral downhill for Susanna, who insisted, "I want to do what I want to do and that does not include anything in show business." She added, "I made a dozen pictures in Hollywood . . . and only in one did I approach—even remotely approach—being in the least satisfied. That was *Phantom of the Opera*. . . . It, at least, had some taste." By the mid-'70s, Susanna, who had been reduced to being (temporarily) a check-in attendant at a Manhattan Turkish bath, returned to Hollywood—this time by bus. There was no welcoming committee to greet her. She later resided in North Hollywood and worked at a non-show-business job.

In the spring of 1989, just as a version of Broadway's *The Phantom of the Opera* was opening in Los Angeles, there were newspaper accounts of how the ex-costar of 1943's *The Phantom of the Opera* was impoverished and forced to live in her car. When ex-child stars Jane Withers and Margaret O'Brien read this article, they came to Foster's financial rescue. The actress, long away from her profession, returned to the screen in 1992 in producer Wade Williams's remake of Edgar G. Ulmer's classic low-budget film noir 1945 feature *Detour*. The original had starred Tom Neal, and the remake had his son, Tom Jr., playing the role his dad made famous—that of a drifter who comes under the spell of a scheming woman (Lea Larish), resulting in murder. Susanna was seen in the part of Evie. In 2000, she appeared as herself in writer-director David J. Skal's *The Opera Ghost: A Phantom Unmasked*, a documentary on Universal Pictures' various screen versions of the Gaston Leroux classic *The Phantom of the Opera*. She also turned up at a showing of the 1943 *Phantom* at Hollywood's refurbished Egyptian Theater complex. Still looking quite striking, Foster talked nonstop during a question-and-answer session, discussing everything from politics to religion.

Filmography

The Great Victor Herbert (Par, 1939)
The Hard-Boiled Canary [There's Magic in Music]
    (Par, 1941)
Glamour Boy (Par, 1942)
Star Spangled Rhythm (Par, 1942)
Phantom of the Opera (Univ, 1943)
Top Man (Univ, 1943)
The Climax (Univ, 1944)

Bowery to Broadway (Univ, 1944)
Follow the Boys (Univ, 1944)
This Is the Life (Univ, 1944)
Frisco Sal (Univ, 1945)
That Night With You (Univ, 1945)
Detour (Wade Williams, 1992)
The Opera Ghost: A Phantom Unmasked (Univ,
    2000) (documentary)

Album Discography

LPs

The Phantom of the Opera (Mac/Eddy JN 124)
    [ST/R]

The Phantom of the Opera (Sountrak 114) [ST]

CDs

The Phantom of the Opera (Facet 8115) [ST/R]

Connie Francis in *Looking for Love* (1964).
[Courtesy of JC Archives]

Connie Francis

(b. Concetta Constance Franconero, Newark, New Jersey, December 12, 1938)

With over 88 million records sold globally, Connie Francis was long one of the world's most popular recording artists. In the late 1950s and early 1960s, she reflected the youth pop-music scene, belting out in her trademark contralto vibrato such hits as "Stupid Cupid" and "Lipstick on Your Collar." She had first risen to popularity with an old standard, "Who's Sorry Now?" and for five years was never off the music charts. Of all the hundreds of songs she ever recorded, she is most closely associated with "Where the Boys Are." The latter was the theme song to her first MGM movie, of the same title (1960), in which she demonstrated a wonderful sense of comedy (like Judy Garland, whose successor she was proclaimed to be). It was a flair her subsequent films sadly never capitalized on.

A songstress can only be a teen queen for so many years before maturity, changing musical styles, and most of all, new talent crowds her from the coveted throne. However, Connie Francis made a successful transition to the major cabaret circles, and if her recordings were no longer chart-breakers, she was certainly not forgotten. But then a series of highly publicized tragedies (the death of her beloved Bobby Darin, her rape, her brother's gangland-style murder, the temporary loss of her voice) in the 1970s and 1980s transformed her into a figure warranting tremendous sympathy rather than high adulation. All this led to emotional breakdowns and several comeback attempts (many of which were engineered by her longtime mentor and friend, Dick "American Bandstand" Clark). Each new emotional milestone in her seesawing life made her fans (now middle-aged) more aware how much time had elapsed since she and they were teenagers rocking at the hop.

She was born Concetta Constance Franconero on December 12, 1938, at Saint James Hospital in Newark, New Jersey, the daughter of George and Ida (Ferrara) Franconero. Her father, the son of Italian immigrants, was a former dockworker turned roofing contractor. Two years later, her brother George was born. Connie was brought up in Belleville, New Jersey, and later in Bloomfield. Because her father enjoyed playing the concertina, he had his daughter take lessons on a miniature accordion when she was three and a half years old. By the age of five, she made her debut singing "O Sole Mio" at a school recital, and was soon singing and playing the accordion at community gatherings. When she twelve, she was four-feet eleven-inches and weighed 135 pounds. As she recalled, "I played the accordion then, and it was a good place to hide behind."

She had already appeared on Paul Whiteman's *TV Teen Club* (ABC-TV), which originated in Philadelphia. In December 1950, her father took her to New York to be on *Arthur Godfrey's Talent Scouts*, where, at Godfrey's suggestion, she adopted her stage name of Connie Francis. She won first prize that night. Later her father brought her to the attention of George Scheck, who produced a New York City–based TV show called *Star Time*, which featured young talent. He was not interested in more kid singers, but he was intrigued that she played the accordion. He hired her to be on his show, the start of a four-year run. Very soon after starting with Scheck, she happily dropped the hateful accordion and concentrated on singing. (She later said, "in 1967 there was a big flood in my basement and the accordion died.") During summers, she performed in entertainments at Catskill resorts, sometimes working backstage as well. Having had a strict Catholic upbringing and being subjected to an overprotective father, she was at a loss how to cope with her new, promiscuous environment. Francis sadly commented, "I never mixed socially with these other kids. I just sat around by myself and ate. . . ."

In June 1955, she graduated from high school (where she was an overachiever). George Scheck, now her manager, negotiated a contract for her with MGM Records after she had been rejected by several labels and had spent years singing demos for music publishers. In a two-year period with MGM, she recorded ten singles, but none of them became hits. Unsure that her career would ever become substantial, she enrolled at New York University, where she had a four-year scholarship. She quit after four months when she decided that show business must be her life. She auditioned for Broadway musicals (including *West Side Story*), clubs, and television, but no one was interested. She sang in cocktail lounges and second-rate clubs, usually chaperoned by one of her parents.

Through George Scheck, Connie had become acquainted with rising young singer Bobby Darin, when he and his partner had tried to sell songs to Scheck for Connie to record. A deep romance developed between Francis and the arrogant, confident, talented Darin, but always her father stood between the two of them. It was the first time she had ever rebelled against parental control. Connie was torn between these opposing loyalties, and her father won out. In her autobiography, written many years later, she asks, "Why didn't my father want a relationship for me with someone he knew was going to be a winner?" Because she abided by her father's wishes, Darin finally broke with her. To insure the tie was cut, her manipulative father pressured George Scheck, who was not only Darin's agent but a father figure for the young man, to cut his ties with the singer, which he did. Francis's abiding love for Darin would carry through his two marriages to his untimely death in 1973, and beyond.

Meanwhile, Scheck finally negotiated Hollywood interest in his client. However, because of Connie's weight, she was not considered screen material, and therefore made her film debut as the off-camera singing voice of Tuesday Weld in *Rock! Rock! Rock!* (1956). It was a slapdash independent picture about a teenaged girl (Weld) wanting a new gown for the school prom and needing to raise money for the big purchase. Of the rock 'n' roll talent involved, which included the Moonglows and Alan Freed, *Variety* thought LaVern Baker, Chuck Berry, and Frankie Lymon and the Teenagers were okay. The trade paper added, "Talent runs out of class after that, except for maybe Connie Francis, who does the offscreen vocalizing for Tuesday Weld. . . ."

Alan Freed (of *Rock! Rock! Rock!*) was more successful as a New York City radio disc jockey. In the summer of 1957, he began a four-week series called *The Big Beat* on ABC-TV. Connie was on the first show (July 12, 1957), along with the Everly Brothers, the Billy Williams Quartet, Ferlin Husky, and others. (Later guests included Bobby Darin.) For her final MGM recording session, her father convinced her to sing one of his favorite old songs, "Who's Sorry Now?" using a contemporary beat. Released in November 1957, the song went nowhere until it was plugged by Dick Clark on his *American Bandstand* TV show in January 1958. It moved onto the charts in March and remained there for fifteen weeks in 1958, climbing to fourth position. It sold over a million copies.

Meanwhile, Connie had returned to Hollywood for another movie quickie, *Jamboree* (1957), made by the producers of *Rock! Rock! Rock!* This time, however, she was in front of the black-and-white cameras, along with a horde of other new rock 'n' roll talent (including Frankie Avalon, whom she had once briefly dated; Carl Perkins; and the Four Coins) and assorted disc jockeys (including Dick Clark). For Twentieth Century-Fox's Western movie spoof, *The Sheriff of Fractured Jaw* (1958), starring Jayne Mansfield and Kenneth More, Connie provided the vocals for a few song numbers that buxom Mansfield lip-synched.

Connie recorded more hits, using such young songwriters as Jack Keller, Neil Sedaka, and Howard Greenfield. She was on the charts in 1958 with several numbers: "I'm Sorry I Made You Cry," "Fallin'," and "My Happiness." She was a frequent guest on *American Bandstand* and soon began crossing over into adult variety TV programming (*The Ed Sullivan Show*, teaming once with Bobby Darin, *The Perry Como Show*, etc.) as a guest performer. She was a regular on *The Jimmie Rogers Show* (NBC-TV) during its March to September 1959 run. In addition, she continued to play nightclubs, performed at Carnegie Hall that November, and as her record sales increased, began concertizing around the world, including Australia, the Continent, and the Far East. Meanwhile, she had been refining her figure, profile, and coiffure.

Her song "Mama" rose to number nine on the charts in the spring of 1960, but it was "My Heart Has a Mind of Its Own" that was her first number-one hit (in September 1960), replacing Chubby Checker's "The Twist" at the top spot. It also made her the first female singer to have two consecutive singles (the other was "Everybody's Somebody's Fool") reach the first position on the charts. By then, another division of MGM Records, MGM Pictures, and producer Joe Pasternak had cast her in *Where the Boys Are* (1960), a youth comedy focusing on the annual college student invasion of Fort Lauderdale, Florida, during spring break. Filled with popular and attractive young performers (George Hamilton, Yvette Mimieux, and Dolores Hart), Connie was seen as a practical-minded whiz, full of self-deprecating humor and thrilled to be wanted by myopic Frank Gorshin. The picture was bright, topical, and entertaining, and even if it was conventionally executed, was extremely popular with young moviegoers. One of the picture's highlights was Connie's singing of the title tune, a song she had persuaded Pasternak could be written in four days by her New York friends, Neil Sedaka and Howard Greenfield. *Variety* decided she sang her two numbers (the title tune and "Turn on the Sunshine") with "zip and style."

Becoming more sophisticated with her wardrobe and makeup, Connie was now a top club attraction globally, earning about $1 million in 1961. She had been the focal subject of Edward R. Murrow's celebrity interview program *Person to Person* (CBS-TV) and the well-known biographical show *This Is Your Life* (NBC-TV), and on September 13, 1961 she starred in her own TV special on ABC-TV. As part of the youth invasion, her managers merchandized her image in every conceivable outlet, from sweaters to diaries and charm bracelets. Although now over twenty-one, she still lived at home (in Bloomfield, New Jersey) with her parents. Her father, retired from the roofing business, controlled the four music-publishing companies that she owned. She won a variety of awards; from being named "Most Programmed Vocalist of the Year" by *Billboard* magazine to being "Best Female Singer of the Year" by *Cashbox* magazine. Four years in a row, she was named "Best Female Singer of the Year" by *American Bandstand*. She was a rarity in a field dominated by young male singers (Elvis Presley, Bobby Darin, Rick Nelson, Frankie Avalon, and Tommy Sands).

One of the most clever merchandizing gambits used by Connie Francis was to record a number of singles and albums sung in foreign languages. In 1960, her albums *Italian Favorites* and *More Italian Favorites* were in the top ten on the charts. She soon produced a string of multilingual albums with assorted ethnic themes, each one of which featured an album cover photograph of her in appropriate native garb. The ploy sold lots of records, made her an international favorite, and did much more for her than the paltry feature films she did under her MGM pact. *Follow the Boys* (1963) attempted to duplicate *Where the Boys Are*, but this time the action was set on the Riviera. It was an anemic romance and an unfunny comedy. Besides performing the title tune (which rose to number seventeen on the charts), Connie sang "Italian Lullaby." *Looking for Love* (1964), produced by Joe Pasternak, cast her as a switchboard operator with her heart set on capturing Jim Hutton's affections. Johnny Carson, Danny Thomas, George Hamilton, and others made meaningless cameo appearances. Her best number was the title tune, and with Thomas she dueted "I Can't Believe That You're in Love With Me." The next year, she showed up in an impoverished remake of the Judy Garland–Mickey Rooney *Girl Crazy* (1943) refurbished as *When the Boys Meets the Girl* (1965). As always Connie sparkled when doing comedy dialogue, but there was no chemistry between her and her leading man (Harve Presnell). The diverse guest-star roster included Louis Armstrong, Liberace, and the popular rock group Herman's Hermits. Besides the title song (by Jack Keller and Howard Greenstein), Francis warbled George and Ira Gershwin's "But Not for Me" and harmonized "I Got Rhythm" with Presnell and Armstrong. It was an inglorious end to her movie career.

By the mid-'60s, the British invasion of singers had changed the American musical scenes. Connie's last charted song was "Be Anything" in the late spring of 1964. She had been performing for several years at the Sahara Hotel in Las Vegas (in 1967 she was named Best Female Entertainer in Las Vegas). During 1967, Connie, who had previously had several cosmetic nasal surgeries, again underwent rhinoplasty to refine her profile. This time the operation produced the unfortunate side effect that she could not sing in air-conditioned facilities. She then underwent another operation. Thereafter, according to Francis: "I went into a recording studio and panicked. It sounded like someone else's voice. I had a range of seven notes. I had no vibrato. I felt like a surgeon who had his hands cut off." As a result, she had a nervous breakdown.

In subsequent years, Connie was twice married and twice divorced. She had unspectacular comeback attempts. She was championed by Dick Clark, who had her as a guest on his special *Dick Clark Presents the Rock 'n' Roll Years* (ABC-TV, September 27, 1973). By 1974, she was wed to Joseph Garzilli (her third husband), who was in the travel business. Over the years and during her various marriages she had suffered three miscarriages and was now seeking to adopt a baby. On November 7, 1974, she was performing at the Westbury Music Fair on Long Island. She had just learned that there was a little baby boy available for adoption, and she intended to become the child's mother. After singing onstage that night, she returned to her motel room, where in the early morning of November 8, she was held at knifepoint for two and a half hours and raped. The felony received worldwide attention. Francis sued the motel for $5 million; the amount was reduced to $2.5 million in court, and she settled eventually for $1.5 million. Her attacker was never found. The trauma of that event and its aftermath halted Connie's career yet again. She adopted that boy, named Joey, and he became the focus of her life, especially after her separation, reconciliation, and eventual divorce from Garzilli.

Living on past earnings and record royalties, Francis remained mostly out of the limelight. In the fall of 1978, she was a much-heralded guest on *Dick Clark's Live Wednesday* (NBC-TV), singing a medley of her hits. Unknown to viewers, her performance "was all tricks" done in the engineer's booth. Because of her severe vocalizing problems, she had prerecorded the songs and then lip-synched them on the air. She did not know how else to get through the ordeal. In 1980, she made a new album in England. She claimed the songs were "done four bars at a time." In November 1981, she was again at the Westbury Music Fair singing her old hits ("Stupid Cupid," "Who's Sorry Now," and "Where the Boys Are") and such personally meaningful newer songs as "I Will Survive" and "I've Made It Through the Rain." She brought her seven-year-old son Joey onstage and she told the audience, "I'm rusty. I'm klutzy. You forget a lot in seven years. I'm an amateur. I have to start all over again." This time she was not staying at a motel, but was being driven back to her Essex Falls, New Jersey, home nightly.

On March 6, 1981, her forty-year old brother George, a former law partner of New Jersey Governor Brendan Byrne, was gunned down in front of his home. Having endured criminal charges of racketeering himself, he had been aiding a federal investigation of mob infiltration into the state's banking industry. Out of that latest tragedy, Francis claimed she gained new strength. For her, it was "the turning point. Suddenly I had a whole family I was responsible for. My mother and father were basket cases. I had to get my sister-in-law's house in order." It led her to realize that, "I'm not a teen-age idol anymore and I'm not a child. I'm a woman with a story to tell." And she did just that in *Who's Sorry Now* (1984), her best-selling autobiography. After writing the book, she stated, "It helped me analyze my relationship with my father, which I really had never done fully before. It helped me put to bed my fear about the rape—it helped me to confront my brother's death."

In October 1985, Connie gave an elaborate two-performance concert in Los Angeles that included her old hits, new songs, clips from her movies and TV appearances, and a tribute to Bobby Darin. Once she got over her initial mike fright, she was in excellent voice. She announced she was going to make new record albums. Instead, a few weeks later, she began to demonstrate extravagant behavior in public, including hysterical outbursts when the slightest thing went wrong. It led to her being committed for psychiatric evaluation in Los Angeles and, later, in Miami. In March 1989, she admitted to the media, as she began a singing engagement at the Diplomat Hotel in Hollywood, Florida: "For the last four years I've been in and out of mental institutions. It has been by far the most distressing experience of my life." She stated that for several of those years she had refused to take the medication prescribed by her doctors and that the resulting chemical imbalance had made her manic depressive.

Upon recovering, Connie set out on her latest comeback bid, which included a successful engagement at the Aladdin Hotel in Las Vegas. The *Las Vegas Review–Journal* reported, "Her voice was powerful and clear, riding lyrical waves to those high, crisp tones. . . . It was immediately obvious that the love and affection the crowd was showing her with a standing ovation would permit acceptance of whatever she chose to do onstage." During her act, she told her audience, "You've always let me know you were there, in good times and bad, and for that I'll always love you."

By the early 1990s, Francis seemed on the road to a legitimate new comeback, with concert dates in Las Vegas, Atlantic City, and elsewhere. In spring 1993, she was in London performing and was planning new recordings, having signed a pact with Sony. In 1994 when Polydor/Chronicles released the four-CD set *Souvenirs* covering the years 1955 to 1969, *Entertainment Weekly* rated the boxed set a "B +," reasoning Francis's "unique catch-in-the-throat voice, intonation, and gift for building performances make even the weaker numbers shine." In 1996, Sony released *The*

Return Concert—Live at Trump's, capturing Connie's performance at the casino club venue. That year, she had to deal with the dying of her cancer-ridden father, age eighty-four. By this period, she had gained a tremendous amount of weight, which made her the subject of several tabloid newspaper articles. By mid-2001, she had blossomed to a reported 185 pounds, which made performing a chore for her. She was a far cry from the bouncy, bubbly, svelte girl who had attracted so many loyal fans decades before. Nevertheless, recompilations of her many recordings still continued to sell well.

Filmography

Rock! Rock! Rock! (Distributors Corp. of America, 1956) (voice only)
Jamboree (Col, 1957)
The Sheriff of Fractured Jaw (20th-Fox, 1958) (voice only)

Where the Boys Are (MGM, 1960)
Follow the Boys (MGM, 1963)
Looking for Love (MGM, 1964)
When the Boys Meet the Girls (MGM, 1965)

TV Series

Star Time (NN, c. 1951–55)
The Big Beat (ABC, 1957)

The Jimmie Rodgers Show (NBC, 1959)

Album Discography

LPs

All Time International Hits (MGM E/SE4298)
Award Winning Motion Pictures (MGM E/SE-4048)
Brylcream Presents Sing Along With Connie Francis and the Jordanaires (Mati-Mor 8002)
Christmas in My Heart (MGM E/SE-3792)
Connie and Clyde (MGM E/SE-4573)
Connie Francis (Metro M/S-519)
Connie Francis and the Kids Next Door (Leo the Lion 935)
Connie Francis Live at the Copa (MGM E/SE-3913)
Connie Francis Live at the Sahara in Las Vegas (MGM E/SE-4411)
Connie Francis Sings (MGM ED/SE-4049)
Connie Francis Sings Bacharach and David (MGM SE-4584)
Connie Francis Sings Favorites (MGM E/SE-3869)
Connie, Italiano (Laurie House LH-8019, CBS Special Products LV-8098)
Connie's Christmas (MGM E/SE-4399)
Connie's Greatest Hits (MGM E/SE-3793)
Country and Western Golden Hits (MGM E/SE-3795)
Country Greats (MGM E/SE-4251) w. Hank Williams Jr.
Country Music Connie Style (MGM E/SE-4079)

Do the Twist With Connie Francis (MGM E/SE-4022)
The Exciting Connie Francis (MGM E/SE-3761)
Folk Favorites (Metro M/S-538)
Follow the Boys (MGM E/SE-4123) [ST]
For Mama (MGM E/SE-4294)
Fun Songs for Children (Leo the Lion 70126)
German Favorites (MGM E/SE-4124)
Grandes Exitos del Cine de Los Años 60 (MGM E/SE-4474)
Greatest American Waltzes (MGM E/SE-4145)
Greatest Golden Groovie Goodies (MGM GAS-109)
Greatest Hits (Mer/Polygram 827-582-1)
Greatest Hits, Vol. 2 (Mer/Polygram 831-699-1)
Happiness (MGM E/SE-4472)
Hawaii: Connie (MGM E/SE-4522)
I'm Me Again (MGM SE-5406)
In the Summer of His Years (MGM E/SE-4210)
The Incomparable Connie Francis (Metro M/S-603)
Irish Favorites (MGM E/SE-4013)
Italian Favorites (MGM E/SE-3791)
Jamboree! (Warner Bros.—no number) [ST]
Jealous Heart (MGM E/SE-4355)
Looking for Love (MGM E/SE-4229) [ST]
Love, Italian Style (MGM E/SE-4448)

Mala Femmena (Evil Woman) (MGM E/SE-4161)

Merry Christmas (Sessions ARI-1023)

Modern Italian Hits (MGM E/SE-4102)

More Greatest Hits (MGM E/SE-3942)

More Italian Favorites (MGM E/SE-3871)

Movie Greats of the Sixties (MGM E/SE-4382)

My Best to You (Cap Record Club 91145)

My Heart Cries for You (MGM E/SE-4487)

My Special Favorites/More Great Love Songs (Suffolk Marketing—no number)

My Thanks to You (MGM E/SE-3776)

Never on Sunday (MGM E/SE-3965)

A New Kind of Connie (MGM E/SE-4253)

Noah's Ark and Other Wondrous Bible Stories (Leo the Lion 1035)

Rock 'n' Roll Million Sellers (MGM E/SE-3794)

Rock, Rock, Rock (Chess/Atlantic 1425/MCA CH-9254) [ST]

Rocksides (1957-64) (Mercury/Polygram 831-698-1)

Second Hand Love (MGM E/SE 4049)

Sessions Presents Connie Francis (Sessions SG-69)

Spanish and Latin Favorites (MGM E/SE-3853)

The Songs of Les Reed (MGM SE-4655)

Songs of Love (Metro M/S-571)

Songs to a Swinging Band (MGM E/SE-3893)

Treasury of Love Songs/Sentimental Favorites (Suffolk Marketing SM-1-50)

The Very Best of Connie Francis (MGM E/SE-4167)

The Wedding Cake (MGM SE-4637)

When the Boys Meet the Girls (MGM E/SE-4334) [ST]

Who's Sorry Now (MGM E/SE-3686)

CDs

All By Myself (Trend 157.021)

All the Best (KRB 1012)

Among My Souvenirs (Malaco MALD-1100)

Award Winning Motion Picture Hits (Pendulum PEG041)

The Best of Connie Francis (Polygram Special Markets 314-520-377-2, Universal Special Markets 520377)

The Best of Connie Francis (Readers's Digest 295960222)

The Best of Connie Francis (Universe UN-1-049)

The Best of Connie Francis: 20th Century Masters—The Millennium Collection (Polydor 547848)

Boy Hunt—The Best of Connie Francis (Polygram POCP-1679)

Christmas Album (Spectrum 554759)

Christmas Cheer (Polygram 314-520208-2, Universal Special Markets 520208)

Christmas In My Heart (Pendulum PEG021)

Christmas With Connie Francis (World Star Collection 99954)

De Coleccion (Polydor Latino 314-527-226)

The Collection (Fremus CDFR-0525)

The Collection (Polygram 5518222)

Connie at the Copa (Pendulum PEG036)

Connie Francis (Castle Masters Collection 37403044)

Connie Francis (The Entertainers 317)

Connie Francis (The Entertainers 357)

Connie Francis (The Entertainers 365)

Connie Francis (Joker 10059)

Connie Francis (Joker 10062)

Connie Francis (MCP 158.648)

Connie Francis & Hank Williams, Jr., Sing Great Country Favorites (Bear Family BCD-15737)

The Connie Francis Collection (Castle Communications CCSCP-325)

Connie Francis on Guard (Jazz Band 2133) w. Mitchell Ayres, Bob Crosby

Connie Francis Performs the Hits of Buddy Holly (Wienerworld Records QED-297)

Connie Francis Sings Screen Hits (Polygram POCP-1509)

Connie Francis, Vol. 1 (TNT 3795/1003)

Connie Francis, Vol. 2 (TNT 5245/3791)

Connie Francis, Vol. 3 (TNT 3795/4945)

Connie Sings Buddy (Castle Pie 262, Musicrama 787442)

Connie's Greatest Latin Hits (Mercury Latino 839924-2)

Country 'n' Western Hits (Pendulum PEG025)

Dance Party (Pendulum PEG042)

The Exciting Connie Francis (Pendulum PEG018)

Folk Song Favorites (Pendulum PEG039)

40 Legendary Hits (Time-Warner 232538-2)

From the Heart (Time-Life R132-04)

Fun Songs for Children (Pendulum PEG040)

Girls Girls Girls (K-tel BU-787-2)

The Great Connie Francis (BCD GLD-63146)

Greatest Hits (Dominion 3346-2)

Greatest Hits (Startrax 511973-2)

Her Greatest Hits & Finest Performances (Reader's Digest RC7-097-1/3)

I'm Gonna Be Warm This Winter (Polydor POCP-1687)

Irish Favorites (Pendulum PEG038)

The Italian Collection, Vol. 1 (Polydor 539556)

The Italian Collection, Vol. 2 (Polydor 539557)

Italian Favorites (Pendulum PEG020)

Jewish Favorites (Pendulum PEG033)

Kissin', Twistin', Goin' Where the Boys Are (Bear Family BCD-15826)

Lass Mir die Bunten Traume (Bear Family BCD-15786)

Die Liebe Ist Fin Seltsames Speil (Polygram 5395032)

Love Songs (Polygram 5500862, Karussell/Pickwick 50086, Pickwick PWKS-540, Spectrum 55086-2)

MGM Classics (Embraceable You) (MCA MCAD-31130)

Minha Historical Internacional (Polygram 527854-2)

More Italian Favorites (Pendulum PEG034)

My Thanks to You (Pendulum PEG019)

Never on Sunday (Pendulum PEG037)

On Guard (Jazz Records 2133)

Party Power (Polygram 513432-2)

Portrait of a Song Stylist (Harmony HARCD-108)

Postcards From America (London 314-525464-2) (ST)

Pretty Little Baby (CeDe International 66135)

The Return Concert—Live at Trump's Castle (Legacy CK-64837)

Robot Man (Back Biter 61011)

Rock 'n' roll Million Seller (Pendulum PEG024)

Rocksides (Pickwick KD-3021)

Schoner Fremder Mann (Polygram 5517442)

Songs to a Swingin' Band (Verve POCJ-2661, Pendulum PEG035)

Souvenirs (Polydor 533382)

Spanish & Latin American Favorites (Pendulum PEG026)

Star Gala (Polygram 5527492)

Sue Thompson/Connie Francis (VCD DEK-027-6)

Die Superhits von Connie Francis (Ariola Express 291036)

The Swinging Connie Francis (Audiophile 286, Style/Voca 286)

Swinging in Japan (Polydor POCP-1687)

36 All-Time Greatest Hits, Vol. 1 (GSC Music 15053-1)

36 All-Time Greatest Hits, Vol. 2 (GSC Music 15053-2)

36 All-Time Greatest Hits, Vol. 3 (GSC Music 15053-3)

Treasury of Love Songs/Sentimental Favorites (The Beautiful Music Company BMD-50)

24 Greatest Hits (Prism PLATCD-3916)

Unforgettable Memories (SPA 66125, Zaiks CD-66125)

The Very Best of Connie Francis (Avon Special Products DPSM-5073)

The Very Best of Connie Francis (Heartland Music HD-1127/28)

The Very Best of Connie Francis (Polydor 827569-2)

The Very Best of Connie Francis, Vol. 2 (Polydor 831699-2, Polydor POCP-1679)

Where the Boys Are (Remember RMB-75069)

Where the Boys Are: Connie Francis in Hollywood (Turner Classic Movies/Rhino R2-75069)

Where the Hits Are (Malaco 2003, Malaco D-134739)

Where the Hits Are: 24 Greatest (Musicrama 680852)

White Sox, Pink Lipstick . . . and Stupid Cupid (Bear Family BCD-15616)

Who's Sorry Now? (Pendulum PEG017)

Who's Sorry Now? (Success 22531CD)

The Wonderful World of Connie Francis (RMB 756009)

The World of Connie Francis (Polygram 5513092)

Annette Funicello

(b. Annette Joanne Funicello, Utica, New York, October 22, 1942)

America saw Annette Funicello grow from an ingratiating little girl on TV's *The Mickey Mouse Club* into a beautiful young woman via the medium of television. Thanks to her support from the Walt Disney organization, Annette not only developed into a popular film, TV star, and role model, but she also had a successful recording career. As she left childhood and became a voluptuous young woman, Annette embarked on a series of highly successful beach-party movies for American International. They forever typed her in the minds of the public as delightfully filling out a (decorous) bathing suit while passing away the hours on the California sands rocking and rolling and being romanced by Frankie Avalon. As the 1960s ended, the actress opted for marriage and a family in deference to a career, although she remained in the public eye with occasional appearances, mostly on the small screen (notably in advertisements promoting peanut butter), which had launched her in the first place.

Annette Joanne Funicello was born on October 22, 1942, in Utica, New York, and when she was four her family moved to California. The next year, she took dancing lessons in hopes of becoming a ballerina. At the age of nine, she won the "Miss Willow Lake" beauty contest and began a modeling career. While appearing in the outdoor production "Ballet vs. Jive," Annette was spotted by Walt Disney, who signed her to appear as one of the original Mouseketeers on *The Mickey Mouse Club* on ABC-TV in 1955. As a result of her cute looks and pleasing personality, Annette was an immediate hit on the children's program and quickly became the most recognizable of the Mouseketeer children, remaining with the program through its four-season run until the fall of 1959. She also appeared in several Disney multipart stories on ABC-TV: "Adventure in Dairyland," "The Further Adventures of Spin and Marty," "The New Adventures of Spin and Marty," and her own starring serial, "Annette," which aired early in 1958. For Disney, she also did guest roles in three episodes of the *Zorro* series. In 1958, Annette (as she was now simply billed) made her recording debut on the Disneyland label, and she had chart singles with "How Will I Know My Love" followed by "Tall Paul," which reached the top ten. In the spring of 1959, Annette was seen on *The Danny Thomas Show* (CBS-TV) appearing in several episodes in the recurring role of Gina. That year, she also made her movie debut for Disney playing Tommy Kirk's girlfriend Alison in the comedy *The Shaggy Dog*.

By now avuncular Walt Disney realized that Annette Funicello—like fellow contractee Hayley Mills—was a valuable star for his studio; a maturing and attractive teenager who was popular on both the big and small screens and on records. To promote her as a teen singing star, Disney switched Annette to the Buena Vista label (the Disneyland label was aimed at younger children). In 1959, she scored well with "Jo-Jo the Dog Faced Boy," "Lonely Guitar," and "First Name Initial," while the next year she had hits with "O Dio Mio," "Train of Love," and "Pineapple Princess." Also during that year she had charted albums for Buena Vista with *Annette Sings [Paul] Anka* and *Hawaiiannette*.

Annette Funicello and Frankie Avalon in *Beach Party* (1963).
[Courtesy of JC Archives]

In the film arena, Annette was also kept busy by singing the title song, with Tommy Sands, for *The Parent Trap* (1961). That year, a now grown-up Annette played Mary Contrary, who is about to marry Tom Piper (Tommy Sands), in Disney's remake of the children's fantasy *Babes in Toyland*. In the movie, Annette sang "I Can't Do Sums," while she was serenaded by Ray Bolger in the "Castle in Spain" sequence. She also starred in several segments of *The Wonderful World of Disney* on NBC-TV, and a quartet of these were issued theatrically in Europe. *The Horsemasters* (1961), filmed in England, teamed her with Tommy Kirk as fellow students at a school who teach young people to become expert riders. With Louis Armstrong, Bobby Rydell, the Osmond Brothers, and Kid Ory, she was part of a tour of Disneyland called *Disneyland After Dark* (1962), and with Ed Wynn she costarred in *The Golden Horseshoe Revue* (1962). The fourth "telefeature" was called *Escapade in Florence*, and in it she and Tommy Kirk portrayed American teenagers who meet on holiday in Italy and try to stop a count (Nino Castelnuovo) from stealing a classic work of art. By now, Annette's popularity was such that she was a prime feature of fan and teenage magazines, and her name was on a wide line of merchandise. In the early 1960s, she was even the subject of a quartet of fiction books published by Whitman: *The Desert Inn Mystery, The Mystery at Moonstone Bay, The Mystery at Smugglers' Cove*, and *Sierra Summer*.

Now billed as Annette Funicello, the twenty-one-year-old performer became an established film player in 1963 when she appeared with Tommy Kirk in Disney's *The Adventures of Merlin Jones*. This crazy comedy's title character (Kirk) can read minds, and with his girlfriend Jennifer (Annette), he tries to prevent a judge (Leon Ames) from carrying out a big robbery. Even more successful with the public were the five sun-and-sand movies, all directed by William Asher, in which Annette starred for budget film studio American International. The first one, *Beach Party* (1964), set the trend for the airy series. The movies offered a lot of fun-loving teenagers romping on the beach (with the nubile teenage girls—except decorous Annette—wearing as little as the censor allowed) with lots of rock 'n' roll music, but *no* violence, sex, profanity, alcohol, nor tobacco. The initial outing had an anthropology professor (Bob Cummings) and his bemused secretary (Dorothy Malone) on the California sands studying the sex habits of teens, with Annette and Frankie Avalon playing teenagers in love. *Variety* endorsed, "It's a bouncy bit of lightweight fluff, attractively cast . . . beautifully set . . . and scored throughout . . . with a big twist beat."

Muscle Beach Party (1964) followed, with Annette becoming jealous when a beautiful contessa (Luciana Paluzzi) pursues her boyfriend (Frankie Avalon) after dumping muscleman Rock Stevens (Peter Lupus). In *Bikini Beach* (1964), Annette finds herself attracted not only to boyfriend Frankie Avalon, but to long-haired British rocker the Potato Bug (also played by Avalon). In 1964, enterprising American International also reteamed Tommy Kirk and Annette for a spin-off called *Pajama Party*, a silly science-fiction comedy about a Martian (Kirk) coming to Earth and lusting for Annette, who sang "Where Did I Go Wrong." During this period, Annette returned to the record charts, thanks to the successful sales of the soundtrack albums of *Beach Party* and *Muscle Beach Party* on the Buena Vista label. The actress also made guest appearances on such TV fare as *Wagon Train, Burke's Law*, and *The Greatest Show on Earth*. In the fall of 1964, she guested on Bob Hope's NBC-TV special.

In the mid-'60s, Funicello continued her reign as queen of the surf-and-sand movies when she and Frankie Avalon became involved with other peers in saving a kidnapped singer (Paul Lynde) from a motorcycle gang in *Beach Blanket Bingo* (1965). She and Avalon also starred in the last of the "Beach" series, *How to Stuff a Wild Bikini* (1965), which found Frankie in the military service based in the South Seas. He hires a witch doctor (portrayed by Buster Keaton in one of his last film appearances) to make sure Annette remains faithful to him. In it, Annette sang "Better Ready" and "The Perfect Boy."

The year 1965 saw Annette rematched yet again with Tommy Kirk (as Merlin Jones) for Disney in a sequel to the very popular *The Misadventures of Merlin Jones*. The film was called *The Monkey's Uncle*, and Annette again played Jones's girlfriend Jennifer. Annette and the Beach Boys sang the film's title theme. She also made a guest appearance in American International's *Dr. Goldfoot and the Bikini Machine* (1965) as a girl trapped in a wood stock. Getting off the beach (which was wearing thin with young moviegoers), Annette and Avalon made *Fireball 500* (1966) for American International, along with singer Fabian. It proved to be a frail drama about race driver Frankie taking part in a cross-country spin, not realizing he is hauling whiskey for bootleggers. For her last American International outing, *Thunder Alley* (1967), Annette costarred with Fabian in a tawdry race-car melodrama as the daughter of thrill circus owner Jan Murray. Her boyfriend (Warren Berlinger) throws her over for a fling with new driver Fabian's gal (Diane McBain). Annette closed out the 1960s by making a guest appearance as Minnie in the freaked-out mod/nostalgia comedy *Head* (1968), starring the Monkees. Little appreciated when first released, this picture later enjoyed a cult following.

Marrying her agent Jack Gilardi, Annette pretty much deserted show business in the 1970s to raise her family. In 1971 she did make a guest appearance on ABC-TV's *Love, American Style*, and the next year headlined the syndicated special *The Mouse Factory*. She and Frankie Avalon were reteamed in the late summer of 1976 for a brief CBS-TV variety series called *Easy Does It . . . Starring Frankie Avalon*, and the next year she reemerged for ABC's *Dick Clark's Good Old Days: From Bobby Sox to Bikinis* and *The Mouseketeers at Walt Disney World* on NBC-TV's *The World of Disney*. Late in 1978, at Avalon's urging, she reteamed with him in the NBC-TV pilot *Frankie and Annette: The Second Time Around*, and in 1979, she guested on *Fantasy Island*. She was also visible on television and in print ads via a nine-year series of commercials for Skippy peanut butter.

In 1980, Annette Funicello had a flurry of small-screen activity, guesting again on *Fantasy Island*, appearing on the CBS special *Disneyland's 25th Anniversary*, and two NBC specials, *Men Who Rate a '10'* and *The Mouseketeers Reunion*. Meanwhile, she made an effort to break into the country-music field with 1984's *Annette Funicello Country*. She then did roles on *The Love Boat* and *Fantasy Island* again, before returning to Disney for the cable TV movie *Lots of Luck* in 1985. She starred as a housewife who has to accept all the inconveniences that arise when she is a big lottery winner. In 1986, she did a few segments of ABC-TV's *Growing Pains*.

Theatrically Annette and Frankie Avalon reprised their "Beach" roles in the delightful Paramount comedy *Back to the Beach* (1987). By this time, the two are wed with teenagers of their own, and Annette is forced to use her sex appeal to win Frankie back after he strays away with her rival Connie Stevens. This minimusical not only generated a profit, but it did much to repopularize Funicello and Avalon in the minds of viewers. Late in 1988, Annette appeared on the CBS-TV program *Pee-wee's Playhouse Special* with Pee-wee Herman, who was a guest performer in *Back to the Beach*.

As the 1980s wound down, the actress was still making an occasional foray into TV. She insisted that she owed all of her success to the late Walt Disney: "I don't think that I would have gone on to do anything else had it not been for my association with Disney. I was the only Mouseketeer to remain under contract. Walt starred me in films, television and recording. He really did a lot for me." Having divorced Jack Gilardi (they had three children), she had married Bakersfield rancher–horse breeder Glen Holt in the spring of 1987.

In 1989, Annette made a cameo appearance in the comedy *Troop Beverly Hills*, and she rejoined with Frankie Avalon for a guest appearance in 1991 on the TV sitcom *Full House*. At the time, it was touted that renewed interest in the screen team would lead to a TV comedy series for them and/or more installments of their popular *Back to the Beach* movie. Nothing concrete transpired. Meanwhile in 1992, when the boxed set *The Music of Disney—A Legacy in Song* was released on the Disneyland label, it contained four selections by Annette from her old recordings. It prompted the media to question her about her singing talents. She denied any real abilities in the field, saying,

"I remember being frightened every time I went into a recording studio. The producers developed an 'Annette sound': double tracking [recording a voice over itself] and lots of echo chambers." The mother of three also admitted publicly that she had been suffering from multiple sclerosis since 1986 but had hidden her plight behind a cheery face. Because of her progressive disease Funicello was no longer able to accept new performing offers, but she was still able to reminisce about her golden past. She recounted in mid-1994 that when she was seventeen and on tour with Paul Anka, she fell in love with the singer. When asked if she had any regrets over leaving show business at twenty-three to wed and start a family, she answered, "I always knew my priorities." As to her battle with MS, she responded, "I feel terrific. From the waist up, people never know anything is wrong. I just don't walk so well."

During 1994, Annette's autobiography, written with Patricia Romanowski, was published. In reviewing *A Dream Is a Wish Your Heart Makes: My Story*, the trade publication *Booklist* advised that the memoir was "so sugary your teeth will hurt after reading it. . . . Her health problems are the most affecting part of the account, especially in contrast to descriptions of the cotton-wrapped life she led before the disease struck." According to *Kirkus Reviews*: "She doesn't have a shred of dirty on anyone. . . . What else would one expect from Annette Funicello but an overly nostalgic portrait of the decade that gave rise to Disneyland, TV shows like the *Mickey Mouse Club*, rock 'n' roll, and teen idols?"

The book was sufficiently popular to lead CBS-TV to base a TV movie on it. Titled *A Dream Is a Wish Your Heart Makes: The Annette Funicello Story* (10/22/95), it cast Andrea Nemeth as the young Annette, with Eva LaRue Callahan as the older version of the star. Funicello's old recordings were dubbed in for the singing moments, and Annette (as well as Frankie Avalon) made an appearance in the production. The subject, a consultant on the made-for-television feature, was insistent that the chronicle *not* have a sad ending. Now wheelchair-bound, she managed to be on the set in Vancouver, British Columbia, when the docudrama was shot.

As the months passed, Annette's condition worsened, and it was obvious from her labored, rare appearances in public that she was in a great deal of pain. Beyond her walking problem, she was having difficulty talking and seeing. However, she insisted, "I'm a fighter—not a quitter. I never have been, and I never will be." As time went on, she tried innovative medication to deal with the MS, but nothing seemed to improve her worsening condition. Years passed, and somehow Funicello hung on as MS further ravaged her body. Despite her poor health, she showed up on September 14, 1998, at Los Angeles's Century Plaza Hotel. The function (Dinner of Champions) was a fundraiser to combat the disease. Frankie Avalon was at the gathering, and when he told his former costar she had everyone's prayers, Funicello sadly admitted, "Prayer isn't working." He responded with the encouraging, "God's delay isn't God's denial."

In late 1999, Annette, who was having difficulty performing even the most menial tasks because of MS, was hospitalized to undergo a thalamotomy. The surgery helped to relieve some of her tremors and allowed her to function better in her daily life. Nevertheless, in subsequent months, her ability to see and to talk further diminished, making even the simplest daily activity a chore or an impossibility. Throughout her ongoing ordeal, she received much support from her family and gained great comfort from messages sent by her legion of fans.

Filmography

The Shaggy Dog (BV, 1959)
Babes in Toyland (BV, 1961)
The Parent Trap (BV, 1961) (voice only)
The Misadventures of Merlin Jones (BV, 1963)
Beach Party (AIP, 1963)
Muscle Beach Party (AIP, 1964)
Bikini Beach (AIP, 1964)
Pajama Party (AIP, 1964)
Dr. Goldfoot and the Bikini Machine [Dr. G and the Bikini Machine] (AIP, 1965)
The Monkey's Uncle (BV, 1965)
Beach Blanket Bingo [Malibu Beach] (AIP, 1965)
How to Stuff a Wild Bikini (AIP, 1965)
Fireball 500 (AIP, 1966)
Thunder Alley (AIP, 1967)
Head (Col, 1968)
Lots of Luck (Disney Channel-TV, 1985)
Back to the Beach (Par, 1987)
Troop Beverly Hills (Col, 1989)
A Dream Is a Wish Your Heart Makes: The Annette Funicello Story (CBS-TV, 10/22/95)

TV Series

The Mickey Mouse Club (ABC, 1955–59)
The Danny Thomas Show (CBS, 1959)
Easy Does It . . . Starring Frankie Avalon (CBS, 1976)

Album Discography

LPs

Annette (Buena Vista 3301)
Annette and Hayley Mills (Buena Vista 3508)
Annette Funicello Country (Starview 4001)
Annette Sings Anka (Buena Vista 3302)
Babes in Toyland (Buena Vista 4022) [ST]
Back to the Beach (Col SC 40892) [ST]
Beach Party (Buena Vista 3316) [ST]
The Best of Broadway (Disneyland 1267)
Bikini Beach (Buena Vista 3324)
Dance Annette (Buena Vista 3305)
Golden Surfin' Hits (Buena Vista 3327)
Hawaiiannette (Buena Vista 3303)
How to Stuff a Wild Bikini (Wand 671) [ST]
Italiannette (Buena Vista 3304)
A Love Like Ours (Playback—no number)
Muscle Beach Party (Buena Vista 3314) [ST]
Pajama Party (Buena Vista 3325) [ST]
Snow White and the Seven Dwarfs (Disneyland 3906)
Something Borrowed, Something Blue (Buena Vista 3328)
Songs From Annette (Disneyland 24)
State and College Songs (Disneyland 1293)
The Story of My Teens (Buena Vista 3312)
Thunder Alley (Sidewalk 5902) [ST]
Tuby the Tuba (Disney 1928) w. Jimmie Dodd.

CDs

Annette (Buena Vista Japan 0065)
Annette: A Musical Reunion With America's Girl Next Door (Walt Disney Records 860-010)
Annette Sings Anka (Buena Vista Japan 0066)
Annette Sings Golden Hits/Annette's Beach Party (TNT Laser)
Annette Sings Golden Surfin' Hits (Buena Vista Japan 0070)
Annette's Beach Party (Buena Vista Japan 0069)
Back to Back (K-tel 3019-2) w. Frankie Avalon
Back to the Beach (CBS SCT-40892) [ST]
Beach Party (Buena Vista Japan 0071)
The Best of Annette (Buena Vista 860735)
The Best of Annette (TNT Laser)
The Best of Annette Funicello (Buena Vista 860-735)
A Dream Is a Wish Your Heart Makes: The Annette Funicello Story (WEA 520564) [ST]
Hawaiiannette (Buena Vista Japan 0067)
Hawaiianette/Annette Sings Anka (TNT Laser)
Muscle Beach Party (Buena Vista Japan 0068) [ST]
Muscle Beach Party/Annette (TNT Laser 3314/3901)
Pineapple Princess (Request 290)
Pineapple Princess (TNT Laser—no number)
The 31 Greatest Hits of Annette (Silhouette Music SME1-10011)